More praise for *Global Cases in Benchmarking:*
Best Practices from Organizations Around the World

"Leaders of improvement around the world are already deeply in debt to Robert Camp for his pathfinding work in defining the processes and uses of benchmarking. In *Global Cases in Benchmarking,* the master now offers a new gift: 28 superbly detailed, specific examples, full of lessons ready for use. The man who helped define benchmarking now helps us benchmark benchmarking, itself."

 —Donald M. Berwick, MD
  President and CEO
  Institute for Healthcare Improvement

"This outstanding collection of knowledge and information is an inspiration and impetus for anyone looking for ways to find performance improvement gaps. Bob Camp led the concept of benchmarking and now has shown it is possible to collect and collate knowledge both internationally and across industries wide range of activities. Competitive intelligence and denial of comparative relevance are no longer the enemies of using Best Practices Benchmarking. It is a must read for those leaders and disciples who are accountable for continuous improvement."

 —David Stringfellow
  CEO, Fuji Xerox Australia/New Zealand
  Director, Australian Quality Council

"As an old-timer, this book is very inspiring and refreshing. It shows you, in a very practical way, how benchmarking can be used and also explains the different attitudes towards benchmarking. You'll find it's a great resource for best practices information.

 —Gunnar Ivansson
  Benchmarking responsible
  Ericsson Corporation

"One of the pioneers of benchmarking takes the reader on a journey across industries and geographies to demonstrate that learning from others, regardless of who and where they are, if done correctly is the most efficient way to improve performance. Camp's book is a rich source of both inspiration and how-to."

 —Andrzej Lubowski
  Senior Vice President, Strategic Planning
  Visa U.S.A. Inc.

"As we approach the third millennium, it is clear that successful companies will need to have a global view to keep pace with the accelerating changes in technology and business processes which is happening at an exponential rate. This book, which includes benchmarking case studies from all over the world, is a must for any successful management team that wants to compete in this ever-changing global environment."

—Stephen L. Tierney
Group Managing Director and CEO
Xerox Business India

"*Global Cases in Benchmarking* represents a significant advance in benchmarking literature . . . edited by Bob Camp whose name is synonymous with sound benchmarking practice. This book offers a diverse array of multi-sector examples from around the world. More importantly, the examples are framed using a well-designed case study methodology which adds appreciably to the book's value. This work is a rich resource for business education as well as for the competent practice of benchmarking in support of the pursuit of organizational excellence."

—Dr. Curt W. Reimann
Mayberry Chair of Excellence
Tennessee Technological University and Director (1987–1995),
Malcolm Baldrige National Quality Award

Global Cases in Benchmarking

Best Practices from Organizations Around the World

Also available from ASQ Quality Press

Benchmarking: The Search for Industry Best Practices That Lead to Superior Performance
Robert C. Camp

Business Process Benchmarking: Finding and Implementing Best Practices
Robert C. Camp

Insights to Performance Excellence 1998: An Inside Look at the 1998 Baldrige Award Criteria
Mark L. Blazey

The Reward and Recognition Process in Total Quality Management
Stephen B. Knouse

Staffing the New Workplace: Selecting and Promoting for Quality Improvement
Ronald B. Morgan and Jack E. Smith

Understanding and Applying Value-Added Assessment: Eliminating Business Process Waste
William E. Trischler

Quality Quotes
Hélio Gomes

The Change Agents' Handbook: A Survival Guide for Quality Improvement Champions
David W. Hutton

LearnerFirst™ Benchmarking 1.0 (Software)
with Dr. H. James Harrington, International Quality Advisor–
Ernst & Young, L.L.P.

LearnerFirst™ Process Management (Software)
with Tennessee Associates International

To request a complimentary catalog of ASQ Quality Press publications, call
800-248-1946.

Global Cases in Benchmarking

Best Practices from Organizations Around the World

Robert C. Camp, editor

ASQ Quality Press
Milwaukee, Wisconsin

Global Cases in Benchmarking: Best Practices from Organizations Around the World
Robert C. Camp

Library of Congress Cataloging-in-Publication Data

Camp, Robert C., 1935–
    Global cases in benchmarking: best practices from organizations
around the world / Robert C. Camp, editor.
        p.   cm.
    Includes bibliographical references and index.
    ISBN 0-87389-388-3 (acid-free)
    1. Benchmarking (Management)   2. Benchmarking (Management)—Case
studies.   I. Camp, Robert C., 1935–
HD62.15.G558   1998
658.5'62—dc21   97-50315
                                                                             CIP

© 1998 by ASQ

10 9 8 7 6 5 4 3 2 1

ISBN 0-87389-388-3

Acquisitions Editor: Roger Holloway
Development Editor: Jane Crouse
Project Editor: Jeannie W. Bohn
Set in Helvetica and Minion by Linda J. Shepherd.
Printed and bound by BookCrafters, Inc.

ASQ Mission: To facilitate continuous improvement and increase customer satisfaction by identifying, communicating, and promoting the use of quality principles, concepts, and technologies; and thereby be recognized throughout the world as the leading authority on, and champion for, quality.

Attention: Schools and Corporations
ASQ Quality Press books, videotapes, audiotapes, and software are available at quantity discounts with bulk purchases for business, educational, or instructional use. For information, please contact ASQ Quality Press at 800-248-1946, or write to ASQ Quality Press, P.O. Box 3005, Milwaukee, WI 53201-3005.

For a free copy of the ASQ Quality Press Publications Catalog, including ASQ membership information, call 800-248-1946.

Printed in the United States of America

 Printed on acid-free paper

American Society for Quality

Quality Press
611 East Wisconsin Avenue
Milwaukee, Wisconsin 53201-3005
800-248-1946
Web site http://www.asq.org

Contents

Part 3: Service Sector

Part 6: Education Sector

Getting the Most from this Book

This case study book has many points of entry. The following guidelines are offered to maximize your reading experience.

First Things First

All readers should start with Part 1: Editor's Analysis. It provides a brief overview of the entire book and explains its goals. Part 1 also details the types of cases included and the organizations represented, as well as describes how the book was developed.

Next

Where you go next is up to you. Here are some suggestions.

Read by Economic Sector

Are you in manufacturing? Service? Nonprofit? Government? Education? Parts 2–5 correspond to each of these economic sectors. Each part stands alone. Start with the Introduction where you'll get a quick overview of the cases included as well as a heads-up alert on what to look for as you read. Then read through the cases, or move ahead to the part's Analysis where you'll find commentaries of the cases in that economic sector and summary tables detailing lessons learned, best practices, and cost savings and benefits.

Look for a Process

Are you interested in a particular process? Do you want to know how other organizations around the world handle similar processes? Look at the "Processes" table at the beginning of each part to see what's discussed in each economic sector. Or check the index for a specific process and go directly to the related cases.

Look for an Industry

In what industry do you work? Where do you want to be? Look at the "Country and Industry" table at the beginning of each part to see what industries are represented in each economic sector. Similarly, check the index for a specific industry and go directly to the related cases.

Travel the World

Do you want to know about benchmarking in another part of the world? Find out which countries have the most experienced benchmarkers in the world. Check the "Case Study Listing Master Table" at the beginning of each part for the global regions and specific countries represented. Throughout the book, there are case studies from six continents.

Look for an Organization

Are you interested in a particular organization? Find out about benchmarking in multinationals and other types of organizations. Check the "Case Study Listing Master Table" at the beginning of each part for the specific organizations represented. Also check the index.

How To Read "Outside of Your Box"

All readers are encouraged to read outside their areas of expertise. This book challenges you to do so. Get the most out of *your* benchmarking efforts by reading about an economic sector, process, industry, and region of the world that is *not* your own. Check the Analysis of the each part to get a quick overview of lessons learned, best practices, and cost savings and benefits. Remember, the Analysis is not just the narrative, but includes the summary tables too. Also check the index to find specific lessons, practices, or monetary benefits. Then read through the related cases.

As you've quickly discovered, there is no one best way to use this book. The best practice is the one that works for you.

Acknowledgments

I would like to formally acknowledge the many friends, acquaintances, benchmarking colleagues and references who made this book possible. Many were contacted for leads to organizations that had studies to showcase. A select few undertook to document their projects, which are now included as cases in this landmark text.

I am indebted also to the organizations that are represented. Their senior leaders are to be commended for sharing their experiences with a worldwide audience. This is the very essence of best practice benchmarking.

Without the able editorial assistance of Ms. Jane F. Crouse, I could not have completed the development of this book. Her attention to detail and professional working relationship with the authors was invaluable.

PART 1

Editor's Analysis of Case Studies

Robert C. Camp, President, Best Practice Institute

As I travel worldwide, the continued high interest in, and demand for, case studies of successful benchmarking investigations strike me as remarkable. This demand is second only to the preliminary interest in performance data. Once the organization understands what the benchmark data reveal about where it stands and what the magnitude of the gap is, then the resulting intense interest is identifying what the best practices are that will close the gap. That information and insight are usually revealed in case studies.

Up until now, most benchmarking case studies were set in U.S. manufacturing environments. Therefore, I ventured to assemble a balanced book of studies that would include cases from around the world and represent various economic sectors. What I had in mind was one case study each from the following representative sectors.

- Manufacturing
- Service
- Nonprofit
- Government
- Education

In particular, I wanted to develop studies from each of these economic sectors for each of the following geographic areas.

- United States
- Europe
- Asia Pacific
- Africa/Americas (North and South America excluding the United States)

I theorized that this profile of economic sector and geography would be a rich source of contrast and learning for readers. I believe you will find that to be true.

1

Benchmarking and the search for best practices have had a wave-like movement across the globe. Benchmarking was picked up and embraced by Europe within years of its significant use in the United States. What has been astounding, however, is the intensity with which it has been pursued in the Asia–Pacific area. Likewise, there has been a distinct lag in application in South and Central America and in Canada. The case studies will reveal that pace of progress. More importantly, however, the pace of progress will show that this business improvement approach can, in fact, be successfully applied everywhere.

There are lessons to be learned across all economic sectors—in education, health, and government applied to manufacturing and service industries and vice versa. The applications show a wide variety, by country and language (where the colloquialisms were purposely not changed), to culture, and process. There is also a rich diversity of research approaches. To name just one approach, there are many examples of questionnaire designs used to show the variety of data gathering instruments. All have something to learn from each other. This book should serve to stimulate organizations—around the globe—to learn from each other, and should bring benchmarking—worldwide—up to a common level of expertise and application.

The challenge of assembling such a book began in early 1996 with extensive correspondence with editors, benchmarking centers, benchmarking competency managers, and colleagues and acquaintances. It has proven to be a very substantial effort to outline the goal of the project; supply a suggested outline; show an example; get someone to personally commit to writing (a challenge that this author knows all too well); and finally get the organization's approval to release and place the information in the public domain for others to learn from. I am, of course, highly indebted to these individuals.

In assembling this book I hope to accomplish several goals. The first is to show that the art and science of sourcing and sharing best practices through benchmarking is universally applicable; and that there are significant results that can occur through reasonably disciplined application of the technique. Second, I hope to show what constitutes a case study: What topics to cover and what structure to use so that the case studies serve as models for others—and hopefully incite them to write by example. That will only serve to continually add to this rich source of learning. Third, I want to show how the benchmarking technique can be successfully applied to a wide cross section of topics, problems, and—most importantly—processes. Finally, I hope the book will provide a safe place where those interested in benchmarking can go and learn—and learn quickly. This will save time, and, therefore, speed the interest in benchmarking and its application.

There are 27 cases included in the book: seven in manufacturing; seven in service; four from nonprofits; six in government; and three from educational institutions. They come from all corners of the globe: seven from the United States; five from Australia; three from the United Kingdom; two each from Italy, New Zealand, and India; and one each from Canada, Brazil, Japan, Norway, Singapore, and South Africa.

The processes are equally diverse. They are from oil well casing delivery (manufacturing); successful improvement and change (service); coronary artery bypass surgery (nonprofits); complaint handling (government); and student advising (education). The diversity is covered in several summary charts that are meant to give an overview and snapshot of their various facets, namely, case summary information, countries and industries, and processes; and, in the "Analysis" sections, charts covering savings and benefits, best practices found, and lessons learned.

There is also considerable variation in methodology. Most cases cover the classic approach to best practice benchmarking of a significant process. A select few cases show how benchmarking was established in a new section of the globe. Some may observe that those are not true benchmarking cases, but they do serve to get benchmarking started. That can be vitally important, and can eventually generate cases from those countries. One common thread among all the cases is the richness of lessons learned for those that study this compendium.

The book has some admitted gaps. The education sector (part 6) is limited to higher education. There is no application to K–12 schools or community colleges. The nonprofit sector (part 4) lacks cases from Europe where they are known to exist. There is little application to small and medium-sized enterprises, or SMEs as they are known overseas. Organizations from these areas were invited to participate and some committed to the project, but were not forthcoming. It is hoped that this book will motivate them to document their experiences in additional case studies.

Readers should also appreciate that the case studies vary from the flexible application of the benchmarking methodology to the rigorous use of the model. There is a wide variety presented. All of the cases are legitimate approaches to benchmarking as this is an adaptable process, evidenced by the innovative approaches in the cases themselves. Those pursuing benchmarking should, however, understand the risks of not finding best practices from the less-rigorous approaches. At the same time, however, they should appreciate the significant opportunities of best practice understanding from the disciplined approaches, where success is predictably higher.

This book has taken nearly two years to prepare. This dates some of the material since time has passed since the projects were completed and the authors put pen to paper. It would have been instructive to provide a last-minute update to all of the cases on what has happened since they were written. That, however, is left to the readers' interest and inquisitiveness. Authors' contact information, including E-mail addresses, are provided at the end of each case study if readers want those final insights. I am certain the authors would welcome feedback and readers' indications of their interest in a particular case study.

Ultimately, the editor is at the mercy of those who want to contribute—something over which I have no control. I can only provide the enthusiasm and passion for wanting to spread the benefits of best practices understanding worldwide.

To the readers I commend this book in your library. May it serve to expand your understanding and interest in this important, globally spreading, improvement approach. To the contributing authors and their supporting organizations, I extend my heartfelt thanks and gratitude for taking the lead and devoting the time and energy to this effort.

May you profit extensively from the recognition you receive. And to the hesitant, but potential, contributors who have a superb case bottled up inside you, I hope this book will show you that it is not that difficult to create a case study, and that you should try it. Keep in touch!

Robert C. Camp, Ph.D., P.E.
Best Practice Institute
625 Panorama Trail, Suite 1-200
Rochester, NY 14625-2432
Telephone: 716-248-5712
Facsimile: 716-248-2940
E-mail: rcampbpi@worldnet.att.net

PART 2: MANUFACTURING SECTOR

Introduction

The manufacturing sector includes seven cases from several industries including petroleum, beverages, wood products, and computer hardware. The geographic reach is into every major area of the globe, and the processes are varied as well. They include crude oil analysis, oil well casing delivery, building products manufacturing processes, mining operations, and computer software manufacture. A brief summary, background information, the rationale for each case, and key points to consider when reading follow.

Country:	United States
Organization:	Chevron Research and Technology Company
Industry:	Petroleum industry
Process:	Crude oil analysis
Case Study Title:	*"Crude Oil Analysis and Process Improvement at Chevron"*

Generally, petroleum companies have not been prominent in benchmarking until the past few years. But the recent work is very well done. Many of the hard lessons that had to be learned by trial and error in the early applications can now be avoided. This application to crude oil analysis is such a study. It was done thoroughly and quickly, and was focused on a key area of high leverage to meet customer requirements.

The study also showcases the focus on a "balanced scorecard" of measures, namely quality (accuracy), cycle time (delivery), and cost. It provides the insight that concentration on cycle time and quality will automatically lead to reduced cost. What is not mentioned is that the reverse is not necessarily true; that is, that concentration on cost reduction will result in quality and cycle time improvements. It is interesting that all steps of the crude oil analysis process were evaluated for consequences in each of these scorecard areas. Differences were found and became a major portion of the findings.

The team deployment flowchart is an excellent example of how a project can be mapped to show the sequence of activities, responsibilities, and time line for consensus and key milestone tracking and reporting. The development of a detailed questionnaire and a walk-through of the process gave the team valuable insight that paid off in the analysis phase.

Country:	Norway
Organization:	StatOil
Industry:	Petroleum industry
Process:	Oil well casing delivery
Case Study Title:	*"Benchmarking the Delivery Process of Casing for Oil Wells at StatOil"*

This case study is an excellent example of the proper execution of the key steps of a benchmarking project for a manufacturer. Many of the lessons learned are transferable to any benchmarking investigation. The cost-effective and timely delivery of the oil well casing or "drill pipe" is a critical process to keeping capital- and operationally intense drilling platforms fully utilized. This has to be a core process for an oil exploration and production department.

Several unique refinements to the classical benchmarking process were pursued by StatOil. One was conducting an initial scoping of project costs and benefits to act as a guide for project selection. This is also important since it was one of the earliest tests of the benchmarking approach. Mapping the process flow to "identify bottlenecks, causal relationships, and improvement areas" and to serve as the basis for "designing a questionnaire" are proof statements of the value of this activity. The questionnaire should be a direct result of, and be directly tied to, the map.

The result of analyzing the findings from the benchmarking partners allowed the construction of three different models of best practice processes. This gave a rich source of insight to the redesign of StatOil's eventual process. And, as is usually found, there were many additional potential improvement areas identified from this resource. It was a time- and objective-controlled project that will continue to add benefits when those follow-on projects are completed.

StatOil also took the opportunity to present and review its project with potential partners for complete understanding and partner qualification. The information exchange meetings with partners, following their questionnaire completion with functionally knowledgeable StatOil personnel who had a "stake in this process," was instrumental in making the analysis quite efficient, with results understood and accepted. These are all excellent extensions of the basic benchmarking approach.

Country:	United Kingdom
Organization:	Allied Domecq Spirits & Wine Ltd.
Industry:	Beverage and spirits industry
Process:	Executive information systems
Case Study Title:	*"Delivering Information at Allied Domecq Spirits & Wine Ltd."*

The focus of this case study is the development of an executive information system through benchmarking. The objective was to provide a process that would "organize, filter, and focus external and internal information critical to success." It is, perhaps, a classic in the lessons learned from the organization and the management of the benchmarking team. Starting from a small, three-person team—including the addition of a consultant, to the involvement of a steering group—task forces focused on specific, critical success factors and the involvement of those affected, such as data custodians. Teams finding that nomenclature between the benchmarking partners was not consistent and "meant different things to different people" reinforced the need for consistent process mapping, definition of terms, and the creation of a glossary to gain a quick and common understanding that would uncover best practices. In this case it was revealing that the benchmarking visits served to confirm "what not to do."

This case study reinforces the opportunity for identifying unique best practices when the project is properly organized and the right participants are involved. The case includes a map that, unlike the standard benchmarking process, procedurally defines what to do as well as why. Because of the need for improving productivity, benchmarking information technology is a major thrust. But many extensive benchmarking projects have been unsuccessful in attaining their desired results. Therefore, this case study should be instrumental in detailing the factors for success.

Country:	Italy
Organization:	3M
Industry:	Manufacturing industry
Process:	General ledger consolidation
Case Study Title:	*"General Ledger and Consolidation Processes: The Experience of 3M Italy"*

The accounting and finance organizations within industrial firms, as well as their associations such as the Institute of Chartered Accountants, have actively embraced best practice benchmarking. This is a commendable approach for a function that is, by its nature, focused on the outcomes and analytical understanding of organizations. This poses, however, some major challenges. Not only would the benchmarking study have to deal with an extreme amount of detail, but it would also have to deal with the rules and regulations of accounting convention; that is, what is known as "commonly accepted accounting practice." While taking these hurdles into account, there is the matter of international focus where conventions vary by country. Thus, the benchmarking task must look insurmountable, and that is why this classic case study has a decidedly international twist.

What this study required was a carefully planned project that detailed and defined the processes upfront. Hastily making comparisons among partners to gain insight into the best practice process differences would most likely have failed in this attempt to transform an accounting information system. The project is commendable in the level of preparation in defining the boundaries and key elements of the process.

This was accomplished by successive levels of detail in defining the process. First, the major boundaries and elements were defined. Second, the major transaction processes were delineated including their rules, data, and activities. Finally, an additional, in-depth definition was developed. This led to the final agreement of the five major subprocesses, with clear activities, boundaries, and a glossary of terminology. This level of process classification and process element definition is an excellent example of what may be required of other complicated processes.

Country:	New Zealand
Organization:	Fletcher Challenge Building Products Sector
Industry:	Wood products industry
Process:	Best practices in manufacturing
Case Study Title:	*"A Journey Without End: Best Practice in the Building Products Sector of Fletcher Challenge"*

Few organizations can look back over the past five years and derive a sense of satisfaction from having a planned, structured set of learning experiences focused on insights to best practices on which to base their operations. Fletcher Challenge's Building Products Sector has pursued just such a journey. In the manufacturing and distribution of its products the Sector's managers know they must achieve excellence to improve shareholder value and retain a superior competitive position. It is instructive as to how this was done through several carefully planned study tours and the capture of the learnings for use internally.

The inaugural study tour was in 1993, and was preceded by extensive collective agreement on the focus areas, research on the best practice partner companies, and the team approach to preparation ensuring ownership of the findings. The first study tour covered five topics and 10 prominent, U.S.-based companies. None was in the same industry as Fletcher Challenge.

A second study tour to one U.S.-based company followed in 1995. And in the same year a third study tour was conducted on a core competency, manufacturing, to eight prominent Australian firms. Six main learning areas were covered in this third tour. In

1996, nine companies in the United States and Europe were visited for the fourth tour with eight focus areas of significant interest. Out of these visits came an internal assessment tool that lead to a newly established Business Improvement Award.

As a result of the assessments, a fifth study tour in 1996—to 16 firms in the United States, United Kingdom, and New Zealand—focused on three additional topics. And again in 1996, the need in a particular distribution network led to yet another study tour through New Zealand and Australia.

This pattern of an initially planned tour leading to six others is a commendable exercise of the best practice benchmarking approach. Each successive set of learnings led to other areas of critical need. In all cases, those with the need participated in the tour planning, partner visits, findings report preparation, and the dissemination of information to their affected organizations. All this was done after the best practices had been thoroughly analyzed.

Country:	India
Organization:	NIIT
Industry:	Software manufacturing industry
Process:	Hardware procurement
Case Study Title:	*"Hardware Procurement at NIIT"*

There are several ways to focus projects. The traditional, if not knee-jerk, reaction is to concentrate on cost reduction. This is a study of the benefits of analyzing the problem or process through the focus on cycle time. That is to say, simplifying the process to reduce the cycle time. Therefore, cost reduction would be a fall out of the analysis.

A preliminary analysis revealed that the price of nonconformance (PONC) was very substantial. This was evidenced by long cycle times, percent promised delivery dates missed, renting replacement machines for the period of the delay and/or project execution delays, and loss of reputation. The last item is extremely important for a software development and manufacturing organization such as NIIT. On-time delivery of software is a vital measurement in that industry.

Country:	South Africa
Organization:	Ingwe Coal Corporation
Industry:	Mining and minerals industry
Process:	Continuous miner delays
Case Study Title:	*"An Internal Benchmarking Study of Continuous Miner Operations Within Ingwe Coal Corporation"*

This case study capitalizes on an opportunity that is available to many organizations, namely to conduct an intensive internal benchmarking investigation as the first step of a comprehensive best practice search project. The internal benchmarking approach can do many things, including the following:

- Prove the worth of benchmarking.
- Provide practice in executing a benchmarking study.
- Prepare the team for external visits and comparisons.
- Identify many "better" practices if not best practices.

With eight underground mining operations and a potential of 25 operating sections per mine, and the operation of 90 continuous miner machines, the opportunity for internal comparisons at Ingwe was pervasive. There were also significant differences in the outputs of these mining operations, varying from 40,000 to 70,000 tons per month. This difference in magnitude created a major opportunity to carefully document the processes and compare them to uncover the differences in practices followed. And that is exactly what Ingwe Coal did!

Ingwe exercised the full rigor of the benchmarking process in applying it to the continuous miner operations. This is exemplified in the project description where the charter, initiative, goals, process focus, scope, and team operations of the study were documented. This included supporting cause-and-effect diagram analyses of the basic problem (which was stated as "continuous miner delays reduced"), a detailed flowchart for the mining cycle, and a questionnaire/checklist to gather data and information during the targeted site visits.

This case study is an exemplary execution of the benchmarking process. It carefully and concisely summarizes what and how the study will accomplish along with its potential justification. Specifically, the use of the project description at the end of the first step of the benchmarking process is highly recommended. By that time the team has conducted some important activities, and has fully delineated the scope and boundaries of the project. It is an excellent place to summarize the now-more-refined view of the project, and gain acceptance for the remaining steps that will consume potentially significant time and resources.

Readers should note well the concise yet thorough treatment of the project description that this case study exemplifies.

Master Table

United States	Europe	Asia/Pacific	Americas/Africa
MANUFACTURING			
UNITED STATES	NORWAY	NEW ZEALAND	SOUTH AFRICA
Chevron Research and Technology Company	**StatOil**	**Fletcher Challenge Building Products Sector**	**Ingwe Coal Corporation**
Petroleum industry	Petroleum industry	Wood products industry	Mining and minerals industry
Crude oil analysis	*Oil well casing delivery*	*Best practices in manufacturing*	*Continuous miner delays*
"Crude Oil Analysis and Process Improvement at Chevron"	"Benchmarking the Delivery Process of Casing for Oil Wells at StatOil"	"A Journey Without End: Best Practice in the Building Products Sector of Fletcher Challenge"	"An Internal Benchmarking Study of Continuous Miner Operations Within Ingwe Coal Corporation"
	UNITED KINGDOM	INDIA	
	Allied Domecq Spirits & Wines Ltd.	**NIIT**	
	Beverages and spirits industry	Software manufacturing industry	
	Executive information systems	*Hardware procurement*	
	"Delivering Information at Allied Domecq Spirits & Wine Ltd."	"Hardware Procurement at NIIT"	
	ITALY		
	3M		
	Manufacturing industry		
	General ledger consolidation		
	"General Ledger and Consolidation Processes: The Experience of 3M Italy"		

Country and Industry

United States	Europe	Asia/Pacific	Americas/Africa
MANUFACTURING UNITED STATES Petroleum industry	NORWAY Petroleum industry UNITED KINGDOM Beverages and spirits industry ITALY Manufacturing industry	NEW ZEALAND Wood products industry INDIA Software manufacturing industry	SOUTH AFRICA Mining and minerals industry

Processes

United States	Europe	Asia/Pacific	Americas/Africa
MANUFACTURING UNITED STATES *Crude oil analysis*	NORWAY *Oil well casing delivery* UNITED KINGDOM *Executive information systems* ITALY *General ledger consolidation*	NEW ZEALAND *Best practices in manufacturing* INDIA *Hardware procurement*	SOUTH AFRICA *Continuous miner delays*

CHAPTER 1

Crude Oil Analysis and Process Improvement at Chevron

Derek L. Ransley, President, Ransley & Associates

Study Purpose

Crude oils vary considerably in their composition, which makes some easier to process than others. Thus, different crudes have different values to the refiner. The analysis of crude oil is critical to the functioning of an oil company. The information from such analysis is used to make crude oil purchasing decisions and on how a refinery is to be run. Although Chevron's budget for crude oil analysis was less than $1 million dollars, the customers estimated that crude analysis impacted decisions totaling more than $50 million annually.

The customers were satisfied with the quality of the analyses but were not satisfied with the time required for the analysis or the cost. After discussions with customers, the study team set itself the goal of reducing costs by 20 percent and cycle time by 50 percent while maintaining quality.

Study Team and Approach

A five-person cross-functional team was formed to conduct the study. Four members were intimately involved with various steps in the crude oil analysis process. One person was from the distillation section, another represented the analytical laboratory, and two others had overall responsibility for the data collection, analysis, and reporting of the final product. The author provided the benchmarking expertise.

There was also an advisory committee of sponsors of the study. This was the management of the various team members.

Chevron has a quality improvement process (QIP), which follows the Xerox model and was well integrated into the organization. Benchmarking was less well understood. The team took a benchmarking training class from the author prior to project initiation.

At the outset, the team recognized that the approach would combine the Chevron QIP, benchmarking, and cycle time reduction techniques. These techniques focus on the details of the existing process and seek ways to eliminate non–value-adding steps. Experience has shown that reduction in cycle time is accompanied by a reduction in cost and an improvement in quality.

An early team activity was the development of a road map (a deployment flowchart) of the team's activities. This is shown in Figure 1.1. This road map is an important tool that acts as a guide to the team, a good communication tool for sponsor/advisory committee meetings, and a record of the study at the end.

Team members agreed on their charter, ground rules, and the boundaries of the project. The charter and boundaries were developed in informal interactions with the advisory committee and client representatives. Team members who had overall responsibility for the crude oil analysis process were often in direct contact with their clients, so those members were aware of customer concerns.

The ground rules were agreed upon within the team. There was a feeling that the team would likely need to make decisions where complete agreement was unlikely. The agreement was to go with the majority vote in those instances.

Next, the team identified customers and stakeholders, and reviewed the crude oil analysis process. The first major class of customer for the crude oil analyses were those people within the company who had responsibility for crude oil purchases. A given crude oil can have different values to different companies because of differences in composition. A difference of one cent per barrel can make a $10 million/year difference to a company spending $20 billion on $20/barrel crude oil. This indicates how valuable the analysis is to a crude buyer and the leverage when dealing with such large volumes.

The second major class of customer is the refinery planner; that is the person who has to decide how the refinery will run the crude oil acquired by the buyer. Different refineries have different equipment, which can handle a different array of crude oils. The ideal situation would be one in which a single crude oil is run for a given refinery. In that case, the refinery could be designed or set up to run a single crude. Most refineries, however, run a mix of crudes, and the analysis shows which ones can be run. As an example, a crude is of lower value if it has a high sulfur content. A refinery that is equipped to remove sulfur would run this crude while another refinery that is not so equipped would not be able to run this material.

The team members also represented others associated with the crude analysis. For instance, there are many different analytical laboratories involved with the crude analysis, and those workers are stakeholders in the process. The team was charged with considering all stakeholder issues during its study.

The team members had varying levels of experience with the crude oil analysis process. The team did a walk-through of the process. That is, the team observed the incoming crude being tested to determine if it was a good sample. Then a crude oil was observed as it was being loaded into the still for distillation, and the operators were questioned about the distillation process and their key issues.

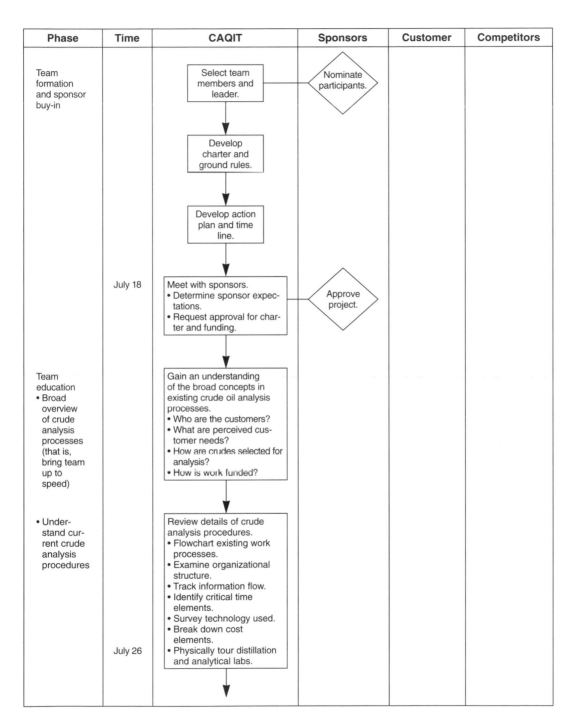

Figure 1.1. Crude analysis quality improvement team deployment flowchart.

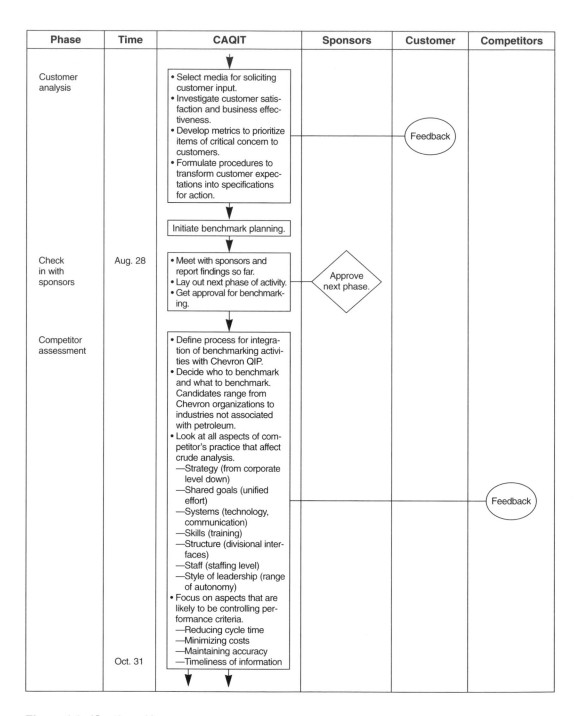

Phase	Time	CAQIT	Sponsors	Customer	Competitors
Customer analysis		• Select media for soliciting customer input. • Investigate customer satisfaction and business effectiveness. • Develop metrics to prioritize items of critical concern to customers. • Formulate procedures to transform customer expectations into specifications for action.		Feedback	
		Initiate benchmark planning.			
Check in with sponsors	Aug. 28	• Meet with sponsors and report findings so far. • Lay out next phase of activity. • Get approval for benchmarking.	Approve next phase.		
Competitor assessment		• Define process for integration of benchmarking activities with Chevron QIP. • Decide who to benchmark and what to benchmark. Candidates range from Chevron organizations to industries not associated with petroleum. • Look at all aspects of competitor's practice that affect crude analysis. —Strategy (from corporate level down) —Shared goals (unified effort) —Systems (technology, communication) —Skills (training) —Structure (divisional interfaces) —Staff (staffing level) —Style of leadership (range of autonomy) • Focus on aspects that are likely to be controlling performance criteria. —Reducing cycle time —Minimizing costs —Maintaining accuracy —Timeliness of information			Feedback
	Oct. 31				

Figure 1.1. *(Continued.)*

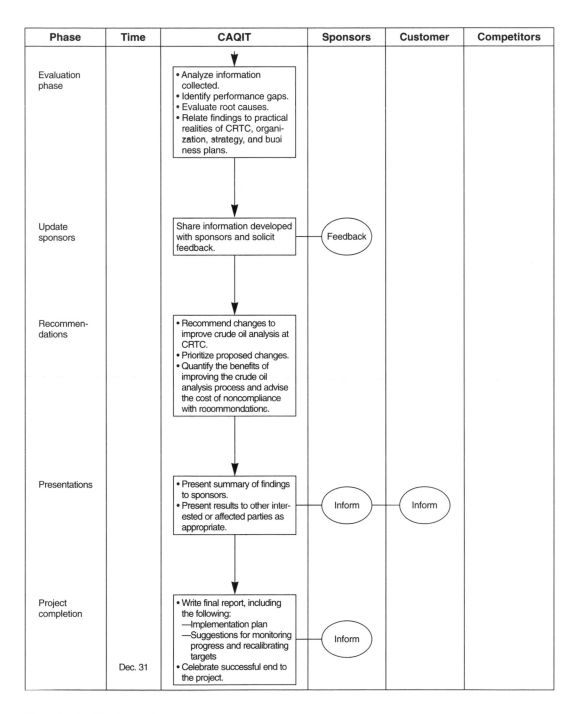

Figure 1.1. *(Continued.)*

In the distillation process the temperature is increased so that different components boil and can be separated. These fractions are then further divided and placed into vials and sent for the specific set of analyses required. The team talked to people in the various laboratories about the issues they faced. The analytical results were accumulated and the sort of information that was built into the final document was observed. Not only did the walk-through give a better overall picture of the process, but it also helped with team building, because various team members took the lead at different stages of the walk-through.

The team set a timetable and methodology that would be used, and targeted some companies for inclusion in the study. The timetable that was established is shown as part of Figure 1.1. After the early stages, this time frame turned out to be too ambitious because it was difficult to build the questionnaire to everyone's satisfaction, and the responses from participants took longer partly because of the length of the questionnaire.

The methodology used in the study was influenced by some success the author experienced in applying cycle time reduction methodology to a different project. In this approach, a process is segmented into its main subprocesses, and each subprocess is examined for its impact on the overall cost of the process, its time requirement, and its impact on the overall quality of the process. Steps in the process that added no value were also sought.

Standard benchmarking techniques were to be applied. The team felt that the necessary data were best gathered through a written response to a questionnaire with follow-up phone calls to clarify any points that were unclear. The team was also influenced by the exposure to the QIP model that routinely was applied to many situations at the Chevron Research and Technology Company (CRTC) (Figure 1.2). The team agreed that combining all three approaches would work well for this project.

The experts on the team were well aware of some of the top performers in crude oil analysis. There is almost a brotherhood of those who do this type of work, and it exists on an international level. Representation from those the team thought to be the best performers was desired so that the best elements from each could be used to reach an understanding of what a best process could look like. Some of the companies that provided crude oil analysis as a service were thought to have some techniques or skills that were not known to the study team. Finally, input from laboratories in different industries, which might have some unique approaches, was sought.

As is common practice in benchmarking, it was agreed that the names of the participating companies would be kept confidential to the group of participants.

Customer data were collected via a written questionnaire. The questions asked were as follows:

1. How important are crude oil assay data to the decisions your organization makes?

2. What is the annual financial impact of the decisions that rely on crude oil assay data?

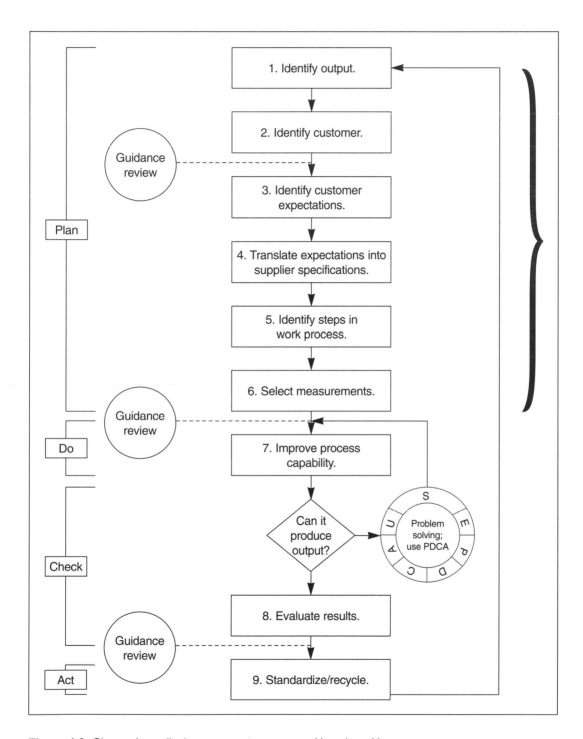

Figure 1.2. Chevron's quality improvement process and benchmarking process.

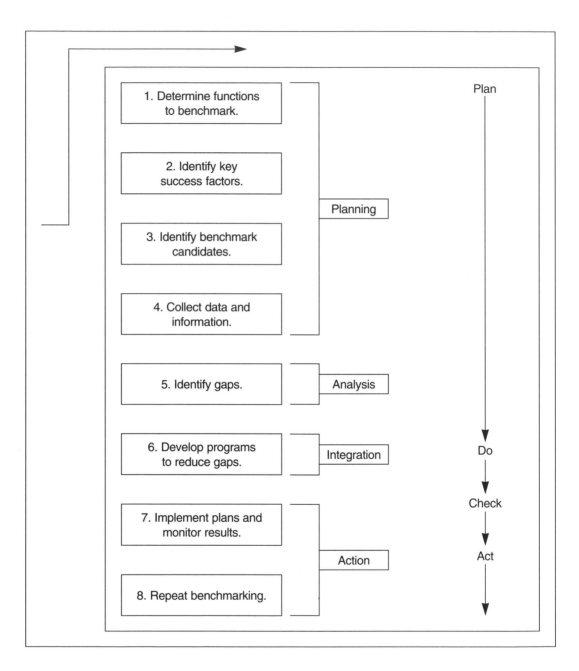

Figure 1.2. *(Continued.)*

3. Rank the following in order of importance in applying crude oil assays to meet your organization's business objectives.

  • Elapsed time to completion

  • Cost

  • Accuracy of data

  • Easy access to data

  • On-time delivery

  • All equally important

4. Is the current crude oil assay process well aligned with your organization's objectives?

5. How are we doing in the elements mentioned in Question 3?

6. Would you be willing to trade off some of your autonomy to participate in a corporate-wide assay program?

7. To what extent are you willing to trade off accuracy for time or cost?

8. Are there specific pieces of information that you would be willing to forgo to improve turnaround time or cost?

9. To what extent would you be willing to sacrifice the proprietary protection CRTC offers for cheaper or faster service by an outside company?

10. What would you do if CRTC stopped providing crude oil assay services?

11. What changes do you foresee in your needs for crude oil assay services?

12. Please provide information on how your organization operates in issues related to crude oil assay services.

  • How are funding decisions made?

  • Who makes the decisions on what assays to fund?

  • Who decides what assay data are needed?

  • Who secures the sample for analysis?

  • How are assay data shared throughout your organization?

  • How is management made aware of these activities?

The responses to these questions indicated that customers were satisfied with the quality of the crude oil assay service but wanted faster turnaround time and lower costs. They also showed some willingness for trade-offs but not much change in the type of information they would need. The team also learned that different organizations had slightly different processes for decision making on issues related to crude oil assays.

In parallel with this effort, the team worked to understand the existing process by interviewing stakeholders, visiting work sites, and process flowcharting. The crude analysis process was viewed as a 10-step process as follows:

1. Contracting for an assay. Discussion with a customer about which crude to analyze and what level of detail was required.

2. Acquiring the crude oil sample. Carefully collecting a representative sample from the well that produced that crude.

3. Verifying the quality of the sample received.

4. Separating the sample into fractions. Distillation.

5. Distributing the samples for analysis. A portion of each fraction is transferred to a sample container, labeled, and sent for one of several different types of analyses.

6. Analyzing the crude and the samples.

7. Accumulating the analytical results.

8. Evaluating the data.

9. Building the database.

10. Reporting the results to the customer.

Although step 1 is not formally part of the process it has such a major impact that it was important that it be included.

The team examined each of these steps from the perspective of time, cost, and quality. This was a very valuable exercise. For instance, the distillation step added very little to cost or cycle time, but without a good quality distillation subsequent work was useless. Thus, more attention was made to ensuring good quality distillation than shaving time or reducing costs for step 4. Similarly, the analyses of the samples were already good quality, but time could be easily lost in testing and tracking multiple samples.

Benchmarking

Those team members who were responsible for the overall coordination of the crude oil analysis effort had developed personal relationships with their counterparts in other major oil companies. This facilitated the participation of these companies in this study. Much time was spent in developing a questionnaire. All participants agreed to complete it. This resulted in a much more detailed document than the team would have wished. The final questionnaire was 33 pages long and contained 116 questions.

Companies that offered crude oil analysis as a service were included in the study. Also included was the clinical laboratory of a local hospital because of its perceived parallel with the laboratories at CRTC. The hospital lab has to deal with multiple samples being sent for a variety of tests, and the results accumulated into an overall record for physicians. Speed and accuracy are critical. The team hoped to learn how the samples were labeled, handled, and tracked. In all, there were 17 participants, including Chevron, in the study.

Besides the walk-through of the process, the team also completed detailed flowcharts of the existing process. This rather tedious process resulted in a 14-page flowchart. It did give the team a way to thoroughly examine the process and the flow between steps, and helped to identify redundancies or time-wasting steps.

Questions were asked about the details of each of the 10 steps of the process. In addition, questions about cost per assay and cycle time and what the team called "project orientation" were also asked. This last item meant that all the distillation cuts and subsequent samples were carried through the process together. This eliminated those situations when a few samples that were trailing through the analysis step held up the overall completion of the assay.

The team used quantitative and qualitative judgments to select best practices. The responses related to cost and cycle time influenced the team's selection of best practices. Other practices were recommended because they seemed to address a problem or issue that had been raised in the team's preliminary work. In other cases what was learned simply made sense.

In some instances, companies were reluctant to tell the team their absolute numbers, particularly on cost, but were willing to break down the cost and time into percentages of the whole 10-step process. Responses for a given step differed by an order of magnitude in some cases. For example, the time to acquire a sample (step 2) was 20 percent to 25 percent of the total time for one company but only 1 percent to 2 percent of the time for another. This type of outcome could lead to an erroneous conclusion if the only focus was on the cycle time for each subprocess. That is, a company that spends 20 percent to 25 percent of its total cycle time on acquiring oil samples might logically conclude that something needs to be done to speed up sample acquisition.

Examination of the benchmarking data, however, led to a far different conclusion. Sample acquisition for best practice companies added little or no time to the analysis cycle. The reason is that these companies plan in advance those crudes that need to be analyzed. Having this plan allows samples to be requisitioned long before this step assumes the role of a detrimental, critical path item. Those companies that do not have a plan are faced with delays associated with obtaining the sample.

A spider diagram was used to identify those companies who were best practice in each of the 10 process steps and in cost, cycle time, and project orientation. A category for research that was being done by the participants to improve the process was also added. Of the 14 categories where judgments were made, one company scored eight bests or shared bests (Company C in Figure 1.3); another scored seven bests (Company E in Figure 1.3); and a third scored three bests. This, once again, demonstrates the value of benchmarking with several partners. No one company is best in all categories, and the accumulation of information provides the opportunity to leapfrog and become better than the best.

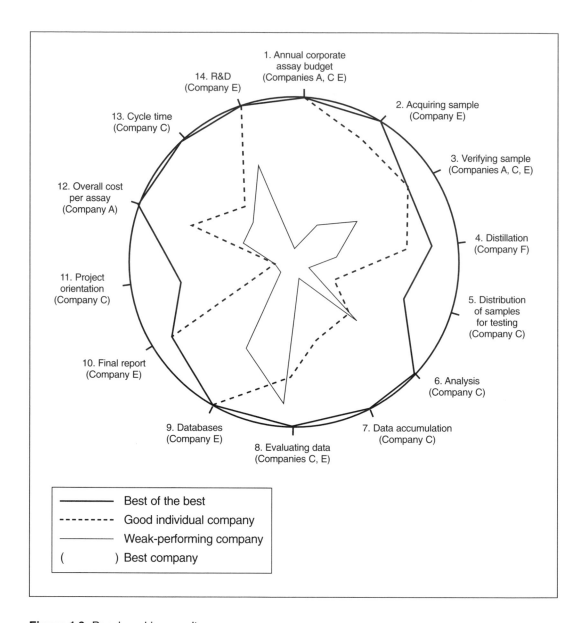

Figure 1.3. Benchmarking results.

A spider diagram for all participants is very complicated. Included in Figure 1.3 are the highest scores achieved in all categories (the best of the best), together with the results from a good performer (Company E) and a weak performer. This again illustrates that no one company is best in every category.

Change Recommendations

The recommendations were presented in tabular form, which identified the study findings, the recommendations, and the impact in a recommended implementation sequence. These included the following:

- Implement an annual funding process for a base load assay program that is aligned with business objectives.
- Adopt a project orientation strategy for all interrelated work associated with crude oil assays. This includes a cross-unit crude assay team, standard assays with fixed time and price contracts, logical sequencing of samples in the information management system, and automation of the process.
- Ally the cross-unit assay team with other teams doing related work.
- Enter into a fixed-price contract with customers for any one of several standard assays.
- Improve the in-house information management system.
- Automate the sample tagging process.
- Use quality manuals to document and control standards for data passed from one work unit to another.
- Implement a quality assurance program in the separations laboratory and investigate the use of state-of-the-art fractionation equipment.
- Create a direct interface between the new crude data system and the laboratory information management system.
- Build the new crude data system with features to computerize most of the crude oil assay data evaluation work.
- Provide the capability to transfer crude oil assay data directly into user systems.
- Improve the turnaround time for those tests that most frequently are on the critical path or replace them with better turnaround time .
- Consolidate the number of different laboratories conducting analyses associated with the process.
- Have meetings between the customers and those doing the analyses so that there is a better appreciation for the importance of the analyses to the company.
- Develop quality assurance testing with standard crudes.

In all, there were 24 recommendations with a suggested timetable for implementation. These were accompanied by suggestions for who should have implementation action and responsibility. Estimates were made for the cost of implementation of each recommendation.

Implementation

There has been ongoing implementation of the study findings. The timetable for implementation depended on the resources and agreements needed. In principle, the annual budgeting process required no additional resources but there was a need for agreement from the various customers to implement the recommendation. This became a political issue, and a senior manager was asked to lead this effort. The team's timetable suggested that this should take no more than three months because the return was so obvious.

The implementation of project orientation could occur within three months although some trial and error was expected before it would run smoothly. It was suggested that a team of people at the working level be responsible for implementation.

Automation of sample tagging was perceived as something that could be implemented almost immediately. A working team was to be responsible and would agree on the process, identify tagging requirements, and communicate its coding suggestions.

There were some long-term implementation items too. There was a significant amount of work needed to be able to build assay data processing features into a new crude data system. This required the time and availability of certain experts and funding for them to provide their services. An optimistic nine months were allowed for this to occur. The work that was needed included analyzing the existing work processes, investigating existing commercial systems, designing and programming a new data processing system, and then testing and implementing it.

Lessons Learned

1. Integration of the QIP, benchmarking, and some elements of cycle time reduction was proven successful during this project.

2. Taking benchmarking training together gave the team a common basis for the study and aided team building.

3. A small, cross-functional team was effective.

4. The development of a road map for the project was very valuable during the study and became a useful record afterward.

5. The project did not meet its timing targets for completion. This created a dilemma as organizational structure and reporting relationships changed during the project.

6. The physical walk-through was useful.

7. Breaking the overall project into its 10 subprocesses was very useful. It established clear boundaries and enabled prioritization of cost, time, and quality issues.

8. The relationships with industry contacts that the team had established ahead of the project facilitated participation.

9. The team would have benefited from active and critical involvement of an industry partner in developing its questionnaire. The questionnaire was too long, and some questions were interesting rather than actionable. An outsider's perspective might have detected these problems.

Acknowledgments

Thanks are due to teammates Mike Henley, Anne Shafizadeh, and Jeff Toman, and team leader Chet James.

References

Furey, Timothy R. 1993. A six-step guide to process engineering. *Planning Review* (March/April): 20–23.

Meyer, Christopher, and Ronald E. Purser. 1993. Six steps to becoming a fast-cycle time competitor. *Research Technology Management* (September/October): 41–48.

Thomas, Phillip R., with Kenneth R. Martin. 1990. *Competitiveness through total cycle time.* New York: McGraw-Hill.

About the Author

Derek L. Ransley recently retired from Chevron Research and Technology Company (CRTC) in Richmond, California, after more than 34 years of service. He currently consults on technology management and benchmarking from Lafayette, California. His work over the last seven years at Chevron was as a senior planning consultant specializing in competitor assessment, benchmarking, best practices, cycle time reduction, and related quality improvement tools, mostly in technology-related areas. Prior to starting his quality work Ransley was involved in research and research management in the petrochemicals sector.

Ransley has published widely on his quality-related work. Recent articles in *Research Technology Management* include "Alignment-to-Partnership" (in press); "Upgrade Your Patenting Process (with Richard C. Gaffney, May/June 1997); "Network More Effectively with This Checklist" (November/December 1995); and "A Framework for R&D Performance Measures" (with Donna Prestwood and Paul Schumann, Jr., May/June 1995). With P. M. Stonebraker and others, Ransley presented "Chevron Material Safety Data Sheet System: The Next Generation" at the Third Annual Fuels and Lubes Asia Conference in Singapore in January 1997.

Ransley is active in the Industrial Research Institute and the Association of Internal Management Consultants. He received a bachelor of science from the University of Wales

(Cardiff) in 1956 and a master's of science and Ph.D. in organic chemistry from Yale University in 1959 and 1962 respectively. He joined Chevron in 1962.

Derek L. Ransley
3125 Withers Avenue
Lafayette, CA 94549
U.S.A.
Telephone: 510-906-0346
Facsimile: 510-906-0376
E-mail: dransley@aol.com

Chevron Research and Technology Company
P.O. Box 1627
Richmond, CA 94802
U.S.A.

CHAPTER 2

Benchmarking the Delivery Process of Casing for Oil Wells at StatOil

Finn Strand, Corporate Advisor–Health, Environment, and Safety Staff, StatOil

StatOil is a company that searches for, produces, transports, and markets petroleum and petroleum-derived products. It is a public corporation that is fully owned by the Norwegian government. Sales in 1996 were approximately $16 billion, with about 15,000 employees. StatOil is divided into 14 business units.

Within the exploration and development (Norway) unit, there is a department named drilling and well technology (D&W). On assignment from management, D&W, in 1994, conducted a benchmarking study of the delivery process of casing for the oil wells.

The Benchmarking Process at StatOil

One possible model of the benchmarking process is described in this chapter. This is obviously just a suggestion for how a benchmarking study can be conducted. Most companies that actively use benchmarking have developed their own models. This is also true for StatOil, who performs its benchmarking studies according to the process shown in Figure 2.1. Another benchmarking model, shown as a wheel, is illustrated in Figure 2.2.

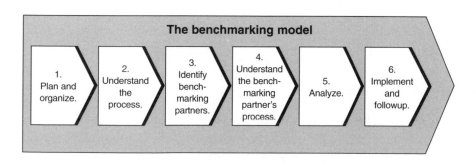

Figure 2.1. StatOil's benchmarking process.

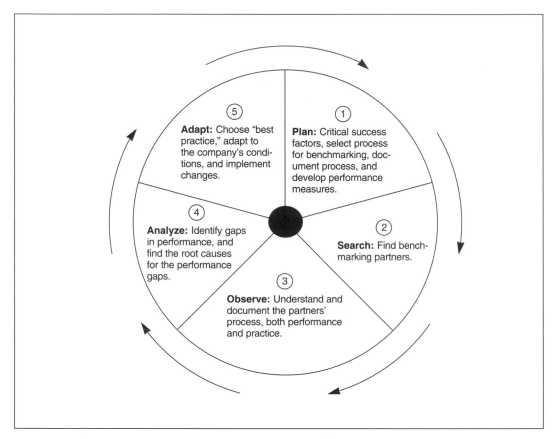

Source: Anderson, Bjørn, and Per-Gaute Pettersen. 1995. *The benchmarking handbook: Step-by-step instructions.* English translation published by New York: Chapman & Hall, a division of Routledge. Used with permission.

Figure 2.2. The benchmarking wheel.

Even though the appearance of the two models is quite different, the content is much the same. The first two phases of the StatOil model roughly correspond to the planning phase of the benchmarking wheel. Otherwise, the content of the last four phases is almost identical.

Plan and Organize

Organizing the Project

The benchmarking study was organized by a steering committee and a project group. The steering committee had the main responsibility for the project and consisted of three persons. The operative unit in the project was the project group, consisting of seven persons, including the project manager. These seven people belong to different departments that all have some connection to this process. As a resource of competency within benchmarking, one person from the corporate quality department participated in the project group. In addition to these people, several others have taken part in the study for various periods of time. To assure the best possible implementation of the identified improvements (step 6 of the StatOil model), the process owner department—operations services (OS)—was made responsible for the project.

The study was started by designing a coarse activity plan for the project, including cost estimates. The duration of the study was estimated to six months, at a cost of about $330,000. Both estimates proved quite accurate; final costs were $340,000.

Selecting the Process to Be Benchmarked

When starting this benchmarking study, the commission and purpose were already given. The D&W benchmarking project's main objective was to reduce the costs of the delivery process of material and equipment to the oil wells. A secondary objective was to accumulate competency and experience in the use of benchmarking as a tool for continuous improvement. As this was a quite wide statement, it was necessary to make a more detailed specification of which process on which to focus. The choice was based on two main concerns: (1) The process must have an impact on customer satisfaction (external or internal customers); and (2) The process must display a potential for improvement and cost reduction.

Thus, the project group conducted an initial mapping of the delivery processes for different types of products, such as mud, well heads, casing, and so on. Based on this, it was decided to benchmark the delivery process of casing, due to the following reasons.

- Customer-supplier relationships and supplier requirements had to be diffused.
- Casing represents a major part of all costs.
- There are many stakeholders involved in the process.
- The delivery of casing has been kept outside another major improvement process within D&W.
- A high priority was to do a good job on one process instead of scattering the efforts over several processes.

Understand the Process

Mapping the Process Flow

A very important and time-consuming part of the benchmarking study was to identify and understand what factors were critical to performance and what results would be compared to other companies. To enable meaningful comparisons against external processes, the processes and systems that form the basis for the current performance had to be understood. The task of understanding StatOil's own process and performance included the following steps.

- Documenting the process through interviews and discussions with persons involved in it
- Representing the process with the help of process maps
- Assessing the use of resources (time and costs)
- Identifying bottlenecks, causal relationships, and improvement areas
- Designing a questionnaire to be used as a basis for comparison against benchmarking partners

The casing delivery process was documented through discussions in the project group and interviews with the persons involved in the process. Main topics for these interviews were as follows:

- Role in the process and relation to other players
- Products and services delivered and received
- Requirements to, and performance measures for, the process
- Cost elements, cost drivers, and non–value-added activities
- Problem areas and improvement suggestions

Interviews were conducted with a total of eight people, who also participated in a one-day seminar with the project group to coordinate findings. This way, agreement on and ownership of the assessment of the current situation were achieved. This assessment also led to the identification of improvements that could be implemented immediately. To visualize the collected information and make it easier to discuss the process, a process map was designed, as shown in Figure 2.3 in a simplified form.

The casing is bought from either Japanese, Mexican, or European manufacturers. All contact with the manufacturers—requests, signing contracts, and placing orders—are handled by a centralized purchasing unit in StatOil—contracts, purchasing, and relations (CPR). The casing is bought for delivery into a European harbor. Casing from European manufacturers is transported to Bremen by rail, while Mexican and Japanese casing is shipped to Antwerp. Reloading and negotiations of freight agreements for transport to the onshore bases in Norway are coordinated by a Norwegian freight company called Nor-Cargo.

The casing is shipped to StatOil's onshore base, which supplies the platforms with casing as the need is reported from the platforms. The reported need also includes backup, where the amount is calculated as a percentage of the total need. Superfluous casing when the drilling is finished is returned to the supply base, Coast Centre Base (CCB).

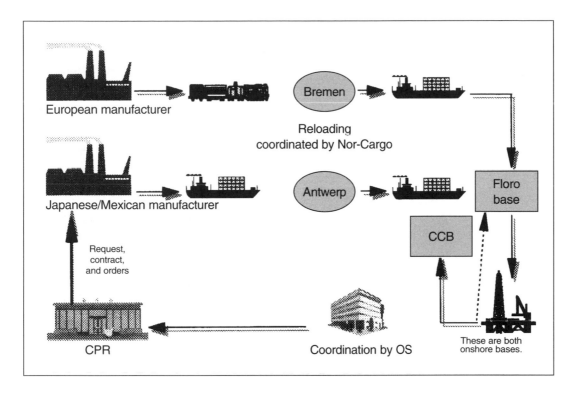

Figure 2.3. The process for ordering and delivery of casing.

Performance Measures for the Process

To be able to make meaningful comparisons against others, it was essential to understand performance. Therefore, in parallel with the process mapping, several performance indicators were identified. Examples are as follows:

- The number of variants of casing
- Lead time from the steelworks to the onshore base
- Turnaround of the inventory
- Price per ton of casing delivered to a European harbor
- Logistics costs for each link of the supply chain
- Inspection costs per ton of casing

Finding the numbers for these indicators for StatOil's process was a rather cumbersome job partly because StatOil had not been using an activity-based costing system.

Problem Areas and Improvement Opportunities

As noted, and as often is the case in benchmarking, the process mapping led to the identification of several problem areas and improvement opportunities. These included the following:

• *Supplier strategy.* StatOil uses five suppliers of casing, dealing directly with the steelworks and assuming responsibility for the casing as it arrives in the European harbors. When buying, the strategies of competitive bidding and lowest price are employed. It could not be documented that these were the best strategies for casing as a whole.

• *Base strategy.* This was identified as a potential cost driver in the process.

• *Specifications.* It can be questioned whether StatOil's requirements for preservation and other issues led to unnecessary costs. Furthermore, questions entail whether all requirements for loading, packaging, protection, and storage in all links were sufficiently cost efficient.

• *Platform operations.* Again, it was questioned whether some of these could be omitted or performed elsewhere.

• *The number of variants.* These were high and led to extra costs.

• *Throughput times.* The time from casing manufacture in Japan until it was used on board was usually about 14 months. Including planning and ordering, it was as much as 16 months. As such, a long throughput time seriously increased the probability that plans and needs would change during transport of the casing. The consequence was often an unwanted increase in inventory.

• *The use of backup.* There were indications that the practice of backup calculations was unnecessary and added substantial costs in the form of tied-up capital, transport, handling, and maintenance. This also applied to equipment other than the casing.

• *Planning/information.* Planning of demand, changes in plans, and poor communication were identified through interviews as driving up costs. The practice made it difficult to optimize process capacity, and the roles of the departments and persons involved were not clearly defined.

• *Financial management and performance measures.* Financial systems provided little opportunity for following up activity-based costs and allocating incurred costs to the casing. Very few measures of effectiveness and customer satisfaction had been established.

• *Continuous improvement of the processes.* The operative communication between all links in the process could be improved. Horizontal cooperation to improve the process had not been formalized, and no one had been given total responsibility for the delivery process.

Identify Benchmarking Partners

The project team faced the choice of finding benchmarking partners internally within StatOil, among other oil companies, or in other industries. The steering committee decided to select other international oil companies as benchmarking partners.

A two-step procedure was used to identify partners. First, five international oil companies were contacted and asked whether they would be willing to participate in a benchmarking cooperation. Four of the five answered positively.

Before making the final decision on whom to use as partners, a visit to all the four companies was performed. During this visit, StatOil and its project were presented. The questionnaire was also handed over to the other companies, who spent one week answering it before returning it to StatOil. After having considered the answers, the final decision on benchmarking partners was made.

Understand the Benchmarking Partner's Process

The next step in the project was to conduct meetings with the partners, with people in the process, to gain full understanding of the partner's process.

The benchmarking team had been composed of persons from most of the departments with a stake in this process. This now proved useful, as the analysis was quite efficient and the results were understood and accepted by all departments.

Before meeting with the partners, it was decided which areas to focus on and what roles the team members would fill during the visits. In the meetings with the partners, which lasted about one day, six persons from StatOil participated. The meetings were held at the partners' location.

The first weekday after such a meeting was spent in a full-day session to collect all material and information, document the partners' process, and analyze the gap compared to StatOil's process. These meetings were very useful and are recommended to avoid information being lost.

During the analysis of the collected information, it also proved necessary to recontact some of the partners to obtain supplementary information and to clear up confusion. This contact was made by phone and fax.

Analyze

Gap Analysis

The purpose of the gap analysis was to identify differences in performance and process content between StatOil and the benchmarking partners. The analysis should provide answers to the questions what is different and why it is so.

Presentations of practice and performance for each of the partners, compared to the corresponding numbers for StatOil, are shown in Figure 2.4. Here, costs in dollar/ton for a more closely specified drill stem are compared. Due to principles of confidentiality, the actual figures are not shown. Statfjord is an oil field operated by StatOil.

The costs of best practice are based on a so-called strawman model; that is, the costs are put together by the best performance of all the partners within each cost element. Thus, best practice does not represent a performance level that has actually been reached by any of the partners, but the level to be obtained by putting the best practice within each area into one single process.

Analysis to Find the Causes for the Gap

There turned out to be rather large differences among the partners with regard to the supply of casing. By studying and analyzing the practice of each of the partners, it was determined that they could be combined into three different main models, called the in-house model, the consignment model, and the outsourcing model.

Each of these models is characterized by certain ways of doing things. There are consequences each of them is supposed to have on the performance of the casing delivery process.

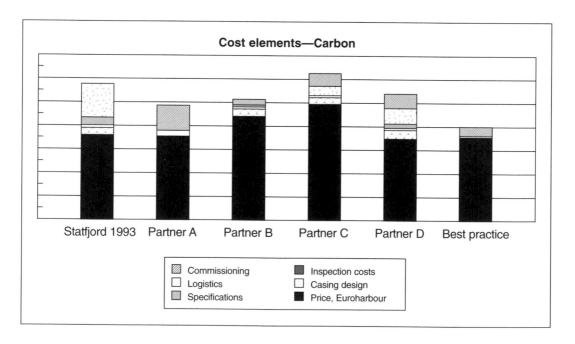

Figure 2.4. Costs of the different partners and best practice.

The in-house model, which is currently used by StatOil,

- Results in long throughput times.
- Gives little flexibility with regard to plans and changes in these.
- Involves many links and ties up large amounts of resources.
- Poses demanding requirements to the monitoring systems.
- Does not take advantage of scale economies in a satisfactory manner.
- Does, however, provide the buyer with the opportunity for direct contact with the steelworks.

The consignment model, which is used by two of the partners,

- Is easy to administrate.
- Results in long lead times.
- Requires the organization to pay for casing in stock.
- Also gives direct contact with the steelworks.

The outsourcing model, used by the remaining two partners,

- Gives short lead and throughput times.
- Is flexible with regard to plans and changes in plans.
- Delivers lower prices to European harbors.
- Is simple to administer, including its required financial systems.
- Frees resources for core activities.
- Gives scale economies as some dealers specialize in chrome casing, others in carbon casing.

Based on this analysis, the team concluded that the principles of the outsourcing model give the best results and should be implemented at StatOil. Figure 2.5 shows costs in dollars per ton for a specified drill stem at the different alternative models.

Based on the recommended improvements, savings are believed to amount to $230/ton compared to the budget for 1994. This means savings of about $6.7 million assuming 32,000 tons are used per year.

Improvement Opportunities

Numerous possible improvements were identified. They cover issues related to the delivery process such as the following:

- Investigate the implementation of a new supply model.
- Assess alternative external suppliers.

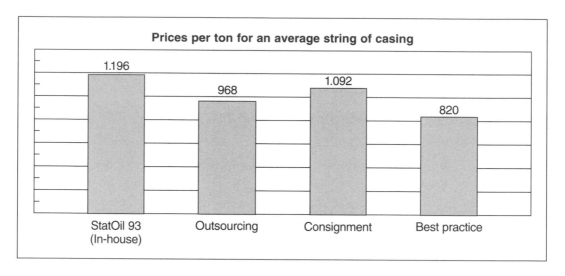

Figure 2.5. Expected costs for using the different models.

• Formalize the supplier-customer relationships.

• Formalize and improve the horizontal process within StatOil.

• Improve the demand planning of D&W.

• Reconsider any specifications that exceed standards from the American Petroleum Institute (API).

• Further standardize variants and types of thread.

• Reevaluate requirements for handling, packaging, and protection.

• Reevaluate the practice for calculating backup of casing.

• Reevaluate the practice of backup for other equipment.

• Simplify operations at the platform.

Implement and Follow Up

Organization

The implementation of the suggested improvements would affect a number of departments and functional areas. Therefore, it was suggested to organize the implementation into several subprojects administrated by a steering committee where the most important process owners were represented.

Schedule

For the casing process, 14 subprojects/activities were defined. They were scheduled for completion during the first quarter of 1995. Although this goal was not quite achieved in the specified time frame, a long range of measures had been implemented by the first quarter of 1996.

Results and Improvements Achieved in the Project

As of the first quarter of 1997, the implementation has been completed. Through a thorough analysis, a realistic potential for improvement was estimated. The gap between StatOil and best practice was identified to be $230/ton. Based on a prognosis of about 32,000 ton per year, the improvements will be approximately $6.7 million per year.

With respect to improvements, this project has been very successful. It is, however, difficult to document the improvements in exact figures. But the savings are in the order of $6.7 million.

The improvement potential for the delivery process for casing, which was the main focus for the project, is shown in Figure 2.6. It illustrates the price per ton for a specified variant in different dimensions.

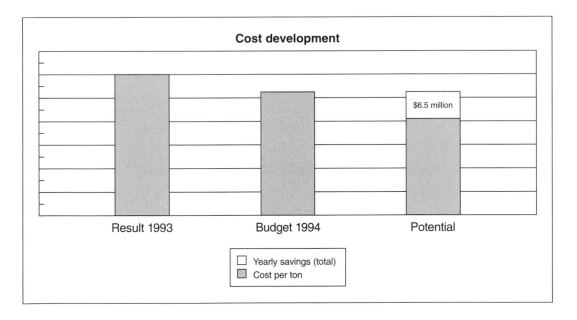

Figure 2.6. Improvement potential for the delivery process.

Lessons Learned About Benchmarking in the Project

The most important experiences learned about benchmarking during this project are summarized in this section. It is the opinion of the project group that benchmarking is a highly powerful and effective tool in a continuous improvement process. StatOil believes it will be very useful in future years, if used in a professional manner.

The most important lessons learned are as follows:

• It is very important to achieve a balance between the ambitions for a benchmarking project, the time set aside for it, and the resources an organization is willing to allocate.

• It is decisive for the result that the project participants fully understand the process that is being benchmarked. Process mapping and establishment of performance measures were new to most people involved in the project, and they all experienced that these activities can take a considerable amount of time to accomplish.

• Academic absorption into measures and numbers can easily lead to stepping into a facts trap; that is, becoming too obsessed with numbers that the practice behind the numbers is forgotten.

• Already during the process mapping, as a direct result of gaining a better understanding of the subject process, substantial improvement potential was identified.

• The project group consisted of persons with different backgrounds and experiences, as well as a mix of operative and staff personnel. A well-composed team is a prerequisite for a good result.

• It is also extremely important to include the people in the process on the team. Especially with regard to process mapping and meetings and interviews with the partners—as well as implementation—this proved to be useful.

• Every member of a benchmarking team must be trained in benchmarking. All projects should start by forming the team, where benchmarking training is an important element.

• Benchmarking is well suited for creating enthusiasm.

• Contact and agreements with benchmarking partners must be based on the terms of the partners. Furthermore, experience has shown that organizing and conducting the necessary activities do take a lot of time. Therefore, the search for partners should be started as soon as possible in the study.

• For a benchmarking study of this extent, the total incurred costs were $340,000. Compared to savings of $6.7 million, this gives a good return on investments.

About the Author

Finn Strand is a former army officer and safety department manager. Presently, he is the corporate advisor on the health, environment, and safety (HES) staff at StatOil. His responsibilities include providing HES best practices—both internally and externally—used in the StatOil group. Prior to this assignment, Strand was a corporate quality advisor who facilitated benchmarking projects, conducted benchmarking training, and participated as an assessor in the process of conferring the European Quality Award. Strand served as a facilitator for this benchmarking project.

He may be contacted as follows:

Finn Strand

HMS

StatOil

4035 Stavanger

Norway

Telephone: 47 51 807932

Facsimile: 47 51 807380

CHAPTER 3

Delivering Information at Allied Domecq Spirits & Wine Ltd.

Bruce J. Rance, Managing Director, i2i Associates Limited

Information is probably the most important asset an organization can own, arguably more important than its employees or brands. Without information the organization is operating, not in the dark, but blindly, and its management thrashes around fire fighting rather than being focused on those few areas critical to success.

Why is it so many organizations are willing to invest a fortune in advertising, but are strangely reluctant to do so when it comes to information systems, an asset with qualities no less ephemeral and similarly lacking tangibility.

This is a case study of seeing is believing; where once having tasted the fruit there was a craving for more. Is this not the same for many benchmark-related process improvement projects?

Background

In 1993, when the information project began, Allied Domecq Spirits & Wine Ltd. (ADS&W) was well on its way to becoming the world's second largest spirits group, measured by volume of the top 100 brands. It achieved this status in 1994 through the acquisition of Pedro Domecq. ADS&W has an annual turnover of about $3.4 billion (£2bn), has a 10,000 staff, and sells a comprehensive range of premium spirits in over 45 countries. In these markets the trading styles vary considerably, but with the competition becoming ever more fierce and sophisticated, it was evident that reliable and timely strategic information was an essential core asset.

The organization is arranged around four executive teams covering the Americas, Europe, Asia Pacific, and special markets. Although these teams have the prime profit growth responsibility, they are supported by two regionally orientated marketing organizations with infrastructure backup in the form of worldwide operations for production and a customer-focused supply chain.

Project Purpose

With a federated structure and matrix style management, it was evident back in 1993 that a key building block to success was information. The finance director then had, for some time, wanted to pull together the disparate forms and styles of information and weld them into a single source—one version of the truth. The author, then director of business process and information, was charged with the responsibility of developing an appropriate information system.

It was evident from the outset that if the company was to flourish, then something more than a simple data presentation vehicle was needed. It had to have functionality and the capacity to change culture. It had to be both focused and comprehensive, and include external information; for example, comparative brand performance in the marketplace and demographic material relating to the major economies. It also had to look inwardly, highlighting areas, when compared with the best in class, which offered business improvement opportunities while at the same time identifying potential threats.

This objective was incorporated within the project's aims, which at the time were articulated as being "To develop an information system that would enable Allied Domecq Spirits & Wine's senior management to focus clearly on achieving the corporate mission and strategy, thereby gaining competitive advantage." This objective was later to be broadened, and was the precursor to the organization becoming involved in benchmarking, and recognizing that for success to be achieved, there had to be a culture that was willing to embrace and implement change. It has to be recognized, however, that change in itself is not sufficient; change must be clearly focused on both the internal and external opportunities. This was the real objective of the information system—to be a vehicle that through a structured process would organize, filter, and focus external and internal information on those areas that are critical to the success of the company. To paraphrase John Rockart (*Harvard Business Review*): "There are a few areas where things must go right for a business to flourish." This author would add: And these things must first be identified!

The project's objectives were agreed after recognizing the critical business need for information and the sponsor's aim of harnessing the different sources and bringing order to the then-current unfocused, uncoordinated, and haphazard processes of information gathering and delivery.

Project and Team Operation

From the outset it was recognized that some form of external help would be required. It appears to be an unwritten truth that, for some reason, consultants bring a form of credibility and legitimacy to the whole exercise and that the organization, sadly, takes it that much more seriously. Putting the cynicism to one side, consultants can also bring focus, drive, and objectivity . Thus, the learning curve is climbed that much faster and the benefits delivered earlier. If consultants don't generate a return and more than pay for themselves, why engage them? It is also important that consultants are not used to abrogate the project director's accountability: They are members of the development team, lending their expertise and adding value as appropriate. The internal members of the development team do the lion's share of the work; however, the consultants' role, although advisory, is important, especially during the early parts of the project.

Prior to the selection of a consultant, an effort was made to review some of those professing to offer skills in the field of (strategic) information system development. It became rapidly evident that there was a dearth of independency. They were either part of a software house, hardware suppliers with consultancy bolted on, or in some way linked obliquely or directly to firms of accountants.

In each case, client inquiries were made to establish some form of satisfaction benchmark. This endeavor was thwarted by the fact that there is very little consistency in what organizations call information systems. It seemed to range from sales analysis to financial performance reporting. There appeared to be few companies attempting to build an overall system that was only bound by the global achievement of corporate success rather than function or silo performance.

An independent firm of consultants was identified and selected. Then the project began, and it is best described as evolutionary. The details of the actual process are described later in this chapter. To set the scene, however, the project began with a resource of the project director, consultant, and a representative from the information technology (IT) department. It matured two years later utilizing a part-time director and IT coordinator, two full-time data managers, and three full-time IT specialists.

At this point it is worth discussing the role of IT. The project, as described, should never be the responsibility of IT. An information system is a commercial and strategic business tool, and as such its development should be the responsibility of a senior manager who has considerable business experience and can thus better relate to the wider business needs.

One other point that became evident as the project progressed was the different meaning people give to the term *information system*. Most seemed to home in on the word *system* and thought *IT*. A few actually got it right and focused on the word *information*. Managers who themselves embark on such a project must ensure that this understanding is clear and that the focus is on information and its use as a critical corporate asset.

The delivery and presentation vehicle as developed by IT is important, but secondary. This is not to decry their contribution; they are vital team members. Deficient delivery and presentation can kill the system no matter how critical the information it contains.

The Process

Developing an information system is a top-down exercise not only in terms of content determination, but also in terms of sponsorship. Sponsorship is key; for this project it was the finance director, a very commercially orientated manager. The chief executive officer was rather ambivalent, though later became an avid user as the system was delivered and its content enhanced over time. Hence, a case of seeing is believing.

Steering Group

It has been clearly stated that the function of the system was to facilitate the company in realizing its objectives by focusing management attention and effort on those few really important areas. To do this a steering group was established. It consisted of key members from the board of directors, with representatives from marketing, sales, production, logistics, and finance. The steering group's role was to ensure the system focus. It was up to this group, through facilitation, to determine what was critical to the organization's success, and it was these areas which were to be the system's cornerstone. These critical success factors (CSFs) were identified as being strategic leadership, core competencies and processes, brand performance, customer satisfaction, and resource management.

Having determined the breadth and scope of the system a prototype was developed based on one of the CSFs. Brand performance was chosen since most management could relate to it and the finance director did not want the system considered as yet another financial reporting tool. The prototype had two key roles: first, to enable the steering group to have some tangible demonstration of what it was buying into so as to ensure its continued support and enthusiasm; and second, to test some of the software.

The role played by such a group cannot be overstressed. If the project is going to be a success there should not be any doubting Thomases in the camp who, by their public stance, will dampen the enthusiasm of others and make a difficult hill even steeper. These early days are critical. Although the project team will be working hard, it frequently has little rapid evidence of its labors. A full, all-embracing system as described here can take several years to develop and will require a considerable financial investment.

This time scale is not so much driven by the information system development, but by the subsystems that it draws upon for the base data. If the right data are going to be accessed electronically, then these subsystems frequently have to be modified or rewritten. Feeding the base data manually is out of the question. The development will fail due to lack of information, breadth, and timeliness, resulting in much of the information being out of date.

Site Visits

From site visits made to other organizations, who had what they termed an "executive information system" and professed rapid delivery, it was evident that such systems mean different things to different people. For this project five site visits were made, and they contributed to the steering group's understanding of what not to do rather than what to do. The benefits tended to be in terms of visual presentation and technical construction. A subgroup of the steering group, consisting of the project director, IT representative, and one other development team member, made the site visits.

The prime issues that came to light were system scope and functional influence of the sponsor. The systems seen tended to focus on day-to-day issues and be inwardly looking. Finance performance reporting was high on the list as was sales achieved compared with budget; all inward looking and near term. There was little attempt to address the much more fundamental issues of corporate objectives and long-term strategies. These systems were not built from the top down, but from the middle out. This lesson was important if the project's aim of being a strategic rather than a day-to-day management tool was to remain intact.

As noted, the prototype's focus was to be marketing, and it achieved both its goals of securing continued support for the project and proving the software selection. At this stage it was far from being an operational system; rather it was held together with glue and string, but it did show what the system would look like. With such a positive response, the next stage was to determine and scope the information that would populate each of the five areas of critical success.

Software Choice

The actual system delivery software utilized for the prototype, and selected for the final system, was LightShip by Pilot. Over 50 processing and delivery packages were evaluated by the consultants, and it was believed, based on their criteria, that the Pilot product would best suit Allied Domecq's needs. It was, however, decided to use a standard IBM 400 machine to store and manage the raw data while utilizing the LightShip professional product as the front-end presenter.

A learning point should be suggested here. The project director had determined that the information system should be portable, and this was one of the criteria used for software selection. The consultant team felt portability was critical and that senior managers would require the ability to access the data wherever they were, such as traveling, in hotels, at home, and so on. Experience has suggested that this is not wholly the case. It is for some of the data, but far from all. Therefore, system development should encompass a review of information to test its role in the management process, strategic or operational. Portability carries a negative in that it tends to slow inquiry response times and restricts the volume of data that can be easily managed. Some inquiries can require considerable amounts of raw information if they are going to be comprehensive. As a rule, it is recommended that information that might be regarded as having library attributes; for example, country demographics, global brand performance databases, and so on, should be accessed via a network and not be resident on a portable PC, which should be reserved for the most critical information.

Task Forces

All along it had been agreed that the information system belonged to the company, not the developers. To further this cultural aspect task forces were established, initially one each for three of the CSFs. These were populated with business unit directors or senior mangers who had actual responsibility for developing the business and, as such, would be key users of the system. Care was put into the structure of these meetings. As members, about 10 per task force were drawn from the different corners of the globe. They gathered in the evening for the following day's meeting. This saved a phenomenal amount of time, and allowed time for people to get used to each other, since several had never met before. Thus, the following day was focused and profitable.

The day was structured such that each task force could debate and fully understand the scope of its particular CSF. Without this they could hardly be expected to determine (1) what the company had to be brilliant at if it were to achieve the CSF; and (2) what were either the measures that would indicate to what extent they were being achieved or the information requirements necessary for their achievement.

Each task force day concluded with a dinner to which the director, or directors, for whom the CSF being discussed had a special interest, were invited. The purpose of the evening was to debate the day's conclusions and keep the directors informed. But more importantly, their active support was maintained by ensuring they were part of the development process and that their views were actively taken onboard.

As an example, under the heading of brand performance, the key performance measures were as follows:

- Quantitative indicators on key brands—Qualities and markets, such as market share, pricing, and so on

- Qualitative data on key brands—Share of media voice, consumer usage, attitude survey data, and the like

- Comparative measures, internal and external, for operational processes—Production, marketing, and so on

- Audit reports on physical product quality at both production and market levels

The key information needs were as follows:

- Worldwide overview of markets, brands, competitors, and ADS&W competitive performance

- Market analysis, for example, politics, demographics, economics, alcohol consumption, and so on

- Data on key competitors, such as size, products, performance, and the like

- Data on emerging or independent competitors (opportunity spotting)

- Brand position within markets

- Information on, and progress of, key projects

- Library information

To aid the discussion and to focus task force members on the types of measure and information, the matrix shown in Figure 3.1 was used.

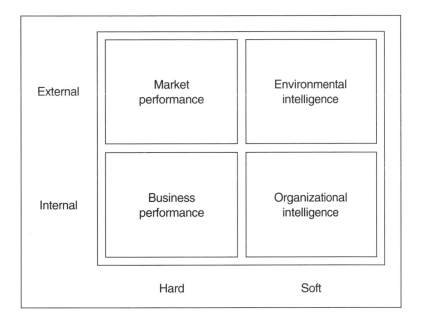

Figure 3.1. Sources of information as the basis of measurement.

This is a simple and well-known pictorial presentation of data but it proved very helpful. For those who were new to the concept, the matrix served as a good framework upon which to develop their thoughts.

The majority of people are very familiar with information that falls within the box labeled "internal and hard"; for example, financial reporting, controls, and similar information that is familiar, readily available, and easily accessible. There was a lot of debate around the other categories, and it highlighted how much businesses tends to focus, not on information they really need, but on that which they are given or that which is easy to retrieve.

The effect of stepping outside the traditional box not only enlivened the discussion, but it also had an effect on the reporting procedures within the organization. There is now a realization that new process and systems development has to take as much account of information inputs and outputs as it does the process itself.

The map shown in Figure 3.2 was the result of site visits and attempts to outline some of the thought processes that evolved and continue to be developed. This map attempts to go beyond the project being described and suggests the next step. It is more embracing and incorporates the need not just to look at key performance measures, but to also include the idea of information inputs that facilitate the effective operation of key activities such as market or sales planning. This is an example of where an information system moves from being an information provider for managing the business to becoming part of its fabric, and is thus fundamental to the whole operation.

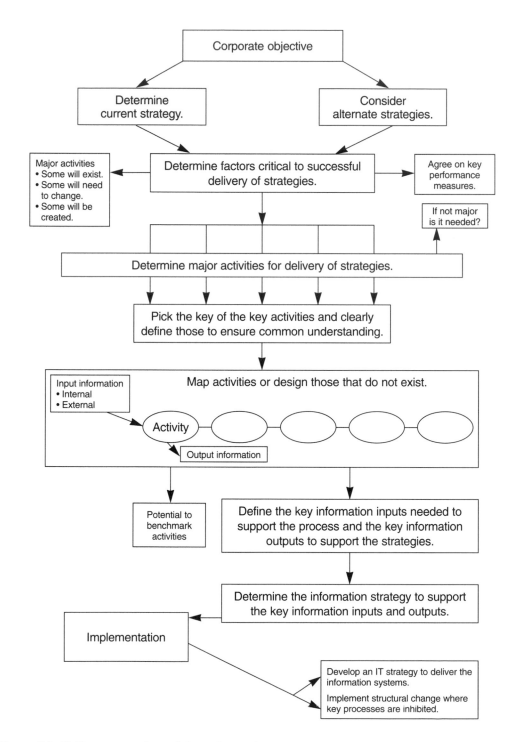

Figure 3.2. Outline process for an information system.

Having now determined the scope and nature of the information to be included in the system, it was appropriate to start the proper development and delivery of a fully functioning information system.

Rollout

Content Focus

Earlier the importance of focus had been stressed, and with so many brands and markets it was important to be selective. Everybody has their favorite, however the team refused to be compromised. Inclusion was determined by one of two indicators, profit contribution or the launch of a key brand in a new market. Without these selection criteria the system would rapidly have been cluttered and been anything but focused, let alone directed to the areas critical to success. One of the early realizations was how cluttered the portfolio was. Analysis showed how few of the brand market combinations generated the vast majority of the profit. This issue is now top of the agenda, and markets are actively refocusing their effort. A further ramification of refocus is a rationalization of the overall portfolio that knocks on to production and logistic facilities. But that is another story. The phenomenon of product and customer proliferation is not uncommon; realization and action to redress the situation are less so.

Automatic Updates

While the selection criteria was being applied, work began on designing the database and working out the system's functionality. The plan was to refresh the system twice a day and force upon users an automatic update whenever they logged on to the network. The reasoning behind this was to ensure, as best as possible, that users always had the most recent version of the information and when colleagues were talking to each other they were viewing the same data. It is appreciated this was log-on dependent, but at least it tried to overcome the problem of out-of-date information. The concept was fine, but in practice this caused much frustration among users. As a refresh could take several seconds, PC users who wanted to switch on and access another application were frustrated by being forced to take a refresh when they had no wish to use the information system at that time. The automatic refresh has now given way to an optional update procedure, either at time of log-on or at any other time by way of an icon.

The process of frequent updates forced other systems to review their own functionality. One of the most significant effects was the company's relationship with its major supplier of market performance data. It had traditionally supplied the data on rather an ad hoc basis. The requirements of the information system forced a change. Consistency was now a requirement and affected content, layout, and structure. New programs were written and the process of handling this type of data became fully automated. The benefit of this to the market information department was that by redesigning their processes it released people from handling data so that they could now add value by the application of their analysis skills; a classic benchmarking outcome.

Data Custodians

During this rollout phase it was further emphasized that the information systems development team had no ownership rights over the data. The ownership was fairly and squarely with the suppliers and the term *data custodian* came into being. One of the most critical aspects of any information system is data integrity. This could not be the responsibility of the team; it had to rest with the providers who themselves, as appropriate, would go further back along the information chain. The effect of this cultural issue was quite startling. The previous practice of, "Well it's Friday; let's fill the forms in and send them to head office" changed. People realized that their data were being used and viewed by many. Data quality and integrity took a giant step forward. This was further enforced by each information screen on the system including the name and telephone number of the custodian so the users knew where to address queries.

Project Review Meetings

The role of the custodians was further reinforced by inviting them to the project review meetings. These were held every eight weeks or so, with the objective of reviewing progress, discussing user comments, and setting priorities for the next few weeks. As with any project the team is very focused and clear as to next steps after a review meeting, but as time goes on the focus becomes a little blurred and tacky round the edges.

These meetings lasted all day and were exhausting; but the benefit was immeasurable. The custodians responded to being fully involved and were keen to make an input, especially when user comments were reviewed, as these often related to the information content for which the custodians had responsibility. There was also a team bonding benefit as members of the data management group, IT representatives, and custodians were able to exchange views and share thoughts in an open forum. The junior members particularly benefited as they were regarded as equal team members and were encouraged to make their input. The trouble was, once given the floor, their enthusiasm was often difficult to manage.

Training

How many senior managers profess computer literacy, but when it comes to it they don't have a clue? With any information system this problem has to be addressed in two ways. One is to train the user, but more importantly it imposes on the developers the need to design a system where the navigation is intuitive and the user does not have to be an expert. Senior managers do not have the time for extensive training in how to use this type of system. If they do, then the system has failed and will be doomed.

Colors

The importance of color should not be underestimated. The development team made use of a color consultant for a day, and the improvements in data presentation were startling. Using a dark background highlights the data and focuses the users' attention on the important detail. For bar charts pastel colors were used, and for line charts primary colors were used. As for those with color sight problems, consistency in color code is critical. The key brand should always be given the same color; this applies equally to key competitor brands included in the chart.

Prototyping

Mention has been made of development times and that the product of considerable effort is sometimes slow to be realized. This was considered by the team to be a serious handicap to the acceptance of the system by users as new applications were slow to appear. The system appeared staid and lacked initial vitality. To get over this problem it was decided to set a target of a new application going live every two or three weeks. This was achieved by prototyping.

Rather than wait until every t was crossed and i dotted, new applications were launched as soon as they were considered to add value for users. The applications may not have had all their functionality, but they worked and, importantly, the data were correct and addressed another key performance measure or information need.

Users responded instantly, frequently switching on to look at the new application previously advised by electronic mail. Overall, the whole system gathered new vigor and life; it was felt that the evolutionary nature of the development had been enhanced.

A Vehicle for Dialogue

One of the most important strengths of any company is its ability to share information and keep people informed. An information system is key in developing this type of culture. As stated at the outset, this author believes information is a company's most valuable asset. The developed system now has the ability for users to add information to a graphical presentation. The function of this is not to develop a dialogue, there are better vehicles for this, but to facilitate explanation and add insight. This is especially important for people in the marketplace. They know what is going on; they now have the ability to share that knowledge.

The Future

As the system becomes ever more part of the organization it will continue to influence culture and be a powerful vehicle for change. This will not be change for change's sake, but because the system was built from the top down and is driven by the corporate objectives. The managerial effort and change are focused at the heart of the major issues—those critical to success.

The system will never be finished. Corporate objectives will change over time, and the information delivered will have to reflect these moves. Applications will come and go, but the focus will remain intact.

What Was Learned

• *The importance of proactive sponsorship.* It has to play much more than lip service; it has to drive and clear the path. The internal development team was lucky with its sponsor, but things can always be done better.

• *Clarity of purpose.* Information systems mean different things to different people. Objectives must be unambiguous and clearly articulated throughout the organization so that there are no misunderstandings.

• *Build from the top down, and stay on track.* The system must be built from the top down, and the team should not be diverted from the project's objectives, however tempting. Once off-track it is very difficult to get back on, and the wrong signals will have been sent out. Just another information system is not being developed. Rather, a strategic tool that will become a core company asset is being developed.

• *Training.* The system's navigation should be intuitive. To help with user understanding, a quarterly newspaper was introduced. It includes user details as well as descriptions of new applications and enhancement to existing ones. There is a "How do I do this" page, details of forthcoming events, and similar information.

• *Portability.* The team should think forward as best as it can. This type of system is never finished; it continually evolves and responds to the organization's needs. The team should think carefully about what should be made portable and what should not. Once a particular path has been chosen, it is very difficult and expensive to change direction.

• *Time.* This type of project takes much longer than imagined and drives right down and through an organization. There is not a stone that won't be overturned, nor a system that will not have to be changed in some way.

• *Quality should never be compromised.* This is probably the only system in the company that will be seen and critically reviewed by so many people.

• *Flexibility.* It is not possible to plan all the actions; as the project develops, so will its needs and demands. The team has to respond to them—providing any changes remain within the project's objectives.

What Was Accomplished

• The greatest achievement was to force senior managers to sit down and review what was critical to the success of the organization and develop a mechanism to highlight where to focus action.

• Management effort within the business is now much more focused with the obvious benefits.

• The system is now part of the company's fabric with more people demanding access. It is regarded as the one version of the truth and is now becoming part of the planning process. Those not on-line feel deprived.

• There is a realization that only the first steps have been taken, and there is still much more to do: not only to deliver the original concept, but also to take it forward onto the next stage.

Afterthought

It is important to stress that although consultants were used for some of the development, their role was very much advisory and dispensed with soon after the initial prototype development and software selection.

Don't expect a revolution. Change will occur, but time must be allowed for users to appreciate the real value of the tool. Hence, seeing is believing. Every now and then something will happen and its origins can be traced back to the system—the one developed as a result of benchmarking.

About the Author

Bruce J. Rance is the managing director of *i2i* Associates Limited, a consultancy that specializes in the initiation and management of consortium studies. Its objective is to help clients identify process improvement opportunities and achieve them through the focused application of benchmarking.

Rance is the former director of business process and information at Allied Domecq Spirits & Wine Ltd. in Bristol, England. There he directed the global development and introduction of process and performance improvement opportunities. Specifically, Rance directed the development of an intelligence system based on key performance measures determined by those areas critical to the company's success; and initiated and directed a corporatewide benchmarking exercise of all financial processes, with the objective of identifying those areas offering the greatest opportunity for process improvement.

Rance has over 20 years of experience in industry where he has principally operated as an internal consultant. During this time he has managed the strategic evaluation of businesses in the United Kingdom and overseas, which as appropriate, led to their significant rationalization and refocusing on core markets and expertise. Rance has also directed the successful acquisition of overseas businesses and the disposal of several in the United Kingdom.

In recent years, Rance's work has focused on both the development of strategic information systems and the initiation and management of process improvement projects. He has spoken on these topics both in the United Kingdom and in North America.

Rance is a Fellow of the Institute of Chartered Accountants in England and Wales. He may be contacted as follows:

Bruce J. Rance
Managing Director
i2i Associates Limited
Rochdale
The Barrows
Cheddar
Somerset
BS27 3BG
England
Telephone: 44 1 934 741102
Facsimile: 44 1 934 741113
E-mail: bjr@customernet.com

CHAPTER 4

General Ledger and Consolidation Processes: The Experience of 3M Italy

Ambrogio Biglia, Logistic and Staff Controller, 3M Italia S.P.A., and
Lucrezia Songini, Assistant Professor, Bocconi University

Background

Minnesota Mining & Manufacturing Company (3M) was established in 1902 to work a corundum mine. (Corundum is a raw material used in the production of abrasives.) Since the 1920s, 3M had pursued a strategy based on continuous technological innovation and product diversification. 3M continuously developed new products, such as the following: Scotch tape (1925); the first audio magnetic tape (1946); the first computer magnetic tape (1952); the Thermofax system (1958); photosensitive products (1964); the Trimax system (1973); Post-It notes (1980); and 640 and 1000 ASA films (1982). Since 1984, 3M has cooperated with NASA to develop space research programs.

In 1992, in order to sharpen its focus on customer needs, 3M began a strategic change process with the goal to transform the organization into a transnational company. According to the publication, *3M Managing Business in Europe in the 90's,*

> *We believe the* Customer *is our reason for being. We believe* Competitive Advantage *is the imperative. We believe we must continue to build on the* Diversity *of our people, technologies and markets—because this truly is 3M's unique strength.*

According to Harry Hammerly, executive vice president of the life sciences sector and international operations,

> *Clearly, 3M is moving away from being a well-defined, traditional, top-down kind of organization. I think we're moving into a new kind of global management structure—the transnational corporation. Unlike the more centralized global corporation, a transnational corporation relies on an integrated network and teamwork. It is driven by the needs of the marketplace; for each business, the company has to create the right mix of global, regional and local components.*

3M has identified eight guidelines that summarize the company's philosophy and that are consistent with the new strategic intent.

1. Focusing on customer
2. Considering human resources as the most important company resource
3. Pushing the individual entrepreneurial spirit
4. Pursuing a strong-minded effort toward technological innovation
5. Using advanced/high-tech technologies
6. Diversifying product lines continuously
7. Evolving organizational structures
8. Turning its eyes beyond the business

As far as the worldwide strategic structure was concerned, three business sectors were identified: (1) industrial and consumer, (2) life sciences, and (3) information, imaging, and electronics (Figure 4.1). They had a global responsibility for basic technological areas and were articulated in groups of divisions and business units. International operations were based on a geographical organization. They cooperated with the business sectors in order to ensure a strong market position. Staff areas were organized on a functional basis and had coordination and support roles.

In 1994, 3M held leadership positions in several market segments; distributed more than 60,000 products all over the world; had subsidiaries in 61 countries; operated more than 200 production sites in 45 countries; had research and development (R&D) centers in 22 countries; employed about 85,000 people; had almost 125,000 shareholders; had net sales of more than \$15 billion; and had net income amounting to \$1322 million.

In July 1996, 3M spun off its data storage and imaging businesses and established a new company—Imation. According to Giulio Agostini, senior vice president and chief financial officer,

> We realized that data storage and imaging technologies were differentiating from 3M's basic technological competencies. It is time-magnetic and photographic products go away in order to follow their faster market development. (Carrer 1996)

As a consequence of the spin-off, 3M sharpened its focus on innovation, customer satisfaction, and international expansion. It consisted of businesses that are global market leaders, held solid growth potential, and earned high returns on invested capital. The industrial and consumer sector is the world's largest supplier of tapes, and is a leader in coated abrasives, specialty chemicals, repositionable notes, home cleaning sponges and pads, electronic circuits, and similar products. The life sciences sector is a global leader in reflective materials for transportation safety, respirators for worker safety, closures for disposable diapers, and high-quality graphics used indoors and out. This sector also holds leading positions in medical and surgical supplies, drug delivery systems, and dental products.

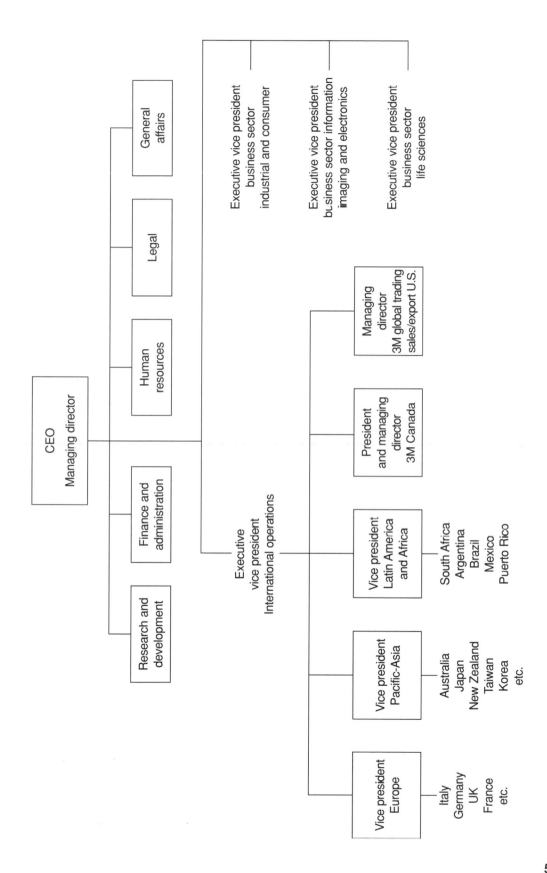

Figure 4.1. Worldwide strategic and organizational structure.

In 1996, 3M had subsidiaries in 63 countries outside the United States; had 170 manufacturing plants in 58 countries and R&D centers located in 22 countries; employed almost 74,000 people; had more than 132,000 shareholders; had net sales of more than $14 billion; and had net income amounting to $1526 million.

3M in Europe

In 1992, 3M restructured its organization in Europe in order to combine strong central business direction with flexible, efficient implementation in response to customer requirements and market opportunities. With a structure of pan-European businesses supported by a strong regional structure, 3M in Europe demonstrates the key elements of a transnational business and integrated network with cross-functional, cultural, and national teams working for the benefit of customers.

Three fundamental elements form the basis of the organization of 3M in Europe: (1) the European Business Centers (EBC); (2) the Regional Subsidiary Organization; and (3) the European Operations Committee (EOC) (Figure 4.2).

Each EBC is a strategic and operational unit, with management responsibility and accountability for the preparation and implementation of the European business plan and for the attainment of the annual European forecast for a business. Each EBC also maintains a direct reporting relationship with its associated U.S. group and, above all, each EBC is customer- and market-driven. Each EBC is a fully integrated business, combining dedicated manufacturing, technical, sales and marketing, logistics, and assigned functional staff. Most EBCs also include one or more European business units (EBUs) for specialized sales and marketing functions at the center and in the regions aligned to specific products and markets. The EBC structure allows 3M to approach European markets in a consistent and strategic manner; significantly reduces the time required to reach business decisions and implement plans; allows 3M to deal with transnational accounts in the way that they desire; and consolidates and focuses marketing, manufacturing, and technical communities on the need to work together to address common business issues.

With business direction provided by the EBCs and EBUs, it is at the regional subsidiary level where things actually happen. This is where customers and employees are located, and where business plans are put into practice. It is where goods are made and sold, where services are provided, and where customers' needs and requirements are satisfied. In its mission to maximize customer and employee satisfaction, key elements of the role of the regional subsidiary are to

- Continue to ensure a strong local presence.

- Provide a local context and a structure for the development, integration, and implementation of EBC and corporate plans.

- Provide efficient and effective use of resources and resource sharing.

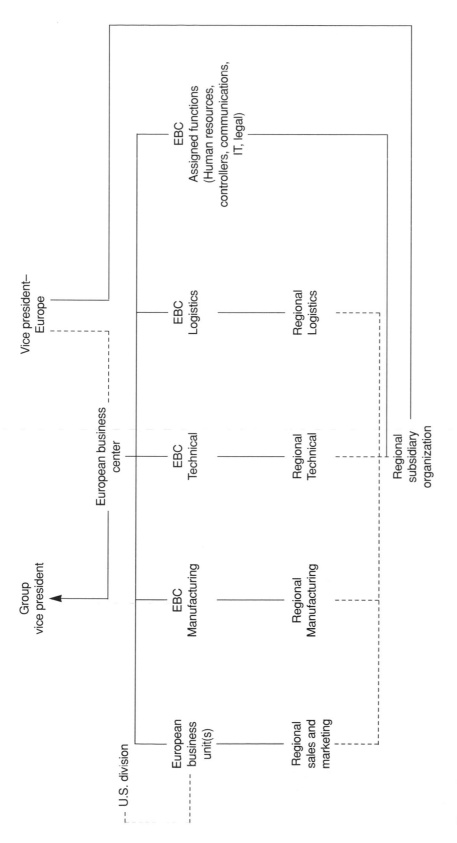

New regions

1. North Atlantic (Denmark, Finland, Ireland, Norway, Sweden, United Kingdom)
2. West Europe (France, Morocco, Belgium, Netherlands)
3. Central Europe (Austria, Germany, Switzerland)
4. East Europe (Czech Republic, Hungary, Poland, Russia, Turkey)
5. Southern Europe (Italy, Portugal, Spain)
6. Greece and Middle East (Egypt, Greece, Gulf, Israel, Pakistan)

Figure 4.2. European business center organization model.

• Provide strong customer focus, and increased product and professional specialization.

• Develop human resource strength and motivation.

• Build key account management.

• Develop customer-focused marketing.

The regions fulfill the role of business service organizations, providing the means to successfully achieve the defined needs and requirements of the EBCs and the corporation in the most effective and economical way.

Eventually, the role of the EOC is to

• Provide strategic direction.

• Manage the total European portfolio.

• Achieve total European profit and loss (P&L).

• Balance the needs of the EBCs and the regions.

• Manage the European structure.

• Allocate resources and investments.

• Direct the course of the future 3M infrastructure across Europe.

The Italian Region

In 1994, 3M Italy was responsible for sales and marketing in Italy, Libya, Malta, and other extra-European countries. The 3M group in the Italian region was composed of six companies, seven production sites, and two R&D centers. It employed about 3600 people, with annual turnover of over $774 million (1256 billion lire).

Within the Italian region the photo color system division was active, with worldwide responsibility for the photo color industry; and two significant EBCs, medical imaging systems and printing and graphic systems.

3M headquarters decided to locate these EBCs in Italy "due to both the recognized experience, capabilities, and competencies in photosensitive products held by the technological and manufacturing center situated in Ferrania and the acquisitions, joint-ventures, and technological investments in adhesive tapes for masking and packaging" (Gruppo 3M Italia 1992, 14). In 1996, after the spin-off of the photo color system division, an Italian subsidiary of Imation was established. It represents the European headquarters for the new company. Imation's main European research center and production sites are also located in Italy.

As a consequence of the spin-off, in 1996, 3M Italy employed about 1600 people. The group structure was articulated in four companies, five plants, and one R&D center. Net sales amounted to about $483 million (781 billion lire) and net income to approximately $16 million (26 billion lire).

The Need for a New European Accounting Information System

As a consequence of business characteristics, shareholders' features, and geographical dispersion, communicating a wide range of data and information in a short time and managing a great number of intercompany relationships have always been common needs at 3M. The move into a transnational company, the European reorganization, and the focus on the same image and service in Europe have emphasized the need to quickly exchange common information among 3M European subsidiaries. It has become absolutely necessary to

- Manage huge volumes of data and information.
- Define common accounting rules and languages.
- Physically and logically integrate various local information systems.
- Define a common European chart of accounts that is accessible by heads of EBCs and EBUs.
- Prepare and communicate reports focused more on product lines than on subsidiaries in order to point out EBCs' and EBUs' global contribution.

In the early 1990s, consistent with these new information requirements, 3M revised all its European information systems. Up to that time, each European subsidiary had local information systems, which were inadequate to sustain the information needs and flows in a European perspective. They had been developed locally, and were focused more on local needs than European needs. Thus, the information systems differentiated in characteristics and innovation.

3M had to transform all local accounting information systems, which emphasized "cross-country," nonstandardized communication flows and personalized reporting activities, into a common, standardized European accounting system. It should be noted that in 1976, GENAC, an advanced accounting information system, had been completely developed by 3M Italy and was implemented throughout Italy. GENAC allowed the automation of data collection, data processing, and information generation. In the late 1980s, 3M Italy was one of the most advanced European subsidiaries as far as accounting information services was concerned. Nevertheless, GENAC was inadequate in a continental perspective.

After an informal internal benchmarking study aimed to compare and evaluate the accounting information systems of main European subsidiaries, the European System of Accounting and Cost Accounting (ESAC) was implemented in 1994. It was developed by different European interfunctional and international task forces and represented the general ledger and financial reporting system, where all subfeeder systems (for instance, the system of order management—EUROMS II), feed inputs. ESAC was connected by batch interfaces to all transaction processing systems, while GENAC was linked by on-line interfaces, because both the transaction processing systems and the general ledger and financial reporting systems (GENAC) were developed locally.

The External Benchmarking Study

As ESAC was implemented in Italy, 3M Italy took part in an external benchmarking study. Its aim was to verify best practices in the general ledger and consolidation processes within a group of Italian subsidiaries of multinational companies (Miroglio 1997).

Study Purpose

The benchmarking study was sponsored by IBM Semea and CESAD Bocconi, a research center of the Bocconi University, specializing in financial and management accounting. IBM Semea was interested in comparing its general ledger and consolidation system with those of a group of first-class companies.

In December 1993, a meeting was held to outline the benchmarking project and to find supporters. IBM Semea and CESAD Bocconi pursued the following goals.

- Share and compare different experiences concerning critical accounting transaction processing systems, most of all the general ledger and reporting processes.

- Identify an ideal process that could better combine cost and effectiveness. To achieve this goal, it was necessary to map out the processes, to describe each single activity, to evaluate the cost linked to each activity, and to compare all companies' findings.

- Identify the best-of-the-breed as a result of the best activity performances among the company sample.

- Identify the actions to implement, in order to improve the actual processes.

Team Operations

During the December 1993 meeting, in addition to IBM Semea and CESAD Bocconi, three companies agreed to the project: Ciba-Geigy, Hewlett Packard, and 3M Italy. The participants in the benchmarking process decided to form a team with a representative from each company. The commitment required that the four companies

- Map out their processes on the basis of the agreed methodology.

- Actively participate in the workshops.

- Measure the critical processes and send information to CESAD Bocconi for consolidation and analysis.

- Actively participate in the interpretation phase, which differentiated the companies' processes, and in the final definition of an agreed model for the general ledger and consolidation processes.

CESAD Bocconi's role was as follows:

- Coordinate and integrate the activities of participants in order to assure common quality standards.

- Provide methodological support during the phases of process mapping, defining process boundaries, and bibliographical research.

- Analyze data and present the results of quantitative analysis.

- Provide and manage the competencies and capabilities required during the different steps of the project.

Steps of the Benchmarking Process

The benchmarking study lasted from December 1993 until July 1994. It was articulated in four steps.

1. *The first meeting (December 1993).* The first meeting was organized by CESAD Bocconi. Companies interested in the initiative were invited to it. During the meeting IBM Semea and CESAD Bocconi presented the goals of the benchmarking study, a proposal concerning the mapping and analysis methodology, a tentative definition of the boundaries of the general ledger and consolidation processes, the schedule, and the commitment required of participants.

2. *The first workshop (January 1994).* One goal was to reach a common definition of the general ledger process and to identify a mapping methodology to be used by each participant company. Another goal was to point out qualitative differences, critical aspects, and performance measures among the general ledger processes of the participants.

3. *The second workshop (April 1994).* This workshop was dedicated to comparing the findings that resulted from mapping and measuring the general ledger systems of each company. ESAC, 3M's accounting information system, seemed to be an interesting benchmark. Significant efforts were spent to understand the link between the way the general ledger process was managed and the performance in terms of efficiency and effectiveness.

4. *The third workshop (July 1994).* The purpose of this workshop was to define the best-of-breed general ledger process; to identify and integrate performance measures; to point out the distance (gap) between each company's process and the ideal process; and to discover reengineering opportunities as well as implementation constraints.

Approach, Conduct, Method of Investigation

Definition and boundaries of the general ledger process. The boundaries and activities managed by the general ledger process were consistently defined with the following generally accepted definition of the major tasks of an information system (Wilkinson 1989, 10–12).

- Data collection involves the collection of data from various sources, their entry, and validation. The typical steps of data collection are: data capture and measurement, recording, validation, classification, and data transmission where they are processed.

• Data processing could involve additional validation and classification activities. Then the data are summarized, transcribed, batched, sorted, and transformed into usable information.

• Data management consists of four steps: storing, updating, retrieving, and canceling. Retrieved data are used in further processing activities or are converted into information for users.

• Data control and security physically and logically safeguard data in order to assure its accuracy. Physical safeguards consist of hardware and files security; logical safeguards consist of organizational, documentary, and bookkeeping controls. Examples of control steps and security measures include validation, authorization, locked cash drawers, reconciliations, verifications, and reviews.

• Information generation places information in the hands of users and involves reporting, analysis, interpretation, communication, and transmission activities.

Figure 4.3 illustrates the major task of an information accounting system.

Consistent with the definition of the major functions of an accounting information system, the general ledger and consolidation process was defined as "the system which collects data from transaction processing cycles and subledgers; contains summary financial data concerning assets, liabilities, revenues, and expenses; [and] assumes the formal accuracy and logical coherence of feeding activities."

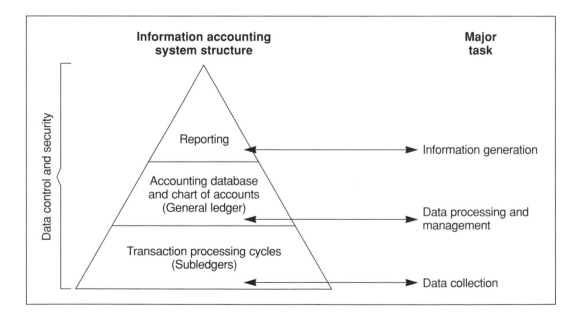

Figure 4.3. Major task of an information accounting system.

The main accounting transaction processes, inside the general ledger, are as follows:

- Begin with data collection from transaction processing cycles (revenue cycle, expenditure cycle, resource management cycle).

- Fulfill the rules that regulate the reporting activity at the consolidated unit level and that manage their updating.

- Include data processing and data management required to assure an accrual basis accounting (data updating and storing, system closing, and so on).

- Include activities related to consolidated processes at various organizational levels (business, country, corporate) and articulated according to different aspects (country, business).

- End with a reporting activity and preliminary results analysis and interpretation.

A more in-depth definition of the general ledger process, as defined by the benchmarking group, involves the following:

- Collect data, which are classified and processed in the functional information subsystems (subledgers).

- Update and record, on an accrual basis, financial data for the period.

- Logically and formally control data.

- Generate information requested to the reporting activity, according to the schemes and rules provided by laws and/or to generally accepted accounting principles.

- Write and distribute external and internal reports.

The consolidation process is included in the general ledger process. It is managed according to headquarters' rules and principles that pertain to the following:

- Systematic collection of operational and financial data, coming from subsidiaries included in the consolidation area

- Definition of qualitative standards (schedule, form, and content) for information that are regularly collected

- Definition and implementation of harmonization methods for consolidated information

- Preparation of consolidated reports and their transmission to upper consolidation levels

Note that at the beginning of the benchmarking study, the team aimed to investigate the consolidation process too. During the analysis, however, the focus was on the general ledger process, while the consolidation process was not studied in depth.

Eventually, defining the activities and boundaries of the general ledger process allowed the team to identify five subprocesses. Each of them combines differently the five major tasks of an accounting information system (data collection, processing, management, control and security, information generation). The five subprocesses are as follows:

1. *System updating* involves the analysis and implementation of rules provided by laws and headquarters; and updating the accounting database, the chart of accounts, the data input procedures from subfeeder systems, the reporting structure, and the document and accounting controls, according to internal and external requirements.

2. *Scheduling* manages the accounting subledgers closing, and schedules the general ledger operations (data adjustments, data allocation and classification, data integration for extraordinary operations, closing of interfaces with subfeeder systems, reconciliations and balancing, communication, and analysis of reports).

3. *Collection of financial data* feeds in and codes records in the general ledger, and involves input coding and controls on data recording, ledger records, and input feeding.

4. *Periodic closing* implies appropriations, manual inputs, allocations, and reconciliations.

5. *Reporting* involves collecting supplementary information, connecting it with subledgers systems, data transmission, preparing internal and external reports, and data analysis and evaluation.

Variables and key performance measures. In order to measure the general ledger process performance of each benchmarked company, the second step of the benchmarking study implied the definition of critical variables and related performance measures. The critical variables were distinguished into context variables and other critical drivers.

As far as the context variables was concerned, the following aspects were identified.

• Organizational position and dispersion of the unit responsible for the general ledger

• Type of activities managed by the general ledger unit

• Involvement of the general ledger unit in information classification

• Range of activities managed by the general ledger unit

• Reports produced

• Employee turnover

• Involvement in analysis and evaluation activities

Other critical drivers of the general ledger process were identified.

• Complexity of activities managed by the general ledger unit

• Resources used

• Efficiency, effectiveness, and information technology support

The most important process drivers and performance measures identified for the general ledger process were as follows:

• Organization of the resources devoted to the general ledger process

—Number of units involved in the general ledger activities

—Percent of the activity that is managed by the unit in charge of the general ledger process

—Activity mix (percent of current activities, maintenance activities, and design and review activities)

—Number and kind of reports produced by the system

—Professional competencies and turnover of human resources.

• Functioning of the general ledger process

—Classification and grouping of information (product, department, function, division, geographical area, and so on)

—Degree and way of involvement in the periodic closing of the units in charge of the general ledger process

—Relevance and deepening of the following:

  • Controls on data coming from subledgers systems

  • Information integration

  • Reconciliations

  • Internal reporting

  • Intercompany adjustments

—Involvement of the unit in charge of the general ledger process in performance evaluation

  • Types of reports

  • Degree of involvement

  • Number of resources involved

  • Person-days

—External influencing factors

  • Number of certified closings per year

  • Volume of transactions coming late from transaction processing cycles

  • Degree of automation of transaction processing cycles

Eventually, the following significant overall performance measures were identified to evaluate the general ledger process performance.

• Cost

—Person-months dedicated to the process

—Total number of people involved in the general ledger process

—Average cost per closing (internal and external)

• Time

——Average cycle time from feeding in transaction processing cycles to reconcilement of accounts for internal reporting

——Average cycle time from the cutoff of the first transaction processing cycle to the overall integration of the general ledger database

• Quality

——Percentage of accounts that are not reconciled later than 60 days

Best Practices, Differences, and Innovative Findings

Similarities and Differences

The identified model for the general ledger process, and its performance measures, allowed each company to evaluate its own process and to compare its findings with those of the other benchmarked companies. The similarities and differences were measured at different levels: context variables, critical drivers, subprocesses of the general ledger process, and performance measures.

Context variables. Some similarities arose as far as the following context variables were concerned: organizational position and dispersion of units in charge of the general ledger (Table 4.1); type of activities managed (Table 4.2); and involvement of the general ledger unit in information classification (Table 4.3).

Table 4.1. Dispersion of the units in charge of the general ledger.

	3M	Alpha	Beta	Gamma
Number of units involved in general ledger activities	2	16	12	5
Percent of activity managed by the unit responsible for the general ledger process	50	42	50	95

Table 4.2. Type of activities managed by the unit in charge of the general ledger.

	3M	Alpha	Beta	Gamma
Current activities	76%	80%	73%	77%
Maintenance activities	14%	10%	15%	10%
Design and review activities	10%	10%	12%	13%

Table 4.3. Involvement of the general ledger unit in information classification.

	3M	Alpha	Beta	Gamma
Legal entities*	6			
Financial accounts*	7000			
Number of accounts that are transferred to the upper reporting level	80	640	1800	5200
Businesses	28		25	7
Divisions	18	30		30
Cost centers*	1200			
Geographical areas			13	
Plants	7			2
Commodity	80		25 (Corresponds to the business.)	30 (Corresponds to the division.)

*Since the information in these categories would reveal the identity of single companies, the data in this aspect are considered confidential.

   In all four companies there was not a unique unit involved in the general ledger activities, but a number of subunits of the accounting and control department. The organizational unit in charge of the general ledger process in all companies had a strong role in the classification of information, while some differences were pointed out as far as the number and type of classifications were concerned.

   Other context variables pointed out significant differences among the company sample; for instance, the range of activities managed by the unit in charge of general ledger (Table 4.4); types of reports produced (Table 4.5); employee turnover (Table 4.6); and involvement in analysis and evaluation activities (Table 4.7).

Critical drivers. As far as the other critical drivers were concerned, significant findings arose with regard to the following aspects: complexity of activities carried out (Table 4.8); resources used (Table 4.9); process efficiency (Table 4.10); process effectiveness (Tables 4.11 and 4.12); and information technology support (Table 4.13). The findings for resources devoted to data control and security are shown in Table 4.14.

Table 4.4. Activities managed by the unit in charge of the general ledger.

	3M	Alpha	Beta	Gamma
Controls on data coming from subledgers	3	4	1	4
Reconciliations between the general ledger and subledgers	3	4	1	4
Database integration with prime entries	2	2	3	4
Integration for adjustments	3	2	3	4
Integration for extraordinary operations	4	2	2	2
Internal reporting	3	1	4	4
Performance evaluation	3	1	3	4
Adjustment of headquarters' rules	4	2	2	4
Adjustment of consolidation principles	4	1	1	4
Intercompany adjustments	3	1	1	3

(1 = not managed, 4 = very important)

Table 4.5. Types of reports produced.

	3M	Alpha	Beta	Gamma
Trial balance	✓	✓	✓	✓
Legal entity balance	✓	✓	✓	✓
Country report	✓		✓	✓
Division report	✓			✓
SBU report	✓		✓	✓

Table 4.6. Employee turnover.

3M	Alpha	Beta	Gamma
9%	8%	20%	37%

Table 4.7. Involvement in the analysis and evaluation of reporting results.

	3M	Alpha	Beta	Gamma
Person-days per year required for the analysis and evaluation of the report results by the general ledger unit	60	0	240	138
People involved in the evaluation process (number)	2.5	0	11	25
Annual evaluation meetings where general ledger units participate	13	0	3	144

Table 4.8. Complexity of activities managed by the general ledger unit.

	3M	Alpha	Beta	Gamma
Number of closing of accounts for internal reporting per year	12 + 1	4 + 1	11 + 1	12 + 1
Number of closing of accounts for external reporting per year	1	1	2	5
Percent of property accounts that are reconciled for internal reporting	100	100	80	100
Percent of property accounts that are reconciled for external reporting	100	100	100	100
Number of subfeeder systems	25	16	7	60
Number of transactionsprocessed monthly*	235,000			
Accounting records carried out by the general ledger unit monthly	24,000	1700	10,500	30,000
Reports prepared monthly	12	0	40	8

*Since the information in this category would reveal the identity of single companies, the data in this aspect are considered confidential.

Table 4.9. Resources used.

	3M	Alpha	Beta	Gamma
Number of people involved in the general ledger activity	17.5	8.5	29	36
Person-months devoted to general ledger activity	200	43	80	430

Table 4.10. Process efficiency.

	3M	Alpha	Beta	Gamma
Average cycle time between subledgers feeding and database reconciliation for internal reporting	3	3	5	5
Average cycle time between last subprocess/subsystem cutoff and periodical external reporting (working days)	7	7	3	6
Average cycle time between first subprocess/subsystem cutoff and overall integration of the general ledger database	10	9	6	7
People involved in keeping accounting records that are directly managed by the unit in charge of general ledger	6	2	18	6.3
Time required for keeping accounting records that are directly managed by the unit in charge of general ledger (person-days)	110	12.5	65	130
Time dedicated to keeping accounting records (directly managed) compared to total person-days used for managing general ledger activities	40%	17%	40% (Includes reconciliation activity.)	40% (Includes reconciliation activity.)

Table 4.11. Process effectiveness.

	3M	Alpha	Beta	Gamma
Percent of entries sent late by subsystems	2	No data	0	2
Percent of transactions rejected by the general ledger system	10	No data	1	0.4
Number of control reports prepared by the general ledger unit during periodic closing	12	0	21	1500
Percent of accounts not reconciled beyond 60 days	0	No data	14	0

Table 4.12. Effectiveness measured with regard to relevance of data control.

	3M	Alpha	Beta	Gamma
Direct controls (on critical areas and analytical)	3	5	5	5
Operational controls (subtotal reconciliations, etc.)	4	5	3	4
Indirect controls (by audits)	2	5	1	3
Physical security	5	1	5	5
Internal audits	3	2	3	4
External audits	5	3	1	5

(1 = not present, 5 = very relevant)

Table 4.13. Information technology support.

	3M	Alpha	Beta	Gamma
Number of subsystems not automated	0	0	0	0
Electronic filing devices	Yes	No	Yes	Yes
Optical filing devices	No	No	No	Yes
Degree of automation of accounting data storing and retrieving	100%	100%	100%	100%

Table 4.14. Control and security activities.

	3M	Alpha	Beta	Gamma
Number of people involved in data control and security activities	12	8.5	18	6
Person-days devoted to data control and security activities	46	48	31	48

General ledger subprocesses. As far as the five subprocesses that form the general ledger process were concerned, some significant findings came out from the comparison.

1. *System updating.* The main differences concerned the following:

   • Input variability was related to differences both in laws and national taxation and in the headquarters' procedures and rules.

   • Depending on the unit in charge of the general ledger, the definition of principles and rules varied. Involvement of the general ledger unit in the definition of principles and rules varied, from a strong involvement to only the implementation of the headquarters' rules.

   • In the general ledger process mostly law and taxation experts were involved, while task forces were responsible for adjustments.

   • The degree of automation and uniformity of group accounting information systems was significantly different.

2. *Scheduling.* The differences were explained by the degree of homogeneity and integration of the accounting systems.

3. *Data collection and control.* The main differences concerned the degree of automation and the interfaces between the general ledger process and the transaction processing cycles.

4. *Periodic closing.* The comparison pointed out differences in the amount of resources used by the general ledger process. These differences were due to

   • The degree of centralization or decentralization of the responsibility for database consistency and completeness

   • The extent of data classification and coding

5. *Reporting.* The differences concerned the number and type of managerial reports and the involvement of the accounting units in the performance evaluation.

Performance measures. Comparing performance among various general ledger processes emphasized a certain uniformity as far as time and quality performance were concerned; however, great differences in the resources allocated to the general ledger process were pointed out. The similarities can be explained by the spreading of advanced integrated information systems, on the one hand, and the high standardization of the process, on the other hand. The differences are related to both organizational position of the unit in charge of the general ledger and the procedures that managed the general ledger.

Best Practices: Characteristics of ESAC

From the comparison of the four companies' general ledger and consolidation systems, ESAC, 3M's system, came out as a significant benchmark.

ESAC is an integrated and on-line system that provides consolidated financial information concerning EBCs, regions, and Europe; facilitates P&L inquiry; compresses cycle time at local, European, and global levels; and assures multilevel security. The most significant features of ESAC can be pointed out, according to the definition of the general ledger process based on the main tasks of an information system (Wilkinson 1989).

Data collection and processing.

Data coding. The chart of accounts was redefined in 1994 to cope with European information requirements. All subsidiaries in Europe have to operate with the European common chart of account, which was driven by the center with limited local flexibility.

The European accounting code is composed of 14 digits: seven digits identify the ledger, four the cost center, and three the subaccount. The following codes are used to feed in the accounting database.

• *Company code.* This is an alphanumerical code that allows the consolidation at company level. It distinguishes among operating companies, consolidated companies, and eliminated companies (which concern accounts for intercompany operations).

• *Main/subledgers.* They identify the P&L and balance sheet accounts. The main ledgers are common to all European subsidiaries, while the subledgers are different according to local laws and accounting requirements. International global consolidation is based on main ledgers, while company consolidation is allowed at main and subledger levels.

• *Operating subaccounts.* They identify operating costs at the cost center level. They are autonomously defined by each subsidiary. At the European level there are two subaccounts: the group subaccount and the condensed subaccount (Figure 4.4). The international and company consolidation is allowed at both levels.

• *Cost centers.* All cost centers are under the responsibility of EBCs, corporate, and regions. Cost centers are consistently articulated with various functions: logistic, information technology, financial services, human resources, legal services, sales and marketing, research and development, and manufacturing. It is noteworthy to point out that ESAC is based on 400 cost centers at the European level, while GENAC, the local Italian general ledger system, was based on 1200 cost centers.

The accounting database. ESAC is an integrated, on-line general ledger system that allows transparence among all European administrative systems. It is a standardized system that allows users to maintain a common chart of accounts, ensure consistent consolidation, provide a common base for costs allocation, and reduce the data volume at the consolidated level. ESAC simplifies and makes more transparent overhead recharges and cost allocation processes, due to homogeneous criteria for cost allocation. It operates in different currencies and carries out variance analysis as far as costs and revenues at commodity, cost center, and subaccount levels are concerned.

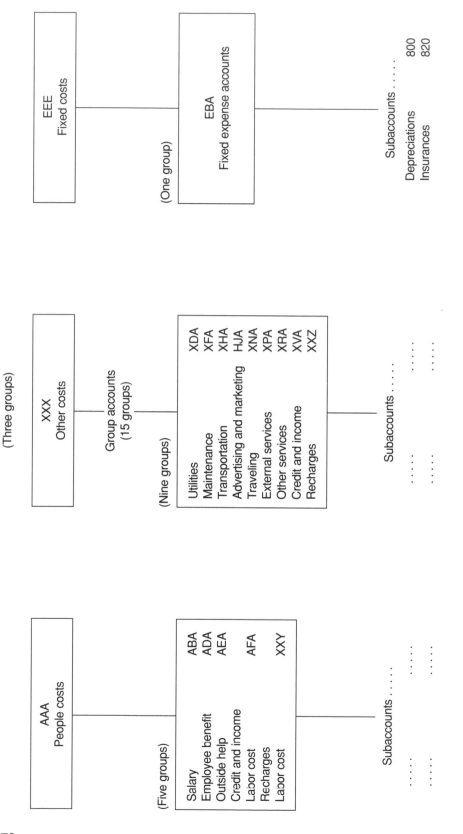

Figure 4.4. Condensed subaccounts.

Data management. ESAC can produce more analytical information than GENAC, because ESAC on-line can process and manage data coming from entries and concerning a 24-month period.

The general ledger database. This contains actual financial data (P&L, balance sheet), while operating data are collected and recorded by the subfeeder systems. The volume of data stored, which are ready for reporting activities, is 20 times wider than the GENAC database.

Inquiry codes. ESAC accelerates the decision-making processes because it enables—in real time—EBCs' managers to readily access P&L results and functional management to exercise greater control on costs. ESAC is focused on business issues, and consequently eliminates discussions on internal recharges. It consistently measures the regional financial performances of local EBC operations with the delegated responsibility.

To assure data control and security at inquiry operations, inquiry codes were defined as follows:

- Responsibility codes are consistent with the responsibility structure and allow each party to access only his or her own data.

- Controller codes enable controllers and other administrative people to access the general ledger database.

Data control and security. Access to the general ledger database is allowed according to various responsibility levels. Each party is allowed access only to the data and information that are under his or her control. To assure data control, three kind of codes were defined: accounting codes, inquiry codes, and reporting codes. Due to its features, ESAC allows a multilevel security as far as access to functions and data is concerned.

Information generation. The need to quickly exchange common information among 3M European subsidiaries and to prepare and communicate reports focused on product lines, EBCs', and EBUs' global contribution, required standardized reporting activities at the European level. ESAC can produce only a specific range of reports, which are useful mostly to EBCs' and EBUs' managers. The financial reports are articulated in commodity P&L consolidation, cost per function consolidation, European contribution gross margin report, balance sheet, and P&L reports.

In particular, the European contribution margin report provides a gross margin-by-product, or product family, on a contribution basis. The European P&L format displays cost per functions; break downs the costs reported in all major P&L lines among three categories facilitating P&L analysis from the EBCs' management viewpoint; focuses on business issues; identifies outsourcing costs for products and services; and allocates costs according to criteria based on cost drivers identification and activity absorption. At the European level, the following reporting codes are used: company, commodity, plant, sales organization, balance sheet, and P&L.

Conclusions and Lessons Learned

As far as the general ledger process was concerned, the comparison between ESAC and the general ledger systems of the other benchmarked companies confirmed the validity of 3M's general ledger and reporting system. In particular, ESAC distinguishes itself on the following aspects.

- It is an integrated and modular system.
- It assures uniformity and transparency among all European accounting systems.
- It is an on-line reporting system.
- It has an easy and flexible inquiry module.
- It allows a multilevel security.
- It defines clear and univocal responsibilities for accounting activities.
- It allows multicompany management and the arrangement of the consolidated balance sheet in real time.
- It will allow the evolution toward a global general ledger and reporting system for all of 3M's subsidiaries worldwide.*

Moreover, analysis of ESAC pointed out that the evolution and updating of the general ledger and consolidation systems is driven by dramatic changes in strategies, company values, and organizational structures. Another significant role is the information technology evolution.

With regard to the benchmarking process, as a consequence of the study, in 1995 CESAD and SDA—the Graduate Business School of Bocconi University—established the Benchmarking Network, which aimed to develop and support benchmarking studies. In 1996 the unit in charge of the Benchmarking Network was articulated in five subgroups, which benchmarked different processes and procedures: (1) financial and management accounting, (2) organization, (3) manufacturing, and logistics, (4) marketing and sales, and (5) banking. The Benchmarking Network organized two workshops and a conference. The associated companies total 56.

References

3M: Managing business in Europe in the 90's. April 1994. Milan: 3M Europe SA.

Agliati, M. 1996. *Tecnologie dell'informazione e sistema amministrativo* (Information technology and administrative systems). Milan: Eaizioni Giuridiche Economiche Aziendali Delí Universitá Bocconi E Giuffré Editori S.P.A. (EGEA).

---

*3M recently launched the "Two-day Close Project," which aims to carry out a dramatic reengineering of all financial processes in order to assure a two-day close worldwide. This project will be implemented by 2001. The new global ledger and reporting system will replace ESAC and all other 3M information accounting systems.

Agliati M., and S. Beretta. 1990. *I sistemi amministrativi nei gruppi di imprese* (Administrative systems in groups). Milan: Eaizioni Giuridiche Economiche Aziendali Delí Universitá Bocconi E Giuffré Editori S.P.A. (EGEA).

Amigoni, F. 1979. *I sistemi di controllo direzionale* (Management control systems). Varese: Giuffrè Editore.

Bartlett, C. A., and S. Ghoshal. 1989. *Managing across borders.* Boston: Harvard Business School Press.

Boisot, M. 1987. *Information and organisations.* Glasgow: Fontana Collins.

Camp, R. C. 1995. *Business process benchmarking: Finding and implementing best practices.* Milwaukee, Wisc.: ASQC Quality Press.

Carrer, S. 1996. *Anche dopo las scissione Italia strategica per la 3M* (Italy is strategic for 3M after the spin-off too). Il Sole 24 ore, 1 June.

Davenport, T. H. 1993. *Process innovation.* Boston: Harvard Business School Press.

Gruppo 3M Italia. 1992. *Rapporto annuale* (Annual report).

Hammer M., and J. Champy. 1993. *Reengineering the corporation.* New York: Harper Collins.

Laszlo, E. 1992. Information technology and social change: An evolutionary systems analysis. *Behavioral Science* 37, no., 4:237–249.

Miroglio F. 1997. Il benchmarking dei processi amministrativi. General ledger: metodologie di misurazione e aconfronto (The benchmarking of accounting processes: Measurement and comparison methodologies for the general ledger process). *Economia e Management* no. 1:111–124.

Morris, D. C., and J. S. Brandon. 1993. *Reengineering your business.* New York: McGraw-Hill.

Nolan, R. L. 1979. Managing the crisis in data processing. *Harvard Business Review,* (March–April): 115–126.

Nolan, R. L., and C. F. Gibson. 1974. Managing the four stages of EDP growth. *Harvard Business Review* (January–February): 76–88.

Prahalad, C. K., and Y. L. Doz. 1987. *The multinational mission.* New York: Free Press.

Songini, L. 1996. Tecnologie dell'informazione, sistema amministrativo e attività amministrative: l'esperienza 3M (Information technology, the administrative system, and the accounting activities: The case of 3M). In *Tecnologie dell'informazione e sistema amministrativo* (Information technology and administrative systems), edited by M. Agliati. Milan: Eaizioni Giuridiche Economiche Aziendali Delí Universitá Bocconi E Giuffré Editori S.P.A. (EGEA).

Songini, L., and L. Gnan. 1996. L'impatto delle tecnologie dell'informazione sulle attività e sulle professionalità della funzione amministrativa: i risultati di un'indagine (The impact of information technology on activities and competencies of accountants). In *Tecnologie dell'informazione e sistema amministrativo* (Information technology and administrative systems), edited by M. Agliati. Milan: Eaizioni Giuridiche Economiche Aziendali Delí Universitá Bocconi E Giuffré Editori S.P.A. (EGEA).

Wilkinson, J. W. 1989. *Accounting and information systems.* New York: John Wiley and Sons.

Acknowledgments

The authors would like to thank, for their support and advice, two CESAD Bocconi's researchers, Prof. Marco Agliati and Dr. Franco Miroglio, who carried out the benchmarking study described. The authors also appreciate the support and advice of Prof. Sergio Beretta, who is in charge of the Benchmarking Network of SDA Bocconi Business School.

About the Authors

Ambrogio Biglia has been employed by 3M Italy for more than 30 years. During his tenure, he has been in charge of various accounting department activities including equity participation and credit. He has also served as controller of the following departments: profit and loss; manufacturing; quality and training; R&D, laboratories, engineering, and environment; support services; and logistic and staff.

Biglia has contributed numerous articles to *Amministrazione e Finanza/ORO,* with topics such as the following: investment planning and control; cost leadership; management control, including challenges for the 1990s; changes in strategic planning; financial reporting; transfer prices; measuring quality; and a decision-making methodology.

Ambrogio Biglia
3M Italia S.P.A.
via S. Bovio, 3 20090 Segrate
Milan, Italy
Telephone: 39-2-7035-3312
Facsimile: 39-2-7035-2111

Lucrezia Songini is an assistant professor of management accounting and of strategic planning and management control systems at Bocconi University and an assistant professor of accounting and control at the SDA Bocconi Graduate School of Management. She is a researcher for the Research Center on Business Administration (CESAD), also at Bocconi University, and served as the coordinator of the 12th annual conference of the Euro-Asia Management Studies Association in 1995. Songini has presented several research papers including the following: "The Impact of Information Technology on Activities and Competencies of Accountants"; "The Crisis of Japanese Management: What Can We Learn from Its Transferability Abroad? The Case of UK and Italian Subsidiaries"; and "Strategic Planning and Management Control Systems of Japanese Companies."

Lucrezia Songini
SDA Bocconi Business School
Area Amministrazione e Controllo
via Bocconi, 8
20136 Milan, Italy
Telephone: 39-2-5836.6850
Facsimile: 39-2-5836.6890
E-mail: lucrezia.songini@uni-bocconi.it

CHAPTER 5

A Journey Without End: Best Practice in the Building Products Sector of Fletcher Challenge

Sue Patterson, Learning and Best Practice Coordinator, Building Products Sector, Fletcher Challenge Ltd.

Background

Fletcher Challenge is a New Zealand-based international company with assets of over $9.46 billion (NZ$13 billion). It is New Zealand's largest company, with more than 20,000 employees worldwide. The company's headquarters are in Auckland, New Zealand, and there are major operations in Australia, South America, China, the United Kingdom, and the United States. Formed in 1981, the company has four main businesses—Fletcher Challenge Paper, Fletcher Challenge Building, Fletcher Challenge Energy, and Fletcher Challenge Forests. The four divisions operate under a common vision of applying similar capabilities to bring "resources to customers better."

The Building Products Sector is one of four sectors comprising Fletcher Challenge Building. The Sector has six operating units with a combined turnover of $509 million (NZ$700 million). It employs 1600 people. The operating units are involved in the manufacture and distribution of wood-, aluminum-, and gypsum-based building materials, building membranes, and residential construction. The Sector has sites situated throughout New Zealand and in Australia, Hong Kong, and Chile.

The fundamental driving force behind best practice in the Building Products Sector is its objective to maximize shareholder value through the achievement of excellence in business operations and the development of a superior competitive position by becoming the best of the best. Further, the Sector's mission statement commits all employees to be "world-class building solutions providers." This mission can only be achieved if the benchmark for world-class, which is constantly and rapidly changing, is aggressively monitored and pursued.

The Building Products Sector recognizes that in order to be the best it needs to know who the best are, how they got to be that way, and why they remain that way. The organization recognizes that the best practice benchmarks of tomorrow will be different from those aspired to today; that the goalpost is constantly moving, and the plank constantly being raised. And so the organization is forced to constantly and aggressively pursue these ever-changing measures of excellence.

The Building Products Sector recognizes the need to benchmark its own work practices and processes against those of best-in-class organizations, and to identify the potential opportunity between what the Sector is currently achieving and the superior levels of performance achieved by others.

The organization has challenged itself to achieve world-class performance levels, which means making changes that really count. By studying best practices and adopting these throughout the businesses in the Building Products Sector—in management and reporting practices, work practices, improvement processes, training, reward, and recognition systems, culture, and operating style—the Sector has a better opportunity of positioning itself for long-term competitive advantage and value creation.

Critical to the success of this best practice journey is ensuring that Building Products Sector employees understand the meaning behind the words *best practice*. From the beginning it was important that the focus on best practice was not perceived as a passing phase—something that was here today but would be gone tomorrow. More importantly, management had to ensure that employees understood that even if they were considered to have achieved best practice in a given area, they would not be allowed to dwell on this success for long. Rather, they would be recognized for their achievements but encouraged to aspire to greater things to ensure they remained best in class.

Management in the Building Products Sector recognized the need to give best practice a profile in the Sector. So an icon was established. It appears on all documentation associated with best practice initiatives and continues to be used today. That icon is illustrated in Figure 5.1.

Figure 5.1. Building Products Sector best practice icon. The skyline reflects the building industry in which the Sector operates; the star is symbolic of excellence; and the circle reflects the globe. Therefore, global excellence/best practice.

Sector managers and employees started talking best practice: what it meant and what it would mean for the Sector. More importantly, they began acting best practice; that is, they adopted a relentless drive for excellence in every aspect of their work. This latter approach has been the key contributor to changing the mind-set of people to focus on wanting to be world-class. This approach is also a testament to the fact that actions speak louder than words and that change has to be driven by the organization's leaders.

This, then, is the story of the Building Products Sector's journey toward best practice. It is a search for those practices that will lead to aggressive internal goal setting and ultimately heightened competitiveness.

How the Journey Began

In 1992, the chief executive of the Building Products Sector, David Sixton, attended an executive development program at the University of Michigan in Ann Arbor. He returned from that program inspired and intrigued by what he had learned from the other participants about the way they worked, their management styles, their business experiences, and what had worked for them in their organizations.

Sixton wanted to learn more about what made other companies successful. He wanted to expose some of the leaders in the Building Products Sector to first-class work practices and new and better ways of doing things. The intention was to open their minds to change and ultimately empower the organization to move forward to achieve world-class performance and international competitive advantage. Thus, the decision was made to embark on the Sector's first best practice study tour.

Learning From the Best

In planning the study tours, the approach has always been to collectively agree to the learning objectives for the tour by deciding which business areas require rapid improvement. This process ensures that all participants have a vested interest, and establishes buy-in to the concept and ownership of the learnings and resulting improvement initiatives.

Once the learning objectives are finalized, those worldwide organizations that exhibit expertise in these areas and who can deliver on the learning objectives are identified. They are then approached as potential benchmarking partners.

Prior to departure, the touring team undertakes extensive research of the companies to be visited, resulting in all team members developing a good understanding of the profile and structure of these organizations. This allows the time during the actual visit to be spent focusing specifically on the learning objectives for the tour rather than on information that is available in the public arena.

The Inaugural Study Tour

The first best practice study tour was undertaken in March 1993, and included visits to 10 of the world's most prominent companies in the United States. The tour lasted two weeks.

As this was the first study tour, and in the interests of ensuring that the participants learned as much as possible about best practice management techniques and how these were being applied in world-class organizations, the learning objectives were broadly formulated. Subsequent study tours have had more defined learning objectives, since, over time, the Sector's management has identified specific areas in the business where improvement has been required.

The learning objectives for the 1993 study tour were as follows:

• *Visionary leadership.* This was defined as the opportunity to gain a greater understanding of the leadership skills and style required to build an effective company culture and to guide people and organizations toward achieving excellence.

• *Human resource strategies.* Specifically, these were employee involvement and empowerment initiatives, reward and recognition systems, training and development programs, internal communication, and motivation.

• *Customer service initiatives.* These included identifying significant step changes and innovations being adopted by other companies and industries to achieve excellent levels of customer service. They also included the development of a customer service focus/culture within an organization.

• *Creativity and innovation.* These were defined as systems and initiatives designed to maximize organizational learning, creativity, and innovation—both in the identified areas and across the broad marketing/operational perspective.

• *Inspiration.* This is the opportunity to broaden participants' horizons and provide firsthand experience that excellence beyond current practices is possible and is being achieved.

A team of 14 general and functional managers undertook this tour. It included visits to the following organizations.

• Beth Israel Hospital, Boston, Massachusetts; 604-bed teaching hospital affiliated with Harvard Medical School

• Boston Edison Company, Boston, Massachusetts; public utility and primarily a retail electric supplier

• Disney World, Orlando, Florida; family vacation and tourist attraction

• DuPont, Wilmington, Delaware; multinational chemical product manufacturer

• Federal Express Corporation, Memphis, Tennessee; courier service

• Fetzer Vineyards, Redwood Valley, California; winegrower

• Hewlett-Packard, Palo Alto, California; computer and office products company

- ITT Sheraton, Boston, Massachusetts; worldwide hotels, inns, and resorts
- Merck & Company, Whitehouse Station, New Jersey; research-intensive health products company
- San Diego Wild Animal Park, San Diego, California; zoo and wildlife park

It is worth noting that none of the companies visited during the study tours operates in the same industry as the Building Products Sector. Thus, their relevance to the Sector might be questioned. Management and employees have learned, however, that regardless of the industry, there are key processes that are common to all. These include such processes as people management and development and customer value creation. Fletcher Challenge's study tours focus on how some of the best organizations in the world manage these and other processes. It is by focusing on the best capability that an organization can stand out from the pack.

During a study tour it is usual for the team to spend half a day meeting with the host company and the other half of the day debriefing the visit. This process ensures the learnings are comprehensively captured and documented, which, in turn, allows implementation plans to be easily and effectively formulated.

On conclusion of the tour, the team produces a manual that encompasses all the learnings from the tour. A copy of this document is shared with the study tour host companies and distributed widely throughout the Building Products Sector. In conjunction with a number of sharing rallies, the manual helps to spread the learning, both sectorwide and throughout other parts of Fletcher Challenge, and it brings about required change.

In the spirit of benchmarking ethics, it is important for Fletcher Challenge to respect the confidentiality of the information that host companies so generously and willingly shared. Therefore, it is not possible to share in this case study the detailed learnings from the study tours. The Sector recognizes, however, that benchmarking relationships will only succeed if the parties involved adopt a sharing philosophy. Accordingly, the Building Products Sector welcomes any approach from organizations that would like to learn from the study tour experiences or discuss the learnings from these tours in more detail.

The 1993 tour acted as a catalyst for further study tours. In 1995 three more study tours were undertaken.

Best Practice in Product Innovation

The first tour of 1995 was to 3M in St. Paul, Minnesota. On this occasion, the touring team was a group of people from the Building Products Sector with responsibility for developing and introducing new products. This tour exposed a different group of people from the Sector to the concept of best practice, and contributed to enlightening people at all levels of the organization as to what can and is being achieved by best practice organizations. The touring team was accompanied by Michael Thomas of 3M New Zealand with whom the Building Products Sector has developed and enjoys a successful benchmarking relationship.

The learning goals for the tour to 3M, formulated by the touring team, were as follows:

• Understand the framework for product development and innovation, including 3M's innovation ethos, processes for maintaining a culture of innovation, allocation of resources, product championing, and measurement systems.

• Understand the techniques and processes by which 3M focuses its efforts on its customers.

• Understand the methods by which 3M extends its product range.

• Understand the way cross-functional teamwork is fostered at 3M.

The Building Products Sector continues to work closely with 3M, sharing experiences and jointly seeking best practices.

Best Practice in Manufacturing

With no fewer than four of the Building Products Sector's six companies being involved in manufacturing, it is obvious that manufacturing is one of Fletcher Challenge's most important processes. The organization's day-to-day performance in manufacturing has a huge impact on the quality of products and so impacts how customers perceive the organization and on their ultimate buying decisions. To be world-class overall, the Building Products Sector must be world-class in manufacturing. Thus, it makes sense to learn from companies that are considered to be best practice in the manufacturing arena.

In March 1995 a study tour to eight prominent manufacturing organizations in Australia was organized. The touring team comprised a cross-section of people from the Building Products Sector whose key responsibility is to manage manufacturing processes. The tour was facilitated by Danny Samson, professor of manufacturing management at Melbourne University, Australia. His expertise in manufacturing best practice and knowledge of Australian manufacturers assisted the study team to identify its learning needs and to select the most appropriate companies to visit.

The companies visited included the following:

• Australian Paper, Sydney, New South Wales; Australian arm of Amcor Paper Group's pulp and paper business

• DuPont (Australia) Fibres Division, Melbourne, Victoria; synthetic fiber maker

• General Motor's Holden Automotive, Adelaide, South Australia; motor vehicle manufacturer, division of GM

• Holden's Engine Company, Port Melbourne, Victoria; engine developer and manufacturer, fully owned subsidiary of GM

• ICI Australia, Sydney, New South Wales; chemical products manufacturer

• Kodak (Australasia) Pty., Melbourne, Victoria; photographic, health, and electronic imaging systems

• South Pacific Tyres, Melbourne, Victoria; tire manufacturer, wholesaler, and retailer

• Uncle Ben's of Australia, Albury, New South Wales; pet food maker

The six specific learning objectives for the tour were as follows:

1. *Best practice in customer focus.* Including the development of a complete customer focus, customer service, customer feedback, and partnerships.

2. *Best practice in quality management and process control.* Including a total quality culture, continuous improvement, measurements, benchmarking, and follow-through.

3. *Best practice in production and inventory control.* Including maintenance, scheduling, inventory management, and logistics.

4. *Best practice in technology management.* Optimizing existing technology, introducing new technology, technology alliances, and the interface between people and technology.

5. *Best practice in managing people.* Including visionary leadership, rewards and recognition, self-directed work teams, communication, health and safety, training, learning and education, workplace environment, and employment practices.

6. *Best practice in using manufacturing as a competitive weapon.* Seeing manufacturing as strategic, developing manufacturing capability, order winners, and core business.

The ordering of these learnings objectives is important. The first four are about particular actions. The fifth describes how the oft-stated most important asset of any company, people, can be managed to enable such actions to be carried out. And the last outlines the aim of the whole exercise.

Continuing the Journey

The senior management team that undertook the inaugural best practice study tour in 1993 traveled again during 1996 to nine companies in the United States and Europe. The companies visited on this occasion were as follows:

• ABB UK (Asea Brown Boveri), York, United Kingdom; global electrical engineering and power generation and transmission organization

• British Airways, Heathrow, United Kingdom; international airline

• Herman Miller, Zeeland, Michigan; furniture systems manufacturer and seller

• Home Depot, Atlanta, Georgia; home improvement retail store chain

• IKEA, Copenhagen, Denmark; Scandinavian-designed furniture, textiles, and household items retailer

• ISS (International Service System), London, United Kingdom; global cleaning organization

• Royal Dutch Shell, London, United Kingdom; oil, natural gas, chemicals, coal, and metals business

- UK Paper, London, United Kingdom; fine paper manufacturer and seller, a wholly owned subsidiary of Fletcher Challenge Ltd.

- Unilever, London, United Kingdom; brand and packaged goods, primarily foods, detergents, personal products, and specialty chemicals

As with the 1993 tour, the learning objectives for this tour were broadly formulated in an effort to capture best practice techniques in a range of areas. They included the following:

- *Customer intimacy.* How to customize products and services to meet unique customer needs.

- *Operational excellence.* How world-class companies combine price, reliability, and hassle-free service to deliver the lowest total cost package to their customers.

- *Product leadership.* How companies generate and market a continuous stream of state-of-the-art products.

- *Creating a supportive environment for learning and growth.* Why some companies learn faster than their competitors; how their people are developed; how risk taking and entrepreneurial behavior are encouraged; how company cultures reinforce visions and values.

- *Customer needs and value understanding.* How world-class companies hear the voice of their customers and, having heard it, how they use this information; how these companies learn with their customers.

- *Strategic thinking.* How companies plan for the future, evaluate growth opportunities, and make the most of their core capabilities; how they achieve a high degree of decentralization, while making the most of synergies.

- *Optimizing logistics.* How companies anticipate customer needs and then build this knowledge into their operations so customer demands are met; how the companies build relationships with their suppliers and their customers; how the companies ensure their business processes are at their best from a functional, organizational, and geographical viewpoint.

- *Reengineering.* How companies capture additional value from their processes through reengineering.

Best Practice in Customer Value Creation

The Building Products Sector has developed an in-house self-assessment process aimed at fostering continuous improvement. It is known as the Business Improvement Awards.

The objective of the awards is to deliver superior value to customers and to Fletcher Challenge by

- Encouraging commitment to business improvement throughout the Building Products Sector

- Objectively measuring the rate of improvement across the Sector

- Recognizing those Sector companies committed to business improvement

- Setting benchmarks annually from which to plan and monitor improvement

- Creating a forum for the sharing of best practice ideas based on a common understanding of key performance drivers

The Business Improvement Awards operate for all companies in the Building Products Sector of Fletcher Challenge, and comprise an annual top award for the overall best performer and one for the best performer in each of seven categories. The inaugural awards in 1995 were used to set the benchmark so future awards could be based on the rate of improvement, rather than the highest score.

The criteria for the Business Improvement Awards are based on the U.S. Malcolm Baldrige National Quality Award and the New Zealand National Quality Awards. The criteria cover seven major categories as follows:

1. Leadership

2. Information and analysis

3. Strategic planning

4. People development and management

5. Process management

6. Business results

7. Superior customer value

Figure 5.2 illustrates how the seven categories of the awards are related.

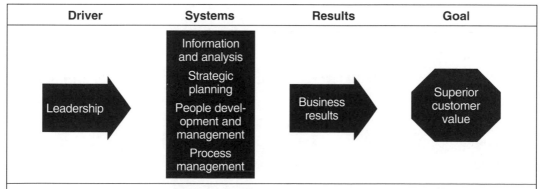

Driver	Systems	Results	Goal
Leadership	Information and analysis Strategic planning People development and management Process management	Business results	Superior customer value

The driver is the company's leadership, which sets direction, enabling the systems to be designed and implemented. These systems then produce business results that are all focused on superior customer value; the primary goal of the company.

Figure 5.2. How the seven categories of the Business Improvement Awards are related.

The assessments undertaken in 1995 identified a sectorwide need for improvement in the superior customer value category. In the majority of cases an appropriate process was already in place but the weakness was in implementation, review, and data validation.

As a result, in 1996 a team of people from the Sector, with responsibility for the marketing activities of their respective businesses, visited 16 companies in New Zealand, the United States, and the United Kingdom. The aim of this tour was to study how these companies learn about their customers and integrate this knowledge back through their organizations to create superior value products and services.

Specifically, the tour learning objectives were as follows:

• Customer market knowledge

—*Approach.* How best practice companies identify their target markets/customer segments and learn about their needs, including the final customer.

—*Hardwiring.* How best practice companies communicate this knowledge back into the organization, identify their order winners, and integrate this into strategy and daily operations.

—*Review.* How best practice companies review the process used and validate the information received.

• Customer partnerships

—*Approach.* The process best practice companies use to receive and record customer feedback and build long-term partnerships.

—*Hardwiring.* How best practice companies integrate this feedback into partnership strategies and daily operations.

—*Review.* How best practice companies review the process used and validate the information received.

• Customer value creation measurement

—*Approach.* How best practice companies measure customer satisfaction and value creation, and benchmark these against competitors and best practice.

—*Hardwiring.* How best practice companies integrate this back into organizational processes, such as strategy, product/service development, and daily operations.

—*Review.* How best practice companies review the processes used and validate the information received.

Companies visited on the tour included the following:

<u>New Zealand</u>

• Ansett New Zealand, Auckland; one of two major domestic airlines
• Clear Communications, Auckland; telecommunications company

- Interlock Industries, Wellington; window and door hardware designer, manufacturer, and supplier

- Stamford Plaza Auckland, Auckland; 322-bed hotel, part of Stamford Hotels and Resorts chain

- Telecom Directories, Auckland; regional and specialist telephone and facsimile directory publisher, division of New Zealand's largest telecommunications company

United Kingdom

- ABB UK (Asea Brown Boveri), Cambridgeshire; global organization with five business segments including power generation, transmission, and distribution, industrial and building systems, and transportation and financial services

- Avis Management Services, Middlesex; worldwide motor vehicle rental services

- British Airways, Middlesex; international airline

- IKEA, London; Scandinavian-designed furniture, textiles, and household items retailer

- ISS (International Service System), Middlesex; global cleaning organization

- SmithKline Beecham, Middlesex; pharmaceutical and health-related products manufacturer and seller

United States

- Dun & Bradstreet, Murray Hill, New Jersey; business-to-business risk management, credit, marketing, and decision support services supplier

- Hewlett-Packard, Cupertino, California; computer and office products company

- Merck-Medco Managed Care, Parsippany, New Jersey; prescription drug benefit program provider, division of Merck & Company

- Miller Brewing, Milwaukee, Wisconsin; second largest brewery in the United States, subsidiary of the Phillip Morris Companies

- State Farm Insurance, Bloomington, Illinois; automobile, home, and pleasure boat insurer

Best Practice in Franchising

In 1996 the Building Products Sector acquired an aluminum extrusion business with an extensive multibrand franchising distribution network. The Sector recognized the need to learn from the experience and expertise of others in the franchising field in an effort to ensure its approach to franchising is an example of best practice.

Accordingly, in 1997, a team of franchising and business development managers visited a range of companies, in New Zealand and Australia, that display expertise in franchising. These companies include the following:

Australia

- Ampol, Australian Petroleum Pty., Sydney, New South Wales; petroleum products and oil industry leader

- Beaurepaires, Melbourne, Victoria; Australia's largest retail tire chain

- Bob Jane T-Marts Pty, Melbourne, Victoria; Australia's largest independent retailer of passenger car tires, wheels, and batteries

- Caterpillar of Australia, Melbourne, Victoria; construction and mining equipment, natural gas engine and diesel engine manufacturer

- Speeds Shoes, Melbourne, Victoria; shoe retailer

New Zealand

- Fastway Couriers, Auckland; courier service with 550 franchise couriers throughout Australasia

- Ford Motor Company of New Zealand, Auckland; car and truck manufacturer

- McDonald's System of New Zealand, Auckland; fast food restaurants

- Stirling Sports Franchises, Auckland; sporting goods retailer

The high-level learning challenge for the touring team was to understand how various franchising models support distribution partnerships that create superior value for both parties today and build an alternative channel competency for tomorrow, in line with the Sector's vision of being a "world-class building solutions provider."

The specific objectives of the tour were to learn how best practice franchising companies do the following;

- Create a sustainable competitive advantage for themselves and their channel partners; in particular

—The management tools used in relation to recruitment, capability development, communication, business support programs, and improving the deal year after year

—Creating a service offer to accommodate differing business needs, specifically differing business sizes and market segments

- Achieve world-class channel management; specifically

—The management of multibrand franchising competing in the same channel

—The approach taken to ensure channels are the most efficient distribution mechanism in the industry

On conclusion of the tour, the team consolidated and reviewed the learnings and prepared an action plan for implementation. This will ensure that the Sector's franchising initiatives are comparable to best practice standards.

Applied Learnings

The pursuit of best practice provides a catalyst to provoke the changes necessary to meet the challenges facing companies today. It creates a unifying purpose, shifting attitudes from complacency to a sense of urgency to become world competitive, and forging a culture that values continuous improvement and major innovation.

A great deal of the study tour learnings have been applied throughout the Sector, and significant improvements in business processes have been achieved. It must be recognized, however, that the best practice journey is a journey for life. Thus, the organization will constantly seek ways to improve itself to create maximum value for shareholders.

The applied learnings range from the implementation of small-step, incremental improvements through to major change programs. The more significant initiatives that have impacted the Sector include the following:

• *Leadership.* Through exposure to the leaders in the companies visited, there is a clear picture of the characteristics and attributes of successful leaders. A leadership profile has been developed, and is used to assess individuals recruited for leadership positions and for recruiting graduates into the organization. This leadership profile is aligned to the vision and values of both the Building Products Sector and Fletcher Challenge. The high-level learnings taken from the studies of visionary leaders are that leadership is an awesome yet rewarding responsibility and that great companies have great leaders.

• *Human resource strategies.* The processes used to recruit, induct, train, and develop people at all levels in the organization have been revised and improved. Studies have reinforced the belief that making sure the right people are in the right jobs is critical to the success of any organization.

The Sector's internal communication strategies have also been revamped, and a range of innovative communication practices introduced. The approach is to ensure that communications with people are frequent, yet simple, informative, and timely; thus ensuring that the message is communicated before employees read it in the newspaper.

The Building Products Sector has also introduced formal programs for recognizing and rewarding people whose efforts and approach to their work mirror the organization's drive for excellence and best practice status. In some cases, these programs have been the catalyst for a complete change of culture in the Sector's businesses.

• *Creativity and innovation (C&I).* On returning from the inaugural study tour in 1993, the Sector embarked on a program to introduce a spirit of creativity and innovation into its culture. This program has resulted in Fletcher Challenge now having a group of some 60 people trained in a range of creative problem-solving techniques that are regularly used to facilitate innovative business solutions. The use of these techniques has resulted in substantial savings being made where the implementation of an employee's idea has meant the apparent need to spend money to fix a problem has been negated. The process is also an effective way of getting people involved and contributing to the success of the business.

• *Customer value creation.* Following the 1996 marketing study tour, the methodologies relating to customer value creation were further researched. The Sector has adopted an approach based on a measure known as customer value added (CVA). This measure and methodology has two parts—the "science" or measurement based on clear, concise, regular questionnaires and econometric models; and the "art," which focuses on understanding the measures and structuring an action program aimed at improving the CVA score and thereby the customer's level of satisfaction. It is believed that this project will improve customer loyalty.

• *Safety.* Learning from DuPont's experiences and expertise in the safety arena, a "Safety First" program has been introduced throughout the Sector with a goal of achieving zero incidents.

• *Learning.* The Sector is continuing to develop itself as a learning organization, skilled at creating, acquiring, and transferring knowledge and modifying behavior to reflect new knowledge and insights. Through developing a supportive environment for learning and personal growth throughout the Sector, people are able to realize the value that can be gained from talking about the way they work and sharing experiences with others. The aim is to offer employability rather than employment by empowering people to take responsibility for their own development and growth. Through changing and challenging times, this has been of great comfort to many Sector employees who recognize that they leave Fletcher Challenge with a greater range of skills than they had when they commenced their employment.

The Importance of the Process

In applying best practices it is particularly relevant to understand the importance of the process within best practice companies. In all the companies studied, it has been apparent that the process used to achieve success in many areas is absolutely critical.

Things did not just happen. They were well planned, and sound processes were put in place to ensure they became a reality. Performance was continually measured to ensure progress was being achieved, and there was an inherent belief that without sound processes, failure would be inevitable.

While the status quo is undoubtedly the most comfortable situation for everyone in an organization, major improvements in productivity, quality, competitiveness, and profitability are not achieved by "Band-Aid®" solutions to deep-seated organizational failings.

Dramatic improvements are only achieved when the complete set of activities that are undertaken to deliver a defined end product are redesigned. That may require the complete dismantling of a process and rebuilding it from scratch.

A handbook on business process reengineering produced by one study tour host company observed that while companies have taken many different approaches to redesigning processes, successful projects have some common elements. These guidelines are also applicable to ensuring the effective implementation of best practice learnings.

• Careful scoping of the business process to be redesigned. If the scope is too small, critical interfaces with larger processes may be missed, limiting the potential impact; if too large, the study may be unmanageable.

• Aggressive quantifiable objectives for improvement; for example, cost reductions, better response and/or delivery times, higher quality products, greater customer satisfaction.

• Cross-functional teams representing all functions and employees at all levels involved in the process to ensure a 360° perspective of the business process redesign and implementation of the rebuilt process.

• Study teams that include customers and suppliers who are integral parts of the process.

• A project manager and study team staff who are recognized as high performers with the vision to define the way business needs to be done in the future.

• Strong, visible senior management support to communicate the project's priority, break through roadblocks, overcome opposition against change, and acquire appropriate resources.

• The entire process is overseen to its completion.

What the Best Practice Journey Has Meant for the Building Products Sector

The study tours and other benchmarking initiatives have enabled the Sector to learn and change at a rapid pace. They have inspired and excited managers and employees about the type of company they can create, and have opened their eyes as to what can be achieved and what is being achieved in best practice companies. The tours and benchmarking initiatives have helped develop better leaders for Fletcher Challenge, formulate a blueprint for the future, and have supported the Building Product Sector's survival by helping to identify its competitive edge.

The study tours discussed in this case study have been undertaken at the Sector level and have focused on those areas where improvement across all Sector companies has been required. Individual businesses within the Sector also undertake study tours and other benchmarking initiatives, usually visiting companies within similar industries to themselves and focusing specifically on identifying best practice within that industry.

This case study would not be complete without mentioning the valuable relationships the Sector has developed with its host companies. The success of the Sector's benchmarking efforts is attributable to the cooperation and willingness of these organizations to openly share their experiences.

The people who have been fortunate to have participated in the study tours, and have had the opportunity to learn from the experiences and expertise of others, recognize the value of such an experience—both in terms of personal growth and in bringing learning to the organization as a whole.

The quest for best practice is indeed a journey without end; however, the Building Products Sector recognizes the limitless value of the learning experience, and the immense inspiration received along the way has been more than sufficient compensation for the fact that the final destination will continue to elude it.

About the Author

Sue Patterson joined Fletcher Challenge in early 1988 as a personal assistant to the managing director of one of Fletcher Challenges' operating companies. She says, "Life with Fletcher Challenge is full of opportunities, and I have been fortunate enough to be able to expand my role and grow with it." Her current responsibilities focus on coordinating the Building Product Sector's initiatives related to learning and its global search for best practices. Patterson may be contacted as follows:

Sue Patterson
Learning and Best Practice Coordinator
Building Products Sector
Fletcher Challenge Ltd.
Private Bag 92114
Auckland, New Zealand
Telephone: 64 9 525 9346
Facsimile: 64 9 579 9615
E-mail: suep@fcl.co.nz

CHAPTER 6

Hardware Procurement at NIIT

Anil Kumar, Vice President, NIIT Ltd., and Ashish Basu, Chief Operating Officer, Institute of Quality Ltd.

Executive Summary

Preamble
As an organization, NIIT has undertaken various quality initiatives, one of them being improving processes using benchmarking. A team embarked upon improving the capital asset procurement process with the objective of reducing cycle time.

Project Scope
The hardware import value is greater than $1.3 million (Rs. 5 crore) for the software exports group (SEG) and the instructional software group (ISG).

Objective
To eliminate the price of nonconformance (PONC) in the area of hardware procurement for SEG and ISG by achieving zero defects on meeting customer requirements.

Process Followed
- Identified the subject for benchmarking: A high-impact area for the organization and one critical to achieving customer satisfaction
- Finalized terms of reference, measurement criteria, and elements of PONC
- Identified benchmarking partners on the basis of speed of procurement (low procurement cycle time) for nonstandard items, approachability, and willingness to share data

- Analyzed data for procurement delay on 58 transactions for the period October 1995–May 1996
- Calculated PONC for 12 transactions
- Determined data collection method
- Presented data to sponsors
- Mapped current procurement process for hardware import, from receipt of purchase intent to delivery at user site
- Identified and analyzed major disconnects
- Mapped "should" or desired procurement process, with a proposed cycle time reduction from 86 days to 19 days
- Mapped current process for installation of hardware and did root cause analysis
- Mapped "should" or desired installation process, with a proposed cycle time reduction from 18 days to 3 days
- Arranged meetings with benchmarking partners

Proposed Solutions

- Standardize hardware configuration with both manufacturers and customers.
- Consolidate requirements bi-annually based on projections at the commercial services organization (CSO) instead of repeating the procurement process for each capital procurement sanction (CPS).
- Eliminate CPS system for hardware import for new projects.
- Neutralize, by advance scheduling, the delay of external influencing factors such as letter of credit opening (10 days), delivery lead time (30 days), and STP licensing (6 days). (In India, an STP or software technology park, signifies an export zone with a different tax structure.)
- Keep an exigency stock of 20 indigenous machines.
- Have the installation certificate linked to issuance of the letter of credit payment to eliminate short shipments.

Major Benefits

- Procurement process reduced from 86 days to 19 days for New Delhi and to 26 days for operations outside of New Delhi
- No time overrun against 41–61 days at present
- No delay in exigency requirements

- PONC reduction
- Better quality of work life
- Internal customer satisfaction
- Avoidance of follow-up costs
- Higher degree of accuracy project estimation

The new process is being piloted for two projects for SEG in Calcutta and New Delhi.

About NIIT

With revenue of $90 million, NIIT is the front-runner and pioneer in information technology education in India. It is also the third largest exporter of software products from India.

NIIT delivers education through classrooms, automated learning centers, multimedia educational software programs, and the Internet alumnus base of over 500,000 students worldwide. It is among the top six educational multimedia developers worldwide.

NIIT has operations in India, the United States, Singapore, Thailand, Indonesia, Malaysia, the Philippines, Hong Kong, Japan, the United Kingdom, Sweden, Germany, Belgium, the Netherlands, and France. Started in 1981, NIIT employs 3200.

The Commercial Services Organization

The mission of the commercial services organization (CSO) is to provide defect-free services to meet the requirements of internal customers on time, every time, through use of robust processes and innovative and cost-effective solutions. One such service is in the area of infrastructure creation, purchasing, and asset management. The purchasing and asset management process is administered by a small team that reports to the vice president of commercial operations.

Customers

There are five strategic business units at NIIT that are CSO customers. Of these, three primary groups are the software services business units, the information technology (IT) solutions business units, and the learning software business units.

Some of the key requirements of these units is for the CSO to build software factories and to procure computer hardware for software development activities in order to service a wide international customer base. The software development activity happens through software factories, notified as 100 percent export-oriented units. The assets imported into export-oriented units and used for developing products for export are exempt from levy of customs duty. To avail itself of this benefit, the purchase department sources computer hardware through international markets.

The creation of infrastructure and software factories is based on annual expansion plans of the strategic business units. Hardware purchasing activities are triggered on getting an approval for asset acquisition. The purchase department, through a formal interface with the user groups, has committed a delivery and installation cycle time of 45 days from the date of obtaining a formal approval for asset acquisition.

Needs/Reasons for Improvement

Every year the purchase department gathers data on customer satisfaction through the formal channel of a customer satisfaction survey and through customer complaints and customer contact. One of the top customer dissatisfiers in the area of purchasing was timely procurement and installation of computer hardware for the software factories. There was enough objective data available on the average cycle time taken to procure and install an asset. Aggregation of the data and time cycle time analysis revealed the following facts.

- Actual procurement and installation time was 110 days against a commitment of 45 days. This resulted in

  —Loss of person-hours (idle time for software developers)

  —Project overrun in terms of software development time

  —Additional cost to the organization to acquire computer hardware

In 1996 as part of its quality journey, NIIT identified benchmarking as a focus area. Within the company, the managing director's quality club took on the mantle of introducing benchmarking and created four teams for carrying out this task. One of the teams was comprised of the vice president of commercial operations, the head of the learning software business unit, and two others from the NIIT education group. This team initiated a project to achieve the following objectives.

- To reduce the procurement and installation cycle time for computer hardware through process improvement

- To negotiate and finalize a mutually agreed cycle time for procurement of hardware with the internal customer

- To ensure zero defects on meeting delivery commitments as per an agreed interface

Methodology

The team decided to use a two-step methodology to achieve the objectives.

The first step provides a process improvement methodology for arriving at some quick-fix solutions. This methodology involves documenting the "is" or current process in a diagrammatic form and then studying it for document flow and the time taken for each flow. The diagrammatic form of the current process is depicted as follows:

- Process 1 is from the time an asset acquisition sanction is obtained to delivery of assets. This is illustrated in Figure 6.1.

- Process 2 is from delivery of asset to installation. This is illustrated in Figure 6.2.

This first step in the methodology also helps in finding the disconnects in the process, which then leads to a "should" process. This should or desired process is a result of a brainstorming session, and is a part of the methodology.

The second step of the methodology is to benchmark the activity to determine the potential opportunity to improve the process and to identify best practices to improve the deliverable in order to satisfy customer requirements.

Observations

The total current process, from capital purchase sanction (CPS) receipt to hardware installation took 110 days. The steps consisted of registering the order, acknowledging the same, negotiating with international suppliers, and sending them a purchase order.

Based on this, a proforma invoice was received, which triggered off the application for an STP license. On receiving the license, the letter of credit was prepared and the details faxed to the supplier. On receipt of the letter of credit, the supplier shipped the hardware via air freight and sent the dispatch documents via courier. Based on these documents, the bill of entry and other documents related to imports were prepared and attested by the bank, which helped clear the hardware through customs. The hardware was then delivered to the user groups.

The analysis clearly revealed the following:

- The cycle time was too long.

- There were more steps than necessary (16).

- There were too many handoffs in line and between internal entities.

- There were too many decision makers at all levels.

- There was a major dependence on external agencies.

- There was a need to make major changes and to make the entire process straightforward.

The brainstorming session started by completely redefining the delivery norms. The question asked was: Why can't we deliver and install computers on customer demand? This was a total paradigm shift. From the purchase department's point of view, it meant building teams capability within the department to service such a requirement; new and innovative thinking; and perhaps a 180° shift in the process.

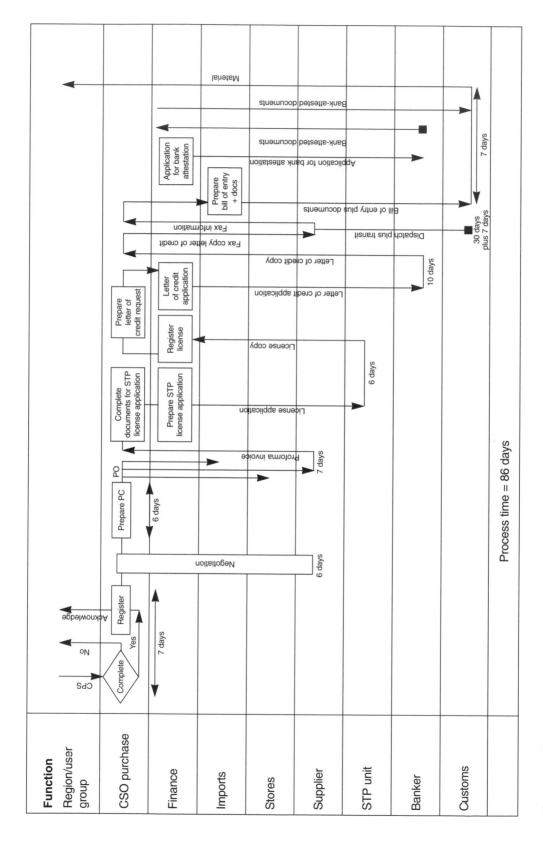

Figure 6.1. Current process 1, from receipt of capital purchase sanction (CPS) to delivery at user site.

106

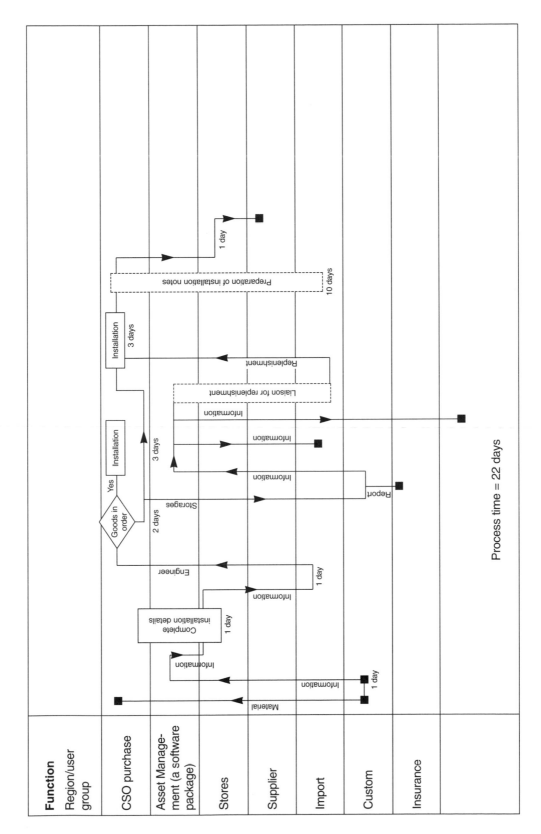

Figure 6.2. Current process 2, from delivery of asset to installation of imported hardware.

On critically scrutinizing the current process, some major disconnects—which were causing major delays—were highlighted. Figures 6.3 and 6.4 depict the should or desired process for procurement and installation, respectively. The following observations are derived.

- Total cycle time reduction from 110 days to 24 days
- Reduction in major steps from 16 to 4
- Reduction of entities in the process
- Major disconnects removed from processes 1 and 2 (Figures 6.5 and 6.6 respectively)

Identifying Benchmarking Partners

Having mapped the current and desired processes, the team set out to identify benchmarking partners. The team looked for functional leaders instead of competitors. The basis for selection was as follows:

- Similarly structured in the purchasing department
- Speed of procurement and effect on cost and quality
- Approachability
- Willingness to share information
- Good process implementation

Data Collection

A questionnaire was designed to capture key data from benchmarking partners on operational issues such as the following:

- Types of items imported
- Number of transactions per annum
- Value of imported goods
- Mode of payment
- Price approvals
- Ordering process
- Profile of people in the purchasing department
- Monitoring and feedback mechanism

Data captured from the benchmarking partners are depicted in Figures 6.7 and 6.8.

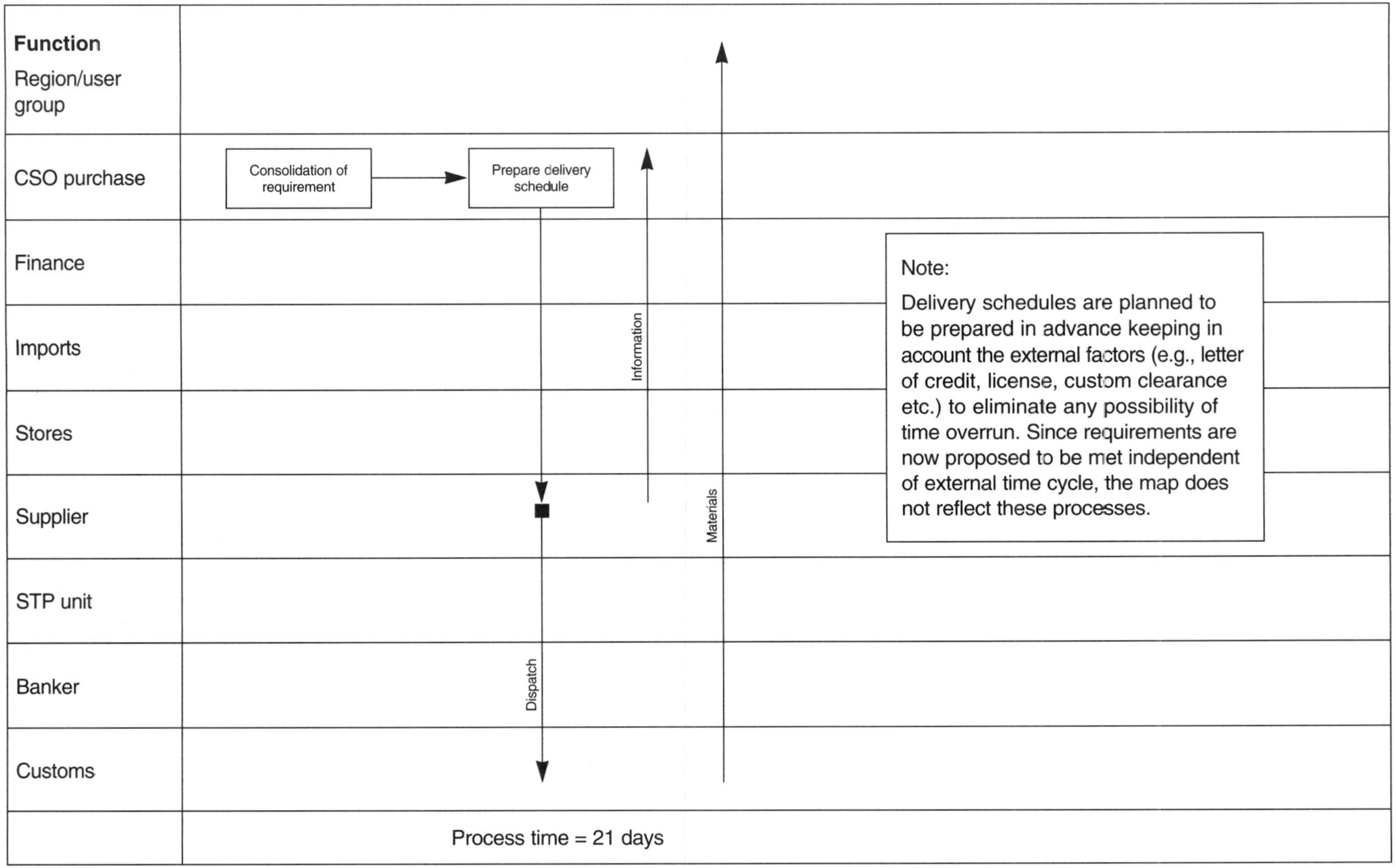
Function
Region/user group
CSO purchase
Finance
Imports
Stores
Supplier
STP unit
Banker
Customs
Consolidation of requirement
Prepare delivery schedule
Information
Materials
Dispatch
Note:
Delivery schedules are planned to be prepared in advance keeping in account the external factors (e.g., letter of credit, license, custom clearance etc.) to eliminate any possibility of time overrun. Since requirements are now proposed to be met independent of external time cycle, the map does not reflect these processes.
Process time = 21 days

Figure 6.3. Proposed process for process 1, procurement.

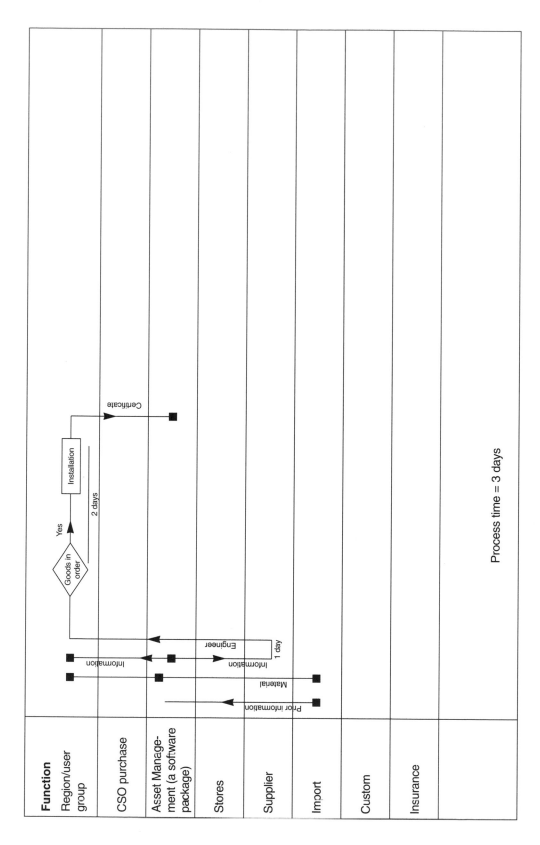

Figure 6.4. Proposed process for process 2, installation.

Disconnects	Duration before benchmarking (days)	Solution	Duration after benchmarking (days)	Action plan
Procurement process triggered on CPS receipt and terminating on purchase	10–30	• Process initiated based on bi-annual requirement; no purchase orders.	0	• Have a standard hardware configuration both with the manufacturer and the customer. • Consolidate requirement for period of 6 months on the basis of projects/infrastructure requirements. • Do not implement CPS system for new projects.
Licensing process	4–10	• Licensing done based on bi-annual plan.	0	• Build the plan with STPs for obtaining license for 6 months' requirements.
Letter of credit opening	7–12	• Introduce a single letter of credit valid for six months' requirements.	0	• Establish a letter of credit valid for 6 months of projected requirements.
Dispatch lead time for supplier	30	• Schedule in advance.	0	• Inform about requirement at least 40 days in advance. • Carry additional stock of 20 indigenous machines to meet emergency requirements.
Procurement process too long	86–110	• Streamline processes.	19	• Follow the new procurement plan.

Figure 6.5. Disconnect analysis for process 1, procurement. Process = capital purchase; scope = hardware (SEG, IEG) import (from CPS acknowledgment to delivery at user site).

Disconnects	Duration before benchmarking (days)	Solution	Duration after benchmarking (days)	Action plan
Information to the representative receiving material at site	3	• Provide prior information to the local representative.	1	• Inform local representative 7 days in advance of possibility of receipt of consignment. • Give local driver final information 2 days in advance of the date on which the consignment is likely to be cleared from New Delhi. • For outstation delivery, inform on the day the consignment is cleared from customs.
Receipt of goods at site and incomplete delivery	5	• Standardize list of accessories to be supplied with hardware. • Have supplier's packing list match NIIT purchase order. • Have installation-linked payment.	0	• Prepare standard checklist of accessories to be supplied along with the order. • Make the checklist part of the purchase order. • Have supplier create a packing list giving a complete description of the item with reference to the purchase order. • Include "release of payment on the basis of installation certificate" as a standard term in the letter of credit.
Integration problems and site installation	14	• Highlight integration problems to suppliers. • Prepare site in advance.	2	• Prepare checklist for compatibility issues. • Make this checklist part of the purchase order. • Prepare checklist for site requirements. • Assign responsibility of preparing site as per requirements to the site representative.

Figure 6.6. Disconnect analysis for process 2, installation. Process = capital purchase; scope = software import for SEG and IEG (from delivery of asset to installation of hardware).

Description	Partner A*	NIIT current	NIIT proposed
Type of items	Standard raw materials	Nonstandard (hardware configuration different in each transaction); software specific	Standardize hardware configuration. Make software specific.
Value (approximate) Import Local	$5.5 million (Rs 20 crore) $8 million (Rs 30 crore)	$2.2 million (Rs 8 crore) $8 million (Rs 29 crore)	$5 million (Rs 18 crore) $15 million (Rs 57 crore)
Number of purchase orders Import Local	400 4000	90 2500	Reduce by at least 25%.
Number of items Import Local	30 2200	20 1500	40 2000
Staff strength	7 officers with bachelor of engineering degrees; 3 assistants with commercial background	3 officers (2 technical plus 1 commercial background); 2 assistants with commercial background	3 officers (2 technical plus 1 commercial background); 1 technical plus 4 commercial background

*Information for Partner B not provided.

Figure 6.7. Comparison of operations.

Process Analysis

It became apparent that the basic approach to hardware procurement was to change from a push system to a pull system. In the case of NIIT, the hardware procurement process was getting triggered on receipt of the CPS. This activity should have actually dovetailed with the sanction for creating new software development capacity in the form of a new software factory, the plan for which is known at least six months prior to requirement. The proposed solution was to consolidate requirements for a period of six months on the basis of projections for projects and infrastructure requirements.

The hardware specification was nonstandard causing a delay of up to 30 days for delivery. The proposed solution to this was offered in the form of specification standardization aligned with the standard products being offered by major hardware manufacturers, which resulted in drastically cutting down the delivery period.

To avail the customs duty benefit, a license has to be obtained from the licensing authorities under India's Ministry of Commerce. This process was being pursued with the authorities on a project-to-project basis and after the software factory was created. There was a clear case of forward planning, consolidating the six months' requirements of creating software factories, and applying to the authorities as a one-time exercise, while the software factory is being created.

Description	Partner A	Partner B	NIIT current	NIIT proposed
Projections	Annual	Annual	No projection	Consolidate requirements bi-annually based on infrastructure service plan.
Purchase approval	Purchase council	As per production plan	CPS	Budget-approved process.
Type of items imported	Standard raw material	Standard engine components	Hardware nonstandard configuration	Standardize configuration.
Release of purchase order	Annual	Annual	Need specific	Bi-annual, based on service plan.
Release of schedule	3 months rolling	3 months rolling	Need specific	Align with project completion.
Letter of credit	Sight draft	Revolving	Transaction specific	Sight draft
Obtain STP license	Not applicable	Not applicable	Transaction specific	Align with project completion.
Mode of shipment	Sea	Sea	Air	Air

Lead time
  Dispatch
  Transit
	
	2 weeks
	4 weeks
		
		3 weeks
		3 weeks
			
			1 week
			1 week
				
				1 week
				1 week

Customs	Bonded warehouse	Bonded warehouse	No bonding	No bonding

Figure 6.8. Process comparison.

By identifying the gap between the current and should processes, overlaps such as those just described could be implemented. This resulted in reducing the procurement process time from 86 days to 21 days (Figure 6.9) and reducing the installation time from 22 days to 3 days.

Best Practices Found

A gap analysis performed against the internal current process, the should process, and external benchmarks indicated the need to include the following best practices in the process.

    • Initiate proactive purchasing, including long-term planning necessary for asset acquisition.

On average per year, NIIT imported hardware worth about $3 million. Hardware was imported on a project-by-project basis, and was aligned with the completion and creation

Activity	Partner A	Partner B	NIIT current—process 1 only	NIIT proposed—process 1 only
Inquiry	Nil	Nil	7 days	4 days
Negotiation	Nil	Nil	6 days	Nil
Proforma invoice	Nil	Nil	7 days	1 day
Purchase order	Nil	Nil	6 days	1 day
Schedule	Nil	Nil	Nil	Nil
License	Not applicable	Nil	6–15 days	Nil
Letter of credit	Nil	Nil	10 days	Nil
Dispatch	15 days	21 days	30–45 days	7 days
Transit	30 days	30 days	7 days	7 days
Custom clearance	3 days	7 days	7 days	1 day (Green channel)
Total process	48 days	58 days	86–110 days	21 days

Figure 6.9. Comparison of procurement process and cycle time.

of the software factory. The hardware procurement process was triggered on receipt of the CPS for creating a new software development facility, the plan for which was known at least six months prior to requirement. Therefore, there was an opportunity to consolidate the bi-annual hardware requirement based on expansion plans, planning the procurement in advance, releasing the letter of intent on manufacturers-suppliers, and deriving price benefit on volume purchase.

Hardware prices tend to be volatile in the international market with prices changing almost every quarter. Thus, there was a risk of committing to a volume purchase spread over six months. To overcome this, a formula was worked out with manufacturers-suppliers to give NIIT access to the price prevailing at the time of import. This long-term procurement strategy also enabled NIIT to look at future trends and invest in emerging technologies to avoid early obsolescence.

• Overlap the subprocesses as far as possible to reduce the total process time.

Various protectionist and regulatory policies have been dismantled in India's import policy to accelerate its transition toward a global economy. Import of goods, however, is still influenced by a number of external factors, and is heavily dependent on government bodies, including banks, licensing authorities, and customs to establish letters of credit, to obtain licenses for duty-free import, and to clear goods, respectively. Each of these activities involves compliance with stringent procedures and documentation, which significantly adds to cycle time. Although most of these activities are independent of NIIT's internal process, in actual practice the external activities were working in tandem with NIIT's internal activities instead of working as process overlap. For instance, the process of applying for and obtaining a license for duty-free import was triggered on completing the software factory. There was an opportunity to overlap this activity while the software factory was being constructed. A 15-day reduction in cycle time was achieved by implementing this.

• Complete transparency of information to entities that are part of the process.

This provides the opportunity for key players in the process to be aware of their inter-linked activities, and enables them to prioritize and plan their own activities.

• Standardize specifications as much as possible.

Global manufacturers and hardware suppliers offer standard hardware configurations almost off-the-shelf. NIIT's hardware requirements were, however, customized to meet the specific needs of its projects. From the manufacturers' point of view, customized requirements mean moving away from the normal product line and manufacturing small volumes (by their production standards). This directly affected deliveries by 30 days. The purchasing team had to go to NIIT end users and negotiate hardware specifications that were aligned to the standard configurations manufactured by suppliers. This resulted in cutting down the delivery period to seven days.

• Build robust processes and necessary controls to reduce the number of decision makers.

It was imperative to build fewer controls in the process by dispensing with the need to get compliance at every stage of the process. For example, the need to get a CPS prior to negotiation was eliminated. Thus, the procurement process was made more robust by introducing only necessary controls and reducing the number of decision makers.

• Reduce dependence on external entities that are part of the process by proactively dealing with them.

Opening a letter of credit involves submitting several documents to a bank, including a supplier's quotation, a copy of the purchase order, the supplier's order confirmation, the supplier's proforma invoice, and so on. Getting these documents from overseas manufacturers was taking as long as 30 days from the date the purchase order was released. The letter of credit was established on an order-by-order basis. Thus, there were as many transactions with the bank as there were orders and shipments. It was decided to open a revolving letter of credit for an amount equivalent to a six months' supply of hardware. Forward planning and consolidating a six-month requirement enabled NIIT to reduce the number of transactions with the bank to only two per year.

Clearing goods through customs involves close interaction with customs authorities from the date the goods arrive at the port of clearance to the date the goods actually clear customs. In all, there are 26 steps, and it takes between eight and ten days to complete the transaction. One major step in the process is the physical examination of the goods. This, perhaps, is the most time-consuming. To help importers reduce the clearance time, customs authorities provide a facility of green channel clearance. This system dispenses with the need for physical examination of goods, and reduces the clearance time to three days. Extending this facility, however, is the sole discretion of customs authorities. It is only for importers who have a good track record. NIIT started availing itself of this facility by maintaining an excellent track record, and thereby reduced the procurement time by another six days.

Actions Taken

• Hardware specification was standardized and aligned with the standard configuration manufactured by suppliers. Add-ons such as memory, hard disc, and so on were stocked as extras. Delivery time was reduced from 86 days to 21 days

• The hardware requirement was consolidated based on infrastructure and software factory needs of end users instead of asset acquisition approval.

• External influencing factors such as time taken for opening a letter of credit and obtaining licenses for duty-free import and product delivery lead time were neutralized by advance scheduling.

• To meet exigency requirements, 20 machines were kept as stock.

• To eliminate short shipments, the installation certificate was linked to issuance of the letter of credit.

Results

Major insights, both tangible and intangible, expected through implementation include the following:

• Procurement process reduced from 86 days to 21 days for the New Delhi operation and to 26 days for operations outside of New Delhi

• No time overruns, compared to 41–64 days with the old process

• No delays in exigency requirements

• PONC reduction

• Better quality of work life

• Internal customer satisfaction

• Avoidance of follow-up costs

• Higher degree of accuracy when estimating projects

Conclusions/Lessons Learned

Major achievements resulting from this benchmarking project include the following:

• Mapping the current or "is" process enabled the team to identify major disconnects.

- Brainstorming enabled the team to weed out the disconnects and refine the process.
- The team gained significant insights into best practices for the hardware procurement process and its related areas.
- Process documentation facilitates replicability across geographies, which is an internal term for regional boundaries. Each geography operates as an independent profit center.
- Benchmarking is critical to achieving customer satisfaction. It facilitates buy-in.
- Process owners should be part of the benchmarking team. This also facilitates buy-in.
- Terms of reference and measurement criteria should be very well defined, and should be kept in mind throughout the project.
- The availability of data is imperative for a good understanding of the situation; however, data should not be overanalyzed or overly precise.
- Mapping the current or "is" process facilitates a clear understanding of the process and helps to identify major process disconnects.
- Brainstorming should be used to generate as many ideas as possible.
- Mapping the desired or "should" process helps to clean up the process and close disconnects.
- In order to gain the most information from benchmarking partners, a list of questions that focus on identifying gaps should be prepared prior to the site visit.
- The team should be prepared to answer the same questions about its operation.
- Each question should have a purpose such that the information obtained is related to the benchmarking study.
- The team should select measurements that are true indicators of performance.
- The team should be thoroughly prepared and should be willing to give what it gets.
- The purpose of the benchmarking visit and what the teams expect to achieve should be well defined before the visit.
- If at all possible, the teams should document findings during the site visit meetings.

About the Authors

Anil Kumar is the vice president (commercial) of NIIT Ltd. He is a member of the managing director's quality club, and served as a project leader for one of its teams. As owner of the procurement process, Kumar was responsible for conducting the benchmarking study, documenting the process, and piloting and implementing recommendations.

Kumar heads the commercial services organization, which has operations in the followings areas and provides the following services: infrastructure creation; vendor development; purchasing and asset management; import and export; stores and inventory management; and administration. Prior to this, Kumar was the general manager (commercial) of the automobile ancillary. This organization provides purchasing services; stores and inventory management; and vendor development for imported and indigenous items, pressure die castings, precision-tuned and machined components, and forgings.

Before joining NIIT, Kumar was the general manager of materials for Tractor Manufacturing Company. He many be contacted as follows:

Anil Kumar
Vice President (Commercial)
NIIT Ltd.
B-234, Okhla Industrial Area
Phase I
New Delhi 110 020 India
Telephone: 91 11 681 7341 or 0801
Facsimile: 91 11 681 7344
E-mail: ank%niit@iris.ernet.in

Ashish Basu is the chief operating officer at the Institute of Quality Ltd., a leading Indian quality management consulting firm. He participates on the steering committee of many organizations including National Insurance, NIIT, Shriram Pistons and Rings, Escotel, and Modi Telstra. Basu is a member of the managing council of the Global Benchmarking Network and of the Philip Crosby Associates II member network.

Before joining the Institute of Quality Ltd., Basu was the head of the instructional software exports group at NIIT—a group he started in 1990. During this time, Basu became formally involved in the quality program at NIIT, and spearheaded many quality initiatives. He was instrumental in obtaining one of the first ISO 9001 certifications under the Tick IT scheme in India. He was part of the direction-setting team for the TQM vision at NIIT in addition to his other job responsibilities.

Basu has a master's in chemistry from the Indian Institute of Management (IIM) Mumbai and a postgraduate diploma in management from IIM Bangalore. He may be contacted as follows:

Ashish Basu
Chief Operating Officer
Institute of Quality Ltd.
K-4, Hauz Khas Enclave
New Delhi 110 016
India
Telephone: 91 11 651 3270 or 3292
Facsimile: 91 11 651 2677
E-mail: iqlsite@giasdl01.vsn1.net.in

CHAPTER 7

An Internal Benchmarking Study of Continuous Miner Operations Within Ingwe Coal Corporation

Alistair Forbes, Benchmarking Manager, Ingwe Coal Corporation

About Ingwe Coal Corporation

Ingwe Coal Corporation was formed in 1994 through the merger of two major South African coal mining companies, Randcoal and Trans-Natal. Both organizations had nearly 100 years of history in the South African coal industry, and were coal exporters to European and Asian markets since the 1970s. As Ingwe, the company now holds the position of the world's largest steam coal exporter, and is the fourth largest private sector coal producer worldwide. Ingwe forms part of the international Billiton group of companies.

Through its subsidiaries and investments, Ingwe owns or has interest in, through joint venture partnerships, collieries situated in Mpumalanga and Kwa-Zula Natal provinces in South Africa and in Australia. The company acquires and exploits coal reserves, finances coal-mining projects, and markets coal products.

Ingwe's total labor force amounts to over 17,000 people on 13 mines on two continents. Over half of its annual output of coal—approximately 75 million tons (68 million metric tons)—is produced by underground mines. Future expansion to coal-producing areas of South America and Indonesia is anticipated to maintain Ingwe's market share of expanding world export steam coal markets.

The formation of Ingwe Coal Corporation occurred when South Africa was going through its major transformation into a fully democratic society. Ingwe is the Zulu word for leopard, and the name reflects the new company's break with the past and its vision to leap into the future with the vigor of the predator embodied in its logo.

Executive Summary

This study is Ingwe's first using the established benchmarking process.

Driven by the strategic objective of increasing the output of its primary producing underground machinery by 10 percent over two years, this internal benchmarking study sought to identify best practices within its continuous miner (CM) operations and to apply these practices to the benefit of all group mines. Ingwe's continuous miners, using a bord-and-pillar technique, annually produce over 55 million tons (50 million metric tons) of raw coal out of approximately 114.4 million tons (104 million metric tons). The remainder is mined from surface operations and underground total extraction techniques. A 10 percent gain in output would be the equivalent to a new mine producing 3.3 million tons (3 million metric tons) of export sales. Thus, the potential benefits of identifying and implementing improvements resulting from a successful benchmarking study are significant.

The study was carried out by a team of six Ingwe personnel, drawn from four of the group's mines and the corporate head office. Nine top sections from seven CM operating mines were benchmarked. The study took nine months, and was carried out on a part-time basis. It also included input from Ingwe's newly acquired COALOPS mines in New South Wales, Australia.

The objectives of the study were to find the best practices within Ingwe and to make recommendations on how to adapt those practices to obtain the increase in performance as per the strategic goal. The study was also a pilot test of the benchmarking process and its suitability for Ingwe as a performance improvement process.

The results of the study identified mine #2B as having the top-performing CM section in tonnage output over the observed period. For the other sections, top performers in their own mines, overall average improvement of 31 percent could be required to match mine #2B's performance. Clearly the potential existed to improve within Ingwe's own mines before looking for business improvement ideas from world-class performers.

The study highlights the main reasons for delays to the coal-mining process, and identifies which mines have tackled each issue in an exemplary way and what can be shared among the group mines. The study also identifies a problem area in information gathering, and makes recommendations for action. The study specifically did not look for ways to improve performance of the CMs once they were actually producing. It endeavored to increase the CMs' working time per shift by finding ways to reduce delays to the mining process.

This report brings to completion step 6 of the 10-step benchmarking process being used by Ingwe. The remaining steps require the following:

- Revision of performance goals
- Development of action plans
- Implementation and monitoring of those actions
- Recycling of the process to identify gaps as the competition improves

The next task is to communicate these findings to senior and general management by means of a workshop or seminar, where the remaining benchmarking steps can be discussed and implemented.

Introduction

Background

This study was commissioned in July 1996 as the result of a specific objective detailed in Ingwe's 1996/97–2000/2001 business plan. The stated objective was to increase CM performance, in effect, output by 10 percent over two years. It was also the first attempt at benchmarking within the group, and thus acted as a pilot project to evaluate the effectiveness of benchmarking in Ingwe.

The project's sponsor was the senior manager of operations, responsible for two mines, #2B and #5, which together produce the majority of coal in the group mined by CM machinery. The sponsor's role includes granting the necessary authorization and resources for the project. The sponsor is also a driving force behind the initiation of the study, and usually stands to benefit from the results in terms of increased performance of the business units involved.

Ingwe has internally applied the benchmarking process among its underground mines employing similar bord-and-pillar mining techniques. This is in keeping with the group's objectives of being a low-cost producer and a leader in the field of overall performance both operationally and financially.

Purpose

The purpose of the study was to identify those best practices employed among seven mines using the CM bord-and-pillar technique, which, when implemented across the group, would significantly contribute to the strategic objective.

Another reason for the study was to examine benchmarking as a performance improvement tool where the benchmarking partners could be easily studied, thus ensuring the best possible chance of success within a reasonably short time. This would enhance the acceptability of benchmarking as an effective process. The internal study was chosen to minimize problems usually associated with wide, international studies. Such problems include

- Distant geographical location and thus access difficulties
- Language differences
- Measurement systems differences
- Difficulty in finding suitable benchmarking partners

The fact that the Ingwe mines had been brought together two years previously through a merger of two former major competitors also contributed to the chances of finding company best practices that had not found their way into the rest of the organization.

Project Description

The Benchmarking Team

The benchmarking team was formed in June 1996 under the sponsorship of one of three senior managers for operations. The author was responsible for the organization of the study, and acted as team leader. Since the study was to cover all eight South African mines in the group, each of the other five team members was appointed from a different mine, ensuring the best range of involvement possible.

Also considered in the make-up of the team was representation of the three disciplines of production, engineering, and human resources. Lastly, a range of job levels, from production managers down to CM operators, was incorporated into the team structure. Thus, a wide range of representation was achieved within the team, all with a direct interest in the CM performance and implementation of the anticipated recommendations. Key players in developing and carrying out the study are shown in Figure 7.1.

To provide additional input and expertise from time to time, internal advisors were invited to assist the team. These involved the functions of health, safety, and engineering. The services of Pieter van Schalkwyk of Benchmarking South Africa (BENSA) were also retained to provide benchmarking facilitation during the course of the study.

The team met weekly for four hours at a centralized venue. The benchmarking involvement was additional to each member's normal duties.

Process and Sequence

The key elements of the benchmarking process were as follows:

- Identifying the need for a benchmarking study on the CM operations

Function	Position	Mine
Sponsor	Senior manager—operations	Ingwe head office
Team leader	Manager—business intelligence	Ingwe head office
Team members	Mining manager	Mine #5
	Shift boss	Mine #2B
	Senior personnel officer	Mine #8 (open cast)
	Mining supervisor	Mine #6A
	Training officer (CM)	Mine #6B
Internal referees	Engineering manager—operations	Ingwe head office
	Area manager—health and safety	Mine #5
	Group manager—risk management	Ingwe head office
External consultant	BENSA	Pretoria

Figure 7.1. Benchmarking study participants.

- Nominating and forming the team
- Training team members through the BENSA three-day workshop in Pretoria
- Identifying and mapping the process flowchart
- Developing the Ishikawa diagram to determine key elements of the study
- Developing the study strategy; that is, to focus on reducing delays to improve cutting time
- Confirming mines to be included in the study
- Developing and implementing the initial questionnaire to highlight mines with potential best practices and analysis of the results
- Developing the second, more detailed questionnaire as the checklist for the site visits; the questionnaire was sent to each mine before the visit
- Visiting underground sites of the top section in each mine
- Evaluating data and identifying the best-in-class
- Identifying gaps between the best-in-class and the remainder of Ingwe mines
- Developing conclusions and recommendations

The need for benchmarking. After senior management's request to investigate the potential of the benchmarking process, it was decided to launch a study focusing on CM operations. An internal study was initiated among the mines using the CMs in a bord-and-pillar technique. The objective was to improve the overall output from the existing resources and to test benchmarking as a viable, effective, and sustainable performance improvement tool. The strength of the benchmarking process is the involvement of Ingwe personnel from start to finish, as implementation would necessarily be carried out by those who took part in the study. The benchmarking process was also designed to support, and be complementary to, existing performance improvement initiatives, as the strategic objective of improving CM performance is being tackled by other processes concurrently at each mine.

Forming a representative team. Team formation was carefully considered, as representation in three aspects was specifically addressed. The team size was restricted to six personnel. This was probably a greater number than actually required, based on reports of other benchmarking studies, but it enabled the representation objectives to be largely met. Nominations for team members were sought from the general managers of the mines involved.

Firstly, the team members came from different mines, thereby making eventual acceptance of the study results more likely across the mines. This also had the spin-off that a potential future benchmarking "champion" could be available on as many mines as were represented. Secondly, a range of relevant expertise was represented, as members were selected from mining, engineering, and human resources functions. Thirdly, members were selected from a range of job levels, from mining manager to the trainer of CM operators, who himself had extensive operating experience. This ensured the representation of officials and workers to get as wide a perspective on the process as possible.

In reality, all team members had occasional problems in joining team sessions through normal work commitments, but it meant that sessions mostly took place on schedule and the momentum of the study was generally maintained. Finally, quite fortuitously, the team consisted of three members from each of the two former organizations that had merged to become Ingwe two years previously.

The training of team members took place in March 1996 at the BENSA facility in Pretoria over a three-day period. BENSA also acted as the consultant for the project.

Determining the scope of the project. Initial team meetings focused on flowcharting and process analysis to establish the terms of reference and scope of the study. It was soon realized that the study strategy would be based on minimizing delays to the mining operation rather than maximizing the cutting rate. Hence, a start-of-shift to end-of-shift focus was adopted, and the flowchart reflects this strategy (Figure 7.2). An Ishikawa diagram (Figure 7.3) was also developed to highlight the key areas of interest for measurement and benchmarking.

The process of identifying benchmarking partners was simplified by including all eight Ingwe mines employing CMs. During the year, the group expanded with the organization of three more underground mines in Australia, but subsequent information obtained on their use of CMs (a total extraction technique not employed in the South African operations) led the team to exclude them from the study at this stage. Certain information on postshift debriefing practices has, however, been included as it was felt that it had some relevance to the study.

At this stage a detailed project description was formulated. This became the guiding document for the study. The entire project description is shown in the chapter appendix (p. 162).

Data collection. Data collection was initiated with a questionnaire circulated to each mine. The survey was designed to assess the level of mechanization and to highlight areas of superior performance on the mines. The matrix of answers from this questionnaire was analyzed prior to the site visits.

From this first survey, a second, more detailed questionnaire was developed (Figure 7.4). It was used as a checklist for the visit, and was sent to the mines prior to each visit. This allowed certain statistical data to be prepared ahead of time, and it allowed section personnel to familiarize themselves with the information required. A matrix of selected answers to the second questionnaire appears in Figure 7.5.

The benchmarking of each mine took place between January 24 and March 12, 1997. Prior to the first visit, the whole team visited mine #5 to develop a uniform visit technique and to test the effectiveness of the final questionnaire.

It was found that although data were in plentiful supply from report sheets, they tended to be unvalidated and variable in reliability. To obtain primary data in certain subprocesses it was necessary to structure the questionnaire to get information based on the

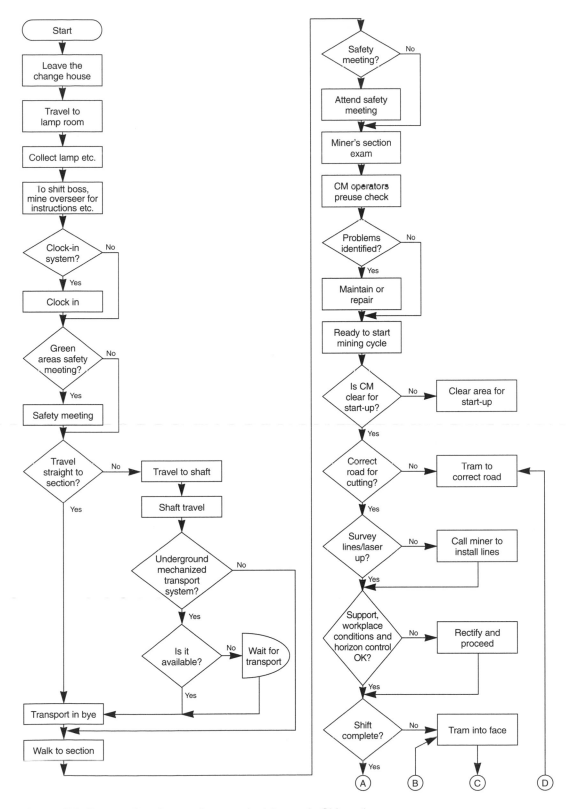

Figure 7.2. Process flowchart underground mining cycle CM section.

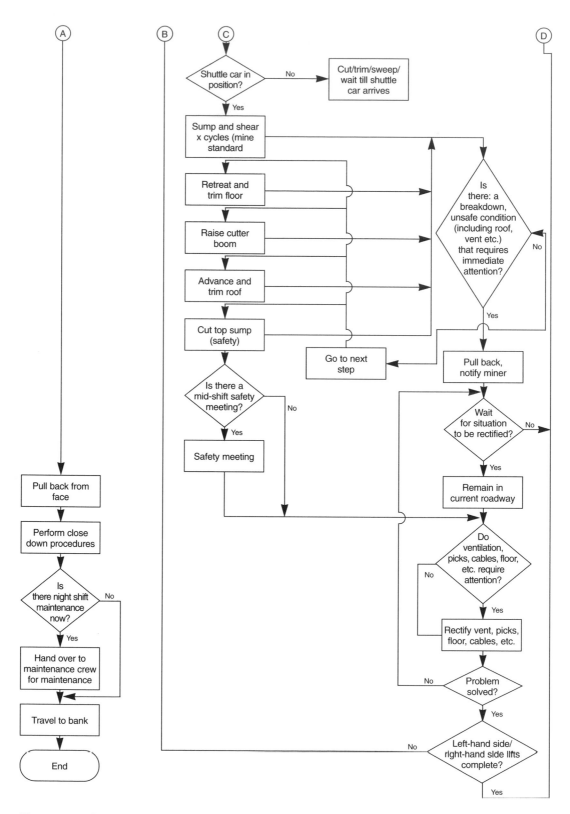

Figure 7.2. *(Continued).*

128

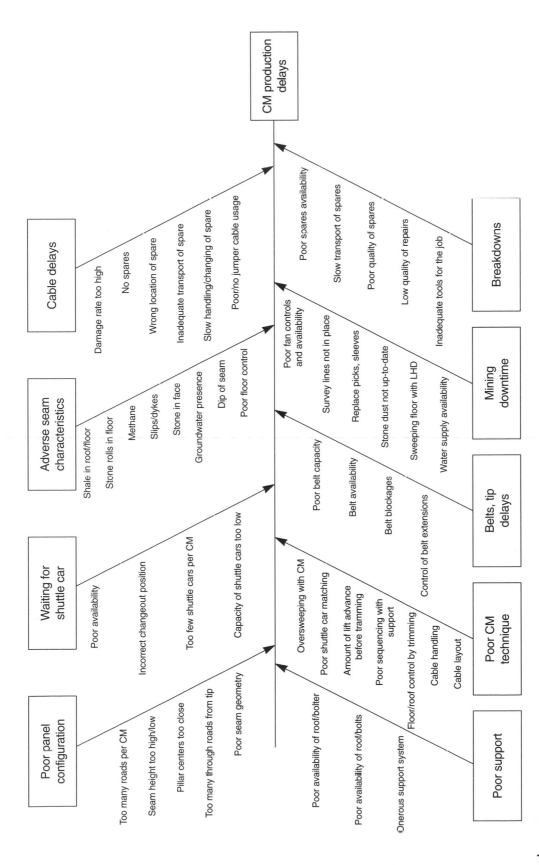

Figure 7.3. Underground CM performance constraints.

129

Mine _____ Section _____ Seam _____ Date _____

1. Section performance parameters

1.1 CM cutting time and production

Data from each mine on CM performance over the previous six month period (July–December 1996 will be required). The following headings apply:

> CM machine
>
> Section (more than one section may apply if CM moved during month)
>
> Mine scheduled operating hours (bank-to-bank hours total) (applicable to CM)
>
> CM cutting motor hours
>
> CM pump motor hours
>
> Survey production tonnage

1.2 Labor in section

Mine overseer	Shift boss	Miner	Operator				
		*		Total labor in section (complement)			
		*		Mining?			
		*		How many fully qualified CM operators in the crew normally?	1?	2?	??
		*		Engineering?			
		*		Other?			

2. Start of shift travel time

2.1. Travel and transport

2.1.1 Start of shift point

Mark on the attached flowchart at what point the shift officially starts; that is, what activities are INCLUDED in the bank-to-bank shift times?

	Start	Finish	Duration
Day shift			
Afternoon shift			
Night shift			
Saturday shift			

2.1.2 Green areas safety meetings

		*		Green areas safety meeting system?
		*		Normal duration of meetings?
		*		Comments: (favorable or unfavorable comparisons with previous system?)

Figure 7.4. Checklist and questionnaire for site visits.

2.1.3 Change house to lamp room travel

		*		Included in shift time?	Yes	No
		*		If yes, distance		km
		*		Time		minutes
		*		Method		
				Comments:		

2.1.4 Travel to shaft

		*		Included in shift time?		Yes	No
		*		Distance			km
		*		Duration of travel			minutes
		*		Method			
		*		Reliability	Never	Sometimes	Mostly	Always
		*		Does this transport take miners straight to their underground section?		Yes	No
				Comments:			

2.1.5 In-shaft travel

		*		Type of shaft	vert / adit / incline
		*		If vertical, whole shift in one lift?	Yes	No
		*		Distance		meters
		*		Normal duration of travel		minutes
				Comments:	

2.1.6 Transport to section

		*		Method		mech. / walk
	*			Distance # bottom to section?			km
		*		Time/duration of transport?			minutes
		*		Transport system employed?			
		*		Normal availability of system?	Never	Sometimes	Mostly	Always
				Comments (floor and vehicle conditions etc.):			

2.2 Inbye procedures

2.2.1 Safety meeting

		*		Is safety meeting held in section?			Yes	No
		*		Normal duration? (average)	<10 mins	10–20	20–30	+30
				Comments:				

Figure 7.4. *(Continued).*

2.2.2 Section inspection

			*	Normal duration? (average)	<10 mins	10–20	20–30	+30
			*	CM roadway inspected first?			Yes	No
				Comments:				

2.2.3 Preuse check by CM operator

			*	When carried out?	During section inspection		After section inspection	
		*		Normal duration? (%)	<10 mins	10–20	20–30	+30
				Comments:				

2.2.4 Daily maintenance of CM

		Artisan		Carried out during day, night, or back shift?	Day	Night	Back
		Artisan		Normal duration?			minutes
				Comments:			

3. Delays in mining cycle

3.1 Health and safety

3.1.1 Presence of gas

		*		Delays in mining cycle because of gas?		Yes	No
		*		If yes, severity?	Never	Sometimes	Mostly	Always
		*		Method of rectification?			
				Comments on effectiveness:			

3.1.2 Ventilation

		*		Delays in mining cycle because of vent controls?		Yes	No
		*		If yes, severity?	Never	Sometimes	Mostly	Always
		*		Method of rectification?			
				Comments on effectiveness:			

3.1.3 Support

			*	Delays in mining cycle because of support controls?		Yes	No
			*	If yes, severity?	Never	Sometimes	Mostly	Always
	*	*		Systematic support?		Yes	No
		*		Type or method (mechanical/resin bolts?)			
		*		Support rule (give main features)?			
				Comments on effectiveness:			

Figure 7.4. *(Continued).*

3.1.4 Stone dusting

		*		Is stone dusting carried out in-shift?	Never	Sometimes	Mostly	Always
		*		Method of rectification?				
				Comments on effectiveness:				

3.2 Mining

A cutting cycle diagram is required. (Do you use a card system?) (A pocket card with information about the cutting standards of the mine)

3.2.1 Pick replacement

			*	Delays due to pick changes?	Nil	<30 mins.	<60 mins.	>60 mins.
*				*Tons per pick?*				
*				Pick type?		Shank size		
				Comments:				

3.2.2 Floor conditions

			*	Delays in mining cycle because of floor conditions?			Yes	No
			*	If yes, severity?	Never	Sometimes	Mostly	Always
			*	Is an LHD permanently assigned to the section?			Yes	No
			*	If yes, how long does it usually sweep for?	Seldom	Sometimes	Mostly	Always
		*		Handling of spillage at tip? Who cleans? How?				
				Comments on types of problems:				

3.2.3 Groundwater in section

			*	Delays in mining cycle because of groundwater controls?			Yes	No
			*	If yes, severity?	Never	Sometimes	Mostly	Always
		*		Method of rectification?				
				Comments on effectiveness:				

3.2.4 Water supply

		*		Delays in mining cycle because of water supply problems?			Yes	No
		*		If yes, severity?	Never	Sometimes	Mostly	Always
				Comments on effectiveness:				

Figure 7.4. *(Continued).*

133

3.2.5 Belts and belt extensions (including switch extensions)

Planning officer				Section belt availability?				%
	*	*		In-shift or back-shift extension?		In-shift?	Back-shift	
*				Time taken?				hours
	*	*		Separate extension crew?		Yes	No	
*				If yes, crew size?				people
		*		Normal number of splits per move?			1 / 2 / 3	
		*		Production time normally lost at start of day shift?				hours
				Are switches pulled during back shift?		Yes	No	
				Comments on method:				

3.2.6 Waiting for shuttle cars

			*	Waiting for shuttle cars?				Yes	No
			*	Severity of occurrence?	Never	Sometimes		Mostly	Always
		*		Roadways?		Pillar centers?		Car in section	
		*		Panel width					meters
				Comments (What are most common reasons?):					

3.3 Engineering

3.3.1 Power supply

*				Section availability?				
			*	Assessment of power delays?	Never	Sometimes	Mostly	Always
				Comments:				

3.3.2 Breakdown/maintenance

		*		Maintenance in or out of production shift			In	Out
*				*Availability of CM? (last 12 months) Formulas ?????*				%
*				*Availability of shuttle cars? (last 12 months)*				%
*				*Availability of feeder breaker? (last 12 months)*				%
*				*Availability of roof bolter? (last 12 months)*				%
		Artisan		Breakdown delays through . . . Poor availability of spares?	Never	Sometimes	Mostly	Always
		Artisan		Lack of transport to section?	Never	Sometimes	Mostly	Always
		Artisan		Poor handling in section?	Never	Sometimes	Mostly	Always
		Artisan		Poor condition of spares?	Never	Sometimes	Mostly	Always
				Comments:				

Figure 7.4. *(Continued).*

3.3.3 Cable damage and repair

Engineering planning				Cables damaged (average) per month—CM?				
				Cables damaged (average) per month—Shuttle car?				
			*	How long does the CM stand when cable is replaced?				
			*	Time taken to change cable—shuttle car?				
		*		Cables: Storage location			Section	Outbye
		*		CM cable in section?	Never	Sometimes	Mostly	Always
		*		Shuttle car cable in section?	Never	Sometimes	Mostly	Always
		*		Handling method (describe)				
		*		Use of jumper cables			Yes	No
		*		Length of jumper cable (if used?)				meters
				Comments:				

4. Travel out of mine

4.1.1 Travel time

		*		Time to reach surface from section at end of shift?	
				Comments:	

5. General

Address the following question to the miner or CM operator in the section.

				What, in your opinion, are the three most important areas where production could be improved?
				What in your opinion, makes your section a top performer?

Figure 7.4. *(Continued).*

		Performance measure	Mine #1	Mine #2B	Mine #3	Mine #4	Mine #5	Mine #2A	Mine #6A	Mine #6B	Mine #7
1.:			Section 12 & 21	Section 41 4 Seam	Section 2	21	44 & 21	23	27	21	2/14B
1.2	Labor	Mining labor	10.33	12	11+2 vent day shift	11	11	10	11	14	12
		CM operators	1	2	2	2	2	1	1	2	4
		CM operators rotation		Weekly			Casual	Casual			
		Engineering	2	3	3	3	4	2–4	2	4	2
		Total	12.33	15	15	14	15	12–14	13	18	17
2.1.1	Travel	Day shift	9.5	9.08	9.5	10.25	9.5	9	9.5	10.5	9.5
		Afternoon shift	9.42	10.15	10.05	10.25	9.5	9	11.25	10.5	10
		Night shift						9			
		Saturday shift	5.5	6.5	9.5	N	9.5		N	N	9.5
2.1.2	Safety meeting	Surface green areas?	Weekly	N	N	N	N	N	Y	Y	N
		Comment							10	15	
2.1.3	Change house to lamp room	In-shift time?	N	N	N	N	N	N	N	N	Y
		Distance in yards (meters)	N/A	N/A	3 (5)	N/A	N/A	N/A	N/A	N/A	.6 (1)
		Time (minutes)	5	5	5	2	5	2	N/A	N/A	10
		Method	Walk	Walk	Bus	Walk	Walk	Walk	Walk	Walk	Bus (contractor)
		Comment									
2.1.4	Travel to shaft	In-shift time?	Y	Y	Y	N	N	N	Y	Y	Y
		Distance in yards (meters)	2200 (2000)	110 (100)	5500 (5000)	22 (20)	55 (50)	22 (20)	550 (500)	8.4 miles (14 km)	5.4 miles (9 km)
		Time (minutes)	10	5	5	2	2	2	2	15	10
		Method	Bus	Walk	Bus	Walk	Walk	Walk	Multipurpose vehicle	Bus	Bus (contractor)
		Reliability	Mostly	Always	Always	Always	Always	Always	Always	Always	Always
		Straight to section?	Y	N	N	N	N	N	N	N	N
		Comment									

Figure 7.5. Selected answer matrix for second, detailed questionnaire.

		Mine #1	Mine #2B	Mine #3	Mine #4	Mine #5	Mine #2A	Mine #6A	Mine #6B	Mine #7
4.1.1	Travel out of mine — Time to reach surface at end of shift (minutes)	15	25	45	45	15 (mech.) 70 (walk)	15 (mech.) 40 (walk)	45	30	5–40
	Comment		Unimog arrives in section at end of shift		Walk				Tractor takes night in and day out	
	General — Three important areas for improvement	LHD in section, maintenance on back shift	Motivation	Multiskilled, teamwork, bonus incentives	Teamwork, bonus incentives	Transportation available, belt/bunker available	Availability of machines, target too high, more transportation	Reduce travel time, no mining stock, communication to operations is poor	Maintenance crew	Cable bin, transportation for spares, start quicker, Sat. off, better car maintenance
	What makes this section good	Motivation, face boss	Teamwork	Monthly bonus	Bonus system	Teamwork + joining	Equipment there	Teamwork	Teamwork	1 belt, teamwork
5.0	Best practices	Excellent road conditions, reliable hour-meters + data capturer, cable bins, section bus, and multiskilling		Food voucher scheme, maintenance in dog shift, dedicated LHD	Bonus system	After shift production, including come out on Sunday nights	Quick shift change, scoop, planned belt maintenance from 6 to 7:30 every morning	Structured safety meeting number of multipurpose vehicles, 1 LHD/section, a Joy contract, artisans have spares book, jumper cable, communication system	Voucher system for cables, monthly maintenance done on Sunday	Cable bonus scheme

Figure 7.5. (Continued).

personal judgment of process "customers." Wherever possible, verification by checks with alternate "customers" of the process was made. In general, complete, accurate, and validated data were in short supply, and as a result, were not widely used by management as a process control tool. This excluded tonnage figures that were checked and validated through the survey function on a monthly basis.

Visit technique. The technique included the following: Each mine was visited once. Usually two or three team members would be joined by the mine overseer or shift boss of the section being toured. The visit would commence shortly before the day shift went on duty when team members assembled at the mining offices. The study team would go underground soon after the main shift and visit the two best-performing sections (by previous arrangement). In order to complete the checklist, interviews were normally held in the section with the miner, artisan, CM operator, and team leader. After reaching the surface, meetings were held with engineering staff to get the statistical data required, and a debriefing session with mining management was held to discuss the main points arising from the visit. Ideas and comparisons were passed on to the mining team at this session.

Following the visits, team meetings were held to evaluate the benchmarking results, compare results, identify the best-in-class, draw conclusions, and develop recommendations.

Evaluation Method

The results of interviews conducted during all the site visits were recorded on questionnaires, and followed by data reduction to a matrix form. Analysis is based on the data collected and the visual observations made by team members at the time of the visit.

Comparison of times attributable to the main delay categories was made between mines to obtain the mine showing the least delay time and, therefore, the best group benchmark in that function. The graphs are formatted to show best practice to the right-hand side of each graph.

Since not every one of the approximately 90 CM sections in the group could be visited, the methodology consisted of sampling the best-performing sections as indicated by mine management before each visit. Where some mines had more than one main operating section, visits were made to each section (hence the reference to mine #2A and 2B). Mines included in the benchmarking survey are shown in Figure 7.6.

Those critical performance areas within the working shift identified and benchmarked in this study were as follows:

- Shift administration

- Transport into the section

- Prestart-up period including safety meetings, section inspections, and prestart maintenance checks; effectiveness of hot seat shift changes

- Delays due to health and safety factors (ventilation, roof support, and groundwater)

Mine	Date of visit
Mine #4	4 March
Mine #3	28 January
Mine #5	24 January 5 March
Mine #6B Mine #6A	6 February 11 March
Mine #2A Mine #2B	6 March 4 February
Mine #1	29 January
Mine #7	12 March

Figure 7.6. Participating Ingwe mines.

- Delays due to engineering requirements
- Delays due to operational techniques

Uses and Limitations

Scarcity of reliable data. The principal issue that arose from this study is the lack of data that are consistent, reliable, and representative of the process being measured. Because of this, comparison between mines was extremely difficult and only truly comparable in terms of tonnage, which is verified and supplied by the various survey functions as per legal requirements.

Data on the delays experienced by the CMs were obtained at the time of the visits through interviews with section personnel and recorded on a four-point scale (always, mostly, sometimes, never). This is necessarily a subjective method of assessment and thus subject to bias that could skew the results. It was, however, felt that results obtained would be sufficiently indicative for the purposes of this study.

The specific area where data reliability needs to be strengthened is in the measurement of cutting time of the CMs. The measurement of actual cutting time during the shift was made by hour-meters positioned in the cutting motor circuits. Hour-meters had been fitted to almost all CMs to measure actual cutting time during the shift. With the exception of mine #1, however, these meters had not been universally fitted until recently, and, due to problems with standardized fitting and calibration, reliable historical data were generally not available to the study team.

Ongoing management use of these data, for process control reasons, is likely to be the only spur to its efficiency in future for comparative purposes.

Survey Evaluation

In presenting the survey findings, the analysis follows in two parts. The first part consists of the overall section performance, where output is directly compared among the mines' best-performing sections. The second part examines and compares the various sub-processes that constitute the most significant delaying processes in the mining cycle, in effect answering the question "Why the gap?" The second part of the analysis commences with a brief comparison of section labor complements and shift formats, as both facets have an impact on overall performance of the sections. This second part continues with the analysis of the delays in the health and safety, engineering, and mining aspects.

Overall Section Performance

The sections visited are compared in terms of monthly tonnage output and cutting rate based on the average of data over the previous six months (where available). This was used to establish benchmark performances of the coal cutting/mining process. Figure 7.7 illustrates these findings, establishing mine #2B as the benchmark performer in both aspects during the period July to December 1996.

Analysis of the gap between the best practice at mine #2B and the individual mines shows a potential improvement of 31 percent if the other mines were to simply close the

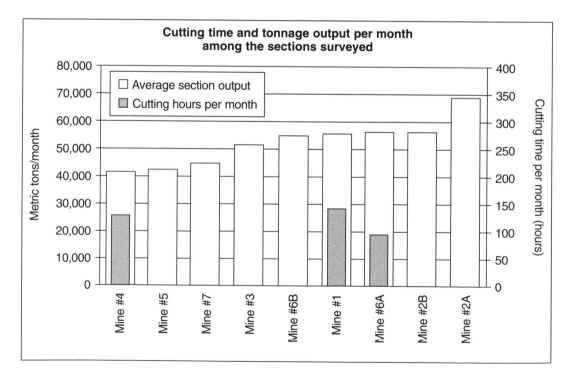

Figure 7.7. CM benchmark performance.

tonnage gap. Although this is highly theoretical, it does put an order of magnitude on the potential to improve just by looking within the organization.

Comparison of cutting times (in terms of hours utilization per month in the coal cutting mode) reveals that shortage of data prevented a complete comparison. This is because some mines either still had to install the cutting head hour-meters or there was insufficient data because the hour-meters had only been fitted just prior to the survey.

The ongoing use of these meters as an in-process means of performance measurement must, at the end of the day, lead to a better understanding of daily deviations from performance targets. Therefore, it is essential that management continue to validate and use the data to give itself a second tool that will be as useful as the tonnage measurements, which have been used as the standard for so long.

Although Ingwe's Australian operations were not included in the data collection phase of this study, communication with David Swan of COALOPS did reveal a practice of reporting that may be transferable to the South African mines. Figure 7.8 shows details of the postshift debriefing at one of the Australian mines. This document is used to impart information to operational staff in order that rectification of problem areas arising in the shift may be actioned. This would need further analysis by local mining staff in adapting it to the particular needs of the South African operations, but it provides insight into information handling that is used in a highly competitive world coal industry.

Analysis of Principal Delays to Production During a Normal Shift

Section labor complements and shift formats. The labor in each section consists of operational and engineering staff. In the operational complement numbers ranged from 10.3 to 14.5 persons per shift, where workers performing duties between multiple sections, such as ventilation or load-hand-dump machine (LHD) operators on clean-up, were apportioned accordingly. The average number of operational staff per section was 12.

The number of CM operators per section was identified in each case. Some 67 percent of sections provided for two operators, the remainder just one. Although it was felt that the presence of two operators was a best practice and allowed for a better continuity and performance due to the facility of leave relief and rotation (to combat fatigue and promote motivation through competition), this was not conclusively borne out in the overall section performance comparisons.

On the engineering side, the staff levels ranged from two to four workers. The difference was the presence of aides (operatives). Some 44 percent of sections did not use aides, and operated with the minimum of two. Further investigation is recommended in this particular area in order to identify a best practice. Figure 7.9 shows the comparison of section labor as identified at the time of the study.

A comparison of shift formats revealed a number of variations between the mines. Figure 7.10 indicates that most mines operate a two-shift rotation system with or without a Saturday shift. Only one mine operates on a three-shift system, which is on a trial basis at

The following data are routinely collected on every production shirt for all units within the group.

A *unit shift plan* (expectation) is initiated at the start of the shift by the shift coordinator, and the crew leader reports back against this plan. The information is collected by crew leaders (supervisor at face) during the shift and recorded on specific *shift reports* for that purpose. These reports reflect the following:

- Safety status
- Unit manning
- Production performance (plan versus actual)
- Supplies and spares status
- Availability (up time, downtime; operational and plant)
- Work orders schedule (plan versus actual)

The data are downloaded into a database "pulse mining systems" by the shift coordinator during the *shift review* (formalized end-of-shift status report). *See system element #30.*

The information is analyzed, and the crew leader is responsible for his team's performance. Shortfalls in performance are highlighted, and actions initiated to prevent reoccurrence. These data are analyzed shiftly, daily, weekly, monthly, annually, and life of panel.

Coal Operations Australia Limited

System element #30: Shift review meeting procedure

Purpose

The purpose of this shift review meeting is to provide a forum for relevant and timely discussion of the previous shift. The review takes place between the shift coordinator and the production coordinator. Major topics covered are as follows:

- Safety report
- Performance and attainment
- Reasons for schedule miss
- Actions required to prevent reoccurrence of schedule miss
- Ideas for enhancing safety and performance

The systematic eradication of causes for "schedule miss" is the key to ongoing improvements in productivity.

Frequency

The shift review meeting takes place daily (exception Thursday) at the following times:

- Night shift: 7:15 A.M.
- Day shift: 3:15 P.M.
- Afternoon shift: 2:20 P.M.

The meeting should take no more than 15 minutes.

Responsibility

It is the responsibility of the production coordinator to ensure that the shift coordinator attends each review at the appointed time. The shift coordinator must be able to discuss his shift in a concise and informed manner.

Figure 7.8. Postshift debriefing at C.O.A.L. Colliery.

Format

The format of the meeting will be in accordance with the shift review meeting agenda.

Agenda

1. Were there any accidents/incidents on your shift?   Yes / No

   Were there any near misses on your shift?   Yes / No

   Were there any breaches of the act, regulations, manager's rules?   Yes / No

2. Is the production delay report (PDR) complete?   Yes / No

   If no, why?

3. Production review by unit

   • Meters driven (plan versus actual)?

   • Total tons?

   • Rip hours?

   • Bolt hours?

   • Number of shuttle cars?

4. Operating time by unit? (8 hours = 480 minutes)

5. Were there any production delays?   Yes / No

   • Operational

   • Mechanical

   • Electrical

   • Other

6. Was the maintenance plan achieved? If no, why?   Yes / No

   • Planned versus actual work orders

7. What action was taken to rectify any safety, production, or maintenance issues?

   Problems?

8. What action can be taken to eliminate reoccurrence of those problems?

9. Outbye project status?

Figure 7.8. *(Continued)*.

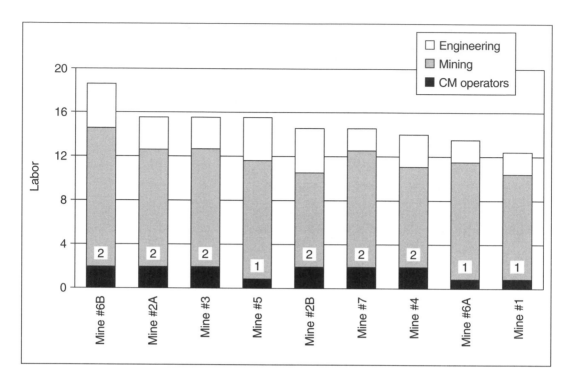

Figure 7.9. Section labor.

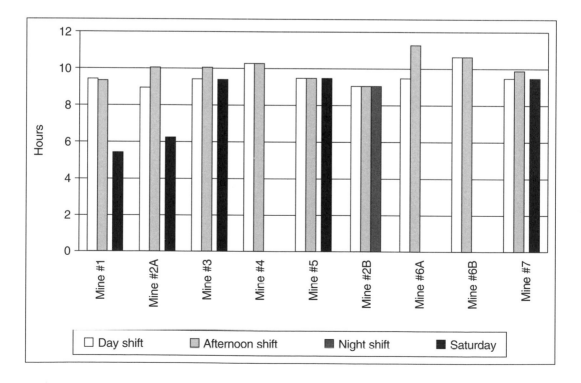

Figure 7.10. Shift format and duration on mines.

mine #2A. Five mines worked a Saturday shift of duration between 5.5 and 9.5 hours. The remainder made up the allotted weekly hours through extending the shifts worked on weekdays.

Given that there is a limit to the amount of hours that may be worked in any fortnight, as a result of the practice of minimizing unproductive traveling and start-up time through using fewer but longer shifts within the constraints of accepted work practices, then mines #6B, #6A, and #4 could be considered best practice examples in this case. The absence of a single Saturday shift in any fortnight adds approximately three hours production time to the section capacity.

It is appreciated that labor legislation is moving to a shorter working week and that mines would have to be particularly thorough and circumspect when considering implementation of changes in this area.

Shift travel times. Unproductive time spent in traveling to the workplace starts in most cases as workers leave the lamp room and, in one case (mine #7), the change house. The phases identified in the study are as follows:

- Change house to lamp room, lamp room to shaft, and in-shaft travel (incline, adit, or vertical)
- Shaft bottom to section (workplace)

In this study the total entry time varied from 22 minutes to 70 minutes, the average being 44 minutes per shift. The breakdown of travel times is shown in Figure 7.11. The mines are grouped into shaft types; that is, inclines/adits (mines #1, #6A, and #7) and vertical shafts (the rest).

Change house/lamp room to shaft bottom. Geographical location plays a major role in the times recorded as far as shaft bottom. Best practices identified here would be of most use to planners of future operations as existing facilities are unlikely to be changed. Best practice for minimizing lamp room–to-shaft times is to be seen at the newer mines, #2A, #2B, #4, and #5, where shift times commence at shaft top because lamp room facilities are located there. Mine #6A is also effectively in this category. Short travel in the shaft is best exemplified by the inclines (two to three minutes) where trackless transport can be used (the best-in-class is mine #6A followed by mine #1), and the whole section crew can be transported at one time. Vertical shafts that were too small to transport the whole section crew at once added significantly to the overall entry time (for example, mine #4 at 40 minutes). The average for vertical shafts access time was 15.3 minutes with the best-in-class being mine #2B with its large shaft capacity, taking only 5 minutes to transport the entire crew.

Underground transport of personnel. Speed and reliability with safety were the main issues in the consideration for reduction of delays in this phase. Additionally, the reliability factor became important when it affected the shift-end timing. Workers who did not trust the reliability of the transport to be available and on-time at the end of shift would be sure

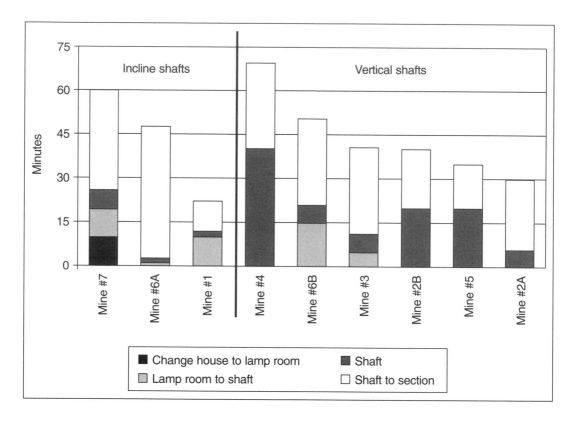

Figure 7.11. Travel times into sections from change house/lamp room.

to exit at the nominated time by starting to walk to the shaft prematurely, resulting in the loss of production time. Dedicated transport that remained with the section crew during the shift, usually flame-proof buses, was considered the most trustworthy system by the section members.

Those mines that have adit/incline access and can utilize buses to transport the section personnel directly from the lamp room to the section via the incline had the potential to reduce traveling time to the minimum. In this respect both mines #1 and #6A have exemplary practices.

Reliability assessment by section personnel was used to formulate the scatter diagram of average speed against reliability. This is shown in Figure 7.12.

A range of vehicles is used for underground transport of personnel. Most mines use a multipurpose vehicle (MPV) system to convey their personnel, but a tractor/trailer combination and flame-proof buses were also used. Two mines have workers walk into their sections every shift. In terms of speed, mine #5's bus system was a leader at 6 mph (10 kph). This was attributable to the relatively straight system of access roadways to the section, which is indicative of the benefits of a new mine developing pit room. Here, good mine layout plays a significant role in speed of access.

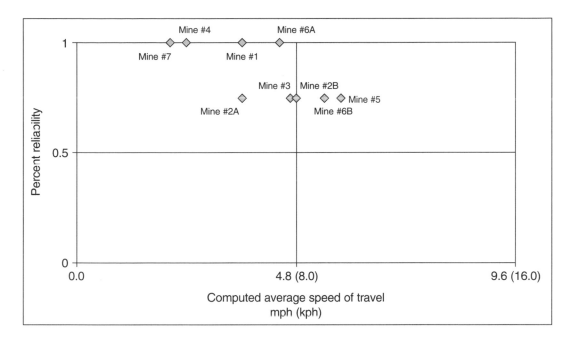

Figure 7.12. Reliability versus speed in underground transport.

With respect to road conditions, the access roads into the sections ranged from excellent, being roads that are well graded, treated for deterioration, dry, and well-illuminated, to roads that were in poor condition. These roads were uneven, water logged, and badly illuminated. Of note were mine #1's road conditions that were well maintained and illuminated.

The prestart-up period. The prestart-up period is defined as the time taken from arriving in the section to the time at which either the pre-use check of the CM or the daily maintenance of the CM has been completed. This time includes the section examination, safety meeting, the pre-use check of the CM, and, if applicable, the routine daily maintenance of the CM. The graphical representation of these times is shown in Figure 7.13.

In general, the start-of-shift procedure took from 30 minutes at mine #6B to 85 minutes at mines #2A, #3, and #5. The average start-up time was 65 minutes. Some 56 percent of the mines surveyed did the necessary tasks sequentially, while the remaining 44 percent of the mines attempted to reduce this time by running one or more tasks consecutively, or transferring them entirely from this time period. For example, mines #6A and #6B perform safety meetings in "green areas" on the surface before the shift.

The best-in-class for these procedures is mine #6B. The time allotted to start-of-shift procedures is reduced to a minimum by adopting two procedures: (1) doing daily maintenance of the CM on the back shift; and (2) completing the safety meeting before the start of a shift. An alternative practice is that initiated at mine #1, where the miners conduct

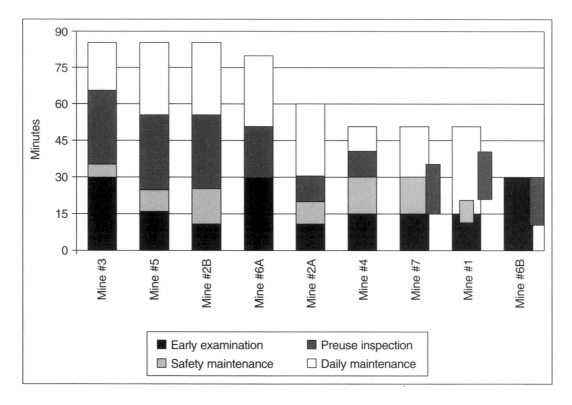

Figure 7.13. Start-of-shift procedures.

their safety meeting with their team while examining their workplace. The potential savings in adopting these best practices would be to increase production time by an average of 35 minutes per shift.

For daily maintenance, most mines do a detailed maintenance at the beginning of the day shift, then do a follow-up in the afternoon shift. As a result of the three-shift operation being carried out at mine #2A, 2.5 hours is set aside for every day shift to do maintenance. Mine #3 performs daily maintenance with special crews on the nonproduction "dog shift," which is between the end of afternoon shift and the start of day shift.

Shift overlaps and "hot seat" changes. Having addressed the prestart-up period, an examination of the overlapping shifts aspect was made in order to identify any best practices within the group. Figure 7.14 depicts the amount of overlap occurring between day shift and afternoon shift in the various mines. The maximum of 90 minutes is practiced at mine #6B, while gaps (negative overlaps) between shifts occur at mines #2B and #6A.

The concept of a "hot seat" changeover is often quoted as the reason for the overlap but are gains really being made in these cases? On further analysis, a comparison of the overlap with the traveling times both into and out of the section should indicate whether crews are actually changing in the section or crossing somewhere on the way in. In theory, to

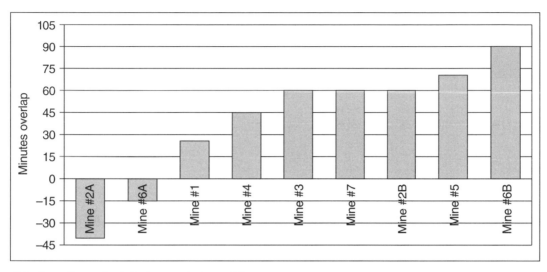

Note: A negative overlap indicates a gap between shifts.

Figure 7.14. Current day shift and afternoon shift overlaps.

change over shift in a hot seat mode will bring advantages through the reduction of time spent by the oncoming shift in the start-up procedures such as section inspection, pre-use checks of machinery, and possibly early safety meeting. Between 30 and 85 minutes of additional time is potentially available if the hot seat changeover is successful. This, of course, is subject to legal requirements regarding inspections, pre-use, and safety meetings being maintained.

Figure 7.15 shows the same shift overlaps as in Figure 7.14 but now compared to the traveling times recorded for each section, ordered in a decreasing gap (between shift leaving and next shift arriving in the section) from left to right. This clearly shows that, while mine #6B actually has a small period in which the shifts are in the section at the same time, the gap between shifts meeting in the section extends to as much as 90 minutes in the case of mine #4, which still has a 45-minute overlap of shifts. Hence, mine #6B and perhaps mine #5 have shift overlaps that will permit a genuine hot seat changeover to take place; the other mines cannot be expected to have such an advantage in potential savings. Therefore, the best practice in this regard would rest with mines #5 and #6B in terms of effective administration of shift overlaps for hot seat changes.

Health and safety issues. These are factors that require imperative actions from a legal aspect in the mining operation, and, depending on their severity, can contribute to the amount of downtime a section experiences.

Gas and ventilation. None of the sections visited claimed to be hindered by delays due to the presence of methane gas, or that there was a problem with the amount of ventilation entering the sections. The method of ventilating the individual headings was consistent, in that the mines either used fans or scoop brattices.

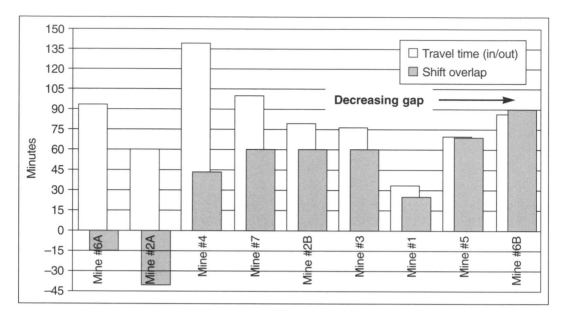

Figure 7.15. Shift overlap versus travel times.

Roof support. Two methods of support were noted, namely systematic and nonsystematic support. Of the mines visited, only sections at mine #4 (nonsystematic), mine #7, and mine #6A (systematic) indicated occasional delays with the roof-bolting operation. Effective supervision was the issue that had the most impact here.

Groundwater. Mines #1, #3, and #6A suffer from the ingress of groundwater into their sections, and as a result, sometimes had delays to the mining operations. The provision of adequate pumping equipment in the affected sections did, however, limit these delays.

Engineering issues. These refer to the mechanical and electrical delays preventing the continuation of the mining operation.

Power supply. Only mine #7 suffered from power supply availability problems, but this was mainly due to outages caused by wet weather conditions and electrical storms experienced occasionally.

Machine availability: Spares-related practices. Strict comparison of machine availabilities from mine to mine was not carried out once it was found that the data were incompatible due to different calculation methods being used. A separate task to review and ensure compatibility of data from group mines would be recommended before any true comparison could be made. It was, however, identified that particular problems in spares availability existed.

Four spares-related factors were identified as affecting the engineering availability of the CM. These factors were the

1. Availability of the correct item in the stores

2. Transport of the required spares underground and to the section

3. Method of handling and fitting heavy items or modules

4. Condition of the replacement item and its suitability for installation

On a four-point scale, interviewees in the sections visited indicated the severity of delays as per the bar chart in Figure 7.16. Following the convention of best practices occurring to the right-hand side of the graph, it can be seen that mine #5 was least affected by spares-related problems causing delays to the engineering downtime. Availability in the store, and transport into the section, were the main reasons for delays in this case.

Transport of spares was rated poorly throughout the sample of mines, because of the time taken to get the spare part from the store to the section. This was attributed to the poor availability of transport when the item was required, as well as the difficulty in communicating with the controllers of the transport for the speedy expedition of spares to the section. No best practice was evident as all the mines struggled with the quick delivery of spares into the section. This is an area that would benefit from further research and innovative solutions at all mines.

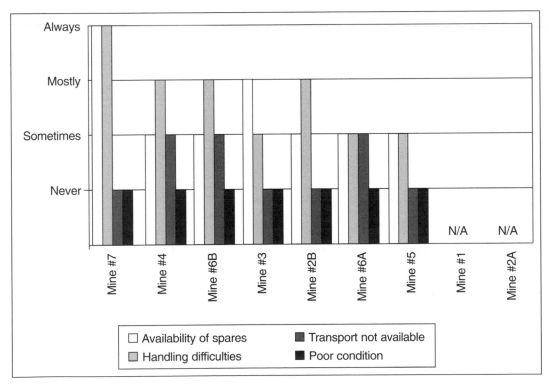

Note: Data for mine #1 and mine #2A were not available at the time of this write-up.

Figure 7.16. Delays in breakdowns due to spare problems.

Delays experienced through the nonavailability of spares was also a problem that was attributable to stocking policies and controls used by each mine.

The two areas where little or no problem arose were the correctness of spares arriving in the section and the handling of spares in the section. Mine #6A reduced the case of the wrong spare arriving in the section by giving a comprehensive set of parts books to the artisans, which can be rated as a best practice. With regard to the handling of spares in the section, mines #2B and #5 have potential best practices. Mine #2B has installed a crane on its section scoops that assists with the handling, whereas mine #5 has a maintenance car with crane facility to aid its artisans.

Electric cable damage. The investigating team focused on three aspects of cable changing, and these were the machine standing time during a cable replacement, the time taken to actually replace the cable, and the method of cable storage. The various mines' performances are shown in Figure 7.17.

Machine standing time is the total time lost as a result of a defective or damaged cable. The time taken ranged from 4 hours at mine #5, which stores fresh CM cables at an outbye location rather than in the section, to 30 minutes at mine #6A, which employs a quick changeout technique based on the use of a short 231 foot (70 meter) "jumper cable" to get the CM back into production with the shortest delay. In the study team's view, this was a time-saving best practice. Studies on the mine have shown that most cable damage takes place within a short distance of the CM, which at mine #6A would occur in its jumper

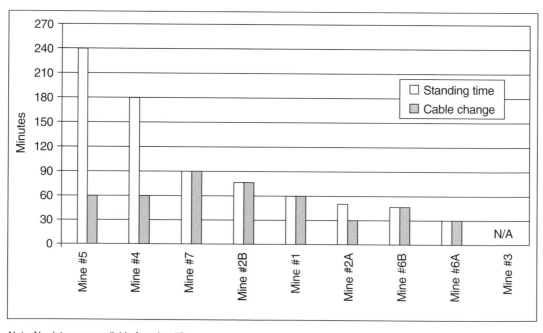

Note: No data were available for mine #3.

Figure 7.17. CM standing time for cable changes.

cable. Delays only result in 30 minutes of downtime as the section personnel pull the normal 660 foot (200 meter) cable forward, having removed the short jumper cable.

Cable change time, shown in Figure 7.17, is the time taken purely to replace the unserviceable cable with a fresh cable. Additional time may be taken to transport the replacement cable into the section. This would constitute the difference between the standing time and the cable change time. In the case of mine #4, cables are repaired in the section, hence the large difference between standing time and cable change time.

In terms of techniques used, the most common method of replacing a defective or damaged cable was by hand, using a number of the section crew. Other methods used were with the use of an LHD, a scoop, a shuttle car, or, on very rare occasions and when available, a cable tractor with a bin.

Cables were stored either in a cable bin, which appeared a best practice as it limited the potential for damage to cables during the transport to the section, or on a cable rack in the section or in a convenient place on the floor in the section. Only mine #5 reverted to storing CM cables outbye, resulting in long standing times.

Advantages gained in improving cable changeout times will be more significant if cable damage rates are high. The reduction of cable damage rates remains an area of concern on all mines. Figure 7.18 illustrates the cable damage rates of both CM and shuttle car cables on the mines. The mines are rated from left to right on CM cable damage rates in cables per section per month. It is noted that shuttle car cable damage rate bears

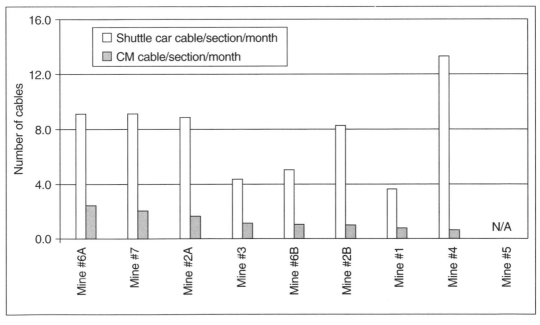

Note: Mine #5 data not available.

Figure 7.18. Cable damage rates per section per month.

little relation to the CM cable damage rates. Mine #1 shows the best all-round performance based on this sample.

A potential best practice exists at mine #7, where the development of a cable bonus system has, in its first month, resulted in a dramatic drop in cable damage. Each section is allotted about $2200.00 (R9 000) at the beginning of the month. If a cable is damaged, the cost thereof, as stipulated in the table below, is subtracted from the $2200.00 (R9 000). What remains at the end of the month is then divided equally among section members.

Cable type	Cable cost (approximate U.S. dollars/R.S.A. Rands)
Continuous miner	$484.00 (R2 00)
Shuttle car	$242.00 (R1 00)
Roof bolter	$121.00 (R5 00)
Feeder breaker	$121.00 (R5 00)

Issues of Mining Technique

The principal reasons for delay in this category were identified as follows:

- Pick replacement during the shift
- Poor floor maintenance
- Stone dusting in-shift
- Shuttle car delays
- Belt extensions
- Water supply problems

Pick replacement during the shift. Time delays due to pick changes were within a narrow range of 30–60 minutes per shift, depending on geological conditions of the coal seam. These delays tend to be unavoidable. A wide range of pick types were identified on the mines with no clear brand leader being outstanding. The most common types seen were Sandvik, Secoroc, Kennametal, Boart, and American Tool.

Floor maintenance (sweeping). A well-swept section has always been regarded as an important contributor to high performance and, as a result, was a focus of attention. Delays of machines that become immobilized by the build-up of coal on the floor of the section are best prevented by a rigorous regime of clean-up by LHD-type machines at regular and frequent intervals. In this study the type of equipment used and the frequency of sweeping were identified.

Only two types of equipment were in use. All sections at mines #2A and #2B use a battery scoop to sweep their sections, while on other mines the diesel LHD prevails as the sweeping tool. The battery scoop appeared to be the more effective application, as the LHD was easily removed from the section for considerable time periods for alternative use in the transport of materials underground. This led to an infrequent use within the sections for the task of sweeping and resultant build-ups of loose coal on section floors. Scoop-equipped sections tended to have superior floor cleanliness. Figure 7.19 illustrates the distribution of sweeping machinery from mine to mine.

Stone dusting. The speed of advance in the cutting cycle of CM machinery has made it necessary to apply stone dust at more frequent intervals. When this action takes place in-shift, it causes delays to the mining operation, and production is lost. Those mines that can perform stone dusting to legal requirements without disrupting the production cycle are those this study was attempting to identify.

It was found that two differences in stone dust application occurred. The first was the method of throwing stone dust and the second was the timing of this job. Figure 7.20 details the extent of delays and the type of machinery used.

A fan-tail stone dusting machine towed by a tractor was used in most instances, except in the case of mine #7 where manual stone dusting is still carried out. When questioned about whether stone dust applications took place in or out of shift, the response ranged between "sometimes" and "always."

No mine in the study successfully practiced after-shift stone dusting completely. Observations revealed that a substantial amount of time was lost doing in-shift stone dusting. Estimates revealed that delays of 30 minutes are common and even up to an hour in some instances. This should be a supervisory priority to minimize on each mine, and at this stage no best practice could be recommended by the study team. It should be noted, however, that the greater speeds of advance by the CMs and the legal requirements for the distance of stone dusting from the coal face prescribe innovative ideas to overcome this situation.

Mine	LHD	Scoop
Mine #7	1 per section	
Mine #2A		1 per section
Mine #6B	1 per section	
Mine #5	1 per section	
Mine #3	1 per section	
Mine #6A	1 per section	
Mine #2B		1 per section
Mine #1	1 per 3 sections	
Mine #4	1 per 3 sections	

Figure 7.19. Distribution of section sweeping machinery.

Belt extensions. This is the act of extending the section conveyor to keep pace with the advance of the mining face. It tended to be done every two pillars. There were two alternatives for the timing of an extension: toward the end of day shift, and immediately after the night shift. Six of the mines preferred the day-shift system, while the remaining three opted for the back-shift system. In both cases production time is usually lost on the day shift. On average, all mines lost about 3.3 hours of production time once every eight to nine days. Day-shift extensions resulted in 3.1 hours of lost time, while back-shift extensions resulted in the loss of 3.6 hours of production. Figure 7.21 depicts the range of delay periods typically experienced by the mines.

The best practice was shown to exist at mine #2B, where there was only a 1.5 hour production loss per extension. This can possibly be attributed to the size of the belt crew (12) and/or better supervision of the extension. Mine #6A, however, with the largest belt crew (14), did not show the same effectiveness in reducing hours lost during the shift.

It is necessary to do a more detailed analysis on belt extensions in the future, since this study was not comprehensive enough to examine all the factors affecting a belt extension (for example, the use of additional equipment). Mine #2A operates a three-shift scheme, and consequently none of the belt extensions is done out-of-shift. This results in a larger time loss being shown in Figure 7.21.

Water supply. The study team found that delays due to water supply problems—although potentially disruptive (a CM requires a water supply for water sprays when cutting coal)—did not feature as a significant delaying factor among the mines. Only two

Mine	In-shift delays*	Method†
Mine #6A	Always	Not available
Mine #1	Mostly	"Fan-tail"
Mine #5	Mostly	"Fan-tail"
Mine #2B	Mostly	Not available
Mine #2A	Sometimes	"Fan-tail"
Mine #3	Sometimes	"Fan-tail"
Mine #4	Sometimes	Not available
Mine #6B	Sometimes	Not available
Mine #7	Rarely	Hand done

*The extent of the delays was obtained from miners via interviews during the site visits. They rated the delays on a four-point scale (always, mostly, sometimes, rarely).

†"Fan-tail" is a spreading device towed behind a tractor to distribute inert stone dust in coal workings.

Figure 7.20. Stone dusting delays and method.

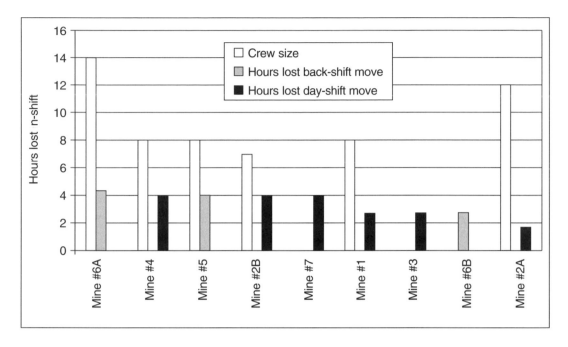

Figure 7.21. Delays due to section belt extensions.

variations in piping type were observed. They were PVC pipes and galvanized piping. Advantages of plastic piping in weight and ease of handling were countered by breakage and damage, which occurred easily in the underground environment.

Conclusions

Overall Performance

• For the section tonnage outputs from like machines and conditions in Ingwe, there is theoretical potential for up to 31 percent improvement overall by all sections in the sample. Thus, this would match production from the highest performer at mine #2B.

• The use of hour-meters on the CM cutting drums to provide additional data through which to measure useful cutting time and actual cutting rates in tons per hour is not yet being effectively implemented. Hence, comparable data from mines in the study were only partially available.

• Postshift debriefing sessions used at Ingwe's Australian operations are a potential best practice, and offer the possibility to improve existing information gathering techniques in the South African operations. These sessions should be analyzed by local staff for use on Ingwe mines.

Shift Formats

Shift hours.

• All mines, except one, operate a two-shift rotation system. One mine (#2A) is operating a three-shift rotation on a trial basis. Shift formats are diverse with regard to the use of the Saturday shift. Some 33 percent do not work Saturday shifts at all.

• Those mines on a two-shift rotation that have eliminated the Saturday shift are minimizing the proportion of traveling time. These three mines—#4, #6A, and #6B—have extended normal day and afternoon shifts during the week to make up the total hours required. Their systems constitute best practice under the existing conditions. Changing to non-Saturday working stands to add approximately three to four hours of useful working hours per section per fortnight.

Travel times during the shift.

• The best practice of minimizing the travel time of section personnel to the shaft bottom occurs when the lamp room is located at the shaft and the section crew can arrive at shaft bottom as one unit. In the case of vertical shafts, this practice exists at mines #2A, #2B, and #5, where large shaft transport capacity enabled the transport of the section crew down the shaft in one cycle. In the case of incline or adit entry mines, mine #6A showed best practice operation with section buses taking each crew underground from the lamp room to the section. Unfortunately, there is little that existing mines can realistically do to improve the situation in the short term. The potential does exist, however, for new mines to take these factors into account at the planning stage to set up a best practice.

• Underground transport into sections was exemplified by the dedicated bus system in use at mines #1 and #5, which was quick and reliable. Speed of entry, however, also depended on road conditions and illumination. Mine #1 showed exemplary road conditions through the use of a road maintenance contractor.

Labor in Sections

• Average labor in sections was 12 people (mining and engineering staff), and varied according to ventilation requirements and various methods of assigning LHD operators to sections for sweeping. Some 67 percent of sections operate with at least 2 CM operators in the crew complement. Engineering labor differs in the use of aides assisting the artisans. No clear common practice with respect to these personnel is apparent.

In-shift Delays

Prestart-up.

• In the four functions of early examination, safety meeting, CM pre-use check, and daily maintenance, mine #6B showed best practice by transferring the safety meeting to a preshift "green area" location, doing pre-use checks in parallel with section inspection, and transferring the daily maintenance to a back shift. This reduced the start-up period to 30 minutes, the best practice. The average start-up time for the mines in the study was 65 minutes. Thus, there exists the potential to reduce the start-up period by an average of 35 minutes daily across sections in this study.

Shift overlaps and hot seat changeovers.

• Seven of the nine sections operated a shift overlap system between day and afternoon shifts. Of these seven, only two sections had the opportunity, based on the overlap time, to actually change over in the section and thereby to make a hot seat changeover a practical proposition. The principal of a hot seat changeover should be to save time (up to an hour should be possible) by reducing the time of normal start-up procedures for the incoming shift. There exists potential for mines to review their overlap times (and abbreviated afternoon shift start-up procedures) to gain up to an hour of additional production time.

Health and safety.

• Although originally thought to be an area of potential for reducing delays, the sections sampled appeared to have the delays for reasons of gas (methane), support, or ventilation well controlled. Considering these were the top-performing sections, it was to be expected that legal issues would have been well dealt with. Potential may exist in other, less well-organized sections, which could not have been picked up in this study, but this should be addressed during the normal course of shift supervision.

Engineering.

• The potential for improvement of machine availability was found to be greatly dependent on the speedy delivery of the correct spares underground to the machine in question during breakdowns. Delays in this delivery chain were identified in the areas of availability of the item in the store; the ability to transport the item in a timely manner from surface to the machine in the section; and the use of equipment provided for handling heavy items during repairs. In this area, mine #5 led the mines in terms of its overall techniques in availability, speed, and handling of spares, based on data obtained from section personnel.

• The other area of delay identified as significant was the changing of damaged cables and the rate at which cables, both CM and shuttle car cables, were damaged. Mine #6A showed exemplary practice in reducing CM standing time to approximately 30 minutes due to the use of a jumper cable that could be quickly removed in order to resume production. Few other mines appear to utilize the jumper cable concept.

• Cable damage rates were difficult to assess as reasons for the damage were not recorded by the study. Transport of cables in containers that would limit transport damage was identified as a best practice at mine #2B. An innovative cable bonus scheme was identified at mine #7. Overall, mine #1 showed the most limited cable damage performance at 0.7 CM cables and 3.6 shuttle car cables per section per month.

Mining. In the areas of delays due to: pick replacement, section sweeping, stone dusting, shuttle car techniques, belt extensions, and water supply interruptions the following conclusions were noted.

• Pick replacement delays were generally 30–60 minutes per shift. No one type of pick was preferred, and five main types were used.

• Delays due to inadequate sweeping of the sections were avoided if a dedicated LHD or scoop could be assigned to the section. Scoops were potentially more effective, as LHDs tended to be removed from sections to perform other transport-related duties to the detriment of the section condition. Mine #2B utilized a scoop per section with a crane fitted, which assisted with the handling of heavy spares in the section.

• Stone dusting during shifts caused frequent delays in most operations. No best practice was discernible, and potential exists for the eradication of time lost this way on all mines except mine #7, which applies stone dust by hand.

• Delays due to shuttle car operating techniques were acknowledged in the study but not quantified. The subject has received considerable attention in past research to which mines are referred in the text.

• Belt extensions constitute regular delays for every section. Neither the day-shift—or back-shift technique appears dominant. Mine #2B shows best performance at under two hours delay per shift experienced, using a crew of 12. The average crew size is 9.5 where recorded, and is normally seven to eight members at the sections in the study. This is an activity that could be further researched to devise an effective best practice.

• Water supply interruptions to the CM spray system and consequential production delays were not found to be significant.

Recurring Themes

In reviewing the results of the analysis two recurring themes came through. The first was as expected, being the data availability problem, of which mention has already been made. The second was the relative diversity of ways in which mines tackled the same problems. This lends itself to comparison and the identification of a best practice. Several have come to light in the study (for example, mine #6A's CM jumper cable and mine #2B's scoop fitted with a crane facility and its cable container system).

Connecting both of these themes is the observation that a single management system has yet to be developed throughout the Ingwe group. This would be experienced by managers who are transferred to sister mines in the group and who have to learn the prevailing system at each mine before they become completely effective in the new position. In addition, a manager returning to a mine after an absence would probably find that the system was different from the one previously known purely because it had changed with the ongoing change of management staff. The development of a universal system throughout the group supported by a standard management information system is a matter that should receive some attention in the organizational development of Ingwe.

Recommendations

Section Performance

It is recommended that

- Measuring CM cutting time through the use of effective hour-meters on CMs should be monitored on a shift basis on all group mines, and should be reported at the highest level in order to measure improvement against the strategic target.

- A culture should be developed in the group that, during each working shift, nothing should be allowed to delay the production from the CM.

- Downtime should be precisely accounted for (to the minute), and should be recorded in a standard report format, which is validated by line management at the end of the shift.

- A system of brief but rigorous, boss-led, postshift debriefing meetings should be introduced to analyze and recommend action on any points that are outstanding at shift end.

Shift Formats

- Shift rosters should be investigated to minimize the effect of traveling time as a proportion of total available working time.

Travel Times In-shift

- The travel chain should be examined to minimize time lost due to excessive distance and waiting time between the different legs of the journey.

- Underground transport arrangements should be aligned so that section crews trust in the reliability of the chosen system through increased reliability and increased safe speed of entry.

- Main roadways used for entry and exit of personnel and materials should be maintained to the best conditions of surface and illumination. This may include the use of road maintenance contractors.

Labor in Sections

- Section labor complements should make provisions for two CM operators per shift.
- Staffing levels for artisans aides (or operatives) should be standardized throughout the group.

In-shift Working

- Safety meetings before shifts start (green areas) should be investigated and implemented where possible.
- Prestart procedures on each mine should be reviewed to take advantage of parallel activities or should be transferred to another time slot.
- The stocking policy of underground spares should be reviewed to minimize outages due to stockouts in mine stores.
- The systems on mines for the transport of spares underground to machines on breakdown should be given top priority for upgrading.
- The introduction of jumper cables on CMs should be implemented on those mines not employing jumper cables.
- Cable transport by container should be implemented where possible.
- Cable preservation schemes, such as the one at mine #7, should be investigated and implemented groupwide.
- Stone dusting during shift, which causes delays to the mining cycle, should be investigated and eliminated where possible.
- Mines should review their shuttle car operating techniques with respect to changeout positions to avoid CMs having to wait for shuttle cars.
- Belt extension crews should be sized to carry out the extension in the least time possible.

Appendix: Ingwe Project Description

Team Charter

A five-person team selected from the production, engineering, and human resources sections of various group mines will be undertaking an internal benchmarking study among Ingwe mines to identify group best practices that will contribute to improved performance in continuous miner (CM) operations. The internal study has been chosen for four reasons.

1. *Payback.* The CM method is responsible for the production of over 55 million tons (50 million metric tons) of run of mine (ROM) coal annually. (ROM is unbeneficiated; that is, straight from the mine.) Improvements resulting from increased productivity as best practices implemented by the mines offer the opportunity of a significant payback for

the benchmarking effort. For example, a 5 percent improvement in output will result in approximately 2.8 million tons (2.5 million metric tons) produced. This, in turn, will result in additional revenue of some $60.5 million (R250 million) to the group.

2. *Alignment with the business plan.* CM performance improvement has been identified in the group's 1996/97 business plan. A specific goal of a 10 percent improvement in output through increased cutting time over the next two years has been set. Thus, the project directly supports the company's strategic goals.

3. *An effective introduction to benchmarking.* Familiarization with the benchmarking process and its 10-step methodology will be readily possible through this internal pilot project. Once the process has been proven, Ingwe can then move to world-class practice benchmarking with confidence.

4. *Greater success with a limited scope project.* This internal study is likely to have the best chance of success due to a relatively limited scope. The study is unlikely to suffer from some of the problems encountered in wide international studies. These problems include the following:

- Large geographical distances between partners necessitating costly travel and communications
- Lack of comparable data
- Language difficulties
- Cultural barriers
- Difficulty in finding suitable benchmarking partners

All of these potential problems can prolong and complicate the study.

Project Triggers

The impetus for this study comes from two sources: the internal analysis of CM performance; and the CM production statistics, which are from mines #1, #2, #5, and #6. These are shown in descending order of performance in Table 7.1. The wide range of outputs can be attributed to a number of influences that may or may not be controllable, but proper investigation will be required to qualify why differences occur in similar types of operations.

Figure 7.22 is a histogram of the data from Table 7.1. This histogram reveals that the mean performance lies in the region 44,000–49,500 tons (40,000–45,000 metric tons) per month per section per machine. Performances over 66,000 tons (60,000 metric tons) per month have, however, been recorded by individual sections.

It is reasonable to assume that these high-performance sections could be the source of best practices, which contribute to the high performance, in certain subprocesses of CM operations. Conversely, those sections at the lower end of the production figures, possibly operating in a physically constraining environment, could also be the source of best practices brought about by a necessity to remain viable. This study will endeavor to identify those practices.

Table 7.1. Average CM output by mine by section (January 1995–July 1996).

Mine	Seam	Average monthly tons/section/machine
Mine #2A	4	64,459 (58,599 metric tons)
Mine #2B	2	58,528 (53,207 metric tons)
Mine #6A	2	53,539 (48,672 metric tons)
Mine #3	2	52,416 (47,651 metric tons)
Mine #5	4	52,298 (47,544 metric tons)
Mine #2C	4	51,366 (46,696 metric tons)
Mine #2A	2	49,931 (45,392 metric tons)
Mine #1	1	47,397 (43,088 metric tons)
Mine #2B	4	46,169 (41,972 metric tons)
Mine #6B	2	45,119 (41,017 metric tons)
Mine #3	1	43,833 (39,848 metric tons)
Mine #5	2	40,430 (36,755 metric tons)
Mine #1	2	38,245 (34,768 metric tons)

Note: Data taken during the period January 1995–July 1996 from mine production statistics data.

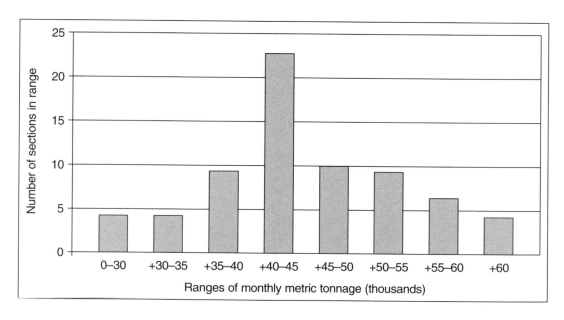

Figure 7.22. Distribution of monthly section output.

Competitive Analysis

Through productivity figures available within the public domain (see Table 7.2), it can be seen that top CM mines' productivity in both Australia and the United States show increases over Ingwe mines of significant proportions, albeit from very small mines that employ less than 100 people. Although the top-performing CM mines in New South Wales and the United States are smaller in output by an order of magnitude, the productivities being achieved show that Ingwe's best has some way to go to match the world's best, and that scope for improved performance exists when measured in world terms. Therefore, this information gives rise to the need to investigate CM performance within Ingwe with the aim, through performance improvement techniques such as benchmarking, to achieve world-class standards.

Project Goals

As the analysis proceeds it is expected that specific targets will be set, but several important outcomes are expected from this study. They are as follows:

- Increased cutting time by each machine. Cutting time is the time the machine spends in the sump or shear mode when the cutting motors are operating in near-full load situation.

- Improved machine utilization. This is defined as the time the machine is working as a proportion of the time available after maintenance and breakdowns.

Table 7.2. International CM productivity comparison.

Mine	Tons/person/year (Based on saleable tons, all personnel)	Annual output (Million metric tons per annum)
Ingwe		
Mine #2	6178 (5616 metric tons)	11.6
Mine #5	5861 (5328 metric tons)	9.7
Mine #6	2693 (2448 metric tons)	5.8
NWS Australia		
Canyon	12,980 (11,800 metric tons)	0.2
Invincible	7452 (6775 metric tons)	0.3
Awaba	7095 (6450 metric tons)	0.4
United States		
Pegasus	20,879 (18,981 metric tons)	0.5
Daniels Branch No. 1	19,207 (17,461 metric tons)	0.8
Select No. 3	16,302 (14,820 metric tons)	0.4

- Improved machine efficiency. This is the productivity achieved by the machine for the period it is working.

- Greater mine productivity and lower unit costs of saleable coal. This is the macro result of the above-mentioned factors that impact on the whole mine performance.

Critical Performance Metrics

In assessing the current processes it was determined that the following critical performance metrics are used to measure CM performance. For each effectiveness measure, the average internal measurement, the company leader, and the target benchmark must be obtained.

- CM cutting time (minutes/shift)
- CM output (tons/month)
- Average loading rate (tons/hour)
- CM availability (percent)
- Shuttle car availability (percent)

Other measures found to be relevant during the study will be included in the final report.

The Benchmarking Topic

The underground mining process consists of four separate phases during a shift.

1. Traveling to the workplace
2. Initial examination, safety talk, preuse inspection, and routine daily maintenance
3. Cutting, loading, and tipping operation, including parallel functions of roof support and services
4. Travel to surface at the end of the shift

For the purposes of this study the terms CM and continuous miner will refer to all mechanical continuous miners in use at the coal face, including road headers. As all of the four factors have a direct impact on the CM achieving its optimal performance, the topic to be benchmarked will include a complete start-to-end shift study of the section mining process.

This project will impact the timeliness of travel into and out of the workplace, the start of shift work steps, and the mining cycle, including the section roof support and services. Engineering performance of those items of production machinery will be examined inasmuch as it directly impacts on the output of the section.

Process Flowchart

The mining process is described as per the process flowchart shown in Figure 7.23. This will form the basis for comparison between the various mines in the study.

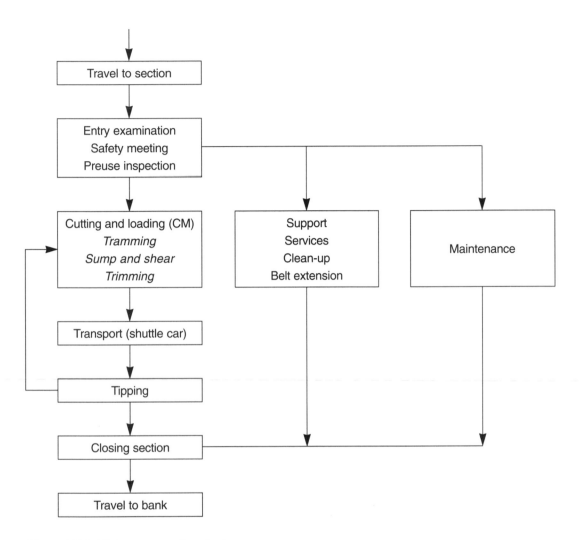

Figure 7.23. Mining process flowchart.

Project Scope

Study duration and resources. The study is expected to be completed within six months of the start date. Thus, the recommendations were expected to be available by end of March 1997. For more details, please refer to the project control chart.

It is estimated that a team of five staff members, plus a facilitator and an engineer will be required to work some 340 hours each to complete the project.

The project will review approximately 90 CM sections on seven of the Ingwe mines within South Africa. Mines included in the study will be: #1;, #2A and #2B; #3; #4; #5; #6A and #6B; and #7.

It is anticipated that costs of the study will be nominal as team members will be working on a part-time basis, and will continue to work in their normal occupation. Team members will operate as a group using a centralized venue (normally one of the mines) for group working sessions.

Methods of investigation. Investigation will be through the use of questionnaires and site visits to all mines operating CM machinery in the group within South Africa. Time will not permit the undertaking of any primary data gathering by the team through work study or observation other than at the (limited) time of a site visit. The historical production data and statistics from the mines' own systems will be reviewed, and analysis shall be done of all data collected through these means by the team. The benchmarking team will issue a final report that will include a summary of observations, analysis, and recommendations arising from the analysis.

Team members. The project sponsor is the senior manager of operations, and the cross-functional team consists of the following members.

	Mine	**Department**	**Position**
Clifford Hulley	Mine #5	Mining	Underground manager
Stephen Ward	Mine #2	Mining	Shift boss
Gideon Thwala	Mine #6B	Training	CM trainer
Tom Coetzee	Mine #6A	Engineering	Maintenance foreman
Brian Swart	Mine #8 (open cast)	Human resources	Senior personnel officer
Alistair Forbes (Facilitator)	Head Office	New business development and strategic planning	Manager business intelligence
Neil Atkins	Head Office	Engineering	Area engineering manager

About the Author

Alistair Forbes is the benchmarking manager for Ingwe Coal Corporation. His responsibilities include the development of benchmarking as a performance improvement tool, aligned with Ingwe's group strategy on all group mines in South Africa and Australia. His position was created in 1997 in order to further the use of benchmarking in the organization. Prior to this, since 1994, Forbes was the manager of business intelligence, where he was responsible for strategic planning and knowledge management for the Ingwe group.

Forbes began his career as a mining engineer with Anglo American in South Africa on the deep gold mines in Welkom (Free State). Through a number of moves, he gained production experience to middle management levels in diamonds, copper, and coal within southern Africa. Forbes joined his present employer, then known as Rand Mines, in 1986 in the project planning department. In 1989 he was transferred to the marketing function as an inland marketing manager.

Forbes received a bachelor of science degree in mining from the Royal School of Mines at Imperial College in London. He obtained a master of business leadership postgraduate degree from the University of South Africa in 1992.

The author may be contacted as follows:

Alistair Forbes
Benchmarking Manager
Ingwe Coal Corporation
6 Hollard Street
Marshalltown, Johannesburg, R.S.A.
P.O. Box 61820
MARSHALLTOWN, 2107, R.S.A.
Telephone: 27 11 376 3212
Facsimile: 27 11 834 3299
E-mail: alistairF@ingwe.co.za

PART 2: MANUFACTURING SECTOR

Analysis

Country:	United States
Organization:	Chevron Research and Technology Company
Industry:	Petroleum industry
Process:	Crude oil analysis
Case Study Title:	*"Crude Oil Analysis and Process Improvement at Chevron"*

Unlike many benchmarking studies, this one started out with a quantitative project goal: that of reducing cycle time by 50 percent and cost by 20 percent while maintaining quality. This set expectations for what had to be accomplished from the benchmarking study, and influenced the investigation during all phases—including the realization that all the best practices would not be found in one firm. Thus, the team had to put a "best-of-the-best" practice process together so that project goals could be met.

The case makes the point of not developing a questionnaire in isolation. Involving benchmarking partners was very productive, and helped sort out those questions that were "nice to have" from the essential, a common failing in these types of investigations.

Country:	Norway
Organization:	StatOil
Industry:	Petroleum industry
Process:	Oil well casing delivery
Case Study Title:	*"Benchmarking the Delivery Process of Casing for Oil Wells at StatOil"*

In this case, the quantitative benefits compared to the project expenditure were very handsome indeed. The initial study had a benefit-to-cost ratio of 25:1, and the identified additional areas of potential would nearly double this again. With the level of preparation, it is not surprising that the best practice findings were very well documented for each of the three operational models: in-house, consignment, and outsourcing.

This carefully selected project was an introduction of benchmarking to an organization that successfully launched this improvement approach. It also proves the dictum of concentrating on the process to gain the insights and "not becoming too obsessed with the numbers."

Country:	United Kingdom
Organization:	Allied Domecq Spirits & Wine Ltd.
Industry:	Beverage and spirits industry
Process:	Executive information systems
Case Study Title:	*"Delivering Information at Allied Domecq Spirits & Wine Ltd."*

Findings were primarily qualitative in nature, although they potentially could be converted to monetary savings. The significant findings included the following:

- Incorporating an intuitive design so that users do not have to be experts
- Using color for ease of understanding and consistency of interpretation
- Prototyping on the fly, as the system was being rolled out
- Avoiding a massive cut over to the new system, thus impacting cultural change
- Emphasizing that the system was the one version of the truth, and that data and information integrity were, therefore, automatically incited to a higher level of accuracy

Country:	Italy
Organization:	3M
Industry:	Manufacturing industry
Process:	General ledger consolidation
Case Study Title:	*"General Ledger and Consolidation Processes: The Experience of 3M Italy"*

Lessons learned and benefits were derived from the usefulness of understanding the processes and practices, as is the focus of most benchmarking today, and from documenting the student and faculty "customer" requirements, expectations, and needs. The perceived difficulties came from those traditionally associated with these types of comparisons, namely that they are credible and comparable. The process focus ensures the later.

While the results were not quantified, they are assumed to be non-inconsequential when all costs of quality are considered. Compared to the nominal expenses for this type of study, the payback must be substantial.

Country:	New Zealand
Organization:	Fletcher Challenge Building Products Sector
Industry:	Wood products industry
Process:	Best practices in manufacturing
Case Study Title:	*"A Journey Without End: Best Practice in the Building Products Sector of Fletcher Challenge"*

The applied learnings are replete with statements of best practices. These cover significant areas such as leadership success attributes; human resource strategies; innovation; customer value creation; safety and learning through creation; and acquiring and transferring knowledge. While all of these core competencies were uncovered through best practice benchmarking during the study tours, it is most likely that the last area—learning—was most strongly understood. All the study tours must have strongly confirmed that an organization like Fletcher Challenge can learn from others and that there is a major opportunity to do so.

One of those major learnings was the importance of understanding the process as a prerequisite for uncovering and understanding best practices. Without sound processes failure would be inevitable. This involved some best practice approaches to good study tours found at the partner companies. These approaches included the following:

- Scoping the process
- Using measurable objectives
- Having cross-functional teams that included customers and suppliers
- Creating a vision for the future
- Having strong, visible senior management support

Fletcher Challenge Building Products Sector did a superb job in all these areas during the structure, conduct, and assimilation of its best practice tours.

Key leanings on the value of these benchmarking visits enabled fast learning and rapid change, an inspired workforce on what was achievable, and the development of enhanced leadership skills for continued survival. Valuable relationships with the benchmarking partners, all from dissimilar industries, did not elude Fletcher Challenge. This is an excellent example of a plan of action and plan for change that can be derived if done right. And Fletcher Challenge did!

This author is privileged to have shared the best practice benchmarking experience with Fletcher Challenge, and visited with the management team that made it possible. It is commendable.

Country:	India
Organization:	NIIT
Industry:	Software manufacturing industry
Process:	Hardware procurement
Case Study Title:	*"Hardware Procurement at NIIT"*

While the analysis focused on the length of the cycle time, the number of process steps, and the number of process step handoffs, best practices were found in the areas of converting from individual pricing to a formula; avoiding the need for letters of credit by agreeing to a credit line; and using the Green Channel for customs clearance. Ultimately breaking the cycle time down into its key elements was the way these best practices were revealed in adequate detail in order to permit implementation.

A preliminary sample of delay impacts from hardware imports was estimated to be of the order of $930,000 (Rs 28.00 lacs). The more telling measure was the total cycle time for the current process of 86 days. A best practice process was developed from benchmarking partner observations that reduced the cycle time to 48 days. Those benchmarking visits gave insight into how the process could be innovatively and creatively improved by the knowledgeable process owners and operators, thus further reducing the cycle time to 21 days.

Country:	South Africa
Organization:	Ingwe Coal Corporation
Industry:	Mining and minerals industry
Process:	Continuous miner delays
Case Study Title:	*"An Internal Benchmarking Study of Continuous Miner Operations Within Ingwe Coal Corporation"*

The original target of this study was to increase mine output by 10 percent. If all sections could be raised to the best-performing section then there was a theoretical 31 percent improvement possible. In spite of these findings, however, the best performers were admittedly only half as productive as the industry leaders. Therefore, there was ample potential for finding best practices internally. A follow-on extension of the study would be to use the preparation in this phase to identify and externally compare to the best-in-class of the industry in order to bring Ingwe operations to world-class status.

Best practices were identified in all of the major phases of the process focusing on the objective of reducing delays. These included travel time to and from the mine site using dedicated buses; more efficient start-up procedures including before-shift safety meetings held on the surface; and enhanced maintenance practices performed out of shift, including the speed of delivery, handling, and extended component life of spare parts. Contributing factors included geological conditions and motivational teamwork factors.

Lessons learned included the ability to gain management acceptance through thorough preparation using a rigorous, applications-tested analysis tool, such as benchmarking, and the proof of its worth in the analysis of existing operations. As a result, the existing study will most likely be expanded to include the external investigation phase. And as a direct reflection of these successes two additional studies of core processes have been launched. The establishment of a position of benchmarking manager at the group level and a network of benchmarking champions at the mines further attest to the value of this technique.

Summary Cost Savings and Benefits

United States	Europe	Asia/Pacific	Americas/Africa
MANUFACTURING			
UNITED STATES	NORWAY	NEW ZEALAND	SOUTH AFRICA
Chevron Research and Technology Company	**StatOil**	**Fletcher Challenge Building Products Sector**	**Ingwe Coal Corporation**
Crude oil analysis	*Oil well casing delivery*	*Best practices in manufacturing*	*Continuous miner delays*
• Cycle time 50% less • Cost 20% less • Quality maintained	• Benefit/cost 25:1 • Additional potential to 50:1	• Learn, change at rapid pace • Inspired workforce • Enhanced leadership • Practices could be quantified and are substantial	• Output range 40–70 tons per month • 10% mine output increase • 31% theoretical increase
	UNITED KINGDOM	INDIA	
	Allied Domecq Spirits & Wines Ltd.	**NIIT**	
	Executive information systems	*Hardware procurement*	
	• Not quantified, but substantial	• Cycle time reduced from 85 days to 48 days • Best practice is 21 days	
	ITALY		
	3M		
	General ledger consolidation		
	• Turnaround 4X (high to low) • Person months 10X • Data control 63% higher		

Key Best Practices Found

United States	Europe	Asia/Pacific	Americas/Africa

MANUFACTURING
 	
UNITED STATES
 	
Chevron Research and Technology Company
 	
Crude oil analysis
 	
• 24 recommendations
• Assay process improvements
• Improved turnaround time
• Lab consolidation
	NORWAY
	
	StatOil
	
	Oil well casing delivery
	
	• Three models used
	  1. In-house
	  2. Consignment
	  3. Outsourcing
	
	UNITED KINGDOM
	
	Allied Domecq Spirits & Wines Ltd.
	
	Executive information systems
	
	• Intuitive design
	• Use of color
	• Prototyping
	• Cultural change toward data integrity
	
	ITALY
	
	3M
	
	General ledger consolidation
	
	• 3M the benchmark
	• Integrated, modular
	• On-line
	• Flexible inquiry
	• Multilevel security
		NEW ZEALAND
		
		Fletcher Challenge Building Products Sector
		
		Best practices in manufacturing
		
		• 26 mentioned including the following:
		  —Customer focus
		  —Process control
		  —Inventory control
		  —Technology management
		
		INDIA
		
		NIIT
		
		Hardware procurement
		
		• Pro forma invoice
		• Standard purchase order
		• Customs clearance
			SOUTH AFRICA
			
			Ingwe Coal Corporation
			
			Continuous miner delays
			
			• Data gathering checklist
			• Focus on reducing delays by examining the following:
			  —Travel time
			  —Start-up procedures
			  —Enhanced maintenance techniques
			  —Spares effectiveness
			• Benchmarking network established

Lessons Learned

United States	Europe	Asia/Pacific	Americas/Africa
MANUFACTURING UNITED STATES **Chevron Research and Technology Company** *Crude oil analysis* • Use deployment flowchart for activity, time line, and responsibilies.	NORWAY **StatOil** *Oil well casing delivery* • Do not become obsessed with data. • Mapping is highly revealing. UNITED KINGDOM **Allied Domecq Spirits & Wines Ltd.** *Executive information systems* • Data accuracy required by central system. ITALY **3M** *General ledger consolidation* • Best practices implementation are a function of the following: —Strategies —Values —Structures	NEW ZEALAND **Fletcher Challenge Building Products Sector** *Best practices in manufacturing* • Creating, acquiring, and knowledge transfer are major opportunities. • Learning objectives for study tours identified. INDIA **NIIT** *Hardware procurement* • Well-documented process entices partner participation.	SOUTH AFRICA **Ingwe Coal Corporation** *Continuous miner delays* • A substantive internal benchmarking opportunity, involving 90 machines, was created. • Management acceptance gained. • Follow-on projects were justified.

Introduction

The service sector includes seven cases. They are drawn from telecommunications, retail, book publishing, home mortgage lending, computers, and service and trade development. The processes covered run the gamut from customer satisfaction management, to store operations, to assessing successful change, to export development, to book distribution, and to procurement process redesign. Again, the geographic distribution shows the applicability of benchmarking to anywhere in the globe. A brief summary, background information, the rationale for each case, and key points to consider when reading follow.

Country:	United States
Organization:	Pacific Bell
Industry:	Telecommunications industry
Process:	Customer satisfaction management
Case Study Title:	*"Applying Benchmarking at Pacific Bell: Skills, Tools, and Techniques"*

The customer satisfaction management process is one of the most heavily benchmarked processes. It is also a vital process for organizations who know the criticality of meeting customer needs as a matter of sustaining revenue if not survival. Thus, gathering, analyzing, delivering, and using customer feedback are essential parts of the customer satisfaction process.

While the importance of the process itself is reason enough for this case study, it is also an example of another key facet of the benchmarking process, namely the gathering of benchmarking information through questionnaires. This was preceded by a comprehensive documentation of the process. But this study also makes the point that the survey questions should be directly tied to the process, most often documented by a flowchart.

179

Some innovative approaches to survey construction were also pursued. The design included the segregation of quantitative (benchmark) information from the qualitative (best practice) information. The questionnaire was internally piloted to debug it and sort the must-have from the nice-to-have information. The team members, however, went beyond these essential steps and involved themselves in data gathering. They trained themselves to be good interviewers and conducted the interviews themselves, mostly over the telephone.

These are excellent lessons for anyone conducting benchmarking studies. They reemphasize the need for care in the planning phase to ensure credible results. Given the level of detail and involvement of the team, the analysis phase should be a snap. And the ability of the team to authoritatively justify its recommendations is grounded on this preparation.

Country:	United Kingdom
Organization:	Boots The Chemists
Industry:	Service industry
Process:	Sales promotion
Case Study Title:	*"Internal Benchmarking at Boots The Chemists"*

This case study is a vivid example of the introduction of benchmarking into an organization that had never used this improvement approach. The objective was not only to showcase the benchmarking approach but to change the culture for information sharing, to objectively face the need for improvement, and to develop an internal commitment to change.

This case study is also a testimonial to the value of internal benchmarking as an important starting point if not an imperative for initiating benchmarking activities. With over 1200 locations, there had to be a rich source of learning among stores and the ability to source better internal practices. All that Boots The Chemists had to do was to organize the project.

In order to gain store managers' interest in the project, the benchmarking team had to be insightful and opportunistic. It selected a critical process—something all store managers had to do to be successful. Thus, the sales promotion process and timing (the run up before Christmas) was chosen as the critical process. This went a long way toward having a winning project, and helped to sell and gain commitment for benchmarking. These are instructive lessons for any organization starting benchmarking.

Country:	Italy
Organization:	IBM Italy
Industry:	Computer industry
Process:	Procurement process redesign
Case Study Title:	*"Application of Benchmarking Techniques for Business Process Reengineering: IBM Italy's Procurement Process Reengineering Model"*

The concept of best practice benchmarking is not difficult. In fact, the simplicity of the concept is one of the major contributors to its longevity. But in its fullest application, benchmarking is detail-rich. And the fullest application is needed in complex situations, especially where the priority process is not known without some objectivity and data. This case study is an excellent lesson in how to uncover, prioritize, and determine the health of a large cross-functional core, if not enterprise, process such as manufacturing.

There are few organizations who give themselves the luxury of analyzing their overall process structure before commencing benchmarking. Often the tendency is to simply select a process and get started. But this is no guarantee that the right process was selected that will best achieve the business results desired and priority customer requirements. That takes some analysis. IBM Italy's case is an excellent example for those concerned with the careful selection of a vital process to benchmark.

The approach preferred and followed in this case is to first identify the very highest-level processes; that is, the enterprise processes. There could be six to eight. For IBM Italy, there were seven enterprise processes for manufacturing. Next, these processes were detailed into five categories, each containing of one to five subprocesses, for a total of 18 subprocesses. Following this, the processes were rated as to their contribution to the organization. This involved an analysis of cost and value. Specific actions or improvement approaches could then be tailored to the health of the processes.

In this case the procurement process was identified as a high-value/high-cost process and a priority candidate for process redesign through benchmarking. This was the process that was mapped for comparison to the best practice processes of others. The contribution to improvement from human knowledge, process practices, and technology could then be compared with confidence that credible results would be obtained.

This is truly the level of detail that should be followed, especially for complex processes. Readers who want to know how to obtain, gain acceptance of, and justify best practices will want to study this case in some detail.

Country:	New Zealand
Organization:	Trade and Development Board
Industry:	International trade and development industry
Process:	Export development
Case Study Title:	*"Expanding Benchmarking to Include an Entire Industry: Tradenz Best Practice Study"*

It is often questioned whether benchmarking can be used for operations that are not easily quantified. The need to identify improved practices for businesses as a group that would make them more internationally competitive certainly meets that criterion. Thus, on the surface, it would seem difficult, if not impossible to benchmark the following objectives.

- Add value to already high-performing companies.
- Promote an industry internationally.
- Provide development for second-tier, supporting companies.
- Understand gaps in competitiveness.

But this case study proves that these difficulties can be overcome. The underlying basics of benchmarking were applied. Namely, the project was first focused on one industry—telecommunications. Next, a targeted set of companies was identified—the high performers. Next, a set of accepted measurement criteria was used to obtain objective information—in this case the Baldrige criteria. And finally, a specific set of eight processes was targeted for improvement. This approach is indicative of the necessary steps to a successful best practice investigation.

Country:	Australia
Organization:	NRMA
Industry:	Service industry
Process:	Assessing successful change
Case Study Title:	*"Benchmarking Improvement and Change: How Quality Award Winners Do It"*

There are quality awards in 20 or more countries around the world, with more continually being established. The evaluation criteria are most often grandfathered to the Malcolm Baldrige National Quality Award established in the United States. In some instances those criteria have been further improved through local adaptation. It is conceivable that thousands of organizations have used the Baldrige Award criteria for internal quality program assessment. The number of successful applicants is a known or knowable number; perhaps one or two per country per year. The achievement is a crowning success for the award recipient. It often is the culmination of many years of quality improvement pursuit.

But how many organizations that have committed to the quality journey and successfully achieved national recognition question and want to benchmark the value derived from such a massive undertaking? NRMA received the Australia Quality Award in 1992, years after institutionalizing a quality program. In spite of the national recognition and the indirect recognition resulting from the queries of organizations that wanted to learn how NRMA succeeded, there was an internal need to quantify the value of the program.

Therefore, NRMA set out to benchmark the success, in tangible terms, of its improvement and change process. But whom does a quality award recipient benchmark? Because of the Australia Quality Council's preeminence in the quality movement in Australia, it seemed appropriate to use the Council to source leading-edge benchmarking partners and facilitate the study. Thus, this approach is indicative of the value of collaborative benchmarking conducted through the services of a benchmarking association or center. More often than not, these organizations provide a mutually secure environment for sharing best practices and can attract the very best participants.

Country:	India
Organization:	Housing Development Finance Corporation (HDFC)
Industry:	Home mortgage financing industry
Process:	Loan management
Case Study Title:	*"Redefining Service Frontiers: Lessons From the Best Practices of the Housing Development Finance Corporation"*

Organizations conducting benchmarking need to identify partners that have best practices. There are several ways to do that. This case study details the traditional way of uncovering these organizations, namely to conduct a careful review of the publicly available information. This would include quantitative information, such as financial indicators, as well as qualitative information, such as statements in annual reports. A careful sifting of performance indicators, over time, to prove consistency was the approach taken here. This winnowed down a large list of potential partners to a manageable list that could be further researched. The approach also included contacting the partner directly.

Then, the follow-on steps would be to have the organization identify why it believed it was a best practice company as judged by sustained, improved performance. In this case, HDFC—a very successful housing finance company—was readily able to categorize its best practices in the areas of leadership, service, staff development, and use of technology. This is a very viable approach to identifying not only potential partners, but also to having them self-nominate themselves for what they believe they do best. This study is replete with narratives of best practices.

Country:	Canada
Organization:	Canadian Book Publishers Association
Industry:	Publishing industry
Process:	Book distribution
Case Study Title:	*"Improving the Profitability of Canadian Book Publishers: An Example of the Application of Performance Measurement and Benchmarking at Both the Firm and Sector Level"*

How is reliable, comparable performance information obtained? Almost without exception the first thing an organization wants is comparable performance data, or benchmarks. A company wants to know where it stands before launching into a formal activity of finding best practices. The need to know performance data may start by baselining the organization's own data and information. For instance,

- What is the firm's performance, such as customer satisfaction levels measured by percent customers satisfied for its own customers?

- What is the customer requirement—the satisfaction of others with competitive products and services?

- What is the performance of the industry's best companies?

- What are the satisfaction levels achieved by the top quartile in the industry?

- What is world-class?

- What is the level obtained by those that are renown for service excellence regardless of industry, geography, product, or service?

For some time, there has been an activity that has tackled this precursor to finding and implementing best practices (benchmarking). It started in the United Kingdom over 20 years ago and has spread to a number of other countries. It is called the Interfirm Comparison Program. In it, the activities of 20 to 30 companies in an industry sector are analyzed and the data are normalized for comparability. Each participant company then has a set of objective information by which to compare and determine performance gaps. The magnitude of the gaps leads the organizations to then consider which products or processes need improvement from incorporation of best practices.

This book would not be complete without a case study from the Interfirm Comparison Program. The one described here involves book publishing activities in Canada. The study led to a focus on one important aspect of book publishing, namely fulfillment operations. Depending on how efficient book publishers are at fulfillment—generally defined as order entry, warehousing, transportation, and the handling of returns—can literally determine profit or loss.

Master Table

	United States	Europe	Asia/Pacific	Americas/Africa
SERVICE	UNITED STATES **Pacific Bell** Telecommunications industry *Customer satisfaction management* "Applying Benchmarking at Pacific Bell: Skills	UNITED KINGDOM **Boots The Chemists** Service industry *Sales promotion* "Internal Benchmarking at Boots The Chemists" ITALY **IBM** Computer industry *Procurement process redesign* "Application of Benchmarking Techniques for Business Process Reengineering: IBM Italy's Procurement Process Reengineering Model"	NEW ZEALAND **Trade and Development Board** International trade and development industry *Export development* "Expanding Benchmarking to Include an Entire Industry: Tradenz Best Practice Study" AUSTRALIA **NRMA** Service industry *Successful change* "Benchmarking Improvement and Change: How Quality Award Winners Do It" INDIA **Housing Development Finance Corporation** Home mortgage financing industry *Loan management* "Redefining Service Frontiers: Lessons from the Best Practices of the Housing Development Finance Corporation"	CANADA **Canadian Book Publishers Association** Publishing industry *Book fulfillment* "Improving the Profitability of Canadian Book Publishers: An Example of Performance Measurement and Benchmarking at Both the Firm and Sector Level"

185

Country and Industry

United States	Europe	Asia/Pacific	Americas/Africa
SERVICE			
UNITED STATES	UNITED KINGDOM	NEW ZEALAND	CANADA
Telecommunications industry	Service industry	International trade and develop-ment industry	Publishing industry
	ITALY	AUSTRALIA	
	Computer industry	Service industry	
		INDIA	
		Home mortgage financing industry	

Processes

United States	Europe	Asia/Pacific	Americas/Africa
SERVICE			
UNITED STATES	UNITED KINGDOM	NEW ZEALAND	CANADA
Customer satisfaction manage-ment	*Sales promotion*	*Export development*	*Book fulfillment*
	ITALY	AUSTRALIA	
	Procurement process redesign	*Successful change*	
		INDIA	
		Loan management	

186

CHAPTER 8

Applying Benchmarking at Pacific Bell: Skills, Tools, and Techniques

Alfred R. Pozos, Manager–Quality Assurance and Quality Business Systems, California State Automobile Association, Joyce Miller, Director–Business Process and Training, Pacific Bell, Peter Cartwright, Manager–Customer Satisfaction Measurement, Pacific Bell

Company Profile

Pacific Bell provides local telephone service and access to long distance services for California residents. It originally provided its services as one of the operating companies of AT&T, but AT&T was dissolved in 1984 in a broader move to deregulate the telecommunications industry. In the wake of this dissolution, Pacific Bell and the regional company that controlled it—Pacific Telesis—restructured so that they could compete in a deregulated market. Significant downsizing has become prominent among the changes at Pacific Bell. In five years, the organization reduced its workforce by 60,000, going from a high of 115,000 employees down to about 48,000. In mid-1997 Pacific Telesis and its subsidiaries, including Pacific Bell, were acquired by Southwestern Bell Corporation.

In the deregulated and increasingly competitive marketplace that followed the breakup of AT&T, Pacific Bell sought ways to improve the productivity and quality of services and products delivered to its customers. In 1989, Pacific Bell began developing an initial framework for a quality improvement process and started a small corporate quality center that quickly began to focus on quality trends and processes, including benchmarking. In the intervening years, the Pacific Bell Quality Center became a true center for benchmarking with ongoing studies, external contacts, and a newsletter.

Because it benchmarks, Pacific Bell is now more competitive. Benchmarking has focused its corporate culture on customer satisfaction and empowered workers to improve services and products. Using benchmarking, Pacific Bell identifies efficient suppliers, stays abreast of changing customer needs, and reveals innovative practices that can improve productivity. In short, benchmarking is a key tool for continuing improvement at Pacific Bell.

In 1992, Pacific Bell analyzed and summarized the systems that it had in place to measure customer satisfaction. The study examined whether Pacific Bell was accurately and efficiently measuring customer satisfaction and appropriately using the results. The benchmarking team discovered more efficient ways to measure customer satisfaction and to use the data, resulting in significant savings to Pacific Bell.

Planning the Study

Background

Pacific Bell has measured customer satisfaction since 1964. Originally, surveys were conducted via mail, but the company moved to telephone interviews in 1971. Questionnaires were modified in 1984 and 1991, but the sampling techniques and methods of analysis have been the same since 1984.

Under the sponsorship of the vice president for quality, the company measuring organization was chartered to conduct a benchmarking study of its systems because of concerns regarding the viability and accuracy of its customer satisfaction process. Essential questions that were the foundation of this project were associated with the methodology for gathering customer satisfaction data.

- Were the processes that Pacific Bell was using for this process state-of-the-art?

- Was the company using the best and most accurate processes to measure customer satisfaction?

During the development of the project, the team also focused on the use of these data. That is, was the company using customer satisfaction data in the best way possible to improve product or services? Although not an original motivator for this study, this area of inquiry proved to be the most valuable to the company.

Strategically, the accurate measures of customer satisfaction and the opposite, customer dissatisfaction, are essential to the functioning of a large corporation. Therefore, the fundamental questions that this study attempted to answer were as follows:

- Was the company obtaining essential customer input using its current methodology?

- If it was, how was this information being used in the company, when compared to best-in-class companies?

A benchmarking team was formed composed of the director of company measures; the four managers from the company measures organization who had direct responsibility for the application, analysis, and refinement of the company's customer satisfaction measurement systems; and the corporate manager for benchmarking, who acted as a facilitator. The team conducted this study in addition to performing its regular duties. The project commenced in May 1992 and was completed in February 1993.

Objective

The objective was to compare Pacific Bell's customer satisfaction measurement process for gathering, delivering, analyzing, and using data with other best-in-class companies.

Purpose

The purpose was to learn from best-in-class companies and to use the learnings to improve Pacific Bell's measures and processes.

Methodology

The director of company measures was the only member of the team who had attended a benchmarking class. Nevertheless, the team, with the assistance of the corporate manager for benchmarking, was successful in following a definitive process and completing the project.

The team undertook the task of outlining its current process. A 17-page document was prepared that delineated all of the processes that the company used to gather, analyze, and disseminate data. Tactically, this enabled the benchmarking team to agree on and to achieve a common understanding of the existing process.

The members of the team—by virtue of their positions in the company measures organization—attended seminars, classes, and consortia meetings associated with customer satisfaction measures. As a result, there was a very high level of understanding of the measurement process generally, and the application of that process within the company and within business generally.

The team determined that having a common understanding of existing processes, and having a general knowledge of those organizations that were determined to be best-in-class, were not sufficient criteria for the selection of benchmarking partners. In a series of meetings, the team evolved the following profile as more definitive, and assigned relative point values to be associated with the importance of each element.

Benchmarking partners' profile.

4 Must

3 Very important

2 Somewhat important

1 Minimally important

Company Profile

4 Profitability. The organization's *Fortune* 500 ranking over the last five years was determined to be one of the most important elements. An analysis of the five-year time frame was deemed to be essential to avoid selecting a company whose profitability appeared to be only a recent, and perhaps, random occurrence. Profitability was viewed as a key indicator because it was perceived that data from "excellent" companies that were not profitable would call into question the validity of the project.

3 Diverse market segments. This was an attempt to partner with organizations who had similar marketing populations so as to examine somewhat comparable organizations.

3 Service industry. Although this element was not a must-have, it was included because the team perceived that service industries function somewhat differently than other industries, and customer expectations of a service industry would be different from their expectations of other types of businesses.

3 Ongoing relationships. The intent of this element was to examine businesses that had ongoing relationships with their customers as opposed to one-time sales relationships that are typical of other businesses. It was perceived that ongoing relationships with the company created a unique type of customer expectation.

2 California presence. This was an attempt to find comparable organizations that dealt with the international flavor of the California market and its economic, ethnic, and language diversity.

1 Technology-driven. This element attempted to establish linkages with organizations that were constantly introducing technological innovations to assist in market share acquisition and to examine how these organizations measured customer satisfaction relative to these innovations.

1 Regulatory climate change. This element was looking for compatibility with other regulated businesses in an attempt to determine the impact of these changes on customer satisfaction and how these organizations dealt with them.

In addition to these company profile data, the team also evolved the following customer service profile criteria.

4 Is a sustained leader in customer satisfaction.

4 Actively uses customer feedback to improve internal processes in a systematic way.

4 Demonstrates that customer satisfaction is improving over time.

4 Has a qualitative and systematic measurement system that measures external customer reaction.

3 Measures service transactions.

3 Successfully integrates internal processes to improve levels of customer satisfaction with external data gathered from customers.

2 Considers customer satisfaction as an integral part of the quality effort.

2 Correlates employee satisfaction with customer satisfaction.

2 Uses a variety of instruments to gather input.

1 Has had a bad history of customer service and expected a positive recovery.

1 Uses measures of employee effectiveness (internal customer satisfaction) and external customer satisfaction that are linked in the organization.

1 Has different types of measurement groups (for example, research oriented versus historical tracking).

1 Conducts internal surveys of how employees evaluate customer service.

After agreeing on the select sort criteria, the team hired a researcher to determine, from the literature, the organizations that best met these criteria. The researcher conducted an extensive and in-depth review of the literature and presented to the team a ranking and rating of the organizations as measured by the select sort criteria.

The team members were then assigned four companies each. They reviewed the literature supplied by the researcher relative to those organizations, and then presented to the entire team company evaluations and point rankings based on their own review. It was from this final ranking that a list of potential benchmarking partners was identified.

Collecting Information

This project surveyed eight organizations representing a cross section of business including those in finance, consumer package goods, insurance, telecommunications, and imaging.

The team constructed a two-tier questionnaire: a qualitative portion and a qualitative one. Within the quantitative portion of the survey were questions associated with the number of people who performed the measurement function within the organization; the annual cost for this function; the number of customers surveyed; the response rate; and the cost per interview.

The qualitative portion of the interview was much more extensive and dealt with such items as why and how the organization measured customer satisfaction; who performs the function and in what organization within the company they are located; whether or not the company compared its results to its competitors; the methods used for gathering the data; how customer samples were selected; whether or not customer loyalty was measured; and the analysis and use of the customer satisfaction data.

After the development of the questionnaire, the team first tried it within the company. Team members were also coached on basic interviewing skills, establishing rapport, and methods of persistent but courteous inquiry. After a successful trial, it was determined that the question set was a viable instrument for the project.

The team, having a limited budget, decided to attempt to conduct this study via telephone and facsimile. Initial contacts were made personally by the benchmarking manager. Those companies that agreed to participate were immediately provided with Pacific Bell's responses to its own question set: This was a multipage document that described, in its totality, the measurement process within the company. Partners were asked to fill out and send back the quantitative portion of the study first. Subsequently, two-hour telephone interviews were arranged with each of the partners. They were asked if the interview could be audio recorded and all but one agreed.

Originally, the team had some concerns regarding the feasibility of telephone interviews and the willingness of interviewees to be audio recorded. These concerns proved to be groundless.

Upon acceptance of the benchmarking proposal by a corporate partner, the organization was assigned to a team of two project members to arrange interview times and schedules. Given the fact that the team members were conducting this study in addition to their normal and ongoing responsibilities, and the interviewees had similar obligations, the process of arranging and completing these interviews was time-consuming.

The benchmarking manager advised the team members to meet and finalize the notes from the interviews within 24 hours of completion. Given the press of other obligations this was not always done, but the team members persisted and the note taking was completed.

Analyzing Data

A series of day-long meetings were scheduled to review and analyze the results of the study.

First, the quantitative data were analyzed and arrayed for the entire team to review. Because they were quantitative data, there was little discussion relative to their merits and they were generally accepted.

The discussion and array of the qualitative data was much more complex. Each question, along with its subsets, was portrayed on an easel. Each two-person interview team was then asked to provide a representative answer for that question for the companies that they had interviewed. Much discussion was held regarding these answers, and representative answers were arrived at by common understanding and consensus. In addition to formulating representative answers agreed to and understood by all, this process also served to bring the entire team to a common level of knowledge and understanding regarding the companies they had not interviewed.

Upon completion of this phase, the data for each question were typed and arrayed on a spreadsheet for easy review by each team member. These documents were then distributed to the team members, and they were requested to review them and to prepare a summary statement for each question. This summary statement was to represent the essential and common answer to each question. A second day-long meeting was held, where, question-by-question, a summary consensus answer was formulated.

The final stage of this analysis asked the team, on a question-by-question basis, to determine—based on this analysis—what changes they would recommend for Pacific Bell.

Summary of Team Analysis

Similarities

- Questionnaire development processes are similar to those used by benchmarking partners.

- In questionnaire content, all of the companies ask the same overall and attribute questions as Pacific Bell.

- All organizations ask strategic questions relating to loyalty, price, value, and competitive comparisons.
- All organizations measure and report results based on market segmentation.
- Transaction surveys, that is, those that are a follow-up to a specific service transaction, are common in the benchmarked companies.
- Most companies use a five-point verbal scale in their surveys. Excellence scales, in various forms, are most common.

Key Differences

Surveyed companies

- Conducted far fewer interviews than Pacific Bell.
- Generally used much longer surveys in order to explore issues more in detail and cover more topics such as loyalty and value.
- Used vendors to do small, focused interviews on a more ad hoc basis as compared to Pacific Bell's regular use of them.
- Excluded very few customers from surveys (only those requesting exemption or those in litigation with the company) as compared to multiple possible exclusions at Pacific Bell.
- Had much simpler data management processes because they provide, by comparison, much fewer reports to fewer employees than Pacific Bell.
- Had much smaller measurement staffs because of far fewer demands, much smaller distribution levels, and much less frequency of data reports than Pacific Bell.
- Spent five times less than Pacific Bell on customer satisfaction measurement because of far fewer data demands.
- Located the measurement staff in organizations having direct responsibility for using the data as compared to Pacific Bell's location in a headquarters' staff.
- Placed more emphasis on results and less on absolute targets than Pacific Bell. The best-in-class emphasized information content and valued satisfaction measurements for strategic information as compared to Pacific Bell's evaluation of it as a quality audit.
- Used satisfaction data to a greater extent than Pacific Bell in corporate and division planning processes, and did not use these data to measure day-to-day operations. The best-in-class companies created internal process measures over which the local field organization had control to measure day-to-day work.
- Used satisfaction data for pay-for-performance purposes only at the executive level, as compared to Pacific Bell's use to pay to lowest level management, because it was determined that only at executive level could management influence processes to improve the metrics associated with the corporate customer satisfaction measurement process.

Essentially this study yielded the following: Several factors stand out as key differences between Pacific Bell's approach to customer satisfaction measurement (CSM) and that which was observed at partners' companies. At the partners' companies there is

- Much more use of CSM data in strategic level planning
- Absence of customer satisfaction results in pay-for-performance for low-level managers
- Reliance on internal process measurements for day-to-day operations management
- Low total expenditures on CSM

These are not independent differences. They reflect a very different approach to applying CSM data and to assuring quality at the front line. At Pacific Bell, measurements seem to reflect a philosophy that customer satisfaction is primarily the responsibility of the customer-facing employees and their supervisor. This leads to tactical improvement efforts at the local level, but little systemic change. Since customer satisfaction measurement is not routinely incorporated into the planning process at Pacific Bell, an opportunity to link policy with customer requirements is missed.

The use of internal measurements as the primary quality assurance tool at the partner companies raised interesting questions for Pacific Bell. It seems that Pacific Bell's intensive use of customer satisfaction data is necessary, at least in part, because there is limited trust in existing internal measurements. A major challenge, if Pacific Bell were to adopt a new model of CSM, would be to develop a new system of internal measurements. This system would have to be based on customer requirements (measuring the right things), and it would have to be viewed by employees as a valid quality tool.

An additional feature of Pacific Bell's current process is what may be viewed as an overdependence on CSM data by first- and second-level managers for subordinate evaluation. If sample volumes were to be greatly reduced, local managers would have to adopt new ways of evaluating the quality of work done by members of their teams.

New Directions

An application of the lessons learned from this project would indicate that there are certain things that should be stopped and others that should be started. These recommendations are as follows:

- Establish an organization that would integrate all customer input and use it to improve products and services and to fine-tune strategic planning.
- Stop producing CSM results below the vice president/general manager level.
- Stop paying first- through third-level managers on CSM results.
- Develop internal process indicators that tie to customer requirements.

• Expand the scope of CSM surveys and reduce the frequency of reporting to quarterly results. Fewer customers would be surveyed, and this would reduce the possibility of over-surveying.

• Survey customers who had recent survey events as well as those who have not. Certain surveys would be targeted to specific segments (for example, the best or "gold" customers from whom the company rarely gathered any input).

• Utilize CSM data at the strategic levels and see improved products and processes as a result.

• Stop the investment that goes into managing the results, and increase investments into managing service and product processes.

• Eliminate the frustration of low-level managers caused by their being held to measurements that are only partially in their control.

• Build internal measurements that resist tampering through designed-in security and that create a new respect among employees for accurate measurements.

Results and Improvements

Within approximately one month of the completion of this project, the company officers agreed to a reduction in the CSM sample size. This reduction resulted in a savings of $1 million. While this savings was gratifying and it repaid manyfold the cost of the study, there are yet other applications that may be more significant.

From a closer scrutiny of these excellent companies it was determined that there was a need for Pacific Bell to have a detailed understanding of what the core customer requirements are that are associated with the attributes of customer service. For example, one of the questions asked of customers relates to speed of answer: the amount of time it takes any employee to answer a customer's call. Specifically, what is the time interval that is acceptable to the customer? Prior to this study the customers' exact requirements were not known. A study is proceeding to further define these requirements for each attribute of service.

Taking the totality of these recommendations to heart, the team leader along with her supervisor, the vice president of quality, obtained the consent of two business units, one each in northern and southern California to trial a new CSM system. This system would not promulgate existing CSM results below the vice presidents and their direct reports. Instead, low-level management would be measured on processes that supported customer requirements. For example, one would be the speed of answer to a customer's call. In offices, employees would be measured on how well they met this objective. In this way local supervisors would be managing a process over which they had control and which would impact the traditional CSM system in a positive manner.

In another example, research indicated that customers would prefer to have specific dates and narrow time frames for appointments. Organizationally the company does not have sufficient employees to meet the optimum expectation: a specific date with a specific time. It can, however, provide a specific date with a two- or four-hour window. Customers have indicated that an eight-hour time commitment is unacceptable. Ways to measure the degree to which the field has met this commitment are in place, and supervisors will manage to attempt to meet these standards.

Before this trial could be implemented, however, the executive committee of the company decided to implement this change throughout the entire company. This represents a tidal shift in the corporate culture since it changes the way customer service will be measured and evaluated at the field levels in the company. It is positive because it holds executives responsible for the traditional CSM results. Since executives control processes and procedures across the organization that impact these results, it is fair that they be evaluated on these. For the majority of the employees this change will be extremely positive because they will now be measured on and rewarded for processes over which they have control and which have been demonstrated to have a positive impact on customer service.

This change is in process and work continues on gathering more data on customer requirements and establishing mechanisms by which these processes will be implemented in the field and processes established to measure them.

An immediate need for a coordinating organization to integrate customer requirement data and develop strategy and policy based on these data has arisen. For example, customers have indicated that they would like to be called when work is completed and informed of its completion. Currently, the company has no policy regarding such a process, and although this practice is currently implemented in different parts of the company, it has not been done systematically. A policy organization would standardize such processes throughout the company. Currently, the establishment of such an organization is being considered.

In summary, almost all of the recommendations originating from this study have been or are being considered for implementation. This represents a significant accomplishment since one of the most difficult aspects of the benchmarking process is the implementation of the changes that have arisen from the recommendations of the project. As has been noted, this implementation is companywide and represents significant cultural change.

Status Since the Benchmarking Study

This study was completed in 1992. This following section reflects the status of this effort as of August 1997.

The long-term impacts of this study can be considered in terms of direct effects, where study findings were immediately turned into actions; and indirect effects, where study recommendations coincided with other business directions that ultimately supported the study's findings.

Direct Effects

Several of the study findings were immediately applied. These included

- Reducing the sample size
- Gaining a detailed and actionable understanding of customer requirements
- Changing reporting and accountability for results in order to de-emphasize the use of CSM for the day-to-day management of frontline operations
- Providing more company-level data analysis and strategic direction

Sample size. Sample size reduction yielded immediate cost savings that have been maintained. There have been some increases in sample to accommodate special market segments, but overall there has been widespread support for controlling cost in this manner. The reduced volume of customer feedback has not reduced Pacific Bell's focus on customer satisfaction or its ability to use the data to maintain and improve quality.

Customer requirements and questionnaires. Following this study, Pacific Bell conducted an extensive customer research project to better understand its customers' service requirements. The goal was to define requirements in actionable terms, and to use those definitions as the basis for new customer satisfaction surveys. The surveys were then completely redesigned to provide feedback that could be related directly to specific process outcomes (such as arriving on time) and specific employee behaviors (such as providing needed information). The surveys and their reports provided ongoing reinforcement to customer-facing employees on the nature of customer requirements and the organization's performance against them.

Changing reporting levels and accountability. The goal of this change was to encourage the use of internal process indicators for the day-to-day management of the process. The elimination of CSM reporting at local management levels was, however, the least popular and least successful change that was made. At the time of this change, the company's work to develop more robust process measures was just getting underway, so that no adequate replacement for the detailed CSM feedback to the front line was currently available. Over time, Pacific Bell has returned to the reporting policies that were in place prior to the benchmarking study. So there is a caution here for the application of benchmarking results. Individual changes need to be considered in a context of the management approach and culture of the company. Change efforts that do not fit with the company's direction and its capabilities will be wasted.

Company-level analysis and strategic direction. The benchmarking study suggested a much more active role for the company measures organization. At that time, the measures group did little data analysis, relying instead on client organizations to interpret data and formulate policy. In the time since the study, the group has added staff and capability to provide information and direction as well as data. Among the group's analytic functions are the following:

- Show which aspects of service are most important to customers.

• Indicate where the important gaps are between expected and delivered service.

• Support process management by linking customer requirements to internal process measures.

Indirect Effects

Several of the study findings indicated that Pacific Bell could do a better job of using CSM data in an integrated approach to product and process improvement. Past practice has held local management with the primary accountability for results, so there was little systematic analysis and change.

Since the study, Pacific Bell has been integrating process management into its management of service delivery. Process management emphasizes the importance of managing the entire end-to-end cross-functional process, and developing appropriate in-process measures that will assure that the process output will meet customer requirements. With the emphasis on process management, new performance measures have been developed that provide direct feedback to process managers. These new measures support a balanced approach to measurement that uses both customer feedback and process measurement to ensure overall quality.

Another study finding was that the customer feedback system itself could be enhanced by supplementing its event-related, follow-up surveys with other surveys that would explore things like competitive position and the overall relationship with the customer. Pacific Bell has been experimenting with surveys of this type, and has gained valuable insight into several areas, including which aspects of overall service (such as sales, repair, billing, and so on) are most influential in customers' overall satisfaction and likelihood to continue as customers; and how Pacific Bell's service compares to that of present and future competitors.

Cost/Savings

A high-side estimate of the costs of conducting this benchmarking project was $70,000. A conservative estimate of the savings realized from reduction of sample size and the implementation of the new CSM plan is $5 million annually, with the potential for more savings as new plans are fully implemented.

Learnings About Benchmarking

The process of benchmarking is an intensive effort in design and execution, demanding a focused intellectual discipline. In this study, although it was determined that there were several things that could have been done better (normalizing data factors, further refinement of the question set), results far exceeded expectations in terms of the data gathered and the applications for improvement at Pacific Bell.

For a study of this type there is a need to have a focused and conversant team leader, such as Joyce Miller, who, although a superior in the hierarchy of the company, flattened the hierarchy and liberated and empowered team members so that all had the opportunity to make their maximum contribution. Further, the continuing support, encouragement, and dogged persistence of the team leader were what caused the project to progress and complete in a relatively short time, given that team members undertook this study in addition to their other responsibilities.

This study was fortunate in having extremely knowledgeable team members: Eric Batongbacal, Dorothy Clary, Peter Cartwright, and Miguel Molina. Their expertise greatly facilitated the process. Their willingness to undertake, persist, and, in actuality, to complete this process in addition to their other responsibilities was a critical factor in the success of the project.

Finally, the results and findings of this study have indicated directions and dimensions relative to this process that, in an aggregated and systematic way, no one had ever previously considered. The ramifications of this study are still being felt to this day and the implications and actuality for the company are revolutionary.

Conclusion

If the purpose and objectives of this study are recalled, it should be noted that these were accomplished. An analysis has led to a validation of some tools and the need to dramatically alter others.

The study provided insight and motivation to pursue several key changes to customer satisfaction questionnaires and measurement practices. These both saved the company money and provided clear definition of customer requirements and the company's performance against them. A few changes did not fit well with existing capabilities and practices of client organizations, and were eventually scrapped. Other findings could not be immediately implemented, and have found application only as client organizations have changed the way they manage the customer service process. Thus, it took more than one benchmarking study and its findings to support the desired change, but the study presented the case and the impetus for change.

In application, the results met the stated goals of the study and, by the implications that were derived from it, far exceeded expectations. The implications noted resulted not only in a significant cost saving by refining the existing process, but also dramatically altered the manner in which more relevant data are gathered and products and processes systematically improved, thereby significantly improving the competitive position of the company.

One of the most potential beneficial outcomes of this study is the introduction of new methods, companywide, of customer satisfaction measurement that improve the quality of work life for the majority of employees. The establishment of a measurement system that allows employees to control and improve activities by which they are assessed, while at the same time being a more accurate indicator of customer satisfaction, liberates and empowers employees to control and improve activities by which they are assessed and which they have to perform. If this liberation and empowerment is even partially actualized, then all of the effort associated with this project will be more than justified. But as has been seen, it is most likely to have this and more.

About the Authors

Currently, Al Pozos is the manager of quality assurance and quality business systems for the California State Automobile Association (CSAA). He is responsible for the development of quality assurance and TQM, and the provision of information and organizational systems that support the underwriting organization. Prior to joining the CSAA in 1997, Pozos served as senior consultant for General Public Utilities in New Jersey. There he was responsible for the development of performance and process improvement strategies and tactics.

In 1993, at the time of this study, Pozos was the manager of benchmarking for Pacific Bell's Quality Center. As director of the International Benchmarking Clearinghouse, from 1994–1995, Pozos provided benchmarking support and related services to all members of the clearinghouse and to the public at large.

Pozos earned a doctorate in psychology from the Saybrook Institute in San Francisco, has a master's degree in education, and an undergraduate degree in history, language arts, and the humanities. He may be contacted as follows:

Alfred R. Pozos
Manager–Quality Assurance and Quality Business Systems
California State Automobile Association
150 Van Ness Avenue
Building 3, 5th floor
San Francisco, CA 94101-1866
Telephone: 415-565-4098
Facsimile: 415-565-4567
E-mail: Al_pozos@csaa.com

Joyce Miller is the director of business process and training at Pacific Bell. She is responsible for: service order design and methods for processing wholesale business unit orders; developing business requirements for the mechanization of ordering systems; and developing and delivering training to business office and account team personnel. Miller earned a bachelor's degree in speech pathology and audiology from Kent State University and an MBA in marketing for Golden Gate University. She may be contacted as follows:

Joyce Miller
Director–Business Process and Training
Pacific Bell
370 3rd Street, Room 201 H
San Francisco, CA 94107
JEMill@pacbell.com

Peter Cartwright is the manager of customer satisfaction measurement at Pacific Bell. He is responsible for the development and analysis of customer and internal client satisfaction measurement. Cartwright earned a master's of science in civil engineering and an MBA from Carnegie Mellon University in Pittsburgh. He may be contacted as follows:

Peter Cartwright
Manager–Customer Satisfaction Measurement
Pacific Bell
2600 Camero Ramon, 2E 150 U
San Ramon, CA 94583
510-867-5647

CHAPTER 9

Internal Benchmarking at Boots The Chemists

Debbie Tolputt, Business Improvement Manager, Pam Squires, Assistant Project Manager, and Jayne Welsh, Project Team Manager, Boots The Chemists

Introduction

Should a benchmarking project be carried out only on a particular process? Or should benchmarking become part of the way the organization's work is done? Should people just implement the outcome of a benchmarking activity? Or should they own and apply benchmarking principles to the everyday things that they do? Should benchmarking be used to find ways to improve the average or should its focus be on becoming the best?

At Boots The Chemists, benchmarking is not a "one-off" project. Benchmarking is used to increase understanding, to encourage ownership, and to change the focus from improving the average to being the best—or even better than the best.

This case study examines the following:

• Changing the culture to encourage internal benchmarking to work

• Communicating benchmarking principles and making them work with a large audience

• Adapting the process of benchmarking to meet the needs of the target audience

What Is Boots The Chemists?

Boots The Chemists (BTC) is a retailer based in the United Kingdom focusing on health care and beauty products. It is market leader in many areas of its business, including health care, cosmetics, toiletries, baby consumables, films, and film processing. BTC has over 1200 stores, which range in size from 216 square feet (20 square meters) to 48,600 square feet (4500 square meters). Turnover during 1995–1996 was about $5050 million (£2944 million), with over 50,000 people employed. BTC has the largest electronic point of sale (EPOS) system in Europe with 13,500 tills. It conducts some 600 million transactions every year. Half the female population of the United Kingdom visit a Boots store every week. For instance, BTC sells a total of 58 million lipsticks a year—about 36 a minute!

The stores are divided up into two chains, large stores and small stores. In the large facilities, store managers report to an area manager in groups of about 20. The area is defined geographically. In small facilities, store managers report to a district manager in groups of about 15, again arranged geographically. A small store area manager will then have 10 district managers reporting to him or her.

Study Purpose

The focus of this study was on cultural change. Early in the project it was recognized that internal benchmarking would only work if those involved were all willing to share information, share how they were achieving success, and be open and honest about those areas that needed improvement. Some traditional barriers that had been created over many years and were still there—"because that's the way we have always done it"—had to be eliminated. A feeling of ownership had to be created so that the store managers and area support staff wanted to make this work and so that benchmarking did not become another "one-off" initiative from the head office.

The original objectives for the project reflected this propose.

- "To introduce the concept of benchmarking to area, district, and store managers."

- "To introduce internal benchmarking into BTC stores and make recommendations on the process of benchmarking, benchmarking groups, and benchmarking practices."

Part of the initial benchmarking study included conducting a benchmarking exercise on a particular process, and this part of the project will be covered in the case study, although at a fairly high level. The main reason for conducting the benchmarking exercise was to use its output and success to sell the concepts of benchmarking and to help encourage the change of culture that was needed.

Problems and Issues

There were three key issues in this study.

1. The benchmarking study sought ways to encourage sharing and learning among store managers and area teams, who were highly competitive. If they found a successful way to do something, they exploited it, but did not necessarily share the knowledge with other stores or areas.

2. The benchmarking study sought ways to increase the availability of information. For store managers, individual performance information on other stores was difficult to access from the stores' point of view. Managers were only given the information they needed to run their own part of the business.

3. The benchmarking study sought ways to increase and diversify comparisons. Most store comparisons were done against the average of a group. The groups were made up of

either their district or area (regardless of size and type of store) or an average of a group purely divided by sales floor size, again regardless of intensity, location, or demographics. This gave little incentive to do more than meet or beat the average. Many store managers felt the groups were inappropriate, and this fueled reasons why their store was seemingly different from the group. Managers used this information to explain level of performance.

Project Origin

The project originated from within BTC's operations improvement department, which is responsible for representing the store view in the development of all its systems and procedures. The original sponsor for the work was the head of the department.

Operations improvement sits under the control of the director of retail stores. One of the key initial tasks was to sell the concept to the director of retail stores to gain commitment and authorization to carry out the project.

The boundaries of the project were set within the store environment, the area directly controlled by the director of retail stores. Outside of the benchmarking team's direct control were functions such as logistics, merchandise, and marketing. The team wanted to work within areas where it could directly influence and control in the first instance. The team recognized that once it had achieved this, it could use its success to sell benchmarking principles and concepts to other areas of the company, thus allowing the team to focus on a whole process in the future.

Why was this started? With over 1200 stores it was recognized that although all BTC's key processes were the same in every store, the performance varied greatly. Therefore, there was an enormous opportunity in using internal best practice benchmarking to focus on critical processes and bring up low performers to achieve the same performance as the best.

With so many stores, there was a wealth of expertise and skill from which to learn. To be successful each store had to be willing to share its method for success, and to learn from others where its performance needed improving.

The study team decided to run two trials to try out two different approaches using benchmarking principles. Both of the trials were ultimately aimed at gaining success and credibility for benchmarking, which would help the team sell the concept and drive the culture change, which was the major objective. While conducting the trials the team also planned to carry out work to analyze the best groups of stores for comparison purposes.

The study started in January 1994. The key stages of the project are shown in Figure 9.1.

Trial 1: The Top 10 Stores

Based on their level of takings, the top 10 stores were selected from the large store chain. The benchmarking team wanted to bring this group of managers together to talk about benchmarking principles, to encourage them to start sharing information and experiences

Start	Activity	Complete
January 1994	Learning, investigation, and planning	Throughout project
March 1994	Formed quality team	Throughout project
April 1994	Investigated resources available from consultants/ benchmarking groups	June 1994
May 1994	Visited other companies learning how they carried out benchmarking	July 1994
August 1994	Joined Benchmarking Centre	August 1994
September 1994	Trial 1: Top 10 stores • Initial meeting—September 1994 • Implemented in store—October 1994 • First regular quarterly meeting—January 1995 • Reviewed against KPIs—March/April 1995	April 1995
January 1995	Trial 2: Sales promotion process • Selected groups—January 1995 • Visited best stores—February 1995 • Amalgamated finding to define best practices—March 1995 • Implemented best practices in stores—April 1995 • Reviewed—May/June 1995	June 1995
February 1995	Introduced concept of benchmarking at annual BTC stores conference—500 area, district, and store managers	February 1995
June 1995	Prepared launch package	June 1995
July 1995	Launched concept and best practices for sales promotion process to stores through area meetings	September 1995

Figure 9.1. Key stages in benchmarking trial and launch.

to learn from each other, and then to apply that learning within their own stores. What could be achieved if these managers could work together, learning from the best for a selected process?

No excuses were made for taking on the largest stores because

- Together, the top 10 stores contributed large sales volume, and a small percentage increase in performance gave the biggest return.

- The top 10 stores were spread around the country and had no detailed information about each other's individual store performance.

- The top stores had no direct comparable store within their own area, so they only had an average of a sales floor group against which to compare their performance. This group included other stores not quite in the same style and size.

- These were 10 of BTC's most influential managers. If they could be convinced of the value of benchmarking, then they could become ambassadors for changing the culture and supporting benchmarking.

Trial 2: Sales Promotion Process

The main focus in the company and its stores is the "Drive for Sales." The benchmarking team selected a process that was critical to that goal. The sales promotion process relates to the regular special offers within the store and focused on how the stores prepared, mounted, and maintained the sales promotion program. This process was also selected because the team knew it could obtain a good result—a winner—to help sell, and gain commitment for, the benchmarking concept. It would also gain store managers' interest as it is something that they all have to do, and effective management is critical to achieving sales targets.

Within the stores, the change needed to focus on those areas under the store managers' control, such as the management of staff resources, customer service, organization of processes, and tasks at most effective times. If improvements in areas outside their control were identified, the team agreed to feed back improvement suggestions to other areas of the company as part of selling the benchmarking process.

Store Comparison Groups

In order to tackle the issue of providing meaningful targets against which stores could aim, the company needed to review how it grouped its stores for performance comparison. Since stores vary so greatly in terms of size, type, location, intensity of sales, customer profiles, and merchandise offering, the benchmarking team needed to identify criteria against which the stores could be divided into meaningful groups for comparison of performance level.

Careful consideration had to be given to how this was sold to senior managers. It was difficult to accurately identify the actual hard benefits that would be achieved through changing the culture and by changing the focus from the average to the best. Getting senior management to buy into the concept and support the project while the benchmarking team underwent a learning process was critical to ensuring that the project was given the necessary resources and support to continue.

The two trials were not only selected to deliver results that would help sell the benchmarking concept into stores, but they were also used to capture the imagination and support of senior management, who would need to give commitment, resources, and support to the benchmarking project. The team targeted a process critical to achieving the company's current goals and objectives. The team selected a group of stores that would give the biggest return.

Throughout the project, the team also took opportunities to involve key influential people in developing the concept, thus getting them to identify the way forward. For instance, the launch process was raised through area meetings and agreed to by the area managers themselves. This ensured that they bought into, and supported, the session at their area meetings.

Team Operations

The Project Team

The initial project team consisted of the author, giving about 60 percent of her time to the project, and an assistant project manager, who was dedicated to the project full time. They were supported by the head of the department, who was the project's sponsor and a project team manager, who was actively involved developing ideas and the project's direction. This team was selected—not because of its benchmarking knowledge—but because of the skills of its individual members, their impact and influence, their desire to seek information, and their open-minded approach.

A quality team was set up to work with the project team. It consisted of three store representatives, one area representative, and one district manager. A representative from operations improvement was invited to the join the quality team. This person was skilled in obtaining and analyzing store data. Similarly, a representative from the implementation department joined the quality team. This person's responsibility was implementing new systems.

The quality team met on a part-time basis only; initially every few weeks and less frequently later in the project. The objectives of the quality team were to

- Maintain a store focus.

- Develop and communicate in a way that will be welcomed by the stores.

- Understand fully the current sales promotion process and the impact of any changes.

As the project progressed, different people with specific skills or knowledge were invited to join the quality team and the core project team in order to meet certain needs. For example, once the top 10 store trial was underway, and the launch date was getting closer, one of the managers from one of the top 10 trial stores worked with the core team to advise it on how to best sell and gain commitment from the area, district, and other store managers.

Research and Investigation

Initially, the core project team spent time learning about benchmarking by reading books and attending seminars and training workshops. The team investigated what expertise was available, including looking at the input and value from consultants, such as KPMG, Pulsar, World Class, and Kaizer. The approach taken by the consultants varied from taking control, to working with the team, to one that offered more of an activity-based costing approach rather than benchmarking. The team also looked at other organizations that offered support and assistance, such as the Best Practice Club and the Benchmarking Centre.

After much consideration the team decided not to use an external consultant, although much was learned from the discussions with the consultants. Thus, the process of investigation was useful. The team did decide to join the Benchmarking Centre in order to gain contacts, advice, and support, when it was needed, from other companies.

The project team also spent time reading about other companies, looking at what they achieved and how they had done it. The team also visited some organizations to learn what they had done, and—just as important—what not to do.

The team also talked to other areas of The Boots Company who had an interest in benchmarking or who could possibly provide the information or data needed for a benchmarking project. The company had an enormous amount of data: The issue was identifying where it was and then obtaining the information required in the right format to enable the team to use it constructively and easily.

Approach, Conduct, and Method of Investigation

Trial 1: Top 10 Stores

In October 1994 the store managers of the top 10 stores were invited to attend a benchmarking day. To demonstrate top-level commitment, the event was hosted by the head of operations improvement and the director of retail stores. These senior managers also provided introductions at the event and participated in the discussions.

Managers were initially asked to share information on the performance of their stores on the run up to Christmas; whether they thought they would meet their Christmas sales budget; and what was helping or hindering them. As the discussion moved around the group it was obvious that the managers found this difficult at first. The table was full of their colleagues and senior management. They were more used to competing against each other rather than sharing information with each other. As the discussion progressed, however, issues were raised, and ideas and support grew. This introductory session, which was planned to last an hour, took over two and was worth every minute. By lunch time the managers really began to share ideas and work together as a team.

The director of retail stores also took away several issues that needed focus to improve Christmas sales performance and actioned them.

The rest of the day concentrated on giving the managers an understanding of benchmarking and deciding how to best use the concept within the team.

The concept of benchmarking was kept as simple as possible, and was communicated to the managers as a four-step process shown in Figure 9.2. The four steps covered the following:

1. *Planning.* Select the subject area; define the process and measures; identify partners and data sources.

2. *Collecting the data.* Include financial information; visit partners; and "feel" and map the process.

3. *Analyzing the data.* Determine the gap; establish process differences; and target future performance.

4. *Taking action.* Develop action plans; implement them for effect; monitor results; and review and recalibrate as needed.

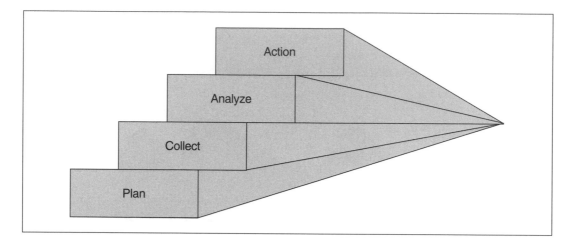

Figure 9.2. Benchmarking as a simple four-step process.

The key outcomes from the benchmarking day were as follows:

• Identify weekly and monthly key performance indicators (KPIs), which would be shared weekly via fax on a Monday morning. The KPIs showed each store's performance. They are detailed in Figure 9.3.

• Gain commitment from the team that the top performer was to share key information on how it was achieving high performance.

• Gain commitment that store managers would brief key members of their management team about benchmarking principles and identify areas for potential use.

• For those areas selected, the store managers agreed to follow through the process of benchmarking and link themselves to the store with the best performance. They would also identify how the top store achieved its performance through discussion and visits.

• Gain store managers' commitment to hold quarterly meetings, each at a different store. The focus of each visit would be a particular process for which that store was best. Prior to the visit the other stores would identify how they carried out the process in their store. Part of the visit would allow time to look at the process in the host store, as well as discussion of the process as a team, to understand how it was carried out in the other top 10 stores. The best practices could then be identified and used by all stores.

The quarterly meetings were set up and commenced. The meetings were also an opportunity to introduce more details and skills relating to benchmarking and assess whether these should be introduced to all stores.

One of the key areas of discussion was process mapping, and one meeting was spent introducing process mapping techniques. The store managers found the detailed knowledge and time required to properly carry this out difficult to accept and apply. They found

KPI	Description
Total stores sales	Percent increase over last year
Business center sales	Percent increase for main groups of merchandise, such as beauty and personal care, gift, baby, food, and heath care
Average transaction value	Percent increase on last year
Sales promotion performance	Selected one key promotion and showed store's increase in sales for promotional period against normal sales level for store
New line performance	Selected three new lines, monitored them for four weeks showing sales value on units for the week and the cumulative over the four-week period

Figure 9.3. KPIs shared with the top 10 stores.

it easier to describe the process through a series of simple statements, such as what happened, when it happened, who had responsibility for it, and what was the outcome.

Process mapping may be a skill employed when conducting a centrally organized benchmarking project, but it became obvious that for store managers focused on driving a fast retail business the procedure was too detailed and, quite honestly, caused them to switch off!

Trial 2: The Sales Promotion Process

The quality team was used to focus on the sales promotion process. The initial key measures identified were based on the rate of increased sales over normal sales for promotional lines over a period of three weeks. The boundaries were clearly set within the store area of responsibility only—from receipt of the goods at the backdoor of the store through to completing the sale to the customer. It was recognized that the process actually commenced right back in the merchandise and marketing area with the selection of the offer. Initially the focus was only on the part of the process that the project team could influence directly; that is, the stores. Then time was spent time brainstorming and defining the team's "official" understanding of the process and mapping it out.

Two groups of stores were selected, and the performance of the sales promotion process was measured in each of these groups of stores so that the best and worst could be identified. From each group the team then visited four stores, and, together with key members of store staff, mapped out the process that actually happened. A project assistant in the department, who was given process mapping skills, accomplished this task. No instruction in process mapping was given to store staff, as they had already reacted negatively to it. The team member watched the process, asked questions, and then documented the process.

This information was then brought back to the center and collated to allow comparison of the process carried out in each store, and comparison against the team's original definition of what "should" be happening. From this, differences and improvements were identified.

A best practice document, combining the key findings from each of the store visits, was then produced. This was put together in a draft format so that the stores could use it, and was issued to all of the trial stores within the two chosen groups (not just those that had been visited).

Store Comparison Groups

Various methods were used to examine how stores should be regrouped into more comparable groups. Factors such as intensity, demographics, and location (out of town, city center, and so on) were examined.

Although all stores have the same process, to ensure comparison of performance levels, stores needed confidence that they could achieve the same performance as the best in their group. Therefore, the team had to be able to confidently sell the reorganized groups.

Best Practices Discovered: Results

Trial 1: Top 10 Team Results

Six months after the initial briefing, progress was reviewed by visiting each of the top 10 stores. The key findings and results were specific areas. For example, sales plan, Sunday trading, and back shop layout had been targeted and investigated by individual stores. All had resulted in changes to the process in the initiating store and improvements in performance.

One of the stores had used the benchmarking information to identify a significant drop in sales promotion performance compared to the group in the run up to Christmas. The store worked with the best performer in the group and identified that the differences were related to changes in space and location due to the merchandising of Christmas stock. The store reviewed this following information from the best performer and immediately regained sales promotion performance as well as maintaining Christmas merchandise sales.

To make the best use of the time managers spent at both their quarterly visits and other individual store visits, a store visit protocols document was prepared by the project team. The document covered the following:

- Preparation prior to the visit for the visiting manager
- Preparation prior to the visit by the store being visited
- Principles during the visit
- Action to be followed after the visit

Trial 2: Sales Promotion Results

The 16 stores involved in the sales promotion trial implemented the best practices, and fed back their comments to the project team both on the actual process and the format of the protocols document. Following further feedback from the trial groups, the combined results of the investigations for sales promotion were put together in a final best practices document, which identified key actions that needed to be taken and when they had to be completed. The consolidated best practice information covered the following:

• Planning prior to offers

• Setting targets

• In-store displays and show material

• Targeting interested customer groups

• Organizing stock

• Setting up at the start

• Maintenance during promotion

• Rundown and clear up

• Review of performance

The resulting evidence indicated that although stores were doing many of the activities, none of the stores actually followed through on all the best practices or completed them at the most effective time. Implementation of the whole process of best practices brought into these areas a coordination of communication, planning, organization, and delivery, which ultimately improved sales performance in the stores.

Implementation and Actions Taken

Extension of Selected Teams

The top 10 store team is committed to continuing quarterly meetings and sending out KPIs weekly and monthly. The team has now taken ownership of its meetings and arranges the dates, location, and focus. The top 10 store team only calls on the benchmarking project team if the former requires specific information or advice.

This framework has been extended to two other groups: the top eight stores in the small store chain and a regional shopping center group of seven stores. Initial meetings, similar to the first meeting of the top 10 stores, commenced. The stores agreed which KPIs are to be shared weekly and monthly, and they are using quarterly meetings to focus on key processes.

The concept of bringing together groups of stores in a similar way has also been extended by some of the area managers following the success seen with improvements on key processes in the top 10 stores. In this instance the KPIs are organized and provided by the area manager.

Launch of Best Practice Benchmarking Principles to All Stores

The launch process started in early 1995 with a session at the annual stores conference. Here, the benchmarking team had the opportunity to talk to 500 store, district, and area managers and senior central personnel.

Although this was the start of the official launch, the team had already begun to introduce the concept of benchmarking as widely as possible. Articles appeared in the company's magazines and, where interest had been expressed, the team attended area and district meetings to talk about the work and how area and district staff could start using benchmarking principles.

If one of the main purposes of this benchmarking project was to change the culture to being more open, then this principle needed to be followed from the outset of the work. This encouraged openness and learning in others.

Therefore, the launch was seen as an extension of the communication and learning that had already taken place. It was a way to gain ownership and commitment by communicating the successes achieved so far in the top 10 store group and the trial stores involved in the sales promotion best practices.

The team visited each area meeting and talked to all large store managers and all district managers. The session lasted about two hours and included the following activities.

• A 10-minute game was used to demonstrate how sharing can benefit everyone involved.

• Only an overview of benchmarking principles was given, because at this stage all the managers had already gained an understanding of benchmarking through previous meetings and articles.

• The details of the two trials and their successes and results were given. Within each area session at least one manager, and preferably more managers, who had been involved in either the top 10 store trial or the sale promotion process trial were involved. These managers talked about their own experiences, their difficulties, and how the trial had affected their own store and its success. This worked well since a colleague gave an honest opinion on benchmarking. It was not just somebody from the head office trying to sell a concept.

• The sale promotion best practices document was issued.

• New comparable groups that were being formed were discussed, and information on the groupings and KPIs was given to area personnel to use.

• Small discussion groups were formed, and each group was asked to consider a question related to the introduction of benchmarking in its area or district and how it could be achieved. The results of these discussions were fed back into the large group, and, as an area, the managers agreed an action plan. Each area presentation was organized and adapted to suit its needs. Full involvement was essential to achieve the objective of encouraging ownership.

The key focus of the sessions was always to

• Gain commitment and encourage ownership.

• Encourage open sharing of success.

• Encourage learning from the best.

The benchmarking team continually stressed at the launch, and all the way through the project, that this was not another "one-off initiative from head office," and that this was not something managers had to do in addition to all the other things that were needed to run their stores. Instead, benchmarking was shown as a tool that can be used to achieve existing goals and objectives.

Key Barriers and How to Overcome Them

There were three main issues identified at the start of the project. These should be reviewed.

Encouraging sharing and learning from others. Sharing and learning were encouraged through the team's open attitude to the project, through senior managers' commitment to share and learn from each other, and through the work the project team did with individual store, area, and district teams. The benefits of learning from each other were demonstrated in the initial ice-breaker game carried out during the briefings and through the shared experiences of the store managers who had been involved in the trials and had gained success through learning from the best store.

Availability of information. Throughout the project, information that had previously been unavailable or denied to stores was made available to them. Information on new comparable groups was shared with the areas, and they were encouraged to share this with their stores. Future developments with a new management information system (MIS) will enable BTC to achieve much more with this process.

Comparison against the average. The focus has been moved away from looking at the average to examining the best of a more comparable group. Thus, store managers are no longer able to claim that their store is different. Managers are reminded that they are all in the same business, and thus, they all have the same processes. The key is to learn from others, and then make their successes work in another environment.

Next steps. Since this case study examined a communication and culture change rather than benchmarking a particular process, it would be wrong to assume that it is finished. As with all good benchmarking projects, this is a continuous process, and BTC has really only started to identify and achieve the results possible from internal benchmarking. So what is next?

Management Information System

One key area of weakness is the easy availability to stores of KPIs, classified in comparable groups and with a focus on the best performance of the group. A new MIS, which will have a benchmarking capability to allow this to be available, is under development. The focus of the management information will change by moving away from the average of inappropriate groups to comparison against the best of a more appropriate group.

For those KPIs critical to the business, this will ensure the focus is always on aiming for the best. The focus used to be on improving the average. As seen from Figure 9.4, if only the average moves up, then only a small proportion of the stores are aiming to improve and the average will change slowly. If, for critical processes, all stores below the best are aiming to improve, and the information on how to achieve that step change is shared, then the effect on performance is more dramatic.

The MIS can also be used to identify those areas with the biggest variance for critical processes—where there are the biggest gains. This could be the focus of future benchmarking activities.

Focusing benchmarking activities. Now that ownership and benchmarking activities within the stores are encouraged, the project team must ensure that it can share success across the company. Thus, ways that individual stores' best practices can be identified and shared are being sought.

From the center's point of view the benchmarking gains can be applied to centrally driven projects, together with the more detailed skills such as process mapping. In the future there will be opportunities to learn through external benchmarking, although currently there are many areas upon which there is opportunity to focus and learn from internal benchmarking.

From current situation	To benchmarking situation
• The current measure is against stores of a similar size only, regardless of location, store, and type.	• Comparison is against a more appropriate benchmarking group to target performance.
• Comparison is against the average of the group.	• Comparison is against the best in the group.
• Average figures can cause complacency for those stores at or above average.	• All stores are aiming to make a step change to achieve performance at or above the best.
• The average improves slowly as those stores below the average aim to improve their performance.	• Continuous improvement by stores increases performance further.

Figure 9.4. Why move the focus from the average to the best?

Conclusions/Lessons Learned

Gain senior management commitment. Careful consideration as to how senior managers are initially sold into the project is critical. Where a change in culture is required this will take time, and hard evidence of success may not be visible for some time. A focus to capture managers' imaginations and keep their support throughout the project is vital. The short-term wins gained through forming the top 10 team helped enormously to maintain interest and enthusiasm while beginning to achieve the long-term goals relating to the concept and culture changes required to introduce benchmarking throughout the company.

Target the audience and keep it simple. Benchmarking principles and concepts must be suited to the audience. For instance, at one point the study team tried to introduce process mapping to the top 10 store managers, who had difficulty coping with it. Therefore, simple statements about what happened, who did it, when did it happen, what the outcome was, and so on were used instead of the formal mapping process. When best practice documents for stores detailing the sales promotion process were produced, they took a similar form so that they would be easily accepted and understood by store staff.

Use success and the people involved to sell the concept. One of the success areas for BTC was involving store managers, from both the top 10 store trial and the sales promotion trial. Getting them involved in the process of communicating and selling benchmarking to other store managers was critical.

Recognize the current company culture and allow time for change to evolve. Culture change does not happen overnight. It takes time, and throughout the change the project team needs to be consistently working toward a definite goal. BTC's goal is to change the focus away from the average to the best. Part of that change is through encouraging openness to identify the best performers and then to learn how they actually carry out the process. The other part of the equation is how the process is measured. The MIS will carry on this focus through changing the reporting of performance away from the average to the best. None of these changes are easy or quick, and throughout the process there must be ways of gaining confidence and commitment.

Recognize the barriers and identify ways to overcome them. The benchmarking team must be open about how people feel, must raise issues, and must discuss them openly. The team must find ways to overcome or disprove concerns. Many store managers felt that it "won't work for me because my store is different—different location, customers, and so on." Managers must be reminded that they are not being asked to copy what someone else is doing, but rather to take the practices and customize them to their own environment.

Involvement and openness are essential. In order to be able to learn from the best, the best has to be willing to share how it achieves that performance. In order to achieve the same performance as the best, each store has to be open to learn and change. Throughout the project the team took every opportunity to involve those who were interested, and shared as much information as possible to encourage an environment of sharing ideas and learning from the best. This change does not happen overnight; it is a matter of continually and consistently creating the right environment and opportunities for that change to grow and expand, until it really does become part of the way work is done.

About the Authors

Debbie Tolputt is a business improvement manager at Boots The Chemists, where she is responsible for improving the efficiency and effectiveness of BTC property areas dealing with purchase, disposal, development, and maintenance. Tolputt earned a professional diploma in management from Open University.

Pam Squires is an assistant project manager at Boots The Chemists. For this study she was part of the project management team responsible for introducing the concept of benchmarking to over 1200 BTC stores and area teams. Squires attended Top Valley School.

Jayne Welsh is also a project team manager at Boots The Chemists, where she provides operational support for over 1000 BTC stores. For this study she was responsible for introducing the initial concept of benchmarking and obtaining company sponsorship for the project. Welsh has a diploma in business management studies from Open University.

Tolputt, Squires, and Welsh may be contacted as follows:

Boots The Chemists
Store Planning
City Gate, Toll House Hill
Nottingham NG2 3AA
England
Telephone: 0115 949 5828
Facsimile: 0115 949 5796

CHAPTER 10

Application of Benchmarking Techniques for Business Process Reengineering: IBM Italy's Procurement Process Reengineering Model

Luigi Redaelli, Material Logistic Architect, IBM Italy, and Paolo Confalonieri, Project Manager, Autofaber

IBM Italy's Reengineering Process Model

During the second half of the 1980s, IBM Italy realized that significant productivity improvements could be obtained through business process reengineering. Thus, the first question asked was how to simplify business processes. Inside IBM Italy's manufacturing environment, managers thought about developing a new methodology to drive reengineering. After some pilot cases, two different methodologies were finalized. They became known as the six steps and the business process reengineering methodology, which is represented by a diamond.

The Six Steps

Shown in Figure 10.1, the six-step methodology allows IBM Italy to identify its critical business processes as well as to prioritize its reengineering efforts. The six steps are as follows:

1. Identify and draw the business process model. That means to represent the activities performed inside a manufacturing environment in terms of a business process; that is, activities tied together from a logical point of view. At the end of this step the managerial team realized that all the activities performed inside IBM Italy's manufacturing environment could be represented with seven macro business processes, as shown in Figure 10.2. Of course, this is the first level of business process; but in order to understand a single business process, it must be broken down into at least two successive, detailed levels. Figure 10.3 shows the list of subprocesses contained inside the materials management process. During this first step the inputs and outputs for each business process, and the relationships among all business processes, must be defined. For this purpose SADT/IDEF 0 methodology, as shown in Figures 10.4 and 10.5, was used. According to Marca and

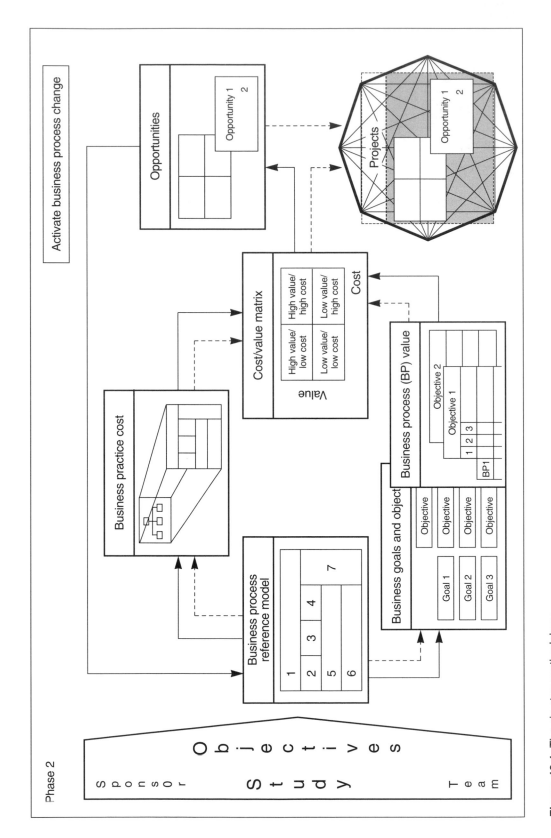

Figure 10.1. The six-step methodology.

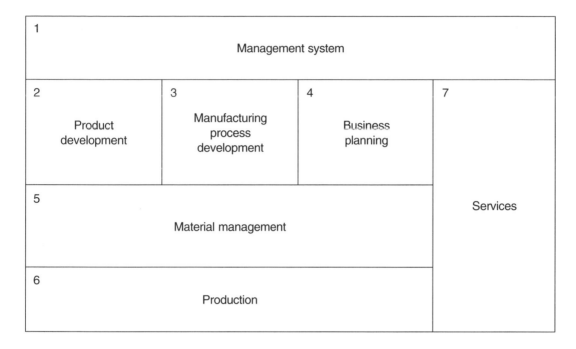

Figure 10.2. IBM Italy's seven macro business processes.

McGowan (1988), the structural analysis and design technique (SADT) utilizes a graphical representation and an approach for the description of systems and processes.

2. Define business process costs. That means to identify the costs—mainly in terms of human resources—related to each business process, while referencing the business process model.

3. Define business goals and objectives. That means to identify the goals and objectives at the enterprise level, with the agreement of top management. At this step, the importance of each goal and objective and its weight must also be defined.

4. Define each business goal's value. That means to define the value in terms of its contribution to reach the goals and objectives for each business process.

5. Develop the cost-value matrix. That means to put all the business processes, at the first level of detail, onto a cost-value matrix, while considering the costs and values identified during steps 2 and 4.

6. Identify opportunities. Following step 5, there is now the possibility of classifying the processes into four categories, as shown in Figure 10.6. These categories are defined as follows:

• *Low value/low cost.* The costs of these processes must be maintained at a minimum level, without other investment, primarily because these processes have a low contribution toward business goals and objectives.

05	Materials management
05.01	Demand planning
05.01.01	Plant demand planning
05.02	Supply planning
05.02.01	Planning factors
05.02.02	Top input
05.02.03	Parts requirements generation (Material plan)
05.02.04	Capacity assessment
05.02.05	Inventory control
05.03	Supply execution
05.03.01	Ordering
05.03.02	Order entry and scheduling
05.03.03	Release to production
05.03.04	Work in process
05.03.05	Cost accounting
05.04	Procurement
05.04.01	Vendor management
05.04.02	Source management
05.04.03	Orders management
05.04.04	Accounts payable
05.04.05	Vendor technical assistance
05.05	Material distribution center
05.05.01	Material handling
05.05.02	Transport and containers

Figure 10.3. Materials management subprocesses.

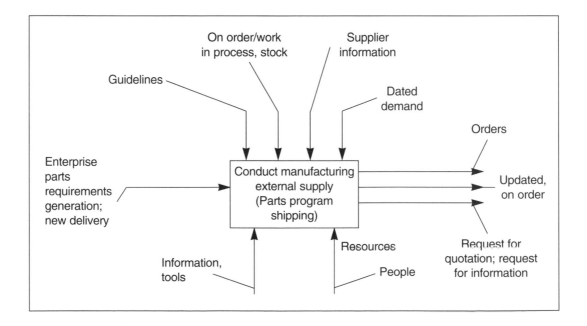

Figure 10.4. SADT/IDEF 0 methodology.

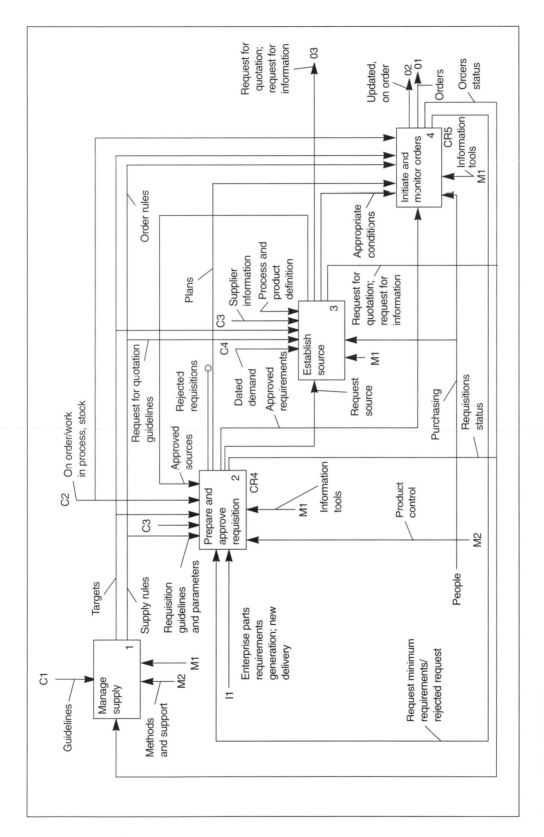

Figure 10.5. SADI/IDEF 0 methodology, detailed.

223

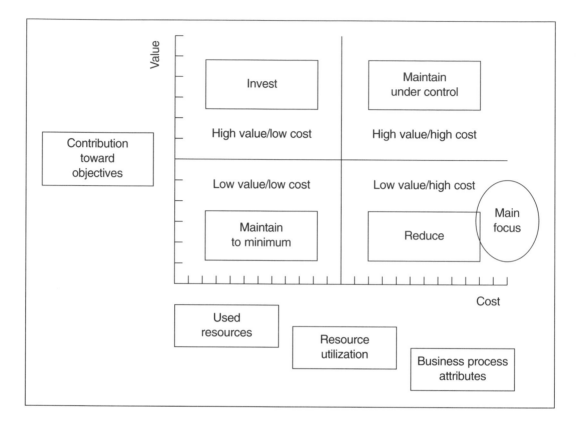

Figure 10.6. Business process value-added matrix.

• *Low value/high cost.* The costs of these processes must be reduced, and the resources moved to the high-value/low-cost processes.

• *High value/low cost.* In order to maintain the high value, or, if possible, increase the value, investments must be made in these processes.

• *High value/high cost.* In order to reduce the costs of these processes, reengineering efforts must be made. From a reengineering point of view, this category of business processes is considered at a high-priority level.

Following the six-step methodology conducted inside IBM Italy's manufacturing sector, the positions of its business processes became evident, and the final result is shown in Figure 10.7. The procurement process was a high value/high cost process; thus, it was the first one approached for reengineering.

Business Process Reengineering Methodology

The business process reengineering methodology is represented by a diamond, and is shown in Figure 10.8. Applying this methodology reengineers a specific business process.

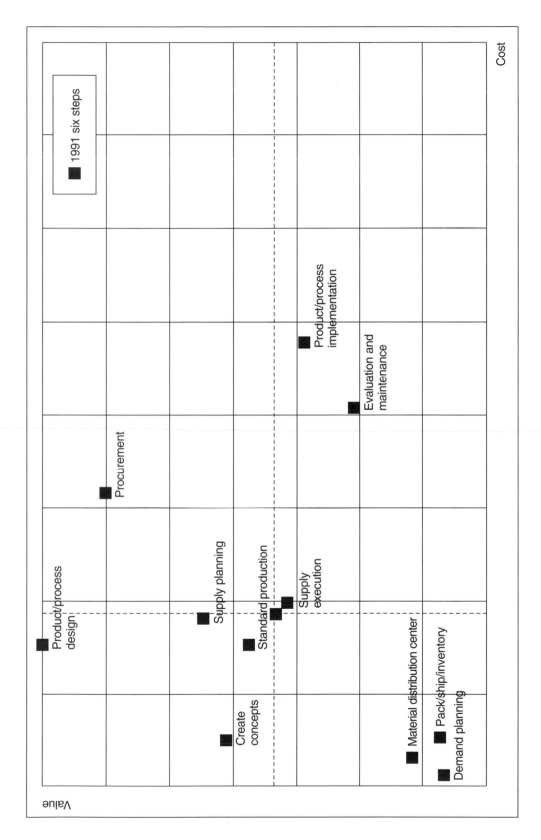

Value

Cost

1991 six steps

Product/process design

Create concepts

Procurement

Supply planning

Standard production

Supply execution

Product/process implementation

Evaluation and maintenance

Material distribution center

Pack/ship/inventory

Demand planning

Figure 10.7. Business process contribution.

225

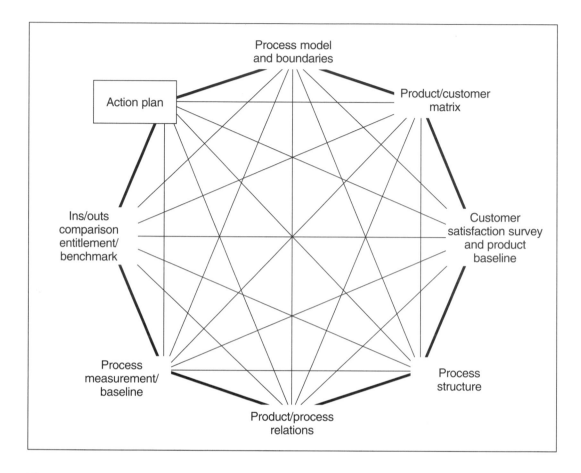

Figure 10.8. Business process reengineering methodology.

The management team applied this "diamond" methodology to the procurement process, which was identified as a critical process using the six-step approach. The steps of the diamond methodology are as follows:

1. Draw the business process model and its boundaries. This first step is the same as step 1 of the six-step methodology. In this case, however, the selected business process (that is, the procurement process) must be detailed and mapped. The SADT/IDEF 0 methodology was used to do this, and the results were previously shown in Figures 10.4 and 10.5.

2. Develop a product-customer matrix. In this step, the products of one specific business process must be identified. The products are the main outputs identified in step 1. From Figures 10.4 and 10.5, the products of the procurement process are orders, and requests for quotations and information. In order to identify the customers of this process, the users of these outputs and products must be identified.

3. Identify customer satisfaction survey and product baseline. Some interesting information about the process can be obtained by performing a customer satisfaction survey. The goal of this step is to gain the perception of the process from the customers' point of view. Thus, the following questions should be asked and answered.

   • How do customers perceive the performance of the process?

   • What do customers perceive as the critical factors?

   • What are the most important products of the process?

4. Develop the process structure. At this point, the process structure should be thought of in terms of its content, as follows:

   • Intelligence—activities left to human intervention

   • Methodology—activities addressed by rules and procedures

   • Technology—activities supported by information system tools

   Another bit of interesting work to do is to evaluate the cycle time of the process and the value-added time against the no-value-added time for each activity. Figure 10.9 shows the value-added time and the no-added-value time for each activity related to the procurement process. Figure 10.9 reveals that only 11.1 percent of the total process cycle time is value-added time; the remaining 88.9 percent is no-value-added time, such as wait time, run time, and so on.

5. Identify product and process relations. With this step, the relationships between the product and the process are discovered. For example, this step revealed that the quality of one product (that is, one order) depends on the total process cycle time or on the content of intelligence of the process. Thus, the process variables (such as cycle time) that influence the process products and outputs should be highlighted.

6. Develop a process measurement and baseline. The goal of this step is to define the process measurements and to measure the current values. The basic measurements are

   • Process quality or defectiveness

   • Process costs, such as human resources needed to obtain one product

   • Process cycle time

   • Process cycle efficiency, such as value-added time and no-value-added time

   The baseline identification allows the management team to measure real improvements against the current situation. This is shown in Figure 10.10.

7. Development in/out comparisons, entitlement, and benchmarking. Now the management team is ready to perform a process comparison against the same process inside the same company (for multinational companies) and against other external companies. The team decided to perform the process comparison against other

Activity	Baseline December 1989		Entitlement September 1991	
	Value-added	No value-added	Value-added	No value-added
Parts requirements generation instruction	3 hrs.		3 hrs.	
Parameters and input preparation	5 hrs.		5 hrs.	
Top input consolidation	8 hrs.		8 hrs.	
System run		40 hrs.		48 hrs.
Requirements analysis	5 mins.	3 hrs. 55 mins.	5 mins.	3 hours 55 mins.
Manual netting by analyzer	10 mins.	1 hr. 50 mins.		
Modify date/quantity—input on job order sizing quantity	2 mins.	1 hr. 58 mins.	2 mins.	3 hrs. 58 mins.
Fill and validate parts program shipping form	31 mins.	11 hrs. 29 mins.	5 mins.	3 hrs. 55 mins.
Send/receive parts program shipping and track	7 mins.	11 hrs. 53 mins.		
Distribute delivery plan to buyer	1 min.	7 hrs. 59 mins.	1 min.	7 hrs. 59 mins.
Previous/current plan comparison	5 mins.	3 hrs. 55 mins.	5 mins.	3 hrs. 55 mins.
Negotiate delta with vendor	5 mins.	15 hrs. 55 mins.	5 mins.	7 hrs. 55 mins.
Manual netting by buyer	10 mins.	3 hrs. 50 mins.		
Communicate delivery plan to vendor	3 mins.	7 hrs. 57 mins.	3 mins.	7 hrs. 57 mins.
Send form parts program shipping to central unit	2 mins.	3 hrs. 58 mins.		
Manual update on order	10 mins.	11 hrs. 50 mins.		
Expedite on vendor activities	3 mins.	3 hrs. 57 mins.		
Send/receive form parts program shipping to analyzer	8 mins.	11 hrs. 52 mins.		
Process time	17 hrs. 42 mins.	142 hrs. 18 mins.	16 hrs. 26 mins.	87 hrs. 34 mins.
Process cycle efficiency	11.1%		15.8%	

Figure 10.9. Value-added time and no-value-added time in the procurement process.

external companies, with the objective to discover the best practices performed in other industries. This step will be discussed in detail in the next section. The benchmarking is not a stand-alone step but it makes sense inside a reengineering process.

8. Develop an action plan. Now the actions or the new practices must be implemented so that processes can be improved, and so those improvements can be measured. Each of the previous seven steps suggests some improvement action to implement. The actions implemented in IBM Italy's procurement process are discussed and detailed after the benchmarking study explanation.

Indicators	Nbr. Int	Nbr. Ext	Details/formula	Drawn by*	Baseline December 1990	Year end 1991	Actual February 1992	Year end 1992	Entitlement xx/9y	Benchmark 1992
Defectiveness			Planned delivery schedule—real need / Planned delivery schedule (quantity)	B	400 k	300 k	300 k			5 k
End-to-end cycle (total cycle time)			From materials requirements planning to delivery plan sent to vendor	B	20	5	5			5
Cycle time distribution (Sigma)			Not applicable							
Cycle efficiency (Value-added time/ total cycle time)			$\dfrac{\text{Value-added time}}{\text{End-to-end cycle}}$	A	11.1	30	30			31.8
Process efficiency (cost/product)			$\dfrac{1}{\text{Cost per lot}} \times \dfrac{1}{\text{End-to-end cycle}}$	A	5	28.5	28.5			44.4
Adherence to commitment			Percentage of delivery plans sent to vendors within end-to-end cycle (enterprise parts requirements generation cycle)	B	80%	95%	95%			100%
Customer satisfaction			To be determined							

*(A) Estimate / (B) Sampling / (C) Manual reporting / (D) Automated reporting

Action plan highlights

Planned	Ongoing	Implemented
Technology	Advanced logistic information system environment utilization (pull request vs. vendors, execution driven)	Information system updated (Advanced logistic information system enhancements / new facilities in delegated support system environment)
Methods		Open orders utilization (Delegated support system)
Individuals	Organization changes / empowerment strategy implementation / training	

Figure 10.10. Improvements versus current situations.

A Methodology for Benchmarking Business Processes

By-process Thinking

By-process thinking means the attitude to consider, in a coordinate flow, a set of activities accomplished to pursue a business goal. Consorzio Autofaber, a joint venture among IBM, Haltel, and Milano Ricercle, has supported many large enterprises in the execution of benchmarking activities aimed at comparing processes of the same kind to settle best practices and optimal attitudes. As an example, processes covering environment, logistics, and purchasing that are common to different enterprises have been analyzed. For IBM Italy, the by-process approach was very helpful to formally describe what contributes to the achievement of business goals.

The Application of By-process Methodologies: Indicators, Measurements, Benchmarking

Having defined the process as a set of coordinated activities carried out to accomplish a given service, it is now possible to move a step forward. A process typically consists of several entities.

- *Activities,* which are carried out by personnel or information systems
- *Events,* which trigger the execution of activities or are triggered at the completion or at the termination of activities
- *Data,* or, generally speaking, *objects,* which are handled by the activities

Depending on the kind of the process, the treatment can be: manual, such as assembly or transformation; conceptual; or check actions, which are carried out continuously with a given periodicity or when specific problems arise.

Once what takes part in a process has been identified, it is helpful to represent the process with standard techniques, such as SADT and ARIS (architecture of integrated information systems) (Scheer 1995). This operation description, universally known as mapping, provides a formal process representation. Attributes related to activities, data, and events, which point out characteristics of interest, can be identified. Attributes include average duration of an activity, variance of that duration, quantities released, and rework cycles. These attributes are eligible to become process indicators.

The identification of indicators related to a significant aspect of the process under analysis is another way to model the process. This means that a consistent set of indicators can reasonably give a complete view of what is managed within the process, as well as the performances, effectiveness, efficiency, serviceability, and so on.

The next step is the evaluation of such indicators. The values assigned to those indicators can be directly assumed from operations, as well as estimated or predicted. When an indicator summarizes minute information it may be difficult to gather numerical values from reality. Often—especially in benchmarking activities—with processes that are quite similar in terms of goals, methodologies, and tools, it is very difficult to derive values that can be directly compared with each other. Therefore, human interventions are usually required to obtain estimations, since some assumptions must be made. So far, the experience gained leads to the conclusion that self-evaluation criteria can also be successfully applied. In this case, the basic premise is that the self-evaluation must be done playing with all cards on the table; that is, the value proposed in the self-evaluation session must rely on considerations already well known by all the participants in the benchmarking activity. In addition, a critical joint discussion held by the different participants can confirm or adjust the proposed vote.

The Benchmarking Conduction

As a general guideline, an external facilitator, with a good knowledge of process modeling and sufficient knowledge on the specific process, can be retained to drive the activity. The facilitator for IBM Italy was chapter co-author Paolo Confalonieri.

As a general way to conduct the benchmarking, an inductive method was chosen by the facilitator. Instead of suggesting a fixed model, a reference model was proposed, thus driving the participants from free presentation to a reference model through a sequence of converging steps. The scheme is detailed as follows:

First, adopt the reference model for the purchasing process. The following items were considered as references.

- General features of the process
- Ordering and call-off procedures (job order lot, frame order, and so on)
- Information management and flow
- Software tools for general support
- Critical areas as argued by participants
- General process indicators

Second, in the first joint meeting, the reference model should be followed. Every participant presented his or her process with a high degree of freedom.

Third, the facilitator analyzed the presentations, and proposed an initial questionnaire to drive all the participants toward the reference model. Only nonconfidential information was asked of participants. Some clusters were identified (for example, electronic manufacturer versus telecommunications manufacturer); that is, enterprises acting in similar industrial domains showed peculiarities in terms of management policies. Nevertheless, the heterogeneous composition of the pool of participants was still considered a strong point. Stimuli presented by enterprises acting on different markets were found appealing for other participants.

Responses to some of the questions from the questionnaire, which was proposed to every participant, are reported as follows:

- Methodologies currently applied
  - —*Job order lot.* Applied or not; shared.
  - —*Frame order.* Applied or not; shared.
  - —*Other.* Applied or not; shared.
- Evolution of the methodologies: Which application is expected for up to one year?
  - —*Job order lot.* Applied or not; shared.
  - —*Frame order.* Applied or not; shared.
  - —*Other.* Applied or not; shared.
- Organizational consideration: Is the purchasing process
  - —Centralized
  - —Distributed by production type
  - —Distributed by line of business
  - —Distributed by commodity
- Which tasks are directly implied in the purchasing process?
  - —Production planning
  - —Engineering changes
  - —Call-off of parts previously ordered
  - —Order emission
  - —Other
- Detail the expected adjustments, needed for up to one year, in the involvement presented in the previous question.
- How can the purchasing process can be characterized? (Answers not mutually exclusive.)
  - —By volumes of parts purchased
  - —By the number of different parts purchased
  - —Organizational aspects
  - —Lead time
  - —Flexibility
  - —Delivery policies
  - —Other
- Explain the application of the information system at the purchasing process.

- Identify the first indication of weaknesses in areas.
- How are the process indicators/measurements used?
  —Not used
  —Only identified
  —Identified and collected
  —Identified, collected, and elaborated
  —Other

The fourth step of the benchmarking process was another joint meeting to discuss the results of the questionnaire. The facilitator commented on what the participants recorded, with the objective to find out an agreed model of the purchasing process, described by a set of indicators. The analysis of the participants' answers allowed the facilitator to propose such a model consisting of 31 indicators to be estimated by each participant, generating a second written questionnaire. Also a benchmark, that is, the optimal attitude, was expressed for each of the indicators. A semiquantitative, self-evaluation was adopted: Each participant was assigned a vote from 1 to 5. This evaluation method was chosen since the indicators collected by the participants were not directly comparable. Nevertheless, the path followed so far, exposed the completeness of the topics chosen for comparison by the participants. Thus, all members of the group knew why a participant declared a certain vote. In addition, each self-assigned vote is explained in a global session, leaving the opportunity to adjust it after a joint discussion. No problems emerged applying this method.

Results and Actions Implemented

The results are presented in Figure 10.11. After using the reengineering methodology and after examining the benchmarking study results, IBM Italy's management team realized that its procurement process was highly unsatisfactory. This is as shown by means of baseline measurements; see the column labeled "Baseline December 1990" in Figure 10.10. The benchmarking study also pointed out that there was one best practice completely unexploited inside IBM Italy's manufacturing environment. That practice is shown as number 14, the complete responsibility of the inventory level to the buyer, in Figure 10.11.

Figure 10.12 shows the new process implemented, which moved the responsibility of the call-off execution directly to the manufacturing lines, with the buyer maintaining responsibility for the contract and related terms and conditions. The main results achieved from such actions are shown in Figure 10.13, and are detailed as follows:

- Cycle time reduction: from 20 days to 2.5 days
- Inventory reduction: $7 million after the first year
- Head count reduction: The equivalent of three positions in the purchasing department
- Defectiveness: from 400,000 ppm to nearly zero

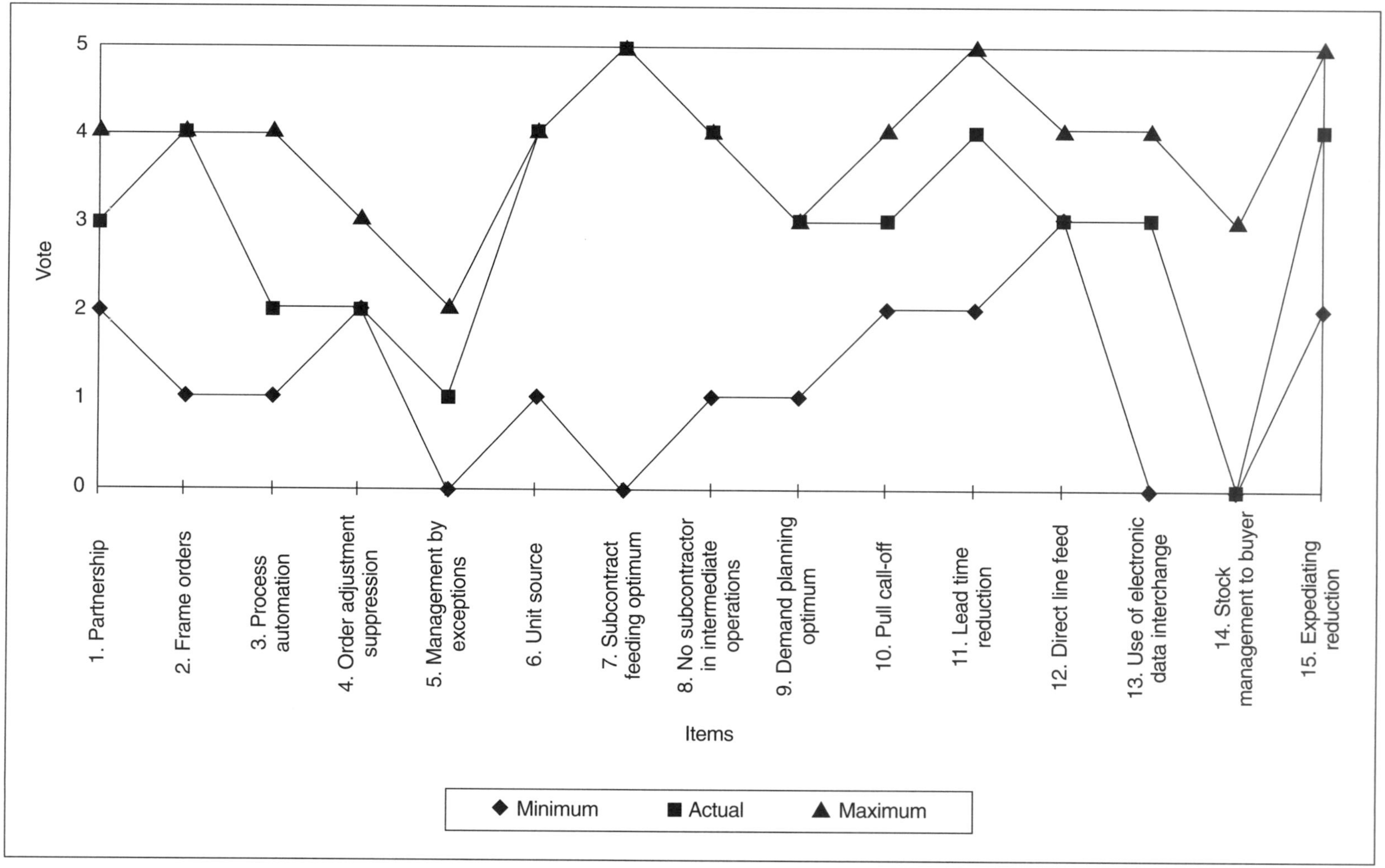

Figure 10.11. Voting results.

234

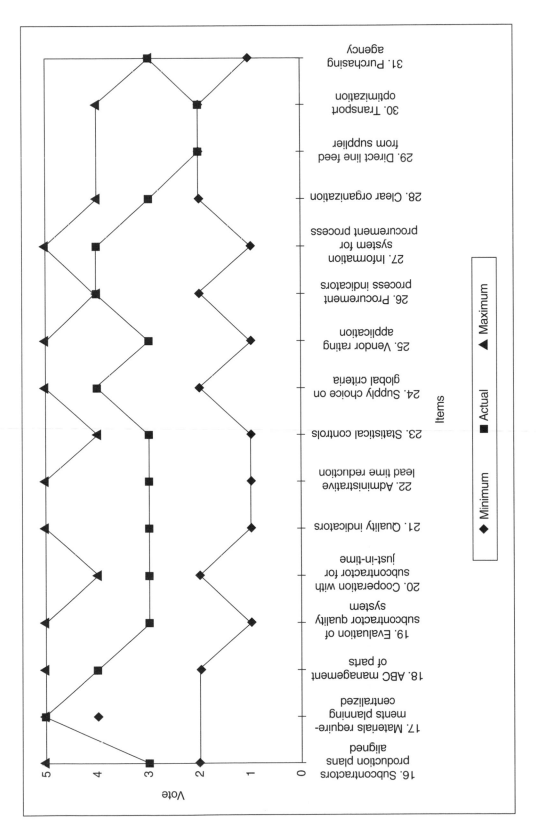

Figure 10.11. *(Continued).*

235

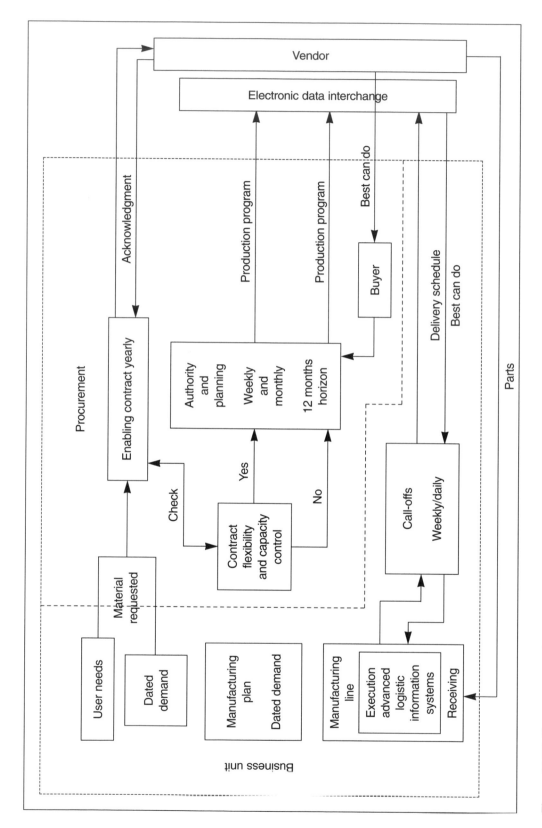

Figure 10.12. New procurement process.

236

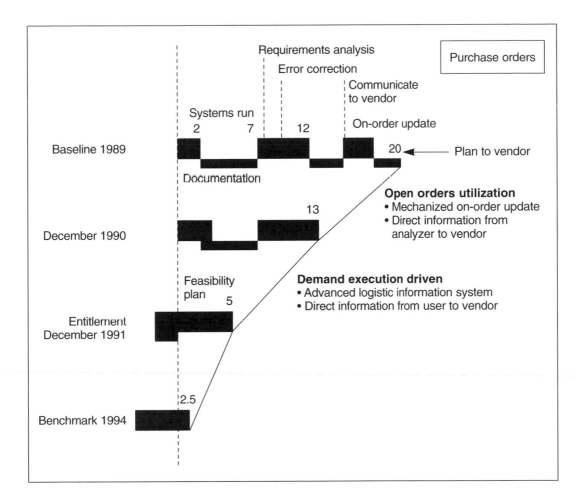

Figure 10.13. Benchmarking results.

Thus, benchmarking has been proved to be a good tool in order to confirm the effectiveness of reengineering activities and to remove internal inhibitors (old internal procedures).

References

Marca, David A., and Clement L. McGowan 1988. *SADT: Structured analysis and design technique.* New York: McGraw-Hill. Reissued in 1993 as IDEF 0/SADT: Business process and enterprise modeling. San Diego: Eclectic Solutions Corp.

Scheer, August-Wilhelm. 1995. *Business process engineering: ARIS navigator for reference models for industrial enterprises.* New York: Springer Verlag.

About the Authors

Luigi Redaelli is a material logistic architect responsible for procurement process reengineering at IBM Italy. He holds a bachelor's degree in electronic engineering from Politecmico of Milan. His work has also appeared in Logistica Management (June/July 1992 and June/July 1993).

Luigi Redaelli
Reengineering Dep. VM 290
IBM Semea via Lecco 61
20059 Vimercate (Mi)
Milan, Italy
Telephone: 39 39 600 4670
Facsimile: 39 39 600 5051

Paolo G. Confalonieri is a project manager at Autofaber. He is responsible for coordinating research projects on process analysis and reengineering and on applied statistics for quality improvement. He holds a doctorate degree in information science from the Università degli Studi di Milano. His work has also appeared in Logistica Management (June/July 1992).

Paolo Confalonieri
Autofaber
via Cicognara, 7
20129 Milan, Italy
Telephone: 39 2 744149
Facsimile: 39 2 7385567
E-mail: palconf@milano.ccr.it

CHAPTER 11

Expanding Benchmarking to Include an Entire Industry: Tradenz Best Practice Study

Chris Simmons, Managing Director, Benchmark Communication Limited, Joanne Douglas, Business Development Manager, and John Duncan, Senior Project Manager, New Zealand Trade Development Board (Tradenz)

Background

Tradenz is the commercial name for the New Zealand Trade Development Board, the government agency responsible for export development and the growth of international business. Tradenz delivers a range of services to New Zealand exporters through its extensive network of overseas offices. Staff in these offices work as contact points for importers, distributors, and other key contacts in the market. Tradenz also works to improve the capability of New Zealand export companies, focusing on issues such as business practice, technology, finance, and investment.

In 1993 Tradenz was working with New Zealand industry joint action groups (JAGs) to address industry capability issues. Key concerns identified included the following:

- How to develop hard evidence of an industry's capability that could be used to position that industry internationally.

- How to identify and measure generic industry capability issues (gaps) and competitive advantages.

- How to develop a platform on which to base industry second-tier development and expansion.

- How to maximize the benefits of collectivism. Informal structures had evolved for information sharing, but the ability of industry members to identify best practice and to leverage from each others' breakthroughs was limited.

Benchmarking, particularly its evolution into best practice, was identified by Tradenz as a mechanism that would effectively address most of the issues raised.

While benchmarking and best practice techniques were well developed at the individual company and the company comparative levels, the concept of a group or industry study, to Tradenz's knowledge, was unique. The industrywide approach required expansion and modification of standard benchmarking methodology. Thus, Benchmark Communication Limited was engaged to facilitate the development of an industry benchmarking model for Tradenz.

Study Purpose

Tradenz identified that, through benchmarking, it could compare critical success factors within a New Zealand industry with the best in the world. This comparison would identify process improvement opportunities for New Zealand businesses that would make them more internationally competitive.

In developing the industry benchmarking model Tradenz identified five key objectives.

1. To add value to high-performing companies

Many of New Zealand's top companies are continually being approached by Tradenz and other groups to disclose their secrets. Through benchmarking best practice, both within New Zealand and internationally, Tradenz can provide the top performers with information to further improve their business. The provision of information will enhance Tradenz's relationship with these companies and encourage networking among New Zealand companies.

2. To provide benefits to national operations and industry directorates

Benchmarking allows Tradenz staff to work together and deliver services seamlessly to their customers. It also helps project managers to understand how the top New Zealand companies operate and gives them access to senior management of the top companies.

3. To promote New Zealand industry internationally

Benchmarking at an industry level allows Tradenz to show how New Zealand industry compares with best practice companies overseas. The comparison could be used to help New Zealand industry attract financial backing, both domestically and internationally, and highlight the joint-venture and investment opportunities that exist.

4. To provide a platform for the development of second-tier companies

Benchmarking will provide case studies highlighting what New Zealand companies could achieve if they perform at world-class standards. Tradenz can use the material to consult with New Zealand companies as they look to develop their processes and excel in the international marketplace.

5. To identify capability issues for specific industries

Benchmarking will identify gaps in international competitiveness among particular industries so that appropriate strategies can be developed to overcome those gaps. This is illustrated in Figure 11.1.

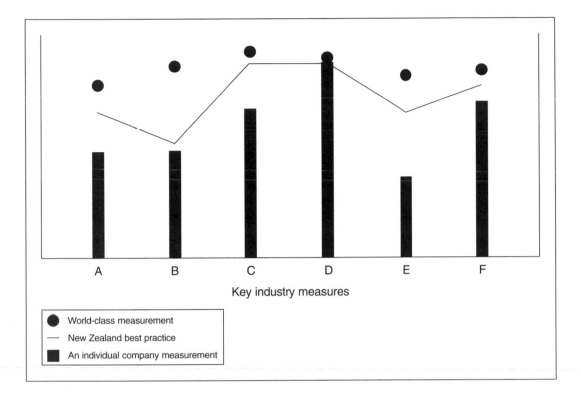

Figure 11.1. Creating industry comparisons.

The Process

Tradenz, in conjunction with Benchmark Communication Limited, developed a four-step process for use in completion of an industrywide benchmarking study. This is shown in Figure 11.2. The model required piloting on a group that satisfied a number of base criteria relating to information disclosure, quality business processes, and auditable best practice attributes.

The telecommunications industry was identified and selected as the group that met the pilot criteria for the benchmarking exercise. Several additional companies, reputed to successfully use advanced business methodology and with similar core competencies, were also invited to join the study.

The participants of the pilot industry benchmarking project were

• Alcatel New Zealand Limited

• Deltec New Zealand Limited

• Exicom International

• Marine-Air Systems Limited

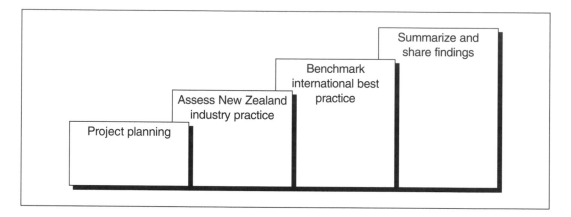

Figure 11.2. Tradenz four-step benchmarking model.

- Production Engineering Company Limited
- Swichtech Power Systems Limited
- Tait Electronics Limited
- Tru-test Distributors Limited

The Four-Step Benchmarking Model

1. Planning and Leading a Benchmarking Project

Tradenz recognized the importance of keeping the project focused. Considerable time was spent on defining the objectives and planning the project before collecting any benchmarking information. To plan and lead the project, Tradenz identified and completed the following steps.

• Identify clearly which companies would participate in the benchmarking project. In this case a group of electronic/telecommunication equipment manufacturers was identified as the pilot site.

• Ensure that everyone involved in the project understood the business reasons for the project.

—Tradenz identified that through benchmarking, it could compare critical success factors within a New Zealand industry with the best in the world, thereby identifying process improvement opportunities for New Zealand businesses that will make them more internationally competitive.

—The electronic/telecommunication equipment manufacturers wanted to develop an industry group that identified and adopted best practice strategies and that enabled the industry to compete internationally.

• Identify the project's key stakeholders and those people whose leadership and support are critical to the project's success. Key stakeholders included senior management from both Tradenz and the participating companies.

Tradenz determined that the project would be completed in six months, thus ensuring that it remained focused.

2. Assessing Current New Zealand Industry Practices

The next step in the benchmarking model was defined as an internal assessment; that is, taking the industry's pulse. The industry's existing practices, strategies, and processes needed to be assessed to

• Provide a foundation for the project by identifying the critical success factors and measuring the top-performing New Zealand companies against those factors.

• Provide a good base for meaningful comparison with international practices.

Both the "value chain," as described by Michael E. Porter in his book *Competitive Advantage,* and the Malcolm Baldrige Award criteria were used as the basis for identifying the industry's critical success factors and establishing a ranking of companies against those critical success factors identified

Identifying Critical Success Factors

The benchmarking team defined the group's existing practices, strategies, and processes though completion of site visits and detailed interviews with senior management at each participating company. The interviews aimed at understanding each organization's vision, values, and general direction through the eyes of senior management. The objectives of this exercise were to

• Understand the commonality of approach across the industry group.

• Determine the level of understanding of critical industry issues.

• Identify the key critical success factors (CSFs) and performance measures.

The methodology involved personal interviews with the key executives of the participating companies using a structured interview guide. The executives completed a worksheet to summarize their thoughts and to prioritize critical issues. Then the companies were approached a second time to gain specific measurements and process approaches to the CSFs.

During the interview, the organization's vision for the future was determined. The components of the business critical to its achieving the vision were identified. A discussion of the current business practices for identifying these components ensued. The following practices were covered.

• Research and development

• Supplier networks

- Sales and marketing
- Distribution
- Organizational infrastructure
- Financial control
- Human resources
- Technology

The next part of the interview included identifying the critical performance indicators and the performance achieved during the past three years. The interview concluded with the completion of the critical success worksheets (Figures 11.3 and 11.4).

Once the group's critical success factors were identified a process had to be developed to ascertain how each of the New Zealand companies rated against the success factors. The Malcolm Baldrige National Quality Award criteria were used to provide a common frame of reference for each company interviewed. By using the assessment criteria as a base, generic questions and interview frameworks were generated. The interview frameworks ensured the questions challenged even the best, and allowed a fair comparison across a range of companies.

Instructions: Use the two worksheets to assist in defining the critical success factors that create value within your company.

Take some time to consider the key processes undertaken by your organization. Reflect upon your vision for the future, consider the supplier and customer relationships and think about the internal infrastructure. Now define the key functions, activities or success factors within your organization (do not attempt to rank the items in any order).

Critical success factors

1. _____

2. _____

3. _____

4. _____

5. _____

6. _____

7. _____

8. _____

9. _____

10. _____

Figure 11.3. Identifying critical success factors—Part 1.

Based on experiences, we have identified three criteria that are useful in focusing on the critical success factors. The three are

• **Criticality**—is the function or activity *critical to execution of company business strategy?* (Value = 5 points)

• **Improvement need**—Does the function or activity represent a *major area for improvement in company business practices?* (Value = 3 points)

• **Cost savings**—Does improving the function or activity offer *significant potential cost savings?* (Value = 1 point)

Reflecting on your personal knowledge and experience, put a check (✔) in the boxes which correspond to the three criteria described above. When you have reviewed each function or activity that you listed on the previous sheet, add the point values of the checks you made by each critical success factor and write them in the column at the right of the page. You may mark more than one criterion if you feel it relates to the critical success factor. The maximum points any one factor can score is 9.

Critical success factors	Criticality (5 points)	Improvement need (3 points)	Cost leverage (1 point)	Total
1. _____	☐	☐	☐	_____
2. _____	☐	☐	☐	_____
3. _____	☐	☐	☐	_____
4. _____	☐	☐	☐	_____
5. _____	☐	☐	☐	_____
6. _____	☐	☐	☐	_____
7. _____	☐	☐	☐	_____
8. _____	☐	☐	☐	_____
9. _____	☐	☐	☐	_____
10. _____	☐	☐	☐	_____

Figure 11.4. Identifying critical success factors—Part 2.

The Value Chain

The value chain (Figure 11.5) describes the various activities performed to design, produce, market, deliver, and support a firm's products. The differences between competitors' value chains often dictate the competitive advantage to be gained. By using the value chain as a reference, the project team was able to ensure all aspects of the business were considered.

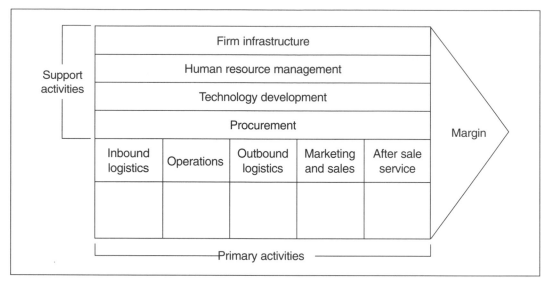

Figure 11.5. Porter's value chain.

Results of the Exercise

The group's CSFs identified from the interviews using the value chain were as follows:

• *Culture and leadership* includes the senior executives' personal leadership and involvement in creating and sustaining a customer focus and clear and visible organizational values.

• *Human resources* includes the systems a company has in place to define its requirements and to attract, develop, and retain high-quality human resources.

• *Customer orientation* is the company's relationship with customers and its knowledge of customer requirements and of the key quality factors that drive market competitiveness.

• *Organizational structure* is the ability the company has developed to ensure that growth (or achievement of vision) is neither impeded nor compromised by organizational or managerial limitations.

• *Planning and control* involve the process that defines the future orientation of the company, its commitment to its stakeholders, and its ability to cope with change while meeting its goals.

• *Product or service innovation* includes the systems a company has implemented to ensure maximum generation, capture, assessment, and development of new product and service concepts.

• *Concept commercialization* is the process the company uses to bring a product concept to market fruition, creating maximum added value from the identified market opportunity.

• *Information systems* are the support mechanisms the company has developed that deliver timely, relevant, and accurate information at a realistic cost, enabling effective decision making at all levels.

• *Management of operations* is the systematic process a company uses to pursue constantly improved quality and operational performance.

Each of the success factors identified during the site visits and interviews was accepted as crucial to the future of the subject company and the industry at large. On completion of the interview process a cross section of New Zealand industry best practice was summarized for publication using the CSFs identified.

Once the CSFs had been determined, each participating company was asked to supply performance measures (metrics) for the past three years (see Figures 11.6–11.8). These metrics would be used as a basis of comparison with best practice international companies.

3. Benchmarking Best International Practices

Benchmark Communication Limited developed a guide to assist in identifying best practice companies to profile. Company publications, trade journals, professional associations, and data searches were all used to identify companies. Once all the primary data had been analyzed best practice companies were selected that

• Were diverse in size and industry

• Believed their practices improved their business and competitive position

• Showed good financial performance

• Were reputed to be innovators or leaders

Using the CSFs identified during the New Zealand companies study, Benchmark Communication identified a range of international companies considered to exhibit best practice in the studies specific areas of interest. Over 20 companies were identified.

Telephone interviews were carried out with senior management of 15 of the companies identified. The interviews completed during this phase were developed using the same criteria developed for the New Zealand company study (see Figure 11.9).

As with the New Zealand companies, each international company was then asked to complete performance measures (metrics) for each of the CSFs determined in the project. It was considered essential that the study team use the same criteria for both the New Zealand and international assessments to ensure consistency of data and so that companies taking part in the benchmarking exercise could clearly see how New Zealand and international practices differ.

		International (sample)	New Zealand group		
			Max	Med	Min
Training hours/employee	1990–1991	10	20	3	1
	1991–1992	10	22	11	2
	1992–1993	30	30	5	4
Training expenditure (percent sales)	1990–1991	1	2.5	0.6	0.2
	1991–1992	1	2.5	0.7	0.2
	1992–1993	5	3	0.6	0.08
Staff turnover (percent)	1990–1991	5.4	47	2.8	0
	1991–1992	13	20	5.0	0
	1992–1993	13	8.3	2.0	0
Absenteeism (hours as percent of payroll)	1990–1991	<0.5	25	0.6	0
	1991–1992	<0.5	15	0.5	0
	1992–1993	<0.5	7.5	0.5	0
Accident rate (hours as percent of payroll)	1990–1991	0.5	10	0.02	0
	1991–1992	0.5	3	0.2	0
	1992–1993	0.5	2	0.2	0
Average length of service (years)	1990–1991	33	10	4	2
	1991–1992	35	11	4	1.3
	1992–1993	27	12	6	2
Internal promotions (percent of each total)	1990–1991	100	70	15	10
	1991–1992	100	75	20	5
	1992–1993	60	80	28	10

Figure 11.6. Metrics collected to validate best practice profiles in human resources.

		International (sample)	New Zealand group		
			Max	Med	Min
Access (employees/workstation)	1990–1991	1	4.6	3.3	1
	1991–1992	1	3.0	2.5	1
	1992–1993	1	3.6	1.25	0.8
MIS investment (percent of sales)	1990–1991	2	2.2	0.72	0.5
	1991–1992	3	2.5	1.0	0.06
	1992–1993	2	2.0	1.2	0.25

Figure 11.7. Metrics collected to validate best practice profiles in information systems.

The benchmarking team then completed a profile for each company interviewed. A summary was also completed for each CSF identified. The summary included a statement of

- The company's vision
- The scope of the operation
- Company best practice
- Impact of best practice

4. Summarizing and Sharing Best Practice Findings

Tradenz, in conjunction with Benchmark Communication Limited, has developed an industrywide benchmarking model, a crucial component of which is the sharing of information and the presentation to both New Zealand industry and international company participants.

On completion of the final interviews with best practice companies, a cross section of best practices was summarized for publication. The summary incorporated an overview of the project, the objectives, and approach; a summary of the key findings from the New Zealand companies study; and a summary of the key findings from the international benchmarking study.

The information provided industry participants with comparative information so they could clearly understand differences between their own company practices and industry best practice. Thus, this helped them to formulate change recommendations based on international best practices.

		International (sample)		New Zealand group		
		U.S. $	NZ $	Max	Med	Min
Sales per employee ($)	1990–1991	138,210	190,000	220,000	123,000	59,700
	1991–1992	156,390	215,000	270,000	99,000	91,000
	1992–1993	112,750	155,000	308,000	158,000	97,000
Growth rate—sales ($)	1990–1991	3.64	5	91	4	−29
	1991–1992	24.00	33	40	10	−29
	1992–1993	14.55	20	179	23	19
Growth rate—net profit ($)	1990–1991	0.58	0.8	223	10	−47
	1991–1992	4.22	5.8	376	26	−12
	1992–1993	4.29	5.9	856	39	27
Net profit margin (net profit/net sales)	1990–1991		2	21	0.9	−16
	1991–1992		8	14	2.5	0.7
	1992–1993		0	16	8.0	1.0
Asset turnover (sales/net assets)	1990–1991		4.5	9.91	2.74	2.09
	1991–1992		5.6	9.4	2.92	1.92
	1992–1993		4.5	5.6	3.26	2.3
Warrantee claim (percent of revenue)	1990–1991		0	2.4	0.08	0
	1991–1992		0	2.1	0.13	0
	1992–1993		0	1.3	0.2	0
On-time delivery (percent)	1990–1991		75	80	70	60
	1991–1992		80	85	75	63
	1992–1993		85	97	85	80
Sales from new products (percent < 5 years old)	1990–1991			90		30
	1991–1992			95		40
	1992–1993			98	74	46
Research and development expenditure (percent revenue)	1990–1991			14	9.05	7.4
	1991–1992			9	7.16	4.7
	1992–1993			12.3	8.03	4.7
Marketing expenditure (percent revenue)	1990–1991			20	6.7	1.5
	1991–1992			21.4	8.16	1.9
	1992–1993			19	7.23	1.8

Figure 11.8. Metrics collected to validate best practice profiles in planning and control/management of operations.

Note: Interviews of companies outside of your study group must include general questions about the company, as this information helps define the context of which best practice occurs.

Organizational structure

• What is the company's vision and scope of operations?

• How many staff does the company have, and how widespread are they?

• What is the company's management structure?

• How easily can the company manage change, especially for restructuring and market repositioning? How is it placed financially to cope with such change?

• What decision making is expected of the board and CEO?

Company culture and leadership

• What is the company's vision and scope of operations?

• How many staff does the company have, and how widespread are they?

• How do senior executives get involved in and lead company activities? Include

　—Customer focus

　—Quality values and expectations

　—Quality and operational performance

　—Employee recognition

　—Communication of quality values outside the company

• How do they regularly communicate and reinforce the company's customer focus and quality values with managers and supervisors?

• How do they evaluate and improve their involvement and leadership?

• What services, facilities, and opportunities does the company provide for staff?

• How often and by what methods does the company determine whether employees are satisfied? What trends have been evident in recent years?

• How is the company a leader in the community? Include how the company

　—Promotes quality awareness and sharing of quality-related information

　—Seeks opportunities to enhance its leadership

　—Promotes legal and ethical conduct in all its activities

Human resources

• What is the company's vision and scope of operations?

• How many staff does the company have, and how widespread are they?

• How does the company plan in the short and long term for selection, development, mobility, and recognition of human resources?

• How does the company promote employee contribution, individually or in groups, and give feedback?

• How does the company's recognition, promotion, reward, and encouragement of staff and managers support its performance goals and plans?

• How does the company evaluate whether its approach to staff performance and recognition works?

Figure 11.9. Generic interview guidelines: Questions for international best practice companies.

Management of operations

• What is the company's vision and scope of operations?

• How many staff does the company have, and how widespread are they?

• How does the company maintain the quality of its production processes in accord with the product design requirements? Include key processes and key indicators of quality and operational performance.

• How does the company define and communicate its quality requirements to suppliers?

• How does the company ensure that its quality requirements are met by suppliers? Describe how these results and other relevant performance indicators are communicated to suppliers.

• What is being done or is planned to help suppliers meet key quality and response-time requirements?

• How does the company assess systems, processes, and practices? How often are assessments made, and by whom? How does the company ensure quality of its measurement and documentation?

• How are all key measures of product quality and operation performance changing?

• What quality comparisons are made with principal competitors in the company's key markets?

Planning

• What is the company's vision and scope of operations?

• How many staff does the company have, and how widespread are they?

• How does the company develop long- and short-term strategies, goals, and business plans to address quality and customer satisfaction? Include

  —Customer requirements

  —The competitive environment

  —Financial market and societal risks

  —Company capabilities

  —Supplier capabilities

• How are data about customer relations and operation performance aggregated, analyzed, and used for change?

• How does the company relate changes in product and service quality and operation performance to overall financial performance? Detail key financial measures over the past three years.

• How are the plans deployed? How are work-unit plans and activities aligned? How are resources committed?

Customer service and contact

• What is the company's vision and scope of operations?

• How many staff does the company have, and how widespread are they?

• How does the company determine its customers' needs and expectation?

• How does the company determine what current and potential customers need or expect? Include customers, the process for collecting information, and product and service features.

• How does the company build and maintain customer relationships?

• What customer-service channels does the company offer?

• How does the company follow up customer transactions?

• How does the company evaluate and improve its customer-relationship management strategies and practices?

Figure 11.9. *(Continued).*

- What commitments or guarantees does the company make to customers?
- How does the company measure customer satisfaction?
- How does the company plan to further improve customer relationships?

Information systems

- What is the company's vision and scope of operations?
- How many staff does the company have, and how widespread are they?
- How are different types of data selected for use in improving quality and operational performance?
- How does the company ensure reliability, consistency, and accessibility in its operations, particularly in relation to software quality?
- How is the scope of information management evaluated and improved on? Include such factors as the following:
  —Customers
  —Product and service performance
  —Internal operations and performance
  —Inventory management
  —Supplier performance
  —Costs and financial performance
- How would you further improve the information system?

Commercialization

- What is the company's vision and scope of operations?
- How many staff does the company have, and how widespread are they?
- How are product designs integrated to include all phases of production and delivery? Outline the key process-performance characteristics selected to suit customer requirements.
- How is product commercialization monitored, and what trends have emerged over the past three years?
- How are designs reviewed and validated for product and service performance, process capability, and supplier capability?
- How is product commercialization monitored and what trends have emerged over the past three years?
- How does the company improve its design processes for new products, services, or modifications?
- What opportunities arise from the company's product commercialization?

Product or service innovation

- What is the company's vision and scope of operations?
- How many staff does the company have, and how widespread are they?
- How does the company encourage and use innovative product and service ideas?
- How does the company translate these ideas early on into the design of products, services, and processes to match customer requirements?
- What technology is being developed for new products and services?

Figure 11.9. *(Continued).*

Conclusions and Lessons Learned

In conducting this study a number of observations were made that should be kept in mind when examining the data and conclusions.

Those mechanisms identified as best practice within one company are not necessarily valid nor appropriate for another. The industry group was looking for lightbulbs—those flashes of brilliance derived from a different emphasis and perspective that may lead to or stimulate new and innovative concepts. In all cases, best practice came down to what worked for a company. Culture and leadership dominated the definition of the CSFs for the group and emerged as the imperative; that is, if the culture and leadership factors were not right, then no other factor had substantial and long-lasting impact on business health. That culture and leadership rose to the forefront was underpinned by the leading companies' emphasis on the importance of qualitative versus quantitative analysis and in particular their attention to human resource principles.

The enablers (the things that companies did to give them good outcome) observed in the New Zealand sample were as innovative and successful in addressing areas of organizational need as any international examples uncovered. From completion of the study it is recommended that companies exhaustively seek local examples and benchmarking partners before embarking on an international benchmarking exercise. Several large and very well regarded international companies that were involved in the study reinforced the findings that best practice often emerges more readily in smaller, more flexible entities.

Pilot Group Outcomes

The primary and most easily quantified outcome of the study, for the participants, is the improvement in the knowledge each holds of the broad practices and attitudes contained within the industry. Information exchange between New Zealand participants is now well established, with innovative and advanced practice being shared and used to address areas of weakness or need identified through the study.

There is now a strong platform for collective decision making on issues relating to capability. There is also potential for joint approaches to concept innovation—improvement of the product commercialization process and encouraging and capturing the right skill sets.

Within the pilot group the study found evidence of innovative, proactive, flexible, people-focused companies, whose practices are reflected in strong business growth and the achievement of business goals, as measured through key performance indicators and demonstrated by the metrics collected.

The benchmarking project has given each company the opportunity to identify CSFs in its industry and analyze its company practices against the industry best, both domestically and internationally. Companies can now learn from the best and develop best practice strategies within their own organization to successfully compete in the international marketplace.

Tradenz Outcomes

Tradenz has developed an industry benchmarking model that has addressed the key objectives outlined in the study purpose. As a second phase, Tradenz has developed an action guide to completing a benchmarking study using the methods and approaches developed during the study. The guide is used by New Zealand companies in benchmarking projects to assist them in identifying and adopting best practice strategies to enable them to compete successfully in the international marketplace.

About the Authors

Chris Simmons is the managing director for Benchmark Communication Limited, a consultancy on benchmarking and change through the use of best practice information. Simmons earned a bachelor of management studies from the University of Waikato.

Joanne Douglas is the business development manager for the New Zealand Trade Development Board. Her responsibilities include facilitating improvement in the quantity and quality of export and related activities within the New Zealand service sector. Douglas is a former marketing manager for national and international sales of petrochemical-based products. She earned a bachelor's of horticultural science from the University of Canterbury.

John Duncan is the senior project manager for the New Zealand Trade Development Board, where he consults primarily in business development, change management, and learning systems. He earned a master's of business administration from the University of Canterbury.

The authors may be contacted as follows:

Chris Simmons
Managing Director
Benchmark Communication Limited
P.O. Box 90624
AMSC
Auckland, New Zealand
Telephone: 64 9 529 2887
Facsimilie: 64 9 524 6569
E-mail: chris@bestpractice.co.nz

Joanne Douglas, Business Development Manager
John Duncan, Senior Project Manager
New Zealand Trade Development Board (Tradenz)
P.O. Box 8680 Symonds St.
Auckland, New Zealand
Telephone: 64 9 366 3768
Facsimilie: 64 9 366 4767
E-mail: joanne.douglas@nro.tradenz.govt.nz

CHAPTER 12

Benchmarking Improvement and Change: How Quality Award Winners Do It

Bruce Searles, Principal, Bruce Searles Consulting Pty. Ltd. and Steve Ambrose,
Process Improvement Manager, Westpac Banking Corporation

Background

The NRMA (formerly the National Roads and Motorists Association) is arguably Australia's largest general insurance company, and is the largest motoring organization. At the time of the study, NRMA employed approximately 5000 people dispersed across 84 branches throughout the east coast of Australia. NRMA's major lines of business include insurance, financial services, and motoring assistance. NRMA has an annual turnover of approximately $1.6 billion ($A2 billion) and assets of approximately $4.9 billion ($A6 billion). NRMA received the Australian Quality Award in 1992.

Introduction and Origins

It seemed entirely appropriate that Australian Quality Award winners should want to question the value of their improvement and change processes. It is, after all, one of those nagging questions that won't go away, and until such time as it is answered— satisfactorily or not—it will continue to fester and cause irritation. If the question is left unanswered, major surgery (change and restructure) may be required, and major surgery should always be avoided where possible.

The origins of this particular study came from two different sources. The original need to conduct such a benchmarking study can be traced back to NRMA achieving an Australian Quality Award in 1992. The Australian Quality Award is very similar to, and have been modeled off, the Malcolm Baldrige National Quality Award in United States. As the first service organization to receive such an award in the large-organization category, the requests from other organizations to find out how improvement and change were handled were great. NRMA was happy to fulfill its obligation, to present its case study, and to provide other organizations with the benefits of its experiences with regard to improvement and change implementation. After all, this was in the spirit of quality.

It must be remembered that in 1992 the Australian Quality Award had only been running for five years. Thus, the list of winners was small, yet the queue to visit these successful quality organizations was long.

In fulfilling its responsibility to assist other organizations in their own pursuit of improvement and change, there were expectations of the chance to learn something from the many organizations forming the queue at NRMA's front door. There was a long history of success in the eyes of the business community and a remarkable reputation for customer service; however, on this occasion there had been public or third party recognition. With this recognition via the Australian Quality Award, there developed a newfound confidence to consult the market and find out how other organizations performed. There was also the consideration within the organization of wanting to stay ahead of the pack, and any complacency the award might bring with it was not to be tolerated. Striving for new and better ways was to be the focus. Partnering this was the desire to find out where the next advances might emanate from, and the best way to do this was to not only respond to those organizations wishing to learn but to also learn from them.

Unfortunately this was not to be. Only limited direct useful information was gained, although many contacts were established. There was a perception within NRMA of being shortchanged. Disappointingly, other organizations were not as prepared or able to share information.

While this highlighted an imbalance and a glaring problem needing to be fixed, it also highlighted an even greater problem within the field of improvement and change. Where do organizations who are advanced in improvement and change gather further information to assist in their pursuits? Unlike many other organizations, NRMA does not have a parent company to whom it can turn. Quality by trial and error can be very expensive, and there are literally thousands of case studies for those organizations who have tried and failed this method.

Also, during the latter half of 1995, questions arose within NRMA about defining the value added to the organization from the improvement and change efforts. After all, improvement and change efforts had been taking place for the last 10 years, and had contributed to achieving an Australian Quality Award; but where were the tangible bottom-line results to show for all the effort?

This is a question all organizations must surely wrestle with, especially when there are opposing forces to quality within an organization wanting it discredited. This, however, was not the situation within NRMA. What was taking place could be regarded as simply a healthy questioning of the value added, just as athletes might want to know how fast they are running or swimming or what benefit the extra training sessions are providing.

Within NRMA, the champions of improvement and change took this issue onboard, and went about demonstrating the value added to the organization. A study was commissioned and carried out by three final year MBA students. The terms of reference for the study were to demonstrate the value added from improvement and change and to evaluate performance. This latter objective was an attempt to evaluate how successful NRMA has been at implementing change.

The findings of the initial study completed by the MBA students found difficulty in actually defining the value added from improvement and change and that it might be easier to demonstrate what would happen without quality. It also found that improvement and change had become so widely accepted as part of NRMA's culture, demonstrating the way in which things were done, that it was difficult to separate the impact of improvement and change on business results. Therefore, to take quality away from NRMA would be to rip away at the system holding together many of the vital parts.

The Need to Benchmark

The internal study

- Recommended the need to benchmark
- Examined how other leading quality organizations structured and operated their improvement and change processes
- Examined how other leading quality organizations tackled the task of implementing change initiatives

This was an ambitious undertaking but nonetheless an extremely interesting and enlightening one, and one that already had endorsement from NRMA's senior executives. One of the tasks undertaken by the MBA students was to interview those senior executives. It was during one of these sessions with the then-acting CEO that the suggestion to benchmark the performance of quality first came to light.

The Role of the Australian Quality Council

The first step to get the benchmarking study underway was to contact the Australian Quality Council. The AQC is the peak body for quality within Australia, and is responsible for administering the Australian Quality Awards. The AQC is widely regarded as the pacesetter for benchmarking studies, and has a very strong track record of bringing organizations together to participate in these studies.

The AQC's involvement in this study would be vital to overall success. It was important that NRMA was not seen to be running the agenda. While the organization had very clear reasons for wanting the benchmarking study in the first place, there was potentially more to be gained from the study than just the immediate objectives of the organization itself. The AQC would provide impartiality to the proceedings by acting as the overall facilitator and administrator of the study.

Setting the Objectives

The success of the ensuing benchmarking study would center around the quality of the organizations asked to participate in it. This would be one of the key roles of the AQC: to ensure that the benchmarking study contained the right mix of organizations so as to obtain the best possible results for all participants. Inviting organizations to commit and participate to the benchmarking study was, at this stage, difficult as the specific scope and objectives had yet to be established. There was general agreement about the study being a good idea, but what exactly would the objectives be and what were the potential benefits from taking part in the study?

With these questions in mind, the first meeting of all the interested parties was convened. This was a crucial meeting in the study's life cycle. This would be the session at which the objectives for the study proper would be set, and where an assessment would also be made on the willingness of each organization to commit to the study. Present at this meeting were up to 12 organization representatives, not all of whom would be participating in the final study. With 12 organizations, finding consensus on the study's objectives was not easy. All 12 organizations were successful, and therefore were eager to assert some leadership. Naturally some organizations were trying to push their own agenda and attempted to set highly specific objectives. It probably comes as no surprise to learn those organizations were not part of the final study. Eventually the six objectives were agreed upon and set as follows. How do organizations

1. Establish and maintain a climate that ensures improvement of processes?
2. Identify, adapt, and deploy new tools, processes, and techniques for improvement of business processes?
3. Ensure improvement is communicated throughout the organization?
4. Work with managers for them to understand their role in improvement and to ensure improvement is sustained?
5. Measure, report, act upon, and sustain value-added results from improvement initiatives?
6. Design structures and strategies to deploy, maintain, and improve process improvement?

The original concept was always going to prove a challenge, but once these objectives were set and agreed upon, there was little doubt remaining it would be a difficult study. However difficult the study objectives appeared they were eased somewhat by the high quality of the participating organizations. The final number of participating organizations totaled eight. A brief description of each organization follows.

The Participating Organizations

• *Company A* is a large multinational Australian company comprising some 59,000 employees worldwide. It is a diversified company primarily involved in mining and manufacturing of steel products. It also offers consulting services for engineering both internally and externally, and has been heavily involved in quality for several years.

• *Company B's* major lines of business are personal communications, radio transmission equipment, line transmission equipment, and switching equipment. This organization takes its lead from the Japanese parent company, and therefore specializes in the Japanese model of quality.

• *Company C* is part of a worldwide car manufacturer. This company is very committed to continuous improvement as well as quality from the top down, right through to the shop floor. The kaizan approach to quality is highly visible, and its JIT manufacturing is a must-see.

• At the time of the study, *Company D* was regarded as the fifth largest bank in Australia. Its success in improvement and change came from having a very lean organization, a style that is most unbureaucratic, and a managing director highly committed to quality. The organization also prides itself on the level of technological advancement over other banking institutions.

• *Company E* is regarded as being one of the "Big Four" in Australia's banking industry. While it is relatively immature with respect to its quality journey, the company's eagerness to learn about quality and therefore participate in the study, together with its sheer size, made the organization an interesting participant. In an organization with 35,000 employees spanning approximately 1500 sites how are change and quality implemented?

• Since *Company F* was a recent (1995) Australian Quality Award winner, its participation was a must. Furthermore, as a government utility involved in reform and deregulation, the organization's approach to these external forces of change would be of great interest.

• *Company G* is a large organization based in Western Australia. Its demonstrated respect of quality equals, and in some instances is more advanced than, many of its more fancied companies on the east coast. As an organization, Company G is highly diversified, having mining and manufacturing as well as retail and services to the rural sector as its major operations.

• *NRMA* is the eighth largest motoring organization in the Southern Hemisphere, and arguably the largest general insurer in Australia. It received the Australian Quality Award in 1992. NRMA was well suited to be the major sponsor of this study. It is widely recognized as a leader in the change and quality fields.

With these organizations participating, the success of the study was assured.

Methodology Followed

In reality it would take more than just the organizations involved to ensure the success of the study. To translate the objectives into meaningful results would require rigor and discipline. To achieve this the methodology employed would need to be sound. This would not be an easy task, as a study of this nature had not previously been undertaken. Thus, there was no recipe methodology to apply. Other studies undertaken and facilitated by the AQC (for example, call center studies) had focused on easily accessible and quantifiable results. For such benchmarking studies the methodology was one of analysis, followed by cause and effect. While this is something of an oversimplification for the actual methodology employed, it is intended to indicate that the methodology was relatively uncomplicated. Quantifying the results of quality and change was not going to be easy.

The final methodology was one agreed upon through a consultative approach, with a commitment to flexibility throughout the study. There were to be a number of checkpoints throughout the benchmarking study to ensure the methodology was achieving the desired results. If at any stage the methodology was failing then a reevaluation was required. While this may be regarded as very time-consuming, it did help to guarantee the success of the study, and made sure the study was not heading "up the garden path."

The first step in the methodology was to assess the strengths and weaknesses of each organization. This was done using the Australian Quality Award's criteria. Each organization prepared a report detailing where its performance was regarded as superior or in need of improvement, as defined in the AQA criteria. The reports were to address the six objectives of the benchmarking study.

These detailed reports served several purposes. First and foremost, this was an objective means by which the participating organizations could judge their performance against a criteria all could apply. For some organizations who had AQA-qualified evaluators examine their organizations the task was even more objective. The detailed reports were also a means by which people could develop an understanding of each organization quickly, without needing to spend time in each of the organizations.

From the reports as well as data from the organizational self-assessments, award evaluations, and organizational knowledge, a matrix was constructed detailing where strengths and weaknesses existed for each organization. This was a very large matrix. Not surprisingly there were some instances where the group shared common strengths and common weaknesses. This, in fact, proved to be a bonus as it would allow study participants an opportunity to see the same practice in differing environments.

The matrix was then used to determine where each of the participants had the greatest interests (or improvement opportunities), thus narrowing the focus even further. From this large matrix was developed a second matrix, which identified the areas and items of operation against each objective each participating organization was going to supply.

It was then determined that the best way to progress the study to the next stage was through a series of site visits. These would allow a much greater depth of knowledge to develop about each organization, and would also allow a firsthand view of the reported superior operations and processes. The coordination of the site visits proved to be a difficult task given the geographically dispersed nature of the participating organizations and their individual workloads. For example, visits around the end of the financial year were definitely not feasible.

Given the detail of what was to be addressed at each site visit, one day at each organization was clearly not going to be adequate. It was stressed and accepted that the site visits were to act as the first contact or as "the foot in the door." If a visiting organization developed a particular area of interest after attending the site visit then it was up to that organization to continue to develop the relationship.

At the highest level, the entire process could be depicted in the diagrams shown in Figures 12.1 and 12.2. Figure 12.1 shows the benchmarking process, and Figure 12.2 illustrates the data gathering process.

Results

The results of the site visits are detailed in Table 12.1. The results for each of the participating organizations naturally vary as does the way in which the results were used. The results provided in Table 12.1 are those identified by the sponsoring organization; that is, NRMA.

The way in which the results were communicated and deployed was crucial to the overall success of the benchmarking study. To assist in this regard NRMA had taken some actions early in the study. As part of the rounds of site visits, NRMA had identified a number of key senior managers from within who could potentially gain a great deal from the site visit and invited them to participate. The additional participants would vary with each site visit depending on the organization being visited. Not surprisingly, the selected

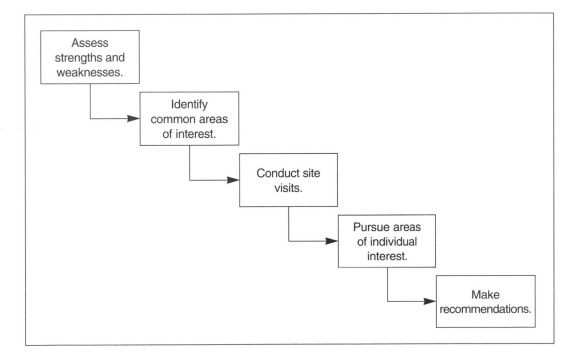

Figure 12.1. Benchmarking process.

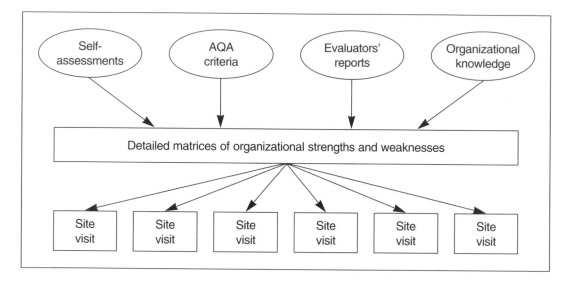

Figure 12.2. Data gathering process.

participants were highly impressed with much of what they were able to see. Their enthusiasm surrounding the visit and the entire process was crucial to communication within NRMA. With benchmarking champions now strategically placed throughout the organization, communication was considerably easier.

The results were compiled into a final report, which was delivered to key individuals throughout NRMA, depending on where in the organization the best practice was deemed to have greatest application. The next step was to complete a round of consultations with the identified areas and to provide further details of the identified best practices. To assist with this activity, those additional senior management who participated in the site visit were "conscripted."

There was naturally a mixed response to a number of these findings and recommendations, but in the main the responses were favorable. The immediate challenge was to try and ensure there was change as a result of this study; but this was not always to be the case. Those areas of NRMA that were eager to change or adopt the best practices required more detailed information to determine exactly how the best practices could be incorporated into current practices. Subsequent visits and consultations with the participating organizations were required.

While this process overall is not fast, it is very thorough. This is an important part of any successful change, and was highlighted through the site visits. Successful improvement and change take time.

One of the most satisfying aspects to evolve from the benchmarking study was the development of a very strong network of equally minded and committed organizations. This ensured a very smooth process for any subsequent site visits.

Table 12.1. Identified best practices.

Practice	Company	Why is it a best practice	Application within NRMA
Market research	Company E	Highly focused on understanding customers, patterns, and behaviors	Market research
Value model	Company E	Same model as used successfully by large telecommunications companies in understanding customers	Retail division and those projects dealing with customer relationships
TV	Company E	Live satellite TV providing daily communication to approximately 1500 branches	None
Communication of vision and mission	Company D	Vision and mission are printed on mouse and desk pads for communication and reinforcement	Could be used in the communication of values
Conversion of mainframe mail to PC mail	Company D	Allows mail communication between head office and branches	Any where there is communication between head office and the branches
Quality council	Company D	Managing director and general managers meet every quarter to discuss quality; is the peak body for quality	Similar structure could operate in our organization
Quality forum	Company D	Monthly meeting of general manager representatives to discuss quality issues and elevate to council if required	Similar structure could operate in our organization
Follow-up on customer closing business	Company D	Valuable information can be obtained from customers and then used as input to product development	Insurance could apply this to obtain information
Centralized processing	Company D	Lowers branch cost structures and ability to provide consistent service and advice	Claims regionalization
Reward	Company D	Small rewards are given weekly for those who have done something well or learned from a mistake	Retail
Quality control committee	Company B	General managers meet every two months to discuss quality issues; is the peak body for quality	Similar structure could be used at our organization
Each policy and plan has performance measures	Company B	Control through measurement and statistics	Throughout organization
Help desk	Company B	Automatic caller identification systems	Telephone service center and road service

Table 12.1. *(Continued).*

Practice	Company	Why is it a best practice	Application within NRMA
Software used for handling complaints	Company B	Software package allows documentating, tracking, and reporting on complaints	Customer relations and quality suggestion system
Employee attitude survey	Company C	Annual staff attitude survey has response rate of 80 percent	Human resources
Self-assessment	Company C	Participation is compulsory	
Supplier support	Company C	Heavily involved in building relationships with suppliers; crucial for their JIT manufacturing	Assessing and purchasing
Supplier assessment program	Company C	Helps to raise the standards of the suppliers and for them to understand what is expected of them	Assessing and purchasing
Strategic planning	Company G	Focus on the six things that matter most to the organization	Strategic planning
Use of targets and forecasting in strategic planning	Company G	Allows organization to better understand its processes and plan for contingency	Strategic planning
Corporate performance indicators (CPIs)	Company G	Only focus on two CPIs 1. Return on capital 2. Earnings before interest and tax	
Strong process focus	Company G	Strong process focus allows actions plans to be cross-functional thus improving success rate of actions	
Electronic documentation system	Company G	All documentation (some 800 documents) to be on-line; substantial cultural change	Internal communication

Conclusions and Lessons Learned

The overall success of any benchmarking study is dependent on the quality of those participating in the study. This is pointed out in numerous texts as a crucial point; yet it cannot be stressed enough. How do you know when you have the best partners? There is no easy answer for this; however, history and track record are useful indicators for the suitability of a participant. It is also useful to follow a "gut feel" when selecting partners. The final test of partnership suitability must be a willingness to contribute and share. This is the key.

Look for diverse partners to benchmark with. In this study there were banks, insurance companies, car manufacturers, mining companies, and telecommunication companies. On face value many of these companies would appear to have nothing in common. Not so. Not only did the organizations share a desire to benchmark together but they were then able to open their doors and share their experiences and operations with one another. Furthermore, the relationships between these organizations have remained in place, possibly increasing their strategic importance.

To benchmark well takes time. Never underestimate the amount of time, work, and effort required. The results will directly correlate to the work put in. Fortunately, in this particular study, sufficient time was allocated to enable the study to be completed.

The availability and use of data are always important features. This benchmarking study could have benefited from more rigorous data analysis. It is not immediately apparent, however, where this could be applied, given the different nature of what was being benchmarked. Where possible, objective data were used in selecting the relative strengths and weakness of each organization via self-assessment results and formal evaluations. It should be remembered this benchmarking study focused substantially on qualitative analysis rather than quantitative analysis.

Improvement and change processes can be difficult to measure. The standard forms of measurement (the balance sheet) do not lend themselves well to measuring this. In evaluating where the greatest impact to the balance sheet is, how can the difference between the change or the process of the change be determined? Too often organizations look to the bottom-line result without consideration of how that result was achieved.

This benchmarking study was an attempt to identify those methods and techniques, which when consciously or subconsciously enacted, allow organizations to see improved bottom-line results across a range of key performance indicators—not just financial indicators. Sometimes the discipline and process of going through a change initiative can be more beneficial than the change or outcome itself.

There are no right or wrong answers from benchmarking studies. The answer is what will best fit within your organization. For example, one organization in the study had a daily satellite TV program beamed to its branches throughout Australia. This was a remarkable achievement, and is surely a world's best practice for internal communication. This does not mean, however, it is suitable for all organizations with geographically dispersed locations, partly due to high costs.

Finally, benchmarking will develop a network of contacts, that if managed well, should remain in place for many years. This allows the facilitation of even greater learning and improvement, an objective we should all be interested in undertaking. Thus, it seemed entirely appropriate that the 1992 Australian Quality Award winners should want to question the value of their improvement and change processes.

About the Authors

Bruce Searles spent most of his working life at NRMA, holding a number of positions within the organization. His last position, at the time of the benchmarking study, was as assistant general manager, international best practice. In this role Searles reported to the chief executive officer, and led business improvement and change across the entire organization. While in this role Searles assisted the Australian Quality Council to develop benchmarking programs for other Australian organizations. Searles also served NRMA as its assistant general manager of public policy, where he lead NRMA's advocacy on behalf of its two million members and the community at large.

Recently, Searles established his own consultancy, specializing in benchmarking and process innovation. He leads national benchmarking studies and process innovation, assisting organizations with cultural change and business improvement. Recent presentations include "Networking with the Best," given at Novo Quality Services at PSB Singapore, and "Implementation of Change," presented at the international benchmarking conference of the Australia Quality Council.

Searles holds bachelor's and master's degrees in civil engineering from the University of New South Wales. He is a licensed quality advisor with the Australian Quality Council.

Bruce Searles Consulting Pty. Ltd.
PO Box 29
Asquith NSW 2077
Australia
Telephone: 61 2 9482 4092
Facsimile: 61 2 9482 4093
E-mail: searles@zip.com.au

Steve Ambrose is a process improvement manager for Westpac Banking Corporation. His responsibilities include developing and maintaining a strategic model for process improvement; establishing and maintaining a framework for product and process measurements; and identifying process measurements.

Prior to this, Ambrose was a senior consultant for Andersen Consulting. His primary responsibilities included project management and designing, developing, and implementing new business processes and solutions.

During the NRMA benchmarking study Ambrose was deeply involved with the day-to-day undertaking. He worked with Bruce Searles in international best practice assisting with business improvement across the organization. He provided consulting advice and assistance to internal and external inquiries, coordinated benchmarking contacts, and supported the CEO and general managers in change initiatives.

Ambrose has presented numerous seminars on quality benchmarking and reengineering, including guest lectures at the University of Technology in Sydney. He holds a bachelor's of science from the University of New South Wales.

Steve Ambrose
Westpac Banking Corporation
Operational Services
Level 7 Shell House, 140 Phillip Street
Sydney 2000
Australia
Telephone: 61 2 9226 0753
Facsimile: 61 2 9226 1733

CHAPTER 13

Redefining Service Frontiers: Lessons from the Best Practices of the Housing Development Finance Corporation

Nasser Munjee, Executive Director, Housing Development Finance Corporation, and D. P. Singh, Principal Consultant, Eicher Consultancy Services

Introduction

In the final decade of the twentieth century, unparalleled total customer satisfaction is becoming the decisive strategic weapon of top-performing companies (TPC's) in India. It is with this perspective that Eicher Consultancy Services (ECS), an Indian management consulting firm, chose to derive some meaningful learnings from the best practices of an outstanding example of customer service in India. For the last four years ECS has been researching the winning management practices of top performers. Each year, ECS ranks the 30 top-performing Indian companies. According to *Business Today,*

> *To identify them [the top 30], ECS operated at two levels: besides initiating extensive background research, it drew up structured, 15-page questionnaires asking for data on the management practices of each company. When they were sent to the CEOs of the 30 TPCs, two-thirds responded by supplying the quantitative and qualitative data they had been asked for.*

Subsequently the CEOs and the top management staff of these top-performing companies were interviewed by ECS consultants. The insights gathered through these initiatives were distilled into a report on the best of the best. For the record, none of the top performers is a client of ECS.

Undoubtedly, service is emerging as a key focus area in their strategies. This focus, however, was most pronounced in the case of the Housing Development Finance Corporation (HDFC), the largest mortgage finance institution in India. In addition, there was a sound rationale in the ECS approach of selecting HDFC as a role model for customer service.

The best practices research initiatives of ECS had a basic premise: Companies that achieve superior financial performance are top-performing companies. To distill the top performers, a rigorous screening criterion was applied to all the corporations listed at

Mumbai Stock Exchange and whose annual revenues exceeded $99.12 million (INR 3000 million) in 1992–1993. Subsequently, six key performance indicators were considered for the past three years.

1. Return on capital employed

2. Return on equity

3. Return on sales

4. Growth in sales

5. Growth in operating profits

6. Growth in asset base

Based on this screening the top 30 companies were considered top performers. Only nine companies made ECS's top 30 list in both 1994 and 1996. HDFC is one of these nine companies, demonstrating superior financial performance on a consistent basis. Its management philosophy is built around a high customer focus intent. It has some very fine service delivery processes in place. A number of these are what might be called "soft" areas, however they are very challenging when it comes to successful implementation. In such a background ECS wanted to find in-depth answers to one overriding question: What is it that really makes HDFC different and its performance so outstanding? Therefore, ECS requested that HDFC collaborate in this learning mission, which it did. What followed was a team deployed by HDFC to join hands with ECS consultants to seek answers to this overriding question.

HDFC's Background

Incorporated in 1977 with a share capital of $3.29 million (INR 100 million), the net worth of HDFC as of March 31, 1997, is $547.42 million (INR 16.63 billion). This corporation commenced operations as a mortgage bank. It raised large wholesale resources and lent retail primarily to individual households. In mid-1991, it entered the retail deposit market by offering savings and investment opportunities to households in competition with other instruments in the financial market. As a result of customer focus and efficient processes, the number of depositors has risen from 56,000 in 1991 to over 867,000 in March 1997. The outstanding amount of deposits as of March 31, 1997, was over $1.15 billion (INR 35 billion). Much of this success is also due to the significant contribution made by HDFC's growing number of authorized deposit agents, who now number over 42,000.

HDFC's performance includes some impressive credentials.

• HDFC pioneered retail housing finance in India.

• It is the undisputed leader with 55 percent market share among the 23 registered housing finance companies.

• It has a top-quality loan portfolio, with a loan recovery rate above 99 percent.

- HDFC has the highest credit rating received for deposits and bonds.
- It has twice been rated as a best managed company in India by *Asiamoney* magazine.
- It is rated as the second most competitive company in India by *Euromoney* magazine.
- HDFC helped one million middle-class Indians buy their homes.
- It is consistently profitable and growing at 30 percent, on average, every year
- Its chairman, Deepak Parekh, was honored with *Business India's* Businessman of the Year award in 1996.
- HDFC's 1997 financials include the following:

  —Income of $416.41 million (INR 12.85 billion)

  —Profit after tax of $81.63 million (INR 2.48 billion)

  —Earnings (fully diluted) per share of $6.68 (INR 203)

  —The declared dividend is 45 percent.

The enablers going behind this performance level of HDFC could be organized into three interrelated groupings: (1) leadership, (2) service management, and (3) staff development.

Leadership at HDFC

Strong and determined leadership is the essence of HDFC's success story. There are some real gains to be made from creative and continuous innovation; and this innovation can only be nurtured by an organization that enjoys leadership of the highest quality. A second key requirement is cultural affinity not only at the top of an organization, but also throughout it. This cultural affinity has been built gradually and systematically over years of sustained efforts. Combined, strong leadership and cultural affinity are the twin pillars of the highly responsive organization.

HDFC chose to use these strengths through a strong service management philosophy. Service became the business. Service became the product. The leadership team realized that service is not an abstract concept but the outcome of a combination of attributes, which, if used in alignment with each other, produces a measurable product.

Top-performing companies are characterized by those that focus attention very specifically on the attributes that combine to make up the service dimension. These companies are constantly competing on ideas, implementation, internal cohesion, learning, knowledge, and indeed leadership. HDFC is setting the right role model.

This organization has spent years growing potential top management talent. The present top management team has come up through the ranks. HDFC has practiced orderly management successions as the first rule of business.

As a result, the top 15 managers have been there for the last 15 years, and no one has left. HDFC has established management continuity. This has resulted in being able to network and build a culture. It has resulted in taking the long-term versus just the short-term view on products, markets, and investments. In 1993 when Deepak Parekh took over as chairman, he had already spent 15 years with HDFC. His projected tenure at retirement is close to 23 years.

Deepak Parekh spends 80 percent of his time on strategy and policy issues. The remaining 20 percent of his time goes into operational issues of HDFC.

The top three areas that take his maximum time are (1) human resource development, (2) joint ventures, and (3) financing.

Figure 13.1 shows the breakup of functional background of HDFC's board of directors. Figure 13.2 provides the management goals of HDFC and other top performers.

Service Management at HDFC

For us, service management both within and without the organization is the yardstick which measures the efficiency with which we are in touch with the changing needs of our employees and customers in terms of both product design and delivery.

—Deepak Parekh
Chairman, HDFC
(Source: Annual Report 1995–96)

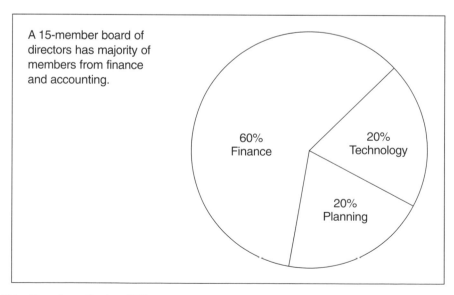

Source: Eicher Consultancy Services 1996.

Figure 13.1. HDFC's board constitution.

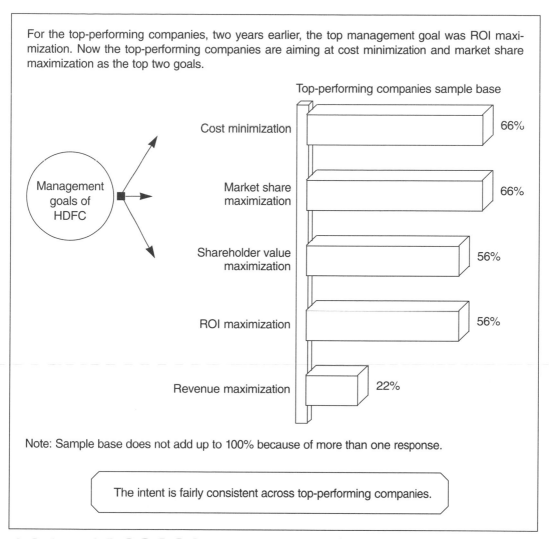

For the top-performing companies, two years earlier, the top management goal was ROI maximization. Now the top-performing companies are aiming at cost minimization and market share maximization as the top two goals.

Top-performing companies sample base

Management goals of HDFC

Cost minimization — 66%

Market share maximization — 66%

Shareholder value maximization — 56%

ROI maximization — 56%

Revenue maximization — 22%

Note: Sample base does not add up to 100% because of more than one response.

The intent is fairly consistent across top-performing companies.

Source: Eicher Consultancy Services 1994, 1996.

Figure 13.2. Management goals of HDFC and other top-performing companies.

Since 1991, HDFC has been redefining its service quality management process. With no local role model available, over the years it has evolved its own quality philosophy: Make it simpler for individuals to take loans and place deposits and offer impeccable service thereafter.

Service management at HDFC has been driven by the service trilogy, which has service strategy, systems, and empowered people as its three apexes and the customer at the center. Process quality has been enhanced by cutting down cycle time, decentralizing loan appraisal and deposit acceptance systems, and increased investment in technology. Figure 13.2 compares HDFC with other top-performing companies on their strategy focus areas.

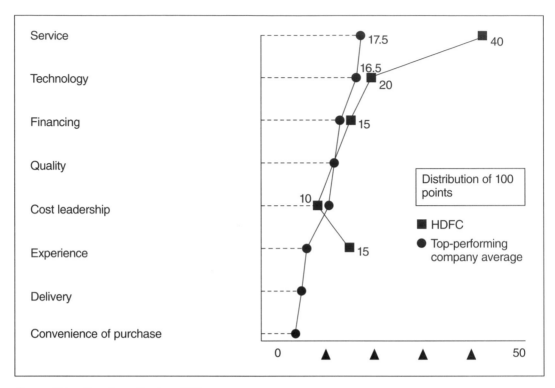

Source: Eicher Consultancy Services 1996.

Figure 13.3. Focus areas of the corporate strategy.

Simplifying Loan Disbursals

Loans disbursal is a key service delivery process within HDFC that has undergone break-through improvements in last four years. This has resulted in shorter cycle times, improved process efficiency, and increased cost-effectiveness.

Until 1990, a loan applicant's paper would be scrutinized by two people: the credit appraiser and the legal appraiser. A technical person would then visit the site for inspection. Each time customers visited HDFC with a new document they would meet a new person and all the previously submitted documents would be reevaluated.

The service enhancement review took into account two factors of the transaction: the financial and the personal. The first one included issues such as the number of visits to HDFC to avail the loan; time spent at the information desk before meeting the concerned person; turnaround time from the application date to the date of the offer letter; reduced paperwork to make it easier for customers; and steps that could be merged or eliminated altogether. The personal dimension looked at staff attitudes, such as the care and attention customers received when they visited HDFC. Obviously, this was the easier aspect to fulfill as it totally depends on employees' people-handling skills.

At the end of this exercise, the credit and legal function were merged into a single window concept whereby customers would meet only one person during the loan availing process. The technical information would be available to the loan appraiser on the computer system and the same would be updated by the technical department after site visits, which would be undertaken for an entire project or an area at one go. A computer package was designed to monitor waiting time at the information desk whereby the customer's arrival time is logged in and the concerned appraisers would have the same displayed on their monitors. The supervisors and the branch manager would also have the same information available on their monitor and if required could reallocate the customers to other appraisers. The need to access physical files was eliminated as the entire current information was now available on the system. Based on need, customers can be interviewed immediately on submission of their application. Then, the offer letter can be issued to the customer on the same day, and the check can be issued in the next 48 to 72 hours. Figure 13.4 illustrates the changes in the process.

The merging of the credit and the legal functions meant that the appraisers had to learn each other's jobs. This was achieved by providing performance support packages on the computer system, proper training, and motivation to learn. People facing change were not left to flounder: They were nurtured and mentored and allowed to learn at their own pace and in a participatory way.

These process redesign efforts were also influenced by the building societies in the United Kingdom and loan institutions in the United States. Over the years, several HDFC teams visited these institutions including the Saving and Loan Institute in Fairfield, Connecticut, and similar institutions in Europe, to study the service delivery systems. In 1996, a team of senior managers from HDFC visited some of the largest building societies in the United Kingdom to study their changing role and product range. The purpose was to understand the latest innovations in the service delivery systems adopted by these institutions, especially those related to the use of technology. Systems were then modified to suit local conditions and subsequently adopted.

Simplifying Deposits

Changes in the environment also necessitated HDFC to consolidate its service management, which until then had relied on bulk funds. With the credit squeeze India faced in the recent past, however, bulk funds were difficult to come by. Subsequently the strategy shifted to raising retail deposits from households. This segment already had existing players in the form of banks, nonbanking finance companies, mutual funds, and the like. HDFC realized that it would derive its competitive edge primarily out of superior service levels in this segment.

HDFC line managers identified a major improvement opportunity when they observed that deposit certificates were issued to investors only on realization of their checks, which would translate into a time gap of a fortnight to a month from the date of

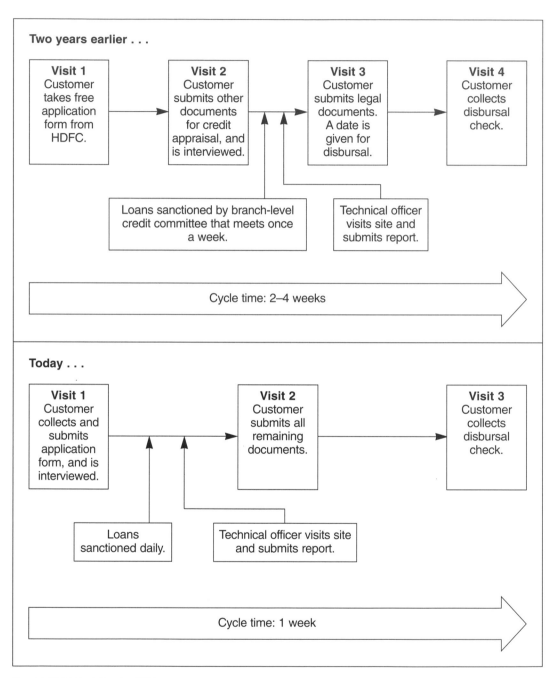

Source: The top performers 1994.

Figure 13.4. Redesigning the loan disbursal process.

deposit. Discussions with agents and depositors revealed that this was an area of concern. On scrutiny, HDFC realized that a very insignificant percentage of checks were returned unpaid by the bankers, more so for technical reasons and hence one of the points of service edge would be "instant deposit certificates." This necessitated a complete reexamination of the existing computer package, process flow, hardware, human resources, approving authorities, and checks and control mechanisms.

The entire deposit processing activity was divided into front office tasks and back office tasks. The front office would be solely responsible for acceptance of deposit and issue of deposit certificates. All subsequent activities, such as the issue of interest warrants, brokerage payments, and reconciliations, would be handled by the back office. This change would not have been possible without a change in the office design, which required approving officers to be seated in close proximity to the front office staff accepting deposits. The front office itself had to be located close to the cash counter for acceptance of cash deposits as well as for security reasons.

Service standards were set up for all tasks in the front and back offices; for example, a deposit certificate has to be issued within 10 minutes of the acceptance of the deposit application form and the check or cash. Currently, renewal of deposits, loan against deposits, as well as repayment of deposits are all on-line. Scanning of depositor signatures has facilitated the process of on-line repayment of deposits.

In 1995–1996, HDFC built on the foundations created earlier to initiate breakthrough process improvements within the organization predicated on service excellence. This has been driven by reshaping and redesigning systems and processes that impact customers directly. Office redesign, process streamlining, and complete automation of systems focusing on the customers' convenience have been important features of this process.

The entire process is based on the rapidly rising retail base of HDFC's operations on both sides of the balance sheet. In order to service this base of well over 1.1 million customers, HDFC is putting in place a state-of-the-art service delivery mechanism with different channels to suit different customers at different periods of time.

Systems at HDFC are helping it to maintain a high asset quality in over 340,000 individual loan accounts. With sophisticated management information systems and loan recovery procedures, arrears amount to a very small proportion (about 0.52 percent) of its outstanding loan portfolio. This has been made possible by a continuous process of introducing increasingly simpler and customer-friendly techniques to ensure that repayments are received when they are due. HDFC's loan portfolio is well diversified both in terms of market segment and geographical spread; however it is HDFC's innovative approach to managerial solutions that is providing an edge for the organization.

Example. An HDFC borrower expired after a prolonged illness, leaving behind his wife and children. The equated monthly installments had not been paid for over a year. The borrower's wife could not be offered employment by his employer as she had no basic qualifications. The borrower's brother was a student doing graduate work at a local college.

After talking to the family, the HDFC branch manager found a suitable job for the borrower's brother. While part of the loan was prepaid out of life insurance proceeds, the balance of the loan is being repaid by the borrower's brother. This unusual act by the branch manager not only helped the family in saving their house but also ensured that HDFC's loan did not go into default.

Staff Development at HDFC

Since 1991 HDFC has increased its business threefold; however, there has been an increase in employees of only 6 percent. Employee turnover has also been very low. And surprisingly, to support 794 people in the organization, there is only a six-member human resource (HR) team.

Organizationally, HDFC looks different than its counterparts by having a flatter, leaner structure and broader span of control. The structure helps in making people accountable, not letting them hide among layers of bureaucracy.

Senior managers at HDFC want a lot of inputs with planning and decision making. They see leadership as a creative process and depend on fluid communication up, down, and across the organization. They seek active contributors to generate new ideas and to build sign-up for improvement initiatives, but not sign-off for decisions without their involvement in subsequent implementation.

Parameters used to measure staff performance include the following:

- Integrity
- Service orientation
- Job knowledge
- Interpersonal skills
- Communication skills
- Leadership skills

The primary goal for the training function is to ensure that staff members are adequately trained in functional and behavioral skills in order to sustain high standards of service.

A workshop—HDFC, Service, and You—was designed and every employee participated in it. The program provided certain fundamentals of service management, such as the distinction between service and manufactured product, service trilogy, gaps in the service delivery process, service delivery cycle, service measurement, service recovery, and so on. At the workshop itself, teams would: make presentations to the senior management; analyze certain high pay-off processes using the service delivery cycle; and identify tasks that could be eliminated, tasks that could be merged, and tasks that would bring added value to a process. The outcome was that 80 percent of the suggestions could be implemented immediately and the rest, which required further deliberations, were implemented within the target date, with one of the team members "championing" the process change up to its ultimate conclusions.

In addition, a number of interventions were made to prepare the service providers within HDFC. Deposit accounting and automation workshops were conducted to improve the systems knowledge of frontline staff to enhance productivity. At the regions, a series of workshops entitled "Negotiative Selling Skills" and "Building High-Performance Teams" were conducted to improve marketing skills and to develop team building. Other programs on creativity and problem solving, time and stress management, as well as interpersonal skills were also conducted.

In recruiting new staff, HDFC believes in hiring the young and the inexperienced. The rationale being that there are no mind-set issues and unhealthy work practices from previous jobs. To such a profile, imparting sustained training inputs becomes most productive.

In addition to these three enablers of leadership, service management, and staff development, the picture of HDFC's top performance would be incomplete without including its deployment of technology and its internal financial management.

The primary source of HDFC's best practices to redesign its processes has been total customer prediction. The rationale being: The customer determines the type of systems and people an organization should have; and then the organization looks at its service strategy. Collecting customer feedback has been a regular feature since the very beginning. Feedback has been collected through surveys—both in-house and commissioned surveys, focus groups, and personal interviews with customers by branch heads and department heads. Feedback collected from customers by frontline staff is also communicated on a one-to-one basis as well as through other forums, thereby enabling modifications in processes. Process design and redesign is normally initiated by frontline staff; the result of which is implementation of changes recommended without much trouble, since there is a sense of ownership of the suggestions made.

In addition, organizations including Federal Express, Marriott Hotels, Scandinavian Airlines, GE Caps, NatWest Bank, Disneyland, Steve Leonard, and Hertz Rent-a-Car also influenced the process changes. The sources of the learnings were through readings, presentations, and discussions at various forums.

Technology at HDFC

For HDFC, technology is about how the gap between the organization and the customer is closed. Technology makes a difference. HDFC staff members realize that they are working not to make a living but to make a difference. This attitude creates and capitalizes on how the company makes a difference. The question "What are we as a company" needs a very specific and unequivocal answer. HDFC has turned technology into an enabler—something that helps to achieve a very specific purpose defined by the service strategy that has evolved.

Falling in love with technology is a major danger. HDFC managers constantly ask themselves what they will do with it and how it improves their service management goals and not how sophisticated it is. Technology is a solid foundation on which HDFC has built a consistent service management system.

HDFC's Management of Internal Finance

In a volatile marketplace, prudent and long-term vision in relation to internal financial management has proved to be a major strength in the financial management philosophy of HDFC. This cautious and middle-of-the-road approach—avoiding the temptations of chasing short-term gains—has steered the corporation well clear of the financial irregularities that have taken place in India's financial sector involving many major players in the market. Investors in HDFC have always benefited by rights and public issues of shares in HDFC, and sister companies as premiums have been pegged at much lower than market value resulting in substantial benefits to shareholders. Shareholder value has been constantly enhanced as a prime objective of corporate vision.

Emphasis has always been in the direction of continuous improvement and learning by doing. An example of this could be the turnaround time from the receipt of a loan application to the dispatch of the loan offer letter. This has improved from four weeks to one week, and currently the turnaround time is 45 minutes if all the required documents are available. Similarly, in the case of deposit mobilization, initially only deposit receipts were offered across the counter. Currently, even repayments are made across the counter. In addition, depositors are provided a facility of direct credit to their respective savings account through an electronic clearing system offered by the central bank of the country. HDFC was among the first few companies to offer this facility to fixed deposit account holders in the country, and capitalized on a new facility offered, thereby saving time and effort for both HDFC and its customers. HDFC's shareholders are also among the privileged few in the country who can get immediate transfer of their shares. This was an internal benchmark set for themselves by the lending and deposits department.

The Future

The process of liberalization, which began in 1991, is systematically continuing across a wide spectrum of India's economy. A major part of this process is the liberalization of the financial sector, which is gradually being undertaken by dismantling the regulated credit system. The impact of these developments will alter the operations of financial institutions dramatically on both sides of the balance sheet. The flow of funds will become a function of market criteria and not an administrative fiat. While these developments will, in the short run, create a more uncertain and volatile financial environment, in the long run they will create the institutional skills with which to deal with some of the problems that emerge in a market-efficient manner.

HDFC is well placed to absorb these shocks as it has been market oriented with respect to resource mobilization as well as its lending program for years. HDFC has developed a retail base of investors—something that the rest of the industry is only now waking up to. Internal systems have been developed to be robust and flexible to take into account changes in the external environment. Staff has been trained in retail financial operations and methods of dealing with individual customers efficiently. Management has been exposed to market-oriented strategies in a difficult and overregulated environment.

Conclusion

Issues like entry of large international players, interest rates, changing technology, privatization, acquisitions, and political turmoil are facing India's economy frequently and severely. In such an environment HDFC is performing on a consistent basis. It is not a result of luck, trick plays, or the misfortune of competitors, but a dogged commitment to fundamentals and execution. HDFC's sustained efforts are yielding superior long-term results.

But perhaps most importantly, for companies that wish to compete in this league, the best practices are not a secret accessible to only a select few. These practices are known and talked about, and it is possible to emulate them—but obviously with great effort. It requires discipline and commitment. That, along with a good dose of inspiration, vision, and faith about where the organization is going, can make it happen.

References

Eicher Consultancy Services Ltd. 1994. *Top-performing companies: Research on the best of the best in India.* New Delhi: Eicher Consultancy Services Ltd.

———. 1996. *Top-performing companies: Research on the best of the best in India.* New Delhi: Eicher Consultancy Services Ltd.

The top performers. 1994. *Business Today* (New Delhi: Living Media India Ltd.), 7–21, June.

About the Authors

Nasser Munjee is a monetary economist by training and has been educated at the London School of Economics and the University of Chicago. He holds a Ph.D. in economics.

Munjee joined HDFC at its inception in 1978 and is currently on its board as an executive director and as its chief economist. He is also on the board of the newly established HDFC Bank. His prime responsibilities include resource mobilization (retail deposits), research, training, human resource development, policy formation, and communications.

Munjee has worked extensively in the field of housing finance and has been a consultant for the World Bank, UNCDF, USAID, Asian Development Bank, and Habitat. He has worked in China, Vietnam, Sri Lanka, Indonesia, Bhutan, and Ethiopia. He also runs the Centre for Housing Finance, a training center for professionals in India and the developing world.

Recently, he has helped to establish Bombay First, a nongovernment corporate effort to contribute to an action agenda for the city's future. Urban development and the future of cities are among his current research interests.

Munjee has authored several articles including "Development of Housing Finance in India" in the *Journal of Indian School of Political Economy* (January–March 1991); and "Resource Flows for Housing: Ideas, Paradigms, and Coalitions" in *Housing Finance International* (September 1992). He also serves as editor of *Housing Finance International*.

D. P. Singh is a principal consultant with the New Delhi practice of Eicher Consultancy Services. His consulting engagement focus is on benchmarking and business strategy. He has over eight years of management consulting and industry experience.

Singh has gained extensive experience in consolidating the Indian market position of his client organizations operating in Indian, South Korean, and North American business cultures. He practices a collaborative approach of consulting.

His innovations in the field of management include developing a summary of best practices of top-performing companies in India. *Business Today* ran a cover story on his findings (June 1994). His current research interests include people-related issues in service quality and managing successful joint ventures.

Singh is a active speaker in leading academic and professional forums. His academics include a bachelor's degree in technology in electronics from Banaras Hindu University and an MBA from Indian Institute of Management, Bangalore.

Nasser Munjee
Executive Director
Housing Development Finance Corporation Ltd.
Ramon House, 169, Backbay Reclamation
Mumbai 400 020 India
Telephone: 91 22 2855049
Facsimile: 91 22 2850078
E-mail: nasser.munjee@hdfc.sprintrpg.ems.vsni.net.in

D. P. Singh
Principal Consultant
Eicher Consultancy Services Ltd.
Eicher House, 12 Commercial Complex
Greater Kailash-II (Masjid Moth)
New Delhi - 110 048, India
Telephone: 91 11 6445521
Facsimile: 91 11 6425799
E-mail: dpsingh.ecsnth@eicher.sprintrpg.sprint.com.

CHAPTER 14

Improving the Profitability of Canadian Book Publishers: An Example of the Application of Performance Measurement and Benchmarking at Both the Firm and Sector Level

Harvey S. W. Goodwin, President, Charles E. Napier Company Ltd.

Prologue

This case will describe a process that has been developed in Canada to provide competitive performance information to Canadian manufacturing and service firms and to develop sector-specific operating models that maximize firm-level performance. The process itself draws on all of the available tools for information gathering and analysis, one of which is benchmarking.

The process begins with a detailed performance audit of a group of firms in an industrial sector. The audit measures firm-level performance and develops a set of sector-specific performance objectives. By comparing each participant's actual performance to the objectives, it is then possible to identify its areas of competitive weakness and recommend remedial action.

Where there are common areas of weakness across a number of participants, external benchmarking studies are arranged to audit the performance of selected state-of-the-art operating practices. The performance objectives generated from these studies are then used to develop firm-level performance improvement plans for the study participants. This information is also used to identify sector-level problem areas and to develop new sector operating models.

Acquiring and Using Competitive Performance Information

To survive in any market requires

- A knowledge of what the customer wants
- A knowledge of the options available to the customer
- A knowledge of the weighting the customer puts on each of the five competitive factors: price, design, quality, delivery, and service

With this knowledge a business should then be able to

• Design products or services to meet its customers' requirements.

• Provide a level of quality to meet its customers' expectations.

• Sell at a competitive price.

• Provide a level of service and delivery that is equal to or better than its competition.

In the real world, however, life, unfortunately, is not that simple. Each competitive factor is related to—and to a large degree dependent on—one or more of the others. Thus, product design, quality, and price are directly related. Delivery and service are also related to price. These factors are also related to the production processes used, to the equipment used, to the materials used, to labor productivity, to sales and marketing strategies, and to all of the other variables that must be controlled in any business.

Knowledge of the competition. While management may have some knowledge of the competition at the market level, managers almost certainly will not have any knowledge of their competitors' operations. Therefore, in attempting to meet their competition, they may well have to modify both their products and their production processes without any comparative information from other suppliers producing similar products. In today's world of intense competition this is a formidable task for any management.

The process of management is, to a major degree, the art of balancing trade-offs. Labor costs must be traded off against investment in equipment and automation. Delivery response and service levels must be traded off against inventory levels of both materials and finished product. Product design and quality must be traded off against manufacturing costs, which in turn relate to the sales price and to profitability.

In any industry sector the most successful companies are those that have made the best overall trade-offs. If the other firms in the sector knew more about these leaders, those other firms could also be more competitive. This would lead to increased demand and market growth.

Thus the information that is most valuable to management is almost certainly comparative operating data. For obvious reasons this is also the most difficult information to obtain. The process of benchmarking was developed as a means of obtaining comparative operating process information from both competitors and, in certain cases, from firms in other industry sectors using similar processes. Benchmarking has great value at the process level but has only limited value at the corporate level.

Generating reliable competitive performance information. The Canadian government introduced an industrial sector performance evaluation process over 20 years ago. The evaluation methodology was developed by the UK government to address the need for industrial renewal after World War II and was later made available to Canada. This methodology was used to develop a performance auditing service called the Interfirm Comparison Program (IFC), which has been operated continuously by the Department of Industry.

IFC studies are sector focused and address 20 to 30 manufacturers or service providers in the same industry sector. Detailed financial and operating information is collected during on-site interviews. This information, after adjustment and normalization, is used to generate a range of performance ratios and to benchmark selected operating practices. The performance ratio results of all participants are then used to generate a set of sector-specific performance objectives. Each participant's performance is then evaluated against these objectives and from this its areas of comparative strength and weakness are identified. Recommendations are then developed to address each participant's areas of weakness. An IFC study report is prepared for each participant and delivered to it during a final on-site briefing.

All IFC studies are carried out by qualified consultants on contract to the Department of Industry. The Charles E. Napier Company has done 10 such studies since 1987.

Information provided by the IFC program. The unique value to management of the IFC program is that it addresses performance at all levels of the business and provides comparative performance information from a substantial group of competitors. In addition, because of the way the data are presented, it ensures complete confidentiality of source information. The performance areas addressed are as follows:

- Return on assets
- Profit margin and asset turnover
- Production costs (materials, labor, overhead)
- Operating expense (sales, marketing, administration)
- Asset utilization (current and fixed assets)
- Labor productivity (staff and production labor)
- Space utilization (office and manufacturing space)
- Production equipment utilization (per employee and per square foot)
- Value added (time, space, investment)

Management is provided with the following:

- An in-depth evaluation of performance in all areas of the business
- Identification of the organization's areas of comparative weakness
- A set of achievable performance objectives
- Recommendations for actions to improve performance
- A set of sector-specific performance objectives

Thus, managers receive a range of detailed comparative performance information that they can use to modify their operating practices so as to be more competitive.

The IFC program has so far addressed over 90 industrial sectors and over 4000 firms. After the first evaluation, sectors are usually reevaluated every three to four years.

Identifying and benchmarking external state-of-the-art operating practices. Where an IFC study identifies one or more process areas that are weak across a number of the participants, and where the participants would like to benchmark the processes against the state-of-the-art, a group benchmarking trip is then organized. These trips normally involve five to 10 Canadian firms. Ten to 15 selected firms in the same industry sector, usually in Europe, are then visited. The consultants prepare all of the information-gathering instruments, identify and arrange for the visits to the firms to be benchmarked, arrange for transportation and accommodations, and lead the visit. The actual on-site information gathering is done by the Canadian participants during the visit.

After returning from the visit, the consultants prepare a comprehensive visit report covering each of the firms visited. The consultants also develop performance benchmarks based on the operating results obtained. Operating practices are documented and best practices identified. In addition, all production processes are photographed, and copies are included in the visit reports provided to the participants.

Meeting global competition. With the advent of the Canada/U.S. Free Trade Agreement, it soon became obvious that, in many sectors, the competitive factors in the Canadian marketplace were being established by imports. To increase the value of the IFC program, mirror studies are now routinely carried out mainly in the United States to provide Canadian industry with comparative U.S. performance. Ten cross-border studies have been done so far, nine in the United States and one in Europe. These studies have provided Canadian industry with detailed performance information about the manufacturers of the imports their products compete with in Canada. They have also provided the U.S. and European participants (as a quid pro quo) with an evaluation of their performance as compared to the other participants in their industry sector and with a general comparison of their performance to that of like firms in Canada and the United States.

The result has been that Canadian industry has been made aware, in detail, of the performance levels of its competition. In some cases the Canadians found that they were more than cost competitive but were weak in marketing their products in export markets. Others were able to identify those areas of their operation where performance would have to be improved if they were to compete successfully. In some cases, Canadian firms found they were performing at levels above both their domestic and foreign competition.

Some industry associations annually publish comparative performance statistics. These are generally based on financial report-level information and provide a range of accounting-type ratios for the sector as a whole. While this level of information is of general interest, it is of little value to managers who have to make detailed decisions about what they will have to improve and by how much to ensure that they can meet their competition. The IFC program is the only source of reliable sector-level performance information available in Canada.

This case will describe how the IFC methodology was initially applied to the Canadian book publishing industry in 1991 and the performance information it generated. It will then describe a follow-on benchmarking study of state-of-the-art book fulfillment operations, which took place in 1992–1993. This, in turn, led to a follow-on IFC study of this sector, which was done in 1995–1996. This study also involved a group of Canadian booksellers in that the consultants felt that to better understand the sector operating model it was very important to evaluate how the book publishers' products and services were seen by their clients—the booksellers.

The findings from this second IFC study led to a second benchmarking trip to evaluate booksellers' management practices and publishers' fulfillment practices. The case will conclude with a discussion of the problems facing the Canadian book publishing/bookselling industry sector and the actions that must be taken to address them and thus generate a more efficient operating model.

1991 Interfirm Comparison Study of Canadian Book Publishers

Purpose of the Study

For some time, the Charles E. Napier Company had been aware of the problems facing Canadian book publishers. The Canadian market is relatively small compared to many other countries, which means that Canadian publishers can not justify the size of print runs and thus take advantage of the economies of scale that are common in the United States and Europe. Most Canadian publishers are located in Toronto and Montreal, which means that many books have to be shipped halfway across the country, both east and west. Because of Canada's two official languages, it effectively has two separate markets. All of this contributes to higher costs and thus to lower profitability.

The federal government, to promote the publishing of Canadian authors, has operated a relatively generous grant program for Canadian publishers. This, however, has come under pressure as the government fights to control deficit.

In the spring of 1991 the Charles E. Napier Company made a proposal to the Canadian Book Publishers' Council, one of the two industry associations, that the company carry out an IFC study of a representative group of the council's members. Its membership generates about 85 percent of the book sales in Canada but only represents about 15 percent of Canadian publishers. The purpose of the study would be to measure individual firm-level performance, to develop sector-specific performance objectives, and to use these to identify each participant's areas of comparative weakness. In addition, this information would be used to identify sector-level problem areas. It was agreed that the study should begin as soon as possible and should be based on the participant's 1990 financial results. The association agreed to recruit the study participants.

Characteristics of the Study Participants

A total of 18 firms participated in the study. Nine of the participating firms were owned in Canada, six in the United States, and three in the United Kingdom.

Total sales of all participants in 1990, the year chosen for the study, was $403 million. Within the group, the highest level of net sales reported was $40.6 million and the lowest was $1.7 million. Two firms had sales below $10 million; five between $10 million and $20 million; eight between $20 million and $30 million; and one above $40 million.

The Study Team

All work was carried out by Harvey Goodwin and William Lemmon of Charles E. Napier Company Ltd., during the second half of 1991. Each participant assigned a senior member of its management to be the contact point with its staff.

Study Methodology

Phase 1: Familiarization. To be effective, each IFC study must be designed around the operating practices of the industry sector. The most effective way of acquiring operating practice knowledge is to spend time in one or more of the participant's operations. To facilitate this, a small advisory group of four of the chief financial officers of the participating companies was formed. They, in turn, arranged for the group to spend time with selected participants so as to expose the group to each of the market areas served; namely, school, college, trade, mass market paperback (MMPB), and professional and reference. In addition the group explored the many differences between indigenous publishing and agency sales. In Canada, individual publishers represent offshore publishers as agents, whereby they stock and sell their books either for a commission or fee, or as principals where they buy and sell in their own name.

From the information gathered during this familiarization phase, the consultants realized that to provide a valid performance comparison between participants they would have to generate performance information not only at the corporate level but also at each of the market levels for both indigenous publishing and agency sales. They would also have to provide performance information at the total indigenous and total agency levels.

Again, based on the findings from the familiarization phase, the consultants developed 44 performance ratios covering all phases of the book publishing business (see Figure 14.1). Also, 19 specific operating practices, for which benchmarking information could be collected, were identified.

Phase 2: Development of information-gathering instruments. All information was collected during site visits to the participants. To facilitate this process, the consultants developed an interview guideline with specific questions covering all areas of interest. These questions cover both qualitative information about operating practices and quantitative information to supplement the participant's financial data. Financial statements and a set of cost center expense printouts were also collected.

A. Return on assets

A-1	Operating profit/operating assets	%

B. Profit margin and asset turnover

B-1	Operating profit/net sales	%
B-2	Gross profit/net sales	%
B-3	Operating expense/net sales	%
B-4	Net sales/operating assets	Times
B-5	Net sales/inventory	Times

C. Book production costs

C-10	Book production	
C-11	Total production costs/net sales	%
C-14	Purchased books/net sales	%
C-15	Net book sales/gross sales + returns	%
C-20	Returns/gross sales	%

D. Operating expense

D-20	Fulfillment	
D-21	Fulfillment costs/gross sales + returns	%
D-22	Fulfillment costs/gross sales	%
D-23	Fulfillment costs/net sales	%
D-24	Fulfillment labor/gross sales + returns	%
D-25	Fulfillment labor/gross sales	%
D-26	Fulfillment labor/net sales	%
D-30	IFC depreciation/net sales	%
D-31	$1000 gross sales + returns/employee	$'000
D-32	$1000 gross sales + returns/square foot	$'000
D-33	Labor costs/hours worked	$
D-40	Administration	
D-41	Administration costs/net sales	%
D-42	Salary and benefits/net sales	%
D-43	$1000 net sales/employee	$'000
D-50	Sales and marketing	
D-51	Sales and marketing costs/net sales	%
D-52	Salaries and commissions/net sales	%
D-53	Travel/net sales	%
D-54	Advertising and promotion/net sales	%
D-55	Complimentaries/net sales	%
D-56	$1000 Net sales/employee	$'000

Figure 14.1. 1990 performance ratios for Canadian book publishers.

E. General		
E-10	Annual net sales increasing (decreasing)	%
E-11	$1000 net sales/total employee	$'000
E-12	Value added/total hours worked	$
E-13	Value added/square foot	$
F. Asset utilization		
F-10	Total operating assets/$1000 net sales	$
F-11	Current assets/$1000 net sales	$
F-12	Inventory/$1000 net sales	$
F-13	Accounts receivable/$1000 net sales	$
F-14	Accounts receivable	Days net sales
F-16	Fixed operating assets/$1000 sales	$
F-17	Capacity utilization (net sales)	%

Figure 14.1. *(Continued).*

The questions in the interview guideline are grouped by corporate function so as to minimize demands on managers' time. Figure 14.2 shows the 1990 interview guide.

Phase 3: Development of the data analysis program. A spreadsheet-based data analysis program was developed specifically for each sector evaluated, because many of the performance ratios are sector-specific and the levels at which the performance ratios are calculated may be very different. As this study was done in 1991, Plan Perfect in DOS was used as the spreadsheet program.

Phase 4: Information gathering. All information was gathered during interviews with senior managers in their offices. In this study, all 18 participants were in the Toronto area. The interviews typically took four to five hours to complete. It was essential that all senior functional managers be involved, as it was this group that would have to address the firm's problems when they were identified.

Phase 5: Data analysis, normalization, and input. To ensure that all of the performance ratios are based on comparable data, much of the financial information received had to be normalized. In doing this,

- The costs of all fixed assets are brought to current value.
- Rented buildings are capitalized at 10 times the annual lease value.
- A common depreciation schedule is used for all classes of fixed assets and replaces the firm's depreciation rates.
- All costs associated with borrowed capital are removed.

Company code:

Interview date:

Interviewer:

1.0 General information

1.1 Is your company **beneficially owned** in Canada, and is it a public company or is it privately owned? If your parent is a book publisher, what are your agency terms regarding costs, price, returns, and corporate overhead allocation?

1.2 Please describe your **management organization** and the distinct areas of responsibility within your company.

1.3 How do you **review the performance** of your company? Is this done on an overall basis?

1.4 How would you describe the **business that you are in?**

1.5 What is your policy for the **write-off of royalty advances?**

1.6 What is your policy for the **write-off of inventory?**

1.7 Have you any **problems finding and hiring** qualified personnel, and if yes in what areas in particular?

1.8 What would be your **average annual turnover** of staff?

1.9 Is your company **unionized?**

1.10 What **hours are worked** by your staff in terms of hours per day, days per week, and weeks per year?

1.11 Do you work and **pay for overtime,** and if so what percentage would this represent per year?

1.12 Have you received **government funding** support in the past, and if so from which levels of government and from what programs?

1.13 What **role** do you feel the **government should play** in the publishing industry in the future?

1.14 Would you list the **major problems** that you see facing the publishing business in Canada?

1.15 How many **equivalent full-time employees** did you have in your last fiscal year by department?

Publishing	Administration
Editorial	Sales and marketing
Fulfillment	

2.0 Sales and marketing

2.1 Please describe how your **books are marketed by market area?**

2.2 What **information systems** do you have in place to monitor how your books are selling?

2.3 What **information do** these systems provide, and how **current** is the information when you receive it?

2.4 How is this **information used** when you receive it?

2.5 How do you **price** your books in each of your market areas?

Figure 14.2. Interview guideline for Canadian publishing industry 1990 IFC study.

2.6 What is your **policy on delivery of books?** Do you pay for delivery and if so how? Is this shown as a separate charge or is it included in the price? What is your practice in each market area?

2.7 Are you satisfied with the way you are now **marketing and selling** your product? Do you see any changes coming in this area?

2.8 What percentage of your **sales by market areas are exported** from Canada, and to what countries?

2.9 Are your **marketing and sales practices** in the export market any different to those in Canada, and if so please explain by market area?

2.10 What limitations by market area do you see to **growth in the Canadian market?**

2.11 What limitations by market areas do you see to **growth in the export market?**

2.12 There are a number of **competitors to the written book** appearing, being video and audiocassettes, software programs, and CD-ROM. What role will these products play in the future, and will they compete directly with books or rather expand the overall market for information?

2.13 What is your policy on **advertising and promotion** with respect to corporate image and individual titles? How do you evaluate its usefulness? How do you carry out these functions?

2.14 How do you physically provide an **acceptable level of service** to your clients across the country in terms of reasonable delivery times for product? Do you treat your own books any differently from agency books?

2.15 Do you use **telemarketing** and if so in what markets? What success have you had and approximately how much would this cost in terms of a percentage of net sales?

2.16 In the college and school markets, do you use **consultants** to provide on-site expertise as a means of providing customer service? If you do has this been successful, and how much does this cost in terms of a percentage of net sales by market area?

2.17 Do you produce a catalogue of your school and/or college books and their associated support material? What is the cost? How many catalogs are produced?

2.18 Do you provide free copies of school or college books? If you do, what is your policy and what are your costs?

2.19 Do you provide desk copies for schools and colleges, and if so what is your policy and what are your costs?

2.20 What is your discount policy for school and college books? Is a discount given on the list price or the net price?

2.21 What is the sales life of each market category of book you produce?

3.0 Editorial

3.1 In what areas do you subcontract work out to others such as printing, editorial, graphics, and so on?

3.2 Do you see the availability of new systems such as desktop publishing altering the way you now do business, and if so how?

3.3 Do you generate the graphics for your covers, etc., in-house, and if so what equipment are you using?

Figure 14.2. *(Continued).*

3.4   Can you estimate the approximate breakdown of your total editorial costs into **development,** which would cover the cost of manuscript creation, **copy,** which covers the costs involved in making the manuscript printable, and finally **R&D,** which covers the costs of verifying the validity of the developed manuscript?

3.5   What is your policy for the write-off of film and plates and does this vary by market area?

3.6   What is your policy toward **piloting new school book/systems?** What would be your average cost over a three-year period?

4.0   Publishing

4.1   How many **books did you print** in the last year?

4.2   How many **books did you purchase** on an agency basis in the last year by market area?

4.3   What were your **gross sales** in terms of **number of books** in your last fiscal year by market area?

4.4   From these gross sales how many **books** were **returned** by market area?

4.5   How many titles **did you publish** in your last fiscal year by market area?

4.6   Of the total number of **titles published** in your last fiscal year how many of these **produced a profit,** and what was the average profit per title by market area?

4.7   Similarly, how many titles **generated a loss,** and what was the average loss per title by market area?

4.8   Who is held **responsible** for the **profit/loss** resulting from your publishing activities?

4.9   Do you prepare some form of **business plan** for each book that you publish, and if so how is this plan monitored and by whom?

4.10   What procedure do you follow that results in your **decision to publish a new book?** Does this vary by market area?

4.11   How do you manage the **printing** of the books that you publish?

4.12   In the event that you purchase a quantity of a book for resale what would be the **normal purchase terms?**

4.13   What are the **terms for** the **purchase of books** on an **agency** basis? Do you pay for the quantity that you buy each time you buy? Can you get books on consignment? Are you paid a commission or do you buy at a discount? What are the normal payment terms? What is the procedure for the disposal of overage?

4.14   What is your **policy for giving advances** to authors?

4.15   Are there any actions that you have taken in the last year to improve your level of **productivity,** and if so what were they?

4.16   Do you see an opportunity to introduce **computer-based systems** into your business to improve performance, and if so where?

4.17   What percentage of your indigenous books are **adapted versions** of acquired books? How do costs of adapted books compare to those of indigenous?

4.18   Of the total number of books sold last year how many were **presold?** Please provide figures for indigenous and agency and by market area.

Figure 14.2. *(Continued).*

5.0 Fulfillment

5.1 Do you **contract out** any of your **fulfillment,** or do you contract to do fulfillment for other publishers? If so what are the terms, who is responsible within your organization, and how is this managed?

5.2 What would be your **average turnaround** time on orders, and what would be your longest and shortest time?

5.3 Can you break down your total fulfillment costs into **customer service and pick-pack and ship** on a percentage basis by market area?

6.0 Management information systems

6.1 What **statistics** do you produce for your managers on a regular basis that provide them with information on the overall operation of the company?

6.2 How is this **information used?**

6.3 Is your **management system computerized,** and if so please describe what functions are now computer based and which functions you intend to computerize in the future.

Figure 14.2. *(Continued).*

- All income and expenses not directly associated with publishing are removed.
- Any extraordinary expense is questioned and adjusted where justified.
- All government grants are removed.

Certain costs have to be adjusted on an individual firm basis to ensure comparability. These include the following:

- Grouped occupancy costs, where necessary, are allocated by function.
- Where fulfillment or other functions have been contracted out, the associated costs are broken down into the normal cost categories and applied to each of the markets served.
- Where particular markets are not included in the study because of too few participants (minimum of three), their associated sales and expenses are calculated and included in the corporate-level totals.
- MIS costs are collected and allocated to the MIS function wherever possible.

After completing the normalization, each firm's information is inputted into the data analysis program, and the resulting financial statements are checked for consistency. This information is then transferred to the performance ratio module, and performance ratios are developed for each market level for each firm. These are also checked for consistency. The ratios are then transferred to the appropriate spreadsheets for each market for indigenous publishing and agency sales, for total indigenous publishing, for total agency sales, and for total corporate. Finally, all ratio results on all spreadsheets are ranked from best to worst to protect the confidentiality of the information. The final task is to highlight each participant's results on each level of spreadsheet.

Phase 6: Development of internal performance objectives. A performance objective should provide a performance target that, if met, would place the firm among the top players in its market area. The objective levels were set at the bottom of the first quartile of all results for a particular ratio after ranking from best to worst. Thus, there are always 25 percent of the participants who exceed every performance objective.

Phase 7: Firm-level performance evaluation. Having developed the sector-specific performance objectives, the actual performance of each participant is then evaluated against the objectives. Any ratio result that is below an objective is highlighted as being an area of competitive weakness. Having also benchmarked many of the operating practices, it is usually possible to identify one or more reasons for the below-objective performance. Where this can be done, recommendations are developed for remedial action that will result in performance improvement.

Phase 8: Preparation of participant study reports. Participant study reports have three sections. The first covers the evaluation of the participant's performance as compared to the sector-specific performance objectives and includes recommendations for performance improvement. The second provides an overview of the study group's operating practices. The third is an appendix that includes all of the applicable performance ratio spreadsheets, the participant's input data after normalization and adjustment, the performance objectives, and a definition of the terms used in the report.

Summary of the Study Findings

It is difficult and dangerous to generalize on the overall performance of the book publishing sector in that each book publisher sells a different mixture of products in different volumes to different markets. It is a common belief in the industry that agency reselling is required to subsidize indigenous publishing. While there were cases in the study where this was true, there were others where the opposite was true. If there was a common thread, it was that successful participants were successful in all product and market areas whereas those who were less successful were less successful in most if not all areas. The problems encountered could be more attributed to management than to markets.

Based on performance comparisons at the total company level, the most successful participant generated an overall return on operating assets of 38.5 percent. This is a respectable level of return in almost any industry sector. The highest overall return on sales was 19.8 percent, again an enviable level of performance. The objective performance levels for these ratios were 13.7 percent and 9.3 percent. These levels would suggest that, in very general terms, the industry should be seen as being financially attractive. To make more meaningful comparisons, however, a move down to the individual market level is necessary.

The trade market would seem to involve the greatest amount of risk in that each book published is a completely new venture. The risk may be reduced somewhat if the author is already recognized and successful. The basic drive in this market, however, is to discover the new author who will become successful under the publisher's banner.

Trade publishing involves a constant search for, and evaluation of, new works. When a decision is taken to publish a book, the author is contracted and in some cases is paid an advance on the royalties to be earned on future sales. The number of books to be printed, or the print run as it is referred to in the industry, is based on a calculated guess as to the potential sales volume. As the shelf life of trade publications is anything from a month to several years, the initial volume of sales is very important in terms of paying back the upfront investment in royalty advances and production and marketing costs.

The objective level of return on assets for the trade market including sales of both indigenous and agency books was 9.5 percent, and the objective for return on sales was 6.9 percent. Similar figures for indigenous sales were 11.8 percent and 13.2 percent, while those for agency sales were 6.2 percent and 5.9 percent. This would suggest that the overall trade market is reasonably healthy and that the indigenous market was slightly more attractive than the agency market.

The school market is unique in that most books are developed to meet the defined requirements of a provincial department of education or regional school board. Individual books in most cases are developed as part of an overall academic program in a particular subject area and are developed for the publisher by selected authors under contract. The upfront development costs are substantial, but because of the defined requirement, the identified client, and the life of most school book programs, the overall level of risk is considerably lower than for trade publishing.

In this area, the objective return on assets was 18.0 percent and on sales was 14.7 percent. This is obviously a profitable market area. At the indigenous level, the objectives were 13.3 percent and 13.2 percent, and at the agency level they were 55.6 percent and 30.8 percent.

The college and university market has characteristics again different from other markets. These books can be texts or reference books. Texts are generally written by a single professor or group of professors in the subject area and are offered to publishers for publication. Reference books are again written by experts in the subject area and are acquired for publication by royalty contract. In this market, books are sold to university and college bookstores, and titles generally have a relatively long life expectancy. The objective return on assets in this area was 20.7 percent and on sales was 15.7 percent. The objective return on indigenous assets was 29.6 percent and on sales was 16.2 percent. In the agency section of the market, the objective return on assets was 28.9 percent and on sales was 17.9 percent.

The MMPB market is again very different from the others in that books are sold through a wide range of retailers and titles have a life expectancy from days to several months. There are, of course, the Dr. Spock-type books that seem to have an unlimited life. Most paperbacks are reprints of hardcovers although some new titles are being published in paperback form to reduce their cost and increase their sales volume. This is a volume market that works on substantially reduced margins. The objective return on assets was 12.9 percent and on sales was 6.7 percent. At the indigenous level the objective return was not calculated as there were too few study participants in this market area to allow for a meaningful comparison to be made. At the agency level the benchmark return on assets was 24.8 percent while the comparable return on sales was 13.1 percent.

While two firms produced professional and reference books, the volume was only marginal. Thus, comparisons were not done.

As a group, the 18 firms in the study generated a combined operating profit of $20.2 million ($27 million Canadian). Had they met all of the performance objectives identified in the study, their combined operating profit would have been $52.3 million ($70 million Canadian). Thus, while the sector as a whole is profitable, it has an opportunity to improve its level of profitability by 159 percent.

Firm-level Problem Areas Identified by the Study

While the overall level of return on assets and sales was generally satisfactory, there were a number of operating areas where performance could be substantially improved. These areas included the following:

- Inventory control
- Production/editorial costs for indigenous books
- Fulfillment costs
- Sales and marketing costs
- Royalty costs
- Advertising and promotional costs
- Book return levels especially in trade
- Accounts receivable levels

The problems in most of these areas were the result of inadequate planning and control and the lack of meaningful objective setting. The performance objectives generated by the study would thus provide management with a basis against which to establish internal performance objectives and to develop action plans to address those areas where performance was found to be below objective level.

Fulfillment costs across the participants varied from a low of 4.8 percent of net sales to a high of 20.3 percent. The comparable results on the basis of gross sales plus returns, or in terms of total books handled, were from a low of 4.0 percent to a high of 19.6 percent. Thus, the relative cost of this function was substantial, and its relative importance varied greatly across participants. In most cases, it was found that participants had overcapacity in this area, which for many was a surprise. Several of the participants, having recognized this, were either already providing a fulfillment service to other publishers or intended to look for opportunities to do so. Thus, fulfillment appeared to offer an excellent opportunity for the publishers to establish a common distribution facility in the Toronto area with satellites in the Maritimes, on the Prairies, and in Vancouver.

1994 External Benchmarking Study of Fulfillment Operations

Study Objective

Having identified fulfillment as both an area of weakness for most of the participants and as an opportunity area for common action within the sector, following the completion of the 1991 IFC study, the advisory group proposed to organize an external fulfillment benchmarking study. The group approached all of the participants who had fulfillment costs above the objective level as well as several other publishers who were not in the 1990 study but who were known to have similar problems. Five firms agreed to participate. The objective of the project was to identify and evaluate advanced book fulfillment technologies that could be used by Canadian book publishers to significantly reduce their costs of fulfillment while increasing their ability to meet the changing requirements of their markets.

Study Participants

Five major Canadian publishers agreed to participate in the study. All were located in the Toronto area.

Establishing Canadian Fulfillment Performance Baselines

To establish a sound basis against which to compare the external performance benchmarks to be generated, a detailed performance analysis of the fulfillment operations of the five participants was first carried out. In doing this, it was found that, because of significant variations in certain operating variables, to generate meaningful performance comparisons, all costs would have to be calculated on the basis of units handled. In this industry, most cost comparisons are based on a percentage of net sales value. As an example of the range in operating variables, the average unit sales value of a book sold by the five publishers went from a low of $2.90 ($3.88 Canadian) to a high of $17.85 ($23.90 Canadian). Returns as a percentage of gross sales went from a low of 2.7 percent to a high of 27.4 percent. The average value per unit of inventory went from a low of $0.66 ($0.88 Canadian) to a high of $5.41 ($7.24 Canadian). For this group, total fulfillment costs went from a low of $0.23 ($0.31 Canadian) to a high of $0.93 ($1.25 Canadian) per unit for gross sales plus returns. At the net sales level, the per unit cost for fulfillment varied from $0.38 ($0.51 Canadian) to $1.27 ($1.70 Canadian).

Organization Visits

It was generally agreed that book fulfillment was most advanced in Europe. Thus a list of European book publishers, book distribution centers, and book wholesalers was developed with the help of the Canadian participants, European book publishers' and booksellers' associations, and the embassies of the Common Market countries located in Ottawa. From this list, 12 firms were selected as having a reputation for excellence in advanced fulfillment technology. All 12 were approached and asked if they would be prepared to host a benchmarking visit. Ten firms agreed; they were

1. Tiptree Book Services Ltd., UK

2. WII Smith Retail, UK

3. Macmillan Distribution, UK

4. International Thompson Publishing Services, UK

5. Bookpoint Ltd., UK

6. Exel Logistics, UK

7. Centraal Boekhuis BV, The Netherlands

8. Koch, Neff & Oetinger & Company, Germany

9. Libri Georg Lingenbrink & Company, Germany

10. VVA-Bertelsmann Distribution, Germany

A trip was then organized for nine representatives of the Canadian publishers to visit these firms during the spring of 1994. To ensure that all of the information required to benchmark the fulfillment operations was gathered, questionnaires for each of the areas to be benchmarked were developed. The questionnaires were assigned to the study participants. They, in turn, gathered the information and returned the completed questionnaires to the visit leader.

All of the firms visited provided a one- to three-hour introduction to their company including a great deal of detailed information on their operating practices, on the equipment they were using, on the products they handled, and on the markets they served. In addition they all answered a barrage of questions during the introduction, during the plant tour, and again in a final briefing session. As much of this information as possible was recorded by the participants and was returned to the visit leader. Many photographs were also taken during the visits. Following the study team's return, a detailed findings report was prepared, and a copy was provided to each of the participants.

Summary of Findings

• All of the fulfillment operations seen were run as independent businesses, some as profit centers, and some as cost centers. They each had their own managements, who in all cases answered to a board of directors. Also, they each had their own individual business plans. This was in sharp contrast to the Canadian scene where the larger publishers operate their own fulfillment facilities as departments of the publishing company.

• It was estimated that a minimum annual sales volume of $74.7 million ($100 million Canadian) would be required to justify a fully automated fulfillment operation.

• Several successful operating models were observed. The first was the publisher-owned independent book distributor. Tiptree, Macmillan, International Thompson, Bookpoint, and Bertelsmann were in this category. The second model was the book publisher/bookseller jointly owned book distributor. Centraal Boekhuis was in this category. The third was the independent book distributor/wholesaler. KNO and Libri were in this category. Finally, Exel Logistics was an independent book distributor that was owned by an international logistics group that expanded into book distribution through the acquisition of its predecessor. Each of these models had the sales volume necessary to justify full automation. This allowed them to offer lower fulfillment costs and a broader range of services than individual publishers would be able to provide on their own.

• Automation was justified on the basis of both reduced fulfillment cost and improved fulfillment service. Both of these factors are critical in the very competitive European market. Improved service covers both reduced delivery times and improved accuracy in the fulfillment process. It was estimated that a mistake cost 10 times as much to rectify as the original fulfillment cost.

• While automation was seen as the obvious route to the future, the problems that are involved with its successful introduction should not be underestimated. Two that were mentioned were the need to radically change the operating culture in the plant and the need to ensure that management has fully bought into the concept before it is brought on-line.

• European book publishers and booksellers collaborate to reduce the overall cost of fulfillment and through better fulfillment service to minimize the total inventory of books in the system.

• Germany and France have legislation to protect the retail price of books. This is monitored and policed by publishers, wholesalers, and distributors.

• Considerable savings have been realized through the consolidation of freight where all of the requirements of individual customers are packaged together rather than shipping individual publisher's books in separate boxes.

• It is important in planning for automation to fully factor in the current and future variables such as the number of orders received, the number of order lines processed, the pattern of units per order line, the number of invoices issued, the number of titles to be held in inventory, and so on. Different combinations of variables will dictate significantly different approaches to the fulfillment processes selected and the equipment used.

• All of the UK firms were using packaged software, although in all cases they had to substantially modify it to meet their own particular requirements. In contrast, all of the continental European firms had developed their own software. The consensus would appear to be to develop software in-house if the capability exists.

• None of the European firms used carousels although several said that they were considering their use for backlist books.

• Three of the firms used sorters. Another firm had a sorter on order. There was not a clear consensus as to the best application of this technology.

• Four of the firms were using cartons with internal poly sheets that were shrink wrapped around the books before the cartons were lidded. While this avoided the use of dunnage many of the stores complained about the difficulty of reusing the box.

• All of the automation seen was based on a centralized computer-based warehouse management system. The corollary to this practice is that if it is to be successful, all plant operations must be controlled by the computer. This requires considerable retraining at all staff levels.

• Three firms were shipping product in plastic returnable totes, thus reducing their shipping material cost and reducing the need for recycling of used cartons.

• All firms measured the dimensions and the weight of all books as they were received and used this information to determine carton sizes for specific orders and to verify pick accuracy by weight.

• The concept of the fulfillment facility acting as a "data warehouse" for the publishers was promoted by one firm. It provided its publishers with statistical information to assist them to cross-sell and up-sell their titles.

• One firm operated what it called "virtual publishers." These were sales agencies to which the firm sent the smaller publishers who came to the firm for fulfillment services. Rather than handle them as individual companies they were treated as groups and contracted at the agency level.

• Most of the bookstores in Europe have electronic point-of-sale terminals.

• If European fulfillment technology were applied in Canada, fulfillment costs could be reduced from 35 percent to 50 percent.

Applying these findings to the Canadian book publishing industry the following conclusions were drawn.

• By providing European-style, just-in-time fulfillment services to Canadian booksellers, it should be possible to reduce returns by up to 70 percent.

• By encouraging Canadian booksellers to routinely provide their publishers with detailed sales information, it should be possible to substantially improve overall inventory management.

Benefits Derived From the Visits

• On their return, all of the Canadian publishers introduced some of the fulfillment practices seen during the European visit.

• Together, two publishers have established a common fulfillment facility in Ontario that is fully automated and is based on the layout of the Exel Logistics plant visited in the United Kingdom. The Canadian facility has been set up as a separate corporation with its own management group. The publishers' intention is to offer a full range of logistics services to other Canadian publishers.

The 1995 IFC Study of Canadian Book Publishers

Early in 1994 the Canadian Book Publishers' Council again approached the Charles E. Napier Company to do a second IFC study. This time, however, the council asked the company to recruit participants. It was agreed that the study would address the 1994–1995 financial year.

Characteristics of the Participants

Fourteen firms agreed to participate in this study. Eight of them had participated in the previous IFC study.

Total sales of all participants in the 1994–1995 study was $294 million. The highest level of sales reported was $56 million and the lowest was $1 million. Four firms had sales below $10 million; three were between $10 million and $20 million; one was between $20 million and $30 million; and five were above $30 million.

The Study Team

This study was again carried out by Harvey Goodwin and William Lemmon of Charles E. Napier Company Ltd. during 1994–1995.

Study Methodology

Many of the problems identified in the first IFC study were found to result in a depreciation of customer service. To better evaluate the effect of this on the relationships between the publishers and the bookstores who sold their books, and to further test the findings of the European fulfillment practices benchmarking study, 21 selected bookstores across Canada were interviewed as part of this second IFC study. All the bookstores interviewed were recommended by the study participants.

The remainder of the study methodology was similar to that used in the 1991 study and described in an earlier section. A list of the performance ratios calculated for this study is included in Figure 14.3. The interview guidelines used to gather information from the publishers are included in Figure 14.4, and those used to gather information from the booksellers are shown in Figure 14.5.

A. Return on assets

  A-1   Operating profit/operating assets   %

B. Profit margin and asset turnover

  B-1   Operating profit/net sales   %
  B-2   Gross profit/net sales   %
  B-3   Net sales/operating assets   Times
  B-4   Net book sales/inventory   Times

C. Book production costs

  C-1   Total production expense/net sales   %
  C-2   Paper, print, and binding/net book sales   %
  C-3   Royalty expense/net sales   %
  C-4   Purchased books/net book sales   %
  C-5   Net book sales/gross book sales + returns   %
  C-6   Returns/gross book sales   %
  C-7   Inventory write-down/inventory   %

D. Publishing/editorial

  D-1   Total publishing and editorial expense/net sales   %

E. Fulfillment

  E-1   Fulfillment expense/gross book sales + returns   %
  E-2   Fulfillment expense/net book sales   %
  E-3   Fulfillment labor/gross book sales + returns   %
  E-4   Fulfillment labor/net book sales   %
  E-5   Net delivery expense/gross book sales   %
  E-6   Material expense/net book sales   %
  E-7   IFC depreciation/net book sales   %
  E-8 $1000 gross book sales + returns/employee $'000
  E-9   Gross book sales + returns/square foot $
  E-10 Labor expense/hours worked $

F. Administration

  F-1   Administration expense/net sales   %
  F-2   Salaries and benefits/net sales   %
  F-3 $1000 net sales/employee $'000

G. MIS

  G-1   MIS expense/net sales   %
  G-2   Salaries and benefits/net sales   %
  G-3 $1000 net sales/employee $'000

Figure 14.3. 1994 performance ratios for Canadian book publishers.

H. Sales and marketing

H-1	Sales and marketing expense/net sales	%
H-2	Salaries, benefits, and commissions/net sales	%
H-3	Travel expense/net sales	%
H-4	Advertising and promotion/net sales	%
H-5	Complimentaries and gratis/net sales	%
H-6	$1000 net sales/employee	$'000

I. Corporate

I-1	Capacity utilization (gross book sales + returns)	%
I-2	Annual net sales increase (decrease)	%
I-3	$1000 net sales/employee	$'000
I-4	Value-added/hours worked	$
I-5	Value-added/square foot	$

J. Asset utilization

J-1	Total operating assets/$1000 net sales	$
J-2	Current assets/$1000 net sales	$
J-3	Inventory/$1000 net book sales	$
J-4	Accounts receivable/$1000 net sales	$
J-5	Accounts receivable	Days net sales
J-6	Capitalized prepublication expense/$1000 net sales	$
J-7	Fixed operating assets/$1000 net sales	$

Figure 14.3. *(Continued).*

1.0 Corporate information

    1.1 In which country is the majority of the ownership of your company held?

    1.2 Is the company publicly of privately owned (annual report)?

    1.3 Is your company unionized?

2.0 Sales

    2.1 What percentage of your agency sales are on the following basis?

        Purchase for resale/no returns   %

        Purchase for resale/returns   %

        Consignment/commission   %

    2.2 If you have return privileges with your agency suppliers what are their terms?

    2.3 How do you treat agency sales revenues and costs in your accounts?

    2.4 What services do you provide to your agency suppliers in terms of total agency sales?

        Sales services   %

        Marketing services   %

        Fulfillment services   %

        Invoicing services using your invoices   %

        Invoicing services using their invoices   %

        Collection services   %

        MIS information   %

        Other services   %

    2.5 How do you monitor the sales of those books for which you provide return privileges?

    2.6 Do you make any effort to manage your clients' inventory levels of those books for which you offer return privileges, and if so how?

    2.7 What is your returns policy by market? What percent of returns are covers only?

    2.8 Have you any system for preapproving returns at your clients' locations before they are shipped back, and if so how does it work?

    2.9 In that returns are a major expense to the publisher in some markets, what can the industry do, if anything, to reduce or eliminate them?

    2.10 What is your policy covering the payment of freight on sales?

    2.11 Do you export any of your indigenous books, and if so to which countries and on what terms (agency vs. direct sales)? What percentage of your book sales are exported?

    2.12 Do you sell subsidiary rights to other publishers outside of Canada, and if so please provide details?

    2.13 Who is responsible in your organization for export sales, and how is this function staffed?

    2.14 Do you exhibit your books at trade fairs in Canada and/or abroad, and if so please provide details?

    2.15 Canadian book publishers do not appear to export many books compared to the number we import. Why is this, and is there anything that could be done to increase exports?

Figure 14.4. Interview guidelines for an interfirm comparison study of Canadian book publishers for the 1994 financial year.

2.16 In your view is there a need for a wholesale book industry in Canada? If yes, please explain what advantages it offers and how it affects your sales.

2.17 How have you used computer technology to increase the efficiency and effectiveness of your sales function?

3.0 Marketing

3.1 For which markets do you produce catalogs?

3.2 Do you now or have you considered putting your catalogs on disk, CD-ROM, or on-line?

3.3 Do you do any telemarketing, and if so into which markets?

For your indigenous books

For purchased agency books

For agency books on consignment (terms)

3.4 If you sell through commissioned sales agents please provide the percentage of sales by market.

Trade	%
School	%
College	%
Professional and reference	%
MMPB	%

3.5 Do you sell to distributors? On what terms do they buy from you? What percentage of your sales are through distributors?

3.6 In your view, is it important to provide a comparable level of service in terms of book delivery and availability to your clients across the country, and if so how do you physically accomplish this? If you do not provide a comparable level of sales, does it affect your sales?

4.0 Production

4.1 Do you track the number of books (units) that are

Printed

Purchased

Consignment-agency

Sold

Returned

Destroyed

4.2 Where do you get your printing done?

Canada	%
United States	%
Other countries/country	%

4.3 Please comment on your experience with the cost, quality, and service of Canadian printers as compared to those in other countries.

4.4 When do you use non-Canadian printers and why?

Figure 14.4. *(Continued).*

4.5   What is included in your preproduction costs?

4.6   What is your policy for writing off your preproduction costs either by capitalizing and amortizing or by expensing in the year incurred?

4.7   What is your policy and practice for writing down inventory?

4.8   How have you used computer technology to improve the efficiency and effectiveness of your production function?

5.0   Editorial

5.1   Do you prepare any form of business plan for each of the books you publish? If yes, how is it used, and is it an effective management tool?

5.2   In which functional areas do you contract out work, and what percentage of the work does this represent?

Manuscript reading

Editing

Graphics

Layout

Other

5.3   How do you establish your royalty levels and the level of advances you give to your authors?

5.4   What is your policy for writing off advances that have not been earned out?

5.5   Do you buy the Canadian publishing rights to books published outside of Canada? If yes, please explain. What percentage of sales would these books represent?

5.6   Do you adapt other publishers' books for the Canadian market? If so please describe. What percentage of sales would these books represent?

5.7   Do you translate any of your own books or any other publisher's books into French, and if so for which markets? What percentage of sales would these books represent?

5.8   Do you publish any works of non-Canadian authors? What percentage of sales would these books represent?

5.9   How have you used computer technology to improve the efficiency and effectiveness of your editorial function?

6.0   MIS

6.1   What MIS functions are included within fulfillment?

6.2   What percentage of your orders are received by

Phone	%
Fax	%
EDI	%
Mail	%
E-mail	%

Figure 14.4. *(Continued).*

7.0 Fulfillment

7.1 Do you contract out your fulfillment? If yes, do you handle your own returns?

7.2 Do you do any contract fulfillment for other publishers? If yes, what services do you provide beyond straight fulfillment?

Marketing and selling

Invoicing and collection

Other

7.3 Do you include with your sales the sales revenue and the book units fulfilled for others?

7.4 When and on what basis do you generate your picking schedules, and can you change a picking schedule once made, and if yes, how?

7.5 What percentage of the books you receive are bar coded?

7.6 Do you use bar coding? If yes, where in the operation? How is this information used? Please describe the monitoring equipment you use.

7.7 How do you check shipments against orders before shipment? What error level did you have in your last year?

7.8 How many people are required to handle your returns? What percentage of warehouse labor hours does this represent?

7.9 On average, how many returns did you handle per labor hour (receiving, inspecting, recording, and restocking)?

7.10 What has been your average order size in terms of lines per invoice and units per line in 1994?

7.11 What has been your average lines picked per hour and your percentage of correct picks?

7.12 What has been your average number of books stocked per hour?

7.13 What computer equipment are you using? Do you operate a LAN?

7.14 What order entry and warehouse management software are you using, and where and when did you acquire it?

7.15 How would you prefer that we address your fulfillment performance? (Choose one)

• We can include your contract sales and returns with your book sales and returns and then develop performance ratios based on your total fulfillment volume.

• We can reduce your fulfillment costs by your contract fulfillment revenues and then develop performance ratios based on your use of *your* fulfillment facilities.

Figure 14.4. *(Continued).*

Firm interviewed: _____

Person interviewed: _____

Location: _____

Interviewer: _____

Interview date: _____

Version date: _____

Note: All weighting will be on a scale of 1 to 10 with 10 being high.

1.0   Corporate information

1.1	Answering as	An independent store	❑
		A store that is owned by a chain	❑
		A store that is a part of a group	❑
		A chain	❑
		A group	❑
1.2	Ownership	Canadian	%
		U.S.	%
		Other	%
1.3	Annual sales in 1994 as a	Retailer	%
		Wholesaler	%
		Distributor	%
1.4	Annual sales in 1994 by market	Total	$
		Trade	$
		School	$
		College	$
		MMPB	$
		Professional and reference	$
1.5	Annual sales in 1994	New books	%
		Remainders	%
1.6	Number of stores in group/chain by geographic area	Maritimes	
		Quebec	
		Ontario	
		Prairies	
		British Columbia	
1.7	Sources of new books sold in 1994	Publishers	%
		Wholesalers	%
		Distributors	%

Figure 14.5. CANPUB 94 book retailers interview guidelines.

1.8 Sources of remaindered books sold in 1994

Publishers	%
Wholesalers	%
Distributors	%
Retailers	%

1.9 Sales value of imported books $

1.10 Value of imported books by source

U.S.	$
UK	$
Europe/other	$
Asia	$
Latin America	$

2.0 Procurement

2.1 Please weight the following criteria as they affect your book buying decisions.

Book promotions (flyers, telemarketing, reps, author tours) ❑

Book appearances (form, size, cover) ❑

Book reviews (Canadian, foreign) ❑

The time of year (summer vs. winter) ❑

Other ❑

2.2 Weight the following criteria in terms of their influence on your selection of the publishers from whom you buy.

The publisher's name and reputation ❑

The authors they publish ❑

The physical appearance of the books ❑

Their book promotion activities ❑

The publisher's list prices ❑

The publisher's terms of sale ❑

The publisher's discount structure ❑

The publisher's delivery history ❑

The publisher's return privileges ❑

The publisher's catalogs ❑

The publisher's sales reps ❑

The publisher's client service capability ❑

2.3 Weight the following criteria in terms of their influence on the number of books of each title you order.

The subject of the book ❑

The author ❑

The unit price ❑

Figure 14.5. *(Continued).*

The publisher's terms of sale	❏
The book's promotion	❏
Book reviews	❏
The sales rep's recommendations	❏
The appearance of the book	❏
The reputation of the publisher	❏
The publisher's delivery history	❏
The publisher's returns policy	❏

2.4 If publishers did not offer return privileges, how would you then weight the same criteria?

The subject of the book	❏
The author	❏
The unit price	❏
The book's promotion	❏
Book reviews	❏
The sales rep's recommendations	❏
The appearance of the book	❏
The reputation of the publisher	❏
The publisher's delivery history	❏

2.5 Weight the following criteria in terms of their influence in your decision as to how many books by title to hold in inventory.

Past sales experience of similar types of books	❏
The publisher's rep's recommendations	❏
The book's unit cost	❏
Your physical space considerations	❏
The publisher's returns policy	❏

2.6 Weight the following criteria in terms of their influence on your decision as to when to return books to their publishers.

The book's weekly sales volume	❏
Shelf space considerations	❏
The book's unit cost	❏
The publisher's returns policy	❏

2.7 What percent of your inventory do you have on display? %

2.8 What percent of your sales are special orders? %

2.9 What percent of your orders do you place by
Mail %
Telephone %
Fax %
EDI %
E-mail %

Figure 14.5. *(Continued).*

2.10 Are purchased books delivered directly to the store or to a central fulfillment warehouse? If the latter, how does the store relate to the warehouse?

2.11 What buying decisions are made at the store level and what centrally?

2.12 What role, if any, do the publishers and their sales representatives play in your buying decisions or in your inventory management practices?

2.13 In what ways could your publishers better support you so that you could decrease your level of returns and your in-store inventory?

2.14 Can you comment on the relationship, if any, between the publisher's delivery times, the quantities you order, and your level of returns?

2.15 In your view, what should be done to reduce the level of returns?

2.16 What difference would a no-returns policy make to your business?

2.17 In the following areas, what do you expect from your publishers?

Delivery	Days from receipt of order
Payment terms	Days
Minimum order size	Books or $

Payment of freight on new books

Payment of freight on returns

Promotional activities (in-store)

Catalogs (markets, updates, paper, and CD-ROM)

Returns policy (time and quantity)

Co-op advertising (conditions and volume)

Rep's experience (services expected)

Frequency of sales calls (in-store, by telephone)

Client services capability (order tracking, returns credit, other)

Telemarketing (to you)

3.0 Sales

3.1 How do you generate your sales statistics (manually, computer, computer/bar code scanner)?

3.2 Which of the following statistics do you generate, and how often are they generated?

	Weekly	Monthly	Yearly
Total sales revenue			
Sales revenue by market			
Sales revenue by publisher			
Sales revenue by title			
Sales revenue by shelf space by title			
Total sales in units			
Sales by title in units			

Figure 14.5. *(Continued).*

3.3 If you are collecting your sales information electronically, what equipment are you using?

Electronic point of sale equipment

Computers (mainframe, PC)

Software

Bar code readers

3.4 What retail sales information do you provide to your publishers, and how often is this provided (sales by title, total sales, returns, units, and $)?

3.5 What additional retail sales information would you be prepared to provide to publishers?

3.6 Have publishers asked you for retail sales information and if so for what specifically?

Figure 14.5. *(Continued).*

Bookseller Survey Findings

The report, "Survey of the Service Requirements and Operating Practices of Canadian Booksellers" was sent to all of the booksellers interviewed, to the Canadian Booksellers Association, to the two associations representing Canadian publishers, to the publishers in the IFC study, and to Industry Canada who had financed the survey. The hypotheses that the consultant team wanted to test with the booksellers were as follows:

• By providing European-style, just-in-time fulfillment services to Canadian booksellers, it should be possible to reduce returns by up to 70 percent.

• By encouraging Canadian booksellers to routinely provide their publishers with detailed sales information, it should be possible to substantially improve overall inventory management.

The conclusions drawn from the survey were as follows:

• The overall performance of the book publishing/bookselling industry in Canada could be substantially improved. Because of the many players involved, however, this was unlikely to happen unless there was a willingness on the part of both publishers and booksellers to work together to address their common problems.

• The critical operating variables for Canadian bookstores were the following:

—Just-in-time fulfillment

—Reliable and responsive service from the publishers

—Publishers' sales representatives who will work with the stores to promote sales

—Competitive book pricing and discounts

—Publishers who research the potential market demand for each of their books before they publish

—Cooperative advertising and promotions with the publishers based on the bookstore's total sales of the publisher's books

To meet the bookstores' requirements, publishers will have to

• Group their fulfillment requirements to generate the sale volume required to justify the fully automated fulfillment operations that can provide just-in-time service.

• Develop a national inventory management system involving regional inventories and centralized inventory management and control.

• Substantially improve customer service to provide accurate, real-time response to client requirements.

• Stock more agency titles so as to provide better order response.

• Reengineer the communications technologies that connect them to the booksellers so as to improve information flow both ways.

• Work with the bookstores to generate a flow of timely sales information on which to base publishing and inventory management decisions.

IFC Study Findings

The principal findings generated from the 1994–1995 IFC study were as follows:

• Operating profit as a percentage of operating assets ranged from a high of 36.6 percent to a low of (–32.6) percent.

• Operating profit as a percentage of net sales ranged from a high of 22.7 percent to a low of (–21.8) percent.

• The total operating profit generated by the 13 firms in the study was $12.3 million ($16.4 million Canadian).

• Returns had increased from the previous study with the median level being 11.5 percent.

• Had all of the firms met all of the performance objectives, their combined operating profit would have been $53.0 million ($70.9 million Canadian). Thus, there was an opportunity to increase overall operating profit by a factor of 3.3. A list of the performance objectives developed for this study is included in Figure 14.6.

• To make the evaluation results of this study more relevant to the participants, for each firm, the increased operating profit it would generate by increasing its actual performance to the level of the performance objective was calculated. The areas in which this additional profit potential was calculated were as follows:

—Labor productivity

• Production—indigenous employees

• Production—agency employees

• Publishing and editorial employees

• Fulfillment

- Administration
- MIS
- Sales and marketing by market area

—Asset utilization
- Total assets
- Current assets
- Inventory
- Accounts receivable
- Fixed operating assets

—Space utilization
- Value added
- Sales per square foot

—Fulfillment performance
- Total expense
- Labor cost
- Delivery expense
- Material expense
- Depreciation
- Sales per employee
- Sales per square foot
- Labor cost per hour worked
- Returns

—Administrative performance
- Total expense
- Salaries and benefits
- Sales per employee

—Production performance
- Total expense
- Purchased books (agency)
- Sales per employee
- Publication and editorial cost (indigenous)

	Performance ratios	Corporate			School			College		
		Indigenous	Agency	Total	Indigenous	Agency	Total	Indigenous	Agency	Total
B-1	Operating profit/net sales				21%	24%		20%	24%	
C-1	Total production cost/ net book sales	50%	53%		43.5%	48%		45%	51%	
C-2	Paper, print, and binding/ net book sales	23%			20.5%			17.5%		
C-3	Royalty expense/ net sales	10%			9%			11%		
C-4	Purchased books/ net book sales		49%			48%			48%	
C-6	Returns/gross book sales			10%	1.5%	1.5%		16%	16%	
C-8	$1000 net sales/production employee—Indigenous	1500								
C-9	$1000 net sales/production employee—Agency		2200							
D-1	Total publishing and editorial expense/net book sales	5%			5%			10%		
D-2	$1000 net indigenous sales/publishing and editorial employee	$ 822 US 1100 C								
E-1	Fulfillment expense/gross book sales + returns			3.2%						
E-2	Fulfillment expense/ net sales			4.5%						
E-3	Fulfillment labor/gross book sales + returns			1.8%						
E-4	Fulfillment labor/net book sales			2.5%						
E-5	Net delivery expense/ gross sales			0.5%						
E-6	Fulfillment material expense/ net book sales			0.3%						
E-7	Fulfillment IFC depreciation/ net book sales			0.8%						
E-8	$1000 gross book sales + returns/fulfillment employee			$1120 US 1500 C						
E-9	Gross book sales + returns/ fulfillment square foot			$635 US 850 C						
E-10	Fulfillment labor expense/ hours worked			$10.08 US 13.50 C						
E-11	$1000 net sales/fulfillment employee			$ 896 US 1200 C						
F-1	Administration expense/ net book sales			5%	5%	5%		5%	5%	
F-2	Administration salaries and benefits/net sales			3.1%						

US = U.S. dollars   C = Canadian dollars

Figure 14.6. Performance objectives for the 1994–1995 study of Canadian book publishers.

Trade			Professional and reference			Juvenile trade			MMPB		
Indigenous	Agency	Total	Indigenous	Agency	Total	Indigenous	Agency	Total	Indigenous	Agency	Total
16%	26%		22%	21%		11%	22%			20.5%	
57%	50%		46%	51%		57%	51%			60%	
29%			20%			38%					
10%			12..5%			15%					
	49%			49%			50%			58%	
16%	16%		8%	8%		5%	5%			28%	
3%			6%			5%					
5%	5%		5%	5%		5%	5%			5%	

US – U.S. dollars   C – Canadian dollars

Figure 14.6. *(Continued.)*

Performance ratios	Corporate			School			College		
	Indigenous	Agency	Total	Indigenous	Agency	Total	Indigenous	Agency	Total
F-3 $1000 net sales/ administration employee			$1867 US 2500 C						
G-3 $1000 net sales/MIC employee			$5975 US 8000 C						
H-1 Sales and marketing expense/net book sales			14%	16%	17%		14%	14%	
H-2 Salaries, benefits, and commissions/net sales			7%	7%	7%		7%	7%	
H-3 Travel expense/net sales			1%	2%	2%		2%	2%	
H-4 Advertising and promotion/ net sales			2.1%	2.1%	2.1%		0.5%	0.5%	
H-5 Complimentaries and gratis/ net sales			1.5%	1.5%	1.5%		2%	2%	
H-6 $1000 net sales/sales and marketing employee			$ 747 US 1000 C						
H-6 $1000 net sales/sales and marketing employee						$448 US 600 C			
H-6 $1000 net sales/sales and marketing employee									$448 US 600 C
H-6 $1000 net sales/sales and marketing employee									
H-6 $1000 net sales/sales and marketing employee									
H-6 $1000 net sales/sales and marketing employee									
I-3 $1000 net sales/total employee			$ 172 US 230 C	$ 149 US 200 C	$ 149 US 200 C		$157 US 210 C	$157 US 210 C	
I-5 Value added/square foot of total area			$ 112 US 150 C						
J-1 Total operating assets/ $1000 net sales			$ 448 US 600 C						
J-2 Current assets/$1000 net sales			$ 235 US 315 C						
J-3 Inventory/$1000 net sales			$ 105 US 140 C						
J-4 Accounts receivable/ $1000 net sales			$ 119 US 160 C						
J-5 Accounts receivable									
J-7 Fixed operating assets/ $1000 net sales			$ 187 US 250 C						
E-2 + G-1 MIS + Fulfillment expense/net book sales				6%	6%		6%	6%	

US = U.S. dollars   C = Canadian dollars

Figure 14.6. *(Continued.)*

Trade			Professional and reference			Juvenile trade			MMPB		
Indigenous	Agency	Total	Indigenous	Agency	Total	Indigenous	Agency	Total	Indigenous	Agency	Total
13%	13%		15%	17%		16%	16%			8.5%	
3.5%	3.5%		7%	7%		7%	7%			3%	
0.6%	0.6%		1%	1%		0.6%	0.6%			0.8%	
3.5%	3.5%		3.5%	3.5%		3.4%	3.4%			2.6%	
-0-	-0-		0.5%	0.5%		-0-	-0-			-0-	
		$672 US 900 C									
					$485 US 650 C						
$224 US 300 C	$224 US 300 C										$ 934 US 1250 C
			$239 US 320 C	$239 US 320 C		$172 US 230 C	$172 US 230 C			$299 US 400 C	
6%	6%		6%	6%		6%	6%			6%	

US = U.S. dollars   C = Canadian dollars

Figure 14.6. *(Continued.)*

—Sales and marketing performance

- Total expense

- Salaries and benefits

- Travel expense

- Advertising and promotion

- Complementaries and gratis

- Sales per employee

The 1995 External Benchmarking Study of the Book Publisher/Bookseller Relationship

Study Objective

The objective of this visit was to evaluate the publisher/bookseller interfaces in four countries in Europe to better understand the particular operating practices they use, which have resulted in their improved operating efficiencies.

Study Participants

Five publishers and eight booksellers participated in the study. The following three Canadian government departments also participated.

1. Industry Canada

2. Canadian Heritage

3. Foreign Affairs and International Trade

Organization Visits

Based on the findings of the 1993 benchmarking study, it was decided to return to Europe as its level of performance appeared to be well above that in Canada and the United States. The primary focus of this visit was to explore in detail the relationships between selected book retailers and the publishers from whom they bought their books. To do this, with the help of several European bookseller associations, visits were arranged to 14 bookstores and three book fulfillment operations. Eight of the bookstores were located in London, two in Amsterdam, three in Paris, and one in Frankfurt. One of the book distribution centers was located in Culemborg in Holland, one in Paris, and one in Gutersloh in Germany. The visit was carried out over two weeks in the spring of 1996.

Summary of Findings

• The relationships between bookstores and publishers are not dissimilar in Europe and in Canada. Europe, however, has an increasing number of large automated fulfillment operations that can, and in most cases do, provide just-in-time service. These may have developed as competition to the larger wholesalers who are setting the standard for fulfillment service. Not having a well-developed book wholesale industry in Canada, its publishers have not had to compete on the basis of fulfillment service.

• Table 14.1 illustrates the fact that short reliable delivery times result in lower levels of returns.

• The level of information that is regularly exchanged between bookstores and publishers is well in excess of that in Canada. This has the result of giving the bookstores more confidence that they can get the information they require when they want it, and it provides the publishers with sales information by title in real time. This, in turn, allows the publishers to better manage their inventories.

• The ultimate in cooperation is Centraal Boekhuis in Holland, which is jointly owned by the Booksellers' and Book Publishers' Associations, and distributes in excess of 80 percent of all books in The Netherlands.

Table 14.1. Short, reliable delivery times result in lower levels of returns.

Country	Bookstore	Delivery, actual	Delivery, desired	Returns
United Kingdom	Books Etc.	2 weeks	1 day	10%–11%
	Stanfords	3 days	1 day	2%
	Dillons	7–10 days	3 days	10%
	Waterstones	2–3 weeks	3–5 days	20%–30%
	Muswell Hill Bookshop	1–2 weeks	1 day	15%
	Compendium Books	1 day	1 day	3%
	Swiss Cottage Books	1–2 days	1–2 days	5%
	Marylebone Books	2 days	2 days	1%–2%
Holland	Athenaeum Boekhandel	1–2 days	1–2 days	5%
	Scheltema Holkema	2 days	1 day	8%
France	Librairie Gallimard	2–10 days	2 days	13%–14%
	Gilbert Jeune Copac	1 day	1 day	12%
	Le Bon Marché	2–3 days	2–3 days	5%
Germany	Hugendubel	1 day	1 day	2%–3%

Benefits Derived from the Visit

• If significant changes are to be made in the book publishing/bookseller relationship in Canada, it will require both groups working together to define a new relationship and then to manage the change process. This trip allowed representatives from both groups to live and work together for two weeks and for both to see the European model at work.

• The information gathered confirmed the direct relationship between fulfillment service levels and returns.

• A subsidiary benefit for the Canadian booksellers was the opportunity to see a broad variety of European bookstores and to be able to discuss their views on floor layout, display techniques, the advantages of providing subsidiary services like a snack bar or a gift wrapping service, their approach to staff training, and similar issues.

Summary of the Activities Undertaken to Improve Performance in the Canadian Book Publishing/ Bookselling Industry

The 1990 IFC study identified a number of areas where the publishers' performance was below objective level. The most significant of these was the fulfillment operation where 14 of the 18 participants reported costs that were well above the objective of 5.0 percent of gross sales plus returns. Three obvious reasons for this were overcapacity; the level of returns, which ranged from a low of 1.5 percent of gross sales to a high of 46.1 percent; and an almost complete lack of fulfillment automation.

To test the consultants' hypothesis that the cost of fulfillment could be substantially reduced by automating the fulfillment operation, they organized the benchmarking trip to Europe in 1994. The information gathered during the visit suggested that by applying the level of automation seen in Europe to Canadian fulfillment operations, the cost of fulfillment would be reduced by 35 percent to 50 percent. To justify this level of automation, however, would require a minimum annual sales level of $74.7 million ($100 million Canadian), well above the sales of the largest Canadian publisher.

Thus, it was recommended that two or more publishers join forces to build common fulfillment facilities based on the European model. Two Canadian publishers subsequently built a common fulfillment facility to handle their distribution requirements and eventually to sell distribution services to other Canadian publishers. There is still ample opportunity for other publishers to follow the same route.

To further explore opportunities for reducing the level of returns, booksellers were included in the 1994 IFC study of book publishers. From the information gathered during interviews, it was discovered that if the publishers could deliver their books within 48 hours from receiving the order, returns could almost be eliminated. In fact, several booksellers suggested that the ability to return books has had a very negative influence on the industry, in that bookstores no longer had to be careful buyers.

To test this hypothesis, the benchmarking trip to Europe in 1996 was organized. Both booksellers and automated fulfillment operations were visited. Findings supported the hypothesis that if deliveries were within two days, returns would be 5 percent or less.

Thus, this series of studies has

- Provided each of the participant publishers with an analysis of their performance as compared to sector-specific performance objectives.

- Identified each participant's areas of comparative weakness and quantified each area in terms of increased profit potential.

- Offered each participant specific recommendations for performance improvement.

- Identified sources of automated fulfillment technology in Europe that could be acquired and employed in Canada.

- Identified operating practices that would substantially improve the level of customer service offered by publishers and thereby reduce the level of returns.

- Provided the industry sector, including both publishers and booksellers, with a proven operating model that, if adopted, would greatly improve the overall performance of both parties, which in turn would lead to lower costs, increased sales, and improved levels of profitability.

About the Author

Harvey Goodwin's career spans over 40 years. During that time he spent 23 years with Alcan in Europe, Africa, and North America; spent five years with Bell Northern Research; and since 1982 has been a management consultant in Ottawa, Ontario, Canada.

Goodwin is the president of the Charles E. Napier Company, Ltd., a management consulting practice. He is also the CEO of two other management consulting firms, and has developed successful practices with the Canadian federal government and small and medium-sized manufacturers in Canada. In addition to directing successful performance benchmarking with clients in Canada, Europe, and the United States, Goodwin has developed a technology acquisition practice as an alternative to in-house product and process development.

The Charles E. Napier Company focuses on industrial performance improvement. The consultancy has managed interfirm comparison (IFC) studies covering many diverse areas including upholstered furniture; residential furniture in Europe, Canada, and the United States; printed circuit board manufacturers; trading houses; and of course, Canadian book publishers. Additionally, the company has served several Canadian government agencies including the Canadian International Development Agency, the Solicitor General of Canada, and the Ministry of Science and Technology.

Goodwin graduated with a bachelor of mechanical engineering degree from McGill University and a diploma in international business from the Centre d'Études Industrial in Geneva, Switzerland. In 1980 he earned a diploma in technology management from the Massachusetts Institute of Technology. Goodwin may be contacted as follows:

Harvey S. W. Goodwin
President
Charles E. Napier Company, Ltd.
180 Howick Street
Ottawa, Ontario, Canada
K1M 0G8
Telephone: 613-747-7643
Facsimile: 613-747-7645
E-mail: harvey.goodwin@sympatico.ca

PART 3: SERVICE SECTOR

Analysis

Country:	United States
Organization:	Pacific Bell
Industry:	Telecommunications industry
Process:	Customer satisfaction management
Case Study Title:	*"Applying Benchmarking at Pacific Bell: Skills, Tools, and Techniques"*

The preparation of the team undoubtedly allowed it to quickly determine similarities and to isolate the key differences, namely better or best practices. And these were significant. But thorough team preparation also allowed for something else crucial to the customer satisfaction measurement process—how the data were used. As noted in the study, it indicated direction and dimension that in an aggregate and systematic way had not ever previously been considered.

Specific best practices were identified. These included the time taken to answer a call that was acceptable to a customer, and what the customer wanted by way of date and time to schedule a service call and what Pacific Bell could offer to satisfy this need. Even aside from these changes in practices, which must be pervasive, the return on project investment was very handsome, resulting in a 70:1 return for the project cost.

Country:	United Kingdom
Organization:	Boots The Chemists
Industry:	Service industry
Process:	Sales promotion
Case Study Title:	*"Internal Benchmarking at Boots The Chemists"*

The team faced all the challenges of getting common understanding of performance data, establishing peer groups for data (the top 10 stores), and agreeing on a logical grouping of stores for credible comparisons. But having done so, the best practice findings were impressive. All locations had the opportunity to implement some best practices not previously known, which ultimately improved sales performance.

The case also presents an innovative, structured way to sensitize the organization to the need for, and opportunity for, sharing. It also makes the case that the appropriate comparison is not to the average—as is the case in most performance reporting systems—but to the best stores, the benchmark! The lessons learned from the barriers Boots The Chemists faced, and its approach to overcoming them, are instructive to all readers.

Country:	Italy
Organization:	IBM Italy
Industry:	Computer industry
Process:	Procurement process redesign
Case Study Title:	*"Application of Benchmarking Techniques for Business Process Reengineering: IBM Italy's Procurement Process Reengineering Model"*

The payoff for such an in-depth analysis to select the priority process was the recognition that the procurement process was unsatisfactory. This was supported by baseline data. And the study further confirmed that there was an unexploited opportunity of significant proportions for IBM Italy manufacturing to pursue.

Country:	New Zealand
Organization:	Trade and Development Board
Industry:	International trade and development industry
Process:	Export development
Case Study Title:	*"Expanding Benchmarking to Include an Entire Industry: Tradenz Best Practice Study"*

While the specific best practices identified are included in a final report and not detailed in the case presentation, a study of the measurement data and sample questionnaire guidelines reveal that significant best practice findings resulted. Overall, this study led to some significant conclusions. A model was developed tailored to the benchmarking need. The findings, while cautioned on their direct applicability, did stimulate new and innovative concepts. This is often the case in benchmarking where the admonition is to "adapt, not to adopt."

Learnings from this study continue to point to the opportunity to do benchmarking locally, before assuming it is necessary to contact and visit organizations around the world. But more subtle and fundamental things were also accomplished. These included understanding the collective wealth of best practice information available, if only marshaled for effective use; and that information exchange is possible. That is especially critical in the worldwide competitive arena that is the marketplace today.

Country:	Australia
Organization:	NRMA
Industry:	Service industry
Process:	Assessing successful change
Case Study Title:	*"Benchmarking Improvement and Change: How Quality Award Winners Do It"*

Twelve organizations originally agreed to participate in the study initiation and scope definition. Eight eventually agreed to participate in the study. They represented mining, communications, automotive, banking, utility, and diversified and insurance industries. Since quantifying the results of quality and change would be difficult, it was decided to use the Australian Quality Council's award criteria, which are objective and provide a common set of definitions. Once the data and information were documented it was instructive to find that organizations had many instances of common strengths and weaknesses. This became the indicator of where best practices would occur. This, in turn, led to contacts, site visits, and eventually long-term relationships. This is often the progression found from these types of collaborative benchmarking initiatives.

Twenty-three best practices are noted in the sample exhibit. Nineteen of these were judged of value to NRMA, for an 83 percent success rate. These best practices were found at six of the eight organizations, or about three per organization. Of the best practices, three each applied to improvements in customer satisfaction, quality, and employee motivation and satisfaction; five focused on improvements in processes; and four sought to increase business results.

Country:	India
Organization:	Housing Development Finance Corporation (HDFC)
Industry:	Home mortgage financing industry
Process:	Loan management
Case Study Title:	*"Redefining Service Frontiers: Lessons From the Best Practices of the Housing Development Finance Corporation"*

It is interesting to note that India is emerging from an era of self-sufficiency and closed borders, to dismantled regulations and liberalized, if not open, borders. In this case, benchmarking is seen as a way to prepare for and become flexible to these changes; to become a market-oriented economy that perhaps shocks the previous ways of doing business.

The preparation for these changes is a meticulous commitment to understanding and adaption of best practices to internal operations. These best practice understandings are available to all.

Country:	Canada
Organization:	Canadian Book Publishers Association
Industry:	Publishing industry
Process:	Book distribution
Case Study Title:	*"Improving the Profitability of Canadian Book Publishers: An Example of the Application of Performance Measurement and Benchmarking at Both the Firm and Sector Level"*

In addition to specific best practices that were found, this case study also developed four different operating models. These could be considered alternative processes. Each firm would have the option of choosing the best practices from these models to construct a best-of-the-best practice process.

Best practices were identified by determining where book fulfillment was done with excellence, in this case Europe. European book distributors had a much higher level of automation to reduce lead times and to improve accuracy, since correcting an error after the fact is an order of magnitude more expensive than doing it right the first time.

Potential savings were substantial. If the best practices and technology were applied to Canadian book publishing firms, their fulfillment cost base would be reduced from 35 percent to 50 percent; and returns—a serious source of non–value-added expense in the book distribution industry—could be reduced by 70 percent.

Summary Cost Savings and Benefits

United States	Europe	Asia/Pacific	Americas/Africa
SERVICE UNITED STATES **Pacific Bell** *Customer satisfaction management* • Benefit/cost 70:1 • $5 million savings • 60% questionnaire reduction	UNITED KINGDOM **Boots The Chemists** *Sales promotion* • Not quantified ITALY **IBM** *Procurement process redesign* • High-value, high-cost enterprise process • Increased cycle efficiency from 11% to 16% • Decreased purchase order time from 20 days to 3 days	NEW ZEALAND **Trade and Development Board** *Export development* • Detailed in —Human resource: 50 vs. 5 hours/employee —Control: 4.5 vs. 3.3 turns AUSTRALIA **NRMA** *Successful change* • Eight AQC leaders involved • 83% of practice transferable • Common strengths and weaknesses identified INDIA **Housing Development Finance Corporation** *Loan management* • 55% market share • 99% loan recover • 30% growth • Highest credit rating	CANADA **Canadian Book Publishers Association** *Book fulfillment* • Cost base reduced 35%–50% • Returns reduced 70%

Key Best Practices Found

United States	Europe	Asia/Pacific	Americas/Africa
SERVICE <u>UNITED STATES</u> **Pacific Bell** *Customer satisfaction management* • Team preparation • Diagnosis and corrective action • Call answer time • Service call scheduling • Actionable questionnaire data • Measures, strategy link stronger	<u>UNITED KINGDOM</u> **Boots The Chemists** *Sales promotion* • Nine best practices identified • Sensitize to information sharing benefits • Barriers overcome • Common data definitions • Top 10 peer group <u>ITALY</u> **IBM** *Procurement process redesign* • Combinations of —Knowledge —Practices —Technology	<u>NEW ZEALAND</u> **Trade and Development Board** *Export development* • Models of innovative concepts • Benchmark locally • Extensive best practices available <u>AUSTRALIA</u> **NRMA** *Successful change* • Site visits build relationships • 18 best practices noted, including the following: —Three each in customer, employee, and quality concepts —Five in process improvement —Four in business results <u>INDIA</u> **Housing Development Finance Corporation** *Loan management* • Leadership • Service • Staff development • Technology use	<u>CANADA</u> **Canadian Book Publishers Association** *Book fulfillment* • Four operating models/ processes 1. Publisher owned 2. Publisher/bookseller 3. Independent 4. Logistics outsource • European fulfillment best practices identified • Higher automation • Reduced lead times

Lessons Learned

United States	Europe	Asia/Pacific	Americas/Africa
SERVICE UNITED STATES **Pacific Bell** *Customer satisfaction management* • Understand core customer requirements for service attributes. • Empower employees to improve activities on which they are assessed. • Analytical partner selection process used.	UNITED KINGDOM **Boots The Chemists** *Sales promotion* • Gain commitment. • Disprove concerns. • Be open to learning. ITALY **IBM** *Procurement process redesign* • Confirm redesign activities. • Remove internal inhibitors.	NEW ZEALAND **Trade and Development Board** *Export development* • Knowledge improvement strategies maintained. • Information exchange value established. • Joint concept/innovations established. AUSTRALIA **NRMA** *Successful change* • Collaborative benchmarking was successful. • Quality Award recipients learn. • Consequences without quality initiative questioned. INDIA **Housing Development Finance Corporation** *Loan management* • Competitive pressures require commitment to fundamentals. • Best practices are not secrets.	CANADA **Canadian Book Publishers Association** *Book fulfillment* • Practices and operating model specific to industry sector can be identified.

PART 4: NONPROFIT SECTOR

Introduction

While this is a small sector, it is encouraging that there is good representation from a few nonprofit groups. These include a U.S. teaching health care facility, associations, and productivity boards. They provide a wide contrast in processes from medical procedures, such as coronary artery bypass surgery, to a mundane process such as on-the-job training, which tends to be taken for granted.

While there is some geographic representation in the United States and Asia/Pacific, it is unfortunate that Europe is not represented because there has been good application of benchmarking there, although in limited areas. Perhaps this is indicative of the potential for this technique.

These four cases provide rich proof that best practice benchmarking is vitally important in the nonprofit sector. A brief summary, background information, the rationale for each case, and key points to consider when reading follow.

Country:	United States
Organization:	Northern New England Cardiovascular Disease Study Group (Dartmouth Medical School)
Industry:	Health care industry
Process:	Coronary artery bypass surgery
Case Study Title:	*"Improving the Outcomes of Cardiac Surgery: A Benchmarking Study by the Northern New England Cardiovascular Disease Study Group"*

A landmark study of mortality rates for cardiac surgery, drawn from medical claims data in the late 1980s, showed significant variation among institutions. This led to a series of voluntary learning interventions for a group of hospitals in the northeast region of the

United States. A study group was established to gather, analyze, and exchange information on the cardiovascular disease treatment process, including benchmarking among six institutions. Each institution formed a team representing seven professions involved with cardiac surgery.

The approach followed a somewhat predictable set of steps normally found in best practice analyses. Initially, a database was established to gather specific patient data. These outcomes data were disseminated, and discussion groups formed to decide on future studies and analyses. It was interesting that after the adjustment of the data for case mix a significant variation still existed among medical centers and surgeons. This then led to the need for improved approaches to examine the process of cardiac surgery.

A three-part approach involved data feedback, continuous improvement training, and structured benchmarking site visits properly called *comparative process analysis*, was established. The site visits went through several phases of continuous improvement, each time further focusing on key core processes and critical outcomes. This involved mapping the process from surgery decision through patient discharge. The first benchmarking teams focused on the process to identify differences, but at the same time observed both substance and style—what was not observed at the "home" institutions, as well as communications and decision making.

The second major phase of the study concentrated on a specific outcome, namely postoperative heart failure. And the benchmarking process was changed to concentrate on specialties, clinical mapping, and a change process called Serial V. Therefore, the six medical centers created a cross-functional structure of center and specialty teams. Eventually, 17 site visits were conducted, and 13 more are planned.

Country:	Singapore
Organization:	Singapore Productivity and Standards Board (PSB)
Industry:	Association industry
Process:	On-the-job training
Case Study Title:	*"Benchmarking On-the-job Training"*

There are some processes that, on the surface, seem so mundane that they would not be candidates for benchmarking because they are so pervasive or are assumed to already incorporate best practices. On-the-job training (OJT) is one such process. But when the productivity of a company, government, or country is at stake, how individuals are quickly and adequately prepared to be effective in their jobs can be crucial. It is instructive that Singapore, a reasonably small city-state, recognized the importance of OJT in its quest for productivity and to become the best. In effect, this is the way organizations ensure that best practices will be mastered, namely by ensuring—not assuming—that individuals are effectively trained on the job.

But what constitutes effective OJT? That was the objective of this benchmarking project: to understand the best practices for OJT of leading Singaporean companies. And, as often is the case, the first obstacle that the team faced was that the OJT process was generally not well documented, even in the peer group of companies. This task was accomplished with reasonable ease and became the baseline for a questionnaire.

Country:	Japan
Organization:	Japan Productivity Center
Industry:	Association industry
Process:	Benchmarking emergence
Case Study Title:	*"Emergence of Benchmarking in Japan"*

How does benchmarking emerge as an initiative in a particular locale, usually a country, bounded by a language? It is instructive to note how this happens, and this case study is an example of that chrysalis-to-butterfly process. It usually involves the following:

• Interest in the topic from the point of view of improving productivity. In this case productivity institutes around the world have recognized best practice benchmarking as a necessary initiative. There are many examples of these from the United States to Singapore to South Africa.

• A crisis; that is, recognizing there is a competitive crisis from ignoring or not fully appreciating the fast-paced changes taking place in the competitive global marketplace. Consequently, there is the need to become more competitive through understanding and incorporating worldwide best practices. This was the case in India and Australasia, and is now emerging in South America.

• The dedication of select individuals who believe in best practice benchmarking and champion the topic. It has been through the dedication of those individuals that much of the interest, initial awareness, and proven sources of benchmarking success have been derived.

This case study is indicative of this emergent process. Initial interest in the topic of benchmarking resulted in 1995 when the Japan Productivity Center for Socio Economic Development (JPC/SED) held one of the first benchmarking conferences. The editor of this book was invited, with all expenses paid, to travel to Japan and give a one-hour presentation to approximately 200 invited industry and other prominent organization leaders.

The crisis recognizing the need to change came in 1996. In the early 1990s, Japan reached the limits of gaining efficiencies through restructuring. Since the collapse of its "bubble economy," Japan struggled to regain its competitiveness in world markets. This was brought home in a shocking way when the World Economic Forum's report on competitiveness showed Japan dropped from first in 1993 to thirteen in 1996, a precipitous change for an economy that had been emulated for years. It is interesting that it took a crisis to shock a country much the way it shocked a company, namely Xerox.

Finally, the dedication of select individuals to raise the awareness of the benefits of best practice benchmarking was evidenced in many individuals. Among the many who could be cited are Yotaro (Tony) Kobayashi, chairman of Fuji Xerox. His sponsoring this business improvement approach among industry leaders and functioning as head of the Business Roundtable have been instrumental to make the case for benchmarking in Japan.

It is also the dedicated efforts of others, working through the infrastructure, to marshal the proof that benchmarking can be conducted in all countries, in any language and in any culture. It simply needs to find the right fit. Tomohiro (Tom) Takanashi, the author of this case study, has been one such individual.

Country:	Brazil
Organization:	The Benchmarking Group
Industry:	Association industry
Process:	Initial benchmarking launch
Case Study Title:	*"The Benchmarking Group in Brazil"*

One of the intriguing questions about benchmarking as it expands around the world is how does it become formally established in a country? Today, there are more than 15 formally established benchmarking centers. These go by various names: centres, clearinghouses, services, institutes, councils, clubs, and associations. These local centers of competency for benchmarking have been established to tailor their products and services to local conditions, typically within a country, and to eventually deal with the delivery of benchmarking to teams in the local language. This case study is the description of one: The Benchmarking Group of Brazil.

It is instructive to see the sequence of events that led to the Group's establishment. Initially, a concern for the quality of citizen life led to an understanding of quality principles, which led to the creation of a national quality award to recognize quality practices, which led to the identification of benchmarking as the preferred vehicle to promote interchange of best practices. The Group's objective became to "foster benchmarking among Brazilian organizations." This is a commendable operating objective tied to a larger countrywide purpose, something that several countries have initiated.

The establishment of a Brazilian model for its operation now gives the Benchmarking Group the opportunity to learn from other benchmarking centers around the world. This continues the benchmarking tradition—learning from others—established at the initial center in Houston, Texas, in 1991.

Master Table

United States	Europe	Asia/Pacific	Americas/Africa
NONPROFIT			
UNITED STATES		SINGAPORE	BRAZIL
Northern New England Cardio-vascular Disease Study Group (Dartmouth Medical School)		**Singapore Productivity and Standards Board (PSB)**	**The Benchmarking Group**
Health care industry		Association industry	Association industry
Coronary artery bypass surgery		*On-the-job training*	*Initial benchmarking launch*
"Improving the Outcomes of Cardiac Surgery: A Bench-marking Study by the Northern New England Cardiovascular Disease Study Group"		"Benchmarking On-the-job Training"	"The Benchmarking Group in Brazil"
		JAPAN	
		Japan Productivity Center	
		Association industry	
		Benchmarking emergence	
		"Emergence of Benchmarking in Japan"	

Country and Industry

United States	Europe	Asia/Pacific	Americas/Africa
NONPROFIT UNITED STATES Health care industry		SINGAPORE Association industry JAPAN Association industry	BRAZIL Association industry

Processes

United States	Europe	Asia/Pacific	Americas/Africa
NONPROFIT UNITED STATES *Coronary artery bypass surgery*		SINGAPORE *On-the-job training* JAPAN *Benchmarking emergence*	BRAZIL *Initial benchmarking launch*

Improving the Outcomes of Cardiac Surgery: A Benchmarking Study by the Northern New England Cardiovascular Disease Study Group

Cathy S. Ross, Quality Improvement Coordinator, Cardiac Surgery Improvement, Joseph F. Kasper, Director of the Benchmarking Project, Gerald T. O'Connor, Research Director, Northern New England Cardiovascular Disease Study Group

Every system is perfectly designed to get the results it gets.

—Paul B. Batalden, M.D.

Background

Outcomes research came suddenly to cardiac surgery in 1987 when the Health Care Financing Administration published its studies of mortality rates by hospital and found substantial institutional variability (U.S. Department of Health and Human Services 1987). These studies were widely reported and quite controversial. There was genuine concern that administratively collected data were inadequate to draw inference on the quality of medical care (Park et al. 1990). Specifically, the reported differences in mortality rates by institution might have been the result of confounding characteristics of patient case mix not adequately described by Medicare claims data. These differences may distort apparent rates of in-hospital mortality and lead to false conclusions about the quality of medical care provided (Dubois et al. 1987; Berwick and Wald 1990; Green et al. 1990). In the aftermath of this data release, a regional voluntary consortium called the Northern New England Cardiovascular Disease Study Group (NNECDSG) was formed with the purpose of studying and improving the medical and surgical management of cardiovascular disease in the region. The group adopted the following mission statement.

> *The Northern New England Cardiovascular Disease Study Group exists to develop and exchange information concerning the treatment of cardiovascular disease. It is a regional, voluntary, multidisciplinary group of clinicians, hospital administrators, and health care research personnel who seek to improve continuously the quality, safety, effectiveness, and cost of medical interventions in cardiovascular disease.*

Members currently include cardiothoracic surgeons, cardiac nurses, cardiologists, perfusionists, anesthesiologists, hospital administrators, and scientists associated with the following six institutions.

1. Beth Israel-Deaconess Hospital, Boston, Massachusetts

2. Dartmouth-Hitchcock Medical Center, Lebanon, New Hampshire

3. Eastern Maine Medical Center, Bangor, Maine

4. Fletcher-Allen Health Care, Burlington, Vermont

5. Maine Medical Center, Portland, Maine

6. Optima Health-Catholic Medical Center, Manchester, New Hampshire

Differences in Clinical Outcomes

On July 1, 1987, the NNECDSG established a regional database for all patients receiving coronary artery bypass grafting (CABG). The data collection used a brief (one-page, one-sided) form and a deep commitment to uniform variable definitions and routine validation of the database. In 1989 regional databases for percutaneous transluminal coronary angioplasty (PTCA) and heart valve replacement surgery were established. Overall, clinical and outcomes data have been collected and analyzed on approximately 65,000 cardiac procedures. NNECDSG meets three times per year to disseminate the data and discuss ongoing improvement efforts and future studies.

Between 1987 and 1989, data were collected on 3055 consecutive CABG procedures. The regional hospital mortality rate was 4.3 percent. The rate varied among centers (range: 3.1 percent–6.3 percent) and among surgeons (range: 1.9 percent–9.2 percent). A number of statistically significant predictors of mortality were identified (for example, age, female gender, small body surface area, greater comorbidity, reoperation, poor preoperative cardiac function, and emergent or urgent surgery). After adjusting for the effects of potentially confounding variables, substantial and statistically significant variability was observed among medical centers ($p = 0.021$) and among surgeons ($p = 0.025$) (O'Connor et al. 1991).

The group concluded that the observed differences in in-hospital mortality rates among institutions and among surgeons in northern New England were not solely the result of differences in case mix as described by these variables. Rather, the differences were likely reflected in unknown aspects of patient care.

Interventions to Improve Cardiac Surgery

This observed variability in outcomes provided the rationale to closely examine the processes of cardiac surgery and to attempt to learn from each member of the NNECDSG.

This knowledge of variability and the comfort that grew during the early years of the consortium led the group to organize a regional effort to improve the clinical outcomes of cardiac surgery. Based on the group's experiences, and guided by advice from Donald M. Berwick, M.D., the NNECDSG planned a three-part intervention consisting of (1) feedback of outcome data, (2) training in continuous quality improvement techniques, and (3) benchmarking site visits to other medical centers. This process constituted phase 1 of the project.

Feedback of Outcome Data

Starting in 1990, reports of risk-adjusted outcome data were distributed to participating clinicians three times each year. Each surgeon received three reports: his or her own outcomes, those of his or her medical center, and regional results. Anonymity of individual surgeons and participating institutions was preserved in the aggregate regional reports. Characteristics of patients and specific fatal and nonfatal outcomes were summarized. Three, two-day meetings each year provided a forum to discuss these results.

Continuous Quality Improvement Training

A two-day training session was conducted for the executive committee of the NNECDSG and two, four-hour training sessions were conducted for the general membership of the group. The theory and techniques of continuous quality improvement were presented and discussed. The approach was based largely on the writings of Deming (1986) and Walton (1986), and the use of these methods in medical care settings as described by Berwick (1989) and Laffel and Blumenthal (1989).

Benchmarking Site Visits

During 1990, the NNECDSG began a series of site visits to observe the processes of CABG surgery (Camp 1989; Spendolini 1992). The site visits in this phase of CABG benchmarking are more properly called *comparative process analysis*. It was agreed at the outset that no single institution was necessarily the *best* in all aspects of CABG surgery. Thus, each visiting team was advised to identify the good elements of process; that is, things the team would like to take home with it, and the elements of process where the team members could offer constructive criticism. Ideally, each visiting team would have consisted of a representative from each relevant discipline—surgeon, anesthesiologist, perfusionist, operating room (OR) nurse, critical care nurse, plus facilitator. This, however, was not always the case. Each team did include a cardiac surgeon and a perfusionist; three teams included a cardiac surgery nurse; and one had an anesthesiologist. All site visits were facilitated by an industrial engineer (Joseph F. Kasper).

The site visits were completed between November 1990 and February 1991, and were conducted in a round-robin fashion—a team from A (with facilitator, an industrial engineer) visited B, a team from B (with the same facilitator) visited C, and so on. A visit consisted of a full day of observation beginning with a preliminary briefing followed by observation of one or two CABG cases and concluding with a debriefing question-and-answer session. The teams observed the entire CABG system, from the cardiac catheterization conference through surgery and postoperative care. By agreement, observers were given free run of the hospital, and were encouraged to seek real-time clarification through questions. Observers were reminded to notice both the substance and the style of activities, to look for what was not there as well as what was there, and to pay attention to communications and decision making along with medical/surgical technique.

No previously prepared data collection forms were used; instead, individuals used tape recorders, note pads, and short-term memory. Observers were strongly encouraged to submit free-form written reports within seven days. Report styles varied considerably—detailed activity time lines, critical commentary, and comparisons with "home"—were all submitted. Overall, the reports were exceptionally dense in content. All reports were shared with all participating institutions. The visitors focused on similarities and differences compared with home institutions. Rather than recording and evaluating the entire day's events, participants paid the greatest attention to corresponding colleagues (for example, the visiting surgeon primarily monitored the activities of the host surgeon). Each host attempted to conduct "business as usual," and provided complete access to all events. The group's enthusiasm for the benchmarking project led to additional visits. A report of these findings has been published (Kasper, Plume, and O'Connor 1992).

Improvement in Clinical Outcomes

Monitoring mortality rates continued, and there were 74 fewer deaths during the 27-month postintervention period (24 percent reduction) than would have been expected based on historical data from this region (Figure 15.1). This reduction in mortality rate was temporally associated with the interventions, was similar across patient risk groups, and was not substantially influenced by surgeon migration. These improved outcomes were not significantly different for men and women or for elective and nonelective patients.

Reductions in hospital mortality rates were observed in four of the five medical centers during the postintervention period. Only the hospital with the lowest adjusted mortality rate during the preintervention period (2.3 percent) showed no substantial change. Since these were simultaneous interventions it is not possible to separate their individual contribution to the improvement observed. A full report of the interventions and the outcomes has been published (O'Connor et al. 1996).

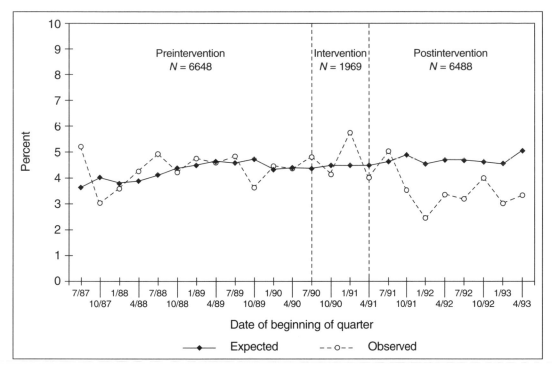

Source: O'Connor et. al. 1996. Used with permission.

Figure 15.1. Expected/observed mortality, all patients (*N* = 15,095).

Current Improvement Initiatives

After the 1990–1991 interventions, the NNECDSG conducted a regional study of the mode of death associated with cardiac surgery. This study indicated that postoperative heart failure was an important distinguishing characteristic between lower and higher surgical mortality rates (Disch et al. 1992). In 1996, the NNECDSG undertook a focused intervention aimed at reducing the rate of fatal heart failure associated with coronary artery bypass graft surgery. Based on prior experience, several changes in approach were made. Notable among them were the following: the development of both center and specialty teams, an emphasis on clinical process mapping, and the use of the Serial V method to effect process change in the participating institutions (Figure 15.2).

Team Structure

Two types of work teams were created: center teams within each of the six NNECDSG institutions, and specialty teams with representatives from all six institutions so that variation in functional process and technique could be identified.

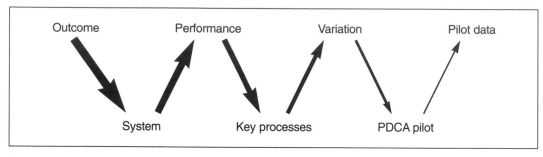

Source: Batalden, Nelson, and Roberts. 1994. Used with permission.

Figure 15.2. Serial *V* method: Time measurement specificity.

Each center team consists of a cardiothoracic surgeon, anesthesiologist, perfusionist, cardiologists, and both operating and cardiothoracic intensive care unit nurses. This allows study of process and patient care both during the procedure and postoperatively through the first two days following surgery. It is during this time frame that most CABG deaths occur. The center teams are responsible for

- Flowcharting the processes of patient care at their own institution
- Site visiting each member institution and analyzing the lessons learned
- Implementing changes at their institution

The specialty teams were organized by function and specialty. These consisted of six surgeons, perfusionists, anesthesiologists, cardiologists, and both operating and cardiothoracic intensive care unit nurses, with a representative from each of the six NNECDSG institutions. These specialty teams allowed for a highly focused study of each functional area, and allowed team members to identify and study differences in technique between institutions. The specialty teams are responsible for

- Compiling a literature review of heart failure
- Developing data collection instruments and a list of site visit questions
- Studying process flow diagrams to identify and study institutional differences
- Identifying possible causes of heart failure

Clinical Process Mapping

NNECDSG members were introduced to flowcharting at one of their meetings. The group was divided into specialty (surgery, nursing, anesthesia, perfusion), and asked to map the process of care from decision to perform the surgery up through discharge from the intensive care (Figure 15.3). This exercise turned out to be a powerful tool to help individuals focus on process and not on each other. From this exercise, high-leverage areas were

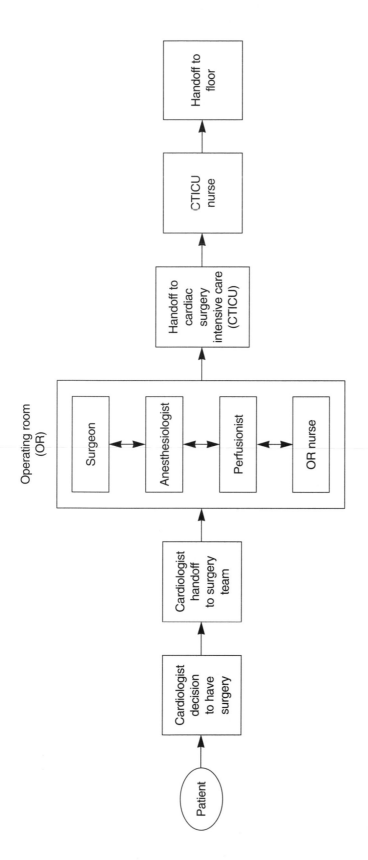

Figure 15.3. Coronary artery bypass surgery process of care.

identified that may be potential causes for postoperative heart failure. These included the following:

- Preoperative management of patients with unstable angina
- Handoffs between different specialties and different functional units
- Different processes used to protect the (nonbeating) heart during bypass surgery
- Separation of the patient from the cardiopulmonary bypass
- Diagnosis and treatment of heart failure in the ICU

During the next few months center teams focused on characterizing their process and discovering where the variability exists. The teams used the following methods.

- Process mapping
- Cause-and-effect diagrams
- Data collection, including anesthesia and perfusion data, literature reviews, and the site visit questionnaire

Teams used the maps for careful process comparative analysis. Once differences were noted, teams further brainstormed on what processes could lead to heart failure. Out of this, a cause-and-effect process flow diagram was developed (Figure 15.4). Through this exercise, data collection tools were developed for anesthesia, perfusion, and the site visits.

Phase 2 site visits differed from phase 1 visits. During phase 2, the intervention was more focused. Instead of viewing the entire process, the focus was on only those processes that may lead to heart failure. The team's narrowly defined aim required a more extensive planning period and the development of a site visit data collection tool. The team members improved how they observed through these simple lessons learned from phase 1.

- Watch peoples' style and substance.
- Ask: Is this transferable back to my place?
- Determine a sense of timing: What are you seeing? Is the pace too slow, quick, or lazy? Or are activities clear and crisp?
- Document communication: What is information transferred? Is there potential for confusion? Is communication ambiguous? Are communication checks used?
- Observe handoffs at key items during the process: Cardiologist to anesthesia or surgeon, anesthesia to ICU nurse. Look for content and ownership of these times. Is ownership clear?
- Review accuracy and completeness of record keeping.
- Ask: Does the ICU nurse get a complete report of events that occurred in the OR?
- What is the one thing that you saw that you would like to bring back to your institution?

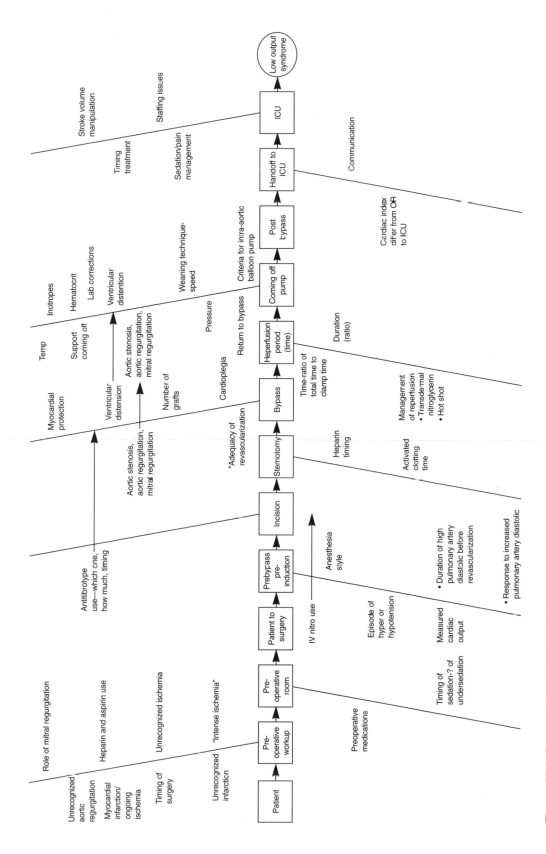

Figure 15.4. Causes of loss (heart failure).

349

Dissemination of valuable information was facilitated by having the teams meet immediately after the visit to debrief and identify key process changes that could be implemented at their own institution. Teams were encouraged to disseminate the information throughout their institution to help promote acceptance of changes. Written reports were again required but the time frame was shortened to three days to increase the quality of the report.

To date, 17 site visits have taken place, with 13 additional visits to begin in the fall of 1997. Upon completion, the findings will be disseminated throughout NNECDSG institutions.

Process Change Methods

The method used for phase 2 was described by Batalden, Nelson, and Roberts (1994). This method links measurement, process knowledge, and continual improvement cycles with outcomes. By linking all three, teams are able to clearly identify where the differences lie and where improvement efforts should focus. Batalden, Nelson, and Roberts state that "Sources of adverse outcome are complex and include variations in policies, procedures, equipment, and techniques, as well as people and their interactions. Improvement in outcome requires that action be taken in the patient care process. Action [should be] based on knowledge and understanding of the complete system of causation and the underlying processes."

To help teams understand and implement the Serial V method, Batalden, Nelson, and Roberts include a practical worksheet used to guide the teams toward an accurate hypothesis. This worksheet is in two parts, and is illustrated in Figures 15.5a and 15.5b.

The NNECDSG believes that this focus on heart failure, as well as the revised team structure, the emphasis on process mapping, and the use of specific techniques to accelerate process improvement, enhances its prior methods. The chapter, however, is a report of work-in-progress, and, at the time of this writing, the NNECDSG has not completed its evaluation of the impact of this approach.

Conclusion

The NNECDSG has gained some experience in developing an infrastructure for improving the quality of cardiac surgery. All cardiac surgeons in the northern New England region contribute data on every case. The data sets are validated regularly; reports are distributed; and they are discussed three times a year. Specific studies and site visits using multidisciplinary teams (Kasper, Plume, and O'Connor 1992) are used to generate and test hypotheses and to effect changes in the processes of care (O'Connor et al. 1996). The teams' participation, for over a decade, has confirmed that clinicians care deeply about the quality of care. They have developed a regional infrastructure to examine processes, to use data for improvement, and to learn from daily practice. They have learned from Deming (1986),

Clinical Improvement Worksheet

Aim: Accelerate clinical improvement by linking outcomes measurements and process knowledge with the design and conduct of pilot tests of change.

① *Outcomes* → **Select a population**

What's the general aim? Given our wish to limit/reduce the illness burden for "this type" of patient, what are the desired results?

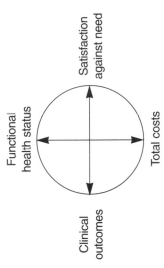

② *Process* → **Analyze the process**

What's the process for giving care to this type of patient?

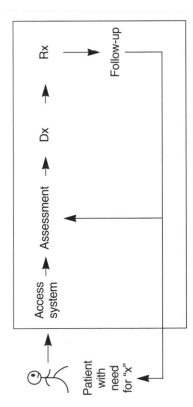

③ *Changes* → **Generate change ideas**

What ideas do we have for changing what's done (process) to get better results?

• • • •

④ *Pilot* → **Select first/next change for pilot testing**

How can we pilot test an improvement idea using the *Plan-Do-Check-Act* method?

Source: Batalden, Nelson, and Roberts. 1994. Used with permission.

Figure 15.5a. Serial *V* worksheet.

Team members → Who should work on this improvement?

1. *Leader*
2. *Facilitator*
3. _____
4. _____
Coach _____

5. _____
6. _____
7. _____
8. _____
Admin. support _____

A. Aim → What are we trying to accomplish? (more specific aim)

B. Measures ↑ How will we know that a change is an improvement?

C. Selected change → How would you describe the change that you have selected for testing?

D. Plan — How shall we PLAN the pilot?
• Who? Does what? When? With what tools and training?

• Baseline data to be collected?

E. Do — What are we learning as we DO the pilot?

F. Check — As we CHECK and STUDY what happened, what have we learned?

• Did original outcomes improve?

G. Act — As we ACT to hold the gains or abandon our pilot efforts, what needs to be done?

Source: Batalden, Nelson, and Roberts. 1994. Used with permission.

Figure 15.5b. Making improvements: Clinical improvement worksheet.

Shewhart (1993), Berwick (1989), and Nelson and Batalden (1993) that there are certain prerequisites for this type of activity. Foremost among these is a safe place to work. The data necessary to improve clinical care cannot be used to punish individuals who participate in the quality improvement efforts. The NNECDSG also needs an agreed-upon metric for outcomes and a forum to discuss results. The number of adverse outcomes in the experience of any particular physician is simply too small to inform subsequent decisions. Lastly, the NNECDSG needs comparative knowledge of the processes of care associated with outcomes so that clinicians can learn from each other. In this group's experience, this process has been multidisciplinary, scientifically rigorous, inexpensive, and enjoyable.

References

Batalden, P. B., E. C. Nelson, and J. S. Roberts. 1994. Linking outcomes measurement to continual improvement: The serial "V" way of thinking about improving clinical care. *Joint Commission Journal of Quality Improvement* 20, no. 4:167–180.

Berwick, D. M. 1989. Continuous improvement as an ideal in health care [see comments]. *New England Journal of Medicine* 320, no. 1:53–56.

Berwick, D. M., and D. L. Wald. 1990. Hospital leaders' opinions of the HCFA mortality data. *Journal of the American Medical Association* 263, no. 2:247–249.

Camp, R. C. 1989. *Benchmarking: The search for industry best practices that lead to superior performance.* Milwaukee, Wisc.: ASQC Quality Press and White Plains, N.Y.: Quality Resources.

Deming, W. E. 1986. *Out of the crisis.* Cambridge, Mass.: MIT Center for Advanced Engineering Study.

Disch, D. L., G. T. O'Connor, J. D. Birkmeyer, D. G. Levy, E. M. Olmstead, and S. K. Plume. 1992. Trend towards increasing predicted mortality among patients undergoing coronary artery bypass grafting. *Clinical Research* 40, no. 2:347.

Dubois, R. W., W. H. Rogers, J. H. Moxley, D. Draper, III, and R. H. Brook. 1987. Hospital inpatient mortality: Is it a predictor or a quality? *New England Journal of Medicine* 317, no. 26:1674–1680.

Green, J., N. Wintfeld, P. Sharkey, and L. J. Passman. 1990. The importance of severity of illness in assessing hospital mortality. *Journal of the American Medical Association* (JAMA) 263, no. 2:241–246.

Kasper, J. F., S. K. Plume, and G. T. O'Connor. 1992. A methodology for QI in the coronary artery bypass grafting procedure involving comparative process analysis. *Quality Review Bulletin* 18, no. 4:129–133.

Laffel, G., and D. Blumenthal. 1989. The case for using industrial quality management science in health care organization. *Journal of the American Medical Association* (JAMA) 262, no. 20:2869–2873.

Nelson, E. C., and P. B. Batalden. 1993. Patient-based quality measurement systems. *Quality Management in Health Care* 2, no. 1:18–30.

O'Connor, G. T., S. K. Plume, E. M. Olmstead, L. H. Coffin, J. R. Morton, C. T. Maloney, E. R. Nowicki, J. F. Tryzelaar, F. Hernandez, L. Adrian, K. J. Casey, D. N. Soule, C. A. S. Marrin, W. C. Nugent, D. C. Charlesworth, and R. Clough, all for the Northern New England Cardiovascular Disease Study Group. 1991. A regional prospective study of in-hospital mortality associated with coronary artery bypass grafting. *Journal of the American Medical Association* (JAMA) 266, no. 6:803–809.

O'Connor, G. T., S. K. Plume, E. M. Olmstead, J. R. Morton, C. T. Maloney, W. C. Nugent, F. Hernandez, R. Clough, B. J. Leavitt, L. H. Coffin, C. A. Marrin, D. Wennberg, J. D. Birkmeyer, D. C. Charlesworth, D. J. Malenka, and H. B. Quinton, all for the Northern New England Cardiovascular Disease Study Group. 1996. A regional intervention to improve the hospital mortality associated with coronary artery bypass graft surgery. The Northern New England Cardiovascular Disease Study Group [see comments]. *Journal of the American Medical Association* (JAMA) 275, no. 11:841–846.

Park, R. E., R. H. Brook, J. Kosecoff, J. Keesey, L. Rubenstein, E. Keeler, K. L. Kahn, W. H. Rogers, and M. R. Chassin. 1990. Explaining the variations in hospital death rates: Randomness, severity of illness, quality of care. *Journal of the American Medical Association* (JAMA) 264, no. 4:484–490.

Shewhart, W. 1993. *Statistical method from the viewpoint of quality control.* New York: Dover Publications.

Spendolini, M. 1992. *The benchmarking book.* New York: American Management Association.

U. S. Department of Health and Human Services. 1987. *Medicare Hospital Mortality Information, 1986.* Washington, D.C.: U.S. Department of Health and Human Services 01-002.

Walton, M. 1986. *The Deming management method.* New York: Dodd, Mead & Co.

About the Authors

Cathy S. Ross is a project coordinator at the Center for the Evaluative Clinical Sciences at Dartmouth Medical School. She holds a bachelor's of science in biology from the University of Denver, and expects to complete a master's of evaluative clinical sciences at Dartmouth College during 1998.

Ross coordinates the NNECDSG's quality improvement project aimed at reducing the rate of fatal low output heart failure and dysrhythmia associated with coronary artery bypass surgery. She is a faculty member for the Institute for Healthcare Improvement Breakthrough Series on Cardiac Surgery and the Volunteer Hospital Association Quality Improvement Series for Cardiac Surgery.

Joseph F. Kasper is the director of the benchmarking projects, an adjunct professor of engineering, and an adjunct professor of community and family medicine at Dartmouth College. He also serves as a consultant in health care improvement, and is the former president and CEO of the Foundation for Informed Medical Decision Making. Kasper received a doctorate in science from the Massachusetts Institute of Technology and an MBA from Boston University.

In addition to the works cited in this chapter, Kasper has authored three books and numerous papers and articles. A selection of recent publications includes the following:

- "Using Comparative Process Analysis to Improve Outcomes of Surgical Procedures" (Proceedings of the 13th Annual International Conference of the IEEE Engineering in Medicine and Biology Society)

- "Developing Shared Decision-making Programs to Improve the Quality of Health Care" (*Journal of Quality Improvement*)

- "Quality Is Not an Adjective" (*Directions*)

Gerald T. O'Connor is the director of the NNECDSG. He has been a member of the Dartmouth faculty since 1987, and is currently professor of medicine and community family medicine. He is chief of clinical research at the Dartmouth-Hitchcock Medical Center and the associate director of the Center for the Evaluative Clinical Sciences at Dartmouth Medical School. Since 1988, O'Connor has been lecturer on medicine at Harvard Medical School.

O'Connor is an epidemiologist. He received a doctorate of science in epidemiology and a master's of arts in public health education from Boston University of Public Health, and a Ph.D. in health services from the Union Institute in Cincinnati, Ohio. O'Connor completed postdoctoral studies in cardiovascular epidemiology at the Channing Laboratory, Brigham and Women's Hospital, Harvard Medical School.

His major areas of study are risk prediction, decision support, and quality improvement in cardiovascular disease. In addition to the publications cited in this chapter, O'Connor has authored hundreds of articles, reports, and papers. His current research support includes the following:

- Health Reform and Small Area Analysis (Robert Wood Johnson Foundation)

- Heart Valve Replacement Surgery: A Quantitative Study of Risk (American Heart Association)

- Outcomes Dissemination: The Maine Study Group Model (Agency for Health Care Policy and Research)

All the authors are associated with Dartmouth Medical School in Hanover, New Hampshire. They may be contacted as follows:

Cathy S. Ross
Quality Improvement Coordinator
Center for the Evaluative Clinical Sciences
Dartmouth Medical School
7251 Strasenburgh Hall
Hanover, NH 03755-3863
Telephone: 603-650-1956
Facsimile: 603-650-1935
E-mail: cathy.s.ross@dartmouth.edu

CHAPTER 16

Benchmarking On-the-job Training

Darshan Singh, Deputy Director, and Benedict Anandam, Senior Officer, Planning and Research Department, Singapore Productivity and Standards Board (PSB)

Background

Companies today can no longer continue doing the same things. The marketplace is always changing. Customers are constantly making new demands. To increase their productivity and profitability, companies need to improve the way their goods and services are produced. Production and servicing costs need to be reduced. New products and services are also required.

Consequently, the workforce needs to be continuously skilled to work on new processes to produce new and better goods and services. With the rapid pace of change occurring at the workplace, external training agencies may not be able to respond quickly or may duplicate actual company conditions, processes, and equipment. Increasingly, the solution for business success is on-the-job training (OJT).

OJT is perhaps best described as a training system where the workers acquire new skills through progression within a workstation or a cluster of related workstations in the company (Pious 1992). Learning is structured, systematic, and conducted within the work environment by the immediate supervisor. Workers learn only those skills that contribute to the production or servicing process. Therefore, OJT is training that is conducted in the context of the work environment and that is geared specifically to developing the skills that workers need to fulfill the job demands. In this way, training is more productive compared to traditional classroom methods. Furthermore, opportunity costs are minimized because workers are not released exclusively for training. Several other significant benefits of OJT are as follows:

• Companies can take advantage of OJT to rapidly skill employees, thus ensuring that worker proficiency and flexibility help to improve the organization's competitive advantage.

• Training can be tailored to meet the needs of individual workers.

• A formal OJT program compels the documentation of an organization's work processes and procedures, which aids in improving the overall level of efficiency.

Objective of the Study

It is important to realize that the gains through a structured and systematic OJT system are within the reach of all organizations, regardless of size or industry. Therefore, developing an effective OJT system can be considered an important component in the management of human assets. It was with this in mind that the Fuji Xerox–PSB Benchmarking Centre teamed up with the Singapore Institute of Human Resource Management (SIHRM) to conduct a benchmarking study on OJT. The objective was to provide participating companies in the study with an opportunity to learn from the practices of leading Singapore companies in the field of OJT. The findings from the study would then help the participating companies develop plans to improve their OJT systems. Other companies can also draw lessons from the findings.

Focus of Topic

The work process selected for the study was defined as the structured OJT process within the company. The study examined the OJT process from job identification and development of training guidelines, to the conduct of training and review of the OJT program. It focused on the factors and practices that could influence the effectiveness and eventual success of an organization's OJT program. The key steps in the process are shown in Figure 16.1.

Team Operations

The Benchmarking Centre and the SIHRM assembled a group of six companies that were interested in participating in the benchmarking study. These companies came from both the manufacturing and service sectors and had an average employee strength of 600.

Benchmarking awareness and training for the group members were provided through briefing sessions, sharing of background materials on benchmarking methodology, and a two-day benchmarking workshop conducted by the Benchmarking Centre. The participants, who were either training or human resource managers, were thus familiarized with the benchmarking methodology that was adopted for the study.

The benchmarking group consisted of a total of 10 individuals including two from the Benchmarking Centre and one from the SIHRM, whose role was that of an observer/resource expert. The persons from the Benchmarking Centre took on the roles of team facilitators for the study.

The first step taken was to have each group member prepare a summary of his or her own OJT processes. These summaries included narratives of the OJT process as well as flowcharts depicting the work flow in each organization. These summaries also highlighted the areas of concern of the group members with regard to their existing OJT processes.

The initial responses from the benchmarking group indicated that all had some form of OJT for their staff. Generally, the type of training tended to be for newly hired staff who

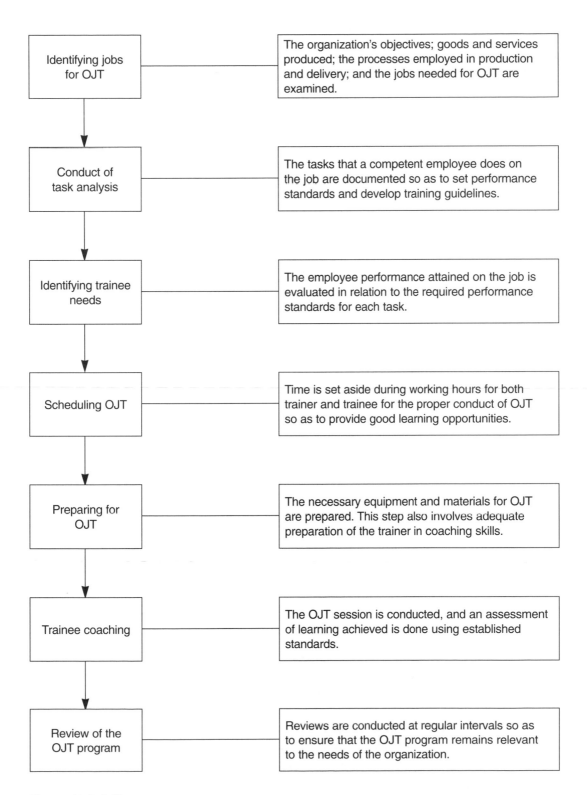

Figure 16.1. OJT process steps.

had to learn some kind of procedural skill, such as the repair or replacement of a machine part. OJT would usually begin upon hire, with the type and length of training depending on the skill to be learned. The skills that the trainee already had were, in many cases, also taken into consideration when planning for OJT. Frequently, OJT was also planned for skills upgrading should it be found necessary. It was found, however, that the framework for the planning, preparation, and the conduct of OJT was generally not very clearly defined among the group members. For instance, the methodology that the trainers used to conduct OJT was often left up to the trainers.

Due to the varied composition of the group, the concerns about OJT were rather wide ranging. These included topics from training for cash collection to the lack of suitable trainers and the scheduling of OJT. Some of the key issues that the group wanted to address in the study were as follows:

- Personnel responsible for the OJT program
- Availability of qualified OJT trainers
- Scheduling of OJT
- Method of conducting OJT
- Identification and development of measures to assess OJT performance

The next step taken was to identify a group of companies with good practices in OJT, which was considered to be a crucial element in the successful outcome of the study. Thus, the criteria adopted in the selection of this benchmark group were first developed around the nature of the study. In this case, it referred to companies with a well-structured and successful OJT program. Secondly, the characteristics of the benchmarking group of companies, as the benchmark partners, had to be comparable companies. Therefore, it was decided that the companies to be included in the benchmark group should be identified based on the following criteria.

- *Company size.* Not more than 1000 employees with a turnover of $170 million or less.
- *OJT program.* A structured and well-recognized OJT program in the company.
- *Work processes.* OJT in the production, customer service, maintenance, or security-related work processes in the company.

Also of importance, the benchmark companies would have to be endorsed by the Institute of Technical Education (ITE) and/or PSB. These two agencies in Singapore can certify organizations that have adopted a systematic and structured approach to the conduct of OJT as certified on-the-job training centers (COJTC). To qualify for the COJTC status, companies must, among other things, demonstrate a commitment to support the implementation of OJT through appointment of trained staff to manage the OJT program; identify trainee needs and develop the appropriate programs; and provide guidance in coaching skills to the supervisors who are required to conduct OJT. Additionally, the organization must have a proper system for documenting training records.

Based on these criteria, a number of companies were invited to participate in the study. Four companies eventually agreed to participate.

Information about the OJT process in both the benchmarking group and the benchmark group was drawn primarily through the use of a questionnaire. The framework and the design of the questionnaire was based on the key steps in a structured OJT system, and took into consideration the issues raised by the benchmarking companies.

A draft of the questionnaire was first sent to the benchmarking group for modification and comments. Subsequently, the finalized questionnaire was prepared and forwarded to the benchmarking group. The finalized questionnaires were also sent to the four benchmark companies for completion. All completed questionnaires were then returned by the companies to PSB for compilation. The responses from the companies were summarized and tabulated. The summary tables were then circulated to all participating companies for process-to-process comparisons and analyses.

The benchmarking group met several times to discuss the results from the questionnaire. While analyzing the results, the team recognized the need to get more details from two of the benchmark companies. The reason was that the performance of these two companies, in particular, was outstanding, as were their stated practices. A list of issues raised by members was forwarded to these two benchmark partners for further clarification and discussion.

In the case of one of these companies, the training manager agreed to meet with members of the benchmarking group for an interview. Members were thus given an opportunity to probe at length about the OJT system in place, as well as the productivity improvements generated through the implementation of its training system. A site visit was arranged by the Benchmarking Centre in the case of the second benchmark partner. During the visit, the host company gave a briefing of the company's OJT management system as well as a tour of the facilities. A question-and-answer session was also scheduled. Furthermore, the host company made arrangements for the visitors to meet the staff—both trainers and trainees—so as to give a complete picture of their OJT system.

As a result of the responses to the questionnaire as well as the interview and site visit, a number of findings were made on the key practices adopted by the benchmark companies in their OJT processes.

OJT Practices in Benchmarking Companies

OJT System

Companies can set up a structured and successful companywide OJT program within a period of one year. This can be achieved even if the program is not confined to one functional area at a time.

OJT covers not only new employees, but also experienced workers and supervisors. Even management staff should undergo OJT.

There is a smooth interface between OJT and off-job training (Off-JT) in the plans. In this respect, both theoretical and practical training are well integrated for maximum benefit. There are plans for a progression of skills to be acquired by employees through both Off-JT and OJT during their working life, so that they can effectively contribute to the organization.

A key factor contributing to the successful implementation of structured OJT systems in the benchmark companies is the training provided to managers and supervisors on the management and administration of the OJT program. This training covers areas such as the planning and implementation of OJT, the evaluation and review of OJT, and the management of OJT development and delivery.

Identification of Jobs for OJT

Change is cited as the major factor in identifying jobs for OJT. Examples of change include new equipment, new staff, and changes in procedures or processes. Additionally, low standards of output or service could serve as a basis for job identification. The priority in identifying jobs for OJT is given to those jobs that have the most significant impact on the company's business or operations.

Conduct of Task Analysis

Various techniques are used to gather data for the task analysis. These include interviews with both job holders and their supervisors, feedback through questionnaires, examination of company records, and observing competent employees carrying out their tasks. Additionally, the benchmark companies gather feedback through discussions with department heads, and review relevant training programs of recognized training institutions. This is done so that the benchmark companies can get a good understanding of the type of skills and knowledge that can be imparted on-the-job for specific jobs, and how OJT can smoothly interface with Off-JT.

Detailed procedures are in place for training in specific jobs as part of the process of task analysis. These training procedures are intended to provide the step-by-step training instructions to impart the skills and knowledge required for the achievement of task standards. These procedures are developed based on data collection, and the expertise of external/internal consultants. They are closely aligned with the detailed steps required for performing a task (or task elements); the key points for error-free, quality work when performing the task; the performance standards to be achieved by the trainee; and the specific skills and knowledge required for performing the task.

Training managers act as internal consultants, or change agents, for developing and delivering OJT. They are trained on consultancy process skills (such as how to diagnose problems, plan action, and facilitate implementation) and OJT development skills (such as how to conduct task analysis, develop OJT course blueprints, implement OJT, and evaluate OJT).

Identifying Trainee Needs

Employees for OJT are identified on the basis of change. For instance, these workers could be new employees or transferred staff. The installation of new equipment, or changes in procedures/processes, are also grounds for workers to undergo OJT. Additionally, OJT is scheduled for upgrading workers or for promotion.

Scheduling OJT

The department and line managers in the benchmark companies are actively involved in preparing the schedule for the OJT program. Supervisors might be involved as well.

OJT is not carried out for all the hours that the trainee is working but only at specific times of the day. The times during which OJT is scheduled are spelled out in the OJT manual. This could vary, however, depending on the pattern of customer traffic or production schedule. The schedule for OJT is planned in advance, and department managers are entrusted with the responsibility to keep track of training and schedule staff for OJT whenever it is required.

Workplace Preparation for OJT

Proper scheduling of training ensures that a suitable work space is available for conduct of the training. Additionally, preparation involves having ready the proper materials and equipment.

Trainer Preparation

Trainers are mostly at the supervisor level in the organization. A minimum educational or skills level is set for trainers. Furthermore, trainers undergo a formal OJT trainer's program at a training institution.

Trainee Coaching

The trainees are provided with documentation on the schedules, expectations, and objectives of the training at the start of OJT.

There is a manual or framework for training that trainers are required to follow. In particular, there is a standard four-step coaching process for OJT. These steps are as follows:

- *Demonstration.* The trainer shows the trainee how the whole task is done.

- *Guided instruction.* The trainer breaks down the task into small steps, explains each step, allows the trainee to practice each step at a time, and provides performance feedback.

- *Skills practice.* The trainee performs the whole task with feedback from the trainer.

- *Follow-up.* The trainee carries out the task independently with periodic monitoring by the trainer.

Clear targets, standards, and time frames are set. These cover areas such as the type of work to be done, the time frame for the completion of OJT, and the number of job rotations to be done.

Regular assessments are made of trainees. These may include an oral or written test as well as observation of the trainee on-site. Additionally, such assessments are made by using mystery guests in the service businesses. These guests would provide input as to whether they were generally satisfied with the level of service rendered.

OJT performance is taken into account in the employee's performance appraisal. Moreover, wages are pegged specifically to the skills level acquired during OJT.

The OJT trainer-trainee ratio varies from 1:1 to 1:5, with an average of 1:3. It should, however, be noted that the actual ratio during a training session is determined by a number of factors. For example, when training new employees a ratio of 1:1 is used whereas a higher ratio is used in the training of more experienced staff. The skill to be trained is also a factor in the actual trainer-to-trainee ratio for a session. This ratio may vary even during the skilling of a particular task; that is, while training on a task, the ratio can change from one session to the next depending on the requirements for the session.

The handling of cash by OJT trainees is carefully monitored and controlled. For instance, OJT sessions are limited to a maximum of four hours to avoid prolonged exposure to the handling of cash.

With workers of low education who may not be able to grasp the course content, trainers use pictorial training documentation and simple flowcharts to explain the work process. Furthermore, language is not regarded as a barrier to training, as it is conducted in the trainees' preferred language.

Review of OJT Program

OJT programs are reviewed regularly, either on a quarterly or an annual basis. In the process of reviewing their OJT programs, the relevant programs of recognized training institutions are also examined, so as to get ideas for improving the content of their own programs.

Performance Indicators

Several performance indicators were included in the study questionnaire. The tabulation of the average performance for the benchmarking group companies and the benchmark group on the various measures is presented as Table 16.1. The significant performance gap between the two groups of companies simply emphasizes the differences in the management and conduct of OJT of the two groups.

Table 16.1. Performance measures.

Measure	Benchmarking group Average	Benchmark group Average
Estimated person-hours spent per quarter per OJT trainer on OJT training	32.2	91.6
Annual percent of workforce that underwent OJT program	16.1	31
Success rate of OJT program (Percent of trainees who successfully completed program)	82.5	100
Percent of workers who have moved up the skills ladder	60	100
Percent of workers who have been multiskilled as a result of OJT	5	65
Percent of workers promoted as a result of OJT	10	75
Annual training expenditure on OJT as percent of payroll	2.5	5.5
Gains achieved by OJT program on the following indicators		
• Increase in output (percent)	20	50
• Reduction in cost of waste as a percent of sales turnover (percent)	5.2	10.3
• Reduction in cost of rework as a percent of sales turnover (percent)	3.2	10.1
• Decrease in the cost of complaint handling as a percent of sales turnover (percent)	16.7	32.5
• Reduction of training cost (percent)	12.5	28
• Reduction in cycle time (percent)	10	20

Proposed Improvements
The findings of the study brought to light the following procedures and processes that the benchmarking group could consider adopting from the benchmark companies to improve OJT systems.

Coverage of the OJT Program
The benchmarking group could widen the scope of the OJT programs to include all functional areas of the organization. A companywide OJT program would have certain advantages over a more limited program. For example, such a step would ensure that there is a greater commitment in the organization to the implementation of a structured OJT program and that performance standards are set for all staff. If companies, as a start, want to limit the scope of the OJT system, then it is important to consider including jobs into the program that have the greatest impact on business goals and profits.

The benchmarking group could consider including employees other than new hires in the program. Such a step would provide an avenue for upgrading of the more experienced staff. Even managers could be included in the OJT program so as to ensure that all new managers know and appreciate the work situation on the shop floor.

Developing an OJT Program

One of the steps that companies could take to develop a structured and comprehensive OJT program is to conduct a task analysis and incorporate the findings into the program. If necessary, the possibility of recruiting consultants for this specific purpose could be considered. Companies could also develop their training managers as in-house consultants to company staff for developing and delivering OJT. As part of their responsibilities, the in-house consultants should facilitate the conduct of the task analysis and the development of the training procedures.

The benchmarking companies, like the benchmark partners, should adopt a systematic framework for the development of comprehensive and detailed training procedures around which an OJT program can be structured. The training guidelines are closely aligned with the skills and knowledge required for performing the task, the performance standards for the task, and the detailed steps in performing the task. Such a competence-based framework requires everyone within the organization to take responsibility for training and development. Managers and supervisors have to be trained to introduce and manage OJT in their work units. In the benchmark companies, such training is provided by sending managers and supervisors for external courses, or conducting training in-house after the internal training expertise in this area has been developed.

Clear and Detailed Documentation for OJT

The development of training guidelines, through task analysis for the conduct of OJT for each task, forms one of the first and critical steps in the development of a structured OJT program. Feedback from the benchmark partners has indicated that without such documentation, the development of a structured and successful OJT program would not be possible.

It is recommended that the development of such documentation be carried out in close consultation with the relevant department/line managers and supervisors; however, the actual preparation of the training documentation can be approached in at least two ways. For instance, in the case of one benchmark company, one person first wrote a draft over a three-month period, and then consulted with the relevant departments. For another benchmark partner, the draft was first written by the appropriate department heads followed by vetting and revision in close consultation with the training manager. The process in this case took about four to five months.

No matter which approach is taken, the involvement of the managers of the various departments plays a crucial role. This is not only because they are the ones who know the tasks best, but also because involving the departments has the advantage of securing the commitment and support of managers for the training manuals. Therefore, managers would feel that they have ownership of the training documentation and are more likely to ensure that the new procedures were followed.

To minimize difficulties posed by language, training documentation—especially that for use by trainees—can be made pictorial as in the case of one of the benchmark companies. Thus, rather than having to read a procedure explaining the steps for a task, illustrations could be used wherever possible to convey the same message. Additionally, flowcharts illustrating the steps required for the satisfactory completion of a task could be considered for incorporation into the training documentation. The training should also be carried out in the trainees' preferred language so as to minimize the possibility of misunderstanding.

To ensure that the appropriate training documentation is carefully developed, and with adequate feedback and consultation, companies may consider having at least four to five months set aside in its development. For example, in one benchmark company, this time period was spent developing OJT course blueprints for 30 jobs covering 630 OJT hours in functions such as administration, marketing and sales, security services, food and beverage services, and engineering services. A longer time period may be necessary depending on the amount of documentation required. Furthermore, once finalized, changes to the training documentation should only be made upon approval at the appropriate levels or departments. Such changes should also be formalized by the training department and promulgated accordingly.

Competent Trainers

Minimum standards should be set for OJT trainers. These standards must include education level, length of service, designation, special qualifications or knowledge, and skill content. The minimum requirements must be clearly specified to ensure that trainers have a suitable level of expertise in the task that they have to train. Importantly, trainers in the benchmark companies are required to attend a formal OJT trainers program. By taking such steps, the benchmarking group can develop a pool of suitably qualified and certified OJT trainers.

The benchmarking companies could also follow the lead of one of the benchmark partners to further improve the quality of the trainers by having them participate in development programs. These programs could cover various relevant areas such as the handling of difficult employees.

The number of trainers in an organization is obviously a factor that cannot be ignored. As a guide, the trainer-to employee ratio in organizations could be between about 1:21 and 1:25, which were the ratios found for two of the better performing benchmark partners.

Conduct of OJT

Companies should consider adopting the four-step coaching method that the benchmark companies have successfully employed in their OJT programs. This would ensure a uniformity of approaches to coaching as well as increasing its effectiveness.

An important component of the conduct of OJT is, of course, the assessment or evaluation of trainees at the end of the program. The conduct of such assessment for all trainees should be formalized in the training documentation and should be closely followed. The benefits of this are that both trainers and trainees know the standards to be met and can then work toward achieving them. A formalized system of evaluation, using oral or written tests together with job performance standards, would also minimize the level of subjectivity in the appraisal of trainees. Furthermore, such a step could serve as feedback on the effectiveness of the OJT program.

An additional method of evaluation that companies in the service businesses may consider adapting is that based on the mystery-guest concept. These guests, who remain anonymous, provide input as to whether they are generally satisfied with the level of service or performance.

The companies could consider adopting a trainer-to-trainee ratio that does not exceed 1:4. This ratio would, of course, have to be determined by various factors such as the skill to be trained; however, the experience of the benchmark partners has been that a ratio exceeding 1:4 results in training that is neither efficient nor effective. In fact, one of the benchmark partners ensures that for new employees this ratio is at 1:1.

The number of hours per quarter that trainers are scheduled for OJT is an important aspect of the program that would directly affect the tempo of OJT in an organization. Based on the indicators furnished by benchmark companies, organizations may wish to consider an average of about 90 hours so as to ensure that sufficient time is allocated for OJT.

OJT should not be scheduled for all the hours that a trainee works in a day, but only at specific times of the day. These schedules, which might be spelled out in the training manuals or planned carefully in advance, ought to provide for adequate training opportunities, as well as to ensure that there is close supervision. In this respect, time frames for the completion of tasks should be made explicit.

Administration of OJT

The administration of the OJT program should be done by staff who have undergone appropriate training in the management of a structured OJT program. These staff may include managers, supervisors, or even the trainers themselves. The benchmark companies utilize such staff not only for program administration, but also for monitoring and providing advice on the conduct of OJT.

The review of training documentation, as well as the OJT program as a whole, form a critical part of the administration of the OJT program in the benchmark companies. The importance lies in the fact that it is only through such a review process that problems are identified and program improvements made. Taking the lead from the benchmark companies, organizations may consider reviewing both the training documentation and the OJT program either on a quarterly or annual basis. It should perhaps be noted that the schedule that is followed is not as important as ensuring that a mechanism is in place for a systematic and periodic review. Additionally, to assist in improving their programs, organizations could consider examining the training programs of recognized training institutions.

Companies may also consider limiting the liability of trainers and trainees in case of missing cash or even damage to equipment or machinery during the OJT period. In this way the concerns of all persons involved are taken into account. To minimize such situations, OJT sessions could also be limited to a few hours at a time.

Integrating OJT with the Performance Management System

An OJT program should not be developed and implemented in isolation. It should, as in the case of the benchmark companies, be considered—at least implicitly—a part of a broader system of performance management. A case in point is that of the system for performance appraisal. All companies in the benchmark group consider OJT performance as an integral part of their annual performance appraisal reports. Therefore, it may be advantageous for the benchmarking group to consider adopting this practice.

Wage level is another area for consideration. In this instance, the benchmark companies have generally linked wages to the skills level acquired during OJT.

Study Report

The report of the OJT benchmarking study that included the recommendations for improvement based on the findings was subsequently sent to all participants.

Implementation and Planned Changes

A follow-up by PSB with the benchmarking group was done about six months after completion of the study. This follow-up, conducted through reports and telephone interviews, focused on the actions taken by these participants to improve their OJT training systems as a result of the study.

In general, the benchmarking companies indicated that the study provided useful insight and increased their awareness into the way OJT programs could be developed and managed. Moreover, the study also provided these companies with an understanding of the performance improvements that could be achieved with a systematic and structured OJT program.

An important finding of the study was that the benchmark companies developed clear and detailed documentation through task analysis for OJT. This was, in fact, a frequent first step taken by the benchmarking companies in developing a systematic and effective OJT system.

The benchmarking group was also following the benchmark partners' lead of adopting optimum OJT trainer-to-trainee ratios for their operations. They have found that such ratios have improved the overall effectiveness of OJT by reducing the amount of time spent in retraining.

One of the benchmarking participants reported that the results of the study served as an added impetus to process improvements already underway in the area of OJT. The organization has since worked with the ITE and has recently become a COJTC. In this regard, another two of the companies in the benchmarking group have also approached the ITE and are in the process of obtaining COJTC certification.

Given the long lead times required for implementation, quantitative measures have yet to be collected on the changes instituted thus far; however, feedback from the benchmarking companies with regard to the steps taken testifies to the value of the benchmarking study toward their OJT process improvements.

Reference

Pious, Joseph. 1992. OJT: A cost-effective way to develop a skilled workforce. *Productivity Digest* (August): 2–5.

About the Authors

Darshan Singh is the deputy director for benchmarking and Benedict Anandam is the senior officer for benchmarking, both in the planning and research department of the Singapore Productivity and Standards Board. Singh received a bachelor of arts from the National University of Singapore, while Anandam received a master's of science from the University of Calgary.

At PSB, Singh and Anandam's responsibilities include promoting benchmarking as a tool to help organizations master best practices; generating and disseminating information on benchmarking and best practices; and assisting organizations to assess their performance against the Singapore Quality Award framework of business excellence. The authors may be contacted as follows:

Singapore Productivity and Standards Board
PSB Building
2 Bukit Merah Central
Singapore 159835
Telephone: 65 279 3844
Facsimile: 65 275 3002
E-mail: atben@psb.gov.sg

CHAPTER 17
Emergence of Benchmarking in Japan

Tomohiro Takanashi, Consulting Director and Deputy Division Director, Research and Consulting Division, The Japan Research Institute, Ltd.

Prologue

Until a few years ago, only a few professionals and businesspeople in Japan knew about benchmarking as a kind of quality management tool. Even then, most professionals did not consider benchmarking as a systematic methodology or as a tool for management revolution.

New methodologies to dramatically change the business processes of companies suddenly appeared in Japan's business world. Examples of such methodologies include reengineering as promoted by Champy and Hammer and the Malcolm Baldrige National Quality Award criteria. Benchmarking, especially, has been one of the most effective methodologies.

Before this, companies often used the term *benchmarking* for comparisons of computer performance. Most likely, the Japanese companies benchmarking against American corporations had merely thought of benchmarking as "a funny English expression" that means "comparison" in Japanese.

This author's first contact with benchmarking was during an international quality study done by the American Quality Foundation (AQF) during 1989–1992. At that time, the worldwide accounting firm of Arthur Young International had undertaken international quality studies for four industries (automobiles, computers, banking, and health care) in four countries (Canada, Germany, Japan, and the United States). The author headed a study team in Japan.

There are several reasons for the emergence of benchmarking in the Japanese business world. They include the following:

• Benchmarking is a new management methodology and tool for Japanese top management. It is seen as a savior or as a magic word. This is mostly because Japanese management has come up against a wall called *limits of restructuring*. The Japanese economy is still sluggish, and many longstanding management methodologies (including restructuring of organizations) had no effect on the remarkable recovery of business performances.

• Entering the 1990s, with the collapse of the notorious Bubble Economy, the Japan economy has been struggling with the Heisei depression and an opaque future after the depression. It is under such conditions that Japanese management has been groping for a solution to the problem. (Note: The Bubble Economy is defined as an unusual and unbelievable economic boom, which started in 1986 and peaked in early 1990. Many indices skyrocketed during the Bubble Economy, including the indices of urban commercial land price and urban residential land price. These indices have been in a downward trend since 1990.)

• A sense of crisis coming from the World Economy Forum (WEF) report on competitiveness. Japan declined to 14th in 1997 from first in 1993.

• The revival of American companies in the middle 1990s, with the corresponding decline of Japanese companies.

The Benchmarking Promotion Conference

History

The Japan Productivity Center for Socio Economic Development (JPC/SED) organized the Benchmarking Promotion Conference in July 1995 in response to the promotion of benchmarking as a successful U.S. management tool and to combat the downward trend of Japanese competitiveness as clearly stated in the WEF report. At the time, the sponsor companies were Fuji Xerox; KK; Asahi and Company (a member firm of Arthur Andersen); the Japan Research Institute (the second largest think tank in Japan, owned by the Sumitomo Group); and Jusco Company (one of the largest supermarket chains).

Purpose and Organization Structure

The purposes of the conference are as follows:

• Benchmarking promotion

• Training of benchmarking advocates

• Creating a benchmarking network

• Establishing a benchmarking information center for international cooperation

To achieve these purposes, the conference was established in July 1995. Its organizational chart is shown in Figure 17.1.

Conference activities from 1995 to 1997 included the following:

Promotional initiatives for diffusion meetings. These are three-hour monthly meetings with the following topics.

• Studies of what benchmarking is through actual case presentation

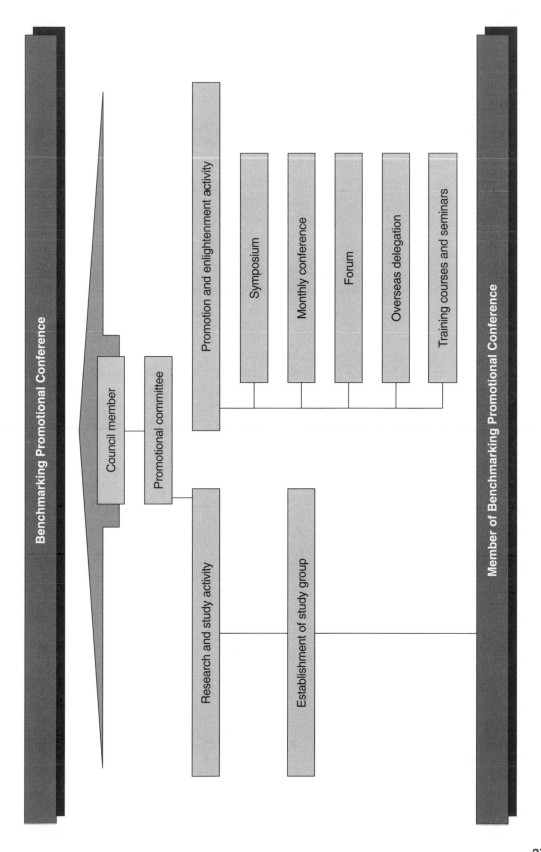

Figure 17.1. Organizational chart for the Benchmarking Promotion Conference.

- How to carry out a benchmarking project and its issues
- New product development and benchmarking
- Benchmarking case studies of Fuji Xerox, GE, NEC Home Electronics, Nippon Hoechst Marion Roussel, and American Express
- A report on the American Productivity and Quality Center's (APQC's) Benchmarking Award sponsored by the International Benchmarking Clearinghouse (IBC)
- A report on the IBC's U.S. conference
- The meaning and purpose of benchmarking in an information-oriented society
- Quality management and benchmarking
- Japan Quality Award criteria and benchmarking
- How to apply benchmarking
- Designing benchmarking research
- Best practices in Japan
- Symposium on how to develop benchmarking, based on monthly meetings' results and studies
- Direction and results of benchmarking in Japan

Research and study meetings. These are also three-hour monthly meetings.

- Benchmarking for new product development, referring to case studies in the United States and to the opinions of American scholars and professionals

- Measurement of new product development, including identifying which metrics to measure, the most appropriate tools and techniques, and how results are fed back into the implementation process

- Innovation and creativity in new product development, including the relationship between innovation and creativity and their effects, how to produce creativity, and its environment and organization in a new system

- Cycle time of new product development, including measurement of cycle time, the goal of cycle time reduction, and reengineering

- A case study on breakeven time (BET) at Hewlett-Packard, which discusses successful performance measurement, characteristics of performance measurement for Japanese companies, and the applicability of the case to Japanese companies

- Relationship between reengineering and the quality of new product development, including points of breakthrough of new product development and a suggested framework and implementation of benchmarking for new product development

- Benchmarking tool study meeting, the purpose of which is to study how a benchmarking project should be undertaken in the real world and how to Japanize and promote the benchmarking training course developed by IBC

• Case studies of Bell Canada and by (Mr.) Jan Massman of the Massachusetts Institute of Technology's Laboratory for Manufacturing and Productivity

Members

The following organizations are members of the Benchmarking Promotional Conference.

Ajinomoto Co., Inc.
American Express Japan
Amway Japan Ltd.
Asahi & Co
Asahi Breweries, Ltd.
Asahi Chemical Industry Co., Ltd.
Bridgestone Corp.
Canon Aptex Inc.
Canon Inc.
Casio Computer Co., Ltd.
Fuji Xerox Co. Ltd.
Fujita Kanko Inc.
Hitachi, Ltd.
Honda Motor Co., Ltd.
Hoya Corp.
IBM Japan, Ltd.
Intel Japan K.K.
Isuzu Motors Ltd.
The Japan Research Institute Limited
Japan Travel Bureau
Jusco Co., Ltd.
Kajima Corp.
Kansai Electric Power Co., Inc.,
Kirin Brewery Co., Ltd.
Kokuyo Co., Ltd.
Kubota Corp.
Matsushita Electric Industrial Co., Ltd.
Matsushita Electric Works, Ltd.
Meidensha Corp.
Meiji Milk Products Co., Ltd.
Mitsubishi Electric Corp.
Mitsubishi Motors Corp.
Mitsui Construction Co., Ltd.

Mitsui Marine & Fire Insurance Co., Ltd.
NEC Corp.
NEC Home Electronics, Ltd.
NEC Planning Research, Ltd.
Nippon Hoechst Marion Roussel
Nippon Motorola Ltd.
Nippon Telegraph and Telephone Corp.
Obayashi Corp.
Oki Electric Industry Co., Ltd.
Omron Corp.
Organo Corp.
Osaka Gas Co., Ltd.
Pioneer Electronic Corp.
Richo Co., Ltd.
Sakura Bank, Ltd.
Sekisui Chemical Co., Ltd.
Sekisui Plastics Co., Ltd.
Sharp Corp.
Sony Corp.
Sumitomo Bank, Ltd.
Sumitomo Chemical Co., Ltd.
Sumitomo Corp.
Sumitomo Heavy Industries, Ltd.
Takashimaya Co., Ltd.
Teijin, Ltd.
Texas Instruments Japan Limited
Tokyo University
Tokyu Construction Co., Ltd.
Toshiba Corp.
Vedatech Corp.
Yakult Honsha Co., Ltd.
Yamaha Motor Co., Ltd.

Benchmarking Case Studies in Japan

The following sections summarize various case studies that have been completed in Japan. These studies were presented at monthly conference meetings during 1995–1997.

Fuji Xerox

Internal benchmarking. In 1994, 32 retail companies of Xerox started benchmarking. They selected 14 metrics, such as percentage of discount, cancellation rate, sales amount per head, number of visits, and so on. The companies competed with each other in these metrics. Every month a ranking was announced, and the top performer in each metric was named. Then, once a year, these top performers presented the reasons why they came out on top. The presidents of the 32 Xerox retail companies attended this presentation, and decided to introduce other companies' best practices. As a result, it was shown that individual profits doubled by the end of 1995.

Benchmarking against C Company. Xerox benchmarked against a partner identified as C Company. It showed a loss in the fourth quarter in 1991 because of another company's (identified as D Company) low-priced computer. Profits substantially increased after C Company undertook restructuring; changed presidents; switched from a high-priced to low-priced structure; and changed its cost determination process from a method of adding up all costs to one of price minus profit.

As a result of benchmarking C Company, Fuji Xerox checked its cost target. Then it started to change how to design, buy, and manufacture machines in order to attain the difficult goal of cost target and to reform the way of manufacturing. By sharing information and adopting novel ideas for design and manufacture, costs were halved in the first phase. By the second phase, costs were again cut in two, thus reducing costs to one-fourth of the original.

New initiatives. Fuji Xerox introduced the ideas of originality, of sensitivity, and of the importance of an individual's personality. These ideas helped to create a high-sensitivity enterprise, which Fuji Xerox calls the "New Work Way." Fuji Xerox believes that benchmarking is one the ways of to realize such a dream.

American Express–Japan

American Express has constructed a database of worldwide benchmarking information at its head office in New York. Since the system in New York is linked to that of IBC, American Express can get IBC's information too.

As part of its internal benchmarking efforts, started in 1993, American Express selected key processes that are common to different operations around the world. Then it decided what to benchmark, and a benchmarking team collected data by visiting selected cities around the world. After all the documentation was collected, a matrix was created and used to compare the best practices of each country. Finally, the possibility of implementing the results was analyzed. The key processes identified were as follows:

- Getting a credit card to members
- Customer management
- Customer service
- Invoicing and collection
- Risk management
- Obtaining members through stores and the management of that system
- Overhead and administrative staff processes

These processes were then divided into about 200 subprocesses. For example, the process of managing sales vouchers is from sales, to approval, to sending sales vouchers, to entry data, to payment, and to inquiry. Each process was ranked into three categories by a matrix so that the status quo in each country could be confirmed.

In this study it was discovered that a system for the accurate measurement of process performance must be created. Also, it is important to introduce activity-based costing and to develop other performance measurements. In the next stage of benchmarking, it is necessary to compare the internal best practices with the best practices that are applied to other industries.

NEC Home Electronics

In 1993, NEC Home Electronics embarked on a benchmarking study for the purpose of reducing head office staff. The head office and administrative sections were a big part of the company's overhead, and it was important to reduce it. The benchmarking team was organized with employees from staff positions and other members in line roles. The study lasted about three months.

At first, the NEC Home Electronics team visited five companies, which were selected as benchmarking partners from publicly available data. It was possible to visit one company after a certain seminar. For the other companies, NEC collected information through business journals. It was quite easy to benchmark because these companies were not competitors. Although the purpose of the benchmarking study was to confirm actual conditions and reduce the size of the head office, the biggest hidden factor was to speed up decision making. Many in the organization felt that rapid decision making requires top-down management. But because NEC management is not like that of an owner-enterprise, there was a need to reduce head office staff in order to achieve the same purpose.

Depending on how some of the conferences were held, some unexpected results were observed. With one company, NEC examined the effect of holding monthly meetings at the end of the month where numerical metrics for business performance were discussed. Usually such meetings were held around the 25th or 26th, and the possible effect of waiting for accurate numbers was surprisingly high.

Nippon Hoechst Marion Roussel

In April 1996, Nippon Hoechst Marion Roussel (N-HMR), a health care management organization, started to consolidate its companies. It had two objectives for its benchmarking project. The first objective was to set quantitative goals and implement a continuous improvement program that could be measured against such goals. This was especially important since there were weaknesses in the areas of company organization, skill levels, productivity, and human resources development. The second objective was to use best practices from the health care industry to integrate the different N-HMR companies into consolidation.

Benchmarking began in February 1996. At the beginning of the process, each division selected task force members. The most important things for the members to understand was why they were selected to the task force and what benchmarking was all about. Additionally, there was a need for cooperation among the performers (employees), observers (managers), and the president or general manager.

N-HMR analyzed competitors to identify main process gaps. For example, what do competitors use for metrics? To focus on one of these processes, a questionnaire about customer satisfaction was sent to wholesalers. Sixty-three companies answered the survey, which revealed that N-HMR was ranked 11th among 11 companies. Part of the reason for its 11th place was that N-HMR was not yet known as a single company.

Generally speaking, it would have been better to ask for comparative interview data after collecting some information from outside sources. But in the case of N-HMR, there was no information about the manufacturing and logistics section of the medical industry.

Nine of the 10 competitors were approached. Of these, three companies understood benchmarking and agreed to participate in the study; three companies agreed to visits and to discuss only open processes; two companies excused themselves from the survey; and one company refused to participate.

After a detailed examination of the benchmarking results, N-HMR's logistics section was able to think in new ways. It discovered that there are other companies interested in participating in benchmarking studies. Although N-HMR's end users are hospital patients, the organization realized it could better serve them by treating its wholesalers as partners.

NEC Semiconductor Business Group

The NEC Semiconductor Business Group is the first winner of the Japan Quality Award, which was established on December 15, 1995. It is equivalent to the U.S. Malcolm Baldrige National Quality Award. The following is adapted from the information and analysis (category 2.2) section of NEC's 1996 management quality report (award application).

In the latter half of the 1960s, the concept for business strategy advancement changed from "a policy of attaching high priority to supplying goods and services between companies under the corporate umbrella" to "the main thrust being concentrated on outward sales." Management leaders at that time promoted a rigorous policy of "a half-step ahead of everyone else" as the fundamental stance on an enterprise's operations. This led companies to shoot for the number-one position in the domestic market, and the number-two position on the global scene. Today, this idea of "a half-step ahead of everyone else" has permeated every corner of the business world, and has found its place as the paradigm in the minds of every rank-and-file employee. "How are the other companies doing?" and "How are we doing compared to other divisions?" are questions that are being routinely asked everywhere.

The NEC Semiconductor Business Group recognized that the market trend and the trends promoted by competitors are very important. In 1971, it organized a task force to gather the latest and the most accurate information on these topics from various credible sources. In addition, comparison data related to major business metrics, such as the level of customer satisfaction, market share, level of technology, manufacturing capability, and price, were collected through a customer satisfaction survey and from questionnaires conducted by external research institutions. All enterprise units analyzed these data in line with their own needs, and utilized the same to set new objectives so that they could outperform their competitors. By assessing their true competitive position, their strengths, and their weaknesses, the enterprise units clarified what elements were needed to succeed and confirmed the things that will be useful for better future planning.

Since then, the NEC Semiconductor Business Group has been utilizing comparative data on competitors as one of the tools to improve company operations. Through its recent activities associated with going through the screening process as a candidate for the Japanese Management Quality Award, the company realized that benchmarking is a powerful tool for management improvement. The past approach of using the question, "How are our competitors doing?" was also understood, at the same time, to be part of benchmarking.

One of the activities that the NEC Semiconductor Business Group has been actively promoting is internal benchmarking among manufacturing units throughout the world. Its quality, cost, delivery date (QCD) parameter is composed of very critical information on which a business's fate (win or lose) depends, and such information is hard to come by from competitors. Therefore, internal benchmarking will play an important role as an organization endeavors to learn the best possible way to improve operations. Naturally, benchmarking will not succeed by competition alone. It is necessary to nourish a kind of relationship in which these independent entities share their own successful practices while leaning about each other. Thus, competition and mutual interactive cooperation are the keys to successful internal benchmarking.

The NEC Semiconductor Business Group conducts process benchmarking during which the processes of other industries are also introduced in an effort to raise the efficiency of manufacturing processes. The practice of benchmarking, normally conducted by individual operational units in the past, will be conducted more on a global basis, and the clarity, strengths, and weaknesses of the core competencies will be made increasingly distinct. The NEC Semiconductor Business Group is currently carrying out its plan to make the benchmarking methodology the best possible practice through intensified improvement and endeavor.

New Movement

Justification for Using Benchmarking

As competition has intensified, Japanese companies have been able to maintain their strength with cost-cutting programs. The potential benefits of restructuring programs focused on cost cutting have, however, reached a limit. Many organizations have turned to automation, and have subsequently

- Increased the efficiency of their production processes
- Lowered costs by shifting manufacturing bases overseas
- Lowered costs of subcontracted processing work
- Increased the share of processes handled in-house
- Decreased the size of their workforce

Companies have also taken steps to increase white-collar workers' efficiency by introducing paperless administrative departments and implementing personnel reductions.

Despite these efforts, there has been a rise in the number of bankruptcies among small and medium-sized companies, a hollowing out of domestic manufacturing industries, and an increase in employees' concern regarding the stability of their jobs. In view of these problems, a growing number of companies are seeking to realize the potential benefits of benchmarking.

Globalization

For many Japanese companies, it is imperative that measures be promptly taken to emulate the example of U.S. benchmarkers in eliminating established practices and introducing new management systems that will allow them to survive even when the yen-dollar rate is less than $83 (¥100). Amid a global society organized on the basis of international competition, Japanese companies cannot simply focus on their current performance. They must adopt long-term global perspectives on their management systems and operations. In other words, to succeed, they must shift from a simple emphasis on competitiveness and quality control–related concepts and give greater attention to issues related to the changing structure and harmonious development of the global economy. Benchmarking programs are a useful tool for instituting the management reforms Japanese companies require.

Benchmarking Questionnaire Tells of the Possibilities

The Japan Research Institute Ltd. developed a research questionnaire during January–April 1997. It surveyed 208 of Japan's largest companies. Some of the questions and their responses are summarized as follows. (Note that some companies did not answer all of the questions.)

- As a management tool for operational reforms, was benchmarking used?

  —Yes: 68 companies (35.6 percent)

- For yes respondents, why do you apply benchmarking?

  —To get breakthrough idea: 33 companies (39.8 percent)

  —To give the field staff a big impact by showing other companies best practices: 30 companies (36.1 percent)

- Do you think benchmarking is effective to the operational reforms for product development, marketing, transportation, sales, warehouse management, finance, accounting, general affairs, personnel matters, and so on?

  —Yes: 182 companies (87.5 percent)

- Are you interested in benchmarking ?

  —Yes: 190 companies (91.3 percent)

- For yes respondents: Regarding benchmarking partners, do you want to include other industry companies with excellent operational processes?

  —Yes: 177 companies (93.2 percent)

- Do you think it is possible to gather information directly from benchmarking partners?

  —Yes: 91 companies (47.9 percent)

- How do you respond when your company is selected as benchmarking partner?

  —Accept: 14 companies (7.4 percent)

  —Accept with condition: 126 companies (66.3 percent)

Examples of Benchmarking Studies in Japan

The following list details the variety of benchmarking studies being conducted in Japan.

- NEC Home Electronics is benchmarking five Japanese companies regarding downsizing headquarters staff.

- American Express–Japan is using internal benchmarking for the operational process of member stores.

- Technische Universitate Dresdenis is conducting a benchmarking study for new product development with companies in the United Kingdom, Germany, and Japan.

- The Japan Research Institute is doing research on the status quo in reengineering and benchmarking initiatives.

- Fuji Xerox is benchmarking a computer company regarding cost management.

- Nippon Hoechst Marion Roussel is utilizing competitive benchmarking against 10 of Japan's largest pharmaceutical companies for its logistics process.

- A British company is benchmarking two Japanese companies regarding a flexible employment system.

- An educational institution known as B University is benchmarking against two other universities about management innovation in the organization.

- An enterprise known as C Computer Company is benchmarking with five foreign companies regarding financial risk management.

- An organization known as D Nonstore Retailer is conducting a benchmarking study based on a database of performance measurements.

- An organization known as E American Company is benchmarking with two Japanese companies regarding total production maintenance.

- An enterprise known as F Computer Company is conducting a benchmarking study with 10 Japanese companies about the accounts receivable and the collection process.

- An electrical equipment company is benchmarking against five Japanese companies regarding a new product planning process.

- An office equipment company is benchmarking its logistics process.

- An electronics/electrical equipment company is conducting a benchmarking study about new product development.

About the Author

Tomohiro (Tom) Takanashi is the consulting director for the Japan Research Institute (JRI), a private think tank formed in 1989 out of the Japan Information Service. The JRI is a knowledge engineering company that combines its expertise in research, consulting, and systems integration to propose high-quality solutions to a variety of global challenges. Established and funded by the Sumitomo group, the JRI employs over 1500 people in offices in Tokyo and Osaka.

For more than 20 years, Takanashi served major clients of Ernst and Young Tokyo (formerly Arthur Young) in an audit and/or consulting capacity, including work on strategic information systems, corporate strategies, operational consulting, and overseas investment.

Takanashi is the coordinator of the Benchmarking Promotion Conference, which is an internal organization of the Japan Productivity Center for Socio Economic Development. He is a member of the supporting committee for the Japan Quality Award, and was a 1996 judge and examiner for that award. He has served as director of many professional and business communities, including the Hong Kong–Japan Chamber of Commerce and Industry, the Japan Association of Business Analysts, the Japan Society for Finance Management, and Japan Society for Risk Management.

Takanashi has been widely published in 32 books (in Japanese) as an author, collaborator, or translator. Recent titles include *An Introduction to Risk Management* (1997, Nihon Keizai Shinbun, Inc.); *Management Quality Revolution?* (1996, Toyo Keizai, Inc.); and *Revive! Management Power* (1994, Chuo Keizaisha).

Tomohiro Takanashi
Consulting Director and Deputy Division Director
Research and Consulting Division
The Japan Research Institute, Ltd.
16 Ichibancho, Chiyoda-ku
Tokyo, Japan 102
Telephone: 03-3288-4791
Facsimile: 03-3288-5540
E-mail: takanasi@ird.jri.co.jp

CHAPTER 18

The Benchmarking Group in Brazil

Rosangela Catunda, Vice President, Grifo Enterprises

Introduction

The Brazilian corporate community has been making ever-increasing efforts to develop and improve the quality of life for its citizens. As a result of this effort, quality and correlate disciplines have become a major concern of organizations.

Within this context, several actions at the national level have been developed by the companies. In 1992, the creation of the Quality National Award, based on the U.S. Malcolm Baldrige National Quality Award criteria, was one such action. Another was the joint venture of 24 corporations to promote the interchange of their best practices.

The main objective of this group is to create a formal channel to foster benchmarking among Brazilian corporations. This chapter describes the formation of the group, its high-order guideline, its functioning methodology, and the benefits derived since its creation.

Formation of the Benchmarking Group

In March 1993, as a result of training given in São Paulo and Rio de Janeiro by David Hutchins, one of the world's largest disseminators of the quality concept, the formation of a concentrated effort to deepen benchmarking studies in several important Brazilian corporations was proposed. From this idea, the corporations involved in the process, prepared—by consensus—a term of reference for the creation of the Benchmarking Group. Today, 24 corporations are associated with the Group.

With the aim to establish the fundamental guidelines for the creation, organization, and functioning of the Group, a document, called "Assumptions for the Implementation of the Benchmarking Group," was prepared and approved. All corporations participating in the Group must agree with the issues established in the document.

Purpose of the Group

The primary interest of the Group is to exchange, in a planned and systematic manner, information about best practices that are known and tested. The Group also provides adequate recording of this information in such a way so as to facilitate its subsequent access by allowed interested parties. The information network can take many forms, including newsletters, books, videos, or any other suitable dissemination channel.

In the beginning, the Group was coordinated by Grifo Enterprises, and intended to become a foundation by integrating itself into other entities (such as foundations and associations) and by congregating benchmark corporations at national and international levels. Today this objective has been reached. The Benchmarking Group is coordinated by the National Institute of Excellence Development (INDE), which is an institution supported by large Brazilian corporations with its own mission to promote its member-companies' development.

In order to reach its purpose during the formation phase, the Benchmarking Group developed its superior order guideline. This is characterized by a set of three large orientations: vision, mission, and critical success factors (CSFs). Through continued strategic planning and critical analysis, the Group's guideline has reached its present form, as shown in Figure 18.1.

Profile and Organizational Structure

The Benchmarking Group is an organization that can fit itself to the conditions and environment surrounding it. This is how it has been successful. In this manner, the Group has

---

Vision of the group

To be recognized as an information and services center, promoter of corporate development, and source of interaction for the implementation of the best practices prevailing in the market.

Mission of the group

To allow the exchange among the corporations in such a manner as to obtain synergy for the continuing development of improvements in the corporate management and to implement an information and services network constantly updated about the best practices being developed in the market, and making them available to the interested corporation.

Success critical factors

• Commitment of the corporations with the Benchmarking Group

• Responsible performance of the management team

• Product development

• Quality of process

Figure 18.1. Superior order guideline of the Benchmarking Group.

a business profile and an organizational structure as shown in Figure 18.2 and described as follows:

1. The business. The Benchmarking Group is an organization comprising several corporations interested in the exchange of experiences to improve their processes.

2. Inputs. The Benchmarking Group receives information on corporate management, sponsorships, and external advisories and new technologies of a supplier market.

3. Outputs. The Benchmarking Group manages the following:

- Monthly seminars
- Information on best practices of the member companies
- A database on corporate management
- Marketing of the associated companies; including the facility of dissemination of corporations (for instance, meeting sponsors, Internet, media) as participants in a group linked to corporate excellence
- Partnership opportunities for benchmarking
- Courses opened to the interested community

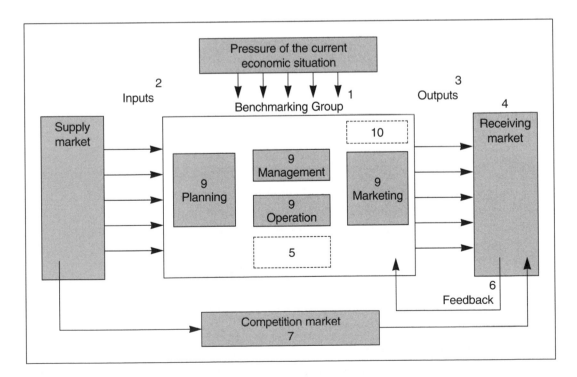

Figure 18.2. The Benchmarking Group as an organization adaptable to the environment: Profile and organizational structure.

- Executive officers meetings
- Evaluation for the Benchmarking Award, which is sponsored by The Benchmarking Group

4. Receiving system. The Benchmarking Group's clients are in the primary market comprised by its member-corporations. They are also clients of other companies and professional societies interested in the products of the Group.

5. Internal feedback process. The Benchmarking Group monitors its codes, rules, and functioning standards through the resources of its members and the INDE, as the coordinating body.

6. External feedback process. The external feedback of clients is made by evaluating monthly meetings and by retaining member-corporations. Periodically, a survey of clients' general satisfaction is done.

7. Competition. The Benchmarking Group's competitors are those that displace their clients, other corporate practices exchange groups, associations, and institutions that act in the promotion of similar events as those of the Benchmarking Group and other business management consultants.

8. Environmental influences. The Group performs within the Brazilian and INDE's political, social, and economical context. It is influenced by international management trends.

9. Internal processes. Basically, the Benchmarking Group establishes the following four processes as its most important.

1. Activities planning
2. Management
3. Operation
4. Marketing

10. Managerial team. The managerial team monitors the internal and external feedback, establishes the objectives, indicates the responsible persons for the inner processes, breaks down the CSFs of the Group, follows up the performance, and allocates resources. This team is comprised of five participants, representatives of the member-corporations, with a term of office of one year. The team is also responsible for the inclusion and removal of corporations from the Group.

Corporation Members

Any company can participate of the Benchmarking Group, provided it formalizes the agreement with the high-order guideline and with what is established in the assumption document and in the Group's code of ethics. The following 24 corporations are members of the Group, as of April 1997.

1. ADP Systems, data processing area

2. Alcoa Alumínio, metallurgical sector

3. Arsenal de Marinha do Rio de Janeiro, from the Brazilian Ministry of Navy

4. Biolab, an analysis laboratory

5. BNDES, a development bank of the Brazilian government

6. Brain, consultants in human resources and creativity

7. Clinica São Vicente, a hospital

8. Empresa Brasileira de Correios e Telégrafos, the Brazilian postal system

9. Foundation for the National Quality Award

10. Furnas, an electric distribution networks supplier

11. Golden Cross, a medical care insurance plan

12. Grifo Enterprises, consulting and quality training

13. Hospital São Lucas, a hospital

14. IBM

15. National Institute for Excellence Development (INDE), maintained by various Brazilian corporations

16. Laboratórios B. Baun, pharmaceutical industry

17. Laboratório Sergio Franco, a clinical analysis laboratory

18. Mills, construction works

19. Petrobrás Distribuidora, a government-owned oil distributor

20. RJ Refrescos, a Coca-Cola bottler

21. Shell Brazil, petrochemical sector

22. Sul América Capitalização, insurance and capital market

23. Varig, an airline

24. White Martins, bottled gases industry

Meetings Development and Information Network Maintenance

As the party responsible for the internal processes, INDE develops the information obtained at Group-sponsored events into a network. This is a database that may be accessed by physical or electronic means, or by the Internet, in accordance with four confidentiality levels, described as follows:

Level 1: Information available only to the participants of the meeting; it may not be released through any media; only those in attendance may benefit from the information presented.

Level 2: Information restricted to the Benchmarking Group; it is retained in the database and accessible only to the participants of the Group.

Level 3: Open information may be kept in the database with access granted to the whole interested community, in accordance with the criteria established by the Benchmarking Group's organizing council.

Level 4: Open information may be kept in the database and granted access to the whole interested community; it can be released in any media such as books, videotapes, and periodicals.

Group meetings are held once a month according to the annual work plan. The place and time are established well in advance and are calendared by the Benchmarking Group's member-companies.

For each meeting, one of the corporations is the sponsor and provides the logistic support. It also presents the subject of the day, with two more facilitators from corporations outside the Group. These guests represent organizations with the best practices in the subject of discussion. In this manner, the information network is fed, and may be accessed in accordance with the defined level of confidentiality.

Each member-corporation must, mandatorily, contribute in terms of information about benchmark processes. Almost any subject is considered interesting and deserving the Group's attention. To participate, the corporations must provide the material resources needed to organize and coordinate the meetings, and must catalyze the information and make it available in the database.

Ethics and Conduct for the Exchange of Information

Benchmarking is a powerful tool for the improvement of several processes found in organizations. It can be used to identify and learn best practices from the corporate world. The commitment of the Benchmarking Group's participants, with its principles summarized in a code of ethics and conduct and adopted by consensus, certainly contributes to the practice of ethic, efficient, and effective benchmarking for all involved parties. The professionals participating in the Benchmarking Group and the organizations they represent are committed to the following principles.

1. Principle of legality.

1.1 In the event of any pending questions on the lawfulness of an activity (for instance, pricing, obtaining of an industrial secret, and so on), that activity should not be practiced until all the legal questions associated with it are fully resolved.

1.2 Discussions or actions that implicate market restrictions or price fixing must be avoided. Also, discussions with competitors involving costs that are part of a product or service's price composition must be avoided.

1.3 Obtaining industrial or trade secrets, through means that may be construed as improper, must be avoided.

2. Principle of information exchange.

2.1 Partners must be willing to supply one another with the same type of information and at the same level of detail. Thus, a benchmarking partner should only require another company to share what the partner is willing to reveal.

2.2 From the onset, benchmarking partners must always try to communicate in the most transparent and clear manner possible. They should aim to avoid misunderstandings and strengthen the mutual interest made available through the benchmarking exchange.

2.3 Partners should never benchmark sensitive or proprietary information from a competitor. If it is necessary to benchmark on an competitive issue, the partners should hire an independent consultant that will maintain the anonymity of the participants or that will report the information solely to those who need it.

2.4 The practice of the reverse engineering or dismounting shall only be considered acceptable in the event that the product or service in question is to be obtained lawfully.

3. Principle of confidentiality.

3.1 In principle, partners should treat the information exchange as something restricted to the professionals and organizations integrating the Benchmarking Group. The information shared must not be passed outside the boundaries of the Group unless prior approval has been obtained.

3.2 The participation of an organization in a benchmarking process must be treated in a confidential manner, and must not be released outside the sphere of activity of the Group—unless prior approval for this issue has been obtained.

4. Principle of use.

4.1 Benchmarking partners must only use the information obtained to introduce improvements in their organization's operations or processes.

4.2 The use or release of data and practices adopted by the benchmarking organizations requires prior consent.

4.3 Benchmarking should not be used as a means to enter the market or a sales segment of a given market.

5. Principle of contact with partners.

5.1 Whenever possible, the benchmarking contacts with another organization should be made through the person accredited by it for this purpose.

5.2 The corporate culture of each benchmarking partner must be respected. Partners should always work with one another according to procedures previously approved by consensus.

6. Principle of contact with third parties.

6.1 Prior and individual approval from each benchmarking partner must be obtained before a benchmarking contact may supply his or her name and organization to a third party.

6.2 Individuals and organizations must avoid communicating the name(s) of their benchmarking contacts in a public meeting or reunion, unless those individuals or organizations are authorized to do so.

6.3 Benchmarking information about competitors should not be obtained during interviews to select former employees of those competitors. Persons must be selected for their knowledge and abilities and not for the competitive information they may possess.

6.4 Partners should try not to use the practice of hiring "independent" consultants to obtain benchmarking information, at any title or pretext.

7. Principle of preparation.

7.1 In order to facilitate the evolution of the exchange process, and prior to contacting organizations, benchmarking partners should demonstrate their personal engagement toward the efficiency and effectiveness of the process through preparation work.

7.2 Organizations should make the best use of the time available to contact their benchmarking partners. Visitors should carefully prepare themselves with data and information, which enables a profitable exchange for all parties involved.

7.3 Organizations should help prepare their benchmarking partners by supplying them with a list of items or issues that would be of mutual interest during a visit.

8. Principle of full compliance.

8.1 Organizations must try to comply with the assumed commitments with their benchmarking partners, at any moment or under any circumstances.

8.2 Organizations should try to perform all the benchmarking processes that may be proposed, in order to satisfy the requirement levels of all involved partners.

9. Principle of understanding and action.

9.1 Each partner should try to have a clear understanding of how the other would like to be treated. Each partner should try to treat the other in this desired way.

9.2 Organizations must try to understand how each of their benchmarking partners would like to see the information they brought to the Group treated and used.

Results Obtained

An undertaking the size of the Benchmarking Group requires a significant amount of work, particularly in its first year. All these large and brilliant corporations are joining efforts and greatly contributing to the success of Brazilian industry and accordingly, to the country's development.

Some especially worthy events should be noted. For instance, during the first three years of its existence, two member-corporations of the Benchmarking Group have won the National Quality Award; namely, Citybank and Alcoa AlumÌnio. This validates the reliability and the seriousness of the work conducted and of the member-companies.

Brazil needs other developmental plans such as this. Many other corporations are willing to participate in the Group. Suggestions to create other, similar groups have been heard. This is how new ideas arise. And these must be supported for Brazil's continued development.

The issues discussed in Group meetings are selected by its members and in accordance with their interest. The Group elected several priority themes to be presented. To this point, the following types of benchmarking exchanges have occurred.

- Quality implementation process of Ticket (a food coupons company), Correios, and Liquid Carbonic
- The benchmarking process, as adopted by IBM
- "Hear the client's voice" process of Grifo, Xerox, Alcoa, White Martins, and Teledata
- Recognition and reward process of RJ Refrescos, ADP Systems, Correios, Biolab, Mills, Banco Garantia, and João Fortes Engenharia (civil construction)
- Organization-based, self-directed work teams at Grifo Enterprises

Selected themes for upcoming meetings include the following:

- Voice of the external client
- Work teams
- Voice of the internal client
- Reengineering/outplacement
- Participative management
- Improvement projects
- Training
- Total quality management

- Information technology
- Internal communication
- Horizontal growth
- Quality in purchasing
- Activity-based costing
- Quality in the small and medium enterprise
- Contribution for the dissemination of best practices tested in the best Brazilian corporations
- Participation in study trips with international benchmarking partners organized by the Group

Conclusions and Lessons Learned

The creation of the Benchmarking Group represented an initiative of Brazilians willing to make a difference in the business world. It shows that it is possible to grow, despite being in an environment heavy with significant economical and political changes, as Brazil is nowadays. But it also shows that this growth can only occur with partnership—sharing the success with others. This is the only way toward total victory.

The Group believes that benchmarking is a great tool for generating an awareness of collective learning. It is through the understanding of what successful corporations do that others may learn. To become a learning organization is the largest benefit brought by benchmarking. Thus, to learn is not only to read, is not only to hear, is not only to practice. To learn is to know how to do.

About the Author

Rosangela Catunda is vice president of the Grifo Center for Executive Training, a division of Grifo Enterprises in Rio de Janeiro, Brazil. Here, she trains hundreds of Brazilian professions in quality issues through MBA-level courses. She is also a management consultant for improvement issues in other, large Brazilian organizations. In 1987, Catunda coordinated PEGQ—Specialization Project in Quality Management, which trained over 400 professionals in quality issues.

Catunda has worked in the quality field since 1979, when she coordinated activities for the Brazilian National Institute for Metrology, Standardization and Industrial Quality, which was linked to the Ministry of Industry and Trade. Here she dealt with civil engineering, automotive, and environmental management issues. Her most recent publications include *Times de Trabalho Autodirigidos* (*Self-Directed Work Teams*) (1995) and a chapter entitled "Benchmarking" in *Reengenharia do Negócio* (*Business Reengineering*) (1993), both published by Editora Pioneira (São Paulo).

Catunda graduated in civil engineering from the Federal University of Brasilia (Universidade of Brasília). She has a master's degree and a doctorate in production engineering. Her Ph.D. was sponsored by the Coordination of Post Graduation Programs in Engineering of the Federal University of Rio de Janeiro-COPPE/UFRJ (Coordenacáo dos Programas de Pós-graduacáo em Engenharia/Universidade Federal do Rio de Janeiro).

Rosangela Catunda
Vice President
Grifo Enterprises
Av. Rio Branco, 1, 16° andar, sala 1602
Rio de Janeiro, RJ, Brazil
Telephone: 021 233 0870
Facsimile: 021 233 7559

Analysis

Country:	United States
Organization:	Northern New England Cardiovascular Disease Study Group (Dartmouth Medical School)
Industry:	Health care industry
Process:	Coronary artery bypass surgery
Case Study Title:	*"Improving the Outcomes of Cardiac Surgery: A Benchmarking Study by the Northern New England Cardiovascular Disease Study Group"*

This best practice benchmarking case study documents significant results. The unadjusted mortality rates initially showed 4.3 percent, with a range of 3.1 percent to 6.3 percent among medical centers and 1.9 percent to 9.2 percent among surgeons. After implementation of some of the findings there were 74 fewer deaths (a 24 percent reduction) than would have been expected based the historical data.

The original three-pronged approach of data, improvement tools, and benchmarking site visits showed significant reductions in mortality rates. Other lessons learned in such a team approach involved a nonthreatening work environment, agreed-upon output/outcome metrics, a forum to discuss results, and comparative process knowledge associated with the outcomes as a basis of learning. This last lesson was an important one because of the sparseness of mortality data for any one surgeon. The number of adverse outcomes in the experience of any single physician is simply too small to inform subsequent decisions.

The teams were trained in and used an improvement approach called Serial V. It is a method to link measurements, process knowledge, and continuous improvement with outcomes. The linking of all three highlights where differences lie and improvement efforts should focus. Other lessons learned involved focus of the projects (postoperative heart failure), the revised, cross-functional team structure, process mapping, and the Serial V technique for accelerating process improvements.

In addition, some best practices for conducting benchmarking were uncovered in this project. These involved how to observe during a site visit. These best practices were converted to a brief list of reminders that included style, transferability, pace, communications, handoffs, and ownership and completeness of reporting. Benchmarkers in other industries can learn from the lessons in health care. And vice versa!

Country:	Singapore
Organization:	Singapore Productivity and Standards Board (PSB)
Industry:	Association industry
Process:	On-the-job training
Case Study Title:	*"Benchmarking On-the-job Training"*

There were several significant findings from the analysis of the process and the comparison to select companies with recognized superior OJT practices. First, organizations can quickly start up a structured OJT process in a very short time, measured in months. Second, the OJT process covers not only individuals new to a process but experienced personnel as well as management. Third, there is correlation and need for off-job training to complement OJT. A fourth key success factor is that training be provided to supervisors in the administration of OJT.

As in almost all benchmarking projects there were also collateral benefits from the study. The most significant of these included the following:

- Using pictures and illustrations to replace text
- Using supervisors and recognized experts to develop the procedures thereby obtaining not only the best practice knowledge transfer but also the commitment
- Using the individual's preferred language during training sessions
- Linking OJT to a specific process
- Linking OJT to performance evaluations
- Linking OJT to wage levels depending on skills

Country:	Japan
Organization:	Japan Productivity Center
Industry:	Association industry
Process:	Benchmarking emergence
Case Study Title:	*"Emergence of Benchmarking in Japan"*

How is the worth of best practice benchmarking proved when it is just emerging? This has been accomplished mostly through conferences and other public, promotional, and informational events. These started as early as 1995 in Japan in a programmed way. Seven promotional initiatives were conducted through 1995 and 1996. Five meetings were focused on one topic only—the product development process. Study tours were organized. Sixteen how-to and case study presentations were carried out between 1996 and 1997.

Sixty-six companies, both manufacturing and service, as well as research institutes and universities participated in these events. Five specific case studies were reported that proved the worth of this approach and confirmed the applicability to Japanese industry. These included Fuji Xerox with internal benchmarking; American Express–Japan with credit card processing; NEC Home Electronics with benchmarking outside the industry; Nippon Hoechst Marion Roussel, which discovered it could "think in new ways;" and NEC Semiconductor Business Group, which used benchmarking to remain "a half-step ahead of everyone else" and shoot for the number-one position domestically and the number-two position internationally.

When benchmarking is launched in a new locale typical comments from many include "We're different; it won't work in our culture" and "We don't share." But invariably when a careful search of evidence of best practice benchmarking is conducted, there is the revealing finding that benchmarking has, in fact, been conducted—even in Japan. This case study cites 15 such studies as proof of the applicability and benefits of benchmarking.

Country:	Brazil
Organization:	The Benchmarking Group
Industry:	Association industry
Process:	Initial benchmarking launch
Case Study Title:	*"The Benchmarking Group in Brazil"*

Several best practices for the establishment of a benchmarking center were appropriately instituted by the Group. These included formal capture of client feedback and surveys of member satisfaction with products and services. One of the success factors found in the establishment of the embryonic organizations is that they tailor their deliverables to the greatest need. The second is a scheme for information security. In this case the Group established a four-level scheme of information protection that obviously will serve to overcome many of the concerns that members have about information security. The adoption of a code of conduct has been instrumental in providing the framework of legal, ethical, and protocol guidelines for successful operation. The code is a product of the earliest center's work but is made available freely to others to foster benchmarking.

While results are not of the quantitative payback type resulting in improved organizational performance, the achievement of the Brazilian Quality Award by two Benchmarking Group's members is a major credit since the award cannot be attained without significant benchmarking. The concentration on a prioritized list of processes, including identifying the needs of small and medium enterprises, suits local conditions and is commendable.

But the fundamental finding of the Group that "growth can only occur with partnership and sharing the experience with others" is pervasive. It proves the worth of best practice benchmarking—a great tool for generating awareness of collective learning—what successful organizations do!

Summary Cost Savings and Benefits

United States	Europe	Asia/Pacific	Americas/Africa
NONPROFIT UNITED STATES **Northern New England Cardiovascular Disease Study Group (Dartmouth Medical School)** *Coronary artery bypass surgery* • 24% reduction in mortality • Improvements range by —Center: 3.1%–6.3% —Surgeon: 1.9%–9.2%		SINGAPORE **Singapore Productivity and Standards Board (PSB)** *On-the-job training* • Not quantified • Significant initiative for Singapore • Best practice mastery JAPAN **Japan Productivity Center** *Benchmarking emergence* • Process demonstrated through the following: —5 case studies —7 promotional events —16 how-to presentations —A focus on one process at a time	BRAZIL **The Benchmarking Group** *Initial benchmarking launch* • Not quantified • Two members received the Brazil Quality Award

Key Best Practices Found

United States	Europe	Asia/Pacific	Americas/Africa
NONPROFIT UNITED STATES **Northern New England Cardiovascular Disease Study Group (Dartmouth Medical School)** *Coronary artery bypass* • Data trends revealed • Improvement tools • Site visit observation techniques		SINGAPORE **Singapore Productivity and Standards Board (PSB)** *On-the-job training* • Fast start-up • OJT training coverage • OJT supervisor • OJT development • Pictures vs. text • SME's knowledge • Wages tied to skills JAPAN **Japan Productivity Center** *Benchmarking emergence* • Benchmarking's benefits revealed • Thinking in "new ways" • "Half-step ahead" mentality	BRAZIL **The Benchmarking Group** *Initial benchmarking launch* • Client feedback • Member satisfaction measure-ment • Information security • SME use and tailoring to local conditions

Lessons Learned

United States	Europe	Asia/Pacific	Americas/Africa

NONPROFIT
 	
UNITED STATES
 	
Northern New England Cardiovascular Disease Study Group (Dartmouth Medical School)
 	
Coronary artery bypass surgery
 	
• Nonthreatening environment established.
• Agreed outcome measures used.
• Forum to discuss results available.
• Comparative process knowledge learning occurred.
• Data sparseness overcome.
		SINGAPORE
		
		Singapore Productivity and Standards Board (PSB)
		
		On-the-job training
		
		• Clear, detailed documentation essential.
		• Value of benchmarking confirmed.
		
		JAPAN
		
		Japan Productivity Center
		
		Benchmarking emergence
		
		• Successful benchmarking launch requires a carefully executed program. It should be done by
		  —Country
		  —Language
		  —Culture
			BRAZIL
			
			The Benchmarking Group
			
			Initial benchmarking launch
			
			• Growth occurs with partnering.
			• Generate awareness and collective learning.
			• To learn is to know "how."

PART 5: GOVERNMENT SECTOR

Introduction

Increasingly, government agencies are pursuing benchmarking as a way of finding best practices on which to base their operations and continue to serve the public. This activity is at the federal, state, or province level as well as at the local city or council level. All of these are represented in the cases, as well as defense agencies that are also very active in benchmarking.

The processes cover complaint handling, engine testing, supply chain processing, water supply, sewerage, and drainage, culture change, and the launch of benchmarking to comply with the directive to conduct compulsory competitive tendering (outsourcing). This truly shows a very creative application of best practice benchmarking to institutions, which, over time, have been a "breed apart."

It is interesting to note that while there is some good geographic coverage from the United States and Asia/Pacific regions, there are three cases from Australia. This is indicative of the leadership shown by the Australian government and its Best Practices Demonstration Project, which encourages the application of benchmarking across a wide spectrum of organizations and activities. It was a commendable initiative!

A brief summary, background information, the rationale for each case, and key points to consider when reading follow.

Country:	United States
Organization:	Vice President Al Gore's National Performance Review, Federal Benchmarking Consortium
Industry:	Federal government
Process:	Complaint handling
Case Study Title:	*"Serving the American Public: Best Practices in Resolving Customer Complaints"*

The President's Executive Order number 12862 directs U.S. government agencies to "Survey customers' (citizens') satisfaction, set service standards, make complaint systems accessible, address complaints, and benchmark customer service against the best in business." As a result of this order and the vice president's initiative—the National Performance Review—teams from various government agencies have formed to benchmark these processes.

This benchmarking study is one of several exceptionally well done best practice benchmarking investigations conducted by the U.S. federal government. Thirteen agencies formally participated in the study and contributed a total of 32 participants to the study team. Eleven organizations were benchmarked. These included six industrial firms in air travel, chemicals, computers, automobiles, insurance, and newspapers. In addition, three government agencies were identified as having leading-edge practices, and were formally benchmarked as was the Revenue Service of Canada.

This formal benchmarking investigation provides a rich source of best practice learnings. In fact, the study uncovered some surprises, which revealed some best-in-class practices were found in government organizations that rival the best in the private sector. The comparison of different practices is summarized in a 12-attribute by 11-organization matrix from which most of the learnings were derived. Therefore, the study continues to emphasize the value of internal benchmarking as well as benchmarking outside the subject industry.

This study also confirms that, not only is best practice benchmarking applicable to government operations at the federal level, but increasingly the same approach is being pursued at the state and city levels as well. Selected countries such as Australia and the United Kingdom have had equivalent success. Therefore, this U.S. study is a "benchmark" in the transfer of this business improvement approach to government operations that want to improve.

Country:	United States
Organization:	U.S. Air Force
Industry:	Department of Defense
Process:	Engine test installation time
Case Study Title:	*"Utilizing Benchmarking to Build Customer-Supplier Relationships: How the U.S. Air Force and Sverdrup Technologies Partnered for Change"*

Benchmarking in the federal government is an accepted fact. Many agencies are required to conduct best practice investigations either as the result of the president's executive order or through the vice president's National Performance Review initiative. What is not so well known, however, is the extensiveness of benchmarking in the Department of Defense and armed forces. This case study is indicative of the successful application to these units, which is commendable.

The case study is interesting because it involved three parties: an Air Force unit, an external customer, and a facilitating third party. The Air Force unit, an engine testing installation, was in jeopardy of losing its existing customers because previous cycle time requirements for military customers were not acceptable to commercial customers.

By conducting a very careful process-to-process comparison with the assistance of a third party, the testing facility was able to not only meet the requirements of commercial customers but it was able also to increase the use of its facilities. Thus, outside revenue was produced in the face of an initially assumed downsizing. This is an exceptional outcome from a benchmarking investigation.

This study required a very detailed process-to-process comparison to carefully identify the differences in practices and tools used. The approach required a total of seven days, again emphasizing the importance of preparation and carefully structured visits. The study proved the basis for keeping existing customers as well as increasing the customer base.

Country:	United Kingdom
Organization:	The Post Office
Industry:	Government
Process:	Supply chain, pipeline processing
Case Study Title:	*"Benchmarking for a First-class Supply Chain: The Post Office"*

Until recent history most of benchmarking successes have been in private, industrial sectors, namely manufacturing and service. There was a sense that the benchmarking process would not lend itself to the public sector, particularly government. That paradigm is now radically changed. It is the experience of such organizations as the UK Post Office and others that have proved the use of this improvement approach.

The journey followed, however, closely parallels that of industrial firms: Start with a pursuit of quality management; recognize benchmarking as an important quality tool; conduct study tours to understand benchmarking's use and successful implementation; and adapt and tailor the benchmarking process to the needs of the organization. Ultimately, however, this quality tool was driven by a need for change and by a recognition that its successful use would concentrate on the work process. The Post Office is a shining example of this journey.

Country:	Australia
Organization:	City of Monash and various municipal governments
Industry:	City government
Process:	Local council processes
Case Study Title:	*"National Australian Local Government Benchmarking Project"*

Australia has had a preeminent success with best practice understanding that is not widely known. At the national level, the Best Practices Demonstration Project was launched to showcase the value of benchmarking. It was truly a major success story for best practice understanding. These initial efforts were heavily focused on the industrial sector but it was shortly followed by interest in government, particularly in local (city) government.

Recently that interest grew to include the mandate that local governments must submit to *competitive tendering,* or putting operations out to bid (outsourcing). What better way to show that a local council should continue to provide the services it does than by showing that it is a best practice operation. This simply intensified the need for this improvement approach. And this case study covers the approach used for the application of benchmarking to these important public sector services. There is major groundwork established here for use around the world.

The case study shows that best practice benchmarking is applicable to operations that benefit citizens, namely rates notification (tax collection), building approvals, library lending, road maintenance, and home care services; and to internal city operations such as payroll and fleet maintenance. This case study also shows that these processes can be flow-charted for understanding and analysis, benchmarked against other local governments, and improved by incorporation of better practices.

Country:	Australia
Organization:	Urban Water Division, Department of Land and Water Conservation
Industry:	Land and water conservation industry
Process:	Water supply, sewerage, and drainage services
Case Study Title:	*"Syndicate Benchmarking: Water Supply and Sewerage"*

Much of the public infrastructure such as roads, power generation, ports, and pure water and waste water treatment are taken for granted by the average citizen. Yet these are major services provided, and most often they are very expensive. Could they be improved? Could sewerage distribution and pumping activities (processes) be improved through benchmarking?

This case study shows the use and value of syndicated (common interest) benchmarking, the value of internal benchmarking, and the success of these approaches in uncovering best practices and significant savings.

Country:	Australia
Organization:	Australia Post
Industry:	Federal government
Process:	Culture change
Case Study Title:	*"Benchmarking Culture Change at Australia Post"*

For many organizations there is a need to benchmark and find best practices in at least three dimensions of their organizations: hardware, humanware, and software. By hardware is meant the organization structures, systems, processes, and rewards. By humanware is meant the roles, skills, knowledge, experience, and attitudes of individuals. And by software is meant the way individuals work together and behave including leadership, interactions, work practices, and culture. Of the three, the software is the "hard stuff." It is the most difficult to define, measure, collect meaningful data, and benchmark.

This case study is directly focused on this most difficult area. It tackles the need for improving the process of planning and implementing strategic culture change through the medium of an employee attitude survey titled "Leadership Excellence Review Self-Assessment." It is interesting that the concept or approach to drive these changes is the medium of focusing on best practices. Australia, of course, has gained worldwide recognition for its Best Practice Demonstration Project fostered by the federal government. But the strategic focus on best practices is insightful, as was the case for Singapore's Year 2000 productivity initiative.

Ultimately all these areas of improvement, whether hardware, humanware, or software, must come from the incorporation of best practices. Therefore, this case study is an instructive classic in how to measure the unmeasurable, namely culture, and how to benchmark its best practices.

Looking for an objective measurement vehicle led the team back to the quality awards, their criteria, and format. In this case the Australia Quality Award was used. But it, in turn, is a close derivative of others and the Malcolm Baldrige National Quality Award, where benchmarking is done in significant ways.

The Australia Post had ample opportunity for doing internal benchmarking. It is the seventh largest organization in Australia with over 32,000 employees, five business units, and obviously many similar entities performing the same process. But in addition, it was able to compare its outcomes with 20 external partners through a network set up by AQC to "measure and compare best corporate cultures." These included automotive, multinational subsidiaries in electronics, chemicals, petroleum, and high-tech industries, as well as large Australian organizations in brewing, airlines, and the armed services.

Master Table

United States	Europe	Asia/Pacific	Americas/Africa
GOVERNMENT			
<u>UNITED STATES</u>	<u>UNITED KINGDOM</u>	<u>AUSTRALIA</u>	
Vice President Al Gore's National Performance Review, Federal Benchmarking Consortium	**The Post Office**	**City of Monash and various municipal governments**	
Federal government	Government	City government	
Complaint handling	*Supply chain, pipeline processing*	*Local council processes*	
"Serving the American Public: Best Practices in Resolving Customer Complaints"	"Benchmarking for a First-class Supply Chain: The Post Office"	"National Australian Local Government Benchmarking Project"	
<u>UNITED STATES</u>		<u>AUSTRALIA</u>	
United States Air Force		**Urban Water Division, Department of Land and Water Conservation**	
Department of Defense		Land and water conservation industry	
Engine test installation		*Water supply, sewerage, and drainage services*	
"Utilizing Benchmarking to Build Customer-Supplier Relationships: How the U.S. Air Force and Sverdrup Technologies Partnered for Change"		"Syndicate Benchmarking: Water Supply and Sewerage"	
		<u>AUSTRALIA</u>	
		Australia Post	
		Federal government	
		Culture change	
		"Benchmarking Culture Change at Australia Post"	

Country and Industry

United States	Europe	Asia/Pacific	Americas/Africa
GOVERNMENT			
UNITED STATES Federal government	UNITED KINGDOM Government	AUSTRALIA City government	
UNITED STATES Department of Defense		AUSTRALIA Land and water conservation industry	
		AUSTRALIA Federal government	

Processes

United States	Europe	Asia/Pacific	Americas/Africa
GOVERNMENT			
UNITED STATES *Complaint handling*	UNITED KINGDOM *Supply chain, pipeline processing*	AUSTRALIA *Local council processes*	
UNITED STATES *Engine test installation time*		AUSTRALIA *Water supply; sewerage, and drainage services*	
		AUSTRALIA *Culture change*	

CHAPTER 19

Serving the American Public: Best Practices in Resolving Customer Complaints

Vice President Al Gore's National Performance Review, Federal Benchmarking Consortium

Executive Summary

The government's customer service revolution started in 1993 with a recommendation from Vice President Gore's National Performance Review, followed by President Clinton's executive order, "Setting Customer Service Standards." The President directed federal agencies to survey their customers to see what kind of service people want and whether they are getting it; to get ideas from frontline workers who deal with customers day-to-day; to give customers choices and easy access; and to develop ways for citizens to complain and get problems fixed. President Clinton set a goal for the government to deliver service equal to the best in business.

In 1995, President Clinton reinforced his order to put customers first. It leaves no doubt that the goal is a revolution in how government does business so that customers are the focus. Customer service standards and measures are to be part of strategic plans, training programs, personnel systems, and anything else that ought to be changed to advance the citizens' satisfaction with government service.

To comply with the president's directive, teams of government agencies embarked on a series of *benchmarking* studies. For purposes of this study benchmarking means determining which businesses—public and private—are doing the best job of customer complaint resolution (request study); understanding the gap between the agencies' own performance; and taking action to close that performance gap. When the best in business were identified, government teams set out to determine why they were the best and then set forth an action plan to make their agencies as good as, or better than, the benchmarked businesses in resolving customer complaints.

Some of the valuable lessons learned during this process are as follows:

• *Make it easy for customers to complain and they will make it easy for the organization to improve.* A dramatic lesson was learned by the teams involved in this study; the best in business want their customers to complain. Informed customers know how services should work. If things are not working, customers are the first to know. Customers who are dissatisfied tell twice as many people about it than those who are happy with service. The best in business use feedback from toll-free calls, letters, and surveys to identify and resolve root causes of dissatisfaction and to change their services to ensure that the customer will be quickly satisfied.

• *Respond to complaints quickly and courteously and with common sense, and customer loyalty will improve.* The study team found that customers reward companies that quickly solve problems by remaining loyal customers. A speedy response can add 25 percent to customer loyalty. One of the study partners adopted a formula for customer satisfaction. Doing the job right the first time + effective complaint management = maximum customer satisfaction/loyalty.

Government agencies can develop the same kind of loyalty and trust from the public if they match or exceed the best in business.

• *Resolve complaints on the first contact and enjoy two benefits: (1) save money by eliminating unnecessary additional contacts that escalate costs; and (2) build customer confidence.* A call back that involves two or more employees always costs more than a call that is handled right the first time. Research in this study confirms that resolving a complaint on the first contact reduced the cost by at least 50 percent.

• *Technology utilization is critical in complaint-handling systems.* Use computers to develop a database of complaints. See if there is a trend. Then fix it! The study team learned that the best in business electronically compiled customer complaint information and presented it to everyone, including management, so that the organization could better align services and products to meet customer expectations.

• *Recruit and hire the best for customer service jobs.* The customer service and complaint resolution specialist positions established by benchmarking partners tend to be highly sought-after positions. Complaint specialists learn the company so well they get promoted. Some organizations built the customer service position into a formal career ladder for advancement in the company. In all instances, frontline employees were valued for feedback in making decisions.

In a nutshell, a manager who wants to have a first-rate complaint system with results within six months should take five steps.

1. Issue a policy statement that says the organization embraces complaints. View complaints as opportunities.

2. Establish an implementation team with representatives from each step in the complaint-handling process and identify each step in the process.

3. Establish a tracking system. Staff should record and classify complaints that will allow them to analyze the complaint data and report to top management. The difference between the subject process and the best in business process is known as the gap—what to improve.

4. Develop recommendations to improve core processes and empower frontline employees to resolve complaints on first contact.

5. Implement. The team should put together an action plan for implementing the approved recommendations.

If this is done right, customers will notice changes within six months.

Overview

All executive departments that provide significant services to the public shall provide a means to address complaints and make information, services, and complaint systems easily accessible.

—President Bill Clinton

Introduction

When Americans have a problem with something, they tell someone about it. They talk about companies that have overcharged them, provided poor service, or who have rude employees. In fact, research shows that people who have a problem are likely to tell eight to ten people about it. Note, however, that fewer than one in 20 people who have a complaint will formally complain to the company itself (Figure 19.1). Best-in-class companies welcome complaints because complaints are customer feedback that can be used to improve service performance and reduce cost, thus improving the bottom line. Best-in-class companies make it easy for customers to complain, even encourage complaints, and then they bend over backwards to set things right and make changes so that future customers do not experience similar problems.

In the past, too many Americans have found a deaf ear when trying to complain about a problem to a government agency. Consider one man's experience when he tried to get a problem solved.

> *I had written in February . . . and again in June . . . Now it is September. I still have not had a satisfactory response . . . What do I have to do to get someone to listen to me?*

This man—legitimately frustrated by his inability to get someone's ear—would be even angrier if he realized how much "handling" his complaint cost. One study estimates that a written response to a single complaint escalated to the Congressional level may cost the agency and the taxpayer over $1000 in staff time.

Fortunately, government agencies are beginning to change the way they look at and treat citizens who have service complaints. Spurred on by Vice President Gore's National Performance Review and its September 1993 report, "From Red Tape to Results: Creating a

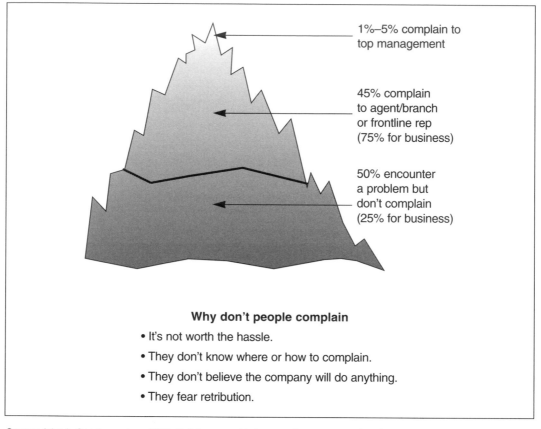

1%–5% complain to top management

45% complain to agent/branch or frontline rep (75% for business)

50% encounter a problem but don't complain (25% for business)

Why don't people complain

- It's not worth the hassle.
- They don't know where or how to complain.
- They don't believe the company will do anything.
- They fear retribution.

Source: John A. Goodman. June 1995. *Building a world-class service system and setting rational priorities.* Arlington, Va.: Technical Assistance Research Programs (TARP), p. 3. Used with permission.

Figure 19.1. The tip of the iceberg phenomenon.

Government That Works Better and Costs Less," government agencies are working hard to make the federal government work better and cost less. Already, the recommendations have resulted in more than $60 billion in savings and elimination of some 200,000 government positions (noted in President Clinton's State of the Union Address, January 23, 1996).

Customer service is an important part of the reinventing government efforts. Directed by President Clinton, government agencies have conducted focus groups and surveys, and set customer service standards to respond to customers' needs. Agencies are starting to eliminate unnecessary regulations, cut red tape, and address other root causes of citizen complaints. And many agencies are taking steps to improve how they deal with complaints. For example,

• The U.S. Postal Service has established a Consumer Affairs Tracking System that records and reports every customer contact. It uses state-of-the-art imaging and database management technology coupled with highly sophisticated correspondence-generation software. This system is comparable to the best-in-business models. The U.S. Postal Service also established a call management initiative to create a single toll-free number available 24 hours a day. It will provide a centrally managed consistent interface to all customers seeking information or problem resolution.

• The Department of Veterans Affairs medical centers have two formats for complaint and complimentary data collection. One is ongoing complaint tracking; the other is the annual survey. Patient representatives throughout the Veterans Health Administration have a tracking system for compliments and complaints. This system identifies trends that are occurring by specific problem, by service, or by individual. The complaint codes are correlated with the National Customer Service standards, which provides ongoing measurement. Alerts are sent to service chiefs identifying more serious problems. This allows the service chiefs prompt notification of the problem and provides expeditious resolution. The national patient feedback program is also correlated with the National Customer Service standards. Annually, surveys are sent to outpatients and recently discharged inpatients. These surveys are used to identify trends that are occurring. Medical centers are responsible for improving the areas where problems exist.

• In 1993, the Comptroller of the Currency established an ombudsman for banks that had problems with the comptroller's rulings on banking regulations.

Citizens are starting to notice and are even writing letters, not to complain, but to compliment the people who work in government.

> *I wish to thank you and your department for your expeditious and thorough consideration and solving of my problem . . . Mr. . . . was able to provide me with the necessary information. In addition, when Mr. . . . received additional information that he thought might be useful, he forwarded it also. Mr. . . . follow-up was a surprise and a good example of real interest in my problem. This kind of thoughtfulness and follow-up is greatly appreciated.*
>
> —Oakdale, Pennsylvania

> *I'm still in shock at how fast FEMA responded to my need. I thought FEMA was just a lot of red tape, to make people feel they could get help.*
>
> —Georgia

> *Human nature, alas, often has us eagerly voice complaints but keep silent when praise is warranted . . . My hunch is I speak for a large number when passing along a deserved* WELL DONE *for the fantastic job you do—often with limited funds and staff.*
>
> —Louisville, Kentucky

Part of the reason for the change is that government agencies are holding themselves to a higher standard. This study represents the efforts of ten government agencies and other interested parties to learn from the best in America's leading companies and to find ways to improve their own complaint processes.

Why Tackle Customer Complaints?

Companies find that effectively handling customers with problems is critical to their reputations as well as their bottom line. When customers complain and they are satisfied with the way their complaint is handled, they are more likely to purchase another product or service from the same company. Companies that resolve complaints on the first contact increase customer satisfaction and product loyalty, improve employee satisfaction, and reduce costs. Companies even encourage complaints. Most dissatisfied customers do not complain. By making it easy for customers to complain, more customers will reveal their problems to the organization, giving it a greater opportunity to correct service delivery or production processes. Customers who get their problems satisfactorily and quickly solved tell their friends and neighbors, and they are not easily won over by the competition.

There is a bottom-line concern for government as well. As noted, complaints can be costly. Repeated handoffs increase costs and waste precious resources. When complaints are not promptly resolved, frustrated customers seek redress in different agencies or at different parts or levels of the same agency, resulting in duplicate efforts and compounding costs.

Just as costs compound when there is a poor complaint system, trust also erodes as citizens become frustrated with a nonresponsive bureaucracy. Indeed, there has been a cumulative erosion of public confidence in government. Thirty years ago, 70 percent of Americans trusted the federal government to do the right thing most of the time. In 1993, only 17 percent of Americans said that they trusted the government (Gore 1995, 27). There are many factors contributing to this decline in trust and confidence, particularly the huge volume of regulations that did not make sense to the public and the high cost of government. The study team learned, however, from the benchmarking partners, that an effective approach to resolving complaints is invaluable in winning the trust and loyalty of the government's customers—the public.

There are costs associated with a poor complaint system, and there are benefits associated with a good one. Studies have shown that handling customer complaints well can be a critical part of a turnaround strategy. If a complaint is handled well, it sustains and strengthens customer loyalty and the company's image as a leader. It also tells customers that the company cares and can improve because of their contact. In government agencies, effective complaint handling promotes public confidence in government services.

Customer complaints also represent valuable information about recurrent problems. They can point the way to understanding the root causes of customer problems and help an organization target core processes that need improvement. If acted upon to improve core processes, customer complaints can be a source of information that can reduce costs as well as improve services.

What Do the Best in Business Do?

Federal employees initiated and led this consortium benchmarking study to learn from the best in business how to design and implement a world-class complaint- and customer response-handling system. That's what benchmarking is all about—systematically learning from the best in business and using that information to improve one's own performance.

The study team asked for help from some of America's leading companies. They had a lot to offer. The customer service revolution means that, today, most companies strive to exceed the expectations of their customers. The study team got a surprise when it looked for best practices; some best-in-business practices were found in government organizations, which have practices that rival the best in the private sector. The team is grateful to all of the businesses and agencies for sharing their experiences.

Study team members reviewed how their agency currently handles customer complaints, and identified key areas where they wanted to learn how the best in business did it. They reviewed written literature, met with experts, and identified benchmarking partners. A team member from each participating agency led one site visit and shared the results with the others; this way the team could benefit from visits to ten companies and agencies at the lowest cost.

The team defined a customer complaint as any indication that the service or product does not meet the customer's expectations. This definition reflects the fact that some companies do not even use the term *complaints,* they call them *problems* or *opportunities.* The team found variation in what companies did, but the best companies used similar approaches to handling complaints. They are as follows:

• Train and empower frontline employees to resolve most complaints during the first contact.

• Make it easy for customers to complain through the extensive use of centralized customer help lines, toll-free telephone numbers, complaint/comment cards at the point of service, and easy-to-use customer appeal processes.

• Enter complaint data in fully automated and integrated information systems, and analyze and use data to identify and fix root causes of dissatisfaction and to determine future directions for product and service improvements. By centrally collecting the data, at the headquarters level, this valuable information can be incorporated into the strategic planning process, assuring future competitiveness.

• Consider complaints as customer feedback and opportunities to improve, alongside other measures of customer satisfaction.

• Use various organizational arrangements, but have important similarities, such as seeking to maximize resolution at first point of contact and dedicating a cross-functional team to collect and analyze data and report complaint information to top management.

• Credit their overall success, at least in part, to a pending organizational crisis, normally related to their survival or significant loss of revenue.

See Table 19.1 for a summary of the benchmarking partners' best practices.

Table 19.1. Complaint resolution practices of benchmarking partners.

How they	Company A	Company B	Company C
View complaints	Resolve problems; retain customers; make improvements	Opportunity to increase repurchase intent	Opportunity to delight the customer and to provide world-class service
Make it easy to complain	Empower all public contact personnel at 13 domestic and numerous worldwide resolution offices	Created a national customer assistance center with 800 number	Created a nationwide call center available 6:30 A.M.–9:00 P.M. using 20 active 800 numbers
Track and analyze complaint data	Code complaints using 113 codes; consumer affairs does analysis	Customer relations network and phone tabulation system	Extensive database with fast trending and dissemination of information
Address root causes	Line departments analyze numerous reports on their service	Analyze customer comment log for problems and trends	Information is routed to appropriate line department for follow-up
Recruit frontline employees to handle complaints	Hire from within; highly sought after position; must have several years of experience	College degree preferred; one-year commitment; salaried position	Resumes reviewed; staff interviews candidates may have as many as 14 interviews
Train frontline employees to handle complaints	Three weeks of classroom and on-the-job training plus one month on "buddy system" plus one week advanced training four weeks later	Initial four-week course plus eight weeks on-the-job technical training	Three weeks training by peers; buddy system
Measure performance of complaint handlers	Tracking system reports cycle time	Call statistics/call monitoring; professionalism review	Track average speed of answering and resolving complaints
Measure the performance of the complaint process	Five to 10 days to answer written correspondence; first contact handles complaint	15-day closure required	An individual is responsible for complaint handling and process improvement
Measure customer satisfaction	Survey high-volume customers; a monthly series of customer feedback reports are given to top management	Developed customer satisfaction survey system	Stand-alone surveys and a set of questions at completion of call
Support employees with technology	Automated systems internally developed using commercial software	Computerized on-line car information system	Sophisticated computer system/internal staff support with on-line instructions
Empower employees to resolve complaints	Agents may give monetary incentives to resolve problems	Customer representative may grant limited payments to resolve complaints	Agents are empowered to delight the customer
Manage customer expectations	Surveys; focus groups; onboard questionnaires and business travel advisory council	Relationship builders; that is, product care clinics, birthday cards, and focus groups	Feedback from customers continually forwarded to the operating people to review customer expectations

Table 19.1. *(Continued).*

How they	Company D	Company E	Company F
View complaints	Complaints are viewed as assets to help improve service	Every contact is an opportunity to improve	Fast track to improving service; catalyst to improvement
Make it easy to complain	Consumer service cards in 40,000 retail outlets; corporate call management 800 number incentive	24-hour access to 800 number; one-third of entire staff are customer reps	800 numbers are in product stating who to contact
Track and analyze complaint data	Maintain several databases that report to top management and inspection service	Every contact tracked separately by research staff	Quality assurance group tracks/trends information from automated system; report to management
Address root causes	All problems are addressed; "Customer Perfect" process adds greater depth	Weekly report on action to fix problems	Complaints are tracked until issue is brought to closure
Recruit frontline employees to handle complaints	Hire best qualified in 85 district offices; high-level position in corporate headquarters	Highly sought after position; college graduate; testing interviews	Train internally and select the best qualified
Train frontline employees to handle complaints	All employees are provided training; modular video program	15 days initial training plus extensive ongoing training with comprehensive curriculum	All employees trained; problems are best handled when first identified by those who own the process
Measure performance of complaint handlers	Monitor calls; weekly report of % on-time; correspondence review	Reps progress through levels; time on job and training	Management measures teams; teams measure individuals; no annual awards for individuals
Measure the performance of the complaint process	Cycle time for phone-written-Internet responses; no handoffs allowed	Cycle time; number of handoffs; one-stop service; 80% of calls answered in 20 seconds	Timeliness of action and end user satisfaction are reported
Measure customer satisfaction	Quarterly customer satisfaction survey (183,000 mail based)	Member surveys every 30 days	Send employees to customer to determine effectiveness of product
Support employees with technology	Computers, with complaint-handling software, for all reps	Automated system to enter each concern; on-line information	Automated problem tracking system, plus all team members kept informed about business
Empower employees to resolve complaints	Reps may refund payments and grant limited goodwill offerings to satisfy customers	Employees are empowered to fix the problem first, then delight customers	Employees/teams delight their customers; see themselves as best-in-world at what they do
Manage customer expectations	Products/services brochure in all offices; advertise clearly; publish service standards	Written surveys; member meetings; focus groups; employee feedback	Publish who they are, what they produce, and for whom

Table 19.1. *(Continued).*

How they	Company G	Company H	Company I
View complaints	A chance to exceed customer expectations	Encourages appeals; assures customers a fair process	Complaints viewed as part of continuous improvement process
Make it easy to complain	Large staff is available to provide immediate response to customer problems	Easy to appeal to examiner, supervisor, ombudsman	Complaint resolution process; reps may go to customer's site to resolve complaint
Track and analyze complaint data	Computer system/mainframe computer records all complaints	E-mail systems used	Sophisticated computer support system; customer satisfaction opportunity system
Address root causes	Corrective action to problem is based on root cause analysis in all areas	Every appeal is carefully reviewed; also by ombudsman	Comprehensive compilation; analysis of root cause data
Recruit frontline employees to handle complaints	Customer advocates are selected based on knowledge of process and communication skills	Highly sought after position; must quality in banking-law-policy-people skills	Complaint handlers not separately recruited; complaints answered by trained specialists
Train frontline employees to handle complaints	Four hours training on problem resolution; all reps have other responsibilities	In-depth training in communication, negotiation, etc.	Every employee gets 100 hours training each year
Measure performance of complaint handlers	Monthly and quarterly reports generated by computer system	Conference interaction; field trips; personal contacts; surveys	Repeat contacts closely monitored
Measure the performance of the complaint process	90% of customers are contacted in eight hours; customer is satisfied within five days of resolution	Field trip; personal contact; customer surveys	Looks at complaint volume and types of complaints
Measure customer satisfaction	Surveys via telephone; all customers are asked if they are satisfied	Customer surveys	Phone and mail surveys; interviews
Support employees with technology	Mainframe computer system with sophisticated report generator	E-mail system	Use a commercially available database management system
Empower employees to resolve complaints	Empowerment is a fundamental principle here	Employees are empowered to resolve any issue; ombudsman provides third-party review	Employees are empowered to resolve all complaints
Manage customer expectations	Specific telephone survey to determine customer expectations	Keeps the customer informed and assures that policy/law are met	Customers participate in product design, development, and support; customer service reps required to contact a percentage of customer base periodically to determine customer needs

Table 19.1. *(Continued).*

How they	Company J	Company K
View complaints	Free market research	Free information to identify needed changes; internal focus groups
Make it easy to complain	Problem resolution program advertised in telephone books, reverse side of notices, and publications	Dedicated complaint staff plus volunteers help with language translation; field offices handle locally where possible
Track and analyze complaint data	PC database used to identify trends and recommend corrective actions	Complaint analysis information sheet used for written complaints
Address root causes	Service enrichment committees that include frontline staff study problems	Annual report reviewed by headquarters; response cards analyzed
Recruit frontline employees to handle complaints	Identify bilingual/customer-oriented personnel	Work in collaboration with union
Train frontline employees to handle complaints	Complaint and recovery workshops	Workshops plus modular training on people skills plus personal development plan
Measure performance of complaint handlers	Monitor the Problem Resolution Program (PRP); activity decreased the last two years	Annual report to review performance
Measure the performance of the complaint process	Reports are generated from the PRP	Independent focus group/survey information analyzed by complaint-handling staff
Measure customer satisfaction	Presently developing action plans	Surveys and focus groups
Support employees with technology	Presently supplying customer account data; plan for on-line help and research	Planning for new computer-based support system
Empower employees to resolve complaints	Every attempt is made to resolve complaints by frontline employees	Employees empowered to resolve complaints at first point of contact
Manage customer expectations	Customer education program in place	Surveys and focus groups used to capture expectation information; the goal is to better educate the public

What's Next?

Agencies that participated in this complaint resolution study are using its results to make changes in their own complaint-handling systems. Indeed, benchmarking that consists only of field trips to world-class companies is known as "industrial tourism." For a benchmarking study to be worthwhile, an organization needs to understand the gap between its own performance and best practices and take actions to close that performance gap. Already,

• The Patent and Trademark Office is using this study's findings along with reengineering efforts to design a Patent Assistance Center and redesign an existing Trademark Assistance Center as one-stop sources for patent and trademark information.

• The U.S. Postal Service is using what it learned from this study as a guideline to reevaluate its complaint-handling function. The U.S. Postal Service is also responding to inquiries and complaints received over the Internet.

• The Department of Interior, in several of its bureaus, has developed and used surveys to obtain customer feedback. They are incorporating lessons learned from this study in their ongoing customer service initiatives, such as customer service standards and customer satisfaction measurements.

• The U.S. Customs Service conducted a gap analysis, designed recommendations, and prepared an action plan for fiscal year 1996 that includes two goals: (1) training for air passenger service representatives, and (2) automating an input system to improve the tracking of complaints and compliments.

• The IRS team prepared a fiscal year 1996 action plan to develop cost estimates of processing the Problem Resolution Program (PRP) and Application Taxpayer Assistance Orders cases and to develop a network of PRP coordinators to better address cross-functional issues that cause problems for taxpayers.

The goal, of course, is for government to listen to its customers (1) routinely through surveys (2) and when products or services do not live up to expectations, through an effective complaint-handling system. This is only the beginning. The American people deserve the best.

It is expected that a number of agencies will use this report to begin reengineering their complaint-handling processes, which will lead to a government that works better and costs less. Other agencies can make use of this benchmarking study as well. See Figure 19.2 for how to use this study to strengthen the complaint system in your organization.

- Get executive buy-in. In order to achieve any real success, senior management must support the team. This should be done early. Include visual material when appropriate.
- Put together an implementation team. This team should include a representative from each step in the complaint-handling process: frontline workers, information systems support, union representatives, management, quality improvement, and so on.
- Map current processes—both for complaints and the core processes they relate to. If the study team is not sure what the complaint system looks like, the team's first activity should be to identify each step in the complaint-handling process, from initial contact to final resolution.
- Conduct a gap analysis. The team should compare its own operations to the best practices listed in this report to understand where there are key differences between the team's organization and world-class performance. The difference between the team's services and the best-in-class processes is known as the gap.
- Develop recommendations. Based on the gap analysis, the team should develop a list of recommended changes in the organization's processes designed to close the gap. Some teams will tackle a large number of recommendations in the complaint-handling report. Others may get better results by focusing on those recommendations that are linked to their core business practices or can provide the largest improvements. The team may ask for input from major organizational components (such as budget, systems, training, and human resources) to identify issues that could affect the implementation of certain recommendations.
- Brief the stakeholders. Senior executives and, where relevant, upper-level union management, should be briefed on the proposed recommendations. Feedback from these sessions should be used to develop final recommendations.
- Implement. The team should put together an action plan for implementing the approved recommendations.
- Achieve measurable results! If the program is done right, customers will notice changes within six months.

Figure 19.2. Reinventing complaint resolution: A checklist for implementing best practices in complaint resolution.

Section 1: Leadership Strategies for Satisfying Customers

The philosophy indoctrinated by the leaders of the company is that every experience the customer has from the time of initial contact, during purchase, and throughout the life of the product, focuses on complete customer satisfaction. All employees have a part in customer relations and ensuring the best quality service and the best product. The emphasis is "Customer First. "

—Benchmarking study partner

There is little question that the leaders in the best-in-business companies see customers as their top priority. The leaders of these organizations practice the following initiatives.

Listen to the Voice of the Customer

One company knew it had begun to hear the voice of their customers when it went from 10,000 letters a year, mostly complaints, to 4,000 a year, mostly compliments. The leaders followed two simple rules: make it easy for customers to complain and make it just as easy for employees to fix problems.

The leaders demonstrate their commitment to customer concerns by investing corporate resources—money for tools like state-of-the-art computers and phone systems, and support, training, and recognition for their employees. The leaders see their job as making it easier for employees to respond to customers. The leaders partner with organized labor to achieve results. They invest a lot of their own time in communication, talking to customers and employees, and recognizing results. They have flattened their organization to cut the number of layers between the customer and the chief executive officer (CEO). Usually no more than three management levels separate frontline workers from the CEO. Leaders of customer service departments are part of the management team.

In all of the best-in-business organizations, customer complaints are seen as opportunities to improve. How complaints are handled reflects the organizations' overall commitment to customer service. Indeed, customer service is a core value in these organizations, reflected in mission statements, plans, performance measures, budget and personnel decisions, and decisions about contractor selection and retention. Leadership communicates its commitment to customers so effectively throughout the organization that the value is pervasive. Customer service does not depend on a single leader; it has been built into the way these organizations do business.

Know That Frontline Complaint Resolution Saves Time and Money and Improves Customer and Worker Satisfaction

It's not rocket science to realize that solving problems when and where they occur is not only better and faster, it's cheaper. If a teleservice representative or a front desk clerk can solve the problem, it saves time and money. Written complaints are similar. If the person who first reads the letter can solve the problem, it costs less and results in a faster response and fewer follow-up letters and phone calls trying to find out what happened. Audits by Technical Assistance Research Programs at over a dozen financial service companies show that poor service and poor customer communication increase the total workload by up to one-third (Goodman, Mar, and Bright 1986).

Smart CEOs recognize that it makes good business sense to empower frontline employees to do what it takes to satisfy customers by ensuring their front line has the authority, the training, and the responsibility for customer recovery. Customer recovery takes a lot of different forms. At one company, frontline employees can offer discount coupons that range in value from $20 to $250. At one government agency, customer representatives can speed up lost refunds or waive penalties that have been inappropriately applied. Sometimes, a careful explanation of the reason for a decision or empathetic listening along with an apology is all that is needed.

Focus on Improving Quality Not Dealing with Symptoms

If routine problems are effectively resolved on the front line, leaders can focus on improving core processes that improve service quality and customer satisfaction. One team member likened the good complaint systems she saw in service organizations to a quality program in a manufacturing plant.

> *The sooner these companies find out about complaints, the faster the core processes can be improved. Good managers don't play "gotcha" with employees. They understand that most complaints are due to procedures and policies that don't meet customers' expectations. Best-in-business companies use complaints to find the problems that had somehow been overlooked. They told us that when employees know that the leadership is focusing on doing a good job for the customer rather than on finding someone to blame, fear and resistance go out the window—the employees want to help find and fix the problems so that next time the job is done right the first time.*

One of the benchmarking partners goes a step further to involve employees and integrate customer feedback. The organization tries to capture customer satisfaction data from every customer contact. It does not believe that a separate complaint-handling system captures the whole picture. Thirty percent of the entire workforce wears the title "customer service representative." These representatives record customer contacts on a sophisticated computer system that allows them to code the root cause of any problem or question. This information is fed to a staff that analyzes the data to look for patterns and trends and for ways to make improvements in systems, procedures, and training. Senior management uses the feedback for planning and communication with employees.

Another company described the transformation of its own customer operations in three phases. In the first phase, customer complaints were seen as a necessary evil, and some customers were considered to be chronic complainers. In the second phase, the company provided "knee-jerk" customer service to pacify complaining customers. Today, the company's response operation not only assures a response in individual cases but collects information and analyzes all customer complaints to understand what underlies them and to identify root causes. When the company identifies a pattern that is causing problems, it introduces broader changes to remove the cause.

Section 2: Information and Analysis

> *We've significantly decreased cycle time and increased consistent and accurate responses with a database of standard letters and core language. Employees can use standard letters to reply to many complaints or inquiries such as the price of a stamp or where a customer can buy a used mail truck.*
>
> —U.S. Postal Service

Not every organization gets frequent requests for used mail trucks, but every organization benchmarked supports its frontline employees with the information and tools they need to respond to customer complaints and inquiries. Every organization sees the information provided by customers with problems as valuable, and collects and analyzes information about customer complaints. One organization described the information as "free market research." The organizations use a variety of approaches to capture and analyze the information and to use it for both routine and strategic management decisions. Best practice organizations use the following techniques.

Support Frontline Employees with Integrated On-line Databases

Companies use integrated, on-line information systems designed to support the performance of frontline employees who interact with customers and assist them in answering customer inquiries quickly and accurately. Characteristics of state-of-the-art desktop computer information systems include the following:

- User-friendly screens equipped with standardized formats to assist the customer service process; including, for example, frequently asked questions with appropriate responses, standard response letters, or actual scripts to reinforce training and prompt the employee

- Unique customer identification and access to customer information so that representatives can give customized service

- Simple on-line procedure manuals, often with help screens

- Avoidance of complex codes and "user-hostile" features in information systems

- Employee participation in development and testing to make sure that systems are accurate and easy to use

- Real-time information exchange and retrieval, and tools (such as electronic mail and fax capacity) so that employees can complete transactions quickly

- Links to fully integrated information databases, including documents submitted in paper form that have been imaged and archived electronically, press releases, new product developments, standard responses, information about hot topics, and performance statistics

- On-line technical support as a first-alarm response to data processing difficulties, to help frontline employees

Capture Information About Customer Problems and Questions

Frontline employees generally enter data to avoid duplication of effort, to improve accuracy, and to avoid backups in obtaining information about customer problems. Data analysis is generally centralized with a dedicated team or department responsible for analyzing data as its primary duty. Analysis groups often identify the most common concerns, analyze hot topics, and facilitate problem solving. For example, determining how to prevent customers from being dissatisfied or from needing to call for information—this leads to a preventive strategy known as *call avoidance.*

Managers in world-class organizations have real-time trend information, rather than end-of-the-period updates. They also get analysis that links frontline performance with corporate goals for customer satisfaction. Menu-driven programs allow users across the organization to develop reports and graphs from data specific to their area of responsibility. Using off-the-shelf software tailored to organizational needs, managers can retrieve and see complaint data displayed by type, region, product or service line, injury or catastrophic event, units responsible, root cause, volume, and so on. Informed management makes better decisions.

Effective analysis groups use integrated and nonduplicative databases. These databases include complaints from all sources, such as telephone calls, surveys, focus groups, correspondence, complaint/concern cards available on site, and/or personal visits. Database records include names, addresses, telephone numbers, individual employee assigned, actions taken, due dates, progress, disposition, and other descriptive information used to enhance all customer contacts.

Use Information to Fix Problems Fast

The first priority of the frontline employee is to satisfy the customer. At the same time, the employee enters the customer's concern into a database along with the action taken to satisfy the customer. In some organizations, the frontline employee also enters a description or codes the root cause of the customer's concern.

Information about customer interactions is then referred to analysis teams and to appropriate process improvement teams that are charged with solving problems. Simple changes are made quickly, often within 24 hours of a problem being identified. The automated tracking system follows the problem to resolution. The features of these systems include precise categories and types of concerns, automated hot topics, automated ad hoc reporting, and competitive information gathering. Frontline employees can also propose changes via the same electronic system.

Address Underlying Causes of Problems

More complex problems or ones with policy implications are prioritized by the analysis group based on customer impact and referred to the area of the organization that can fix the problems or to a team of employees that is charged with solving it. Some companies prioritize customers and attack the core complaints of the most frequent or highest-volume customers. Where there is a fully integrated automated complaint system, core problems are automatically routed to action agents.

Action agents further analyze the data and refer problems to the area of the organization that can best fix the problems, and organize cross-functional teams of employees from all levels in the chain of command to get at the root cause and correct it. By fixing root causes, future problems of the same nature are avoided, resulting in improved customer loyalty and organizational productivity. For example, critical analysis of data at one organization found that a large percentage of the 35,000 calls it received each month were simple billing questions. Now a voice response system can answer these questions, decreasing the number of calls representatives receive and giving customers faster access to the information they need.

There are regular activity reports on actions taken to fix problems. Information on actions taken and overall improvements are communicated to top management, staff employees, and frontline employees through briefings, newsletters, bulletin boards, direct interaction, complimentary letters, and, especially, an interlocking team structure. Information is communicated to customers through corporate media publications, telephone calls, and letters. As problems may relate to either lost productivity or lost revenue, the responsible department's budget may be charged for activities (root causes) for which they have been made aware of and that have not been corrected. Thus, there is a financial incentive for corrective action.

Track Contractor and Supplier Performance

Organizations that rely on contractors for customer interactions measure how well they perform. These companies track the performance of contractors and suppliers' products and services against customer satisfaction factors. An analysis is made to determine if corrective action is needed by these outside sources in order to prevent future complaints. Some companies are using shorter contracts and expecting greater accountability for performance. Some are moving to performance contracts that specify expected performance levels with the parent organization conducting surveys of customer satisfaction and monitoring other measures of contractor performance.

Section 3: Planning

The benchmarked organizations would not be where they are today if they operated the same way they did five years ago—or even last year. And they do not expect to be operating the same way next year—and certainly not five years from now. Information generated from complaints is an important component of customer feedback that drives business decisions and strategic planning in these companies. They integrate information and effectively use it to serve customers. The organizations implement new lines of business because their customers ask for it. The age and needs of their customers are changing so they are making changes to respond to new customers' needs. The best-in-business organizations all do the following.

Use Customer Feedback for Decisions About How Resources Are Used

Finding the best way to acquire new customers and maintain long-term customer loyalty is the reason for the planning process. Obviously complaint data are only part of customer feedback, but it is the importance of all forms of customer feedback, including complaint data, that characterizes planning. Using this information, these organizations make decisions about the use of people, technology, and other resources to meet customer needs. Officers and departments responsible for customer service are part of the planning team. Senior management uses customer feedback to identify opportunities for improvement and to align the organization's services and/or products to meet customer expectations.

Communicate Their Strategic Plans Throughout the Organization

There is no question about how important customers are at every level in world-class organizations. Mission and vision statements about the importance of customers are only as good as their impact on behavior from the boardroom to the mail room. Managers need to walk the talk. All employees need to know how their work contributes to the organization's goals and performance plans. For example, one Baldrige Award–winning company has a single objective, "customer satisfaction through total quality." The policy requires that all employees understand the customer-related requirements in their job and meet those requirements. Company policy emphasizes listening to customers before designing new products or services, through production and beyond the sale, to ensure customer satisfaction. This theme is communicated throughout the company and is clear to every employee. The corporate culture applies all of its creativity and intellect to delighting customers.

Have Dynamic Planning Processes

Best-in-business organizations look to the future and recognize that the way they do business has to change to keep the competitive edge. They project information about customers, as well as other aspects of the business environment, to develop future scenarios and determine what changes are needed in products, services, and other aspects of their business. One company has projected changes in membership into the next century and is already making changes in how it responds to young customers. Constant assessment of customer feedback, as part of the planning process, leads to new product lines and services, notably the 24-hour telephone service that is now common. One government organization uses customer data from the appeals process to identify trends and problems and to reassess its strategic and business plans, leading to changes in policy, guidelines, and procedures.

Section 4: Human Resource Development and Management

Resolving complaints on a regular basis can be extremely stressful. Successful organizations know that and treat their customer service representatives with respect and dignity. The companies carefully select people for the job, train them, and foster a supportive working environment. Frontline employees matter in these companies. The best-in-business organizations do the following.

Recruit and Hire the Best for Customer Service

The customer service and complaint resolution specialist positions established by the benchmarking partners tend to be highly sought-after positions; sometimes there are over 100 applicants for each open position. Complaint-handling employees are considered complaint-handling professionals or customer service professionals. Companies who fill openings from within the organization draw only from a list of highly qualified employees with a demonstrated interest and skill in working with the public. One benchmarking partner did not have a separate customer service position, but trained its technical experts to handle complaints as part of their job. Another company hires from outside the organization, but has a highly selective screening process and a competitive starting salary.

The most important factor in hiring was selection of individuals who fit in with the customer service culture and have a demonstrated skill and interest in working with the public. Organizations used a variety of selection techniques, including temporary assignments to determine the suitability of an employee for resolving customer complaints, initial telephone interviews for call center employees, and extensive staff and peer interviews—up to 14 interviews in one company. Companies look for a variety of character traits, skills, and experience for customer service jobs. These include the following:

- Problem-solving ability
- Skill in handling tense, stressful, and multitask situations
- Strong sense of responsibility
- Good communication skills and voice clarity
- Business writing skills
- Knowledge of relevant processes
- People skills with customers and coworkers
- Compassionate, customer-oriented attitude
- Strong desire to help customers
- Computer skills or aptitude
- College degree desired (sometimes required)
- Typing and other diagnostic tests (may be required)

Promote and Pay People Who Satisfy Customers

Some organizations build the customer service position into a career ladder for promotional advancement in the company. At one company, the customer relations position is an 18-month to two-year assignment, with the employee advancing to higher levels within the company. In other organizations, progression is built into the position via skill-based pay systems. That is, new skills and improved performance result in increased pay and responsibility. Another company develops the representative's expertise within certain areas of complaints, and the individual handles all the complaints in that specific area. The turnover rate for these positions tends to be in the single digits. Individuals generally leave because they are excelling in their careers, which is a cause for celebration. Government agencies need to review and revise their policies and procedures that limit rewarding results; legislative changes are not needed.

See Training as a Critical Investment Not an Expense

Best-in-business leaders consider training an investment, not an expense. They use complaint trends/data to identify training needs. One organization increased training from 17 to 71 hours per person per year. Another, with 70 hours of training per employee, devotes 3 percent of its personnel budget to training. One company gives approximately 100 hours in training to all employees. Most world-class organizations fund college courses. One organization visited provides space for evening classes sponsored by local colleges and universities. Typically, new employee training consists of classroom instruction and on-the-job training—working with someone more experienced. New employees are educated in the underlying principles and mission of the organization, and in the performance expected of them to maintain those principles and mission.

Ongoing training for different categories of skills is crucial. To enhance individual interpersonal relationships, training offerings cover active listening, behavioral interviewing, communicating across cultures, correction (assertive ways to give and accept criticism to and from peers), and building relationships. To develop group relationships, courses cover facilitation, negotiation, leading teams, and coaching. Personal growth skills benefit from offerings such as effective writing, software training, personal presentations, and *The Seven Habits of Highly Successful People* (Covey 1989). Other categories deal directly with business operations. One category teaches process management skills; for example, process mapping (especially in the employee's processes), developmental processes, problem solving, quality improvements, and gap analysis. Another area covers measurement skills, such as operation effectiveness, surveying, and measuring. Lastly, organizations educate their employees on the mission statement, and how their jobs relate to it.

Create a Performance Culture

The organizations visited have a performance-focused culture. Organizational vision, values, goals, and objectives reach all the way down to the front line. The work environment may be casual or formal, but customer and quality concerns are always present. In this atmosphere, complaints are viewed as an opportunity to improve rather than as an indictment of performance.

Employees feel encouraged to contribute their ideas for improving processes, regardless of rank or function. A well-developed feedback loop lets employees know the disposition of their recommendations. Employee feedback is also valued in focus groups, customer online comments, assessment tools, internal surveys, and management information sessions.

Use Teams and Teamwork

A team-oriented culture is the norm in world-class organizations. Teams accept ownership of complaints, and work together to handle complaints, analyze problems, and generate new ideas. All employees are involved in the vision. Everyone is part of the team.

At one organization, there is no hierarchy, no job titles, and everyone works on the front line on a schedule determined by the team. It has state-of-the-art equipment. The information technology staff that developed the software spend time on the telephone with customers so the staff learn what is needed to satisfy customers. Workstations are designed as a neighborhood environment, partnering employees with different skills into self-managed work teams. Morale has soared; turnover dropped from 106 percent to 5 percent, and more work is being done with 76 employees than was previously done by 126 in the headquarters and at distant locations. The goal of the operation is to delight the customer in world-class fashion, and the customer service professionals on the front line work together to do so.

Give Employees Authority and Responsibility to Resolve Complaints

Empowerment of customer service representatives is crucial to providing customers on-the-spot, just-in-time resolution to their problems. Company representatives must have the authority to do what it takes to make things right in the customer's eyes. Also crucial is arming those employees with the resources to properly handle complaints.

Employees with a feeling of ownership in the company help each other for the good of the organization. They take responsibility for improving their own skill levels, solving problems, and sharing information. They share information via newsletters and town meetings so the same mistakes do not recur.

Recognize and Reward Success

World-class organizations recognize their employees' individual and team accomplishments frequently and in a large variety of ways, both monetarily and nonmonetarily. These organizations use employee appreciation events, celebrations, representative- or team-of-the-quarter/year awards, bonuses, and merchandise. At one organization, nonsalaried employees participate in profit sharing based on merit, with their share of the profit determined by their team's performance against company goals.

Evaluation methods are geared toward customer recovery and performance improvement. For example, supervisors use call monitoring as an evaluation tool to help employees perform better, not to give them a poor appraisal rating. At one organization, peers are responsible for monitoring calls and are trained to give constructive criticism. At another organization, individuals rate themselves by listening to their own audiotaped calls. A comprehensive 360-degree performance system includes the supervisor, customer, and peer input into the evaluation. Feedback is continuous throughout the year rather than at one time, and is both oral and written. Performance measures tie back to the company's mission, goals, and customer satisfaction. One company rewards its employees for results that fix something, not for suggestions.

Involve Frontline Employees in Solving Problems

In these companies, managers value feedback from frontline employees, to the point of using the feedback in making decisions. Frontline employees are held accountable, but are given authority to go with accountability. They are encouraged to tell management about their customers' concerns. These employees buy into the system because they can see results based on their suggestions and input. Documenting customer calls helps to decrease the number of dissatisfied customers by determining the root cause of the problems. The company brings frontline employees in from the field to analyze problems, to recommend alternatives to management, and to implement the accepted solution. Employees embrace the corporate culture that complaints are opportunities to improve. All employees feel responsible for solving problems.

Managers take care and pride in positively motivating employees. Managers recognize the importance of the job of frontline employees by listening to and acting on the employees' ideas, rewarding their efforts, highlighting the position on the company's career ladder, and offering training for growth. Frontline workers' personal well-being is also important, and management provides benefits such as child care centers and fitness facilities. These organizations adhere to the policy that employee satisfaction is as important as customer satisfaction to the success of their business.

Section 5: Customer Focus, Expectations, and Satisfaction

In every tank purchased from the Red River Army Depot, there's a toll-free number in the glove compartment so customers know who to call if they have a problem with the vehicle. At Red River, customer calls come into the 24-hour production control center. Here the officer on duty coordinates customer response by initiating, tracking, and evaluating the quality of support provided by the organization. If a customer has serious trouble with a tank, a customer service team can be mobilized to fly out to the customer's site to fix the problem.

While troubles with a tank are not a typical customer problem, organizations like Red River, a winner of the 1995 President's Quality Improvement Prototype Award, go out of their way to make it easy for customers to complain. They organize to respond rapidly when their customers have a problem. These organizations understand what their customers need and expect. The best-in-business organizations practice the following.

Encourage Customer Complaints

One public agency found that three quarters of its customers had no idea who to talk to if they had a problem. Many customers think it's simply not worth the hassle to complain. They are skeptical that the organization will do anything or they may even fear retribution.

Best-in-business organizations actively encourage customer complaints. Some companies even refer to what they do to encourage complaints as "marketing" their complaint system. Companies make consumer service cards available at the place of business. Many solicit feedback wherever they post or publish customer service standards such as on all correspondence, on bills, and in the telephone directory. Some offer discount coupons to encourage customer feedback. Many publish information on how they can be contacted in more than one language. They publish toll-free and other numbers for the company where consumers are most likely to see them; for example, on product packaging. Companies also market their complaint-handling systems during conferences and meetings, in annual reports, newspapers, association circulars, videos, audiotapes, letters, press releases, speeches, training sessions, and via electronic mail.

Seek to Delight Their Customers

The benchmarking partners often use the phrase "delight the customer," and go out of their way to exceed customer expectations. Often this means a compassionate ear. An insurance company has a special team that deals with the needs of grieving spouses. Companies give frontline employees the authority to award customers who have complaints with products, coupons, or even cash when it is necessary to resolve a complaint. Even public sector employees are able to give certain products and services to customers with complaints. For example, the U.S. Postal Service can give up to $20 in stamps when it is appropriate. One service company sets no limits on the frontline employees' authority but tracks company norms for what it takes to resolve particular types of problems. Team leaders look at and discuss variances from these norms. Additionally, employees share ideas for ways to resolve complaints creatively within or below company norms.

Understand Their Customers

These organizations demonstrate a commitment to understanding the customer's perspective. Most of the benchmarking partners send surveys to customers who have complained recently to see how satisfied they were with how the complaint was handled. Some call the customers to determine satisfaction. One organization surveys every fourth customer with a complaint. Another organization described complaints as "free information" about its customers' needs and expectations.

These organizations supplement surveys of people who complain with routine and often extensive data collection tools in order to understand their customers. Customers are surveyed to determine their level of satisfaction with existing services. Surveys are sent with questions, often in a Likert-scale format where the customer can select the degree of satisfaction on a scale, say, from 1 to 5.

These surveys assess customer satisfaction with existing services, delivery of services, helpfulness of employees, and overall performance of the organization. Some companies add a few short questions to the end of customer calls or correspondence. Companies also survey their frontline employees for their attitudes as well as for their ideas for improved service, asking their employees to take the customers' perspective. After the nearby community complained about noise levels, the Red River Army Depot changed the times it detonated ammunition and put "listeners" (members of the community) at checkpoints throughout the surrounding area to monitor noise levels.

The partners focus on clear customer target groups. One company that serves a wide variety of customers decided to focus on its high-volume business customers. Three months after a high-volume business customer has complained, the company follows up to find out whether the customer is still using the organization's services and, if not, the reasons for dissatisfaction. In addition, the company routinely solicits feedback before, during, and after service. It conducts focus groups and has established a customer advisory council to drive decisions related to this key target group.

Manage Customer Expectations

These organizations do not wait for complaints to come in the door. They try to anticipate customers' needs and problems and to set realistic expectations through customer education and communication strategies. Research shows that 40 percent of complaints come from customers having inadequate information about a product or a service. Using customer feedback to understand customer expectations and needs, organizations educate their customers and/or the public on what they can expect from products and services and what obligations and responsibilities customers have. For example, one enforcement/regulatory partner has extensive education on the requirements and reasons for utilizing its services.

Know How to Say No

Both companies and government agencies, especially regulatory agencies, need to draw limits. When it is not possible to give customers what they would like, it is still possible for customers to feel that they have been heard and have been treated fairly. A number of techniques convey concern—calling customers and telling them the company understands; giving customers the best explanation possible; and being open and honest with customers concerning laws and policies of the organization. Being professional and considerate of customers enhances their view of the organization—even when they may be disappointed with the outcome. A recent taxpayer letter to the Internal Revenue Service shows these techniques work.

> *For the first time in a long time, a communication from IRS is clear, concise, informative, and user-friendly . . . The attached—while I'd preferred not to have made the mistake—points out exactly what happened and what needed to be done.*

In a small percentage of cases, it will be necessary to close a complaint when it is felt that the company or agency has done everything that can be done. Recognizing that it is not always possible to satisfy a customer, having procedures and trained staff to handle these cases, is part of an effective complaint-handling system.

Keep the Human Touch

One company found that it made a major mistake when it introduced enhanced information technology. Employees lost eye contact with their customers. Keep the human touch—don't let automation get between the frontline employee and the customer. Eye-to-eye contact may be lost with computers.

Section 6: Complaint Process Management

World-class service providers, which is what Americans expect their government to be, have a carefully developed complaint-handling process. That process is customer-focused, is clearly understood by all employees, has performance standards, and is linked to the core operation. Without a well-designed and well-managed process, complaints are often handed off to different offices for response, delaying and generally increasing the cost of the response. The best-in-business organizations do the following.

Really Know Their Processes

Each and every one of this study's benchmarking partners had a process map for its complaint-handling processes. They told the study team that the map was key to understanding what was going on and was invaluable in perceiving the gaps between the goal of delighting the customer and what was currently taking place. Many companies begin by using simple flowcharting methodology. Some have subsequently developed more complex and more graphic maps, but they all map their process.

Customer representatives and complaint process managers clearly understand the services and products offered by their company or agency. They study and understand the customers' expectations. For example, at one company, customer telephone surveys are used to monitor the expectations of customers who call with a problem. At one public sector organization, managers analyze, verbatim, comments from complaints when they set performance goals for customer representatives. Another, with a client feedback program, surveys and analyzes information from recent clients, and forwards all comments anonymously to the client representative at each facility. These concerns are included as part of each facility's client representative program performance.

Research by this benchmarking team indicated that the best complaint departments have immediate goals to fix the problem at hand, satisfy the customer to the extent allowed by company policy or the law, and make systemic improvements to prevent the problem from recurring. They strive to prevent problems through revised procedures and support for on-the-spot and postevent complaints recovery by frontline staff, and managers. All of the offices visited knew how well they were meeting this goal.

There are different processes for meeting the goal depending on how the customer contacts the organization. For example, customers contact service providers by telephone, letter, in person, or via the Internet. The goals, resources, personnel, and results varied, but universally the best in business knew their processes thoroughly and they made it easy to complain. They provide one-stop resolution and if handoffs are necessary, they are seamless (transparent to the customer). First-call problem resolution while the customer is on the telephone is an element of world-class complaint handling.

Use Customer and Employee Input to Design Processes

Developing a world-class complaint process begins and ends with customers. At one company, customers participate throughout the process of product design, development, and support in order to express concern at the front end of product delivery. Program managers respond to customer problems directly, and senior executives maintain ongoing, personal contact with customers. The U.S. Postal Service has more than 1700 active Customer Advisory Councils that advise on the public's needs for both delivery and problem resolution. The U.S. Postal Service used focus groups of both customers and employees from various areas of the country and feedback from customer satisfaction surveys to develop its complaint resolution process. As a result of using extensive customer and employee input, the U.S. Postal Service found that it was able to improve the quality of responses and reduce cycle time and costs.

The best in business design their complaint process with input from both customers and employees. They develop a culture that supports teamwork—with the customer as part of the team. They design the process with top management commitment, performance measurements, and a direct link to core processes. At one of the benchmarking partners, the customer relations personnel monitor customer feedback. They select a small number of items the customers complained about most often as target issues. Once these issues are identified, individual customer satisfaction committees are formed that link those issues with mission objectives. The complaint process is monitored to correct root causes of dissatisfaction, and the results for these target customer satisfaction issues are reported to the executive committee.

Use Technology to Support and Improve the Complaint Process

The benchmarked companies and agencies had built a technologically advanced infrastructure to answer complaints and other customer inquiries. They use toll-free numbers, sophisticated telecommunication systems, automated call distributors, caller ID, imaging systems, and office automation for state-of-the-art, on-line customer support systems. For example, one company has an automated system that allows service representatives to capture information about each member contact and make it accessible to everyone in the organization.

Practice Continuous Process Improvement

In business as in the Olympics, the bar is constantly being raised. Whether it be foreign competition, technological innovation, or more effective management and teamwork, each organization must produce more and better results with fewer resources. The key to beating the competition and keeping up with the times is continuous improvement. The key to continuous improvement is to refine, redesign, and improve processes while putting the customer first.

All of the benchmarking partners focused their attention on process improvement, and they were good at it. Customers were kept involved, employees were recruited and trained with long-range improvement in mind. Top management was kept informed along with the front line. Best practices were developed by benchmarking and were carefully implemented and recorded. Performance measures were constantly monitored to identify gaps that could lead to opportunities to make things better. Employees were empowered to suggest and make process changes that help customers. Improvements were recognized. The complaint process was viewed as a loop, with the customer at the beginning and at the end and with the core operating processes in the middle. Constant feedback from both customers and employees and constant reevaluation based on satisfaction measurement assure constant improvement. These incremental improvements lead to service excellence, which is a winning strategy that can make government work better and cost less. Everyone wins!

Section 7: Business Results

> *If you don't measure results, you can't tell success from failure.*
>
> —David Osborne and Ted Gaebler

Success for commercial companies is long-term profitability, generated by maximizing customer satisfaction and loyalty. The primary goal of government is to provide services to citizens. Over the long-term, however, success is also generated by maximizing customer/citizen satisfaction and loyalty and earning the public trust. In both arenas government agencies must know what customers expect. Agencies must know how well they are meeting those expectations; they must know what problems customers encounter; agencies must know how much these problems cost to respond to and how much they impact

customer satisfaction. Finally, government agencies must change their processes to eliminate those problems. The best-in-business organizations reduce their costs and increase
their profits by using the following.

Key Performance Measures

The benchmarking partners use a variety of measures to assess the performance of their
complaint-handling systems. These measures are part of a balanced scorecard—a set of
organizational performance measures that include such bottom-line measures as return on
investment and sales; compliance rates for regulatory agencies; measures of overall customer satisfaction; and financial and other measures.

Performance measures are dynamic. They change as goals are met, as improvements
are made, as priority customer segments are identified, and as more predictive measures
are developed. Companies with more mature measurement and complaint-handling systems described changes over time in the measures that they used. In the past, individual
employee performance was measured, and individual awards were given. Today, performance is more often measured for groups or teams, and individuals receive team awards.
Many companies and agencies began measuring customer satisfaction several years ago.
They measure customer satisfaction not only with their products and services, but also
with their complaint resolution process.

The benchmarking partners had accomplished significant changes in key measures.
For example, one highly technical organization decreased the average number of days it
takes to resolve a complaint from 55 to 19 days. A second organization reduced the time
required to resolve cases from 27 to 6 days, well below its standard of 15 days.

Timeliness and Efficiency

The best-in-business organizations measure timeliness with a strong focus on first-call resolution or on-line resolution. They average an 85 percent resolution on the first contact for
all calls received. Timeliness standards vary by complexity and by industry but were specific; for example, resolution within 14 days and response within five business days. At one
company, the customer is asked to set the deadline for an answer to the problem. The deadline is entered in the system and becomes part of the company's commitment to the customer. The customer is notified if the deadline cannot be met. A tracking system monitors
the status of open cases. Preventive measures are more difficult, although some organizations quantified "calls avoided" and other complaint-prevention strategies. Examples of
measures and some high-end norms include the following:

- First call/contact resolution—85 percent average for all calls/contacts received
- Backlog—0 percent
- Cycle time—based on customer expectation
- Call avoidance—through customer education

Customer Satisfaction

Benchmarking partners see quality and customer satisfaction as their first priority, and a variety of measures are used to track the performance of the complaint-handling system from the customer's perspective. Overall levels of satisfaction with how a complaint was handled are often tracked using survey responses from customers who have made complaints. A variety of other qualitative characteristics are measured, such as whether the parties understood the decision and whether they felt that they had been treated fairly. The best in business continually monitor customer expectations for and satisfaction with their complaint resolution system.

Call Center Measures

Organizations responding to complaints through call centers use a variety of measures, such as the following:

- Average speed of answer: for example, 10 seconds or less
- Abandoned call rate: 2 percent to 3 percent
- Busy rate: less than 1 percent
- Service level (total calls less busy signals and abandoned calls): 98 percent
- First-call resolution: one agent/no transfers
- Queue waiting time: less than 60 seconds
- On hold waiting time: less than 15 seconds
- Team leaders typically monitor 5–10 calls per month for each frontline employee

For further information see NPR's benchmarking report titled, "Best Practices in Telephone Service."

Correspondence Center Measures

Organizations responding to written complaints use the following measures.

- Average response time for standard or information responses
- Average response time for specialized/individual responses
- Cycle time for each type of response

Workload Measure

All the benchmarking partners track workload through measures such as numbers of calls, complaints, or letters. The organizations are, however, cautious about how these numbers—especially numbers of complaints—are interpreted. Is it good or bad that the number of complaints goes up in a given time period? Does it reflect more effective marketing of the complaint system? The introduction of a new product? A problem with educational material? Repeat calls from people trying to get a response?

If it has been difficult to complain and an organization makes it easier, the number of complaints should increase initially. Then, as complaint data and other customer feedback are used to eliminate underlying problems, the number of complaints should decline. The best companies do everything they can to encourage complaints, and as a result they greatly reduce the number of complaints received.

Employee Satisfaction

Employee satisfaction is considered to be a key indicator of productivity and customer satisfaction. Best-in-business organizations track employee satisfaction through the use of employee satisfaction surveys and/or through predictive indicators, such as the following:

- Employee satisfaction survey results

- Attrition rates of employees

- Training hours in customer service per employee

When service is good and the organization's culture encourages teamwork, both customers and employees are happy.

References

Covey, Steven. 1989. *The seven habits of highly successful people.* New York: Simon and Schuster.

Federal Benchmarking Consortium of the National Performance Review. 1995. *Putting customers first: Serving the American public: Best practices in telephone service.* Washington, D.C.: National Performance Review.

Goodman, John A. June 1995. *Building a world-class service system and setting rational priorities.* Arlington, Va.: Technical Assistance Research Programs (TARP).

Goodman, John A., Ted Mar, and Liz Bright. 1986. Customer service: Costly nuisance or low-cost profit strategy? *Journal of Retail Banking* (fall): 7–16.

Gore, Al. 1995. *Common sense government.* New York: Random House.

Osborne, David, and Ted Gaebler. 1992. *Reinventing government.* Reading, Mass.: Addison-Wesley.

Technical Assistance Research Programs (TARP). June 1990. *Maximizing customer satisfaction and directly linking to the bottom line.* Arlington, Va.: Technical Assistance Research Programs (TARP).

Acknowledgments

The Federal Benchmarking Study Team thanks the corporate and government partners who willingly shared their best practices with us. Special thanks are also due John A. Goodman of Technical Assistance Research Programs, Laura Longmire of KPMG Peat Marwick, LLP, and Carl Thor of Jarrett Thor International who assisted in planning this study.

About the Authors

Vice President Al Gore's National Performance Review, Federal Benchmarking Consortium is a network of self-managed benchmarking study teams. Federal employees lead and participate in benchmarking studies to systematically learn from the best in business and then use this information to improve their own agency's performance.

The study team focuses on benchmarking a specific organizational process, such as strategic planning, establishing a consumer help line, and resolving customer complaints. At the conclusion of the study, the team develops a comprehensive report, which is published by the National Performance Review. This report emphasizes best practices and is disseminated throughout the U.S. government.

The Federal Benchmarking Consortium receives additional support from the President's Management Council and the Council for Excellence in Government. The President's Management Council is made up of all the Cabinet Deputy Secretaries. They provide leadership by identifying, prioritizing, and nominating processes for benchmarking. The Council for Excellence in Government supports the consortium by providing people to conduct research in support of the study teams. The key personnel for this study are as follows:

Benchmarking study partners.

> Delta Airlines
>
> Eastman Chemical
>
> Office of the Comptroller of the Currency
>
> Red River Army Depot
>
> Revenue Canada
>
> Texas Instruments
>
> Toyota Motor Sales
>
> USAA
>
> USA Today
>
> United States Postal Service

Participating agencies.

> U.S. Department of Veterans Affairs
>> Veterans Benefits Administration
>> Veterans Health Administration

U.S. Department of the Interior
   National Park Service
U.S. Department of Agriculture
U.S. Department of State
U.S. Department of the Treasury
   Internal Revenue Service
   U.S. Customs
U.S. Postal Service
Federal Emergency Management Agency
National Security Agency
U.S. Department of Transportation
U.S. Department of Commerce
   Patent and Trademark Office
   Office of Consumer Affairs

Benchmarking study organizers.
   Pamela Johnson, National Performance Review
   Dan Curtis, National Performance Review

Benchmarking study team leaders.
   Scott Beck, U.S. Department of Veterans Affairs
   Pat Heringa, Veterans Health Administration
   Frances Walinsky, National Performance Review

Benchmarking study team members.
   Shirley Arico, U.S. Department of Veterans Affairs
   Gypsy Banks, U.S. Department of Agriculture
   Kathleen Bell, U.S. Customs Service
   Doris Branch, U.S. Department of the Interior
   David Clippinger, Internal Revenue Service
   David Cook, Internal Revenue Service
   Fay Flournoy, U.S. Postal Service
   Jack Frost, Veterans Benefits Administration
   Rose Gates, Veterans Health Administration
   Norma Jo Greenlee, Patent and Trademark Office
   Stuart Haggard, U.S. Department of Veterans Affairs

Jannie Harrell, U.S. Department of the Interior

Alexander Havas, U.S. Department of Veterans Affairs

Melanie Howell, U.S. Department of State

Rich Howell, Veterans Benefits Administration

Roy Ingersoll, U.S. Department of the Interior

Jan Jamil, U.S. Department of the Treasury

Pamela Johnson, National Performance Review

Bonnie Jones, Federal Emergency Management Agency

Paige Lowther, U.S. Department of Veterans Affairs

Julie Mason, U.S. Department of the Treasury

Lee Monks, Internal Revenue Service

John O'Malley, U.S. Customs Service

Betsy Passuth, U.S. Customs Service

Estelle Rondello, U.S. Office of Consumer Affairs

Melissie Rumizen, National Security Agency

Mary Beth Saldin, U.S. Department of Veterans Affairs

Sharon Sellers, U.S. Department of the Interior

Henry Schaefer, U.S. Department of Transportation

Sandra Wiggins, National Park Service

Colette Wickman, Federal Quality Institute

Ray Wilburn, U.S. Department of Veterans Affairs

For More Information

Vice President Al Gore's National Performance Review
750 17th St. NW
Washington, D.C. 20006
Telephone: 202-632-0150
Facsimile: 202-632-0390
E-mail: www.npr.gov

CHAPTER 20

Utilizing Benchmarking to Build Customer-Supplier Relationships: How the U.S. Air Force and Sverdrup Technology Partnered for Change

J. T. Northcutt, Sr., Quality Engineering Technical Specialist, and David Yoest, Quality Officer, Sverdrup Technology, Inc., Arnold Engineering Development Center, Arnold Air Force Base

Introduction

This chapter describes how a benchmarking activity improved the business relationship between a supplier and its customer. The results obtained both in the primary area of interest—turbine engine installation time—and in the general business relationship between the two firms are documented. The trust and understanding that were established during the benchmarking activity will be discussed along with the resultant business opportunities that have developed.

Sverdrup Technology, Inc. (SvT), in conjunction with its U.S. Air Force (USAF) partner, has successfully utilized benchmarking techniques that were of significant benefit to the Arnold Engineering Development Center (AEDC) and its test customer, United Technologies, Pratt and Whitney (P&W).

SvT is a technical contractor for the USAF, performing propulsion testing at AEDC, which is a national test facility for aerodynamic and engine propulsion technologies. Most of the aircraft designs, along with the propulsion systems that have been developed for the USAF, have been tested at AEDC. It has also performed work for other government agencies and commercial clients. There are over 40 active test cells at AEDC providing testing in aerodynamics (wind tunnels), ballistic ranges, and altitude testing for both full-scale jet turbine engine and rocket motor propulsion. Two recent additions are the J-6 rocket test cell and the DECADE radiation test facility.

Purpose

As is the case with most established organizations, the changing marketplace is forcing AEDC to look at how it conducts business, and has challenged AEDC to review who its primary customers are. In the past, SvT focused on the local Air Force personnel as its primary customer, and was evaluated and rewarded on local perception of performance. Accomplishing tasks and projects on schedule was paramount to nearly all other evaluation factors. In recent years, more emphasis has been placed on cost and user satisfaction. This encouraged a more external focus.

In 1988, federal regulations changed, allowing the end users of AEDC's test services to use outside facilities or their own facilities to satisfy the ground testing requirements of government-procured weapon systems. Due to this change, the end user's satisfaction has become much more prominent and important. The relationship between the local Air Force and SvT also changed. A partnership developed between the two organizations when it became apparent that survival of AEDC was threatened in the late 1980s.

Cost-of-testing pressures built up during this period, and the threat of loss of business to other test facilities was apparent. AEDC reacted by incorporating modern management methodologies. Benchmarking was examined and initially accepted as an area that SvT would try and then evaluate. The first attempt to formally use benchmarking was unsuccessful because of the approach taken. A quality improvement team was given an objective to include benchmarking as part of its work. The team's focus was too diverse, however, and its other objectives distracted the team from doing any formal benchmarking activities.

Operations

Meanwhile, SvT, along with USAF managers, was seeking to develop a closer working relationship with P&W, one of the world's largest jet aircraft manufacturers. P&W, with its military engines, has been a major source of revenue for AEDC. AEDC's capabilities and reputation were not widely known in the commercial engine division, and relations between AEDC and P&W commercial divisions were not close.

Fortunately for AEDC, P&W was seeking a way to altitude test a new family of jet turbines that required large amounts of air mass flow. Very few facilities in the world have the capability to perform these tests at the high air mass flows required. P&W had the option of building its own facilities or using the existing ones at AEDC. Thus, AEDC recognized the potential of this business and decided to pursue it.

One of P&W's concerns centered on the amount of time AEDC needed to install an engine the first time in a test cell. This process is tedious, complex, and very labor intensive. Normal cell installation times for new engines, such as the P&W 4084, have taken approximately six weeks to bring in, inspect, instrument the engine, instrument the test cell, install, hook up, and check out the engine. While all installations require these activities, AEDC was taking much longer than the time P&W claimed it could do the same work. This is important because of the overhead charges that are accumulating against the project. The longer a project is open and running, the more expensive it is because of the applied overhead. Six weeks of installation time is six weeks of project time. Any way to shorten the installation process will shorten the project by the same amount of time.

Shortly after the decision was made by P&W to pursue testing at AEDC, the AEDC test team and P&W representatives began to address the estimated engine installation time. Constant communication by the SvT project manager and the P&W liaison resulted in a good understanding between the supplier and customer. A perception of the need to analyze the differences in P&W and AEDC test facilities, and the installation process, evolved.

Team Investigation

Seven employees from the AEDC test team were selected to travel to the P&W test facility in Willgoos, Connecticut. The team consisted of the USAF project manager and six SvT employees, one from each internal organization involved in the process. They represented the following departments: project engineering; test operations; instrumentation; plant operations; project management; and Air Force project management.

It is significant to mention that all team members were selected for their knowledge and expertise in applicable process techniques. The team was tasked with the goal of comparing the P&W and AEDC installation process for possible improvements to either or both.

Upon arrival of the benchmarking team at the P&W facility, a kickoff meeting was held. The purpose of the meeting was to

- Establish ground rules about which facility areas the AEDC team could access.
- Confirm the activities that would be performed.
- Establish a time line for accomplishment of the activities.

The team was organized into a two-shift operation so that 20 of every 24 hours could be observed.

A separate mechanical logbook and electrical/instrumentation logbook were continuously kept by appointed team members to thoroughly document the processes they observed. Documentation was very detailed and all encompassing. The types of tool used, and comparison of work practices at AEDC and P&W, were also noted. A daily turnover meeting was held between the first and second shift crews to ensure transfer of knowledge. Discussions to assure understanding of the observations of each team member were held daily. This on-site visit lasted seven days.

After the benchmarking team returned to AEDC, an official trip report was written. It detailed the significant differences in the installation process and practices of the two organizations. Some of the differences included the following:

- Test cell preparation prior to engine arrival was different at the two facilities.
- The female lab seal at P&W's facility was designed and located for easier hookup and accessibility.
- All test cell electrical connectors were located outside the inner cell wall at P&W, and data system channel assignments were standardized in the types of measurements.

- The hardware and tools used in the process of fitting and engine alignment were indexed and labeled at the P&W facility.

- P&W deployed a more modular instrumentation hookup design and capability at its facility.

- P&W staff differed from SvT staff in terms of accepted responsibilities and authority of the craft, including differences among hourly employees at the two facilities.

Management acceptance of the findings was obtained within three months after the site visit and a formal report was issued.

Functional goals were established; action plans were formulated with each organization (process owners) to implement the needed changes; and a timetable for accomplishments was constructed. Note: Due to the sensitive nature of this benchmarking effort and national defense testing capability security, the goals and plans are stated generically.

The goal was to reduce overall engine installation time and the applicable resources associated with that process. Actions plans included the following:

- Establish cross-functional, continuous improvement teams to implement the approved changes.

- Establish a steering committee to provide management support and to monitor progress.

- Provide resources and upper management support for the needed improvements and changes.

- Restructure specific union guidelines that restrict the way certain tasks have to be performed by designated craft trades. This could eliminate a major cause of inefficient processes and reduce the overall cycle time and cost of the engine installation process.

No formal timetable for accomplishment was established. All recommendations were implemented and accomplished within 14 months. Some of the recommendations included the following:

- Broaden the craft personnel's tasks and responsibilities.
- Establish common interconnections for instrumentation.
- Develop common connections for fuel, oil, and cooling.
- Request the arrival of inlet rakes prior to the engine's arrival to enhance the proper connection and the leak and continuity checks.
- Standardize the control room configurations.
- Relocate all the electrical connectors to outside the inner cell wall.
- Redesign the bell mouth to make it easily removable.
- Index, label, and locally store all the associated hardware.
- Enhance planning activities and test cell preparation prior to the engine's arrival.

Results

Direct Results

The direct savings associated with this project are at the program level. Due to the efforts of the benchmarking team and others, such as engineers and craftspeople who were not team members, the installation time was reduced from an estimated six weeks (42 days) to 11 days. Thus, the program was shortened by 31 days. Further improvements resulted in installation time being reduced to four days.

The customer, P&W, was extremely pleased with the performance of the program. Ray Lemaire, manager of P&W's commercial engine business and engineering operations, stated,

> *This is a significant milestone. It shows the ability to bring a commercial engine into a government facility. . . . Bringing a new engine to a facility that we had no experience with was an unknown quantity. There was a lot of concern. Those concerns were put to bed when the engine arrived in September and you people mounted it and got it running in 10 days. . . . This has been a very successful program. It's made believers out of a lot of people. Be proud of what you have done because it is a very significant achievement.*

Estimates for the reduction of program costs are conservatively placed at over $20 million.

The success of the venture has encouraged AEDC to expand the activity. Recently, AEDC was visited by a benchmarking team from the Naval Air Warfare Center Aircraft Division. Liaison personnel have been exchanged. A U.S. Navy representative is now a resident at AEDC, and an Air Force officer is located in Trenton, New Jersey, to facilitate information exchanges.

Key Results

The key result is the 20-year agreement that has been signed with the commercial division of P&W to develop the 4000 series of engines. AEDC and SvT were able to prove to P&W that they could do the work. This agreement is valued at $387 million for the facility. Testing at AEDC has been agreed on with Rolls Royce to test the Trent 800 engine—a comparable turbine in weight, size, and thrust. Knowledge gained has also been applied to several military engines as well.

An indirect result of this benchmarking project is the change of focus the Sverdrup Design Section has undertaken. Consideration of user interfaces, connection, and support requirements is now paramount in decision making on design approaches rather than design based on AEDC experience and preferences.

Conclusion and Lessons Learned

AEDC has found that benchmarking with its customers on similar business processes not only can enable productivity gains, but it can also cement the basic business relationship between a customer and a supplier. Thus, both parties have an opportunity to gain. One major lesson learned was to establish a team to specifically obtain benchmark information and not to make it a part of a larger mission. Another lesson learned was to keep the effort focused on a specific process, and not allow it to get broad and out-of-hand. The benchmarking effort should be the primary focus of a team, not an objective of many.

About the Authors

J. T. Northcutt, Sr. is a quality engineering technical specialist for Sverdrup Technology, Inc., located at the Arnold Engineering Development Center (AEDC) on Arnold Air Force Base near Nashville, Tennessee. His job responsibilities include benchmarking training and overseeing the audit program at AEDC. He is also a facilitation, performance measurement, and metrics trainer and consultant and lead auditor. Northcutt's previous positions include serving as an auditor for software quality assurance and as an engineering associate with responsibilities for data analysis, operational procedures development, and technical schematics development.

Northcutt has authored articles and proceedings for the 1996 and 1995 Measuring and Monitoring Performance conference, sponsored by the Institute for International Research; for IMPROV95 and IMPROV94, sponsored by the Juran Institute; and for the 1994 Air Force Quality Symposium. He is a charter member of ASQ's benchmarking committee.

J. T. Northcutt, Sr.
Sverdrup Technology, Inc.
675 Second Street
Arnold AFB, TN 37389-4500
Telephone: 615-454-4771
Facsimile: 615-454-3751
E-mail: northcuttj@hap.arnold.af.mil

David Yoest is a quality officer for Sverdrup Technology, Inc., at AEDC. He directs the quality program and has worked as a quality methods facilitator and senior quality engineer. He also serves Trevecca Nazarene University and Middle Tennessee State University as an adjunct professor.

Yoest holds an MBA from Middle Tennessee State University, and has authored articles in ASQ's Quality Progress and for the Juran Institute's IMPROV93, 94, and 95.

David Yoest
Sverdrup Technology, Inc.
MS 4500
AEDC, TN 37389
Telephone: 615-454-4769
Facsimile: 615-454-3751
E-mail: yoest@hap.arnold.af.mil

CHAPTER 21

Benchmarking for a First-class Supply Chain: The Post Office

Sylvie Jackson, Director, Sylvie Jackson Associates

Background

The Post Office is made up of three major businesses: Royal Mail, Post Office Counters Ltd., and Parcelforce. Within The Post Office corporate group, there are several smaller group service units that provide support services for all three businesses: for example, Welfare, Occupational Health; Training and Development; Information Technology; and Purchasing+Logistics Services (P+LS).

The Post Office introduced benchmarking in 1990 as part of total quality management (TQM). Other significant dates are as follows:

1988	TQM introduced.
1990	Benchmarking process developed.
1990	U.S. benchmarking study tour conducted.
1991	Two strategic tours conducted.
1992	Low-level (process) benchmarking continued.
1993–1994	Benchmarking process reviewed.
1994	Use of competitive benchmarking initiated.

In late 1987–1988 The Post Office recognized the need for change. Royal Mail, the largest business in the group, was continuing to grow, but its market share was declining. There was also significant, explicit customer dissatisfaction, often shown through direct complaint and bad press coverage. Employee dissatisfaction was clearly demonstrated through high turnover, industrial disputes, and a national strike in August 1988.

The combination of customer dissatisfaction and poor performance caused the government to threaten basic changes or reserved services, which would have been disastrous to the business.

Benchmarking Introduced and Developed

During 1988, a number of elements were established for the development of a total quality direction. These included clear definitions of the current state of the business and the future desired state; the creation of a mission and values; an agreed definition of total quality; and establishing the interdependence between achieving and maintaining long-term customer satisfaction and employee satisfaction.

By 1990 it was felt that benchmarking activities were needed to confirm the validity of Royal Mail's approach and to provide a major learning opportunity for key managers. A benchmarking process was developed (Figure 21.1), which was tested by a party of directors and senior managers. This study group visited four companies in the United States, all of whom had won the prestigious Baldrige Award and had been involved in TQM for approximately 10 years. Interestingly, The Post Office benchmarking process was developed by the contributor of this chapter as a research thesis for her MBA.

Once the process was developed, the author benchmarked the process with Xerox Corporation to test whether or not it would work. One of the people the author consulted was Robert C. Camp, who gave the okay for use.

The following year, there were two more study tours and implementation work began on analyzing and using the information gained. Significant outputs from these tours included the following:

- Development of a leadership charter

- Restructuring the business

- Development of a self-assessment model

- Development of a business planning process

Benchmarking, as a useful tool/technique for all employees, was not communicated as well as it might have been, and there was only low-level activity for a while. In late 1993, a group of quality managers started an initiative to relaunch benchmarking in the businesses by reviewing the original benchmarking process and by developing training materials and workbooks. In 1994 The Post Office began to use competitive benchmarking as a way to set new challenging targets and to aid change.

The Post Office defines benchmarking as, "A structured process of learning from the practices of others, internally or externally, who are leaders in a field or with whom legitimate comparisons can be made."

The International Benchmarking Clearinghouse has a far better definition: "The practice of being humble enough to admit that someone is better at something and being wise enough to try to learn to match and even surpass them at it."

How Benchmarking Is Used at The Post Office

As an organization, The Post Office believes that benchmarking

- Allows organizations to learn from the best, who are not necessarily competitors.

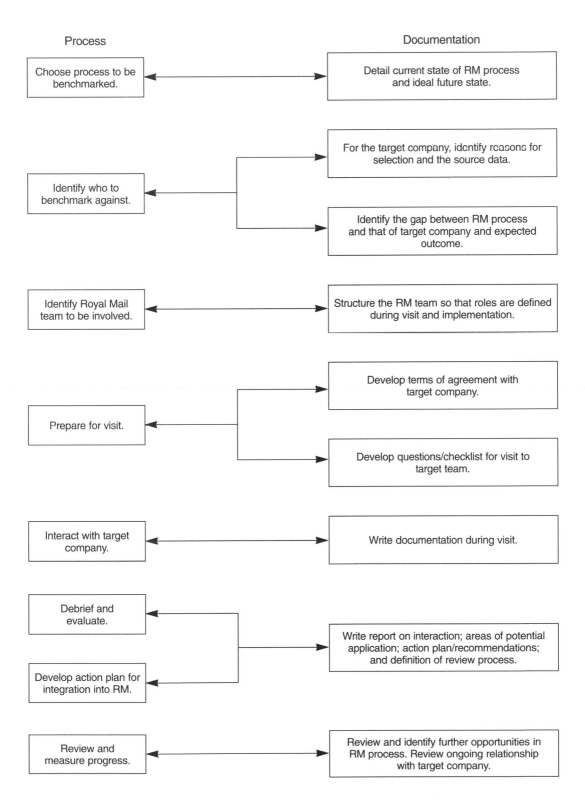

Process

Documentation

| Choose process to be benchmarked. | Detail current state of RM process and ideal future state. |

| Identify who to benchmark against. | For the target company, identify reasons for selection and the source data. |
| | Identify the gap between RM process and that of target company and expected outcome. |

| Identify Royal Mail team to be involved. | Structure the RM team so that roles are defined during visit and implementation. |

| Prepare for visit. | Develop terms of agreement with target company. |
| | Develop questions/checklist for visit to target team. |

| Interact with target company. | Write documentation during visit. |

| Debrief and evaluate. | Write report on interaction; areas of potential application; action plan/recommendations; and definition of review process. |
| Develop action plan for integration into RM. | |

| Review and measure progress. | Review and identify further opportunities in RM process. Review ongoing relationship with target company. |

Figure 21.1. Benchmarking, the strategic approach.

• Improves all areas of the organization, such as process and function.

• Identifies areas for improvement.

• Adopts new and better practices.

• Sets new targets and goals.

• Aids change.

• Challenges the way things are done.

The Post Office has used benchmarking in three different ways.

1. *Strategic.* To provide direction, often long-term direction: Where should the organization be going? What should it be doing?

2. *Competitive.* How well is the organization doing compared to others? The comparison is not necessarily to a similar business, although The Post Office has compared itself with other administrations. It may be comparable in such areas as levels of sick absence, accidents per vehicle, pay scales, and similar measures.

3. *Process.* How do the best or world-class organizations do things? For example, how do they bill customers? How do they deal with customer complaints?

In any of these types of benchmarking there is a simple, basic process.

• What processes are going to be benchmarked?

• Who is the organization going to benchmark against?

• How will information be obtained?

• How will information be analyzed?

• How will information be used?

The initial benchmarking work in 1990 and 1991 was at a strategic level. The Post Office visited four companies in the United States, with the objective of benchmarking its TQM process with their achievements. The four companies, Miliken Industries, IBM, Motorola, and Westinghouse, were all renowned for their achievements in implementing TQM. All four companies had implemented total quality in the early 1980s, and The Post Office directors wanted to identify areas for attention in the future. The key areas brought back were

• To introduce and implement a focus on leadership that included developing a measurement and feedback process for team members to comment on their team leaders. This has now been in operation for more than two years.

• To develop and introduce a self-assessment review of the organization based on the European Foundation for Quality Management (EFQM) model. EFQM shows how strategies are linked together to form a whole change program, rather than a series of unrelated initiatives. This has also been in operation for two years.

• To realize that the basic structure of the business was too complex to manage in a way that was sufficiently customer focused. Therefore, the structure was simplified under the banner of business development—planned in 1991 and implemented in 1992—with the aim of increasing the emphasis on strategic vision and freeing up employees at all levels to implement change consistent with achieving the vision. This was a radical organization change that reduced the number of business units from 70 to only 9; reduced the size of headquarters by 90 percent; and introduced special customer-facing strategic business units whose sole role was to understand the markets in which the business operates and to develop products and services that clearly satisfy customer requirements. Aligned to this change was the introduction of a business planning process and goal deployment.

Competitive benchmarking reveals the performance gaps between the subject organization and the world-class status organization. This presents the management team with a "tangible agenda for change," according to Martin Christopher of Cranfield University.

This is a new area of attention for The Post Office. Recently, the whole organization has been part of an international benchmarking study on financial data. Approximately 65 organizations took part in a survey conducted by a third-party consultancy. This is the third year The Post Office has been involved. The information from the study confirmed that action was required in this area. Although there were already several initiatives planned in this area that would close some of the performance gap, it also highlighted other areas for improvement.

Purchasing+Logistics Services has joined a benchmarking forum that allows for competitive benchmarking with other organizations in the logistics/supply chain process. No direct competitors belong to the forum, so participants are willing to share information.

Apart from some low-level activity, for example, looking at how other organizations deal with activities such as customer complaints, the process benchmarking activities have been confined to sharing best practices within The Post Office. This has led to some improvements in cycle time, cost, and quality of service. The power of looking at the business as a series of linked cross-functional processes has now been recognized, and process benchmarking is likely to be The Post Office's key area of emphasis in the future.

At a major U.S. logistics conference in January 1995, benchmarking was a key topic. A delegate has reported that there was a clear message that process benchmarking is now the most important type of benchmarking that all organizations should be using.

There are pitfalls with benchmarking, and a brief summary of The Post Office's learning points is given in the following:

• Companies should beware of industrial tourism. It is easy for people to say that they have been benchmarking when actually they just had a nice day out visiting another company. The purpose of benchmarking is to learn something, which, hopefully, can be implemented (possibly after adaptation) into the subject organization.

• Large organizations should consider gate keeping because it is easy for several different groups from the organization to end up visiting the same company for benchmarking initiatives. Gate keeping allows information learned to be shared with others and avoids duplication.

• Benchmarking partners must be honest and upfront as to why they want to benchmark and what they hope to gain. There are very useful codes of practice available from places like The Benchmarking Centre.

• Partners must remember to consider what they are willing to share and what they consider to be commercial in confidence. It is less embarrassing to have decided this in advance than to be put on the spot during the visit. Similarly, partners should not expect to share things unless they can offer reciprocal data in that area.

Purchasing+Logistics Benchmarking Study Purpose

The Post Office initiated a review of the supply chain process in June 1993 as a result of the appointment of a new director of purchasing and supply, Jeff Prince. He thought that there were significant improvements to be made in terms of quality of service, customer satisfaction, and value for money. Early diagnostic information showed bought-in costs of $2.6 billion (£1.5 billion), with operating costs of $74.8 million (£43.6 million). It was believed that there were in excess of 30,000 suppliers, of which only 6000–7000 were active. Purchasing and supply activity had been established throughout the various businesses with different degrees of professionalism and status. Inventory was held at 1144 locations, with a total of 1089 full-time staff involved in supply chain activity (0.57 percent of total staff). Additional staff requisitioned supplies from internal suppliers and stores as part of their duties.

The diagnostic work revealed the following supply chain characteristics.

• Internally focused

• Duplication of activity

• Local suboptimization of cost

• Poor communication

• Poor transaction control

• Islands of excellence

Early attention was given to developing a supply chain operational vision as follows:

> *The management of the supply chain will proactively support the group operations through constant monitoring, review and continuous improvement of processes, systems and organization focused on customer requirements. We will adopt industry best practices in supply chain management, which will contribute to improved support of business performance.*

The key features of the operational vision are as follows:

• Identify specific supply chains to meet different product characteristics.

• Optimize costs and service across the supply chain(s).

• Identify and satisfy appropriate customer end-to-end service needs.

- Provide an effective information and communication network.
- Establish a customer-focused organization supporting supply chain best practices for purchasing supply.

Stretch goals were introduced to deliver the supply chain vision. These included the following:

- Reduce supplier base by 90 percent.
- Reduce inventory by 25 percent.
- Reduce excess/obsolete inventory by 50 percent.
- Reduce lead times by 10 percent.
- Increase productivity by 10 percent.
- Reduce overall supply chain costs by 25 percent.
- Improve customer service by 10 percent.

It has often been suggested that the logistics activity accounts for a considerable proportion of total costs, but also locks up assets such as working capital, and can have a considerable impact on customer service. Benchmarking provides the opportunity to identify the areas where real improvement opportunities exist and to leverage those improvements into competitive advantage and thus profit.

Cranfield University, in conjunction with Logistics Consulting Partners who run the Logistics Benchmarking Network, suggests the following reasons for benchmarking logistics.

Objectives

- Time out of the supply chain and thus working capital
- Cost out of the chain from simplification and productivity
- Improving/maintaining/achieving customer satisfaction

By

- Reengineering processes
- Setting balanced objectives
- Engendering trust across the chain
- Developing logistics as a competitive weapon

Not forgetting

- Properly positioned and endorsed management of change
- Focus on time-based objectives
- Clear objectives—the eventual vision
- Empathetic performance measures
- Change pilots

Professor Martin Christopher and Alan Braithwaite of the Logistics Benchmarking Network state that before starting a benchmarking exercise it is essential to be well organized and to prepare thoroughly. The aims and objectives of the exercise must be understood; the appropriate measures must be selected; and the resources and processes that impact the desired outcome must be identified. This is shown in Figure 21.2.

Christopher and Braithwaite state that the key parameters for logistics performance are

• Customer service

• Cost to serve

• Asset investment utilization

In 1992 Cranfield University organized a short course on benchmarking logistics performance. There was considerable interest generated, and the oversubscription led to a second course. The idea of a benchmarking network was raised at the time and was well received. So Cranfield University decided to set up the Logistics Benchmarking Network. The Cranfield Centre for Logistics and Transportation, under the chairmanship of Professor Martin Christopher, acted as the coordinating body and managed the network through Logistics Consulting Partnership.

Membership of the network is contingent on total confidentiality of all shared information between the participating member organizations. Each member nominates one person within his or her organization as the prime point of contact with Cranfield, although this does not preclude participation in the network activities by others in the organization. The Post Office is one of the dozen or so member companies, and the author is the prime point of contact.

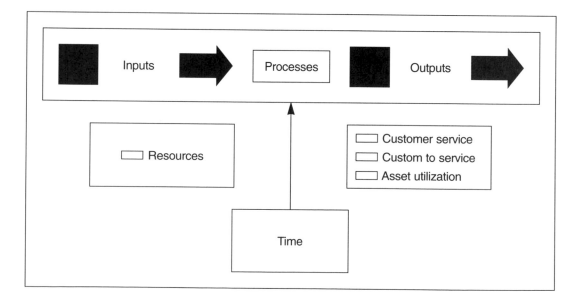

Figure 21.2. What to benchmark.

During the early stages of membership, it was necessary to spend a lot of time data gathering using a common methodology to analyze the organization's logistics processes. This first phase could last between six weeks and six months, depending on available resources.

The data for self-analysis are in six key areas.

1. Material flows and geographic infrastructure

2. Timing and value added

3. Supply performance

4. Business processes and organization control

5. Key business data

6. Self-assessment of capabilities

The output is a benchmarking data set describing the principal supply chain(s) of the member organization. The initial output from one of The Post Office's supply chains is shown in Figure 21.3. This only includes part of the supply chain, as the organization did not have measurable information to cover its internal customers' holding of stock before usage. The Benchmarking Network also ran several special interest groups that were defined as, "A subset of benchmarking network members who have a common interest to understand best practice as it is being achieved, both by members of the network and world leaders in a specific aspect of the supply chain."

The special interest groups met every four months, with the meetings covering the following types of areas.

• Presentations of the concepts and distinctive characteristics of best practice

• Internal discussion groups to determine and share the levels of current achievements by members

• Contact and discussion with outside organizations, arranging for them to share their experience

Each interest group's aim was to answer the question of how to get beneficial change. There were five special interest groups with the following themes.

1. Forecasting

2. Customer service management

3. Supply chain network design

4. Accuracy in the supply chain

5. Managing change in logistics

Regrettably this workload was not sustainable and the network has now been reorganized into a research club, which will continue with benchmarking activity.

The Cranfield Logistics Network is used by The Post Office to benchmark the central warehouse and supply chain processes.

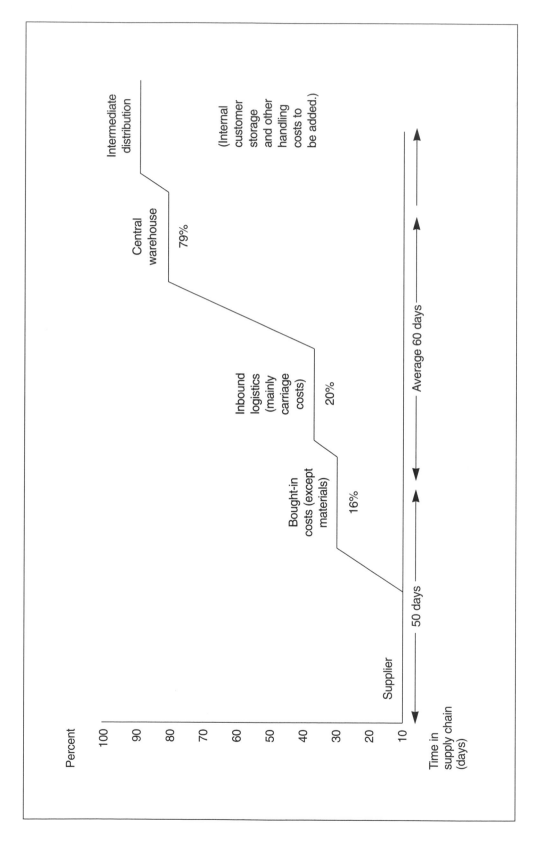

Figure 21.3. Initial output from one of The Post Office's supply chains (for uniforms).

What Has Been Achieved

The completion of the data set identified considerable gaps in The Post Office's knowledge where there were no measurements in place for the supply chain. It has persuaded the study team to identify and prioritize a few key areas for attention and action. In particular, the team was introduced, via the customer service special interest group, to the concept of the perfect order. This idea was developed by Professor Martin Christopher and is used successfully by other organizations.

His views is that "There are only two levels of service as seen from the customer's viewpoint—100 percent or 0 percent." He proposes that organizations choose four to six key measures and aim for 100 percent target on these.

The four measures The Post Office initially chose, which will be linked to service level agreements with customers, are as follows:

1. Internal end-to-end measurement (time to fulfill order)

2. Order fulfillment (availability of stock)

3. Customer satisfaction (response card enclosed with order)

4. Order picking errors

In addition, the customer satisfaction measures currently in place have been reviewed as has the process of how the information is gathered, used, and the results communicated.

The change management special interest group introduced the transition curve, and the study team later went on to run interactive workshops on change management for all the frontline managers in the warehouse. Since P+LS has been undergoing a considerable amount of change, the managers found this an invaluable help because despite all the talk about change management, few people actually understand what it is and their role.

WINWIN

The Logistics Network also helped the teams understand the need for the major transformation change required if The Post Office is to satisfy its customers. In February 1995, the operations warehouse management team initiated a business process reengineering exercise, which became known as project WINWIN. (Warehouse Improvement Now, Which Is Noticeable).

The launch workshop involved the warehousing operations top team, suppliers, customers, and two experts on world-class warehousing from Cranfield University. Figure 21.4 shows the methodology used. The outcome of the workshop was the 26 subprojects listed.

1. Reduce overhead costs; for example, administration support.

2. Move to a can-do culture.

3. Raise productivity.

4. For suppliers, introduce a range of projects, including receipt of goods.

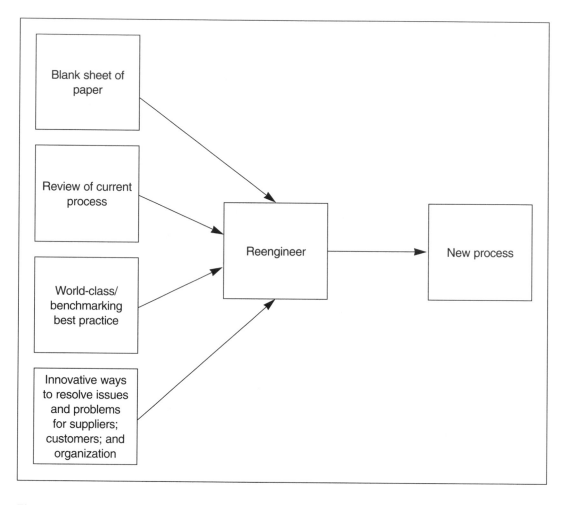

Figure 21.4. Business process reengineering methodology.

5. Strive for perfect fulfillment and 100 percent accuracy.

6. Introduce end-to-end measurement.

7. Reengineer returns procedure.

8. Extend operating hours.

9. Improve client relations and become better, cheaper, and faster.

10. Make client stock level improvements for Post Office Counters.

11. Obsolete stock procedures.

12. Reduce inventory levels to live stock.

13. Improve use of accommodation in the warehouse.

14. Develop an employee skills matrix with training and development.

15. Establish two-way communication.

16. Reengineer the complaints procedure.

17. Introduce service level agreements with customers.

18. Introduce customer satisfaction cards and customer care.

19. Improve telephone responses.

20. Extend pricing menu for different warehouse goods.

21. Reengineer new product launches for early warehouse/purchasing involvement.

22. Review and recommend new management information requirements.

23. Develop an action plan to move to a paperless process warehouse.

24. Establish electronic data interchange (EDI) paperless processing for orders and invoices.

25. Develop invoicing for third-party work

26. Improve information flexibility.

The progress on these projects has exceeded all expectations. Customers have indicated their pleasure at the improvement in performance and service.

The WINWIN project was reviewed and rejuvenated in July 1996 with a second workshop. The Post Office's world-class warehousing experts also joined the project to share their view of the progress made and the new tranche of improvement areas on which to work.

Using Benchmarking for Strategic Purchasing

The other key area of activity at Purchasing+Logistics Services is strategic purchasing. A very different type of benchmarking was chosen for this area.

The Post Office is aiming to be a leader in this field, so it has chosen to join more of a blue-sky type forum. To help to confirm current activity and to determine priorities for future action, The Post Office has joined the Global Procurement and Supply Chain Electronic Benchmarking Network (GEBN) at Michigan State University.

It is a two-pronged research effort in purchasing and supply chain management, focusing on the firms' overall value/supply chain. The research focuses on establishing a worldwide network of over 200 firms, electronically linked, to develop an ongoing global procurement and supply chain benchmarking initiative, which focuses on current and emerging strategies and most advanced practices; and to develop a worldwide field research study to establish best-in-class purchasing, a supply chain, and management strategies and practices throughout the product value/supply chain, from product inception through product discontinuance to improve finished product competitive performance.

Specific objectives of the research are as follows:

- Establish current and future performance data for key purchasing and supply chain management effectiveness performance indicators.

- Establish linkages between purchasing/sourcing and supply chain management strategies, approaches, and measurable performance.

- Develop a longitudinal set of performance and strategy information to identify what really works, what doesn't, and why.

- Identify the leading and/or most advanced strategies and practices throughout the supply chain, from product inception through product discontinuance.

- Establish a best-in-class reference library.

The Post Office has been invited to be one of only 35 contributing organizations to the research, with the extra benefits of

- Being provided with key findings of the comprehensive and ongoing literature review every six months

- Being able to influence the research approaches and key issues and questions to be addressed

- Participating in a series of roundtables every six months to share information about purchasing and supply chain issues and best practices

- Being provided with interim and full reports for all studies, which should provide insightful strategy and best practice and performance benchmarking data

Key Areas of Achievement

Confirmation, focus, and prioritization on two key areas have been achieved.

Supplier Accreditation and Management

A supplier accreditation program, which includes partnerships, was introduced in 1993 (Figure 21.5). This has now been through three annual accreditation and award cycles. The measurement criteria, supplier questionnaire, and marking proformas criteria are the subject of continuous improvement. The supplier management and partnership area is now being developed using best practices identified in the feedback material.

Product Group Teams

As shown in Figures 21.6 and 21.7, these are cross-business, cross-functional teams to manage purchasing, acquisition, and supply strategies as a process. The product group teams are tasked to reduce costs; improve profitability; manage the supplier accreditation

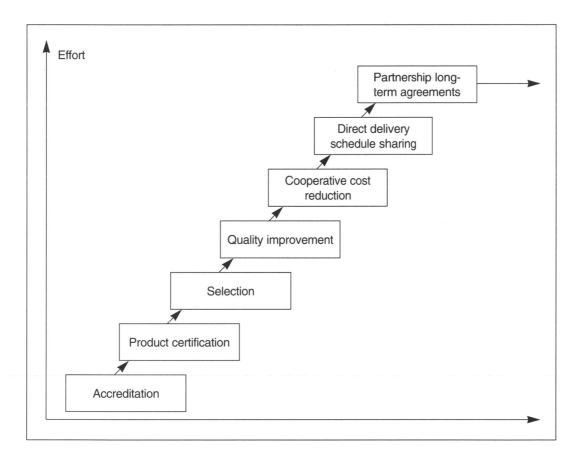

Figure 21.5. A supplier accreditation program.

and management program; map and improve their processes to make them better, cheaper, and faster; consider the environmental impact of their products/services; and help, where appropriate, to improve customer and employee satisfaction. To date, few organizations have introduced this way of working, so there are no real comparisons to make but there is confirmation that this is a best practice.

The detail previously given is an indication of two of the key benchmarking initiatives currently being undertaken by Purchasing+Logistics Services. For instance, the Cranfield Logistics Network

• Is very detailed performance and process related.

• Emphasizes traditional logistics elements (for example, distribution cycle).

• Has useful special interest groups.

• Proves useful to help some product group teams understand and illustrate their processes.

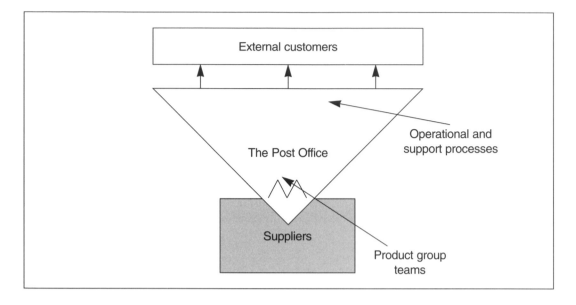

Figure 21.6. Total supply chain process, showing product group team "fit."

Michigan State University's GEBN

• Is primarily at the strategic level.

• Relies totally on participating companies' input.

• Selectively develops company questionnaire responses through case studies.

• Is more purchasing biased.

In addition P+LS is also involved in the following benchmarking forums/clubs/initiatives.

• Centre for Advanced Purchasing Studies (Arizona)—Jeff Prince, director and general manager, attends six monthly roundtables on blue-sky strategic purchasing.

• Profit Impact of Market Strategy/Chartered Institute of Purchasing and Supply (PIMS/CIPS)—Helps companies compare best practice in supply chain management by measuring aspects of business performance.

• Bath University (sponsorship of CIPS chair)—Provides feedback from research; for example in supplier partnerships.

• Purchasing Directors Network Club—Provides informal networking on key issues.

• Best Practice Club—The Post Office recently joined this organization, which runs training days and special topic workshops.

• Ad hoc relationships with organizations—Provide one-on-one benchmarking for specific processes and activities, such as the supplier accreditation program with ICL,

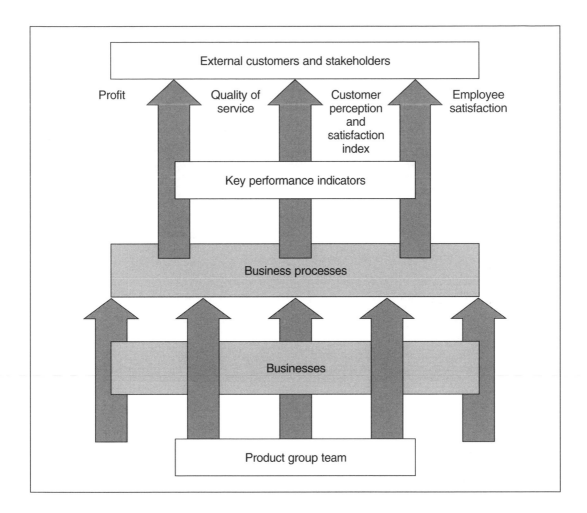

Figure 21.7. Product group teams.

Kodak, and Dowty; operations warehousing and distribution with the Body Shop Lane Group; and the frontline managers/culture change initiative with the Rover Group.

The Post Office views benchmarking as a two-way process and tries to give something back into its community by providing

- Supplier debriefs
- Secondments of staff
  —Partnership sourcing through the Department of Trade and Industry to promote customer supplier partnerships
  —Supply Network Southwest (1 of 20), which was initially funded by the Department of Trade and Industry to promote benchmarking for small and medium-sized enterprises
  —Michigan State University's GEBN research team

• Conference speaking

• Publications about The Post Office's experiences

• National committees such as CIPS

Conclusion

Interestingly, benchmarking can also bring benefits when the organization is the one being benchmarked. Last year, The Post Office was approached for a benchmark visit to its warehouse operation. At the preliminary meeting, the study team was shown a diagram to explain why the other organization was benchmarking. The diagram was a strategic framework for world-class performance, stating the company mission, business objectives, key result areas, measurements, and strategy. At the time, the team recognized a need to be able to simply communicate to The Post Office employees how all its initiatives were moving the organization toward fulfilling its vision. With the benchmarking partner's permission, its framework diagram was adapted to make one suitable for use as The Post Office's supply chain business plan (Figure 21.8).

Benchmarking is one of the most powerful tools around because it not only tells organizations what they should be doing (strategic benchmarking), but it also tells organizations how well they should be doing it (competitive benchmarking), and how to achieve that standard (process benchmarking).

There is no doubt that The Post Office will continue to use benchmarking. After all, The Post Office's vision is "To become a world-class benchmark."

About the Author

Until the end of 1996, Sylvie Jackson was the quality and business process director for Purchasing+Logistics Services at The Post Office in Swindon, England. Her responsibilities included ISO 9002, environment, total quality, benchmarking, and supply chain management. Jackson also led a small team in reengineering the whole Post Office's supply chain. With the team, she developed methodologies and frameworks for managing the supply chain as a process instead of a set of discrete functions.

Jackson joined The Post Office in 1976, where she held a variety of positions including counter clerk, instructor, sales representative, and customer care manager. She was the total quality manager for Royal Mail until her move to the position as quality and business director of Purchasing+Logistics.

Jackson is also a director of the newly formed Institute of Business Process Reengineering. She has written several reengineering and supply chain–related articles and is on the editorial board of the journal *Focus on Change Management* (Armstrong Information Ltd.).

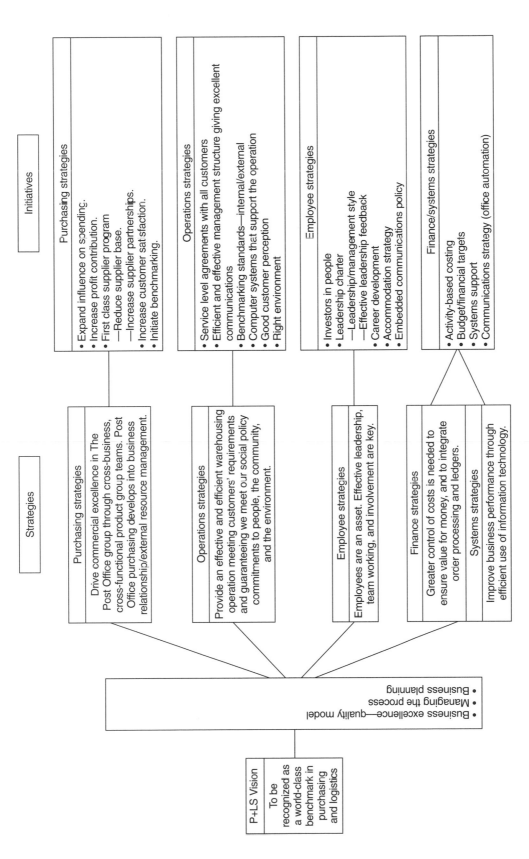

Figure 21.8. The Post Office's supply chain business plan.

Jackson earned a diploma in management studies and another in marketing. She holds an MBA from Staffordshire University. Recently, she received her doctorate at Cranfield University, and is doing research in business process reengineering.

Jackson is now running her own consulting company, Sylvie Jackson Associates, and is a member of the Supply Chain Executive Team. She may be contacted as follows:

Sylvie Jackson

Sylvie Jackson Associates

Westbrook Barn

Lower End

Piddington

Bicester

Oxfordshire

OX6 OQD

England

Telephone and facsimile: 18 44 237248

CHAPTER 22

National Australian Local Government Benchmarking Project

Susan E. Williams, Manager, Benchmarking, City of Monash

Introduction

In an era of rising community expectations and increasing budgetary constraints, one of the most important issues facing local government in Australia is the improvement of performance through the pursuit of best practice standards. An article in the *Australian Financial Review* stated that "Information available to the Federal Government is understood to suggest that $A300 million [about $244 million U.S.] in costs could be removed from the business sector nationally if performance of local councils were lifted to the best practice standards" (Gill 1994, 4).

In 1993, a review of the Commonwealth government's local government financial assistance grants allocation program was undertaken. Specifically, the role of these grants to encourage the primary objective of horizontal fiscal equalization was examined. The pursuit of horizontal equalization attempts to ensure that every local council can function at a standard not lower than the average standard of other councils in the same state. Issues relating to efficiency, cooperation, environmental management, access to services, and increased cost recovery were also addressed. A discussion paper, *Financing Local Government*, was subsequently released by the Commonwealth.

This paper canvassed several approaches toward the incorporation of efficiency goals into the allocation of financial assistance grants. One of these methods is the benchmarking approach, which is defined as setting "targets for performance based on available international, national, and local data and reward councils who meet targets with an allocation of funds in proportion to the council's achievement" (Australian Urban and Regional Development Review 1994, 112).

In March 1994, about $81,300 ($A100,000) in funding was allocated by the Local Government Ministers' Conference (LGMC) to the Victorian State Office of Local Government to undertake an Australia-wide benchmarking study. The LGMC is a group of local government ministers from all states of Australia, the Australian Local Government Association, the Commonwealth, and the respective minister from New Zealand.

The purpose of the study was to encourage benchmarking in local government. This was to be achieved through the demonstration of a practical benchmarking project and the development of a manual and several aids to undertake independent projects without the use of consultants.

A national steering committee was established to fully develop the study. The committee membership was drawn from the Commonwealth government, peak local government organizations, and the Australian Quality Council. The consulting firm, Australian Continuous Improvement Group (ACIG), in association with the firm, Econsult, was engaged by the committee to assist with the project.

The project was divided into two parts. The first involved the development of benchmarking methods and a trial of these methods with a number of councils. This part of the study was designed to address the first requirement to demonstrate the applicability of benchmarking to local government. The second component involved the development of aids to benchmarking.

An Eight-step Model for Benchmarking in Local Government

In *The Benchmarking Book,* Spendolini developed a generic benchmarking model that may be applied to any benchmarking project by any type of organization. He decided on a circular model to represent the process, because most benchmarking models include a directive to recycle or recalibrate. Information needs to be reassessed periodically since products and processes being benchmarked are dynamic and will change with time. Thus, a circular image is the most appropriate means of demonstrating this.

This model was further adapted, developed, and used as a basis for the process of benchmarking by council teams involved in the LGMC benchmarking project. The cycle is described as an eight-step process (Figure 22.1).

LGMC Benchmarking Project Pilot Study

The pilot study comprised three phases: mobilization, subject definition, and data collection. These phases relate to steps one through six in the eight-step model.

Mobilization

In June 1994, at the start of the project, local government officers consulted to decide what to benchmark and how to select councils to be involved in the study. Peak local government bodies in each state canvassed member councils to volunteer to participate in the pilot study. Over 60 written expressions of interest were received.

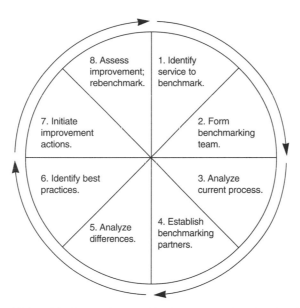

Source: Local Government Ministers' Conference Benchmarking Project. 1995. *Benchmarking for local government: A practical guide.* Canberra: Australian Government Printing Service. Commonwealth of Australia copyright reproduced by permission.

Figure 22.1. The benchmarking cycle.

It was decided to use the Draft Australian Classification of Local Government as a source to group the councils for the study. Urban, urban fringe, urban nonmetropolitan, and rural categories were chosen. Figure 22.2 shows a list of councils in the study.

Defining the Service

Defining the service was the most critical task of the entire process. It is very important for the scope of the service to be well defined and clearly understood.

Subject definitions were developed for seven services. These activities included fleet maintenance, home care services, library services, payroll production, rates notification and collection, residential building approvals, and unsealed roads maintenance. It was decided that six lead councils would be used to develop these service activities. One council undertook to develop two subjects—rates notification and collection and payroll production.

The benchmarking subject definition phase required the development and completion of a service summary, process map (flowchart), key performance indicators (KPIs), and costing worksheets for each service activity. KPIs are best developed through a process that links corporate and program goals to the business plan and key success areas for each service. This approach was used by each of the six lead councils that defined the selected activities.

Council	State	1992 population	Area per Square miles	Area per Square kilometers	Density per Square mile	Density per Square kilometer
Rural						
Carpentaria (S)	Queensland	3399	27,580.4	68,950.9	0.0	0.0
Johnstone (S)	Queensland	18,391	657.6	1644.0	28.0	11.2
Tambo (S)	Victoria	10,770	4091.4	10,228.6	2.6	1.1
Narrabri (S)	New South Wales	14,800	5215.2	13,037.9	2.8	1.1
Young (S)	New South Wales	11,210	1077.6	2694.0	10.4	4.2
Urban developed						
Bankstown (C)	New South Wales	161,900	30.4	75.9	5325.7	2131.9
Manly (M)	New South Wales	36,250	5.7	14.2	6359.7	2558.2
Rockdale (M)	New South Wales	87,900	11.8	27.7	7449.1	3168.7
Enfield (C)	South Australia	63,300	22.7	56.7	2788.5	1115.8
Broadmeadows (C)	Victoria	107,900	26.0	65.1	4150	1115.8
Croydon (C)	Victoria	48,950	13.7	34.2	3573.0	1432.1
Knox (C)	Victoria	129,450	44.8	112.1	2889.5	1154.5
Springvale (C)	Victoria	93,950	39.2	98.1	2396.7	957.9
Urban fringe						
Sutherland (S)	New South Wales	196,300	133.5	333.8	1470.4	588.0
Munno Para (C)	South Australia	34,152	130.1	325.3	262.5	105.0
Noarlunga (C)	South Australia	87,086	67.7	169.3	1286.3	514.5
Werribee (C)	Victoria	78,100	263.2	658.1	296.7	118.7
Swan (S)	West Australia	57,654	416.9	1042.3	138.3	55.3
Urban nonmetropolitan						
Wollongong (C)	New South Wales	181,110	272.9	682.2	663.6	265.5
Rockhampton (C)	Queensland	60,715	74.3	185.8	817.2	326.8
Devonport (C)	Tasmania	24,144	48.1	120.3	502.0	200.7
Launceston (C)	Tasmania	64,029	644.0	1610.1	99.4	39.8
Warrnambool (C)	Victoria	25,040	14.3	35.7	1751.0	702.2
Greater Geelong (C)	Victoria	188,180	509.9	1274.7	369.1	147.6

(C) = City   (S) = Shire   (M) = Municipality

Source: Australian Classification of Local Governments Steering Committee 1994.

Figure 22.2. Council profiles.

For each of the seven services, internally and externally focused indicators were developed and data were collected where possible. The level of customer satisfaction was also determined in each case with the use of a standard questionnaire. Results ranging from 1 to 5 were recorded for the level of satisfaction with a particular service.

Scorecard approach. A number of chief executive officers of the councils involved in the study expressed a desire for the indicators for each subject to be combined to arrive at a benchmark figure. A scorecard approach was proposed. It was at this stage that a group of indicators relating to quality, timeliness, customer satisfaction, and cost was decided upon using the relevant indicators from the internally focused and externally focused indicators chosen in the subject definition phase. This meant that all types of indicators, particularly those for quality and timeliness, were not available for each service in this study.

It was thought that equal weighting between the four types of measurements should be adopted. The combined indicator should be sensitive to movements in all four sets of primary indicators.

Three different approaches were considered for presentation of the benchmark data. These included the following:

Simple tabulation. All performance indicators are presented in tables, which are organized so that councils are shown, in rank order, based on one key indicator. A qualitative judgment is made by each reader of the report based on the combination of indicators.

Value index. Noncost indicators of quality, timeliness, and customer satisfaction are multiplied together when timeliness is expressed as a percentage. This figure is then divided by cost to arrive at an index for ease of comparison.

When timeliness is expressed as the number of days to undertake a task, and the shortest number of eight-hour days is indicative of best practice, then the quality and customer satisfaction indicators are multiplied together. The resulting figure is divided by time, and this result is then divided by cost to deliver a value index. This process was used in this study for the subject of rates notification and collection.

Naturally weighted index. An overall index is computed for the data, combining all four indicator groups based on comparing each council's result against the best result in the pilot group for every indicator. This could be referred to as comparison with the best respondent as a step toward an eventual comparison with best practice.

After consultation, the value index was chosen to express the relative "scores" of the councils involved in the study. The value index could only be applied to two services in the study; namely, payroll production and rates notification and collection.

Data Collection

In the expanded part of the pilot study or data collection phase, 24 councils, including the first six councils, each examined some of the seven service activities. Representatives from all 24 councils were introduced to this phase of the pilot study through a series of workshops.

Over a six-week period, the participating councils collected the relevant data and undertook costing analyses of the activities being benchmarked. Further meetings were held to review the data collection process and discuss outstanding issues. All participating councils indicated a strong desire to remain in the project and to review their information.

The data were then reassessed and analyzed at the council level prior to resubmission in mid-December 1994. A final report on the pilot study was published in January 1995.

The data collection phase is an example of an industry benchmarking study when a group of organizations benchmark against each other in the same industry. After the data are analyzed and collated, best practices among the sample of 24 participating councils are identified for some of the services benchmarked using the value index.

Benchmarking Training Kit

In the final phase of the project, several aids to benchmarking were produced. These included a team workbook and a manual on how to benchmark. Both hard copy (paper) and electronic (computer disk) copy were available. The products were focused toward the workplace team and were published in October 1995.

Benchmarking Methodology

A number of key principles formed part of the benchmarking method for this project. These included the following:

- Customer focus
- Maximum participation to foster ownership and commitment
- Measurable results through tangible outcomes
- Effective communication and consultation
- Shared understanding of expected processes and effects

It is evident that for acceptable benchmarking, customer satisfaction and service quality must be measured. The best way to obtain the basic information to formulate these indicators is by surveying the customers of council services. Traditionally, council information systems in Australia had not previously been focused on delivering these sorts of measures. The study confirmed this, and significant work was undertaken to develop a comprehensive set of guidelines for the pilot councils to use.

Services Benchmarked

Each of the seven services examined in the pilot study is discussed in detail in the following sections. The services are

1. Payroll production
2. Rates notification and collection
3. Fleet maintenance

4. Residential building approvals

5. Library lending services

6. Unsealed roads maintenance

7. Home care services

Payroll Production

Subject definition. The activities associated with payroll production for this study included: production and control of employee payments including input for job costing; time sheets; processing of payroll data; maintenance of leave and associated registers; payments to staff; payments of associated deductions; and the generation of related management reports. The process map is shown in Figure 22.3.

Key performance indicators. The customer satisfaction survey was conducted on a regular basis using a scale of 1 to 5 to indicate the overall satisfaction rating. Response times were measured for the number of pay advice slips that were delivered within the standard response time. The quality indicator was expressed as the number of complaints as a percentage of the total number of pay advices issued. The total cost of the payroll process divided by the number of pay advices issued related to the cost of the service. It was decided to use the cost per employee per annum for the cost indicator for payroll production, since the previous indicator was dependent on pay frequency and not a universal indicator.

(Note: Pay advice slips are not payroll checks. Advice slips are documents that provide details of payment made to employees for work performed in each pay period. Pay checks are rarely issued in Australia, as most pays are electronically placed in each employee's bank account. The pay advices notify employees that this has occurred.)

As expected, the timeliness indicator was 100 percent for most councils. One council reported a lower rate for this indicator due to difficulties with its computer system.

It seems that most councils estimated their data for the quality indicator. Most councils do not keep records of the number and type of complaints with the payroll service.

Results. Figure 22.4 shows the scorecard analysis for payroll production. The analysis for the three better-performing councils in this study shows that the City of Enfield achieved the highest score, indicating a best practice in this specific sample. Despite this, it is worth noting that Enfield did not demonstrate best practice in all four indicators. It did not achieve 100 percent for the quality indicator nor did it achieve the lowest cost. The components of the value index have provided the City of Enfield with goals to achieve a better practice. The City of Enfield learned that it needs to improve on the quality indicator and reduce its cost for payroll production.

Economies of scale were evident for four rural councils in the study. There seems to be some correlation between the size of the council and the costs for payroll. The largest cost

Mapped by: City of Bankstown

Date: July 1994

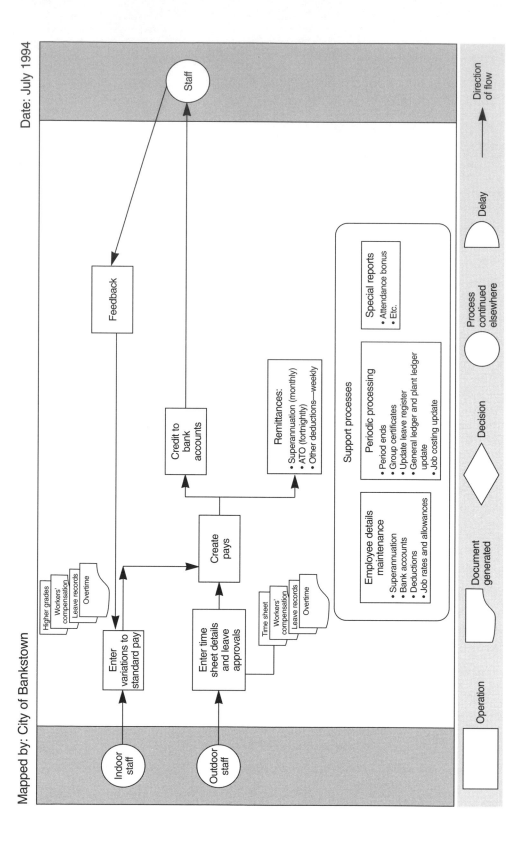

Figure 22.3. Process map for payroll production.

Indicator	Council					
	Enfield		**Broadmeadows**		**Swan**	
Customer satisfaction	5		3.3		4.3	
Quality (%)	99.6		95.3		100	
Response time	100		100		100	
Unit cost	U.S.	Australia	U.S.	Australia	U.S.	Australia
	$190.24	$A234.00	$126.07	$A155.00	$213.82	$A263.00
Value index	212.8		202.9		163.5	

Source: Local Government Ministers' Conference Benchmarking Project. 1995. *Benchmarking for local government: A practical guide.* Canberra: Australian Government Printing Service. Commonwealth of Australia copyright reproduced by permission.

Figure 22.4. Scorecard analysis for payroll production.

in this sample is probably due to this council including the time spent by nonpayroll staff completing their time sheets. During the study no personal contact occurred with this council. It is extremely remote in far north Queensland. Difficulties were experienced in interpreting the requirements for the data collection phase by this council. Figure 22.5 shows the comparison of payroll data for the four rural councils.

Rates Notification And Collection

Subject definition. This subject comprised ordinary rates only. It did not include the fire levy, rural water and sewerage levies, domestic waste management service charges, or the state deficit levy applicable only to the State of Victoria at the time of the study. Valuations were excluded from this study. The process map for rates notification and collection is shown in Figure 22.6.

Council	Cost		Number of staff
	U.S.	**Australia**	
Young	$246.34	$A303.00	103
Johnstone	348.78	A429.00	180
Narrabri	152.84	A188.00	180
Carpentaria	761.79	A937.00	68

Source: Local Government Ministers' Conference Benchmarking Project. 1995. *Benchmarking for local government: A practical guide.* Canberra: Australian Government Printing Service. Commonwealth of Australia copyright reproduced by permission.

Figure 22.5. Comparison of payroll data for the four rural councils.

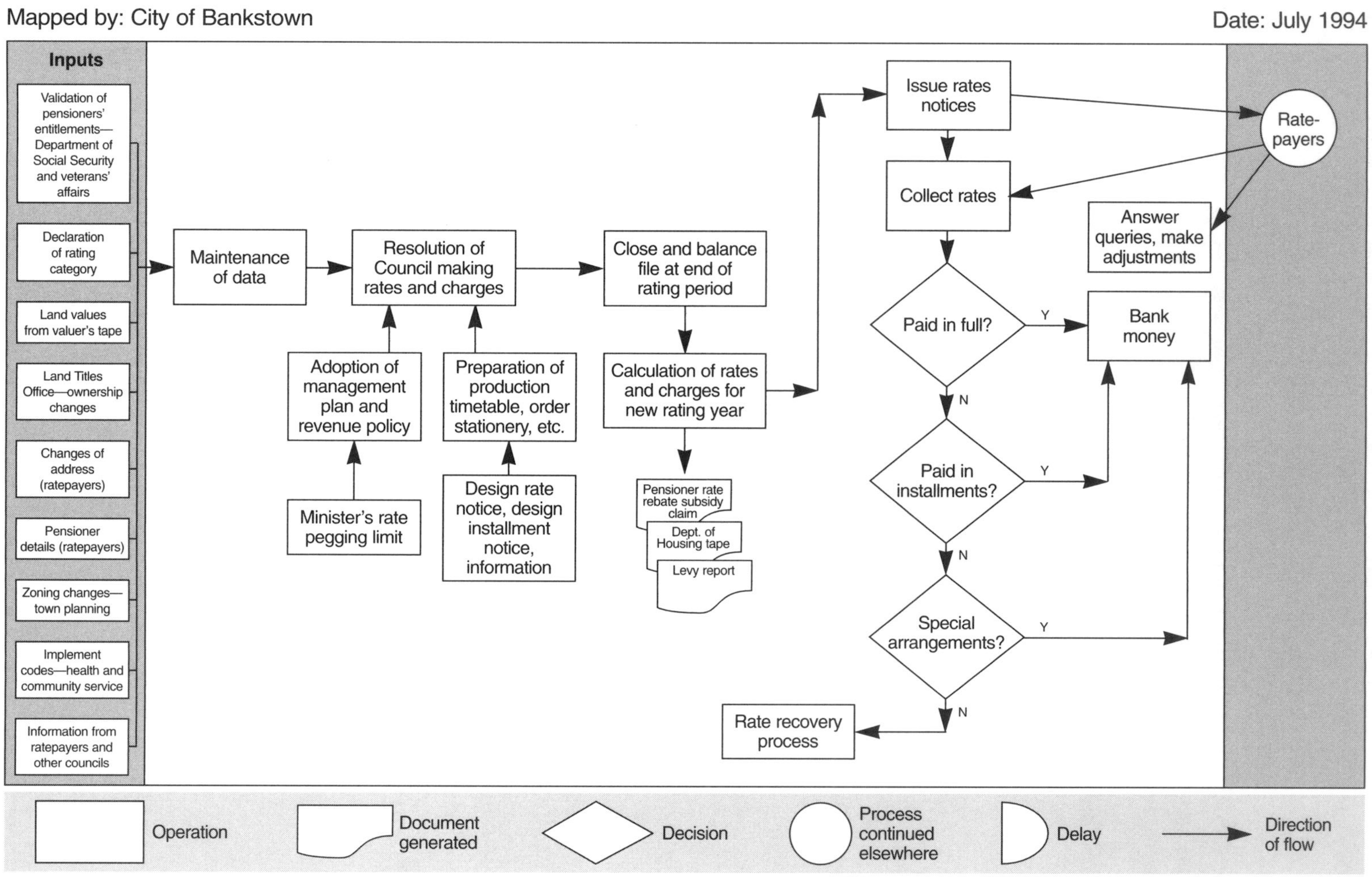

Figure 22.6. Process map for rates notification and collection.

Key performance indicators. The customer satisfaction survey rated aspects of the service relating to the process; for example payment facilities, payment periods, and ease of understanding the rate notice. Response times related to the number of working days between the closing of the rate file and the date of posting the notices. A number of councils did not consider this indicator to be significant; however, some councils recognize that the sooner rate notices are delivered, the sooner payments will be made. Some ratepayers pay their bill when they receive their rate notices, and this assists councils with cash flow.

The accuracy of the rate notices provided an indicator for quality. Data for the number of rate notices returned for correction over the total number of rate notices issued were collected. The total cost for the rates process divided by the total number of rates notices issued, in dollars, was used for the cost indicator.

Results. Figure 22.7 shows the scorecard analysis for rates notification. For this sample, the City of Launceston demonstrated a best practice by achieving the highest score for the value index. The City of Launceston also achieved the best results for each component of the value index.

Response times varied widely from one day to 40 days. Eight councils of the 20 that provided data on rates notification and collection reported the number of days for this indicator to be less than 10. The average cost per rate notice in the sample was $10.50 ($A12.92).

Fleet Maintenance

Subject definition. At first it was decided to benchmark heavy vehicle fleet (HVF) maintenance and light vehicle fleet (LVF) maintenance. HVF included trucks, graders, loaders, backhoes, and rollers; whereas LVF comprised cars, utilities, light vans, and small community buses.

Indicator	Council					
	Launceston		Munno Para		Manly	
Customer satisfaction	4.5		4.3		3.8	
Quality (%)	99.9		99.1		99.5	
Response time	3		14		14	
Unit cost	U.S.	Australia	U.S.	Australia	U.S.	Australia
	$2.27	$A2.79	$2.40	$A2.95	$8.77	$A10.79
Value index	53.7		10.3		2.5	

Source: Local Government Ministers' Conference Benchmarking Project. 1995. *Benchmarking for local government: A practical guide.* Canberra: Australian Government Printing Service. Commonwealth of Australia copyright reproduced by permission.

Figure 22.7. Scorecard analysis for rates notification.

In the data collection phase it became apparent that it would be difficult to benchmark HVF. Despite the small sample size, a number of councils had a variety of equipment in several HVF classes. Data were not gathered for this study.

The activities to be included in fleet maintenance were routine servicing of vehicles and breakdown maintenance. The purchasing of plant and equipment was not to be included. Insurance costs, registration fees, and tire replacements were also excluded. The process map for fleet maintenance is shown in Figure 22.8.

Key performance indicators. The customer satisfaction indicator was obtained by surveying customers when they presented their vehicles for routine maintenance. Quality was represented by 100, less percentage downtime due to unplanned maintenance. Response time was not available for this study. Two measures, however, would have been appropriate: service turnaround time and the percentage of services completed within the manufacturer's standard time. Service turnaround time was considered to be impractical for this study. Whenever a vehicle is serviced it is programmed out-of-action for one day, and the actual service time is not recorded. Data were gathered for the second indicator for response time but were incomplete for this study.

Results. For fleet maintenance, the three best results obtained from a sample of 20 councils are shown in Figure 22.9. No scorecard analysis could be undertaken for fleet maintenance.

Residential Building Approvals

Subject definition. This subject comprised building rules and development plan assessments for new residential dwellings and additions to existing dwellings throughout Australia. The process did not include building inspections. The process map is shown in Figure 22.10.

Key performance indicators. Response times for residential building approvals were recorded as the number of notices issued within the target response time as a percentage of the total number of notices issued.

The customer satisfaction survey assessed the process with a score from 1 to 5. The total cost for the application process per annum was recorded and divided by the number of building approval notices issued for a cost indicator.

No service quality measure was defined since there are a number of potentially different customer groups. These groups would consider the quality process differently. Builders and developers would assess the quality of the process according to the speed with which they obtain an approval; whereas, local residents would make a judgment on whether the building was acceptable. The number of appeals against decisions would not be a valid quality measure since several factors would impact on the process.

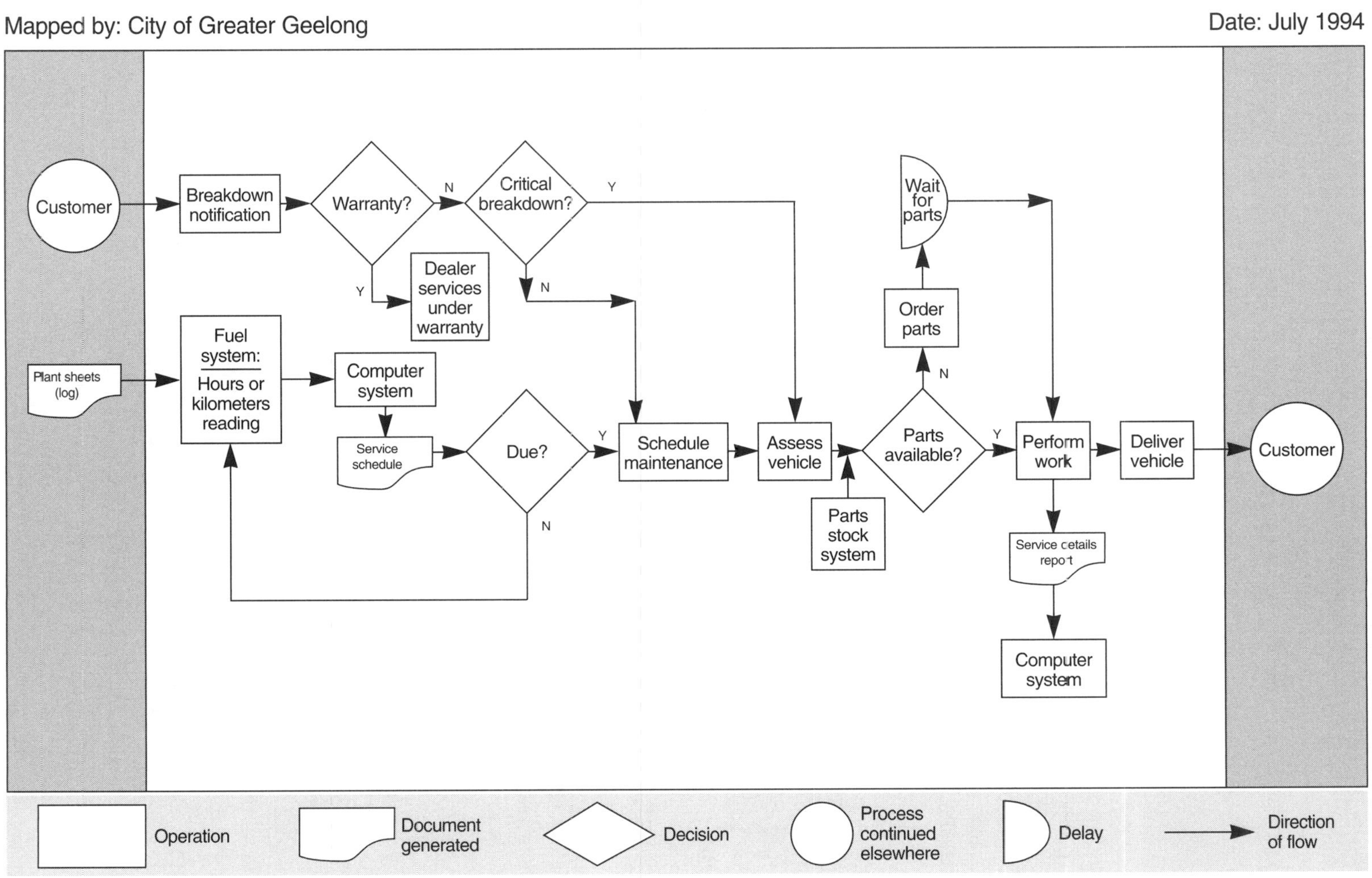

Figure 22.8. Process map for fleet maintenance.

Indicator	Council					
	Knox		Johnstone		Broadmeadows	
Customer satisfaction	4.5		3.4		4.1	
Quality (%)	100		93.4		99.9	
Unit cost	U.S.	Australia	U.S.	Australia	U.S.	Australia
	$238.21	$A293.00	$335.77	$A413.00	$513.82	$A632.00

Source: Local Government Ministers' Conference Benchmarking Project. 1995. *Benchmarking for local government: A practical guide.* Canberra: Australian Government Printing Service. Commonwealth of Australia copyright reproduced by permission.

Figure 22.9. Results for fleet maintenance.

Results. Figure 22.11 shows the results for residential building approvals. No scorecard analysis could be performed for building applications.

It was found during the study that differences in legislation impacted response times. Varying mandatory notification periods had to be subtracted from response times before meaningful comparisons could be made between councils from the different states of Australia in this study.

Library Lending Services

Subject definition. The activities benchmarked included lending an item from the collection to members of the public for a specific period of time, assisting in the location of stock, processing loans, processing returns, shelving stock, and registering new borrowers. Reference materials were not included, nor were purchasing and the addition of items to the collection. The process map is shown in Figure 22.12.

Key performance indicators. No quality or response times indicators could be developed within the time frame of this study. The customer satisfaction survey was used to assess a number of aspects of the service with a score of 1 to 5. The total cost for the lending process divided by the total number of loans issued for the year was used for the cost indicator or cost per issue.

Results. Figure 22.13 shows the results for library lending services. No scorecard analysis could be undertaken for these services in this study. Data provided by the councils involved in the study showed costs ranging from 41 cents (50 Australian cents) per loan to more than $2.44 ($A3). The lower cost councils showed greater rates of lending per borrower.

Mapped by: City of Munno Para

Date: July 1994

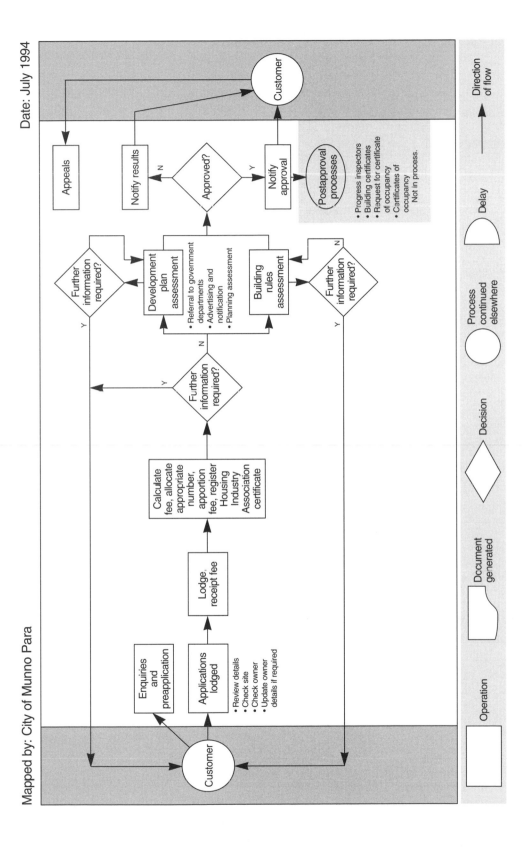

Figure 22.10. Process map for residential building approvals.

487

Indicator	Council					
	Launceston		Knox		Croydon	
Customer satisfaction	4.0		3.5		4.8	
Response time (%)	95		95		55	
Unit cost	U.S.	Australia	U.S.	Australia	U.S.	Australia
	$165.04	$A203.00	$162.60	$A200.00	$207.32	$A255.00

Source: Local Government Ministers' Conference Benchmarking Project. 1995. *Benchmarking for local government: A practical guide.* Canberra: Australian Government Printing Service. Commonwealth of Australia copyright reproduced by permission.

Figure 22.11. Results for residential building approval.

Unsealed Roads Maintenance

Subject definition. Several activities were included in the benchmarking project for unsealed roads maintenance. These included gravel resheeting, drainage, grading, stabilization, pavement modifications, signage maintenance, guideposts, fire hazard reduction, and trimming of overhanging trees. Process maps were developed for reactive and programmed maintenance (Figures 22.14 and 22.15).

Key performance indicators. One quality indicator was the ratio of the number of accidents recorded per annum on the total length of unsealed roads within the municipality, versus the total length of unsealed roads, in kilometers. Other quality indicators registered the number of customer complaints received per year concerning the condition of the unsealed roads within the municipality, and the conformance to service or intervention standard, expressed as a percentage.

The response time for customer complaints was expressed as a percentage of the number of customers' concerns that were responded to within seven calendar days over the total number of customer concerns. The number of kilometers of unsealed roads maintained during the year was expressed as a percentage of the total number of kilometers of unsealed roads within that municipality. The total expenditure on unsealed roads maintenance was recorded and expressed as a ratio of the total number of kilometers of unsealed roads within the municipality.

During the pilot study, the Shire of Swan mailed a customer satisfaction survey (Figure 22.16) to 41 residents who lived near or used unsealed roads within the Shire. The questionnaire sought residents' views on the condition of the unsealed roads and the users' level of satisfaction with maintenance practices and procedures. Seventeen (41.5 percent) responses to the survey were received.

Overall satisfaction with the service provided by the Shire in maintaining unsealed roads received a score of 2.6 out of a possible 5. In the opinion of the respondents, the condition of the unsealed roads was ranked as poor with the average score of approximately 2.

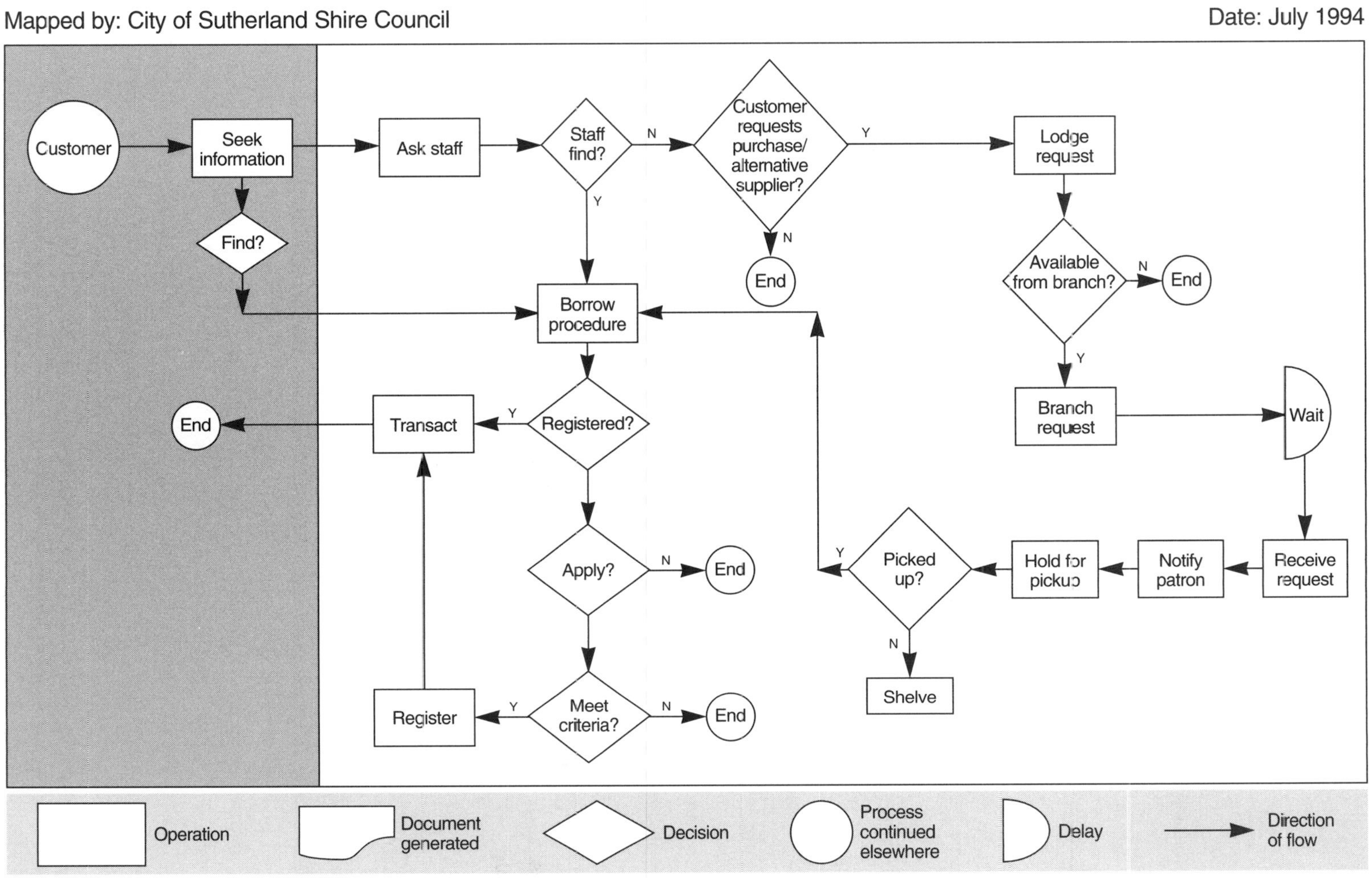

Figure 22.12. Process map for library lending services.

Indicator	Council					
	Enfield		Manly		Sutherland	
Customer satisfaction	4.6		4.2		4.6	
Unit cost	U.S.	Australia	U.S.	Australia	U.S.	Australia
	$0.41	$A0.50	$0.59	$A0.73	$1.09	$A1.34

Source: Local Government Ministers' Conference Benchmarking Project. 1995. *Benchmarking for local government: A practical guide.* Canberra: Australian Government Printing Service. Commonwealth of Australia copyright reproduced by permission.

Figure 22.13. Results for library lending services.

On the other hand, the respondents considered information in letters from the Shire easy to understand, giving that question an average score of 3.6.

Results. No scorecard analysis could be performed. Nine councils gathered data for this subject. The City of Devonport co-opted the Shire of Midlands, a rural council in the State of Tasmania, to join this part of the study,

After analyzing the data collected, it became apparent that there are many local weather conditions that significantly impact on the quality indicators described. The nine councils collecting data for this subject are quite disparate, coming from very diverse geographical regions of Australia; that is, from a tropical climate at the northernmost tip to a temperate climate in southern Tasmania. In the future, it would be preferable to undertake this study with a number of municipalities in a similar geographical area and climate.

It was discovered during the study that customer complaints were mainly prompted when a particular section of road was being maintained. Additional requests for service and customer complaints rose for that area due to the high visibility of maintenance equipment.

Home Care Services

Subject definition. Home care services are only provided by councils in the State of Victoria. For the purposes of this study, home care included general home help, specific home help, and respite care. Home care was deemed to include the assessment of referrals; the handover process from assessment to home care supervisor; allocation of caregivers; service provision; monitoring and reviewing the budget process; payments to suppliers and caregivers; billing for services; and collection of payments. The process map for home care services is shown in Figure 22.17.

Mapped by: Shire of Tambo

Date: August 1994

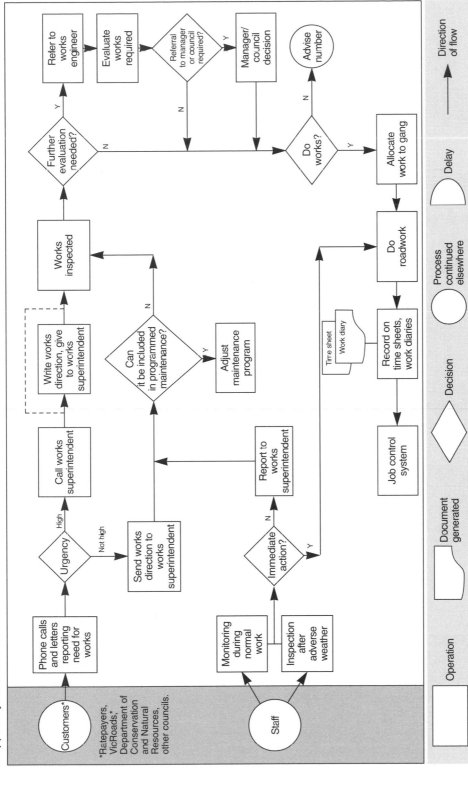

*VicRoads = The State of Victoria's road and traffic agency responsible for managing the State's declared roads. The Roads Corporation is a Victorian Statutory authority operating under the registered business name *VicRoads*.

Figure 22.14. Process map for unsealed roads maintenance—reactive.

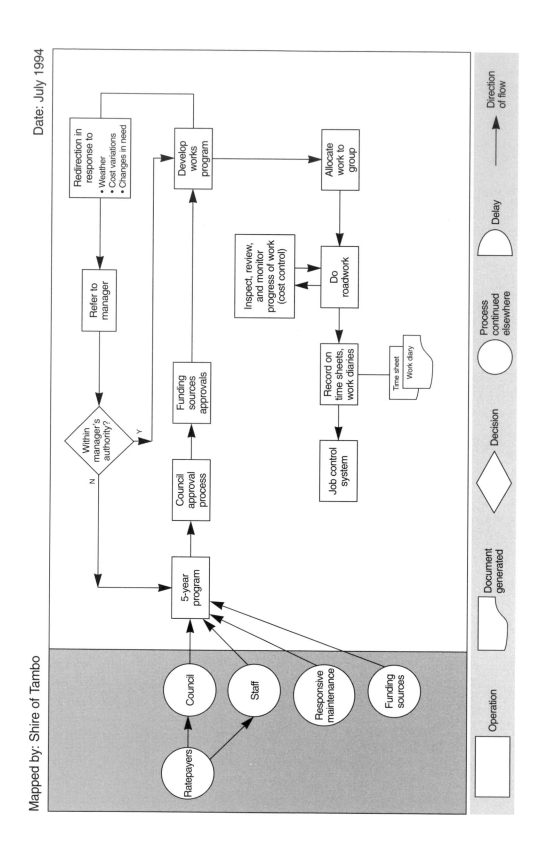

Figure 22.15. Process map for unsealed roads maintenance—programmed.

	Strongly disagree	Disagree	Neither agree nor disagree	Agree	Strongly agree
Staff are available when needed to answer queries concerning maintenance of unsealed roads	1	2	3	4	5
Staff are quick to respond when I ask for assistance concerning unsealed road maintenance	1	2	3	4	5
Staff are courteous	1	2	3	4	5
Staff are helpful	1	2	3	4	5
Telephone queries I have made were dealt with promptly	1	2	3	4	5
The Council responded promptly in dealing with any matters I raised concerning unsealed road maintenance	1	2	3	4	5
Information in letters from the Council was easy to understand	1	2	3	4	5
Unsealed roads within the Shire are graded often enough	1	2	3	4	5
	Very poor	Poor	Neither good nor poor	Good	Very good
Please rate the condition of unsealed roads within the Shire	1	2	3	4	5
	Very dissatisfied	Dissatisfied	Neither satisfied nor dissatisfied	Satisfied	Very satisfied
When unsealed roads are maintained, how satisfied are you with the standard of work carried out?	1	2	3	4	5
Overall, how satisfied are you with the service provided by the Council in maintaining unsealed roads in the Shire?	1	2	3	4	5

Comments:_____

_____

_____

_____

Source: Shire of Swan.

Figure 22.16. Unsealed road maintenance survey.

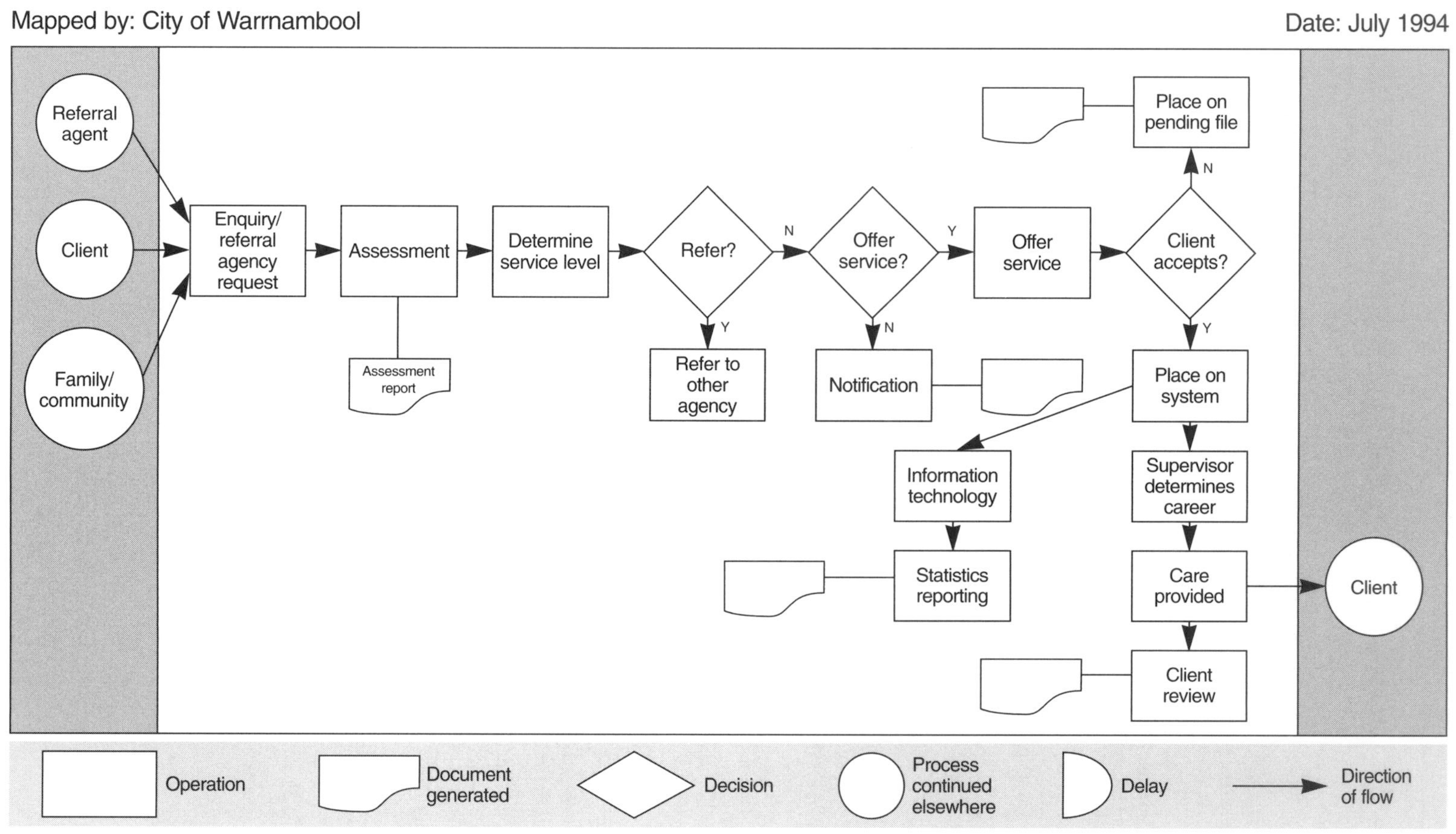

494

Figure 22.17. Process map for home care services.

Key performance indicators. Response times were assessed for the time elapsed from the initial inquiry to the time of the first service call. Similar response times were also assessed for the time between the registration of an emergency request to the time of service delivery. Results were then obtained for the average response time for regular requests for service, in hours.

Two indicators were developed for an assessment of the quality of service delivery. These included the number of requests for a change in caregiver as a percentage of the total clients and the number of verified complaints as a percentage of the total number of clients.

Information on the number of hours of delivered care per annum per total number of clients was collected. Data on the number of delivered hours of care per annum over the number of requested hours of care per annum were also collected.

The total cost of delivering this service per annum divided by the number of hours of delivered care for each of the three types of home care was used for the cost indicator.

A customer satisfaction survey using a random sample of users over the last 12 months was developed. It was used to determine an overall level of satisfaction with the service provided, with a score from 1 to 5.

Results. Figure 22.18 shows the results for home care services. As this subject was restricted to Victoria, there were only six councils involved. The City of Broadmeadows was the only council able to undertake a community survey during the time of the project. Insufficient information was obtained for a quality indicator relating to the percentage of verified complaints. Thus, this was not reported.

For the remaining councils that provided data, a lower response time was noted for the Shire of Tambo at 16 hours. Also, lower unit costs were reported for the City of Knox at approximately $12.03 ($A14.80).

A much larger sample was required and a longer study period is needed to obtain more data and to produce a valid scorecard analysis.

	Broadmeadows (C)					
Indicator	**Specific**		**Respite**		**General**	
Customer satisfaction	4		4		4	
Response time (%)	96		96		48	
Unit cost	U.S.	Australia	U.S.	Australia	U.S.	Australia
	$20.57	$A25.30	$20.57	$A25.30	$15.37	$A18.90

Source: Local Government Ministers' Conference Benchmarking Project. 1995. *Benchmarking for local government: A practical guide.* Canberra: Australian Government Printing Service. Commonwealth of Australia copyright reproduced by permission.

Figure 22.18. Results for home care services.

Lessons Learned

Key Principles for Successful Benchmarking

The work undertaken through the course of the pilot study indicated the need for six key elements for a benchmarking exercise in local government to produce tangible results. These are as follows:

1. Total support, commitment, and leadership from the chief executive

2. Effective training for staff involved in benchmarking

3. Reallocation of resources to allow staff involved to undertake the work required

4. Clear definitions of the services to be benchmarked

5. A balanced set of indicators that cover customer satisfaction, quality, timeliness, and cost

6. Effective communication and networking

Constraining Issues

Significant issues the steering committee confronted during the course of the project included the availability of data, allocation of indirect costs, interpretation of results, and disclosure of information.

The state government of Victoria was implementing a major local government reform program in 1994. Several Victorian councils in the pilot study underwent amalgamation during the course of the benchmarking study. Unfortunately, these councils were unable to provide a full set of results. The City of Knox, however, despite suffering a major fire at its civic center and massive disruptions to service delivery afterward, continued with the study and made a significant contribution.

Positive Outcomes

Many positive outcomes were recognized by the participants in the study. These include the following:

Subject definition.

- Greater understanding of benchmarking by team members, coordinators, and senior management

- Better knowledge of own practices through process mapping and performance indicator analyses

- Identification of areas for improvement in present data gathering and performance reporting

Pilot study.

- Improvements in intra- and interdepartmental team work
- Improvements identified for processes being studied
- Networking with other councils in the pilot study
- Enthusiasm generated by team members working on the study
- Need for better use of data and customer surveys

Conclusion

Any organization, regardless of size or industry, may undertake benchmarking and adapt the technique to its own requirements. The pilot project described here has clearly demonstrated that benchmarking processes can be applied to local government in Australia.

Local government interest in benchmarking has increased since the publication of the *Practical Guide.* A number of benchmarking projects have been conducted, some of these receiving funding from the Local Government Development Program. Benchmarking training programs based on the *Practical Guide* have been conducted for local government practitioners in New South Wales. During 1996, the Commonwealth government sponsored a series of local government benchmarking workshops by Robert C. Camp throughout Australia. A recent survey undertaken by the Victorian Office of Local Government indicated that 47 percent of councils in Victoria were involved in benchmarking projects.

References

Australian Classification of Local Governments Steering Committee. 1994. *Australian classification of local governments.* Canberra: Australian Government Printing Service.

Australian Urban and Regional Development Review (AURDR). 1994. *Financing local government: A review of the Local Government (Financial Assistance) Act 1986, (Discussion Paper #1).* Melbourne: AURDR.

Gill, Peter. 1994. Government wants councils to lift their game, *Australian Financial Review,* 6 January, 4.

Local Government Ministers' Conference Benchmarking Project. 1995. *Benchmarking for local government: A practical guide.* Canberra: Australian Government Printing Service.

Spendolini, Michael J. 1992. *The benchmarking book.* New York: Amacom.

Victorian Office of Local Government. 1996. *Benchmarking by Victorian councils.* Melbourne: Department of Infrastructure.

Williams, Susan E. 1994. *Benchmarking in local government.* Melbourne: Alpha Publications.

About the Author

Susan E. Williams is the manager of benchmarking for the City of Monash in Melbourne, Australia. She is responsible for performance reporting, training teams in benchmarking, undertaking community needs and satisfaction surveys, and updating the city government's corporate plan. She has initiated and implemented the introduction of benchmarking in each division and established a benchmarking and quality group to oversee all benchmarking and quality projects.

Prior to this appointment, Williams worked as the project manager for the Australian national government's benchmarking project. Funding obtained for this project was a direct result of Williams' original research. During her tenure, she oversaw the development of the *Practical Guide* for implementation of benchmarking in local government in Australia and New Zealand, and managed the pilot study with 24 councils throughout Australia.

Williams spent several years working in the Victorian Public Service in the Department of the Premier and Cabinet, the Department of Labour, and Community Services Victoria. Before joining the public service, Williams undertook medical research developing and testing vaccines and was part of a team that analyzed the French nuclear atmospheric tests for the World Court.

Williams earned a bachelor of science degree from Melbourne University and a master of business administration from the Royal Melbourne Institute of Technology. In addition to *Benchmarking for Local Government*, Williams has written numerous articles for local governments and public sector journals, and has presented a number of papers on benchmarking at national conferences.

Susan E. Williams
Manager, Benchmarking
City of Monash
293 Springvale Road (P.O. Box 1)
Glen Waverley, Victoria 3150
Australia
Telephone: 61 3 9518 3526
Facsimile: 61 3 9518 3444
E-mail: suewill@ozemail.com.au

CHAPTER 23

Syndicate Benchmarking: Water Supply and Sewerage

*Roger Patrick, Chief Operating Officer and Director of Specialty Consulting, WRc inc.,
and Peter Mackenzie, Director, Urban Water Division, Department of Land and
Water Conservation*

Executive Summary

Working as a syndicate, seven municipal government organizations used benchmarking to
identify cost and other improvements in sewage collection and transport. The syndicate
approach shared costs, and allowed pooling of talent from small organizations, which
would have been impossible acting individually.

The key results and findings of the project were as follows:

- Cost reductions of an average 18 percent were identified.

- Numerous service and environmental improvements were identified.

- Payback on the total investment (including all time and cash costs) was 100:1.

- Forty percent of the benefits were identified by comparisons between syndicate
  members.

- Many best practices were organization-specific.

- Even for commonly accepted best practices, benefits varied widely among individual
  organizations.

Study Purpose

Water supply, sewerage, and drainage services in nonmetropolitan New South Wales,
Australia (NSW), are provided by 128 municipal councils. Pressure to reduce costs and justify price levels lead the industry bodies to consider benchmarking.

To avoid duplication of effort, the NSW Department of Land and Water Conservation
(DLWC) together with the Local Government and Shires Associations (LGSA) decided to

initiate a pilot project involving a number of councils working together as a syndicate. The goals of this pilot project were to

- Assess the benefits of syndicate benchmarking for local government councils providing water supply, sewerage, and drainage services in NSW.

- Prepare guidelines for these councils on syndicate benchmarking.

- Make recommendations on how councils might undertake benchmarking of these water services.

Because of its high labor content and significant impact on costs, customer levels of service, and environmental performance, a steering committee selected *operation and maintenance of sewage collection and transport* as the pilot process for benchmarking. Sewage collection and transport involve the conveying of domestic and industrial sewage, through pipe work and pumping stations, to waste treatment plants. Sewage treatment processes were not part of the pilot project.

Team Operation

The project syndicate comprised seven councils, which were selected from 24 respondents to an expression of interest sent to all councils in country NSW. The syndicate was assisted by a facilitator and a specialist consultant. The facilitator handled the logistical requirements of the team, and the consultant provided the methodology, training, and analytical tools. Without preempting the project outcomes, the consultant also provided some insights and guidance based on similar benchmarking studies.

The project was conducted over a six-month period from September 1995 to March 1996, and followed the methodology shown in Figure 23.1. It progressed through a series of syndicate workshops and individual efforts by syndicate members. Most analysis was done individually by members. The workshops were held every three weeks or so. They were mainly used for training, to review and analyze work done individually by syndicate members, to reach common decisions, and to prepare for the next phase of the project. The team members held each other mutually accountable for adhering to deadlines.

Approach and Conduct of the Study

Financial and customer analyses were undertaken individually by each syndicate member

- To understand how resources are expended within the key processes for their organizations

- To understand customer needs and expectations and link these to the key processes

- To identify priority areas within the key processes that have the greatest impact on financial performance and customer service

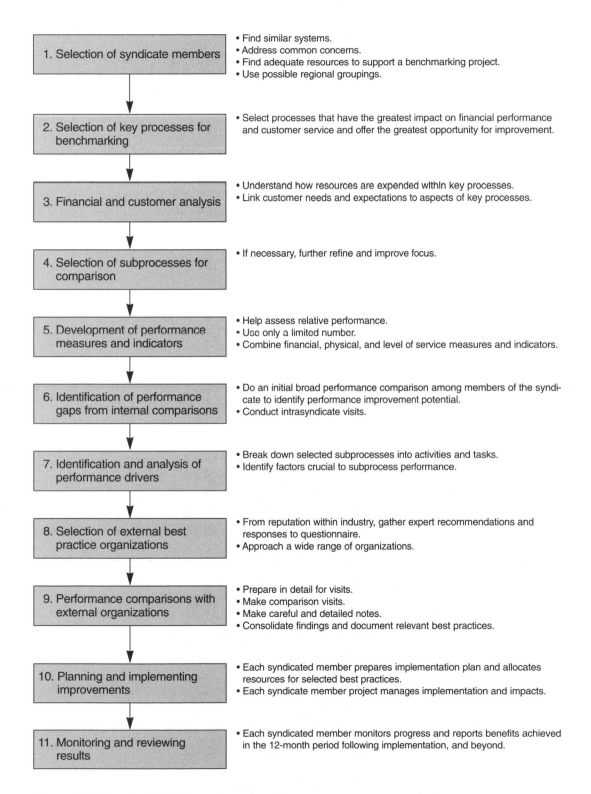

Figure 23.1. Syndicate benchmarking methodology.

Financial Analysis

A common framework for describing the main activities within the sewerage process was agreed, and each syndicate member allocated costs within this framework. It was similar to those used previously by the consultant for other water/wastewater industry clients. This allowed on-paper comparison to similar organizations outside the syndicate, as well as between syndicate members. Due to the absence of commonly accepted activity-based costing systems within the industry, and variations in overhead allocation methods, estimation was needed in many cases to allocate costs.

Customer Analysis

Customer needs were established by devising a questionnaire based on a range of eight probable needs, and each member conducting a telephone survey of several hundred customers. The results were analyzed for three customer types: (1) general community/domestic consumers, (2) commercial customers, and (3) industrial customers.

Once a ranked list of needs was developed, each member team linked delivery of needs against how well each main activity was performed. Strong links were rated 9, moderate links 3, weak links 1. The total scoring and prioritization for the general community/domestic customer group is shown in Figure 23.2.

In this example, the highest customer need was for a safe, healthy system. Therefore, this was rated an 8. The strong links were to the activities "operate SPS" (sewage pumping stations) and "inspect sewers." These links are shown as 9s. Examining Figure 23.2 reveals how the weighting system works to give a total score for each activity. The most important activity turned out to be operate SPS, with a score of 258. The lowest was eliminate WWF (wet weather overflows), with a score of 62.

It was not considered necessary to flowchart the process, since the work carried out was comprised mainly of a set of activities to maintain system operations, rather than a sequentially linked series of steps to produce a product.

On the basis of these analyses, syndicate members divided the sewerage process into two subprocesses for detailed investigation and analysis.

1. Operation and maintenance of sewage pumping stations

2. Operation and maintenance of sewer reticulation mains

Key Performance Measures

Performance measures were developed for the key processes and the selected subprocesses. These were used to identify performance gaps within the syndicate via internal performance comparison among the syndicate members, and to compare against existing external benchmarks.

The performance measures and results for each syndicate member, and the best known results, are shown in Figure 23.3. The syndicate members and the consultant used their

Main activities

Customer needs	Rank	Operate SPS		Inspect sewer		Clean sewer		Preventive maintenance		Reactive maintenance		Improve system performance		Eliminate WWF		Customer service	
Safe healthy system	8	9	72	9	72	3	24	9	72	3	24	3	24	1	8	1	8
Environmentally responsible system	7	9	63	1	7	1	7	9	63	1	7	1	7	1	7	1	7
Reliable system	6	9	54	3	18	3	18	9	54	9	54	3	18	3	18	3	18
No odors	5	9	45	3	15	9	45	3	15	3	15	3	15	3	15	1	5
Efficient customer service	2	1	2	3	6	1	2	1	2	3	6	1	2	3	6	9	18
Appropriate pricing	3	3	9	1	3	1	3	3	9	1	3	1	3	1	3	1	3
Timely understandable bill	1	1	1	1	1	1	1	1	1	1	1	1	1	1	1	9	9
Rapid response to problems	4	3	12	1	4	1	4	3	12	3	12	1	4	1	4	3	12
Weighted total			258		126		104		228		122		74		62		80
Weighted rank			1		3		5		2		4		7		8		6

Figure 23.2. Domestic consumer/community segment priority needs ranking against activity performance.

Performance measures	Council 1	Council 2	Council 3	Council 4	Council 5	Council 6	Council 7	Best known practice
Total cost/kilometers pipe/year	U.S. $ 1136 Australia $A1398	$ 2423 $A2980	$ 2272 $A2795	$ 2065 $A2540	$ 1704 $A2096	$ 1214 $A1493	$ 2894 $A3560	$ 967 $A1190
Nontrades hours/SPS/year	90	220	88	233	180	47	142	N/A
Mechanical and electrical maintenance hours/SPS/year	19	52	66	54	34	71	85	30
Dry weather overflows/year	177	Negligible	Very low	Very low	2.00	6	10	Negligible
Pipe blockages/100 kilometers/year	173	380	60	183	37	59	49	13

Figure 23.3. Performance measures: Sewer operations and maintenance.

503

combined experience to identify the major performance drivers; that is, the key factors that influenced performance under the following domains.

- Planning and scheduling
- Technology
- Organization
- People
- Other

For the high-priority activities, a range of performance drivers was identified by the syndicate. Examples of performance drivers for cleaning down walls in pumping stations (a preventative maintenance activity) included the following:

- How often the work was done (planning and scheduling)
- Type of equipment used (technology)
- Whether the work was done in-house or contracted out (organization)
- Experience and skill of work team (people)
- Physical structure and design of pumping station (other)

These performance drivers were then reviewed against the current work practices and experiences of individual syndicate members, and best practices among the syndicate members were identified. A list of practices and issues considered to have the greatest impact on costs and customer needs was prepared. Then the syndicate decided what data would be required to compare performance with other organizations, and how these data would be collected prior to the benchmarking visit. Syndicate members also estimated potential benefits should it be possible to bridge on-paper performance gaps.

On this basis, the syndicate developed guidelines and a questionnaire to aid in the selection of external benchmarking partners. This questionnaire was forwarded to 31 councils along the east coast of Australia and in New Zealand. The councils were chosen on the basis of the following:

- Having a good reputation in the industry
- Serving a similar size population to the syndicate members
- Operating sewage collection and transport systems of a similar type to those operated by the syndicate members
- Demonstrating an interest in the project

The syndicate selected eight councils as external benchmarking partners on the basis of the quality of their responses to the questionnaire and follow-up inquiries, relevance of their activities to the syndicate members, and their high level of performance. Three of the selected councils were from southeast Queensland, one was from NSW, and four were from New Zealand.

Prior to visiting these external benchmarking partners, syndicate members undertook dry run, or practice, site visits to two councils within the syndicate to gain experience and confidence in the process as well as to fine-tune the approach and conduct of external visits. Following these site visits syndicate members

- Reconfirmed performance drivers

- Estimated additional benefits to the operations and maintenance of their sewage collection and transport through implementation of best practices identified during the dry run visits

- Refined the approach for selecting and visiting external benchmarking partners

- Finalized the guidelines for conducting site visits to benchmarking partners and prepared a detailed questionnaire covering specific issues and aspects to be discussed during these visits

After each trip, the visit team held debriefing meetings to discuss and select those best practices that offered the greatest potential for improvements to syndicate members. Each member then estimated the costs and benefits to his or her individual organization from adapting the observed practices considered to offer the best returns and presented the analysis and results at a syndicate workshop.

Best Practices Discovered and Results

The seven councils in the syndicate estimated that they could collectively achieve net annual savings of about $1.1 million ($A1.4 million) through the introduction of identified best practices requiring either no or minimal initial outlays. This represents about 18 percent of the total annual cost of $6.5 million ($A8 million) for operation and maintenance of the sewage collection and transport systems for the seven councils. The annual savings of $1.1 million ($A1.4 million) have a present worth in excess of $18.7 million ($A23 million) using a 6 percent discount rate. A summary of these savings is shown in Figure 23.4.

The level of estimated cost savings increased as the project progressed. Of the total estimated annual cost saving of $1.1 million ($A1.4 million),

- Initial comparisons between syndicate members yielded estimated annual cost savings of $211,0000 ($A260,000) or 18 percent of $1.1 million ($A1.4 million).

- Dry run visits by the syndicate to two of its members yielded additional potential annual cost savings of $236,000 ($A290,000) or 21 percent of $1.1 million ($A1.4 million).

- Visits by syndicate members to the eight external benchmarking partners yielded further potential annual cost savings of $700,000 ($A860,000) or 61 percent of $1.1 million ($A1.4 million).

Figure 23.4. Estimates of net annual savings during course of project.

		Sewer reticulation mains ($'000)			Sewage pumping stations, nontrades ($'000)			Sewage pumping stations, trades ($'000)			Other ($'000)	Total ($'000)
		Initial comparison	Internal visits	External visits	Initial comparison	Internal visits	External visits	Initial comparison	Internal visits	External visits		
Council 1	U.S.		$57			$8					$57	$122
	Australia		$A70			$A10					$A70	$A150
Council 2	U.S.	$32		$41	$8		$32	$8				$122
	Australia	$A40		$A50	$A10		$A40	$A10				$A150
Council 3	U.S.		$65	$16			$65			$114		$260
	Australia		$A80	$A20			$A80			$A140		$A320
Council 4	U.S.					$41					$16	$57
	Australia					$A50					$A20	$A70
Council 5	U.S.				$81		$163					$244
	Australia				$A100		$A200					$A300
Council 6	U.S.	$81					$57			$8		$146
	Australia	$A100					$A70			$A10		$A180
Council 7	U.S.						$16		$65	$49	$65	$195
	Australia						$A20		$A80	$A60	$A80	$A240
Subtotal	U.S.	$114	$122	$57	$89	$49	$333	$8	$65	$171	$138	$1146
	Australia	$A140	$A150	$A70	$A110	$A60	$A410	$A10	$A80	$A210	$A170	$A1410
Total net annual savings ($'000)	U.S.											$1146
	Australia											$A1410
Annual process costs ($'000)	U.S.											$6504
	Australia											$A8000
% potential savings												17.6%

% identification of savings — Initial comparisons: 18%   Initial comparisons: 18%   Interval visits: 21%   External visits: 61%

The source of savings is interesting, in that approximately 40 percent of the ultimate value was identified *within the syndicate.* This shows that for organizations such as multinational conglomerates, substantial benefits can be expected through internal benchmarking alone. Therefore, if time or budget is short, organizations may consider this route.

Details on best practices are shown in Figure 23.5; however, some of the most significant ones identified as having potential for cost savings and improved customer service include the following:

- Increased use of telemetry not only as a control system for pumping stations but also for monitoring condition and performance

Domain	Area	Best practice
1. Planning and scheduling	• Integrated management systems	Greater use of integrated databases and other computer systems (for example, asset registers, complaints registers, maintenance management, renewals, and capital works program) to identify resource priorities, control work and expenditure, monitor performance, and achieve objectives.
	• Maintenance scheduling	Maintenance programs and activities based on impact of failure (for example, reliability-centered maintenance approach).
2. Technology	• Closed circuit television (CCTV)	Use of CCTV for inspection of new pipe work prior to commissioning, for identification of blockages, and for checking cleared blockages.
	• Root foaming, etc.	Injection of chemicals into sewer mains to reduce blockages from tree roots.
	• Telemetry	Wider use of remote systems such as telemetry for monitoring condition and performance as well as control. Can lead to greater use of reactive servicing/maintenance of sewage pumping stations, reduced operator involvement, and rationalization of available resources. Alarms should alert and identify equipment failures and resulting impact.
	• Raw sewage pumps	Use of grinder pumps and recirculation to reduce buildup of fats, etc. in wet wells. Use of mechanical seals for improved performance.
	• Standardization	Standardization of equipment and procedures (for example, pumps, operating procedures).
	• Pump controls	Use variable range of set points in wet wells to reduce buildup of fats, etc.
	• Wet well linings	Coating of wet wells with, for example, epoxy, pine oil, etc. to reduce adherence of fats and to protect structure.
3. Organization	• Contracting out noncore business activities	Directing internal resources only at core business and contracting out noncore activities such as grounds maintenance, mechanical and electrical repairs, etc. Responsibility for scheduling can also be contracted out.
	• Contract administration	Issuing longer-term maintenance contracts to take advantage of contractor's accrued knowledge of organization's specific systems and equipment.
4. People	• Reduced demarcation	Removal/reduction in work and skills barriers. Identified accountability of work groups for output.
	• Skills	Introduction of higher skill levels and multiskilling.
	• Training	Appropriate and effective programs for training and skill development as identified by business units.
5. Other	• National standardized system	Introduction of uniform performance indicators, training, accreditation, asset management programs and systems, accounting and activity-based costing.
	• Community consultation	Extensive and ongoing consultation with the community to determine needs and willingness to pay.

Figure 23.5. Selection of identified best practices in sewage collection and transport.

- Introduction of energy management practices such as power shedding and time-of-use tariffs
- Use of contractors for noncore business activities
- Greater reliance on reactive maintenance for sewage pumping stations (supported by telemetry)
- Greater reliance on proactive maintenance for the reticulation system
- Use of closed-circuit television (CCTV) inspection for reactive and proactive maintenance of the reticulation system
- Lining of wet wells
- Training and multiskilling for operation and maintenance personnel
- Greater workforce accountability and ownership of assets, systems, and levels of service
- Greater use of computerized management systems

Implementation and Actions Taken

The individual syndicate members are now planning and implementing the best practices that are most cost effective for their organizations. Note that the savings estimate of 18 percent was based on changes that could be implemented within 12–18 months, and that required little if any investment. Further benefits from the adoption of more of the best practices identified during the pilot project would be possible in a longer time frame. Examples of specific implementation projects and their costs and benefits are shown in Figure 23.6.

The councils have agreed to monitor and report on their impact in order to verify the benefits estimated during the pilot project. Feedback from syndicate members is that some have already achieved a substantial portion of the benefits identified.

The Department of Land and Water Conservation is also circulating a report and encouraging all 128 councils in the state of New South Wales to adopt syndicate benchmarking as a practical means of performance improvement.

Conclusions and Lessons Learned

The pilot project has demonstrated the value of syndicate benchmarking. For the total one-off cost of around $162,600 ($A200,000), the pilot project identified net annual cost savings of $1.1 million ($A1.4 million) or about 18 percent of the total annual cost of $6.5 million ($A8 million) for operation and maintenance of the sewage collection and transport across the syndicate. Since the present worth of these savings is in excess of $18.7 million ($A23 million) at a 6 percent discount rate, the readily achievable benefits are about 100 times the project cost.

Council	Examples of best practice initiatives	Potential annual cost saving ($)		Cost of initiative ($)	
		U.S.	Australia	U.S.	Australia
Council 1	• Proactive maintenance of sewers to reduce blockage rate	$65,040	$A80,000	—	—
Council 2	• Reduction in cleaning visits to pump stations through use of mechanical flush valves, reprogramming of pump starts and stops to minimize buildup of scum, and use of automatic well washers	$8130	$A10,000	$97,561	$A120,000 (one off)
	• Reduction in condition visits to pumping stations through use of amp meters on all pump motors and telemetry	$6504	$A8000	$81,301	$A100,000 (one off)
	• Remote switchover of pumps to reduce changeover visits to pumping stations	$6504	$A8000	$40,650	$A50,000 (one off)
	• Use of CCTV for sewer inspections	$48,780	$A60,000	$28,455	$A35,000 annually
	• Requirement for a CCTV report for all new pipes prior to commissioning	$32,520	$A40,000	—	—
	• Scheduled inflow and infiltration program	$20,325	$A25,000	$81,301	$A100,000 (one off)
Council 3	• Use of variable speed pumps in major pumping stations	$16,260	$A20,000	$48,780	$A60,000 (one off)
	• Sewer crew on preventative maintenance	$73,170	$A90,000	—	—
	• Energy management, "power shedding" and "time-of-use" tariffs	$94,309	$A116,000	—	—
	• Epoxy lining/pine oil lining of wet wells	$65,040	$A80,000	$16,260	$A20,000 annually
Council 4	• Refine sewage pumping station operating procedures	$40,650	$A50,000	—	—
	• Review and renegotiate electricity tariffs	$16,260	$A20,000	—	—
Council 5	• Pump choke clearing by nontrades people; review of the amount of grass mowing and landscaping around pumping stations; cleaning of pump wells from surface rather than entry into the confined space	$97,561	$A120,000	—	—
	• Energy audit of pumping station operations	$52,846	$A65,000	$8130	$A10,000 (one off)
Council 6	• Proactive maintenance of sewers to reduce blockage rate	$162,602	$A200,000	$81,301	$A100,000 annually
	• Reducing scheduled cleaning visits to pumping stations	$48,780	$A60,000	—	—
Council 7	• Energy management, "power shedding" and "time-of-use" tariffs	$81,301	$A100,000	—	—

Figure 23.6. Potential savings estimated by individual syndicate member.

Syndicate members felt that additional savings and benefits were possible with further experience in the benchmarking process and if

• The search for best practice partners extended into a wider geographical area and a wider range of industries, including the private sector.

• The pilot project was not limited to maintaining or improving the current levels of service but also considered reductions in the levels of service where overservicing had been identified.

Although the likely savings will be smaller for smaller councils, these results indicate that it would still be highly cost effective for all NSW councils to carry out syndicate benchmarking of their water supply and sewerage services. Also, smaller councils may choose not to proceed to searching and visiting external best practice organizations because, as the pilot project demonstrated, significant cost savings can be identified from internal performance comparisons within the syndicate.

It is estimated that the total annual operation and maintenance expenditure by local government councils throughout NSW on water supply and sewerage services is about $130 million ($A160 million). Taking into account fixed costs for items such as materials and chemicals, and the probability that not all councils will have the opportunity to achieve the same level of savings, it is estimated that statewide annual savings in the order of $12.2 million to $16.3 million ($A15 million to $A20 million) can be achieved in operation and maintenance expenditure through the application of syndicate benchmarking techniques. The present worth of these savings would be from $203 million to $ 268 million ($A250 million to $A330 million) using a 6 percent discount rate.

At the conclusion of the pilot project, members considered that the syndicate approach to benchmarking had great potential for local government and offered significant advantages over single council benchmarking. Benefits included the following:

• Costs, such as for a facilitator, specialist, and/or consultant, can be shared and thereby reduced.

• The syndicate benefits from the synergy created by a range of people with different specializations and background.

• The syndicate can be split up to visit a larger number of external best practice organizations in a given period of time than would be possible for a single council.

• The workload can be shared among syndicate members and thereby reduced.

About the Authors

Roger Patrick has a background in chemical engineering, process industry management, and management consulting to a wide range of industrial and government clients. In recent years he has specialized in performance improvement consulting to water and wastewater utilities, including Sydney Water, Melbourne Water, the Water Corporation of

Western Australia, Brisbane City Council, and the NSW Department of Land and Water Conservation.

Patrick's assignments have included best practices and benchmarking; industry and utility restructuring to emulate private sector performance; process reengineering; outsourcing; business planning; and project management of improvements. His work in the area of best practices and benchmarking has been recognized internationally, through publications, speaking engagements, and workshops.

Patrick was the benchmarking specialist consultant for this project. Currently, he is chief operating officer and director of specialty consulting at WRc inc., a leading water and wastewater management consulting, specialist engineering, research, and information company.

Roger Patrick
WRc Inc.
2655 Philmont Ave.
Huntingdon Valley, PA 19006 U.S.A.
Telephone: 215-938-8444
Facsimile: 215-938-1410
E-mail: patrick_r@wrc-info.com

Peter Mackenzie was the sponsor of this project. He is the director of the Urban Water Division of the Department of Land and Water Conservation in Sydney, Australia. He is responsible for the management of a program to assist country water supply and sewage authorities in New South Wales, Australia. Previously, Mackenzie served as the director of technical services for the NSW Public Works Department. There he was responsible for civil and structural engineering services, surveying, and CAD and laboratory services.

Peter Mackenzie
Urban Water Division
Department of Land and Water Conservation
Level 10, McKell Building
2-24 Rawson Place
Sydney, NSW, 2000, Australia
Telephone: 61 2 9372 7512
Facsimile: 61 2 9372 7566

CHAPTER 24

Benchmarking Culture Change
at Australia Post

Penny Darbyshire, Research Assistant, and Johanna Macneil, Senior Lecturer,
Deakin University

Introduction

Australia Post is Australia's national postal service. Since 1989, changes in government policy have increased the degree of competition Australia Post faces for many of its services. In response, the organization has implemented a series of changes designed to lift performance and customer service, increase efficiency and accountability, and change employee attitudes and organizational culture. In August 1995, the human resources (HR) group at Australia Post supervised the administration of an organizationwide employee attitude survey, designed to assess culture change in Australia Post and provide information for the purposes of benchmarking with leading Australian companies. Although senior management were privy to the results of the survey relatively quickly, reporting back to the organization as a whole began in June 1996. At the time this chapter was written, Australia Post was just beginning to assess the outcomes of this exercise. At this stage, the lessons of Australia Post's benchmarking project relate primarily to improving the process of planning and implementing strategic change.

Australia Post and Its Environment

Australia Post is among Australia's top 40 corporations with revenue of approximately $2.2 billion ($A2.9 billion) and assets valued at over $1.7 billion ($A2.2 billion). In 1997, Australia Post was Australia's seventh largest employer, with 32,040 full-time and 5689 part-time employees responsible for delivering about 14 million letters and carrying millions of parcels every working day. It also provides the country's leading overnight delivery service and offers Australia's largest electronic bill-paying and money-transfer service. The five key areas of Australia Post's business are shown in Table 24.1.

In 1975 the federal government split what was then the Post-Master General's Department into two national communications organizations—Australia Post, Australia's

Table 24.1. Australia Post business units.

Mail services	Letter, parcel, and international post services.
Retail services	Post offices providing access to mail and financial services, collectibles, faxpost, postal-related products, and passport services for the federal government.
Financial services	Services include "Pay It at Post" bill payment, "giroPost" banking, "TaxPackExpress" for the Australian Taxation Office, and money orders.
Collectibles	Including stamps, philatelic products, and books.
Fulfillment services	Also called Store, Pick, Pack, and Send and including mail-order and warehousing services.

national mail service; and Telecom (now Telstra), Australia's national telecommunications carrier. In 1989 the status of Australia Post was changed again to a wholly owned government business enterprise, introducing the obligation to operate commercially, pay government taxes and charges, and make appropriate returns on assets.

The organization's charter also requires that it fulfill a community service obligation to provide a world-class, single-priced letter service, and do so without taxpayer subsidy. Australia Post has been assisted in this goal by legislated monopoly protection on basic postal services. In 1994–1995, however, the federal government decreased protection levels again, opening up more than $203 million ($A250 million) worth of business to competitors. The legislation reduced price protection levels from ten to four times the standard letter rate (currently $0.36 [$A0.45]) and reduced weight protection levels on domestic carriage of letters from 17.5 to 8.75 ounces (500 to 250 grams); deregulated outward-bound international mail, mail carriage within organizations, and mail movement within document exchanges; and allowed competitors to carry bulk letters between cities, interconnecting with Post's network for delivery.

With the limits set on Australia Post's monopoly on standard mail, and the removal of protections in other areas of communications service, greater competition now exists in the market. The federal government is currently reviewing the reserved service again.

Years of Change at Australia Post

According to its annual report (1995–1996, p. 2), Australia Post's corporate objectives are to

- Increase profitability while investing for growth.

- Increase customer satisfaction and maintain customer loyalty.

- Provide all Australians with a universal letter service for domestic standard letters at a uniform price (that is, fulfill its community service obligation).

• Increase returns to shareholders (the Australian people, represented by the government).

• Support Australian businesses.

• Build an enthusiastic and skilled workforce through a participative work culture.

In order to achieve these objectives over the past several years, the organization has implemented a series of organizational change projects, focused on reaping the perceived financial and competitive benefits resulting from improved customer satisfaction and a more highly skilled and responsive workforce. The concept that has come to drive these changes is best practice. Indeed, Australia Post has a dedicated best practice group that supports both staff and line management and workers in implementing change.

The model currently communicated within the organization and that which drives the pursuit of best practice identifies three critical drivers or enablers: industrial participation, two interrelated quality service initiatives (QS1 and QS2), and leadership development. These are explained briefly.

Introduced in 1989, the industrial participation program is designed to involve employees in decision making about their workplace by progressively removing the constraints on workplace flexibility and initiative. The program's purpose is to help capture perceived potential that exists for workplace improvements, which benefit customers, staff, and the enterprise.

The two quality service initiatives, QS1 and QS2, are internal quality accreditation programs established to assist in the effective transition to a more flexible workplace through industrial participation. QS1 was introduced in 1992–1993 and QS2 was introduced in 1995 to help support continuous improvement for all internal and external customers. QS2 has seven criteria based on the criteria for the Australian Quality Awards (AQA), Australia's version of the Malcolm Baldrige National Quality Award. This relationship is outlined in Table 24.2. Each QS2 criterion area has 10 performance levels against which workplaces develop measures and assess themselves. The objectives of QS2 are to develop best practice processes within the workplace; facilitate continuous improvement; and recognize and reward employee achievements.

The leadership excellence project, initiated in 1995 by the head office and designed for business units, aims to develop leadership skills crucial in responding to future challenges. The leadership excellence review process is a self-assessment process to gauge and accelerate business units' progress toward total quality and best practice. It includes a revised performance appraisal system, recognizing leadership capabilities and business performance outcomes, and a succession planning process. It should be noted that this project was introduced simultaneously with the culture change assessment. Therefore, the project's benefits were not expected to be measurable until the assessment was repeated at a later date.

The progressive but integrated nature of these projects is shown in Figure 24.1, which is Australia Post's model for the pursuit of best practice. The model clearly demonstrates that benchmarking of employee attitudes was the process devised to assess organizational cultural change expected to result from these related programs.

Table 24.2. Quality service (QS2) criteria and Australian Quality Award categories.

Australian Quality Awards categories	Australia Post's quality service (QS2) criteria	Description of the QS2 criteria
1. Leadership 2. Policy and planning 3. Information and analysis	1. Quality commitment	Planning for improving quality in all aspects of work
4. People	2. Staff involvement	Effectiveness of workplace team operation
	3. Training and development	Commitment of the workplace to providing ongoing training and development for all to work to the best of their ability in their job
	4. Safety improvement	Effectiveness in ensuring safety, health, and well-being of the people in the workplace
5. Customer focus	5. Customer focus	Demonstration of commitment to meeting the changing needs of customers
6. Quality of process product, and service	6. Innovation	Encouragement and implementation of new ideas and improvements in the workplace
7. Organizational performance	7. Quality achievement	Performance in measuring success against quality improvement plan

Twice before this project, Australia Post had made attempts to measure cultural change, and each time was met with limited success. The attitude surveys were not clearly linked to their other best practice initiatives such as QS1, QS2, and industrial participation. The use of 15 percent sample surveys made employees suspicious about the results and the ability to extrapolate them to each individual work center. Further, the statistics reported were difficult to interpret and therefore difficult to act upon.

The idea to benchmark employee attitudes as a process improvement measure was incorporated into the human resources corporate plan in 1994, and seen by HR staff as requiring national coordination. While the desired workforce culture was clearly a critical part of the best practice model as it developed, the decision, however, to use this particular employee attitude survey was quite serendipitous. Senior managers in the head office HR group were approached by a manager at Toyota to consider joining Toyota in conducting a benchmarking study of employee attitudes. The timing and content of the approach were extremely fortunate, for four reasons.

First, managers at Australia Post had no direct objective evidence to indicate what broad impact their change programs were having on organizational culture, although anecdotal evidence suggested that culture was becoming increasingly conducive to the

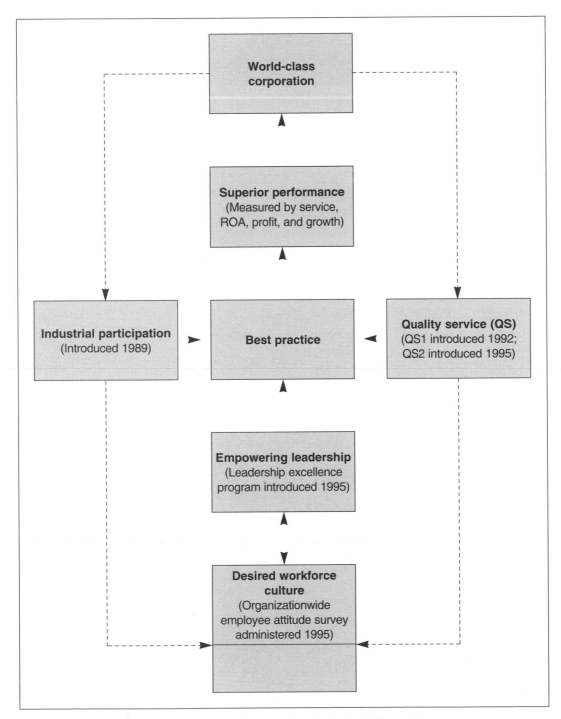

Source: Australia Post Corporation, 1994. *QS2 quality service handbook.* Used with permission.

Figure 24.1. Australia Post's model for the pursuit of best practice.

corporate objectives. Second, Post managers had been considering ways to conduct organizational diagnostics that not only evaluated the effectiveness of current programs but also pointed to emerging challenges. Third, the attitude survey that Toyota was proposing was framed around the criteria for the Australian Quality Awards, which were also the basis for QS1 and QS2. Finally, the instrument was designed to cope with a large sample and, therefore, would give everyone the opportunity to participate.

The potential value of the tool was immediately recognized by various people within the organization, including representatives from the HR group and from the best practice group, who began to lobby for its application. Said a senior HR manager, "We wanted to shift away from tools that measure whether people are 'happy,' to a tool that could actually tell us whether the culture was changing." Further, an organizationwide survey could assess achievement of organizational goals more effectively than initiatives developed at the business unit level.

Planning for the Project

In order to drive the project, the HR group formed a steering committee. The 10 members of this committee were selected by the HR group on the basis of their power, knowledge, and influence. They were

- Two senior state managers from Victoria and New South Wales (the two largest states of operations)

- Two representatives from corporate communications at the state level (Victoria and New South Wales)

- A representative from corporate communications at the head office level

- A member of the best practice group within Australia Post

- Two representatives from the HR group (head office)

- One representative from each of two major unions—the Public Sector Union (PSU) and the Communications, Electrical, Electronic, Energy, Information, Postal, Plumbing, and Allied Services Union (CEPU)

A senior manager in the HR group said that, of the steering committee, the active approval of the state line managers and the union officials was the most critical because of the level of influence they exert over employees. It was a representative from the HR group who acted as the executive arm of the steering committee, and helped the committee to formulate the objectives of the benchmarking study and tailor the existing consultant's version of the survey to better suit Australia Post's needs.

The agreed goals of the steering committee were to

- Measure employee attitudes across a range of key factors.

- Feed back results so that expectations for improvement are broadly agreed.

- Benchmark results against other like work groups so strategies for improvement can be shared.
- Create an environment in which business managers and staff recognize improvements will be measurable and measured over time.

Thus, the survey was expected to provide all business units within the organization with a consistent guide to achieving best practice. Further, the survey was expected to provide general information on the impact of cultural change programs, and allow comparison of performance across organizations so lessons could also be learned outside the organization.

The Benchmarking Instrument

The employee attitude survey used at Australia Post in 1995 was developed by a consulting firm using the criteria for the Australia Quality Awards (AQA). Since the AQA criteria describe aspects of management practice in generic and nonprescriptive terms, the survey questions were conducive to cross-industry benchmarking comparisons. The steering committee and HR staff, however, were also able to work in conjunction with the consultants to tailor the survey to help achieve Post's organizational and human resource goals. The survey's power, in the opinion of the HR group managers, derived from its ability to provide a measure of the company's culture, at individual work center level and overall, at a certain time and (when repeated) over a period.

The survey was simple in design and was divided into four parts. Part 1 asked questions about the respondent, in order to identify like groups of employees for reporting purposes. Parts 2 and 3 listed in alphabetical order 50 factors pertaining to work, conditions, and processes at Australia Post, with a corresponding seven-point scale. As stated, these 50 factors were based on the AQA criteria, and fell into 12 areas.

1. Senior leadership
2. Local leadership
3. Policy and planning
4. Information and analysis
5. Employee development
6. Empowerment
7. Well-being and morale
8. Communication
9. Performance management
10. Customer focus
11. Quality of processes, product, and service
12. Organization performance

The survey was introduced with the following statement: "We would like to know how you feel about a number of factors in the working environment at Australia Post. This will help us identify ways to improve." The first page of the survey also explains that "Part 2 asks you to tell us how IMPORTANT you think various factors are to the success of the company; Part 3 asks you to tell us how you think the company is PERFORMING across these factors; and Part 4 gives you a chance to tell us your views in your own words" (Rodski Behavioural Research Group).

Table 24.3 shows how the three items relating to performance management were presented in Part 2. Part 4 asked for open-ended responses to three questions.

1. What can we do to improve Australia Post?

2. Do you have any other comments regarding Australia Post?

3. What can we do to improve this survey?

These questions were included to gain further information on the perceived effectiveness of the instrument by employees, and any further comments that may not have been drawn out through rating the 50 factors. Employees were assured that responses were confidential, and no data identifying individual respondents would be released by the consultants to Australia Post.

Table 24.3. Examples of factors in part 2 of the Employee Attitude Survey.

Part 2: Importance							
IMPORTANCE: How important do you think each factor is to the success of your work area in Australia Post?							
Rating: 1 = least important and 7 = most important							
STATEMENTS							
How important to the success of your work area in Australia Post over the next twelve months is . . . *Please cross one box (X) for each statement*	**IMPORTANCE** Least — Average — Most						
	1	2	3	4	5	6	7
. . . . . .							
8. Career path							
. . . . . .							
30. Opportunity to make change							
40. Recognition for effort							
. . .							

Survey Administration

Once the final format of the survey was agreed by the steering committee, the administration team was brought together. This team comprised representatives from several levels of authority, within each state division, corresponding with their level of involvement in either administering the survey, or analyzing and communicating the results. Those involved in development and administration were as follows:

- The steering committee, which was previously described, drove the project.
- At the head office level, a project leader/coordinator was appointed.
- At the state division level, liaison officers coordinated the project in each state.
- In the HR group, work group/business unit liaisons coordinated all delivery centers in a delivery area network; all mail centers in a metropolitan area; or all departments at a state head office.
- From within the work center, facility managers coordinated activities for each delivery center, mail center, or head office department.
- Operations managers coordinated the actual completion of the survey by employees on a given shift.

Australia Post head office staff foresaw that it would be difficult to coordinate all employees completing the survey simultaneously. So, the staff allowed a period of two weeks for employees to complete the survey during work time. Survey completion was largely the responsibility of facility managers to coordinate without presenting major disruptions to work and productivity. Employees in each work center were briefed on the purpose of the survey by the facility manager, and provided with instructions on how to complete the survey by the operations manager. Once completed, surveys were collected by the facility manager and posted to a delivery center in New South Wales. Each survey was then scanned and the results collated by the consulting group so that standard reports could be prepared according to the work center reporting specifications developed by the state divisions.

In August 1995, the "Make Your Mark" survey was completed anonymously by 23,000 Australia Post employees, or approximately 61 percent of the workforce.

Survey Results Benchmarked Internally and Externally

In terms of internal benchmarking, reports were generated that enabled comparisons to be made so processes were analyzed at three levels: (1) the work center level; that is, all delivery centers in a delivery area network; (2) all mail centers in a metropolitan area; and (3) all departments at a state head office, as well as the state division level and the national level. Work centers were only identified, and, therefore, compared with other work centers, if 10 or more employees completed the survey. The purpose of this was to preserve the anonymity of respondents.

The external comparisons were with a database holding results from over 200 Australian organizations from various industries and sectors, each of which had completed the same survey within their own organization. In addition, a network under the auspices of the Australian Quality Council was established in 1995. Network One was the "first benchmarking network to measure and compare the best corporate cultures around the country" (Forman 1995). The initial network was with six major Australian organizations including Australia Post. This network expanded later in the same year to 20 companies, all of which regarded the use of the employee attitude survey to gauge cultural change as an ongoing initiative to eventually expand to include international benchmarking partners. The network included the following:

• Several automotive industry organizations, including three of Australia's four motor vehicle manufacturers—Toyota Australia, the Holden Engine Company, and the Ford Motor Company of Australia Ltd.

• Several Australian subsidiaries of multinational corporations including Siemens Ltd. (Germany), ICI Australia (United Kingdom), Shell Australia (The Netherlands), and NEC Australia Pty Ltd. (Japan)

• Several large Australian organizations, both private and government-owned, including Carlton & United Breweries, the Royal Australian Air Force (RAAF), and Qantas Airlines

Many of these organizations were much smaller than Post, in terms of both number of employees and geographical coverage. Very few chose to administer surveys to all employees within the entire organization, as was the case with Australia Post. Instead they opted to survey only a limited number of sites. In addition, the 20 organizations used the employee attitude survey to uncover different things within their organizations. For example, Toyota used the survey as a method for evaluating its corporate strategy from the employees' perspective.

Some suggest that differences in corporate culture make it difficult to learn lessons from other companies. But, considering the underlying consistency embedded in the survey by the AQA criteria, it is possible to effectively benchmark among organizations using this technique.

A number of the reports described later in this case were used to make the external, macro comparisons. Specifically, Australia Post relied on the best practice benchmarking graphs (an example of which is shown in Figure 24.2) for importance, performance, and improvement, with all the results for each work center and state consolidated into a total pool of information describing Australia Post overall.

Survey Analysis and Feedback

Once employees completed the survey and posted it back, the next step was collation of data, analysis, and reporting, which was undertaken by the consulting firm. Reporting back

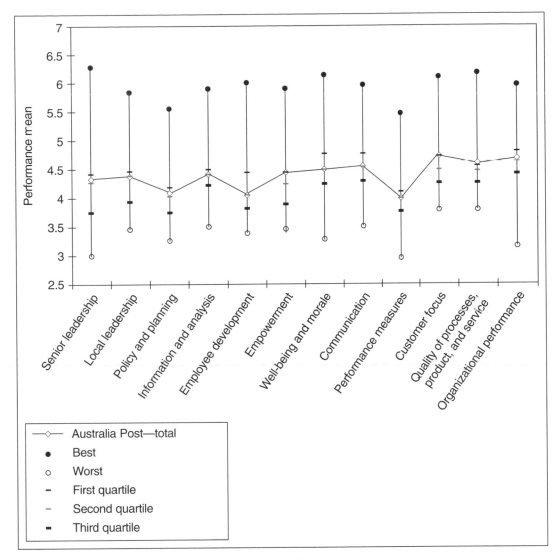

Source: Rodski Behavioural Research Group. Used with permission.

Figure 24.2. Australian Quality Council best practice benchmarks—"How we are performing."

to employees was the responsibility of facility managers, who were seen to play a key role in dealing with survey outcomes. Responsibilities of managers at this level were to

- Distribute reports to staff and initiate the review process by staff.
- Assist staff in understanding the reports; that is, how to read them.
- Obtain additional information that may be required; for example, comparative information.
- Identify major areas for improvement along with facilitators.

- Develop an improvement plan in conjunction with staff and facilitators.
- Be accountable for implementing the improvement plan with facilitators.

Facility managers were supported by facilitators, who were primarily responsible for assisting with the implementation of workplace change, and are viewed as "change agents." Their role was to work with management and union officials to coordinate change at the shop floor using reporting materials and aids. In developing an improvement plan, managers and facilitators were encouraged to use the industrial participation process, and/or QS2 and best practice processes.

Managers of business units, or groups of work centers, particularly within the HR group, had a different role to play. They were required to

- Monitor the progress of subordinate work units and provide any necessary support; for example, provide further information or explain how to understand reports.
- Identify key weaknesses/strengths of work groups.
- Invoke best practice processes to secure improvements.

This level of management focused on the most critical issues instead of trying to address all areas. Important areas requiring attention were identified by examining the reports that summarize the survey results, and are described in the following sections.

Results for Employees

Employees received four of the seven reports of employee attitude survey results. This was so they would understand the key areas but would not be flooded with too much information at once. The remaining three reports were available for employees' perusal upon request. The four reports received by employees included the survey scores report, the gap report, the improvement grid, and the best practice benchmarks chart.

Survey scores report. This report summarizes the scores of all 50 factors, and grouped them according to work center. All those work centers eligible (that is, with 10 or more respondents) received a table that ranked the mean scores of the 50 factors on importance and performance.

Gap report. The gap report summarizes the information of the survey scores report by illustrating the difference between what was seen as important by employees, and how they think Post is performing; that is, **Importance – Performance = Gap.** The larger the gap between importance and performance, the greater the scope for improvement.

Improvement grid. Together with the gap report, the improvement grid focuses on the most important areas to be tackled. This grid graphs the relationship of what employees saw as important, and how Post is performing, based on the rankings of each of the 50 factors. In this way, the report clearly shows those factors that are seen to be important, but on which the relevant area or work center is performing poorly, and alternately where performance is high on important factors.

Best practice benchmarks chart. This chart illustrates how the work center is performing compared with others in the group for each best practice category. As noted, there were 12 categories, with three or more of the 50 factors corresponding to each. (For an example showing the factors relating to performance management, see Table 24.3.) These charts provide the basis for learning across comparable work sites or functions.

Results for Managers

Managers received not only the four reports but also three additional charts that assist in identifying areas for improvement. The three additional reports include the best practice benchmarking importance graph, the best practice benchmarking improvement graph, and charts of Australia Post–specific factors.

Best practice benchmarking importance graphs—"What you said was important." The structure of this report is similar to the performance chart, but uses the importance ratings rather than the performance ratings.

Best practice benchmarking improvement graphs—"Where we can improve." Again, this follows a similar structure to the importance and performance graphs, but in this report, the lower the work center's "line," the smaller the improvement "gap." Additionally, the scale is different on this chart as it represents the difference between importance and performance, not the mean rating of performance or importance.

Charts of Australia Post–specific factors. Australia Post–specific factors are areas that the HR group at the head office felt were important enough to include in the survey, but were not part of the AQA/consultancy methodology. The information contained in this chart is only provided on a state/division basis.

Overall Results

The previous sections outlined how the results generated from the survey were reported, while this section explains the results that were obtained. First, the graph of "what you said is important," illustrated that all of the 50 factors were fairly important to the success of Australia Post. In terms of looking at the 12 best practice categories, those that were considered by employees to be most important were

- Well-being and morale, including specific issues such as job satisfaction and trust in the workplace
- Performance management, including recognition for effort

- Customer focus
- Communication
- Empowerment
- Quality of processes, products, and services

The second report, examining "How you feel Post is performing" based on the 50 factors, demonstrated that employees felt that Post is performing at a level above the average for all the best practice categories. The areas in which employees feel that Post is performing best include the following:

- Organizational performance, which covers aspects such as productivity and knowing how the company is performing
- Customer focus
- Quality of processes, products, and services
- Well-being and morale
- Communication

The third report represents "Where you feel Post can still improve," by graphing the size of the gap between importance and performance. A gap of 2.00 or more shows an issue where there is significant need for improvement, and a gap of 1.50 to 1.99 indicates an issue that is important to improve. For Australia Post nationally, there were no areas with a gap of 2.00 or more. The categories with gaps of 1.50 or more are those that employees felt there is most room for improvement, and included the following:

- Employee development, including training in my area and developing new skills
- Performance management

The results indicate that Post employees feel additional improvement is also required in the areas of empowerment, leadership, and well-being and morale.

The final report looks at how Australia Post measures against other Australian companies. Figure 24.2 compares Australia Post against its external benchmarking partners in the benchmarking network. It shows that Post is above average in all AQA categories, and is doing particularly well with customer focus; quality of processes, products, and services; and empowerment and organizational performance. While the graph does not mention specific organizational participants, Australia Post had access to the information on which were the best performers in each area so that it could pursue the reasons on an organization-to-organization basis. It is also interesting to note that no one organization consistently outperformed the others in all categories; each had individual strengths and weaknesses.

Communication Strategy

At the time when results were released, each work center was provided with a slide presentation, a video presentation, or a computer presentation to accompany the results reports and guides for employees. These audiovisual aids were designed by the HR group in the head office to help explain the results in each of the reports.

As noted, it was the responsibility of the facility managers, with the assistance of facilitators, to communicate the results and embark on improvement processes using QS1, QS2, and industrial participation. Therefore, the results of the survey were used differently in each business unit within each state division. For example, the letters business unit in the Victorian state division chose an approach unlike that of other business units by employing additional measures in the approach to information dissemination. This involved setting up two test sites (mail centers) where focus groups were conducted to reaffirm verbally from employees the key areas that they perceive as being problematic. This was to reinforce the results of the Victorian Health Survey that was conducted in 1994 (by the letters business unit) in addition to the current employee attitude survey. Following this, the letters business unit began developing continuous improvement programs before the results of the employee attitude survey were even released. When the results were released, they supported the action that had been taken by the letters business unit (which will be discussed further in a later section).

Australia Post's Response

Australia Post sees the key performance measures (at the macro level) that link back into best practice as being improved financial performance and improved customer satisfaction.

It is these two goals that Australia Post was striving to achieve through cultural change and the use of best practice initiatives. To realize these objectives, it was important for the HR group to identify the key areas to achieving these two goals. Therefore, despite the vast amount of information produced by the employee attitude survey, the HR group chose to focus on two key issues from the corporate level that are seen as integral to achieving best practice and are consistent with QS2 and industrial participation objectives—including reward and recognition issues and leadership issues.

In terms of reward and recognition issues, postsurvey discussion suggested that employees differentiate between reward and recognition issues. Employees saw base pay as adequate but still desired a variable pay component as a reward; however, the organization's three enterprise bargaining agreements gave across-the-board increases with no variable compensation. Recognition issues were perceived in need of greater improvement than pay. Employee feedback suggested that there was concern about the lack of nonfinancial recognition of good performance. While the survey found that employees see variable pay as important, it is not as important as being told by a superior that they are performing well. Therefore, pay is not seen as a driver for recognition, but verbal encouragement is.

Leadership development, from senior management down to supervisor level, has been an important issue for Post, even prior to the survey being conducted. This is evident with the introduction of the leadership excellence program, and was seen as something that could be reinforced by the survey results.

Implementation Planning

Australia Post has effective systems in place that help facilitate the devolution of information and training for the purpose of implementing proposed changes with relative ease. At the business unit level, however, these channels were not considered comprehensive enough to implement change programs alone. Australia Post's best practice model (Figure 24.1) illustrates that there are three drivers to achieving best practice (that is, QS1/QS2, industrial participation, and leadership excellence reviews). It is these three enablers that assist in the communication of quality initiatives, and, therefore, change. But, as noted, it is the activities of individual business units that are actually responsible for designing the specific implementation approach.

Once again, using the letters business unit of the Victorian state division as an example, it is possible to see how results were maximized by using them to support the initiatives that it was currently conducting. This business unit developed what it called the "Leadership and Change Program." Managers discovered several problem areas within their business unit, first through the Victorian Health Survey, then through the focus groups set up at test sites. These were later confirmed by the results of the employee attitude survey. The areas that needed improvement in this business unit included the following:

- Leadership

- Communication

- More say in decisions

- Safe workplace

- Recognition and reward

- Job security

- Balanced workload

- Noncompetitive practices

Addressing these issues was seen as an important factor in achieving the people-focused goal of ensuring a commercially competitive workforce. It involved three phases shown in Table 24.4.

Before the letters business unit implemented these three phases, it first had to pave the way for change by performing four preliminary tasks. Initially this involved setting up two test sites at mail centers in Victoria and conducting focus groups at the shop floor level to confirm those areas where improvement is most needed. Then, in association with consultants, the business unit performed a job analysis of all positions within the mail centers, ranging from the mail officer (the most junior position in the mail center) to the facility manager (the most senior position). Change programs, however, focused only on the top three levels of authority (that is, facility manager, operations manager, and mail processing controller).

Based on the job analyses, employees at work centers were subsequently surveyed on current performance, in order to create a platform for the conduct of job evaluations and

Table 24.4. Three phases used to achieve best practice in the letters business unit.

Phase 1 **Education and involvement**	1. Get the relationship right (industrial participation and quality life programs). 2. Educate and involve employees about the business and cultural differences.
Phase 2 **Problem solving and gaining commitment**	3. Identify barriers to improved performance. 4. Create teams to eliminate barriers and improve processes.
Phase 3 **Continuous improvement toward best practice**	5. Focus teams on work process improvement. 6. Continue all phase 1 activities. 7. Achieve empowered work teams and trial incentive schemes. 8. Obtain improvement toward best practice.

performance appraisals. The final step is training, and is planned to follow the evaluation of current performance. It will emphasize changing behavior through a combination of classroom teaching and courses/modules. Facilitators will conduct training programs in individual work centers by following the three phases of achieving best practice shown in Table 24.4.

The approach to the project was in keeping with Australia Post's commitment to best practice, which has been built on an extension of the industrial participation and QS1 and QS2 programs. The primary focus of best practice, which emphasizes cross-functional redesign, is directed toward the improvement of the operational, support, and managerial processes.

Industrial Participation

The strength of industrial participation in the context of this project is its ability to underpin QS1, QS2, and leadership development by educating employees and helping to remove the barriers to workplace flexibility, particularly in the first phase of change described in Table 24.4. This is a particularly relevant program at the business unit level, and ties in perfectly with the leadership and change program being implemented in the letters business unit.

Quality Service

QS1 and QS2 are both firmly established process improvement tools that Australia Post uses to drive best practices within the organization. At the business unit level (for example, letters business unit) quality service training can be implemented using the leadership and change program described. The three phases each involve a number of different training initiatives and continuous improvement initiatives, and are outlined in Table 24.4.

Leadership Excellence Reviews

The leadership excellence review process creates numerous opportunities for senior management to actually coach business units and employees to achieve world-class performance. Its development was initially seen as a logical continuation of QS1 and QS2 initiatives developed for Australia Post. QS1 and QS2 featured self-assessment processes for use by managers and staff to advance quality at the local level. Leadership excellence is seen as a tool to guide that quality advancement from the top down. This scheme fits neatly within the leadership training strategy developed by Post, where actual participation in the leadership excellence review process converts leadership training into leadership practice.

Including the AQA criteria in the leadership excellence review process has the advantages of keeping an appropriate internal-external balance in the methodology; assessing Post's quality advance against world best practice; and signaling the organization's readiness to submit an AQA application.

A key feature of Post's self-assessment strategy is flexibility for local managers and their staff. Local process improvement teams can see the leadership excellence review processes to regularly check progress of their facility, section, or unit. Any performance gaps disclosed become the priorities for the local improvement teams. Thus, the leadership excellence review methodology provides another powerful tool for use at the local level in Australia Post's changes.

The national training aim is to secure a gradual, but affordable, buildup of quality, industrial participation, and leadership skills over the three years of this corporate plan. The objectives for state and corporate groups are to achieve the target of 25 percent of staff trained by the end of June 1999.

Lessons Learned

To fully understand what Australia Post was able to achieve from assessing employee attitudes, Post's hopes of what it wanted to achieve must be reviewed, and the problems encountered in this process must be discussed. The first level of goals and objectives were directly linked to the use of the survey and included the following:

- Measuring employee attitudes across a range of key factors

- Feeding back results so that expectations for improvement are broadly agreed

- Benchmarking results against other like work groups so strategies for improvement can be shared

- Creating an environment in which business managers and staff recognize that improvements will be measurable and measured over time

From its inception, the employee attitude survey was seen as a tool to facilitate continuous improvement. Therefore, it was foreseen by Australia Post that another employee attitude survey would be administered in the future. This is planned for the end of the

1997–1998 financial year. With the next stage of the employee attitude survey imminent, Australia Post sees a number of changes it will need to make to improve the initial process and maximize the gains it receives in terms of information and participation. Some of the issues, which arose for the HR group, are discussed shortly.

There are opportunities to improve the organization's feedback mechanisms in relation to the performance of operational processes at the local level. Without adequate feedback, staff have only a limited basis on which to judge the adequacy of their own group's or facility's performance. This inhibits the effective pursuit of productivity improvement and calls for rapid rectification. Australia Post is working to develop these essential performance feedback loops. Development work is proceeding on two levels—isolating the operational processes and developing the appropriate process benchmarks. The introduction of performance feedback loops is expected to stimulate and ensure continued productivity improvement.

Australia Post sees an 85 percent response rate as a realistic and achievable target, although the response rate received for the first survey was about 61 percent. In order to raise the response rates when the survey is replicated, the HR group has discussed the possibility of administering the survey on-line. It is thought that this will overcome the problems of missing responses due to staff being out sick and on annual leave during the two-week survey period. Additionally, an on-line survey will automatically identify all work centers correctly, which was not the case in the first survey. Incorrect identification resulted in many of the surveys not being included in local level benchmarking comparisons.

Conclusion

Although the benchmarking exercise is viewed as very successful, it is still too early to assess the outcomes of the change program at Australia Post. Managers in the HR group were pleasantly surprised at how much Australia Post's culture had changed in a relatively short period of time; from 1989 when the industrial participation program was introduced, to 1995 when the survey was administered. Quality and customer service have improved too, although Australia Post managers believe there is still some way to go. The internal benchmarking data were also very pleasing, as business units and their managers showed an enormous amount of interest in the data and its application to continuous improvement. Benchmarking culture change at Australia Post has provided senior managers with a picture of their organization relative to some of Australia's best-performing organizations, as well as supplying information about the specific best practice initiatives implemented at Australia Post.

Appendix: Methodology of this Case Study

Three research methods were used for this case study. The first was to review published sources on Australia Post, including annual reports, supplementary promotional material, and reports publicly released by Post; and newspaper and journal articles relevant to Post's operations.

The second method was conducting face-to-face interviews. Several members of the staff at Australia Post who played a direct role in conducting the employee attitude survey, generating results, and implementing change were interviewed; as was a member of the best practice group, a former member of the human resources group (who departed in 1995), a consultant who had conducted workplace change training for the organization in recent years, and the consultant responsible for developing the employee attitude survey.

The third research method was the analysis of internal organizational material provided to the researchers by Australia Post. This information included enterprise bargaining agreements, quality service manuals, the employee attitude survey, associated results for managers and employees, details of best practice programs, and so on.

References

Australia Post Corporation. 1996. *Annual Report, 1995–6.* Melbourne: Australia Post.

———. 1994. *QS2 quality service handbook.* Melbourne: Australia Post.

Forman, D. 1995. Toyota's culture quick paves the way to performance reform. *Business Review Weekly,* 3 April, 74–76.

Rodski and Falls Behavioural Research Group. 1995. *Employee attitude survey.* South Yarra, Victoria: Rodski Behavioural Research Group.

About the Authors

Penny Darbyshire is a research assistant with the Centre for Change Management at Deakin University, where she assists with the completion of a variety of research projects. She received a bachelor of administration in tourism from James Cook University of North Queensland.

Johanna Macneil has extensive experience in conducting contract research and training for industry and government clients. These projects have been conducted both at Deakin University, where Macneil is a senior lecturer in management, and at the National Key Centre in Industrial Relations, where she was project director for the Monash University Benchmarking Group and senior research fellow (1992–1995).

Macneil is the co-author of two books including *Benchmarking Australia: Linking Enterprises to World Best Practice* (1994 Longman Professional) and *Reinventing Competitiveness: Achieving Best Practice in Australia* (1996 Pitman). Other relevant publications include *Encouraging Strategic Thinking at Ericsson Australia: Linking Behavioural Styles to Creativity* (in press, Macmillan) and *The Best Practice Experience* (1997 Pitman).

Macneil earned a master's in business administration from the University of Melbourne. Her research interests include best practice management in manufacturing and fostering strategic creativity.

The authors may be contacted as follows:

Ms. Johanna Macneil
Senior Lecturer
Deakin University
221 Burwood Highway
Melbourne, Victoria 3125, Australia
Telephone: 61-3-9244 6270
Facsimile: 61-3-9244 6967
E-mail: macneilj@deakin.edu.au

Analysis

Country:	United States
Organization:	Vice President Al Gore's National Performance Review, Federal Benchmarking Consortium
Industry:	Federal government
Process:	Complaint handling
Case Study Title:	*"Serving the American Public: Best Practices in Resolving Customer Complaints"*

Many of the best practice findings and lessons learned were pervasive of when organizations "put customers first." For example, dissatisfied customers tell twice as many acquaintances about their unhappy experience than those who are satisfied with the service. Thus, organizations should put customers first by making it easy to complain, so the dissatisfied customers talk to the organizations. Companies should respond to complaints quickly, because a speedy response can add 25 percent to customer loyalty. Also, organizations should resolve complaints on the first contact, because it reduces expensive follow-up by at least 50 percent.

The results are being implemented in government organizations with good results. For example, the U.S. Postal Service established a tracking system comparable to best-in-business and a central call management 800 number to resolve problems 24 hours a day. The Veterans Affairs medical centers established a complaint tracking and annual survey to identify problems and trends by service for prompt detection and resolution. The Comptroller of the Currency established an ombudsman for problems with bank regulations.

Why tackle citizen complaints? The government is learning that, much like its business counterparts, effectively handling complaints is critical to its reputation. Not only are complaints costly, but where there is poor handling, trust erodes as citizens become frustrated.

It is probably true that not all the best practices are currently in place in all agencies of the government. But the agencies now know what the best practices are for those operations, and they know what performance levels are the benchmark and achievable. Therefore, this case study is the road map by which each agency can achieve these levels of performance, and, over time, better serve it citizens and create a government that works better and costs less.

Country:	United States
Organization:	U.S. Air Force
Industry:	Department of Defense
Process:	Engine test installation time
Case Study Title:	*"Utilizing Benchmarking to Build Customer-Supplier Relationships: How the U.S. Air Force and Sverdrup Technologies Partnered for Change"*

Very impressive results were obtained from this study. Engine installation time for testing was reduced from 42 to 4 days. The process-to-process comparison was key to how this would be accomplished, thus giving the customer the confidence of being able to realize the new process. This was the basis for the customer committing to a long-term contract for engine testing.

Overall, the program resulted in an estimated $20 million savings. It was instrumental in securing several large multiyear contracts. This case study showed that benchmarking with customers can not only show significant productivity gains but also build an enduring relationship where both parties have an opportunity to win.

Country:	United Kingdom
Organization:	The Post Office
Industry:	Government
Process:	Supply chain, pipeline processing
Case Study Title:	*"Benchmarking for a First-class Supply Chain: The Post Office"*

While most of the benefits from this study are qualitative statements of best practices, it is quite evident that much was achieved with benchmarking. It is insightful on The Post Office's part that this project was titled WINWIN. It was focused on the supply chain process, the fifth most heavily benchmarked process. That, in and of itself, would indicate that there is a rich source for finding best practices, and this was the experience of The Post Office. There was an extensive list of partners that were tapped.

One further important source of best practices was uncovered when The Post Office was itself benchmarked. For it is the insightful organization that sees this as a major benchmarking opportunity for itself.

Country:	Australia
Organization:	City of Monash and various municipal governments
Industry:	City government
Process:	Local council processes
Case Study Title:	*"National Australian Local Government Benchmarking Project"*

Each process benchmarked shows significant differences between selected local councils and the best. This pilot project clearly demonstrated that benchmarking is applicable to local government operations. It even led to the provision of funding at the federal level to see this important improvement tool expanded.

This is an important finding in this era of low- and no-growth government spending, and the need to reverse the tax rate increases that affect all. Eventually, it should serve to have a more productive dialogue about what "processes" and what "best practices" are desired, and, therefore, citizens are willing to pay for.

Country:	Australia
Organization:	Urban Water Division, Department of Land and Water Conservation
Industry:	Land and water conservation industry
Process:	Water supply, sewerage, and drainage services
Case Study Title:	*"Syndicate Benchmarking: Water Supply and Sewerage"*

Somewhat surprising, perhaps to citizens, is that these activities lend themselves to measurement in spite of the lack of consistent activity-based costing and the quantification of major savings. A significant finding was that the bulk of the savings was identified within the syndicate, arguing for the continuing value of internal benchmarking.

In this instance the local councils agreed to some audit requirement for verifying the savings. This level of follow-up is often lacking in benchmarking, and is a commendable undertaking. Ultimately it proved the value of syndicate benchmarking where the costs and activities to conduct the studies are shared, and, therefore, kept within reach of government units' budgets.

Country:	Australia
Organization:	Australia Post
Industry:	Federal government
Process:	Culture change
Case Study Title:	*"Benchmarking Culture Change at Australia Post"*

Overall results were quantitative in that 12 best practice categories were compared to the first, second, and third quartiles of the 20-partner data. In this comparison Australia Post was either in the second or higher quartile. In three categories it was in the first quartile. The data further ranked two attributes—importance and performance. In the first the feedback was how important the category was to the individual. In the second the feedback was how Post was performing. The difference, or the gap, showed the greatest need for improvement. There were five categories that needed attention.

In terms of what Post hoped to achieve, much was accomplished. Measuring attitudes, obtaining agreement on expectations, benchmarking other cultures, and establishing that this organizational area is, in fact, measurable, were confirmed. In addition, improvements for the process were identified and incorporated in the ongoing measurement process.

Summary Cost Savings and Benefits

United States	Europe	Asia/Pacific	Americas/Africa
GOVERNMENT UNITED STATES **Vice President Al Gore's National Performance Review, Federal Benchmarking Consortium** *Complaint handling* • Easy to complain: dissatisfied reduced 2X • Speedy response: 25% increase in customer loyalty • First call resolution: 50% reduced follow-up UNITED STATES **United States Air Force** *Engine test installation time* • Reduced from 42 to 4 days • Program cost reduction, $20 million	UNITED KINGDOM **The Post Office** *Supply chain, pipeline processing* • Not quantified, but easily done from qualitative statements	AUSTRALIA **City of Monash and various municipal governments** *Local council processes* • 50% value index difference • Tax rate reduction AUSTRALIA **Urban Water Division, Department of Land and Water Conservation** *Water supply, sewerage, and drainage services* • Benefit/cost 100:1 • 18% cost reduction AUSTRALIA **Australia Post** *Culture change* • Second or higher quartile of 25 companies • 12 best practice categories	

Key Best Practices Found

United States	Europe	Asia/Pacific	Americas/Africa
GOVERNMENT UNITED STATES **Vice President Al Gore's National Performance Review, Federal Benchmarking Consortium** *Complaint handling* • Learning; 12 attributes × 11 companies UNITED STATES **United States Air Force** *Engine test installation time* • Benchmarking can prevent outsourcing • Benchmarking cements business relationships • Both customers and suppliers gain	UNITED KINGDOM **The Post Office** *Supply chain, pipeline processing* • Supplier accreditation • Product teams	AUSTRALIA **City of Monash and various municipal governments** *Local council processes* • Rates notification • Payroll production • Road and fleet maintenance • Building approvals AUSTRALIA **Urban Water Division, Department of Land and Water Conservation** *Water supply, sewerage, and drainage services* • Service and environment • Telemetry use • Energy management • Subcontract • Reactive maintenance AUSTRALIA **Australia Post** *Culture change* • Attitudes and expectations measured • Reject/confirm change programs	

Lessons Learned

United States	Europe	Asia/Pacific	Americas/Africa

<u>GOVERNMENT</u>
 	
 <u>UNITED STATES</u>
 	
 Vice President Al Gore's National Performance Review, Federal Benchmarking Consortium
 	
 Complaint handling
 	
 • Listening to customers leads to governments that work better and cost less.
 	
 <u>UNITED STATES</u>
 	
 United States Air Force
 	
 Engine test installation time
 	
 • Establish a dedicated team.
 • Stay focused.
	<u>UNITED KINGDOM</u>
	
	 The Post Office
	
	 Supply chain, pipeline processing
	
	 • Being benchmarked has benefits.
	 • Know what process should be.
	 • Know how well organization is doing.
	 • Know what to target.
		<u>AUSTRALIA</u>
		
		 City of Monash and various municipal governments
		
		 Local council processes
		
		 • Use six key elements to success.
		 • Data can be a constraint.
		 • Method is applicable to local governments.
		
		 <u>AUSTRALIA</u>
		
		 Urban Water Division, Department of Land and Water Conservation
		
		 Water supply, sewerage, and drainage services
		
		 • Syndicate benchmarking potential includes the following:
		  —Cost
		  —Synergy
		  —Information gathering
		  —Workload sharing
		
		 <u>AUSTRALIA</u>
		
		 Australia Post
		
		 Culture change
		
		 • Improved feedback systems ensure productivity	

PART 6: EDUCATION SECTOR

Introduction

There has been application of benchmarking to education. There are three examples here, two from the United States and one from Australia. They treat some unique processes such as enrollment, student advising, and law school faculty assignment. It is a tribute to these institutions to want to showcase what they have done.

Because this section is the least represented, perhaps the few cases will pioneer more interest in applying benchmarking to the administrative, academic, and research areas of higher education and other schooling institutions. It obviously can be done!

Country:	United States
Organization:	Babson College
Industry:	Higher education industry
Process:	Enrollment management
Case Study Title:	*"Enrollment Management at Babson College"*

Babson College, in the suburbs of Boston, Massachusetts, is a business specialty school serving the major metropolitan area but also attracting students from a wide geographic area. The college has a history of improvement of its processes through benchmarking. Of course, this may not surprise many if they knew that Bill Glavin, previous vice chairman of Xerox and an advocate of benchmarking, was president of Babson for many years. Obviously the lessons of how best practice benchmarking could change an organization for the better were transferred from industry to education. And that is a major lesson in this case.

Many administrative processes that have parallels in industry have been benchmarked in colleges and universities. This would include billing, information technology, and facilities. But it is the application of best practice to processes unique to an educational institution's operation that is still in its infancy. These would include many academic and research processes.

So the improvement of the enrollment process is important if not critical to such a institution, especially when it considers itself a business specialty school. This means that Babson College must precisely segment its markets and understand the customer's (potential student's) need. This must be done with significant insight in order to diagnose and create action plans for strategic recruiting and to deliver programs and services meeting student expectations.

The attrition from those who inquire about Babson, to those who apply, to those who are admitted, and finally to those who attend is a compelling need for some comprehensive competitive benchmarking. That is what this case describes. It is interesting to see how data and information—which are readily available—are given some careful thought, are assembled and then analyzed to formulate action plans to overcome dissatisfiers, much like many of the customer satisfaction management processes. Often it is assumed by those interested in benchmarking that "there are no data." This, obviously, is far from the truth.

Country:	United States
Organization:	Oregon State University
Industry:	Higher education industry
Process:	Student advising
Case Study Title:	*"Collaborative Benchmarking in Higher Education"*

One of the purposes of this book is to show the applicability of benchmarking to areas of economic endeavor where there has, to date, been little benchmarking, or to areas that are very difficult to benchmark. I would put three areas on the difficult-to-benchmark list: industrial research and development; health care/medical delivery; and academic processes in education. These have proven to be not intractable but difficult from two points of view. One, the processes are diagnostic in nature and often situation-dependent. And two, translation, of the basics of benchmarking, seems to be needed into the language of these arenas.

Some of these challenges have been overcome, and others—like this case study reveals—are still evolving. The industrial R&D arena has had some benchmarking, especially in the management of research centers and in technology transfer. The health care and medical delivery arena, while not subscribing to the term *benchmarking*, has embraced the need to understand best practices. A case study on coronary artery bypass surgery included in this book shows the progress in that field. In this case study from Oregon State University, the approach is applied to an important academic process, namely student advising.

The same issues found in industrial settings were evidenced in this best practice benchmarking project: Defining the "process" and getting agreement on the process measurements were challenges. Adjusting the scope to what was accomplishable in a reasonable time frame was also part of the definition phase. This case study is an example of how these thorny issues were tackled and solved for what could have been a very extended process, as student advising starts before matriculation and ends after successful graduation. This extended time line consideration adds another level of complexity that is not usually experienced in the industrial world, except for large capital projects.

Country:	Australia
Organization:	Queensland University
Industry:	Higher education industry
Process:	Law research supervision
Case Study Title:	*"Law Research Supervision at Queensland University"*

The office of general counsel (law departments) of major corporations, as well as law offices of independent attorneys, have conducted successful benchmarking studies to improve their processes. Would the same improvement approach lend itself to a law school faculty and a higher education process? In this case, the law school, justice studies, legal practices, and research and postgraduate programs of a major university were examined.

Some 14 potential benchmarking projects were identified within the research category alone. Among these, the highest priority was felt to be the enrollment and supervision of postgraduate research students. It is interesting that this process included the upstream activity of enrollment.

On the surface, the connection between enrollment and supervision could be dismissed. This connection, however, was considered essential because the research interests of the student should coincide with those of the faculty supervising the thesis. And some advance notice of the match, or potential mismatch, was crucial to an overall effective learning experience. That match should be revealed before the student matriculated. These are typical findings and decisions that any best practice benchmarking team must tackle; namely where does the process begin and end? What are the boundaries of the process?

The research was conducted with the essential principle for successful benchmarking but applied to the educational setting. The project was conducted by a team of process-knowledgeable individuals, in this case from each of four faculty units. Processes were cataloged, discussed for effect on priorities, and prioritized for selection. Surveys were conducted to determine the customers' requirements. In this case that included views from faculty and students through a survey document and focus groups.

Lastly, the benchmarking partner was selected and given a set of predetermined critical parameters. These included similar size staff and tenure of faculty, research record, publications and grant performance, and research topics undertaken. While the language is that of education and of a particular course of study and instruction, the basic benchmarking process is still applicable. It proves the process. It only has to be adapted to the circumstances. In this case an overseas partner from the United States was also considered.

While the results were qualitative in nature, best practices were definitely found. One was already mentioned: the need to match student research interests with those of faculty early in the process; in fact, prior to matriculation. This would ensure a mutuality of interests and ensure the proper support, often front-end loaded in a student's career. Collocated facilities and the proper computing equipment as well as 24-hour access to buildings and libraries were also high priorities, given student expectations and requirements.

The right of refusal on the part of a faculty member whose research interests do not coincide, in some way, with that of the students is somewhat surprising, if not a completely logical best practice. It would be interesting to find the analogous industrial applications of this best practice. Finally, it was recognized that research skills and supervisory skills were not necessarily the same, and that some coaching was required to ensure that they were properly considered.

Master Table

United States	Europe	Asia/Pacific	Americas/Africa
EDUCATION			
UNITED STATES		AUSTRALIA	
Babson College		**Queensland University of Technology**	
Higher education industry		Higher education industry	
Enrollment management		*Law research supervision*	
"Enrollment Management at Babson College"		"Law Research Supervision at Queensland University of Technology"	
UNITED STATES			
Oregon State University			
Higher education industry			
Student advising			
"Collaborative Benchmarking in Higher Education"			

Country and Industry

United States	Europe	Asia/Pacific	Americas/Africa
EDUCATION UNITED STATES Higher education industry UNITED STATES Higher education industry		AUSTRALIA Higher education industry	

Processes

United States	Europe	Asia/Pacific	Americas/Africa
EDUCATION UNITED STATES *Enrollment management* UNITED STATES *Student advising*		AUSTRALIA *Law research supervision*	

CHAPTER 25

Enrollment Management at Babson College

Susan West Engelkemeyer, Assistant Professor of Management and Director of Quality, Charles S. Nolan, Dean of Undergraduate Admission, and C. J. McNair, Professor of Management Accounting, Babson College

About Babson College

Founded by financier and entrepreneur Roger W. Babson in 1919, Babson College grants the bachelor of science and master of business administration degrees, and offers advanced training for corporate managers through the School of Executive Education. Babson's undergraduate and graduate programs are accredited by the American Assembly of Collegiate Schools of Business (AACSB) and the New England Association of Schools and Colleges. Babson enrolls approximately 3000 students, including over 1600 undergraduate students, 320 full-time graduate students, and 1100 evening MBA students. Nearly all 50 states and over 75 countries are represented by Babson's student population.

Recent undergraduate rankings include Babson College as the only independent business school named among the 50 best AACSB-accredited undergraduate business programs. In 1996, according to *U.S. News & World Report,* Babson received the number-one ranking in entrepreneurship as well as the designation as among the top three business specialty schools in the United States (Popular programs 1996). Recent graduate rankings include number-one in entrepreneurship (The business school rankings 1997) and the best business school for entrepreneurs (The 25 best business schools 1996). The School of Executive Education has been designated as one of the top providers for custom programs by the *Wall Street Journal.* Babson is a college on the move, seeking to secure its position among the business school elite.

Background

One of the major components of any school's ranking, or reputation, is the quality of its students. Recognizing this fact, Babson College has placed major emphasis on efforts to attract and retain top-caliber candidates for its various programs. Specifically, since 1990 Babson has mailed an Admitted Student Questionnaire (ASQ) to all students who have applied to and were accepted into Babson's undergraduate program. The survey group includes students who enrolled at Babson as well as those who chose to enroll elsewhere. The resulting survey data are compiled and analyzed by The College Entrance Examination Board, which supplies basic statistical analysis of the data. Previously collected data include competitive information on attributes that prospective students deem important in their choice of colleges.

In 1996, the undergraduate admission management team leader decided that the administration of the survey would be expanded. More detailed analysis of the data was completed than had been done in prior years, driven by the team leader's belief that it would support a more strategic approach to the enrollment management process at the college.

Over the years, then, Babson College's traditional ex-post analysis of student preferences has transitioned from "interesting information" into a competitive benchmarking study. Additional data have been collected to provide a comprehensive analysis of Babson's performance against its key competitors in attracting and retaining top-caliber business students from across the United States and around the world. This additional information is being combined with other sources of data, such as that from the Enrollment Planning Service, to better inform the college about its competitive position, and to provide strategic direction.

The Enrollment Planning Service (EPS) is a geodemographic database tool that is also sponsored by The College Entrance Examination Board. Data on regions of the United States and around the world that have high concentrations of students with strong SAT scores and an expressed interest in studying business are combined with ASQ data to create strategic opportunities for Babson. In addition, ongoing changes to the college's existing programs and services are made based on the data in order to better meet student needs and expectations. In total, this broad-based competitive benchmarking effort seeks to ensure that Babson College identifies, attains, and retains the best and brightest business-oriented undergraduate candidates.

Study Purpose

With the costs of higher education growing faster than the rate of inflation, it is becoming harder for families to afford the cost of a private college education. And, while it is the case that there is promise for an increase in the traditional college-aged population due to baby boomers' children and an influx of recent immigrants, the proportion of students entering college who have designated business as their area of interest has declined during the last 10 years. Add to these troublesome trends Babson College's determination to improve the quality and reputation of its undergraduate program, which places the college in a new competitive set, and the depth and intricacy of the enrollment challenge emerges. The goal, namely attracting, gaining, and retaining top-caliber students, underlies the drive to understand what factors influence students' choice of institution and how to improve Babson's performance on this critical dimension.

Just as in manufacturing, yield is important in the college admission process. Annually, a large number of students inquire about Babson, a smaller number choose to apply, an even smaller number are admitted, and even fewer of those actually enroll. For example, in the class entering during the fall of 1996, Babson had 13,275 inquiries, 2,394 applications, 1,089 admits, and 369 enrolled, for a 34 percent yield rate. Since identifying, soliciting, and responding to potential candidates is not a cost-free endeavor, it is critical that the college finely tune its enrollment strategy and carefully target available funds to those segments and candidates that offer the highest potential of success.

Not only is there a tremendous cost associated with attracting students to the college, an even more important issue is attracting the right students—ones that fit the college's targeted profile, are interested in business, are poised to meet the rigors of a demanding curriculum, and are able to contribute to the vitality of cocurricular life. While comprehensive universities can attract students to the institution who have the luxury of deciding on their degree area after their first year or two, Babson is a business specialty school. Students who choose Babson must be highly certain they want a business degree. The enrollment management process, then, must first identify and attract students who already know that business is their chosen area of concentration.

Winning the competitive battle for this unique group of students is the key to long-term survival. As Babson becomes more effective at attracting these students, the college is better able to achieve its strategic goals and make progress toward mission attainment.

The Mission Statement of Babson College

According to Babson College's strategic plan (1996),

> *Babson College is committed to being an internationally recognized leader in management education. Through its programs and practices, the college educates innovative leaders capable of anticipating, initiating, and managing change. In a climate of entrepreneurial spirit, creative and analytical thinking, global perspectives, continuous learning and social responsibility, men and women of different cultures, origins, and life stages learn together to define the opportunities of the future.* (pp. 15–16)

Successful recruitment strategies for the undergraduate program are key to the college's ability to achieve its mission. Recognizing this fact, Babson College has embarked on a three-year strategic recruitment plan entitled "Campaign 3000/50." As a result of the findings from the ASQ and the EPS, this plan targets to attract 3000 applicants and accept less than 50 percent of those applicants by the year 2000. The following are the goals of this effort.

- Attract a larger applicant pool: goal 3000 (currently about 2400).
- Maintain selectivity in admission: admit less than 50 percent (currently at 50 percent).

- Enroll a stronger class: 50 percent in top 10 percent of graduating class, 1250+ average combined SAT.

- Achieve a greater diversity in student population: women, AHANA (African American, Hispanic, Asian American, and Native American), geography.

- Enroll students who really want business, will take advantage of the curriculum, and will make Babson a better place in and out of the classroom.

- Solidify the college's place in top 50 undergraduate business schools in the United States.

- Reduce attrition: currently about 85 percent of students graduate.

These goals shape the ongoing competitive benchmarking process at Babson College, as well as define the objectives and efforts of the undergraduate admission management team.

Other elements of the Babson culture and competitive challenge, however, need to be understood and addressed by the admission strategy. For instance, the current cost to attract one undergraduate applicant to Babson is approximately $360, and the cost per enrolled student is approximately $2200. Yet, Babson College is committed to annually increasing tuition by only 1 percent to 1.5 percent above the Consumer Price Index. These facts underlie the institutional imperative to reduce administrative costs, improve service, and redirect savings to enhance the academic programs. In addition to major reengineering efforts, the college also vigorously pursues improving its business processes using quality principles. Uniquely focused on putting the principles taught in the classroom into operation on the campus, Babson College is constantly looking for new ways to understand its competitive environment, the needs of its varied stakeholders, and to improve continuously against these standards.

In addition to pressure to reduce ongoing administrative costs in order to increase the total funds dedicated to the classroom, the college faces additional financial considerations. Specifically, financial aid, in particular grant funds, has become even more important as the college attracts increasing numbers of high-quality students. Attracting these students often comes down to simple economics: the school with the best "offer" will dominate. These facts combine to create two specific questions that the undergraduate admission team must address: "What additional investment is needed for a successful recruitment campaign?" and "Why should the investment be made?"

To answer these questions, the undergraduate admission team leader merged the findings of ASQ and EPS to determine key characteristics of current Babson enrollees, as well as where similar prospective students are located by state, country, market, and secondary school. The data clearly indicated the need for greater support of a successful recruitment campaign; a funding request that was subsequently approved.

Having passed the first hurdle in focusing Babson's undergraduate admission strategy, the undergraduate admission team leader now turned his attention to putting the plan into motion. The essential next step in the implementation of the overall benchmarking process that would shape future enrollment strategies required active involvement of the entire admission team.

Team Operations

The undergraduate admission management team is organized around the fundamental tenet of customer service. Figure 25.1 is a model that places prospective students and their families at the center of the enterprise. The next layer represents secondary customers that communicate with and influence the primary customers. The third layer represents admission team members (assistant directors) who, beyond their face-to-face contact with primary and secondary customers, have designated responsibility for organizing admission volunteers, managing the international and transfer candidate process, and coordinating print and electronic publications. The fourth layer includes the team member (assistant dean) who is responsible for ensuring that day-to-day operations are successfully executed. The outside layer is the team leader (dean) who, in addition to providing guidance and overall team direction, conducts research that informs the planning process.

The undergraduate admission management team leader partners with the dean of student affairs, the dean of undergraduate curriculum, and the director of undergraduate studies to serve as an enrollment management team. This group seeks to understand students from the point of initial inquiry contact with the college, throughout their undergraduate years, until they leave the college or graduate. The directors of student financial services and the center for career development serve this team in ex-officio but influential capacities. These permanent teams pool expertise and insights in creating and implementing effective recruitment policies that support attainment of the college's mission. Benchmarking plays a pivotal role in knitting the efforts of these diverse teams together, directing their attention to the critical success factors in the admissions process.

Competitive Benchmarking: The Babson Experience

Competitive benchmarking focuses on the core business processes that can provide a competitive advantage to an organization over its direct competitors. It is the most similar to the traditional competitive assessment techniques of all the benchmarking approaches, yet it is markedly different. The target isn't knowing the score but rather changing it. If Competitor A can attract and retain 20 percent of its pool of potential candidates, while Competitor B only reaches 5 percent, Competitor A has a competitive advantage. Knowing this fact is not comforting, but it is undoubtedly action-generating.

Competitive benchmarking looks for problems in the way the work is done, not the people doing it. The objective is to catch up and surpass competitors' performance.

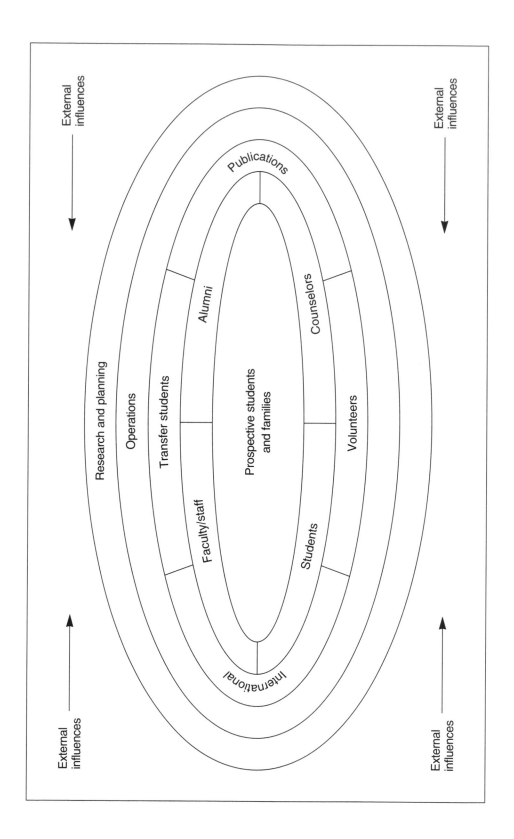

Figure 25.1. Undergraduate admission management team structure.

Utilizing the knowledge of existing employees to drive the change process, competitive benchmarking supports learning at the organizational level, which leads to continuous innovation and change.

The key aspect of competitive benchmarking is that it is narrowly focused on the organization's performance against two or three organizations that compete for roughly the same customers. At Babson College, these competitors include other colleges that are attractive to the target student population—the market segment defines the college's competitors, not the management of the college.

While attaining competitive information is an obvious strategy for any organization seeking to improve its overall performance in the market, it is nearly impossible for an organization to conduct this type of study without the help of an external party. The more sensitive the competitive information being sought, the more important it becomes to elicit the professional support of an objective outside party to actually obtain and analyze the benchmarking data, as suggested by the following comments (Biesada 1991).

> *While some companies have had good experiences benchmarking within their own industry, it is usually in staff, not line, functions. Bentzel (of Alcoa) says he was surprised by the easy access he had to competitors. But the functions he was benchmarking should be taken into consideration. "In the nonmanufacturing areas, direct competitors have little problem talking about topics such as closing the books, order entry, or any other processes or subprocesses."* (p. 30)

Applying these concepts to the college setting, competitive benchmarking that is *not* focused on core business processes is easier to do. The question would be, of course, why use competitive benchmarking in these situations? Best-in-class approaches provide a more meaningful array of data for improving the performance of noncore business processes. According to McNair and Leibfried (1992, 125), then, competitive benchmarking should be used whenever

- Products or customer segments are the focal point of current questioning.
- The process is related to an inherent feature, such as a rule, regulation, or strategic element of the industry.
- Competitive problems are making it difficult for the firm to reach its performance goals.

These characteristics were a match for the situation facing Babson's undergraduate admission management team. In order to effectively implement competitive benchmarking, Babson turned to The College Entrance Examination Board to gather, analyze, and report the key data points influencing the choice of a college or university by the target undergraduate candidate population.

Conduct of the Study

The *Babson College Strategic Plan 1996–2000* recognizes the vital role new student enrollment plays in the college's future success.

> *Inextricably linked to the perceived stature of a college or university is the quality of the students. Further, the new undergraduate curriculum requires that students be capable of meeting its rigor and challenges. Therefore, a principal goal is to attract and enroll students of exceptional quality who are clearly interested in pursuing the unique learning opportunity that Babson's undergraduate program provides. We look to attract students who are already interested in business, rather than attract students who want to come merely to think about studying business. We also want a student body that is gender balanced and from a wide range of ethnic and geographic backgrounds. Bright and diverse students engaged both in and out of the classroom, developing the full extent of their intellectual and social skills, will add to the growing reputation Babson enjoys.* (pp. 15–16)

In the college's strategic plan, specific goals and measures have been established for the undergraduate program. Attainment of these are heavily dependent on an effective enrollment management process. These goals include the following:

• *Class size.* 350–400 first-year students (size of incoming class will remain relatively stable; there are no plans to grow enrollment).

• *SAT scores.* 1250+ combined scores.

• *Test of English as a Foreign Language* (TOEFL) mean score for non-native English speakers: 630 (95 percentile).

• *"Win" measures.* Monitor progress against schools with whom Babson shares common applications. These are in two groups: (1) Business schools over which Babson traditionally enrolls a majority of common acceptances; and (2) Schools from which Babson aspires to win a larger share of common acceptances.

• *Diversity measures* (class of 2000 statistics in parentheses). Goals: 50 percent (37 percent) women; 15 percent (16 percent) AHANA (African American, Hispanic, Asian American, and Native American); 15 percent (24 percent) international; 50 percent to 55 percent (46 percent) non–New England.

• *Selectivity measures.* Select less than 50 percent of the applicant pool. Although only 45 percent of the first-year applicant pool was admitted to the class of 2000, the challenge will be greater in the future as the college regularly competes with institutions of greater prominence and prestige.

Achieving these objectives is the goal of current recruitment efforts at the college.

New student recruitment is orchestrated by the undergraduate admission management team. The world is literally divided up among team members, each responsible for all recruitment activities in assigned territories: secondary school visits, college counselor cultivation, candidate interviews, and alumni admission volunteer training. Approximately 20 percent of the team's time and 30 percent of the operational budget are devoted to off-campus recruitment. Another 40 percent of the team's time and 40 percent of the operational budget are allocated to on-campus marketing efforts: open houses; campus tours; candidate interviews; prospective student overnight visitation; telecounseling conducted by current students, staff, and faculty; and campus day visits to attend classes, speak with students, faculty, coaches, and so on. These efforts are ongoing throughout the year, all leading to that critical day when the candidates' choices become known.

May 1 is the national candidates reply date—the date by which accepted students must respond to colleges and universities with their intention to enroll. The standardized ASQ is mailed to all admitted students by June 15. The questionnaire examines the following:

• The importance of 16 college characteristics

• Comparative college ratings on important characteristics

• Images associated with comparative colleges

• Sources and quality of information provided

• College costs and financial aid data

• Demographic data

• Local questions (up to three)

Figure 25.2 shows a copy of the questionnaire that is mailed to all students who "deposited" (that is, sent required initial funds to hold their place in the incoming class) with Babson. The questionnaire mailed to nondepositors is essentially the same, except it asks if the applicant plans to enroll in college within the next 12 months, and includes questions on the student's top three choices of institutions, as well as specifics on the college attended.

In 1996, Babson's local questions included information on the effect of rankings and curricular changes on the final college choice, and a question on choice of business majors for nonenrolling students.

The college mails the surveys, while The College Entrance Examination Board compiles and analyzes responses. Babson's ASQ questionnaire is accompanied by a personalized letter from the dean of undergraduate admission explaining the need for students' assistance, an assurance of confidentiality, and an incentive to return the questionnaire—a donation to a charity that treats children with cancer. A follow-up mailing is done on July 15, and by August 15 the questionnaires are returned to The College Entrance Examination Board for processing. Within four weeks of receipt of completed surveys, executive summaries and full reports of the data are returned by The College Entrance Examination Board to Babson. Data disks are also included. The raw data can then be merged with institutional files to perform customized studies. Data cited here are from the standardized reports.

Many characteristics of colleges are important to students in making college choices. Some of these characteristics are listed below. Please indicate below how important each college characteristic was to you in choosing the college that you will attend. Circle the numbers that best represent your ratings.

College characteristics   **Importance to you**

	Not important	Somewhat important	Very important
1. Academic reputation	1	2	3
2. Availability of majors of interest to you	1	2	3
3. Availability of special academic programs (independent study, honors programs, etc.)	1	2	3
4. Personal attention to students	1	2	3
5. Quality of academic facilities (library, laboratories, etc.)	1	2	3
6. Availability of recreational facilities on campus	1	2	3
7. Quality of on-campus housing	1	2	3
8. Surroundings (neighborhood, town, or city)	1	2	3
9. Attractiveness of campus	1	2	3
10. Cost of attendance—how much you and your family would have to pay after financial aid (if any) is applied to total college costs	1	2	3
11. Quality of social life			
12. Access to off-campus cultural and recreational opportunities	1	2	3
13. Opportunities to participate in extracurricular activities	1	2	3
14. Preparation for career following graduation	1	2	3
15. Reputation of college with potential employers	1	2	3
16. Emphasis on business and management	1	2	3

Please provide the following information about the colleges to which you applied.

17. Including our college, to how many institutions did you apply? _____

18. Including our college, to how many of these institutions were you admitted? _____

19. On the lines below please list your top three choices among all the colleges **to which you were admitted.** Include our college only if it was one of your top three choices.

First   (Name) _____   (City/State) _____

Second   (Name) _____   (City/State) _____

Third   (Name) _____   (City/State) _____

20. On the remaining lines please list any other colleges to which you applied. Circle YES for each college from which you have received formal notification of admission.

		Admitted			Admitted
_____		**YES**	_____		**YES**
College name	City/State		College name	City/State	
_____		**YES**	_____		**YES**
College name	City/State		College name	City/State	
_____		**YES**	_____		**YES**
College name	City/State		College name	City/State	
_____		**YES**	_____		**YES**
College name	City/State		College name	City/State	

Figure 25.2. Admitted student questionnaire.

From your list of colleges in question 19 above, in columns A and B below print the names of two other *colleges to which you were admitted.* Using the scale shown below, please rate our college and colleges A and B on each of the college characteristics. If you were admitted to our college and one other college only, do not use column B. **If you can't rate a characteristic for one of the colleges or it does not apply, please circle zero for that college.**

1 = Poor/fair   2 = Good   3 = Very good   4 = Excellent   0 = Can't rate

College characteristics	Our college	A: _____	B: _____
21. Academic reputation	1 2 3 4 0	1 2 3 4 0	1 2 3 4 0
22. Availability of majors of interest to you	1 2 3 4 0	1 2 3 4 0	1 2 3 4 0
23. Availability of special academic programs (independent study, honors programs, etc.)	1 2 3 4 0	1 2 3 4 0	1 2 3 4 0
24. Personal attention to students	1 2 3 4 0	1 2 3 4 0	1 2 3 4 0
25. Quality of academic facilities (library, laboratories, etc.)	1 2 3 4 0	1 2 3 4 0	1 2 3 4 0
26. Availability of recreational facilities on campus	1 2 3 4 0	1 2 3 4 0	1 2 3 4 0
27. Quality of on-campus housing	1 2 3 4 0	1 2 3 4 0	1 2 3 4 0
28. Surroundings (neighborhood, town, or city)	1 2 3 4 0	1 2 3 4 0	1 2 3 4 0
29. Attractiveness of campus	1 2 3 4 0	1 2 3 4 0	1 2 3 4 0
30. Cost of attendance—how much you and your family would have to pay after financial aid (if any) is applied to total college costs	1 2 3 4 0	1 2 3 4 0	1 2 3 4 0

Please continue to rate the same colleges as A and B throughout the questionnaire.

College characteristics	Our college	A: _____	B: _____
31. Quality of social life	1 2 3 4 0	1 2 3 4 0	1 2 3 4 0
32. Access to off-campus cultural and recreational opportunities	1 2 3 4 0	1 2 3 4 0	1 2 3 4 0
33. Opportunities to participate in extracurricular activities	1 2 3 4 0	1 2 3 4 0	1 2 3 4 0
34. Preparation for career following graduation	1 2 3 4 0	1 2 3 4 0	1 2 3 4 0
35. Reputation of college with potential employers	1 2 3 4 0	1 2 3 4 0	1 2 3 4 0
36. Emphasis on business and management	1 2 3 4 0	1 2 3 4 0	1 2 3 4 0

From the lists below, please circle all words or phrases that you would say are the most widely held image of our college and colleges A and B.

37. **Our college**
Isolated   Career-oriented   Selective   Average   Small
Prestigious   Not well-known   Athletics   Challenging   Difficult
Fun   Comfortable   Friendly   Conservative   Expensive
Intellectual   Back-up school   Partying   Intense   Other _____

38. **College A:** _____
Isolated   Career-oriented   Selective   Average   Small
Prestigious   Not well-known   Athletics   Challenging   Difficult
Fun   Comfortable   Friendly   Conservative   Expensive
Intellectual   Back-up school   Partying   Intense   Other _____

39. **College B:** _____
Isolated   Career-oriented   Selective   Average   Small
Prestigious   Not well-known   Athletics   Challenging   Difficult
Fun   Comfortable   Friendly   Conservative   Expensive
Intellectual   Back-up school   Partying   Intense   Other _____

Figure 25.2. *(Continued).*

This section asks you to compare our college with colleges A and B on the quality of information provided to you. For each source listed, rate the quality of information provided to you by our college and by colleges A and B. **If a given type of information was not available from one of the colleges or not used by you, circle zero for that college.**

1 = Poor/fair   2 = Good   3 = Very good   4 = Excellent   0 = Can't rate

Sources of information	Our college	A: _____	B: _____
40. Visits by admissions staff at your school	1 2 3 4 0	1 2 3 4 0	1 2 3 4 0
41. College-sponsored meetings in your home area	1 2 3 4 0	1 2 3 4 0	1 2 3 4 0
42. College publications (catalogs, brochures, etc.)	1 2 3 4 0	1 2 3 4 0	1 2 3 4 0

Sources of information	Our college	A: _____	B: _____
43. College videos	1 2 3 4 0	1 2 3 4 0	1 2 3 4 0
44. Communications about financial aid (not the aid decision)	1 2 3 4 0	1 2 3 4 0	1 2 3 4 0
45. Campus visit	1 2 3 4 0	1 2 3 4 0	1 2 3 4 0
46. On-campus admissions interview	1 2 3 4 0	1 2 3 4 0	1 2 3 4 0
47. Contact with the college after you were admitted	1 2 3 4 0	1 2 3 4 0	1 2 3 4 0
48. Contact with faculty from the college	1 2 3 4 0	1 2 3 4 0	1 2 3 4 0
49. Contact with coaches	1 2 3 4 0	1 2 3 4 0	1 2 3 4 0
50. Contact with graduates of the college	1 2 3 4 0	1 2 3 4 0	1 2 3 4 0
51. Contact with students who attend the college	1 2 3 4 0	1 2 3 4 0	1 2 3 4 0

Please provide the following information about college costs and financial aid, if applicable, at our college and colleges A and B.

52. Was either financial aid or the cost of attending a significant factor in your decision to enroll in our college?

    1. Yes   2. No

	Our college	A: _____	B: _____
53. Did you apply for need-based financial aid?	1 Yes 2 No	1 Yes 2 No	1 Yes 2 No
54. Were you offered need-based financial aid?	1 Yes 2 No	1 Yes 2 No	1 Yes 2 No
55. Were you offered a non–need-based scholarship by the college in recognition of your athletic, musical, artistic, or academic talent?	1 Yes 2 No	1 Yes 2 No	1 Yes 2 No
56. Did your financial aid package include:			
Grants or scholarships?	1 Yes 2 No	1 Yes 2 No	1 Yes 2 No
One or more loans?	1 Yes 2 No	1 Yes 2 No	1 Yes 2 No
A work package or campus job?	1 Yes 2 No	1 Yes 2 No	1 Yes 2 No

57. After subtracting financial aid offers, if any, please rate the cost of attending each college from very low to very high. Place an X in the appropriate box on each college's scale.

Our college: 8 Very high / 7 / 6 / 5 / 4 / 3 / 2 / 1 Very low

A: _____ 8 Very high / 7 / 6 / 5 / 4 / 3 / 2 / 1 Very low

B: _____ 8 Very high / 7 / 6 / 5 / 4 / 3 / 2 / 1 Very low

Figure 25.2. *(Continued).*

Please provide the following information about yourself.

58. Which of the following categories best represents your average grades in high school? (Circle one answer)

    1. A (90–100)   2. B (80–89)   3. C (70–79)   4. D (69 or below)

59. What were your highest scores on the following college admissions tests?

    SAT-Verbal _____ (200–800 scale)

    SAT-Mathematical _____ (200–800 scale)

    ACT Composite _____ (1–36 scale)

60. How do you describe yourself? (Circle one answer)

    1 American Indian or Alaskan Native
    2 Asian, Asian American, or Pacific Islander
    3 Mexican American or Chicano
    4 Puerto Rican
    5 Latin American, South American, Central American, or other Hispanic
    6 Black or African American
    7 White
    8 Other _____

61. Are you a resident of the state in which our college is located?

    1. Yes
    2. No

62. How far is our college from your home? (Circle one answer)

    1. Less than 50 miles
    2. 51–100 miles
    3. 101–300 miles
    4. 301–500 miles
    5. More than 500 miles

63. Which of the following best describes the type of high school you attended? (Circle one answer)

    1. Public
    2. Independent, not religiously affiliated
    3. Independent, Catholic
    4. Other independent, religiously affiliated

64. What was the approximate income of your parents or guardians before taxes last year? (Circle one answer)

    1. Less than $20,000
    2. $20,000 to $29,999
    3. $30,000 to $39,999
    4. $40,000 to $49,999
    5. $50,000 to $59,999
    6. $60,000 to $79,999
    7. $80,000 to $99,999
    8. $100,000 or higher

65. What is the zip code of your home address? _____

66. What is your gender?

    1. Female
    2. Male

67. If you were aware of the recently implemented curriculum at Babson, how did it affect your final college choice?

    1. It made me more inclined to enroll at Babson.
    2. It made me less inclined to enroll at Babson.
    3. It had no effect on my choice.
    4. I was unaware of the new curriculum at Babson.

68. If you were aware of Babson being ranked among the top 50 undergraduate business programs in the country, according to *U.S. News & World Report,* how did it affect your final college choice?

    1. It made me more inclined to enroll at Babson.
    2. It made me less inclined to enroll at Babson.
    3. It had no effect on my choice.
    4. I was unaware of the rating.

Figure 25.2. *(Continued).*

69. How important was the gender balance at Babson (60% male/40% female) in your decision to enroll/not enroll at Babson?

    1. Very Important
    2. Important

    3. Not important
    4. No effect on my decision

Please use the space below for any comments you would like to share with us about our college's admissions program.

Thank you very much for taking the time to complete this questionnaire.

Figure 25.2. *(Continued).*

83 percent of the enrolling and 38 percent of the nonenrolling students for the fall of 1997 returned the questionnaires. The response rates for enrolling and nonenrolling students in this study "equal or exceed those typically found in studies of this type. Weighting of responses was done to express all results as estimates of the groups of admitted, enrolling and nonenrolling students surveyed" (The College Entrance Examination Board 1996).

The ASQ study provided information to the college on attributes deemed important by students accepted to Babson. In addition, survey data indicated the win rate with competitive schools. In 1996, the undergraduate admission management team leader requested additional in-depth analysis that provided information on key competitors. Detailed information on five of Babson's top seven cross-admission schools was provided.

The top seven cross-admission school data and Babson's win rate are shown in Table 25.1. Win percentage indicates the proportion of cross-admits that Babson enrolled if the student chose to attend Babson or the other school. It was determined that the five schools used for this study would include two schools that were numbers six and seven, respectively, in cross-admissions. The fourth and fifth ranked cross-admission schools (Schools D and E) were not studied in detail because the college already wins a large proportion of cross-applications with these schools, and the reputation of these schools is below that of the institutions the college wants to compete with in the future. On the other hand, Babson currently has limited success enrolling students from Schools F and G; they are the schools with which Babson wants to steadily improve its win rate. School C is a prestigious institution that Babson is currently somewhat competitive with, and the goal would be to also increase Babson's win rate.

Table 25.1. Top seven cross-admission schools: Win percentage and rating.

	# Cross-admits[1]	Win %[2]	Barron's rating[3]
1. School A	375	60%	Competitive
2. School B	206	72%	Highly competitive
3. School C	203	29%	Most competitive
4. School D	162	79%	Less competitive
5. School E	150	70%	Competitive
6. School F	53	8%	Most competitive
7. School G	34	11%	Most competitive

[1]The number of students that were admitted to Babson College and the school listed

[2]Proportion of cross-admits Babson College enrolls if the student chose to attend either Babson or the school listed

[3]From *Barron's Profiles of American Colleges, 20th edition*. These data are provided to indicate school reputation. Barron's rankings (in decreasing order) are: most competitive, highly competitive, very competitive, competitive, and less competitive. Babson is rated very competitive.

For all the factors rated by admitted students, detailed information was provided on each of the five selected competitors, including the following:

- Demographic profiles of the subset of students comparing Babson to the competitor
- Characteristics/demographic data (for example, test score results, importance of cost) and yield
- Comparative ratings for Babson and the competitor on important college characteristics
- Images most frequently associated with Babson and the competitor

Best Practices Discovered and Results

The study identified 16 important college characteristics that admitted students rated by importance to the candidate's final choice of institution. These factors represent a composite of student preferences for a college environment. Table 25.2 details the college characteristics rated very important by all admitted students.

The six most important characteristics are all academic-related. A majority of students also value the social life and surroundings as well as personal attention and cost factors.

Table 25.3 indicates the importance characteristics where there was a significant difference between enrolling students and nonenrolling students. These data indicate that enrolling stu-

Table 25.2. College characteristics rated very important.

Characteristic	% Admitted students
Preparation for career	92%
Academic reputation	88%
Availability of majors	86%
Quality of faculty	80%
Quality of academic facility	69%
Internship opportunities	66%
Personal attention	65%
Quality of campus housing	53%
Cost of attendance	53%
Surroundings	53%
Quality of social life	51%
Extracurricular opportunities	47%
Availability of recreational facilities	46%
Attractiveness of campus	44%
Access to off-campus activities	33%
Special academic programs	26%

Table 25.3. Significant college characteristics for enrolling and nonenrolling students.

<table>
<tr><td colspan="2" align="center">**Factors reported very important by significantly larger percentages
of enrolling students, where + (*p* < .05), and ++ (*p* < .01)**</td></tr>
<tr><td>++</td><td>Preparation for career</td></tr>
<tr><td>++</td><td>Internship opportunities</td></tr>
<tr><td>++</td><td>Personal attention</td></tr>
<tr><td>++</td><td>Quality of campus housing</td></tr>
<tr><td>++</td><td>Availability of recreational resources</td></tr>
<tr><td>++</td><td>Quality of faculty</td></tr>
<tr><td>++</td><td>Extracurricular opportunities</td></tr>
<tr><td colspan="2" align="center">**Factors reported very important by significantly larger percentages
of nonenrolling students, where − (*p* < .05), and −− (*p* < .01)**</td></tr>
<tr><td>−−</td><td>Cost of attendance</td></tr>
</table>

dents place more importance on a variety of characteristics, ranging from career preparation to the availability of recreational facilities. The only characteristic in Table 25.3 that was rated significantly more important for nonenrolling students was cost of attendance.

In order to better understand Babson's relative rating on college characteristics, data were provided on which of the characteristics considered very important by all admitted students that Babson was rated relatively high versus relatively low. Table 25.4 indicates that Babson compared favorably on factors rated very important primarily in academic-related areas. The factors rated very important that Babson rated lower on were related to cost and social factors.

These factors have implications for cost and competitive reasons. In Table 25.4, the upper right quadrant, factors rated very important where Babson is rated higher, indicate areas where the college can emphasize these factors for recruitment advantages. The lower right quadrant indicates significant opportunity areas for the college. If social and cost factors can be improved, Babson would have a competitive advantage in all of the factors rated very important by its applicants.

Since the college has clear strategic goals regarding improving the quality of incoming students and its competitive position, data were provided on characteristics considered important by high-achieving students (students whose self-reported admissions test scores were in the top 25 percent for all admitted students). Table 25.5 indicates those characteristics considered very important by at least 50 percent of the high-achieving respondents, and where Babson's mean rating was either higher or lower than that for all other colleges.

The data indicate that different factors are very important to high-quality students. For instance, social and environment factors are less important to top students; however, all the academic-related factors very important to all applicants are also very important to

Table 25.4. Importance and rating of college characteristics.

Less important—Babson rated higher	Very important—Babson rated higher
Attractiveness of campus	Personal attention
Special academic programs	Surroundings
	Preparation for career
	Quality of on-campus housing
	Internship opportunities
	Academic reputation
	Quality of faculty
	Quality of academic facilities
	Availability of majors
Less important—Babson rated lower	**Very important—Babson rated lower**
Access to off-campus activities	Cost of attendance
Availability of recreational facilities	Quality of social life
Extracurricular opportunities	

Table 25.5. High-achieving students: Importance and rating of college characteristics.

Less important—Babson rated higher	Very important—Babson rated higher
Surroundings	Personal attention
Attractiveness of campus	Preparation for career
Quality of on-campus housing	Internship opportunities
Less important—Babson rated lower	**Very important—Babson rated lower**
Quality of social life	Cost of attendance
Access to off-campus activities	Availability of majors
Availability of recreational facilities	Quality of academic facilities
Extracurricular opportunities	Academic reputation
Special academic programs	Quality of faculty

high-achieving students. Babson did not compare as favorably on all of these factors with the high achievers.

Another important finding is that financial aid is a significant factor influencing the enrollment decision for high-achieving students. Aid or cost was a significant factor for 36 percent of enrolling students, and 63 percent of nonenrolling high-quality students. Given that cost is a significant characteristic, and Babson is rated unfavorably on cost, it can be assumed that a different pricing structure might be necessary to attract more high-achieving students. Another statistic that supports this conclusion is the win percentage against School A in Table 25.1. Across all cross-admitted students, Babson has a 60 percent win percentage against School A. With high-achieving students, however, the win percentage drops to 26 percent. Since this college is rated lower than Babson by Barron's and also rated lower on all academic-related factors by students responding to the ASQ, it can be assumed that School A is winning a higher proportion of high-achieving students with more attractive financial aid/cost packages.

The data indicated overall competitive information. Statistics were also generated on five of Babson's top competitors. This provided specific information on how Babson was comparatively rated on the importance factors—factors where there was the largest ratings difference—and demographic information. Table 25.6 details the importance and rating factors for School A.

School A is similar to Babson in its educational mission and shares the largest number of cross-admits. As Table 25.6 indicates, Babson is rated higher on all very important academic-related characteristics. The important factors where Babson is rated lower include cost and quality of social life. Without additional information, what is meant by social factors can only be speculated. Since School A has over twice the undergraduate enrollment of Babson, a favorable social perception could be due simply to size. On the other hand, perhaps School A provides more social opportunities than Babson.

Presently, School A's total costs are approximately 20 percent less than Babson. Although cross-admits perceive Babson is superior academically, cost is considered very important by more students than social life. In 1996, Babson's win percentage was 60 percent against School A. This figure is considerably lower than the previous five-year average of 71 percent. ASQ findings indicate that "cost of attendance"—defined as "net price after financial aid"—was the most negative characteristic of Babson when compared to School A, significant at $p < .01$. It seems clear that the primary method for improving competition with School A is through more advantageous pricing and financial aid.

There is a paradox, though, inherent in this strategy. On average, Babson's applicant pool is stronger than School A. Each school employs a "preferential financial aid strategy," which means that institutional scholarship funds are awarded on the basis of "merit within need." Therefore, the strongest-admitted students with demonstrated financial need receive the most attractive financial aid packages. The lowest-admitted Babson candidates will not have their full need met, and will be "gapped." Again, on average, a middle-quality accepted student at Babson will be School A's top candidate, and consequently will receive School A's best financial aid award. In recent years, this trend has been exacerbated as

Table 25.6. School A: Importance and rating factors.

Less important—Babson rated higher	Very important—Babson rated higher
Surroundings	Academic reputation
Attractiveness of campus	Quality of on-campus housing
Availability of recreational programs	Preparation for career
Special academic programs	Internship opportunities
	Quality of faculty
	Quality of academic facilities
	Availability of majors
	Personal attention
Less important—Babson rated lower	**Very important—Babson rated lower**
Access to off-campus activities	Cost of attendance
Extracurricular opportunities	Quality of social life

Babson has become more selective, admitting less than half of its candidates. School A admits about 70 percent to 75 percent of its candidates. It could be argued that the more recent win percentage is reasonable in view of this trend.

Figure 25.3 demonstrates the four factors that experienced the largest ratings differences between Babson and School A. Babson has a significantly more positive rating for "surroundings," "attractiveness of campus," and "academic reputation." Again, "cost of attendance," however, is rated significantly more favorable for School A.

Strategic questions can be addressed by examining the data from four of the five competitors in two groups. Group 1 includes Schools A and B. These are schools where Babson currently wins over 60 percent of the cross-admittances. Barron's rates School A lower than Babson and School B higher than Babson. Group 2 includes School C. Babson is fairly competitive with School C, and Barron's rates School C as "most competitive." Group 3 includes Schools G and F. Both of these schools are rated in the "most competitive" bracket by Barron's, and are schools that Babson aspires to be more competitive with in the future; at this time Babson's win rate is less than 11 percent for either school. Table 25.7 details the very important factors where Babson is rated lower for each group.

These results indicate that a much different set of factors are important to students who choose to attend institutions in each of these competitive groups. In group 1, Babson is rated lower in social life and cost factors. Group 2 has a mix of academic and social factors. In group 3, Babson is rated lower primarily on academic-related factors. This presents a significant challenge for the undergraduate admission management team as it develops marketing programs and services that address the needs of these very different groups.

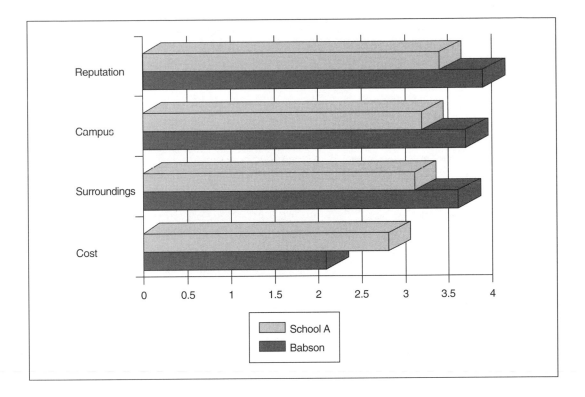

Figure 25.3. School A: Four factors with largest rating differences.

Table 25.7. Competitive factors for strategic groups.

Group 1: Strong competitive position	Group 2: Weak competitive position	Group 3: Aspire to compete with
Very important—Babson rated lower	**Very important—Babson rated lower**	**Very important—Babson rated lower**
School A	School C	School F and school G
• Cost of attendance • Quality of social life	• Quality of social life • Quality of academic facilities • Surroundings • Extracurricular opportunities • Availability of majors • Academic reputation	• Academic reputation • Quality of social life • Availability of majors • Preparation for career • Quality of faculty • Internship opportunities
School B		School G only
• Quality of social life • Availability of majors		• Availability of majors • Quality of academic facilities

Perhaps the greatest opportunity can be found when examining School C. It drew 300 cross-applications in 1996, second only to School A, which had 383 cross-applications. School C also enrolls the highest percentage (15 percent) of cross-admits of all competitors, and other than Schools G and F, wins the strongest students. The win rate for Babson against this medium-sized university with a highly regarded business school is 29 percent for 1995 and 1996. Table 25.8 details competitive factors for School C.

These findings are very revealing. Where cost of attendance with School A was a statistically significant negative factor, cost of attendance is very important, and Babson is rated more favorably than School C. Babson's published costs are virtually identical to School C. The data in Table 25.8 suggest that Babson should distinguish itself against School C on the basis of small size, quality of faculty, personal attention, preparation for a career, and internship opportunities, and not necessarily on the basis of costs or through more attractive financial aid packages.

School C is rated "most competitive" by Barron's and is known to be very selective in the admission process. If Babson could increase its win percentage against this institution, it would subsequently improve the overall quality of Babson students.

Armed with this data, the undergraduate admission team could now turn its attention to crafting a strategy that would increase its win percentages against target institutions. Turning the benchmarking data into action became the focus of all involved.

Table 25.8. School C: Competitive factors.

Less important—Babson rated higher	*Very* important—Babson rated higher
Special academic programs	Personal attention
	Internship opportunities
	Quality of on-campus housing
	Cost of attendance
	Preparation for career
	Attractiveness of campus
	Quality of faculty
Less important—Babson rated lower	***Very* important—Babson rated lower**
Access to off-campus activities	Quality of social life
Availability of recreational programs	Quality of academic facilities
	Surroundings
	Extracurricular opportunities
	Availability of majors
	Academic reputation

Implementation and Actions Taken

Campaign 3000/50 is perhaps the most significant outcome of the ASQ and EPS data. The 1996 ASQ data indicate that over 21 percent of the admitted students did not plan to study business, that cost was a very important characteristic for the majority of admitted students, and that high school visits was the lowest-rated source of information from Babson. These data provided the foundation for a more focused recruiting campaign for the 1997–1998 academic year, but were not enough to support a detailed implementation of a new recruiting strategy. To achieve this goal, the admission team leader turned to other sources of benchmarking and statistical data.

EPS data, which segments the country into 304 geodemographic markets, were used to identify specific "markets" for potential Babson students. These markets were then mapped according to the number of students interested in business, SAT scores above 1200, and family incomes that could support private college tuition. This stratified sample detailed specific geographic areas and secondary schools where Babson's targeted student existed in relatively large numbers. Based on this information, the undergraduate admission management team was given funding for three years for two additional staff members. The team was also given additional travel money to target these areas with more school visits and local interviews, in order to increase the number of applications that would be likely to convert to admitted and enrolled students for the fall of 1998. In addition, a direct mail campaign has been implemented for all students who, according to EPS data, fit Babson's targeted profile.

The following strategies for allocating Babson's funds have been developed in support of the strategic enrollment goals previously listed.

- Babson grants are awarded on the basis of merit and need; within a particular level of need, proportionately more dollars are offered to higher-qualified students and to women.

- Presidential scholarships are awarded to students regardless of their financial circumstances, providing an additional incentive for the highest-qualified candidates to enroll at Babson.

- "Endeavor" scholarships are awarded to African-American students selected on the basis of academic achievement, leadership potential, and financial need.

The ASQ study triggered further investigation when the college discovered that it was losing some of its best applicants to schools that were ranked lower than Babson. One key finding was that financial aid packages at these lower-rated schools were attracting away some of the college's top applicants. As a result, a change in the financial aid policy was made to better attract these high-quality students.

Research indicated that adding scholarship funds to Babson's strong but not strongest-admitted students would have a positive impact on the class of 2001. A "beef-up-the-middle" strategy was employed during 1997, judiciously awarding $300,000 additional scholarship dollars to students more likely to enroll at Babson if the college offered a competitive total cost. This initiative reduced or eliminated the gaps where there was demonstrated financial need not funded by financial assistance. The change in policies worked. Overall, yield of accepted students increased by almost 25 percent, and the overall quality of the class increased on all measures.

On another key recruitment dimension, ASQ data showed that quality of social life was a predominant issue for many prospective students. Since Babson does not have Division I or II athletics, which are a draw for many of the college's competitors, it was believed that a student center might provide opportunities for more activities and facilitate more school spirit. As a result, in June 1996, ground was broken for a new Campus Center Quadrangle, which will include a chapel, the campus center, and center for the arts.

On other fronts, the college announced in June 1997 that the F.W. Olin Foundation will build an independent engineering school on property owned by Babson. This new school will broaden academic program offerings and attract a new group of students to the campus who are looking for expanded curricular opportunities. In addition, anchor schools for study abroad, and cross-registration with Wellesley College, Brandeis University, the new Franklin W. Olin College of Engineering, and other local colleges are enabling Babson to address student needs related to availability of course work outside of traditional business disciplines, with minimal financial consequences to the college.

Complementing these changes are fund-raising activities. The largest capital campaign in the history of the college was completed in June 1997. This effort will reduce the level of tuition dependency and provide funds for strategic initiatives at the college. In other attempts to free up funds to support improvement against student expectations, reengineering of student-based administrative services has been undertaken. This project was initiated in September 1994 in order to simultaneously improve customer satisfaction and reduce operating costs. Cost savings attributed to reengineering will be redeployed to academic areas of the college.

In total, the refinement of the college's recruitment efforts has facilitated a more targeted approach to recruiting. In 1994, Babson had 17,000 inquiries and 2,100 applications, a 12 percent conversion rate. Research determined the sources of "soft" inquiry generation. This knowledge combined with more targeted geodemographic recruiting resulted in 10,090 inquiries in 1997 and 2,415 applications, a 24 percent conversion rate.

While gains are being made in many areas, barriers remain that may impede Babson's ability to make rapid progress against the competitors it aspires to "win" against as well as against other current competitors. These barriers include the following:

• *Mission factors.* Babson is a business specialty school. It has experienced tremendous success as a niche player in the higher education market. At this time there are no plans to expand the range of majors offered. Therefore, the college will continue to be challenged with the prospect of attracting new students who are fairly certain they want a business education.

• *Financial concerns.* Babson College is a tuition-driven institution, so responding to student needs for additional financial aid, services, and extracurricular life places a strain on the budget. The college's latest major capital campaign raised over $120 million for the institution. This funding will provide some cushion against high-tuition dependency, but will not allow a vast expansion of services, given the simultaneous pressure to contain costs. New fund-raising initiatives directed toward specific institutional needs will need to be implemented to address these areas of opportunity.

• *Faculty issues.* Diversification of the student base has placed additional strain on faculty and the curriculum. A focus on enrolling more high-achieving students creates additional demand for more advanced curricular offerings. In addition, increasing numbers of international and minority students have necessitated greater attention to cultural issues, relevant discussion topics, and classroom dynamics, given a more diverse student population.

• *Financial aid.* As higher education costs increase, and federal loan funds decrease, financial aid pressures mount across higher education. Given Babson's goals to recruit the most qualified students from diverse backgrounds, its financial aid pressure is even greater.

Additional initiatives and next steps are planned to facilitate attainment of Babson's goals and to strengthen the college's competitive position. This includes further integration and analysis of existing studies and greater focus of efforts outside enrollment on key strategic issues that were highlighted by the competitive analysis.

Conclusions and Lessons Learned

The competitive benchmarking process at Babson College mirrors the basic concern with continuous improvement that defines the college. Reflecting the beliefs of Robert Camp (1989), the Babson experience is driven by the following philosophy.

> *Benchmarking is a self-improvement and management process that must be continuous to be effective. It cannot be performed once and disregarded thereafter on the belief that the task is done. It must be a continuous process, because industry practices constantly change. Industry leaders constantly get stronger . . . In an environment of constant change, complacency is fatal.* (p. 10)

Studying its benchmarking competitors using validated research methods has been a useful institutional process for Babson College. Senior administrators, trustees, faculty, and others now better understand the opportunities and challenges that face Babson as it positions itself for making progress against its prestigious and highly visible counterparts.

Recognizing that the only way to ensure improvement in the competitive recruitment and admission arena is to better meet student expectations and outperform competitors on all attributes deemed critical by the target undergraduate population, Babson College plans to continue its benchmarking efforts. This decision has been reinforced by the following key lessons, or insights, gleaned from this study.

• Careful targeting of recruitment efforts is the key to the effective use of scarce resources available to the college for this activity.

• Identifying core target areas is an essential first step in improving win percentages.

- Top-ranked candidates differ in the nature and magnitude of the gap perceived between Babson's offer/position and that of the chosen institution.

- Carefully pinpointed action plans can be used to close these gaps.

- The information learned during benchmarking is only the starting point. To be truly useful, the data have to be integrated with the college's mission, goals, and honest assessment of weaknesses to craft an overall recruiting strategy that will enhance Babson's competitive position.

- Achieving the goals that shaped the benchmarking effort is a continuous process of improvement and learning.

In the final analysis, it would seem that a college is not much different than any other organization. It has to be focused on a clear mission, understand how it compares with its competitors on defined critical success factors and "product" attributes, carefully and honestly address the performance shortfalls, and craft action plans that will close key performance gaps. While the product—a well-educated, successful undergraduate population is unique—the definition of good business practice is not. Gaining and sustaining a competitive advantage begins with understanding the challenges and opportunities for improvement that benchmarking identifies, but is a process that can never end.

> *We know what we are, but know not what we may be.*
>
> —William Shakespeare

> *Whatever you cannot understand, you cannot possess.*
>
> —Johann Wolfgang Von Goethe

References

Babson College Strategic Plan 1996–2000. Babson Park, Mass.: Babson College.

Biesada, Alexandra. 1991. Benchmarking. *Financial World,* 17 September, 30.

The business rankings: Top schools. 1997. *U.S. News & World Report,* 10 March, 82–83.

Camp, Robert C. 1989. *Benchmarking: The search for industry best practices that lead to superior performance.* Milwaukee: ASQC Quality Press and White Plains, N.Y.: Quality Resources.

The College Entrance Examination Board (The College Board). 1996. *Babson College highlights report 1996.* New York: The College Entrance Examination Board.

McNair, C. J., and K. Leibfried. 1992. *Benchmarking: A tool for continuous improvement.* New York: Wiley & Sons.

Popular programs: Ranking business, engineering, and the arts. 1996. *U.S. News & World Report,* 16 September, 121–122.

The 25 best business schools. 1996. *Success* (September): 40.

Acknowledgment

Special thanks to Jacqueline Giordano, assistant dean of admission and a member of the undergraduate admission management team, for providing data and information for this case study.

About the Authors

Susan West Engelkemeyer is an assistant professor of management and the director of quality for Babson College. She holds a Ph.D. in industrial management from Clemson University and an MBA from East Carolina University. Her consulting and research areas include operations and total quality management. She has published in *Quality Progress* and other journals and books in the area of quality management. She has served as a senior examiner for the Malcolm Baldrige National Quality Award and as a senior evaluator for the the the award's 1995 Education Pilot.

Charles S. Nolan is the dean of undergraduate admission and team leader for undergraduate admission management at Babson College. He has held this position since 1991. Prior to coming to Babson, Nolan served as assistant provost and dean of undergraduate admission for Washington University in St. Louis from 1989–1991, and also served as director of undergraduate admission at Boston College from 1980–1989. He holds a Ph.D. in higher education administration from Boston College.

A certified management account, C. J. McNair is a professor of management accounting at Babson College. A noted expert in the design and development of cost management systems, McNair has published numerous books and articles in this area, including *The Profit Potential: Taking High Performance to the Bottom Line* (Wiley & Sons, 1995), *World-Class Accounting and Finance* (Business One Irwin, 1993), and *Benchmarking: Tool for Continuous Improvement* (paperback version; Wiley & Sons, 1992). She recently completed a monograph for the Institute of Management Accountants on capacity cost management with Professor Richard Vangermeersch of the University of Rhode Island, as well as *Management Accounting Guidelines* on capacity cost management, redesigning the finance function, and process management, for the Society of Management Accountants of Canada.

The authors may be contacted as follows:

Babson College
Forest Street
Babson Park, MA 02157-0310
Telephone: 617-239-5017
Facsimile: 617-239-5230
E-mail: Engelkem@babson.edu

CHAPTER 26

Collaborative Benchmarking in Higher Education

Stefan D. Bloomfield, Professor of Management, Oregon State University

Introduction

Benchmarking as carried out in manufacturing industries and much of the service sector is, in principle, relatively straightforward. An organization decides on the process to be benchmarked, studies the process as it is currently carried out, establishes process performance measures and other metrics to be used in benchmarking the process, identifies and solicits cooperation from a benchmarking partner, and gathers the relevant comparative information.

Collaborative benchmarking is an extension of this standard model in which a group of organizations jointly selects a process that is important to all members of the group and simultaneously attempts to benchmark the chosen process. Usually, such a group will first benchmark the process within the group itself, with each participant serving simultaneously as both a benchmarker and a benchmarking partner. Then, based on its newly developed expertise, the group may seek external organizations whose leading practices can be studied by all group members.

This chapter reports on a collaborative benchmarking effort initiated by a consortium of higher education institutions in the United States. Although the benchmarking effort is only partially complete as this report is being written, the project illustrates both the difficulties inherent in collaborative benchmarking and the additional obstacles commonly encountered in higher education benchmarking.

The Challenge of Collaborative Benchmarking

Exposing entire industry groups to examples of best practices is nothing new; in fact, this is a standard feature of many industry conventions and similar conferences. A relatively recent development, however, is applying the rigorous approach of formal benchmarking so that all participants of an industry group can recognize key differences and best practices among their own processes.

Initial efforts in this direction have taken the form of systematic data comparison studies among similar companies. Commonly called "interfirm comparison studies," these are often based on lengthy questionnaires that gather detailed input and output data relating to key processes of the industry. A coordinating entity, frequently a third-party organization, then collects and analyzes the data and reports back to the participating companies. Confidentiality is usually maintained by coding the identity of the respondents and reporting many results in the form of ratios to both disguise and account for differences in company size.

As commonly carried out, such studies have been prone to two shortcomings. First, except in operational areas that must adhere to such externally imposed frameworks as tax codes or mandated reporting rules, the supplied data may not, in fact, be truly comparable. Cost or expense data may be difficult to compare depending on the idiosyncrasies of each company's accounting practices, and even straightforward "count" data (number of employees, customers, orders, and so on) can differ by virtue of each organization's internal record-keeping practices. Surmounting this problem requires developing a detailed data dictionary that carefully defines each requested item. The challenge then shifts to providing assurance that each of the participating companies is actually converting its in-house data to the specified format.

The second common shortcoming, more difficult to overcome, involves identifying managerially useful comparative performance measures and metrics. Particularly in non-manufacturing sectors, comparative measures of efficiency and productivity often suffer from a lack of accompanying quality measures. So, for example, such ratios as number of customer service representatives per 1000 customers or the number of information requests handled per hour provide useful information only if accompanied by data indicating the resulting degree of customer satisfaction. Lacking such effectiveness measures, an extreme value for a ratio might reflect extraordinarily efficient operations or extraordinarily poor service. Although financial ratios, such as return on investment or return on equity or assets, can be less ambiguous (assuming the underlying accounting methods are essentially the same), such global measures may not be tightly linked to the effectiveness of the specific processes under consideration.

Collaborative benchmarking attempts to circumvent some of these difficulties by closely adhering to the steps of the classic benchmarking process. As with any benchmarking project, a collaborative effort starts with deciding upon a specific process to jointly benchmark. The process must be one that is both common to each of the participants and of sufficient importance in each of their operations to be worth studying and improving. Additionally, the process cannot be so proprietary nor of such competitive advantage that it would be difficult for organizations within the same industry to jointly study. Once such a process is identified and agreed to at the appropriate organizational levels, each organization then systematically studies its own process in a manner similar to ordinary process benchmarking.

The crucial step in a collaborative benchmarking project is the development of performance measures and metrics for identifying superior performance. As discussed, outside of manufacturing and certain well-regulated service processes, the search for comparable metrics can be quite challenging. Even when there is agreement on the type of measure to be used, differing accounting procedures and measurement protocols, compounded by disparities in data collection and analysis practices, can lead to compromises that weaken the comparability of resulting data. This becomes especially challenging when dealing with effectiveness data because differences in methods and capabilities for gathering information are often most pronounced when it comes to soliciting evaluations from external and internal customers. Nevertheless, by incorporating the discussion of performance measures and metrics as an explicit part of the collaborative benchmarking process, participating companies have the best possible assurance that the resulting information will be both reasonably comparable and managerially useful.

The Challenge of Higher Education Benchmarking

Since the late 1980s, various higher education institutions have tried to apply principles of quality management to their operations. To assure success, the first higher education applications involved quasi-industrial and routine administrative operations that most closely resembled successful applications in the private sector. For the same reason, benchmarking in higher education has been carried out predominately in operational and administrative areas—as opposed to the academic side of the institution.

Process improvement techniques tend to be most effective with processes that are routine and repeatable and have readily available process performance measures. This is rarely the case with higher education teaching and research. Although classroom instruction may appear to be a routine and repeatable process, it can be a surprisingly variable activity—often developed independently and performed differently by each instructor. The creative processes of basic and applied research are even more resistant to the normal analytical procedures of process improvement. Compounding the problem is the fact that process performance measures in teaching and research have been notoriously difficult to define. As a result, the academic operations of colleges and universities, with only a few notable exceptions, have remained largely unaffected by benchmarking and other quality management techniques.

The AQC Benchmarking Project

Starting in the late 1980s, led by the ground-breaking work at Oregon State University, a number of higher education institutions began experimenting with quality management principles and techniques. By the early 1990s several institutions had become nationally recognized for their commitment to applying quality management to various aspects of their operations. To capture the enthusiasm and experience of this leading group of institutions, in 1992 the American Association of Higher Education, in collaboration with the Norris Institute, jointly founded the Academic Quality Consortium (AQC). As shown in Table 26.1, the the AQC now comprises 21 institutions spanning all levels of higher education from two-year colleges to major research universities, including both publicly supported and privately funded institutions. The purpose of the consortium is to support its member institutions in their commitment to quality management and continuous quality improvement, and to share their learning with the rest of the higher education community.

Consistent with its mission of leadership in applying quality management principles and techniques to higher education, one of the first major projects of the AQC was to encourage its member institutions to perform self-assessments using the criteria of the Malcolm Baldrige National Quality Award. The results of this study helped shape the Baldrige Award's 1996 pilot award process for educational institutions.

Table 26.1. Academic Quality Consortium (AQC) members.

*Alverno College	Milwaukee, Wisconsin
Babson College	Babson Park, Massachusetts
*Belmont University	Nashville, Tennessee
Clemson University	Clemson, South Carolina
*Dallas County Community College District	Dallas, Texas
*Delaware County Community College	Media, Pennsylvania
Fox Valley Technical College	Appleton, Wisconsin
Georgia Institute of Technology	Atlanta, Georgia
*Maricopa Community College District	Tempe, Arizona
*Marietta College	Marietta, Ohio
*Miami University	Oxford, Ohio
*Northwest Missouri State College	Maryville, Missouri
*Oregon State University	Corvallis, Oregon
*Pennsylvania State University	University Park, Pennsylvania
Rutgers University	New Brunswick, New Jersey
St. John Fisher College	Rochester, New York
*Samford College	Birmingham, Alabama
University of Michigan	Ann Arbor, Michigan
University of Minnesota, Twin Cities	Minneapolis, Minnesota
*University of Minnesota, Duluth	Duluth, Minnesota
*University of Wisconsin	Madison, Wisconsin

*Denotes institutions participating in the collaborative benchmarking project.

As its second major project, the AQC decided to explore the use of benchmarking in academic operations. Consortium members were aware of the many efforts by higher education institutions to apply quality management principles, including the occasional use of benchmarking, to their administrative and support functions. The unanswered question was the extent to which benchmarking could also be used to improve the key processes of higher education teaching and research. To learn more about benchmarking techniques, consortium members in early 1995 attended a special workshop on benchmarking sponsored by the DuPont Company. On the basis of this experience, the AQC agreed to develop a pilot project to demonstrate the usefulness of collaborative benchmarking for academic activities. Ultimately, 13 consortium members agreed to participate actively in the collaborative benchmarking project.

The first task of the consortium was to select an academic process that all participants carried out in common and that would be amenable to a benchmarking project. Because of the diverse nature of the AQC, some important activities (such as basic research or vocational education) were applicable to only a few of the consortium members. Other commonly shared activities such as classroom or laboratory instruction were simply too varied and idiosyncratic—even within a single institution—to be considered for the project. After prolonged discussion, three possible focuses for a benchmarking project were identified: student advising, curriculum development, and new faculty hiring. Although none of these three activities is part of the direct instruction and research that is the heart of the academic enterprise, each is a key support activity that closely affects the success of teaching and research. At a consortium meeting in late 1995, student advising was chosen as the process with the greatest potential for revealing best practices usable by all participants, as well as providing the best chance of successful and timely project completion.

Studying the Process

In the typical industrial benchmarking project, the next step would be for each participant to closely study their process: mapping it as appropriate, then deciding upon the key metrics and collecting process performance data. To accomplish this in the context of student advising, the consortium members first had to agree on what student advising actually consists of, and then decide what constitutes the key performance measures for that process.

The consortium's attempt to identify metrics and key performance measures for student advising illustrates the difficulty of applying benchmarking to the academic environment. There are a large number of different types of activities that could be considered part of student advising, some of which may take place when a prospective student first expresses interest in a given institution and others of which may take place upon ultimate graduation—as much as five or six years later. The advising can be done by mail or electronic communications, or through personal interactions with professional advisors, faculty members, other students, or a variety of other informal contacts. The content of the advising can include information about the institution, information about a student's individual progress, recommendations for course work and curricula, career advice, and even personal counseling.

Scope of the Process

To start, the consortium identified 35 activities commonly recognized as part of student advising (see Table 26.2). It quickly became clear that no benchmarking study could encompass such a wide variety of activities spread over a student's entire academic career. Therefore, to provide a focus for the benchmarking study and to assure that all interested AQC members would be able to participate, the study was restricted to include only those advising services delivered from the time a student first arrives at the institution as a freshman to the end of that student's first year of study.

Process Performance Measures

Defining key process performance measures and their corresponding metrics proved to be the most challenging aspect of this benchmarking exercise. The basic question can be most simply stated as follows: If one were to examine two higher education institutions, how could the better student advising process be identified? The question is not unlike one that might be asked about personal stock brokers or general practice physicians, both of whom make their living by suggesting courses of action deemed to be in the best personal interests of their clients. Presumably, the best stock brokers, physicians, and student advising systems would be those for which the clients made the most money, stayed the healthiest, and graduated on time. In the case of student advising, however, performance of the system is especially difficult to evaluate because of the number and complexity of intervening factors that can affect the ultimate "success" achieved from the recommendations.

To recognize superior performance in any process, the assessors must understand what the process is trying to accomplish. Also, the degree to which those goals or objectives are being met must be measured. For many years, practitioners have understood the difficulty of defining appropriate performance measures for the process of teaching. Developing such performance measures is complex, in part because much of a student's ultimate success in a course is outside the control of the instructor. Even so, students can be evaluated at the end of a course and some tentative, if largely statistically based, conclusions can be drawn about the relative effectiveness of instructors. These results can then be used as part of a search for best practices in teaching. With student advising, however, the ultimate measure of success—a student's timely graduation, and perhaps demonstrated capability in a degree-related job—occurs after a period of up to six years of contact with advisors. Given the enormous variety of internal and external influences on students in the course of their academic careers, how can it be said that any observed outcomes result directly from particular aspects of the advising system?

Table 26.2. The many activities of student advising.

Working with prospective and new students
- Pre-application institutional-fit advising
- Postapplication/pre-enrollment orientation advising
- Transfer student advising
- Clarifying expectations the institution has of its students
- Helping students through the mechanics of course registration
- Getting students to have continuing contact with the advising system

Working with students on their academic program
- Providing institutional information
- Exploring academic programs
- Assessing student needs, skills, and values in connection with possible majors
- Developing learning plans based on student goals
- Helping students choose courses for the coming term
- Advising on available resources
- Monitoring progress throughout the academic year
- Helping students identify and change majors
- Advising students with special needs
- Reassessing study plans throughout the academic year
- Performing graduation audits

Working with students on skills
- Giving students self-assessment skills
- Helping students learn to recognize their needs
- Teaching students how to go about achieving their potential

Working with students on nonacademic matters
- Placement testing
- Financial aid advising
- Career advising
- Personal counseling
- Crisis counseling
- Informal student-to-student advising
- Co-curricular advising
- Extracurricular advising

Administrative activities
- Selecting student advisors
- Training advisors in institutional information
- Training advisors in relationship skills
- Clarifying for advisors the role of advising
- Monitoring effectiveness of the advising process
- Using appropriate technology for graduation audits
- Using appropriate technology for making information available

Because the collaborative study was focused on student advising during a student's first year at the institution, it appeared that the only way to derive any timely "outcome" information would be to ask the students themselves. That is, the performance measures would have to be the students' own evaluations of the degree to which the advising system had met their needs. That decision led the consortium to an exploration of the ways in which advising systems might be considered to be meeting students' needs. Discussions in late 1996 with students and advising professionals identified six principal characteristics that students look for in an advising system. More or less in priority order, students gave the greatest value to advising systems that:

1. Provided accurate and understandable information about the institution and its programs

2. Provided accurate and understandable information about the student's own progress.

3. Offered advisors who cared about the students and treated them as adults.

4. Provided the students with good accessibility to advisors and information.

5. Provided helpful employment and career-related guidance.

6. Gave students the ability to take ownership of their own academic decisions.

Consortium members agreed that, for purposes of this demonstration project, it would be advantageous to select the most objective of these customer-identified performance measures. For that reason, the AQC focused on just three general measures of advising system performance, each of which actually evidences itself in several ways. These three areas of focus were:

1. The extent to which students received accurate and timely information about the institution, its academic requirements, and its curricular choices.

2. The extent to which students were informed in an accurate and timely manner about their own academic progress, and

3. The extent to which students felt that advising personnel and information was easily and appropriately accessible.

The consortium members believed that these three characteristics of an advising system not only help determine the satisfaction of the student-clients, but also are directly tied to the students' academic success—the ultimate performance measure of student advising.

The Satisfaction Survey

The overall goal of the collaborative benchmarking project was to identify, within the group of participating institutions, demonstrably more effective advising systems, which could then be studied to determine the specific practices and processes that allowed them to achieve their superior results. Accordingly, a survey instrument was developed that would allow students to relate performance of the advising system in the three activity areas with their overall assessment of advising system performance. A key design characteristic of the instrument was that it be relevant to all consortium participants—independent of the type of advising system used or the type of institution being surveyed. The preliminary survey instrument, developed in early 1996, is shown in Figure 26.1.

At the beginning of summer term 1996, the survey was pilot tested at four institutions: a community college, a private liberal arts college, a state-supported four-year college, and a major research university. Preliminary results indicated that students at the test institutions gave different ratings to various elements of the three main focus areas, but the sample sizes were insufficient to determine the extent to which statistically significant differences existed in any systematic fashion.

The next step will be for all participating institutions to administer the survey sometime during the fall 1997 term. The survey will be targeted to students just starting their second year of study. The hope is that some advising systems will be evaluated by students as being superior to others, and that some systematic pattern of system characteristics will emerge as explanatory factors. That will set the stage for further examination of the exact processes that brought about superior system performance.

Conclusion

As with most pilot tests and demonstration projects, this collaborative benchmarking study has been a learning experience for its participants. The problems encountered have reflected both the relatively inefficient organizational context of the project and the great difficulties inherent in dealing with academic processes.

The Project Context

In the typical business benchmarking project, the company starts by identifying a key process that has clear bottom-line significance. The economic significance of the process gives the company the incentive to focus organizational resources on benchmarking and subsequently to implement the improvements that it discovers. In traditional nonprofit higher education—particularly as it involves the instruction function—the customary incentive of bottom-line improvement is largely absent. Additionally, because institutional power is often extremely diffuse, the decision to focus resources on an academic benchmarking project is frequently made on a local level only.

The business sector has found that companies trying to implement benchmarking projects in a half-hearted manner—as a local decision without strong top-level commitment and as an activity somewhat low on the priority list—often end up abandoning the effort or, at best, deriving only minimal benefit from their work. The institutions making up the Academic Quality Consortium have voluntarily come together to explore the value of quality management principles, but their common interest in these managerial

We need your help to further improve the advising services we offer to students. This survey asks questions about the advising that you experienced during your <u>first</u> year of study at this institution.

This section asks about the information you received from advisors.

1. Before you started attending this institution, how helpful was the advising information you received?

   ☐ I didn't receive any information ☐ Not at all helpful ☐ Not very helpful ☐ Somewhat helpful ☐ Quite helpful ☐ Extremely helpful

2. After you began your studies here, how helpful was the advising information you received?

   ☐ I didn't receive any information ☐ Not at all helpful ☐ Not very helpful ☐ Somewhat helpful ☐ Quite helpful ☐ Extremely helpful

3. In your first year of studies at this institution, how many times did you meet with an advisor?

   ☐ Never ☐ Once ☐ Twice ☐ Three times ☐ Four times ☐ More than four times

4. How knowledgeable were advisors about this institution and its programs?

   ☐ I'm not sure ☐ Not at all knowledgeable ☐ Not very knowledgeable ☐ Somewhat knowledgeable ☐ Quite knowledgeable ☐ Extremely knowledgeable

5. How knowledgeable were advisors about you and the courses you had taken?

   ☐ I'm not sure ☐ Not at all knowledgeable ☐ Not very knowledgeable ☐ Somewhat knowledgeable ☐ Quite knowledgeable ☐ Extremely knowledgeable

6. How accurate was the academic information you received from advisors?

   ☐ I'm not sure ☐ Not at all accurate ☐ Not very accurate ☐ Reasonably accurate ☐ Very accurate ☐ Extremely accurate

7. How useful was information from advisors about specific academic majors?

   ☐ I didn't need any information ☐ I didn't receive any information ☐ Not at all useful ☐ Somewhat useful ☐ Quite useful ☐ Extremely useful

8. How useful was information received from advisors about career choices?

   ☐ I didn't need any information ☐ I didn't receive any information ☐ Not at all useful ☐ Somewhat useful ☐ Quite useful ☐ Extremely useful

9. How helpful were advisors in referring you to appropriate information sources when needed?

   ☐ It was never needed ☐ I was never referred ☐ I was seldom referred ☐ I was often referred ☐ I was usually referred ☐ I was always referred

This section asks how you were treated by advisors.

10. How frequently in your meetings with advisors did you feel that advisors cared about you as a person?

    ☐ I didn't notice ☐ Virtually not at all ☐ Only on rare occasions ☐ Some of the time ☐ Most of the time ☐ All of the time

11. How easy was it to obtain information from advisors on how well you were doing academically?

    ☐ I never tried ☐ It was almost impossible ☐ It was very difficult ☐ It was not too hard ☐ It was pretty easy ☐ It was very easy

Figure 26.1. Student advising survey.

12. How long did you have to wait for an appointment to obtain advising information?

☐ Appointments are not always needed ☐ The same day ☐ One day in advance ☐ Two days in advance ☐ Three days in advance ☐ More than three days in advance

13. How long did you have to wait at the advisor's office to obtain advising information?

☐ I never tried ☐ I never had to wait ☐ At most 10 minutes ☐ At most 20 minutes ☐ At most 30 minutes ☐ More than 30 minutes

14. How frequently in your meetings with advisors did you feel that advisors treated you with respect?

☐ I didn't notice ☐ Virtually not at all ☐ Only on rare occasions ☐ Some of the time ☐ Most of the time ☐ All of the time

15. How frequently in your meetings with advisors did they "personalize" the service they provided to you?

☐ I didn't notice ☐ Virtually not at all ☐ Only on rare occasions ☐ Some of the time ☐ Most of the time ☐ All of the time

16. How frequently in your meetings with advisors did they make you feel more "at home" at this school?

☐ I didn't notice ☐ Virtually not at all ☐ Only on rare occasions ☐ Some of the time ☐ Most of the time ☐ All of the time

This question asks for your overall evaluation of the advising system.

17. Taking all your experiences into account, how satisfied are you with the advising services we provide?

☐ I never used the advising system ☐ Very dissatisfied ☐ Somewhat dissatisfied ☐ Neither satisfied nor dissatisfied ☐ Reasonably satisfied ☐ Extremely satisfied

Information you give us in this section will help us further improve our advising services to you.

18. Once classes started, where did you end up finding the best information about programs and courses?

19. What do you think is the greatest strength of the advising system we provide to you?

20. What frustrated you most about the advising system we provide to you?

21. Is there anything else you would like to tell us?

22. How many credit hours of instruction have you completed at this institution?

_____ ☐ Semester hours

_____ ☐ Quarter hours

Figure 26.1. *(Continued).*

techniques is motivated more by intellectual curiosity than by financial necessity. To the extent that the incentive for participating in this project is more altruistic than economic, it is difficult for the consortium to muster the institutional resources needed for a classic benchmarking effort. Additionally, because the AQC meets only twice a year, it is, by nature, an inefficient mechanism for coordinating a project requiring detailed planning, committed participation, and tight deadlines.

Collaborative benchmarking, moreover, starts with all the difficulties and pitfalls of traditional benchmarking and then imposes the additional burden of coordinating simultaneous activities by participating organizations. The author's experience leading industrial projects in collaborative benchmarking is that success can be achieved only if all participants believe they have a substantial personal interest in the project results, and are pushed by top management to fully participate in project activities. To the extent such top management commitment is less evident in the AQC project, there is decreased assurance that the project will be carried out to full completion.

Academic Benchmarking

The great difficulty of applying benchmarking techniques to instruction and research was discussed earlier in this chapter. In summary, the problem is two-fold: adequate process performance measures are often not available or difficult to measure, and the complexity and interacting nature of academic processes—compounded by the long-term horizons involved—make it extremely hard to connect individual processes with their purported performance measures. By grappling with these problems now, however, the AQC is helping better identify the extent of the challenge and is blazing a trail that will almost certainly be followed by other institutions. As the world of higher education becomes more competitive, spurred in part by the increasing success of for-profit educational institutions and web-based instructional opportunities, the economic incentive may become strong enough to encourage more focused institutional effort on individual and collaborative benchmarking projects.

About the Author

Stefan D. Bloomfield is a professor of management in the College of Business at Oregon State University, where he teaches graduate and undergraduate courses in quality management and the decision sciences. He serves as the project director for the AQC collaborative benchmarking effort described in this chapter.

Bloomfield earned his master's degree and Ph.D. in operations research from Stanford University. His current research focuses on the application of quality management concepts and techniques to the service sector and governmental organizations. For several years he has served as an examiner for the Oregon Quality Award, and has directed over 40 comprehensive quality assessments of industrial, service-sector, and governmental organizations.

Bloomfield's international consulting focuses on managerial aspects of quality management. He works with senior management to plan the organization's approach to quality management and helps mobilized the workforce to achieve it.

The author may be contacted as follows:

Stefan D. Bloomfield
College of Business
Oregon State University
Bexell Hall 200
Corvallis, Oregon 97331-2603
Telephone: 541-737-6056
Facsimile: 541-737-4890
E-mail: bloomfld@bus.orst.edu

CHAPTER 27

Law Research Supervision at Queensland University of Technology

Helen Stacy, Research Fellow, Queensland University of Technology

Overview

The tertiary education sector in Australia has undergone radical changes in the last decade, precipitated by changing federal governments, each pursuing different ideological agendas. The first upheavals occurred in the late 1980s under a Labour federal government, when the two-tier system of universities and teachers' colleges and Colleges of Advanced Education were amalgamated. The result was that the number of Australian universities almost tripled. In Queensland, three separate tertiary campuses amalgamated in 1989 to become Queensland University of Technology (QUT). The second upheaval came in 1996 when a new conservative Liberal/National Party Coalition federal government delivered a budget that slashed government spending to the tertiary education sector. For QUT, this placed an acute emphasis on achieving the highest quality outcomes in its core activities of teaching and research.

Common to the otherwise quite different approaches within the Australian tertiary education sector has been the need for university processes to become more competitive in the globalized economy for the discerning student dollar and for competitive research funding. At QUT, emphasis needed to be placed on academic and postgraduate research as a new area of excellence that had been less emphasized in its pre-amalgamation days as a College of Advanced Education and Institute of Technology. In 1995, the university allocated funds to each of its 10 faculties to undertake benchmarking exercises into their research-related processes. In the faculty of law, an area of desired improvement was the need to increase numbers of postgraduate research students (that is, students enrolled as master's, doctor of juridical science (SJD), and Ph.D. candidates) within the context of limited resources, and at the same time, ensuring that the quality of postgraduate education was not compromised.

Background

The faculty of law seeks to encourage meritorious research. This is developed in postgraduate students through supervision of postgraduate degrees by research (Ph.D., SJD, and master's of law by research). It is potentially facilitated through external granting agencies that allow project-related research teams and individuals to be based within the faculty. The outcomes of these activities are publications of research by academic staff and research students in journals, monographs, and conference papers.

Early in the process, three topics for benchmarking were identified. They lie broadly within the federal government portfolio that administers the higher education sector, the Department of Employment, Education, Training, and Youth Affairs (DEETYA) Competitive Research Index (CRI). The CRI sets out the criteria for good research outcomes within Australian universities: the number of postgraduate research students who complete their postgraduate degrees; success in attracting funding for competitive research grants; and research publications. When contemplating the benchmarking topic to assess the law faculty's performance within the CRI, the direction and focus of the benchmarking exercise were guided by the law faculty's own planning objectives that reflect the university's broader objectives, but also articulate objectives that are specific to the law faculty.

Under the faculty of law's strategic plan for 1995–2000, the faculty aims to be within the top 10 law schools in Australia, and aims to achieve a significant international profile in research endeavors. In benchmarking the faculty of law's performance in the areas of postgraduate (by research) students, research grants, and research publications, an objective of the benchmarking process was to produce recommendations of ways that its research performance may be enhanced in line with faculty goals. These goals lie within the context of the QUT law faculty's competitive position relative to other Queensland and Australian law schools. The goals also lie within the funding and infrastructure opportunities and constraints offered and provided by the QUT universitywide context.

The initial step in the benchmarking process was to select a benchmarking topic that would further one of the faculty's primary goals: to increase the numbers of postgraduate research students. This goal is based on the rationale that encouraging greater numbers of excellent students to engage in postgraduate research would enhance the research profile of the faculty. The objectives of the benchmarking exercise were to understand the processes that attract and retain research postgraduates to the faculty, that result in postgraduate completions, and that contribute to the quality of faculty research.

Team Operations

Expressions of interest in the benchmarking exercise from academic staff in the faculty of law were called in July 1995. The need to have representatives from the faculty office and from each of the four recently created faculty organizational units (law school, justice studies, legal practice, and research and postgraduate programs) was emphasized because of the divisions and rivalries that had sprung up within the faculty following this organizational restructure. A team of eight academic staff from across the faculty, assisted by the senior administration officer and chaired by the acting director of research, was formed.

Three members of the team attended a benchmarking workshop organized by the university in May 1995. An information base, consisting of articles and videos about benchmarking processes, was also gathered to supplement the workshop. Since benchmarking has, to this point, been primarily an industry practice, this material needed careful examination for aspects that would be most usefully adopted in the higher education sector.

Approach, Conduct, and Method of Investigation

Current Processes Reviewed

A subgroup of the benchmarking team collated and documented the formal and informal processes and practices relating to the enrollment, supervision, and examination of research postgraduate students (Figure 27.1). Related activities such as advertising postgraduate degrees and the faculties available for postgraduate students were also canvassed.

Additional information from research postgraduate students about their reasons for electing to study in the faculty, their perception of facilities and supervision, and the particular needs generated by their postgraduate research was gathered using two methods.

1. All research postgraduate students were surveyed by mail. The survey document (Figure 27.2) asked both multiple-choice and open-ended questions. About 64 percent of all enrolled students answered the survey. Respondents included 75 percent of the Ph.D. and LLM (master's of law) students, 67 percent of the SJD students, and 25 percent of the MLP (master's of legal practice) students. Results of the survey are detailed in a later section of this chapter.

2. Two focus groups were held to discuss the survey questions, and to have a forum on any other matters students wished to discuss. Again, the results of these discussions are detailed later in this chapter.

Academic staff were also surveyed with a separate document (Figure 27.3) that asked questions related to supervision and support of research students, as well as faculty and university support for academic staff in their supervisory role. Thirty-three responses were received from faculty, representing 47 percent of the staff. See the "Results" section for further details.

Student and Faculty Profiles

Student profile. A summary of statistics profiling the research postgraduate students at QUT in 1995 is shown in Figure 27.4.

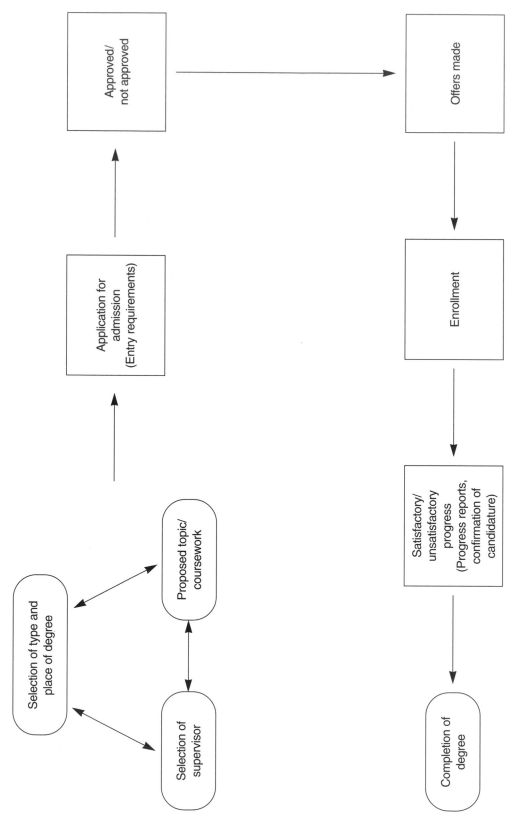

Figure 27.1. Enrollment, supervision, and examination processes at QUT.

Survey of Postgraduate by Research Students
Faculty of Law
Queensland University of Technology

Name: _____

Directions: Please circle your answer for each of the following questions. Use the back for additional space.

1. Why did you decide to pursue a postgraduate by research degree?
   A. Inspired by a class taken in undergraduate degree or other studies
   B. Will be helpful in practice
   C. Strong interest in a particular subject
   D. Interested in pursuing a career in academia
   E. Inspired by a researcher
   F. Other. Please explain.

2. Why did you decide to pursue your postgraduate degree at QUT?
   A. Desire to work with a particular academic (supervisory strengths)
   B. Perceived research strengths of faculty
   C. Quality and prestige of faculty
   D. Resources (i.e., library, computing, office, etc.)
   E. Grant offer
   F. Scholarship offer
   G. Location
   H. Other. Please explain.

3. Was the availability of child care facilities on campus significant to your ability to undertake or complete postgraduate studies?
   A. Yes
   B. No

4. If you have used them, have the child care services at QUT been adequate?
   A. Yes
   B. No

5. What sources of information regarding institutional requirements did you use to help you with your decision to apply to QUT? (Circle all that apply.)
   A. Application
   B. QUT Ph.D. handbook
   C. Faculty of Law Postgraduate Student Information Booklet
   D. Administrators
   E. Other. Please explain.

6. What sources of information regarding faculty research and supervisory strengths did you use to help you with your decision to apply to QUT? (Circle all that apply.)
   A. Application packet
   B. Word of mouth
   C. Continuing education programs, seminars, conferences, etc.
   D. Other. Please explain.

Figure 27.2. Survey of postgraduate research students (October 1995).

7. What sources of information, if any, regarding financial resources, i.e., scholarships and grants, did you use while applying for admission to QUT? (Circle all that apply.)

A. Application packet

B. QUT staff

C. Law faculty staff

D. Did not inquire about grants and scholarships

E. Other. Please explain.

8. Did you consider your research skills prior to entering the postgraduate program to be adequate for the purposes of postgraduate study?

A. Yes

B. No

9. If no, were you able to enroll in a course or otherwise secure further tuition to improve your research skills?

A. Yes

B. No

10. Is tuition as mentioned above essential to undertake and complete postgraduate studies?

A. Yes

B. No

11. Were you involved with an already existent, ongoing research project at QUT before beginning your post-graduate studies?

A. Yes. Briefly describe your involvement.

B. No

12. How did you identify your supervisor when you decided to pursue a postgraduate degree at QUT?

A. Discussions with the head of the school

B. Discussions with the director of a center or research concentration

C. Contact through your own professional experience/previous work with him/her

D. A third party's recommendation

E. Had taken a class with him/her as an undergraduate

F. Read a publication of his/hers or seen him/her give a presentation

G. Other. Please explain.

13. How often did you meet with/speak to your intended supervisor prior to approval of application (regarding your application and research interests)?

A. One time

B. 2–3 times

C. 4–5 times

D. More than 5 times

14. How did you decide upon your proposed topic of research?

A. Long-standing interest

B. Previous research

C. Wanted to work with a particular faculty member that was interested in that topic

D. Involvement in an ongoing research project at QUT

E. Inspired by a class taken for undergraduate degree or other studies

F. Relationship to your job

G. Other. Please explain.

Figure 27.2. *(Continued).*

15. What academic resources are available to you as a postgraduate student? (Please tick all that apply.)
    A. Office
    B. Computing
    C. Library access
    D. Administrative support
    E. Telephone
    F. Other. Please explain.

16. What other resources are available to you as a postgraduate student?
    A. Staff common room
    B. Tea/coffee-making facilities
    C. Other. Please explain.

17. Do you use these resources?
    A. Yes
    B. No

18. What is the frequency of face-to-face contact that you have with your supervisor?
    A. More than once a week
    B. Once a week
    C. Once a fortnight
    D. Once a month
    E. Less than once a month

19. What other contact do you have with your supervisor?
    A. Telephone
    B. E-mail
    C. Other. Please explain.

20. Has involvement in collaborative projects with the staff ever been suggested to you?
    A. Yes
    B. No

21. Would you like to be involved with an existing, ongoing research project in collaboration with a member of the QUT law faculty?
    A. Yes
    B. No
    C. Am already involved. Briefly describe your involvement.

22. How do you find the research environment?
    A. Supportive/helpful
    B. Lonely
    C. Competitive
    D. Not supportive

23. Do you have contact with postgraduate students from other universities?
    A. Yes
    B. No

Figure 27.2. *(Continued).*

24. To what extent are you involved in law faculty activities?
    A. Attend staff seminars
    B. Have given/have been invited to give a paper at a staff seminar
    C. Minimal involvement
    D. Other. Please explain.

25. Is there encouragement from people within the department for postgraduates to publish their work?
    A. Yes
    B. No

26. Since your enrollment as a postgraduate, has any of your work been published?
    A. Yes
    B. No

27. Is there encouragement from people within the department for postgraduates to present papers at conferences or seminars outside the department?
    A. Yes
    B. No

28. Since your enrollment as a postgraduate, have your attended conferences relevant to your research or field?
    A. Yes
    B. No

29. During your course of study at QUT, have you been invited to present a paper at a conference or seminar outside the department?
    A. Yes
    B. No

30. Are you involved in or associate with a research concentration or center?
    A. Yes
    B. No

31. If yes, which concentration/center? Please explain your involvement.

32. What formal or informal systems do you think ought to be implemented to further assist you while pursing your degree? (Please specify formal or informal.)

33. Please add any additional comments.

Figure 27.2. *(Continued).*

Survey of Academic Staff
Faculty of Law
Queensland University of Technology

Name: _____

Directions: Please circle your answer for each of the following questions.

1. In what way are you involved in influencing people to enter into a postgraduate by research degree?
    A. Assign a research paper as part of the assessment for an undergraduate class
    B. Employ undergraduate research assistants to help on projects
    C. Vocal encouragement to undergraduate students who show promise
    D. Encouragement through networking with people who are practicing in the profession
    E. Other. Please explain.

2. If an undergraduate student approaches you with interest in pursuing a postgraduate by research degree, what encouragement to you give him/her?
    A. Speak to the student myself
    B. Refer the student to someone else. Who? _____

3. If a student approaches you with questions about institutional requirements for postgraduate by research study, what resources do you refer him/her to?
    A. Application packet
    B. QUT Ph.D. handbook
    C. Faculty of Law Postgraduate Student Information Booklet
    D. Administrators
    E. I am unfamiliar with the available resources.
    F. Other. Please explain.

4. Have you involved potential postgraduate by research students in research projects that you are working on?
    A. Yes. Briefly explain their involvement.
    B. No.

5. If you have involved potential postgraduate by research students, have those students entered postgraduate by research studies?
    A. Yes
    B. No

6. Have you involved postgraduate by research students in existing, ongoing research projects that you are working on?
    A. Yes. Briefly explain their involvement.
    B. No

7. Do you consider there to be a research culture in the law faculty?
    A. Yes
    B. No

8. How would you define "research culture" in a way that would respond to your needs?

Figure 27.3. Survey of academic staff (October 1995).

9. How do you consider postgraduates (by research) are perceived by the staff?
   A. As peers
   B. As students
   C. Other. Please explain.

10. In what areas of research are you willing and consider yourself competent to supervise postgraduate research?

11. At what level?
   A. Masters
   B. SJD
   C. Ph.D.

12. Please add any additional comments on the back.

The following questions are for people who are currently supervising or have previously supervised postgraduate by research students at QUT.

13. How many (approximately) QUT research students have you previously supervised?

14. Have you ever had formal training to be a supervisor of a postgraduate by research degree?
   A. Yes
   B. No

15. How often do you have face-to-face contact with the student(s) you are supervising?
   A. More than once a week
   B. Once a week
   C.   Once a fortnight
   D. Once a month
   E. Less than once a month

16. What other contact do you have with the student(s) your are supervising?
   A. Telephone
   B. E-mail
   C. Other. Please explain.

17. What percentage of teaching time do you spend on research student supervision?

Figure 27.3. *(Continued).*

18. Has a student you have supervised ever discontinued his/her postgraduate degree?
    A. Yes. Please explain the reasons.
    B. No

19. Have you ever encouraged a student to discontinue his/her postgraduate degree?
    A. Yes. Please explain the reasons.
    B. No

20. Do you encourage postgraduates to seek publication for their work?
    A. Yes
    B. No

21. Do you encourage postgraduates to seek invitations to give papers at conferences?
    A. Yes
    B. No

22. Overall, from a personal and professional perspective, how do you rate your experience of research supervision at QUT?
    A. Very poor
    B. Poor
    C. Fair
    D. Good
    E. Very good
    F. Excellent

Figure 27.3. *(Continued).*

Number of students enrolled as of November 1995.

Degree	Female			Male			Totals		
	Part-time	Full-time	Total	Part-time	Full-time	Total	Part-time	Full-time	Total
Ph.D.	1	3	4	3	1	4	4	4	8
SJD	3	1	4	4	1	5	7	2	9
LLM	2	0	2	2	0	2	4	0	4
MLP	1	0	1	2	1	3	3	1	4
Totals	7	4	11	11	3	14	18	7	25

Students by gender and study time.

Gender	Percentage of research postgraduates	Study part-time	Study full-time
Female	44	63.6	44
Male	56	78.6	21.4

Degree type.

Degree	Percent of research postgraduates
Ph.D.	32
SJD	36
LLM	16
MLP	16

Employment.

Organization	Number of students
QUT	8
University of Queensland	2
Griffith University	2
Government services	6
Private practice	1
Unknown	6

Scholarships.

Scholarship	Number of students
QUT Postgraduate Research Awards	2
Australian Postgraduate Awards	1

Average years of completion.

Degree	Part-time	Full-time
Ph.D.	4.5	3.3
SJD	5.2	2.8
LLM	2.6	Not applicable
MLP	3.7	1

Figure 27.4. Summary of statistics of research postgraduate students at QUT.

Faculty profile. The faculty of law at QUT in 1995 consisted of 69 academic staff members, of which 52 percent are female and 48 percent are male. The centers or areas of concentration include the following: center for commercial and property law; center for crime prevention; research concentration in environmental law; research concentration in public law; and research concentration in civil litigation. A summary of law faculty policies and support structures for postgraduate research students follows:

Procedures established

- Research and Postgraduate Studies Committee
- Manual of procedure for Master's of Laws students
- List of academic supervisors of postgraduate students and their areas of academic specialty
- Policy on resourcing research students
- Six monthly supervisors and students reports for master's of laws (by research), SJD, and Ph.D. students
- Ethics advisors within the faculty (senior academics)
- Examiners provided with copy of course regulations

Developing procedures

- Seminars and workshops on supervision
- Review of monthly reports for master's students

Informal procedures

- Funding for students to attend conferences
- Scholarships and tutorial assistance
- Seminars on ethics
- Candidate appeal process against nominations of an examiner
- Advice and support to English-as-a-second-language students and to international students

Study Topic

An initial list of more than 14 benchmarking topics within the broad category of "research" was eventually narrowed to two. These were recruitment of high-quality postgraduate students; and external competitive grant development within the law faculty.

Recruitment of high-quality postgraduate students included the following: the progression of honors undergraduates to postgraduate study; selected focus and groupings of course work masters of laws subjects; directed research of students within identified faculty research concentrations; targeted scholarship databases; infrastructure support; adequacy of student supervision and student progress; inclusion of postgraduate students in grant application processes; and the development of a "laboratory," or group, research ethos within a discipline that historically conducted sole-researcher activities.

External competitive grant development included the following: mechanisms to increase academic staff grant-writing abilities; enhancing information flow between the law faculty and the University Office of Research; increasing staff collaborative research knowledge and information flow; increasing the focus of research grants within faculty areas of research concentration; and staff time management strategies to enhance grant application quality (and hence enhance the rate of successful grant applications).

The team wanted to use the benchmarking activity to review processes that were generically applicable across each of the four faculty functional units. Ultimately, it was decided to benchmark the processes related to the enrollment and supervision of research postgraduate students. The reason for this undertaking was threefold: (1) within the broader university context, there were relatively few law research postgraduate students; (2) a master's in justice studies was introduced in 1995; and (3) the master's of legal practice was being phased out by 1998.

Selecting a Benchmarking Partner

Using a variety of publicly available information, at least three other Australia law schools were profiled for comparison with QUT. The criteria for selection were matters such as similarity in numbers of academic staff and similarity in

- Faculty age

- Research record

- Variety of research topics undertaken by the interstate law faculty

This latter consideration was important to ensure that the information from the benchmarking partner would be relevant across QUT faculty organizational units.

The faculty of law at the University of New South Wales (UNSW) was selected as the preferred benchmarking partner, with the law faculty of another Australian university selected as an alternative if UNSW was not disposed to participate in the benchmarking activity. A brief comparison of QUT and UNSW is shown in Figure 27.5.

The benchmarking team also considered the utility of benchmarking with an American institution. It was felt that a second or subsequent benchmarking exercise might usefully look at overseas jurisdictions. It was the opinion of the benchmarking team, however, that the highly jurisdiction-specific nature of legal research would make the practices of Australian law schools more directly relevant to the QUT law faculty in the short term.

Benchmarking Visit

Initial contact with the UNSW law faculty was made in October 1995. They were favorably disposed to QUT's request, but senior law faculty staff changes at UNSW meant that the project could not be further pursued until early 1996.

Key measure	QUT	UNSW
Australian Research Council grant ($A)	(1995) $15,188 ($A18,663)	(1993) $73,849 ($A90,746)
Other research grants ($A)	$50,456 ($A62,000)	Unknown
Postgraduate research students	(1995) 18	(1994) 25
Publications	(1994) 62	Unknown Unknown

Figure 27.5. Comparison of law schools: QUT and UNSW.

The formal benchmarking visit occurred in July 1996. Two members of the QUT study team met with UNSW law faculty's director of postgraduate studies, the director of research, and a faculty administrator. Over the course of one day, the respective teams from QUT and UNSW discussed the UNSW procedures relating to enrollment, supervision, and examination of research postgraduate students. Relevant documents were exchanged, and Ph.D. student office facilities were toured.

Results

From the Site Visit

QUT team members describe the site visit as "illuminating." They found that the relative maturity of UNSW's law faculty postgraduate research provided many opportunities to adopt and/or adapt UNSW processes to those at QUT. Best practices with regard to serving overseas students and the time spent prior to formal student enrollment to ensure a match between student and supervisor were shown to pay dividends in terms of completion rate of research degrees.

International students. The first international students enrolled in law research degree programs at UNSW in the early 1990s. When considering admission for international students, UNSW borrowed from a model at the University of Adelaide, which requires international students to go through an orientation process. The cut-off scores for examinations testing English proficiency are the same for postgraduate international students and UNSW's international undergraduate students. Students with no Australian background are encouraged to enroll in a course called "Australian Legal Systems." The university, not the UNSW faculty, offers facilities to non-English speaking students, who are encouraged to undertake research subjects at either the postgraduate or undergraduate level.

At UNSW, international students are admitted on the basis of a written application only. The director of postgraduate studies conducts the admission process by evaluating the candidate; finding a suitable supervisor; and assisting the student to find the right research topic. Students are not admitted until their topic is approved by their supervisor. Some international students are encouraged to enroll in the master's by thesis program, and then upgrade to a Ph.D. if they demonstrate that they are capable of the next level of research and scholarship.

Student enrollment. An increase in the number of full-time students at UNSW demanded enlarged and improved facilities to house them. A postgraduate students' room is available to all full-time research students. The room can accommodate 10 students, offering each student a desk, lockable file cabinet, a computer, as well as a communal telephone. Postage and stationery is paid for by the faculty, and yearly assistance is given to enable students to attend conferences. Advice about the availability of these funds is provided to students prior to enrollment. Upon request, external students of the faculty have after-hours access to the faculty and law library.

Student admission. At UNSW, postgraduate research students are required to provide two referees; describe their research project; note who they would like as a supervisor; and detail with whom they have discussed their potential enrollment. Students do not submit any formal paperwork until they are ready to start their research. Students who do not have anyone prepared to supervise their project do not submit their application. This procedure differs from other faculties, such as science, where students frequently select their topic from the research group's current topics.

UNSW stresses that applicants must provide referees, and reports from the nominated referees are called for at the beginning of the application process. Students may be rejected on the basis of a referee's report. The UNSW faculty's quick response to applications at this early point in the enrollment process accounts for the high number of postgraduate students enrolled in the faculty.

References are not called for international students because of the delays in chasing overseas reports. The series of checks and balances is, however, quite intense. For example, potential supervisors will often check the veracity of the qualifications of potential overseas students.

Review process. A review process is initiated three months into a full-time Ph.D. and master's (by research) enrollment and six months into part-time enrollment. Review documents are not submitted to the law faculty's Executive Committee of the Research and Postgraduate Studies Committees until they are acceptable to the student's supervisor(s). The executive committee consists of the director of postgraduate studies as the presiding member of the faculty; an academic staff member to the law dean; and a representative of postgraduate studies in the university administration. Any member of the executive committee may stop the review process; however, reviews are automatically on the committee's meeting agenda. After this initial review, reports are provided to the research committee by the student every 12 months for a Ph.D. student and every six months for a master's student.

Confirmation of candidature. Confirmation of candidature at UNSW does not take the form of a one-off seminar, as it does at QUT. As part of the review process, UNSW students are initially expected to present a faculty seminar, and then a university rule requires that, thereafter, students do one seminar once a year. Frequently, however, that is not practicable, and usually one or two will be presented throughout the course.

From the Student and Faculty Surveys and Focus Groups

Results from the QUT postgraduate student and law faculty surveys and focus groups revealed a wide variety of recommendations to better meet the needs of research postgraduate students. They included the following:

Preadmission.

- Have the faculty research program profile in print and freely available (for example, on the Internet).
- Include in the profile the rules for entry, potential supervisors' research profiles and supervisors' current postgraduates' topics, and resources available to postgraduate students.
- Have a formalized structure in place whereby potential postgraduates must meet with their supervisors during the application process.

Orientation/induction.

- Conduct these sessions during the lunch hour or during the evenings, but not on the weekends when staff are not available.
- Have orientation sessions last two to four hours.
- Provide a tour of the library and law faculty building.
- Provide a library induction.
- Provide a research postgraduate packet that includes information on thesis word limits, style guide, faculty's usual form of supervision, available resources, and important telephone numbers.

Computing.

- Develop a home page on the Internet. It should provide the packet information to potential postgraduates and should announce upcoming seminars and updated lists of grants and scholarships.
- Provide E-mail addresses to postgraduates.
- Encourage supervisors to use E-mail.
- Provide postgraduates access to computers and CD-ROMs.

Culture change.

- Encourage postgraduates to apply to be tutors within the law faculty.
- Invite postgraduates to faculty research-in-progress and visiting academic seminars.

Research postgraduate seminars.

- Form a postgraduate law student association.
- Have voluntary presentations of research topics.
- Provide food, wine, and a keynote speaker at seminars. Some staff may attend as well.
- Make attendance mandatory.
- Hold seminars during the week, not on weekends.

Resources.

- Give photocopy/reproduction rights to postgraduates or provide access to inexpensive photocopying.
- Provide more information about available grants.

Coursework.

- Continue the "Advanced Legal Research" class; it is excellent.
- Encourage cross-institutional and cross-faculty courses.

Best Practices Discovered

Three aspects of the UNSW practices stood out as examples that ensure successful conduct and completion of a research postgraduate degree. They are

1. Careful match of the research student with the supervisor(s), bearing in mind the student's anticipated career path, the academic's research interests, and the academic's ability to spend the requisite time with the particular student. For example, non-English speaking background (NESB) students frequently require more assistance in the first 12 months of their enrollment, and young (as compared with mature-age) students require close supervision for the first two-thirds of their enrollment.

2. The provision of desk and computing facilities for full-time students in one location so that students can provide support for each other, and 24-hour access to faculty facilities, including the library.

3. A perception that it is proper to refuse enrollment and supervision for a proposed thesis topic that does not fall, at least tangentially, within available academic professional expertise.

Other points to note were as follows:

• NESB students would ideally be assigned a faculty contact prior to their arrival in Australia. Refinement of their thesis topic could, therefore, commence at an early stage.

• Because of the particular historical trajectory of legal academic professional promotion, it was not correct to assume that a law academic who had written a thesis had adequate supervisory skill; nor was it correct to assume that an academic who had not written a thesis had inadequate advisory skills. Thus, supervisory skills were, in part, a faculty obligation to ensure regular training of academic staff.

Implementation Actions Taken

When the full benchmarking report was completed it was submitted to the faculty's Research and Postgraduate Studies Committee for consideration of its recommendations. This report was submitted in September 1997 and is currently under consideration. The major suggestion concerned ongoing training for academic staff embarking on research supervision. The recommendations encompassed the following:

• Enhancing the supervisory skills of the faculty of law. Two workshops were held to aid in staff development. The first, held in early July 1996, was conducted by the Queensland Higher Education Staff Development Consortium and Southern Cross University. It was the latest in a series of "train the trainer" programs on postgraduate supervision, each dealing with different target groups: that is, female staff, veteran university staff, and staff in the post-1987 amalgamated university. The general aim of the program was to empower staff from Queensland and north New South Wales universities with skills, knowledge, and positive attitudes, thus enabling them to feel more competent and confident to supervise NESB postgraduate students. One delegate from the QUT law faculty attended this workshop

The second workshop was held in the law faculty in April 1997, and was conducted by an associate professor from Griffith University in Queensland. The presenter is a world-renowned staff developer in tertiary education, particularly in the field of academic postgraduate supervision and research. Her skills in training the trainer in relation to postgraduate supervision are considered unique in Australia. Sixteen members of the faculty of law attended this workshop.

• Purchasing the videotapes and accompanying manuals that were shown at the workshop so that the entire faculty and staff could use them. This was done in August 1997.

• Provisioning infrastructure, resources, and information, similar to the structure in the undergraduate teaching program, that allows sufficient academic time for the provision of high-quality research supervision. This would require that a clear formula be devised, vis-à-vis the university and law faculty, for the provision of infrastructure for research students from the student fee base. Action under this recommendation presently lies with the faculty's director of research and director of postgraduate studies.

• Providing a rolling series of workshops in the law faculty to allow academic staff to constantly upgrade both their general supervisory skills, and skills that are specific to conducting research in the discipline of law.

• Devising and distributing, to all supervising academics, a booklet that contains the agglomeration of the Australia Vice-Chancellors' Committee (AVVC), QUT, and faculty rules, regulations, and recommendations at they relate to supervision. The Griffith University model, shown at the April 1997 workshop, was commended as a possible precedent for the QUT law faculty, provided it was tailored to QUT's specific needs. Action under this recommendation lies with the director of research and the director of postgraduate studies.

• Recognizing academic supervisory duties in the allocation of teaching responsibilities in the undergraduate teaching program. The action for this recommendation was assigned (via the report on the second workshop handed to the director to research) to the acting associate dean.

• Provisioning a faculty "supervision methods" course for academic staff and research students. The action for this recommendation was assigned to the director of research-in-programs.

• Provisioning a workshop for the supervision of LLM research projects. The action for this recommendation was assigned to two faculty lecturers.

• Reconsidering the current LLM coursework research paper examination arrangement, which has the supervisor also examining the paper. The action for this recommendation was assigned to the director of postgraduate studies.

Conclusions and Lessons Learned

The collation of QUT's faculty processes and practices related to research postgraduate students for the benchmarking exercise provided a useful opportunity to view them in total. The focus groups held with the postgraduate students provided a great deal of useful information about student perceptions of the benefits of a research postgraduate degree undertaken at QUT's law faculty. The staff survey emphasized the need for regular workshops relating to student supervision.

There was some concern that the specific activities of the faculty (for example, justice studies) could not be assisted unless the benchmarking partner also delivered a justice studies program. Part of the this concern was addressed by having two representatives from justice studies on the benchmarking team; however, they were unable to attend the site visit.

To date (August 1997) about $7500 ($A10,000) has been spent on this benchmarking exercise. The perceived benefits are

• An understanding of benchmarking as a tool of comparison of similar processes in a comparable law school in relation to postgraduate research degrees

• The opportunity to view the UNSW law faculty's approach toward enrolling, accommodating, and supervising its postgraduate students

• The opportunity to understand the different perspectives of the organizational units of the QUT law faculty to a benchmarking topic that held varying perceptions of relevance to those units

About the Author

Since 1990, Helen Stacy has served Queensland University of Technology (QUT) in a variety of roles, including lecturer-in-law, director of research, editor of the *QUT Law Journal*, and currently as research fellow in the faculty of law. Prior to joining QUT, Stacy worked throughout Australia as a solicitor, industrial lawyer, and legal officer. During the mid-1980s, she served as a senior legal advisor and senior crown prosecutor in England. In 1992, Stacy returned to Europe as a doctoral fellow at the Max-Planck-Institute for Comparative and Public International Law in Heidelberg, Germany. There, Stacy did most of her research for her doctoral thesis, *Environmental Law: Modernity to Postmodernity*. This is a comparative analysis of environmental legislation and policy in Australia, the two Germanies, and the united Germany.

Stacy has been involved in numerous competitive research grants, for most of which she was the sole researcher. Credits include the following:

• Australian Research Council Collaborative Grant: *Inquisitorial Skills and Fact Finding: Educating Judicial and Administrative Decision Makers*

• Australian Research Council Small Grant: *The Challenge of Poststructural Theory to the Legal System*

• University of Stellenbosch Research Program Sustainable: *Development and Environmental Justice: Participation and Minority Rights of the First Nation Peoples of South Africa*

• Canadian High Commission Faculty Research Program: *Sustainable Development and Environmental Justice: Participation and Minority Rights of the First Nation Peoples of Canada*

Stacy has authored many publications, including monograph chapters, journal articles, reports, and conference papers. Recent, selected titles include the following: *Feminism/ Postmodernism/Postfeminism* (Oxford University Press); *Postgraduate Supervision of Non-English Speaking Students* (Kogan Page); "Lacan's Split Subjects: Raced and Gendered Transformations" (*Legal Studies Forum*); and *Comparative Drought Paradigms: Australia and the Mid-West of the United States* (Natural Disasters Forum, Brisbane).

Stacy may be contacted as follows:

Dr. Helen Stacy
Research Fellow
Faculty of Law
Queensland University of Technology
G.P.O. Box 2434
Brisbane, Queensland 4001, Australia
Telephone: 61-7-3864 1101
Facsimile: 61-7-3864 4253
E-mail: h.stacy@qut.edu.au

PART 6: EDUCATION SECTOR

Analysis

Country:	United States
Organization:	Babson College
Industry:	Higher education industry
Process:	Enrollment management
Case Study Title:	*"Enrollment Management at Babson College"*

The benchmarking findings from comparing Babson College to five out of the seven top cross-application schools were crucial to success. Financial aid packages had to be adjusted to continue to attract some of the best applicants. The quality of social life led to the construction of a new campus center. A new engineering school being added to the campus will broaden offerings. And studying abroad, cross-offerings with other local institutions, helped overcome the limited availability of course work outside business disciplines.

Only a longer time line will tell if the best practices implemented through this traditional competitive benchmarking will lead to improved student enrollment. This could come either from attracting and retaining higher-quality students as well as reducing the cost of the enrollment process. But it is probably safe to observe that if the benchmarking had not been conducted the consequences would continue to show themselves in declining performance measures, if not more severe consequences.

Country:	United States
Organization:	Oregon State University
Industry:	Higher education industry
Process:	Student advising
Case Study Title:	*"Collaborative Benchmarking in Higher Education"*

The care in structuring the data and information collection instrument—in this case a survey sent to students—shows the meticulous application of the basic benchmarking principles to an academic process. This involved care in process definition, documentation, focus, and management; which, while academically difficult, was successfully accomplished. While the results are preliminary, in a pilot test, the survey was able to identify differences in three main focus areas of importance to students. And the results are not dependent on the type of academic institutions, of which four were covered in the survey.

The translation of the terminology from the industrial setting to the academic required some change in language. The following is the statement of the objective in academic terms: "The survey is being used to identify advising systems that are more effective to their customers, in this case the student, and, therefore, to determine the characteristics of these systems that lead to positive results."

In an industrial setting the statement could have been: "The critical core process of student advising, and its vital subprocesses, were identified and inventoried. Performance data from customers of the process will be used to identify those best practices that improve output results." This change of terminology from the industrial to academic setting shows that the translation can be made. After all, the benchmarking process itself is heavily related to the scientific method.

Country:	Australia
Organization:	Queensland University
Industry:	Higher education industry
Process:	Law research supervision
Case Study Title:	*"Law Research Supervision at Queensland University"*

Lessons learned and benefits derived from this study include the usefulness of understanding the processes and practices, as is the focus of most benchmarking today; as well as documenting student and faculty customer requirements, expectations, and needs. The perceived difficulties came from those traditionally associated with these types of comparisons, namely that they are credible and comparable. The process focus ensures the later.

While the results were not quantified, they are assumed to be non-inconsequential, especially when all costs of quality are considered. Compared to the nominal expenses for this type of study, the payback is substantial.

Summary Cost Savings and Benefits

United States	Europe	Asia/Pacific	Americas/Africa
EDUCATION UNITED STATES **Babson College** *Enrollment management* • 50% in top 10% of graduating class • Place in top 50 business schools • More selective application • Greater diversity • Lower attrition UNITED STATES **Oregon State University** *Student advising* • Academic process application • Promising pilot study results		AUSTRALIA **Queensland University** *Law research supervision* • Higher quality postgraduate intake	

Key Best Practices Found

United States	Europe	Asia/Pacific	Americas/Africa
EDUCATION UNITED STATES **Babson College** *Enrollment management* • Improved financial aid • Quality social life • Broader course offerings • Study abroad • Nontraditional course work UNITED STATES **Oregon State University** *Student advising* • Variability in three focus area 1. Institution information 2. Academic progress 3. Accessible advisors		AUSTRALIA **Queensland University** *Law research supervision* • Match student and faculty advisors prior to admission • Provide support facilities and access • Supervisory skills an obligation	

Lessons Learned

United States	Europe	Asia/Pacific	Americas/Africa

EDUCATION
 	
UNITED STATES
 	
Babson College
 	
Enrollment management
 	
• Benchmarking useful for educational processes.
• Challenges and opportunities are better understood.
• Six insights for enrollment identified.
• A college is not much different from other organizations.
 	
UNITED STATES
 	
Oregon State University
 	
Student advising
 	
• Collaborative benchmarking applicable to this process.
• Academic process difficulties overcome by
  —Using performance measures
  —Examining process complexity and time line
		AUSTRALIA
		
		Queensland University
		
		Law research supervision
		
		• Collation of processes helped overall view.
		• Student perceptions provide useful information.
		• Comparability concerns revealed during study.	

Case Study Sources

As noted at the beginning of this book, benchmarking is now global in that it touches nearly all, if not all types of, organizations, institutions, and industries. Thus, readers of this book may want references to finding additional case studies.

There are two categories covered in this section. One are the specific books, magazines, and other references where case studies, of equivalent length and coverage to those included in this book, are known to exist. The other is a search process that can be used to potentially find additional case studies, or mini-case descriptions that will serve as leads to the details.

Known Case Study References

Books

Several authors have included case studies in their books. Most of the more prominent are as follows:

Camp, Robert C. 1989. *Benchmarking: The search for industry best practices that lead to superior performance.* Milwaukee: ASQC Quality Press and White Plains, N.Y.: Quality Resources. Two case studies.

———. 1995. *Business process benchmarking: Finding and implementing best practices.* Milwaukee: ASQC Quality Press. Six case studies.

Codling, Sylvia, T. 1992. *Best practice benchmarking: An international perspective.* Houston, Tex.: Gulf. Seven case studies.

Mohammed Zairi. 1996. *Effective benchmarking: Learning from the best.* London: Chapman & Hall. Twenty case studies.

Magazines

Several magazines have made a practice of covering case study examples. Many of these are of a much abbreviated version than those included in this book, covering only a page or more. But they are useful none the less. Most prominent would be the following:

The Benchmark Magazine (Kempston, Bedford, UK: IFS International Ltd.)

Continuous Journey (Houston, Tex.: American Productivity & Quality Center)

Chief Financial Officer (CFO) (Boston: Economist Group)

Journal for Quality and Participation (Cincinnati, Ohio: Association for Quality and Participation)

Quality Progress (Milwaukee: American Society for Quality)

Target: Innovation at Work (Wheeling, Ill.: Association for Manufacturing Excellence)

Videotapes

There are a limited number of videotapes that cover benchmarking. They can be further researched by those interested. The most prominent are

The Harvard video series: Benchmarking outside the box. 1995. Cambridge, Mass.: Harvard Business School Video. Videocassette.

To be the best. 1995. London: British Broadcasting Company.

Benchmarking Centers

Currently, there are 17 centers spread throughout the globe, typically one per country. These are centers of competency for benchmarking and as such either catalog case studies from their members, publish case studies in their newsletters, or offer benchmarking awards that are published. A list of the benchmarking centers known to date of this book's release is as follows:

Global Benchmarking Organizations

AUSTRALIAN BENCHMARKING SERVICE
Australian Quality Council
69 Christie Street, Level 3
PO Box 298
St. Leonards, New South Wales 2065
AUSTRALIA
Internet   www.benchnet.com/AQC
Mr. Robert Mann, Project Manager
Telephone   61 2 9901 9999
Facsimile   61 2 9906 3286

EUROPEAN FOUNDATION FOR
QUALITY MANAGEMENT
Avenue des Pleiades 19
B–1200 Brussels
BELGIUM
Mr. Geoff Carter
Telephone   32 2 775 3511
Facsimile   32 2 775 3535

THE BENCHMARKING GROUP
c/o Grifo Enterprises, Secretary
Av. Rio Branco, 25, 16° Andar
Rio de Janeiro, RJ
BRAZIL
Dr. Rosangela Catunda, Vice President
Telephone   55 21 233 0870
Facsimile   55 21 233 7559

FINNISH BENCHMARKING CENTER
Nokia Telecommunications Oy
PO Box 44, Fin 02601
Espoo
FINLAND
Mr. Matti Lankinson, Manager
Complementary Systems Customer Service
Telephone   358 0 5112 2621
Facsimile   358 0 5122 2597

FINNISH SOCIETY FOR QUALITY
Mannerheimintie 160
00300 Helsinki
FINLAND
Internet   www.sly.fi
Ms. Marja Turunen, Program Director
E-mail   marja.turunen@sly.fi
Telephone   358 9 436 2218
Facsimile   358 9 436 1077

INSTITUT DU BENCHMARKING
8 Avenue Delcassé
75008 Paris
FRANCE
Mr. Jacques Errard, President
Telephone   33 1 53 77 35 60
Facsimile   33 1 53 77 35 61

INFORMATION ZENTRUM
BENCHMARKING
Fraunhofer Institute
Production Systems and Design
Technology
Pascalstrasse 8–9
D–10587 Berlin
GERMANY
Internet   www.izb.ipk.fhg.de
Mr. Martin Carbon, Manager
E-mail   martin.carbon@ipk.fhg.de
Telephone   49 30 390 06 264
Facsimile   49 30 393 2503

INSTITUTE OF QUALITY LIMITED
K–4, Hauz Khas Enclave
New Delhi 110 016
INDIA
Mr. Ashish Basu, Chief Operating Officer
E-mail   iqlsite@giasdl01.vsnl.net.in
Telephone   91 11 651 3270 or 3292
Facsimile   91 11 651 2677

EXCELLENCE IRELAND
Merrion Hall
Strand Road
Sandymount
Dublin 4
IRELAND
Mr. Sean Conlan, Chief Executive
E-mail   iqa@iol.ie
Telephone   353 1 269 5255
Facsimile   353 1 269 8053

THE BENCHMARKING CLUB
Business International
Via Isonzo 42/c
00198   Rome
ITALY
Internet   www.business-italy.it
Ms. Irma de Rie, Direttore
E-mail   i.derie@business-italy.it
Telephone   39 6 841 36 08
Facsimile   39 6 884 20 34
Facsimile   39 6 853 542 52

JAPAN PRODUCTIVITY CENTER FOR
SOCIO-ECONOMIC DEVELOPMENT
3–1–1 Shibuya, Shibuya-ku
Tokyo 150
JAPAN
Mr. Tomoo Koike, Executive Director
Industrial & Economic Development Div.
Telephone   81 3 3409–1117
Facsimile   81 3 5485–7750

NORWEGIAN PRODUCTIVITY AND
QUALITY CENTER
Norwegian University of Science &
Technology
SINTEF Industrial Management
Production Engineering
Richard Birkelandsv. 2B
N–7034 Trondheim
NORWAY
Internet   www2.protek.unit.no/sintef/
             index.htm
Dr. Bjorn Andersen, Head of Group
E-mail   Bjorn.Andersen@
             protek.ntnu.no
Telephone   47 73 59 05 61
Facsimile   47 73 59 71 17

FUJI XEROX-PSB BENCHMARKING CTR
Singapore Productivity and Standards Board
PSB Building
2 Bukit Merah Central
SINGAPORE 159835
Mr. Darshan Singh
Telephone   65 278 6666
Facsimile   65 278 6665/7

BENCHMARKING SOUTH AFRICA
Prodinsa Building, 7th Floor
Corner Beatrix and Pretorius Streets
Post Office Box 3971
Pretoria 0001
SOUTH AFRICA
Internet   www.benchnet.com/bensa
Mr. Pieter van Schalkwyk
E-mail   bensa@iafrica.com
Telephone   27 12 341 1470
Facsimile   27 12 341 2380

KOREAN BENCHMARKING CENTRE
Paradigm Consulting Associates
Seochoworld Building—Suite 1104
Seocho Dong–1355–3
Seocho-ku
Seoul 137–072
SOUTH KOREA
Mr. Taebok Lee
Telephone   82 2 3473 7220
Facsimile   82 2 3474 7734

CLUB GESTION DE CALIDAD
Avida de Burgos, 9-1Dcha
Madrid 28036
SPAIN
Ms. Inés Gomis
Telephone   34 1 383 6218
Facsimile   34 1 383 8258

SIQ BENCHMARKING CENTER
Swedish Institute for Quality
Fabriksgatan 10
S–412 50 Göteborg
SWEDEN
Mr. Gerth Forlin, Program Director
Internet   www.siq.se
E-mail   gf@siq.se
Telephone   46 31 35 17 04
Facsimile   46 31 773 06 45

THE BENCHMARKING CENTRE
Truscon House
11 Station Road
Gerrards Cross
Buckinghamshire SL9 8ES
UNITED KINGDOM
Internet   http://www.benchmarking.co.uk
Mr. Stuart Allan, General Manager
E-mail   info@benchmarking.co.uk
Telephone   44 1753 890 070
Facsimile   44 1753 893 070

GLOBAL **B**ENCHMARKING **N**ETWORK
136–140 Bedford Road
Kempston
Bedfordshire MK42 8BH
UNITED KINGDOM
Internet   www.gbnpubli.com
Mr. Tom Brock, Secretary General
E-mail   teb@staturb.demon.co.uk
Telephone   44 1234 405 028
Facsimile   44 1234 841 843

THE BEST PRACTICE CLUB™
The Benchmark Magazine
IFS International Ltd.
Wolseley Business Park
Wolseley Road
Kempston
Bedfordshire MK42 7PW
UNITED KINGDOM
Internet   www.benchnet.com/bpc
Mr. Rory L. Chase
Telephone   44 1234 853 605
Facsimile   44 1234 854 499

APQC INTERNATIONAL BENCHMARK-
ING CLEARINGHOUSE
123 North Post Oak Lane
Houston, TX 77024–7797
UNITED STATES OF AMERICA
Ms. Carla O'Dell, Director
E-mail   carlao@apqc.org
Telephone   713-685-4661
Facsimile   713-685-4613

BENCHMARKING COMPETENCY
CENTER
American Society for Quality
611 East Wisconsin Avenue
P. O. Box 3005
Milwaukee, WI 53201-3005
UNITED STATES OF AMERICA
Internet   www.benchnet.com/bcc
E-mail   bcc@benchnet.com
Telephone   414-272-8575 or 800-248-1946
Facsimile   414-272-1734

THE BENCHMARKING EXCHANGE
Suite 356
7960–B Soquel Drive
Aptos, CA 95003
UNITED STATES OF AMERICA
Internet   www.benchnet.com
Mr. Tom Dolan
E-mail   tdolan@benchnet.com
Telephone   408-662-9800
Telephone   800-662-9801
Facsimile   408-662-9800

BEST PRACTICE INSTITUTE™
625 Panorama Trail, Suite 1-200
Rochester, NY 14625-2432
UNITED STATES OF AMERICA
Dr. Robert C. Camp, Chairman
Global Benchmarking Network
E-mail   rcampbpi@worldnet.att.net
Telephone   716-248-5712
Facsimile   716-248-2940

The SPI COUNCIL ON BENCHMARKING
1030 Massachusetts Avenue
Cambridge, MA 02138
UNITED STATES OF AMERICA
Internet   www.spinet.org
Mr. James E. Staker, Vice President and
Director of The Council
E-mail   jstaker@gti.net
Telephone   617-491-9200 (Cambridge)
or   908-953-9007 (New Jersey)
Facsimile   617-491-1634 (Cambridge)
or   908-953-9010 (New Jersey)

How to Further Search for Case Studies

Key Electronic Databases

Trained benchmarking professionals make a practice of searching the relevant databases for any study. These would certainly include the Dialog and ABI Inform databases and others as required.

When searching the databases the approach is to search on a topic or focus area of interest, preferably a process such as product development, supply chain, billing, and customer service. The search would further include key word descriptors such as *benchmarking, best practices, world-class,* and *benchmarks.* Finally, the key to sourcing cases is to further include the key word descriptor *case studies.* What this last search item does is source company names mentioned in the abstracts. These are either full case studies or mini-cases that contain very abbreviated mentions of the actual benchmarking topics or findings results. The burden is on the researcher to contact the subject company for the details.

The Internet and World Wide Web

Benchmarking professionals have the option of accessing the Internet to search any web site for information on case studies. There is no pattern or guarantee for these efforts. The point is they should not be overlooked. One database, however, is almost always required access by benchmarkers. It is The Benchmarking Exchange, Aptos, California, www.benchnet.com.

The remaining sources are left solely to the inquisitiveness, imagination, and resourcefulness of the researcher. Good hunting!

If the readers can add to the list of case studies, please send that information to the editor at rcampbpi@worldnet.att.net. It would be greatly appreciated in the context of furthering the art and science of best practice benchmarking.

APPENDIX B

Case Study Outline

The following is the recommended outline and topical subjects for submission of a case study. An author is at liberty to modify, expand, or contract this outline; however, these topics cover what would be considered a comprehensive treatment of any best practice benchmarking project.

A. Study purpose

- *General: Why was this study undertaken?*
- How were the project goals or charter stated?
- What background events initiated the study?
- Why was this process selected?
- How were process boundaries established?
- How were problems or other facts about the current process defined?
- Were the charter or problem impacts related to goals and objectives?

B. Team operation

- *General: What were the sponsor's requirements?*
- How were project team participants and roles established?
- What benchmarking process was followed?
- What research techniques were used?
- Was outside assistance used? What type?
- What was the study duration?
- What were the costs and benefits of conducting the study?

C. Approach, conduct, and method of investigation

- *General: How was the investigation conducted?*
- Was the current process documented?
- How were process problems and opportunities analyzed?
- Were the processes key performance measures established?
- How were the requirements of the process customer taken into account?
- What were the organizations, industries, or partners benchmarked?
- How were the site visits conducted?
- What were the process-to-process comparisons and analyses?

D. Best practices discovered, results, and summary of findings

- *General: What were the process changes and benefits?*
- Was a composite best-of-the-best practice process determined?
- What best practices and key innovative findings were described?
- What were the major performance and value of gains?
- What was the overall, potential opportunity for improvement?
- What was the benefit/cost ratio?

E. Implementation action taken

- *General: How will the best practice process be implemented?*
- How were the findings communicated to those affected?
- What were the implementation approach and planned changes?
- What implementation barriers and opportunities were encountered?
- What next steps were planned?

F. Conclusions and lessons learned

- *General: Review what was accomplished and key insights gained.*
- How will the organization benefit from the changes?

G. Documentation figures, charts, and references

- *General: Include key figures, charts, and tables.*
- Include any of the following, as applicable.
  —Questionnaire
  —Site visit reports
  —Comparative work flowcharts
  —Quantitative cost analysis
  —Best practice descriptive comparisons and summaries

Index